Rediscovering the American Republic

Biographies, Primary Texts, Charts, and Study Questions— Exploring a People's Quest for Ordered Liberty

Volume 2: 1877–Present

Ryan C. MacPherson, Ph.D.

MANKATO, MINNESOTA

INTO YOUR HANDS LLC

2013

Into Your Hands LLC

Mankato, Minnesota

www.intoyourhandsllc.com

Rediscovering the American Republic: Biographies, Primary Texts, Charts, and Study Questions—Exploring a People's Quest for Ordered Liberty, Volume 2: 1877–Present, by Ryan C. MacPherson, Ph.D.

ISBN–10: 0–9857543–1–1

ISBN–13: 978–0–9857543–1–0

Library of Congress Subject Headings

Presidents—United States—Biography

Presidents—United States—Inaugural Addresses

United States—History

First printing, December 2013.

Second printing, May 2014.

Contents

(The extra white space between certain items suggests possible breaking points for assigned readings when this book is used for course instruction.)

Introduction

Part 1: America in the Gilded Age, 1877–1901

Part 2: Progressive Reform and Human Nature, 1901–1929

Part 3: The Emergence of the American Superpower, 1929–1953

Part 4: The Cold War and Civil Rights, 1953–1981

Part 5: The Triumph and the Vulnerability of the World's Only Superpower, 1981–Present

Epilogue

Back Matter

Introduction

A People's Continuing Quest for Ordered Liberty

Liberty is second only to *life* in the American creed. As Thomas Jefferson wrote in the Declaration of Independence in 1776 (p. 21):

> We hold these truths to be self-evident, that all men are created equal, that they are endowed by their Creator with certain unalienable rights[,] that among these are life, *liberty* and the pursuit of happiness.

Liberty has remained a perennial concern of Americans. In 1787, America's founding fathers drafted the U.S. Constitution to "secure the Blessings of *Liberty* to ourselves and our Posterity" (p. 26). In 1863—"fourscore and seven years" after the Declaration of Independence—Abraham Lincoln commemorated in the Gettysburg Address how "our fathers brought forth on this continent a new nation, conceived in *liberty* and dedicated to the proposition that all men are created equal" (p. 46).

When the men who have made America great spoke of liberty, they did not intend an unbridled free-for-all, for that would result in chaos, ultimately destroying liberty. The American people, from colonial times to the present, have instead sought an *ordered liberty*. In their quest, they have debated how best to foster and preserve liberty—fearing on the one hand the danger of imposing order arbitrarily, while also being wary of the danger toward disorder.

Biographies and Primary Texts: Keys to Historical Understanding

Volume 1 of *Rediscovering the American Republic* included classic biographies of five of the most influential people in American history through the era of the Civil War: William Penn, George Washington, Thomas Jefferson, Andrew Jackson, and Abraham Lincoln. Each of these men sought to establish both order and liberty in America, though they differed with their contemporaries as to the proper mix that would foster a *lasting* ordered liberty. Although none of them fully represented the era in which they lived, all of them interacted sufficiently with people of alternative persuasions to ensure that a focused study of their lives reveals a broad diversity of American experience. Primary source documents included in Volume 1 shed additional light on the challenges, triumphs, and tragedies experienced by the American people, particularly as to issues involving religious liberty, racial equality, and property rights. The proper relationship among the three branches of the federal government, and the dividing line between federal jurisdiction and states' rights, also received significant attention.

Volume 2 continues the same tradition of historical inquiry through a combination of biographies—this time including every U.S. president from 1877 to present—and primary source documents. Once again, the analysis focuses on the proper relationship among the three branches of the federal government, and the dividing line between federal jurisdiction and states' rights. Once again, religious liberty, racial equality, and property rights present perennial questions to which Americans give varied responses. And, once again, the overarching concern is to strike the proper balance between order and liberty—to discover that precious combination known as *ordered liberty* that uniquely can sustain the American Republic for generations yet to come. Through it all, a recognition of human nature, and the rights inherent in each person to life, liberty, and property, must never be forgotten.

Inaugural addresses, public policy documents, and other primary source texts, plus time lines and explanatory tables, have been interspersed among the presidential biographies and organized into five distinct periods of American history. The result is full coverage of the most fundamental content essential to any advanced placement (AP) high school or introductory college survey course. Six "Deep Analysis Questions for Historians" guide the reader in probing the texts for historical significance (see p. 20). Hundreds of specific study questions bring distinct historical episodes into sharper focus. For example:

1. What was [Calvin] Coolidge's conception of human nature, and how did this shape his political philosophy? (p. 337)
2. What role did [Franklin D.] Roosevelt envision for the government amid the economic struggles of the Great Depression? (p. 383)
3. What motivated the United States and the Soviet Union as each nation took part in events that resulted in the division of Germany? (p. 426)
4. How did the political philosophies of Martin Luther King, Jr., and Malcolm X differ, and which of these two men proved more successful in accomplishing his goals? (p. 576)
5. Define "civic virtue" and explain its role in the preservation of a republic. (p. 740)

Volume 1 concluded with a period known as Reconstruction (1865–1877). The Civil War (1861–1865) had ended. The republic was rebuilt—partly upon the old foundations of the Declaration of Independence and the U.S. Constitution, but also with a new twist. Three Reconstruction Amendments solved on paper problems with which Americans long had struggled: henceforth, all slaves would be free, all persons of African descent would have equal rights with whites, and all men—regardless of race— would would be permitted to vote on equal terms. In practice, however, it remained to be seen whether Americans would honor their new creed. Moreover, the old debate between federal jurisdiction and states' rights was not resolved by the Civil War; it only was channeled away from bloody conflict back to the pens which are mightier than swords.

The introductory section of this present volume reviews the founding documents of the American Republic, including the amendments made to the Constitution during Reconstruction and the unifying message of Lincoln's famous address at Gettysburg.

The remainder of this volume continues the story of the American people's quest for ordered liberty in five parts, as previewed below.

Part 1: America in the Gilded Age, 1877–1901

During the decades following the Civil War, the U.S. population shifted from east to west as homesteaders settled the frontier. By the end of the nineteenth century, cities also were expanding rapidly as immigrants sought work in factories. The industrial revolution brought unprecedented wealth to a new class of shareholders and corporate officers. A handful of Americans, including the Scottish immigrant Andrew Carnegie, literally worked themselves up from rags to riches during this period that historians call "the Gilded Age." The government mostly left businesses to compete against each other under the principle of *laissez faire*—French for "let it be." The main regulation the government placed on commerce was the protective tariff, a tax on imports that guarded local producers from foreign competitors.

Who prospered in the political economy of the Gilded Age? Clearly Andrew Carnegie did, and with him John Rockefeller, J.P. Morgan, and other captains of industry and finance. Arguably, the laborers whom they hired also benefited. Senator (and later President) William McKinley supported a high protective tariff not only because it favored domestic business owners, but also because it fostered broader employment and higher wages for the working class, even as the efficiency of the "managerial revolution" reduced the costs charged to consumers. In times of economic growth, people at both ends of the socioeconomic spectrum prospered; however, in times of economic contraction, wage workers suffered from declining wages and unemployment. Was there a better way? Popular writer Edward Bellamy foretold the coming of a socialist utopia if only Americans would learn to accept government regulation for the common good. At the other extreme, Yale economist William Graham Sumner promoted "social Darwinism," an unregulated market in which successful companies became monopolies and unsuccessful ones went bankrupt—just as species survive or else go extinct under the fierce law of the jungle. Seeking to negotiate within the capitalist system rather than overthrow it, Samuel Gompers paved a middle path when founding the American Federation of Labor, but neither his union movement nor anyone else's carried much weight in the *laissez-faire* Gilded Age.

The federal government also took an increasingly *laissez-faire* attitude toward racial conflicts in the South. As southern whites regained control of the South, the regime of "Jim Crow" barred blacks from voting through a combination of clever laws and intimidating mobs. Although most Gilded Age presidents at least paid lip-service to the rights of equal citizenship (including the right to vote) for African Americans, rarely did the federal government take steps to ensure that the Reconstruction Amendments would be honored nationwide. The government's relationship to Native Americans similarly suffered from a disconnect between promise and fulfillment, in part because layers of bureaucracy and broad spans of geography separated policymakers in Washington from western citizens, Indian agents, and diverse tribal groups who negotiated on their own terms. Ultimately, the U.S. military intervened, forcing most Native Americans onto reservations. For a time, the military had no broader scope of activity but than to pacify the western frontier. In 1898, however, the United States went to war against Spain concerning human rights and world trade interests in both the Caribbean and the Pacific. The nation—now an industrial giant—thereby exchanged the isolationism of the Monroe Doctrine for an interventionist posture that would remain characteristic throughout much of the following century.

Part 2: Progressive Reform and Human Nature, 1901–1929

The early decades of the twentieth century marked a firm rejection of the *laissez-faire* economy of the Gilded Age. Leaders from both the Republican and Democratic Parties now championed "progressivism," a set of political ideas calling upon the government to regulate corporations in the name of the common good and to re-engineer society on the basis of modern social science. Under Presidents Theodore Roosevelt and William Howard Taft, the federal government broke up large monopolies. Other progressive reformers were optimistic that immigration, urbanization, and industrialization all could be guided by experts who knew what it took for civilization to evolve to new heights. Woodrow Wilson, whose presidency marked the pinnacle of progressivism, called for a "Darwinian" reading of the U.S. Constitution according to which the strict limitations placed on government could be adapted into a looser interpretation allowing for greater regulation of the economy. In Wilson's first year, 1913, the constitution was formally amended to license a federal income tax upon the rich in order to redistribute wealth to the poor. Another amendment established the direct election of U.S. senators by the people of each state, rather than by the state legislatures. Thus, America transitioned from a republican federation of states into a grand democracy of national citizens. With the national government assuming new responsibilities for individual prosperity, it seemed that anything was possible.

The progressives finally met their match in World War I—a transcontinental conflagration revealing that government cannot so easily re-engineer human nature. Wilson, however, learned this lesson slowly. He hoped that the war would make the world "safe for democracy." He envisioned the postwar League of Nations as a cooperative enterprise by which nations could peaceably settle their differences. He found instead that the U.S. Senate rejected the League. The remainder of the twentieth century would reveal that the sources of militant conflict run too deep in the human heart to be controlled by well-minded policymakers. Americans also discovered that prohibiting the production and sale of alcohol by a constitutional amendment, as was attempted in 1919, cannot end drunkenness or other vices associated with it.

As progressivism failed, Americans returned to their roots for tried and true methods. During the 1920s, a revival of *laissez-faire* economics coincided with full employment, rising wages, falling prices, lower tax rates, and unprecedented profits on the stock market. Meanwhile, fundamentalist Christians warned against Darwinism and called America back to the laws of the Creator. But not everyone took the moral path toward prosperity. Flappers put on make-up, purchased birth control, and frequented speakeasies. Gangsters monopolized the bootleg market. America was as turbulent as ever during the "roaring twenties."

Part 3: *The Emergence of the American Superpower, 1929–1953*

In 1929, the United States reached the height of the industrial revolution. The nation demonstrated its true greatness, however, not by what had already been achieved, but by the ability to rise to prosperity again after loosing nearly everything in the Great Depression. By 1933, the stock market had been decimated, literally, down to 11% of its 1929 value. Unemployment touched one out of four Americans. A worldwide depression manifested itself by similar symptoms elsewhere. In Germany, the people embraced Adolph Hitler and his National Socialist, or Nazi, Party. In America, a more moderate leader emerged: Franklin Delano Roosevelt. Prompting Congress to enact a barrage of progressive reforms, collectively called the New Deal, Roosevelt resisted the urging of leftist pundits who advocated full-scale socialism and contented himself simply to place the capstone on the progressive edifice that had been constructed before World War I. Congressional conservatives nonetheless recognized Roosevelt as the most socialist president the nation had yet seen. Capitalism survived both the Great Depression and the New Deal, but henceforth it would be a mixed form of capitalism—an entrepreneurial market regulated by government agencies chartered to restore and maintain economic balance. The people's perception of the proper role of government had permanently been changed.

What caused the Great Depression? And, how did America recover it from it? Scholars remain divided on both of these questions. Fans of FDR blame speculation on Wall Street for artificially inflating stock prices and thereby setting the nation up for a fall. In this telling of the story, Roosevelt's New Deal saved capitalism from itself by imposing government-initiated discipline on the economy. On the other hand, it may have been congressional foolishness that brought on the Depression, since the stock market fell steeply, briefly recovered, and then fell steadily all in step with news concerning the Smoot-Hawley Tariff—an extraordinarily high tax on imports that threatened to slow world trade. As for recovery, the New Deal had few immediate effects. By the time full recovery was underway, another contributing factor had upstaged FDR's recipe for reform. American factories were mobilizing to support the Allies against Nazi Germany and Fascist Italy in World War II.

After the Empire of Japan bombed the American naval base at Pearl Harbor in 1941, the United States entered the war against all three Axis Powers: Japan, Germany, and Italy. U.S. and British forces together liberated northern Africa, southern Europe, and France. Meanwhile, the Soviet Union repelled Germany from Stalingrad through Poland. By the spring of 1945, the western Allies occupied one side of Europe and the Soviets occupied the other, with Germany squished into surrender. Japan proved more recalcitrant, as her soldiers fought to the bitter end and preferred suicide to surrender. President Harry S. Truman recognized that Japan's refusal to surrender would result in millions of additional lost lives—on all sides—unless a decisive blow would force Japan's hand. That decisive blow came in the form of an atomic bomb in August 1945.

Victorious on three continents, and with a booming economy at home, the United States had become a world leader—a superpower. However, the Soviet Union also wielded considerable power. With its military still occupying eastern Europe and parts of Asia, communist governments appeared in East Germany, Poland, Czechoslovakia, Hungary, Romania, and Bulgaria with other nations also falling behind the "Iron Curtain" as time went on. By 1950, both North Korea and China had communist governments, thereby amplifying the threat posed to the free world by the Soviet Union. Determined to prevent the communists from conquering the globe, the United States committed itself to a policy of containment—a promise to intervene anytime and anywhere that communism was spreading. In instances where diplomacy failed, the so-called "Cold War" turned hot, as, for example, in Korea, where U.S. troops fought from 1950 through 1953 to preserve the borderline between the communist north and the democratic south.

Part 4: The Cold War and Civil Rights, 1953–1981

The containment policy shaped America's course of foreign relations for decades. After Korea, there was Vietnam. Whereas Korea ended in a stalemate, Vietnam was a slow and painful defeat. After a decade of fruitless military efforts, the United States withdrew and the North Vietnamese communists took over the entire country. The Vietnamese people had their own reasons for fighting, but more than anything they had gotten caught up into a global chess match between the Soviet Union and the United States. Other "pawns" in this game included Cuba, where the Soviets planted an arsenal of nuclear missiles aimed at the United States. Unfortunately, it was not always clear that the United States was on the side of freedom. In Greece, for example, America supported a monarchy against a democratic movement due to evidence that the "democracy" had been fostered by Soviet communists. Similarly, the United States supported a harsh regime in South Vietnam simply because the alternative was to allow the communists from the North to take over. According to President Dwight Eisenhower, Vietnam was not so much a chess pawn as a domino— and if the communists knocked over one domino, then all of Asia would topple. Therefore, communism had to be contained at all costs.

The paradoxes of the Cold War also touched upon domestic matters. Even while America was fighting for freedom overseas, African Americans suffered a systematic denial of their liberties at home. The Declaration of Independence had claimed that "all men are created equal." The U.S. Constitution had guaranteed, in its Fourteenth Amendment, "equal protection of the laws" to all persons. Why, then, could black children not attend the same schools as white children? Why did black adults have to work, shop, or eat in different places than white adults? Why were hardly any blacks in the Deep South registered to vote? Why did local law enforcement authorities look the other way when lynch mobs hunted down blacks who dared to assert their rights?

The civil rights movement sought to restore the benefits of Reconstruction and ensure equality before the law for all people regardless of race. Lawyers from the National Association for the Advancement of Colored People persuaded the Supreme Court that schools and bus stations should be racially integrated. Ministers such as Martin Luther King, Jr., won over the sympathy of northern whites in a crusade to evict Jim Crow from the South. Although initially more popular among Republicans, the civil rights movement managed to gain favor among the national leadership of the Democratic Party. In 1964, Democratic President Lyndon B. Johnson persuaded Congress to adopt legislation outlawing racial discrimination in education, employment, and public accommodations of all sorts. At last, the nation delivered its longstanding promise to treat blacks and whites equally, but in the process another promise was broken: public policy should be determined by the local government unless the U.S. Constitution explicitly delegates authority to the federal government.

Seeing the federal government as the best solution to almost any problem, Johnson envisioned the Great Society, in which poverty would be eradicated and Americans would live peaceably with one another. Instead, poverty worsened and racial violence increased. During the 1970s, America struggled over its identity as inflation and unemployment conquered people at home and the military suffered defeat in Vietnam. Neither Richard Nixon, Gerald Ford, nor Jimmy Carter found a way to turn the corner.

Part 5: The Triumph and the Vulnerability of the World's Only Superpower, 1981–Present

Inaugurated in 1981, President Ronald Reagan breathed new life in to the American Republic. Although he once had supported the liberal-progressive platform of the Democratic Party, he now was a conservative Republican. Reagan summoned forth the *laissez-faire* policies of the past, urging Congress to cut taxes, slim down federal regulations, and devote most of America's energy to winning the Cold War. Like FDR, Reagan had a gift for communication. His words instilled confidence. More than FDR, Reagan also produced results. The economy rebounded in short order, giving the free world a distinct advantage against the stagnation of communism. In 1989, communist

East Germany caved in, allowing a democratic reunification with West Germany. Two years later, the Soviet Union disintegrated into several independent states. Triumphant, the United States now stood alone as the world's only superpower.

Democrats learned a lesson from Reagan: the liberal-progressive agenda must be moderated in order to remain in step with the American people. In 1992, Bill Clinton won election to the presidency by styling himself a "New Democrat." He promised to slim down the welfare state rather than pursue Johnson's Great Society. During the Clinton administration, Congress also balanced the budget. Economically speaking, it seemed American prosperity would have no end. However, three problems lingered beneath the veneer of success.

First, Americans were losing their moral compass. During the 1990s, conservatives called for a revival of Judeo-Christian values while liberals championed abortion as a woman's right and homosexuality as a matter of personal liberty. Clinton himself repeatedly fell under investigation for sexual misconduct; although the Senate chose not to convict him of impeachment charges, the evidence of his character lapse became known to everyone.

Second, Congress had achieved a balanced budget in part by downsizing the military. Although this may have appeared prudent insofar as communism no longer posed the threat it once had, a reshuffling of the geopolitical deck now put America at risk against other parties. On September 11, 2001, al-Qaeda terrorists attacked both New York City and Washington, DC. In response, President George W. Bush declared a "war on terrorism," vowing the United States to uproot terrorist groups anywhere in the world where they may be found. This meant invading Afghanistan in 2001 and Iraq in 2003. As renewed militarism pushed the budget back into the red, Democratic challengers faulted Bush for squandering America's prosperity.

Third, in 2007 housing prices began to plummet, revealing mistakes dating back to the 1990s. Subprime mortgage lending, low interest rates, and tax incentives for both home buyers and home sellers had stimulated a frenzy of real estate transactions, resulting in many American families owning homes they could not afford. Once the bubble burst, they found themselves owing the bank more than their homes were worth. As foreclosures and bank failures filled newspaper headlines, the Federal Reserve Board dropped the target interest rate virtually to zero. Congress appropriated what soon amounted to trillions of dollars to bail out major banks and insurance companies while also taking over Freddie Mac and Fannie Mae (the top two transactors of mortgage-backed securities). As a result, the national debt more than doubled during the first decade of the twenty-first century. In 2010 and again in 2012, bailouts sponsored by the European Union attempted to stabilize the economy of Greece, which was collapsing under the pressure of its national debt. Would the United States also need to be bailed out?

With neither the national economy nor the federal budget in sound shape, Congress boldly adopted President Barack Obama's national healthcare proposal in 2010. Scheduled for full implementation in 2014, "Obamacare" required that virtually all Americans purchase health insurance. This sweeping package of progressive reform included taxes on the rich to pay for healthcare for the poor as well as regulations defining the kind of coverage that insurers must provide. In 2012, the Supreme Court concurred that Congress has the authority to fine individuals—in the form of income-tax penalties—if they refuse to purchase government-approved insurance.

With socialism being so openly endorsed by all three branches of the federal government, the quest for ordered liberty finally has reached a dead end. Somewhere along the way, the founding principles of the American Republic were exchanged for a promise of equal prosperity for all. Time will tell whether such a promise can ever be fulfilled—or whether the old ways will be rediscovered. But for the moment, America's experiment with ordered liberty ends here.

Deep Analysis Questions for Historians

Historians are scrutinizers. They question the past. They also question our present beliefs concerning the past. They expect that worthwhile conclusions can be backed up with evidence. In this book, you will explore some of the documents that historians have employed as evidence when studying different eras of American history. The following questions may assist you in deepening your thinking while reading those documents.

1. What does the author argue?

An argument consists of a *conclusion* (the main claim the author wants you to accept) supported by one or more *premises* (reasons, or statements of evidence). First, identify the conclusion. Then, look for the premises offered in support of it.

2. How compelling is the author's argument?

Look at the *premises* to identify what evidence is provided in favor of the *conclusion.* Then ask:

    2a. What makes that evidence persuasive, or not?

    2b. Can I think of counter-evidence? Would the author be able to handle that?

3. From what viewpoint does the author write?

    3a. What sort of prior knowledge does the author assume of his or her readers?

    3b. What sort of values or prejudices does the author assume of the readers?

4. How does the author's specific viewpoint compare to that of other writers?

5. How does this author challenge my previous conceptions?

6. What does the author's argument suggest about deeper issues, such as:

    6a. What does it mean to be an American?

    6b. What are the fundamental traits of human character?

    6c. What is liberty? What is justice?

    6d. What can I learn about myself by studying the lives of other people?

Second Continental Congress, *The Unanimous Declaration of the Thirteen United States of America* (1776)

While the Second Continental Congress was busy planning the diplomatic, military, and financial details of the American Revolution, a small committee was assigned the task of writing up a formal declaration of independence from Britain. The committee delegated to Thomas Jefferson, a rather shy member of Congress, the task of drafting the document. What he produced stunned the world: not only were the colonies declaring themselves independent of Britain, but they also were asserting the natural right of any people to abolish their government whenever the government repeatedly abuses and threatens to destroy their God-given claims to "life, liberty, and the pursuit of happiness."

In CONGRESS, July 4, 1776
A DECLARATION by the
REPRESENTATIVES of the
UNITED STATES of AMERICA, in
GENERAL CONGRESS assembled.

[1] WHEN, in the course of human events, it becomes necessary for one People to dissolve the political bonds which have connected them with another, and to assume among the powers of the earth, the separate and equal station to which the laws of Nature and of Nature's God entitle them, a decent respect to the opinions of mankind requires that they should declare the causes which impel them to the separation.

[2] We hold these truths to be self-evident, that all men are created equal, that they are endowed by their Creator with certain unalienable rights that among these are life, liberty and the pursuit of happiness—That to secure these rights, Governments are instituted among men, deriving their just powers from the consent of the governed, that whenever any form of Government becomes destructive of these ends, it is the right of the People to alter or to abolish it, and to institute new Government, laying its foundation on such principles, and organizing its powers in such form, as to them shall seem most likely to effect their safety and happiness. Prudence, indeed, will dictate that Governments long established should not be changed for light and transient causes; and accordingly all experience hath shewn, that mankind are more disposed to suffer, while evils are sufferable, than to right themselves by abolishing the forms to which they are accustomed. But, when a long train of abuses and usurpations, pursuing invariably the same object, evinces a design to reduce them under absolute despotism, it is their right, it is their duty, to throw off such Government, and to provide new guards for their future security. Such has been the patient sufferance of these Colonies, and such is now the necessity which constrains them to alter their former systems of Government. The history of the present King of Great-Britain is a history of repeated injuries and usurpations, all having in direct object the establishment of an absolute tyranny over these States. To prove this, let facts be submitted to a candid world.

[3] He has refused his assent to laws, the most wholesome and necessary for the public good.

[4] He has forbidden his Governors to pass laws of immediate and pressing importance, unless suspended in their operation till his assent should be obtained; and when so suspended, he has utterly neglected to attend to them.

[5] He has refused to pass other laws for the accommodation of large districts of people, unless those people would relinquish the right of representation in the Legislature, a right inestimable to them, and formidable to tyrants only.

[6] He has called together legislative bodies at places unusual, uncomfortable, and distant from the depository of their public records, for the sole purpose of fatiguing them into compliance with his measures.

[7] He has dissolved Representative Houses repeatedly, for opposing with manly firmness his invasions on the rights of the People.

[8] He has refused for a long time, after such dissolutions, to cause others to be elected; whereby the legislative powers, incapable of annihilation, have returned to the people at large for their exercise; the State remaining in the meantime exposed to all the dangers of invasion from without, and convulsions within.

[9] He has endeavoured to prevent the population of these States; for that purpose obstructing the laws for naturalization of foreigners; refusing to pass others to encourage their migration hither, and raising the conditions of new appropriations of lands.

[10] He has obstructed the administration of justice, by refusing his assent to laws for establishing judiciary powers.

[11] He has made judges dependent on his will alone, for the tenure of their offices, and the amount and payment of their salaries.

[12] He has erected a multitude of new offices, and sent hither swarms of officers to harass our people, and eat out their substance.

[13] He has kept among us, in times of peace, standing armies, without the consent of our Legislature.

[14] He has affected to render the military independent of, and superior to, the civil power.

[15] He has combined with others, to subject us to a jurisdiction foreign to our constitution, and unacknowledged by our laws; giving his assent to their acts of pretended legislation:

[16] For quartering large bodies of armed troops among us:

[17] For protecting them, by a mock trial, from punishment for any murders which they should commit on the inhabitants of these States:

[18] For cutting off our trade with all parts of the world:

[19] For imposing taxes on us without our consent:

[20] For depriving us, in many cases, of the benefits of trial by jury:

[21] For transporting us beyond seas to

be tried for pretended offenses:

[22] For abolishing the free system of English laws in a neighboring province, establishing therein an arbitrary Government, and enlarging its boundaries, so as to render it at once an example and fit instrument for introducing the same absolute rule in these Colonies:

[23] For taking away our charters, abolishing our most valuable laws, and altering fundamentally the forms of our Governments:

[24] For suspending our own Legislatures, and declaring themselves invested with power to legislate for us in all cases whatsoever.

[25] He has abdicated Government here, by declaring us out of his protection and waging war against us.

[26] He has plundered our seas, ravaged our coasts, burnt our towns, and destroyed the lives of our people.

[27] He is, at this time, transporting large armies of foreign mercenaries to complete the works of death, desolation and tyranny, already begun with circumstances of cruelty and perfidy scarcely paralleled in the most barbarous ages, and totally unworthy the Head of a civilized nation.

[28] He has constrained our fellow citizens taken captive on the high seas to bear arms against their country to become the executioners of their friends and brethren, or to fall themselves by their hands.

[29] He has excited domestic insurrections amongst us, and has endeavoured to bring on the inhabitants of our frontiers, the merciless Indian savages, whose known rule of warfare, is undistinguished destruction of all ages, sexes and conditions.

[30] In every stage of these oppressions we have petitioned for redress in the most humble terms: Our repeated petitions have been answered only by repeated injury. A Prince, whose character is thus marked by every act which may define a tyrant, is unfit to be the ruler of a free people.

[31] Nor have we been wanting in attention to our British brethren. We have warned them from time to time of attempts by their legislature to extend an unwarrantable jurisdiction over us. We have reminded them of the circumstances of our emigration and settlement here. We have appealed to their native justice and magnanimity, and we have conjured them by the ties of our common kindred to disavow these usurpations, which, would inevitably interrupt our connections and correspondence. They too have been deaf to the voice of justice and consanguinity. We must, therefore, acquiesce in the necessity which denounces our separation, and hold them, as we hold the rest of mankind, enemies in war, in peace, friends.

[32] We, therefore, the Representatives of the UNITED STATES of AMERICA, in GENERAL CONGRESS assembled, appealing to the Supreme Judge of the World for the rectitude of our intentions, do, in the name, and by the authority of the good People of these Colonies, solemnly publish and declare, That these United Colonies are, and of right ought to be, FREE and INDEPENDENT STATES; that they are absolved from all allegiance

to the British Crown, and that all political connection between them and the State of Great-Britain, is and ought to be totally dissolved; and that as FREE and INDEPENDENT STATES, they have full power to levy war, conclude peace, contract alliances, establish commerce, and to do all other acts and things which INDEPENDENT STATES may of right do. And for the support of this Declaration, with a firm reliance on the protection of divine Providence, we mutually pledge to each other our lives, our fortunes, and our sacred honor.

Study Questions

1. Look up "sovereignty" in a dictionary. Rewrite the definition in your own words.

2. In view of your response to #1, above, write a definition for "national sovereignty."

3. Upon whose laws does the principle of national sovereignty rest (Declaration, para. 1)?

4. What is meant by "self-evident" (para. 2)? (Consult a dictionary if necessary.)

5. What four self-evident truths are listed in para. 2? (Hint: look at the phrases that follow the word "that" each time it is repeated, except for the "that among these are" instance.)

6. What is meant by "unalienable" (or "inalienable") rights? (Consult a dictionary if necessary.)

7. What three specific rights are listed as being inalienable? (This is the place where you refer to the "that among these are" section of para. 2, which you skipped in #5, above.)

8. Quote the four instances in which the Declaration of Independence refers to God (paras. 1, 2, and twice in 32).

9. Summarizing #8, what can be inferred about the religious convictions of the founding fathers?

10. What is the most significant thing you learned by studying this document?

Constitution for the United States of America (1787)

After July 4, 1776, two things became certain for the thirteen original states. First, they had declared independence from Great Britain. Second, they somehow remained interdependent upon one another. Throughout most of the Revolutionary War, the Continental Congress served as an emergency government. Although Congress had adopted a formal political arrangement, the Articles of Confederation, in 1777, the states did not unanimously agree to it until 1781, by which time the war was nearly finished. In the years that followed, the Confederation successfully established a federal lands policy through the Northwest Land Ordinance and related legislation, but failed to hold the founders' confidence as a sustainable arrangement for uniting the states. Congress authorized a convention to draft proposed revisions for the Articles of Confederation during the summer of 1787.

The convention, meeting in Philadelphia, instead wrote an entirely new charter of government, the U.S. Constitution, which today is the longest-serving written constitution in world history. The delegates to the convention drew upon their knowledge of history, philosophy, law, and human nature (informed by Christian theology) to craft a system of government that they hoped would "establish a more perfect union" than the Articles of Confederation had provided. Along the way, the delegates debated many points and forged several compromises in an effort to foster an ordered liberty that would safeguard both the nation's security and the people's rights.

Preamble

We the People of the United States, in Order to form a more perfect Union, establish Justice, insure domestic Tranquility, provide for the common defence, promote the general Welfare, and secure the Blessings of Liberty to ourselves and our Posterity, do ordain and establish this Constitution for the United States of America.

Article I

Section 1.

[1] All legislative Powers herein granted shall be vested in a Congress of the United States, which shall consist of a Senate and House of Representatives.

Section 2.

[1] The House of Representatives shall be composed of Members chosen every second Year by the People of the several States, and the Electors in each State shall have the Qualifications requisite for Electors of the most numerous Branch of the State Legislature.

[2] No Person shall be a Representative who shall not have attained to the Age of twenty five Years, and been seven Years a Citizen of the United States, and who shall not, when elected, be an Inhabitant of that State in which he shall be chosen.

[3] Representatives and direct Taxes

shall be apportioned among the several States which may be included within this Union, according to their respective Numbers, which shall be determined *by adding to the whole Number of free Persons, including those bound to Service for a Term of Years, and excluding Indians not taxed, three fifths of all other Persons* [modified by **Fourteenth Amendment**, Section 2]. The actual Enumeration shall be made within three Years after the first Meeting of the Congress of the United States, and within every subsequent Term of ten Years, in such Manner as they shall by Law direct. The Number of Representatives shall not exceed one for every thirty Thousand, but each State shall have at Least one Representative; and until such enumeration shall be made, the State of New Hampshire shall be entitled to chuse three, Massachusetts eight, Rhode-Island and Providence Plantations one, Connecticut five, New-York six, New Jersey four, Pennsylvania eight, Delaware one, Maryland six, Virginia ten, North Carolina five, South Carolina five, and Georgia three.

[4] When vacancies happen in the Representation from any State, the Executive Authority thereof shall issue Writs of Election to fill such Vacancies.

[5] The House of Representatives shall chuse their Speaker and other Officers; and shall have the sole Power of Impeachment.

Section 3.

[1] The Senate of the United States shall be composed of two Senators from each State, *chosen by the Legislature thereof* [modified by **Seventeenth Amend-** ment], for six Years; and each Senator shall have one Vote.

[2] Immediately after they shall be assembled in Consequence of the first Election, they shall be divided as equally as may be into three Classes. The Seats of the Senators of the first Class shall be vacated at the Expiration of the second Year, of the second Class at the Expiration of the fourth Year, and of the third Class at the Expiration of the sixth Year, so that one third may be chosen every second Year; *and if Vacancies happen by Resignation, or otherwise, during the Recess of the Legislature of any State, the Executive thereof may make temporary Appointments until the next Meeting of the Legislature, which shall then fill such Vacancies* [modified by **Seventeenth Amendment**].

[3] No Person shall be a Senator who shall not have attained to the Age of thirty Years, and been nine Years a Citizen of the United States, and who shall not, when elected, be an Inhabitant of that State for which he shall be chosen.

[4] The Vice President of the United States shall be President of the Senate, but shall have no Vote, unless they be equally divided.

[5] The Senate shall chuse their other Officers, and also a President pro tempore, in the Absence of the Vice President, or when he shall exercise the Office of President of the United States.

[6] The Senate shall have the sole Power to try all Impeachments. When sitting for that Purpose, they shall be on Oath or Affirmation. When the President of the United States is tried, the Chief Justice

shall preside: And no Person shall be convicted without the Concurrence of two thirds of the Members present.

[7] Judgment in Cases of Impeachment shall not extend further than to removal from Office, and disqualification to hold and enjoy any Office of honor, Trust or Profit under the United States: but the Party convicted shall nevertheless be liable and subject to Indictment, Trial, Judgment and Punishment, according to Law.

Section 4.

[1] The Times, Places and Manner of holding Elections for Senators and Representatives, shall be prescribed in each State by the Legislature thereof; but the Congress may at any time by Law make or alter such Regulations, except as to the Places of chusing Senators.

[2] *The Congress shall assemble at least once in every Year, and such Meeting shall be on the first Monday in December* [modified by **Twentieth Amendment**], unless they shall by Law appoint a different Day.

Section 5.

[1] Each House shall be the Judge of the Elections, Returns and Qualifications of its own Members, and a Majority of each shall constitute a Quorum to do Business; but a smaller Number may adjourn from day to day, and may be authorized to compel the Attendance of absent Members, in such Manner, and under such Penalties as each House may provide.

[2] Each House may determine the Rules of its Proceedings, punish its Members for disorderly Behaviour, and, with the Concurrence of two thirds, expel a Member.

[3] Each House shall keep a Journal of its Proceedings, and from time to time publish the same, excepting such Parts as may in their Judgment require Secrecy; and the Yeas and Nays of the Members of either House on any question shall, at the Desire of one fifth of those Present, be entered on the Journal.

[4] Neither House, during the Session of Congress, shall, without the Consent of the other, adjourn for more than three days, nor to any other Place than that in which the two Houses shall be sitting.

Section 6.

[1] The Senators and Representatives shall receive a Compensation for their Services, to be ascertained by Law, and paid out of the Treasury of the United States. They shall in all Cases, except Treason, Felony and Breach of the Peace, be privileged from Arrest during their Attendance at the Session of their respective Houses, and in going to and returning from the same; and for any Speech or Debate in either House, they shall not be questioned in any other Place.

[2] No Senator or Representative shall, during the Time for which he was elected, be appointed to any civil Office under the Authority of the United States, which shall have been created, or the Emoluments whereof shall have been encreased during such time; and no Person holding any Office under the United States, shall be a

Member of either House during his Continuance in Office.

Section 7.

[1] All Bills for raising Revenue shall originate in the House of Representatives; but the Senate may propose or concur with Amendments as on other Bills.

[2] Every Bill which shall have passed the House of Representatives and the Senate, shall, before it become a Law, be presented to the President of the United States: If he approve he shall sign it, but if not he shall return it, with his Objections to that House in which it shall have originated, who shall enter the Objections at large on their Journal, and proceed to reconsider it. If after such Reconsideration two thirds of that House shall agree to pass the Bill, it shall be sent, together with the Objections, to the other House, by which it shall likewise be reconsidered, and if approved by two thirds of that House, it shall become a Law. But in all such Cases the Votes of both Houses shall be determined by Yeas and Nays, and the Names of the Persons voting for and against the Bill shall be entered on the Journal of each House respectively. If any Bill shall not be returned by the President within ten Days (Sundays excepted) after it shall have been presented to him, the Same shall be a Law, in like Manner as if he had signed it, unless the Congress by their Adjournment prevent its Return, in which Case it shall not be a Law.

[3] Every Order, Resolution, or Vote to which the Concurrence of the Senate and House of Representatives may be necessary (except on a question of Adjournment) shall be presented to the President of the United States; and before the Same shall take Effect, shall be approved by him, or being disapproved by him, shall be repassed by two thirds of the Senate and House of Representatives, according to the Rules and Limitations prescribed in the Case of a Bill.

Section 8.

[1] The Congress shall have Power To lay and collect Taxes, Duties, Imposts and Excises, to pay the Debts and provide for the common Defence and general Welfare of the United States; but all Duties, Imposts and Excises shall be uniform throughout the United States;

[2] To borrow Money on the credit of the United States;

[3] To regulate Commerce with foreign Nations, and among the several States, and with the Indian Tribes;

[4] To establish an uniform Rule of Naturalization, and uniform Laws on the subject of Bankruptcies throughout the United States;

[5] To coin Money, regulate the Value thereof, and of foreign Coin, and fix the Standard of Weights and Measures;

[6] To provide for the Punishment of counterfeiting the Securities and current Coin of the United States;

[7] To establish Post Offices and post Roads;

[8] To promote the Progress of Science and useful Arts, by securing for limited Times to Authors and Inventors the exclusive Right to their respective Writings

and Discoveries;

[9] To constitute Tribunals inferior to the supreme Court;

[10] To define and punish Piracies and Felonies committed on the high Seas, and Offences against the Law of Nations;

[11] To declare War, grant Letters of Marque and Reprisal, and make Rules concerning Captures on Land and Water;

[12] To raise and support Armies, but no Appropriation of Money to that Use shall be for a longer Term than two Years;

[13] To provide and maintain a Navy;

[14] To make Rules for the Government and Regulation of the land and naval Forces;

[15] To provide for calling forth the Militia to execute the Laws of the Union, suppress Insurrections and repel Invasions;

[16] To provide for organizing, arming, and disciplining, the Militia, and for governing such Part of them as may be employed in the Service of the United States, reserving to the States respectively, the Appointment of the Officers, and the Authority of training the Militia according to the discipline prescribed by Congress;

[17] To exercise exclusive Legislation in all Cases whatsoever, over such District (not exceeding ten Miles square) as may, by Cession of particular States, and the Acceptance of Congress, become the Seat of the Government of the United States, and to exercise like Authority over all Places purchased by the Consent of the Legislature of the State in which the Same shall be, for the Erection of Forts, Magazines, Arsenals, dock-Yards, and other needful Buildings;—And

[18] To make all Laws which shall be necessary and proper for carrying into Execution the foregoing Powers, and all other Powers vested by this Constitution in the Government of the United States, or in any Department or Officer thereof.

Section 9.

[1] The Migration or Importation of such Persons as any of the States now existing shall think proper to admit, shall not be prohibited by the Congress prior to the Year one thousand eight hundred and eight, but a Tax or duty may be imposed on such Importation, not exceeding ten dollars for each Person.

[2] The Privilege of the Writ of Habeas Corpus shall not be suspended, unless when in Cases of Rebellion or Invasion the public Safety may require it.

[3] No Bill of Attainder or ex post facto Law shall be passed.

[4] No Capitation, or other direct, Tax shall be laid, unless in Proportion to the Census or Enumeration herein before directed to be taken.

[5] No Tax or Duty shall be laid on Articles exported from any State.

[6] No Preference shall be given by any Regulation of Commerce or Revenue to the Ports of one State over those of another; nor shall Vessels bound to, or from, one State, be obliged to enter, clear, or pay Duties in another.

[7] No Money shall be drawn from the Treasury, but in Consequence of Appropri-

ations made by Law; and a regular Statement and Account of the Receipts and Expenditures of all public Money shall be published from time to time.

[8] No Title of Nobility shall be granted by the United States: And no Person holding any Office of Profit or Trust under them, shall, without the Consent of the Congress, accept of any present, Emolument, Office, or Title, of any kind whatever, from any King, Prince, or foreign State.

Section 10.

[1] No State shall enter into any Treaty, Alliance, or Confederation; grant Letters of Marque and Reprisal; coin Money; emit Bills of Credit; make any Thing but gold and silver Coin a Tender in Payment of Debts; pass any Bill of Attainder, ex post facto Law, or Law impairing the Obligation of Contracts, or grant any Title of Nobility.

[2] No State shall, without the Consent of the Congress, lay any Imposts or Duties on Imports or Exports, except what may be absolutely necessary for executing its inspection Laws; and the net Produce of all Duties and Imposts, laid by any State on Imports or Exports, shall be for the Use of the Treasury of the United States; and all such Laws shall be subject to the Revision and Controul of the Congress.

[3] No State shall, without the Consent of Congress, lay any Duty of Tonnage, keep Troops, or Ships of War in time of Peace, enter into any Agreement or Compact with another State, or with a foreign Power, or engage in War, unless actually invaded, or in such imminent Danger as will not admit of delay.

Article II

Section 1.

[1] The executive Power shall be vested in a President of the United States of America. He shall hold his Office during the Term of four Years, and, together with the Vice President, chosen for the same Term, be elected, as follows:

[2] Each State shall appoint, in such Manner as the Legislature thereof may direct, a Number of Electors, equal to the whole Number of Senators and Representatives to which the State may be entitled in the Congress: but no Senator or Representative, or Person holding an Office of Trust or Profit under the United States, shall be appointed an Elector.

[3] The Electors shall meet in their respective States, and vote by Ballot for two Persons, of whom one at least shall not be an Inhabitant of the same State with themselves. And they shall make a List of all the Persons voted for, and of the Number of Votes for each; which List they shall sign and certify, and transmit sealed to the Seat of the Government of the United States, directed to the President of the Senate. The President of the Senate shall, in the Presence of the Senate and House of Representatives, open all the Certificates, and the Votes shall then be counted. The Person having the greatest Number of Votes shall be the President, if such Number be a Majority of the whole Number of Electors appointed; and if there be more than one who have such Majority,

and have an equal Number of Votes, then the House of Representatives shall immediately chuse by Ballot one of them for President; and if no Person have a Majority, then from the five highest on the List the said House shall in like Manner chuse the President. But in chusing the President, the Votes shall be taken by States, the Representation from each State having one Vote; a quorum for this Purpose shall consist of a Member or Members from two thirds of the States, and a Majority of all the States shall be necessary to a Choice. In every Case, after the Choice of the President, the Person having the greatest Number of Votes of the Electors shall be the Vice President. But if there should remain two or more who have equal Votes, the Senate shall chuse from them by Ballot the Vice President [modified by **Twelfth Amendment**].

[4] The Congress may determine the Time of chusing the Electors, and the Day on which they shall give their Votes; which Day shall be the same throughout the United States.

[5] No Person except a natural born Citizen, or a Citizen of the United States, at the time of the Adoption of this Constitution, shall be eligible to the Office of President; neither shall any Person be eligible to that Office who shall not have attained to the Age of thirty five Years, and been fourteen Years a Resident within the United States.

[6] In Case of the Removal of the President from Office, or of his Death, Resignation, or Inability to discharge the Powers and Duties of the said Office, the Same shall devolve on the Vice President,

and the Congress may by Law provide for the Case of Removal, Death, Resignation or Inability, both of the President and Vice President, declaring what Officer shall then act as President, and such Officer shall act accordingly, until the Disability be removed, or a President shall be elected [modified by **Twentieth Amendment**].

[7] The President shall, at stated Times, receive for his Services, a Compensation, which shall neither be increased nor diminished during the Period for which he shall have been elected, and he shall not receive within that Period any other Emolument from the United States, or any of them.

Before he enter on the Execution of his Office, he shall take the following Oath or Affirmation:—"I do solemnly swear (or affirm) that I will faithfully execute the Office of President of the United States, and will to the best of my Ability, preserve, protect and defend the Constitution of the United States."

Section 2.

[1] The President shall be Commander in Chief of the Army and Navy of the United States, and of the Militia of the several States, when called into the actual Service of the United States; he may require the Opinion, in writing, of the principal Officer in each of the executive Departments, upon any Subject relating to the Duties of their respective Offices, and he shall have Power to grant Reprieves and Pardons for Offences against the United States, except in Cases of Impeachment.

[2] He shall have Power, by and with

the Advice and Consent of the Senate, to make Treaties, provided two thirds of the Senators present concur; and he shall nominate, and by and with the Advice and Consent of the Senate, shall appoint Ambassadors, other public Ministers and Consuls, Judges of the supreme Court, and all other Officers of the United States, whose Appointments are not herein otherwise provided for, and which shall be established by Law: but the Congress may by Law vest the Appointment of such inferior Officers, as they think proper, in the President alone, in the Courts of Law, or in the Heads of Departments.

[3] The President shall have Power to fill up all Vacancies that may happen during the Recess of the Senate, by granting Commissions which shall expire at the End of their next Session.

Section 3.

[1] He shall from time to time give to the Congress Information of the State of the Union, and recommend to their Consideration such Measures as he shall judge necessary and expedient; he may, on extraordinary Occasions, convene both Houses, or either of them, and in Case of Disagreement between them, with Respect to the Time of Adjournment, he may adjourn them to such Time as he shall think proper; he shall receive Ambassadors and other public Ministers; he shall take Care that the Laws be faithfully executed, and shall Commission all the Officers of the United States.

Section 4.

The President, Vice President and all civil Officers of the United States, shall be removed from Office on Impeachment for, and Conviction of, Treason, Bribery, or other high Crimes and Misdemeanors.

Article III

Section 1.

The judicial Power of the United States shall be vested in one supreme Court, and in such inferior Courts as the Congress may from time to time ordain and establish. The Judges, both of the supreme and inferior Courts, shall hold their Offices during good Behaviour, and shall, at stated Times, receive for their Services a Compensation, which shall not be diminished during their Continuance in Office.

Section 2.

[1] The judicial Power shall extend to all Cases, in Law and Equity, arising under this Constitution, the Laws of the United States, and Treaties made, or which shall be made, under their Authority;—to all Cases affecting Ambassadors, other public Ministers and Consuls;—to all Cases of admiralty and maritime Jurisdiction;—to Controversies to which the United States shall be a Party;—to Controversies between two or more States;—between a State and Citizens of another State [modified by **Eleventh Amendment**];— between Citizens of different States;— between Citizens of the same State claiming Lands under Grants of different States,

and between a State, or the Citizens thereof, and foreign States, Citizens or Subjects.

[2] In all Cases affecting Ambassadors, other public Ministers and Consuls, and those in which a State shall be Party, the supreme Court shall have original Jurisdiction. In all the other Cases before mentioned, the supreme Court shall have appellate Jurisdiction, both as to Law and Fact, with such Exceptions, and under such Regulations as the Congress shall make.

[3] The Trial of all Crimes, except in Cases of Impeachment, shall be by Jury; and such Trial shall be held in the State where the said Crimes shall have been committed; but when not committed within any State, the Trial shall be at such Place or Places as the Congress may by Law have directed.

Section 3.

[1] Treason against the United States shall consist only in levying War against them, or in adhering to their Enemies, giving them Aid and Comfort. No Person shall be convicted of Treason unless on the Testimony of two Witnesses to the same overt Act, or on Confession in open Court.

[2] The Congress shall have Power to declare the Punishment of Treason, but no Attainder of Treason shall work Corruption of Blood, or Forfeiture except during the Life of the Person attainted.

Article IV

Section 1.

Full Faith and Credit shall be given in each State to the public Acts, Records, and judicial Proceedings of every other State. And the Congress may by general Laws prescribe the Manner in which such Acts, Records and Proceedings shall be proved, and the Effect thereof.

Section 2.

[1] The Citizens of each State shall be entitled to all Privileges and Immunities of Citizens in the several States.

[2] A Person charged in any State with Treason, Felony, or other Crime, who shall flee from Justice, and be found in another State, shall on Demand of the executive Authority of the State from which he fled, be delivered up, to be removed to the State having Jurisdiction of the Crime.

[3] No Person held to Service or Labour in one State, under the Laws thereof, escaping into another, shall, in Consequence of any Law or Regulation therein, be discharged from such Service or Labour, but shall be delivered up on Claim of the Party to whom such Service or Labour may be due [modified by **Thirteenth Amendment**].

Section 3.

[1] New States may be admitted by the Congress into this Union; but no new State shall be formed or erected within the Jurisdiction of any other State; nor any State be formed by the Junction of two or more

States, or Parts of States, without the Consent of the Legislatures of the States concerned as well as of the Congress.

[2] The Congress shall have Power to dispose of and make all needful Rules and Regulations respecting the Territory or other Property belonging to the United States; and nothing in this Constitution shall be so construed as to Prejudice any Claims of the United States, or of any particular State.

Section 4.

The United States shall guarantee to every State in this Union a Republican Form of Government, and shall protect each of them against Invasion; and on Application of the Legislature, or of the Executive (when the Legislature cannot be convened), against domestic Violence.

Article V.

[1] The Congress, whenever two thirds of both Houses shall deem it necessary, shall propose Amendments to this Constitution, or, on the Application of the Legislatures of two thirds of the several States, shall call a Convention for proposing Amendments, which, in either Case, shall be valid to all Intents and Purposes, as Part of this Constitution, when ratified by the Legislatures of three fourths of the several States, or by Conventions in three fourths thereof, as the one or the other Mode of Ratification may be proposed by the Congress;

[2] Provided that no Amendment which may be made prior to the Year One thousand eight hundred and eight shall in any Manner affect the first and fourth Clauses in the Ninth Section of the first Article;

[3] and that no State, without its Consent, shall be deprived of its equal Suffrage in the Senate [arguably modified by **Seventeenth Amendment**].

Article VI

[1] All Debts contracted and Engagements entered into, before the Adoption of this Constitution, shall be as valid against the United States under this Constitution, as under the Confederation.

[2] This Constitution, and the Laws of the United States which shall be made in Pursuance thereof; and all Treaties made, or which shall be made, under the Authority of the United States, shall be the supreme Law of the Land; and the Judges in every State shall be bound thereby, any Thing in the Constitution or Laws of any State to the Contrary notwithstanding.

[3] The Senators and Representatives before mentioned, and the Members of the several State Legislatures, and all executive and judicial Officers, both of the United States and of the several States, shall be bound by Oath or Affirmation, to support this Constitution; but no religious Test shall ever be required as a Qualification to any Office or public Trust under the United States.

Article VII

The Ratification of the Conventions of nine States, shall be sufficient for the Establishment of this Constitution between the States so ratifying the Same.

Attest William Jackson
Secretary
done in Convention by the Unanimous Consent of the States present the Seventeenth Day of September in the Year of our Lord one thousand seven hundred and Eighty seven and of the Independence of the United States of America the Twelfth In witness whereof We have hereunto subscribed our Names.

Study Questions

1. How are the Declaration of Independence, para. 2, and the Preamble to the Constitution related?

2. The framers, in general, believed that the best government would consist of distinct powers that were kept separate ("separation of powers"). How does the Constitution separate the legislative, executive, and judicial functions of the federal government (refer to Articles I, II, and III)? (The answer may seem obvious, but keep in mind that the U.S. was the first nation in the history of the world to establish an independent judicial branch of government.)

3. The framers, in general, also believed that various parts of government should be prevented, by "checks and balances," from assuming too much power. Complete the following statements, which give examples of "checks" and "balances" built into the Constitution. To become a law, a bill must first be passed by both the _____ and the _____ (Art. I, Sec. 7). All revenue (or spending) bills must originate in the _____ (Art. I, Sec. 7). If the President _____ a bill, then _____ can over-ride it with a _____ vote in both houses (Art. I, Sec. 7). The President cannot declare war; only _____ can do that (Art. I, Sec. 8). When the President makes a treaty with another nation, it must be approved by a _____ vote in the _____ (Art. II, Sec. 2). The _____ can declare laws unconstitutional (Art. III and Art. VI). The _____ appoints judges to the Supreme Court and other federal courts, but these appointments must be approved by the _____ (Art II, Section 2). Supreme Court Justices do not serve for life, but rather may remain in their post during _____ (Art. III, Sec. 1), which is to say that they can be _____ by the House of Representative and removed from office if convicted by the _____ (Art. I, Sec. 2 and Sec. 3). The President may be removed from office if impeached by the _____ and convicted by the _____ (Art. I, Sec. 2 and Sec. 3; Art. II, Sec. 4).

4. According to Article I, Sections 2 and 3, of the Constitution (prior to any amendments), how are members of the House and the Senate to be elected? What does this reveal about the framers' original understanding of who or what should be represented in the federal government?

5. According to the Constitution (Art. II, Sec. 2 and Sec. 3; later altered by the Twelfth Amendment) who elects the President? Explain how this works.

6. What do the Declaration of Independence and the Constitution say, whether implicitly or explicitly, about slavery? (See esp. Art. I, Secs. 2 and 9; Art. IV, Sec. 2; and, Art. V of the Constitution, comparing these sections to the Declaration of Independence, para. 2.)

7. What does the Constitution say about religion (Art. VI)?

8. People today often say that Supreme Court Justices are "appointed for life." What does Article III, Section 1, of the Constitution say about this matter? (Hint: see also the final two paragraphs of Article I, Section 3.)

The Bill of Rights (proposed, 1789; ratified, 1791)

Many Americans opposed the ratification of the U.S. Constitution for fear that it would empower the federal government to the detriment of the rights of the states and their people. Although these "anti-federalists" lost the debate over ratification, their concerns led directly to the adoption of the Bill of Rights, or first ten amendments to the Constitution. Initially, Congress proposed twelve amendments. One of them, dealing with the formula for congressional representation, never was ratified; another, ensuring that no congressional pay raise would be effective until after the next election, was finally ratified in 1992 as the Twenty-Seventh Amendment.

Congress of the United States, begun and held at the City of New-York, on Wednesday the Fourth of March, one thousand seven hundred and eighty nine.

THE Conventions of a number of the States having at the time of their adopting the Constitution, expressed a desire, in order to prevent misconstruction or abuse of its powers, that further declaratory and restrictive clauses should be added: And as extending the ground of public confidence in the Government, will best insure the beneficent ends of its institution

RESOLVED by the Senate and House of Representatives of the United States of America, in Congress assembled, two thirds of both Houses concurring, that the following Articles be proposed to the Legislatures of the several States, as Amendments to the Constitution of the United States, all or any of which Articles, when ratified by three fourths of the said Legislatures, to be valid to all intents and purposes, as part of the said Constitution; viz.:

ARTICLES in addition to, and Amendment of the Constitution of the United States of America, proposed by Congress, and ratified by the Legislatures of the several States, pursuant to the fifth Article of the original Constitution.

ATTEST: Frederick Augustus Muhlenberg, Speaker of the House of Representatives

First Amendment

Congress shall make no law respecting an establishment of religion, or prohibiting the free exercise thereof; or abridging the freedom of speech, or of the press; or the right of the people peaceably to assemble, and to petition the Government for a redress of grievances.

Second Amendment

A well regulated Militia, being necessary to the security of a free State, the right of the people to keep and bear Arms, shall not be infringed.

Third Amendment

No Soldier shall, in time of peace be quartered in any house, without the consent of the Owner, nor in time of war, but in a manner to be prescribed by law.

Fourth Amendment

The right of the people to be secure in their persons, houses, papers, and effects, against unreasonable searches and seizures, shall not be violated, and no Warrants shall issue, but upon probable cause, supported by Oath or affirmation, and particularly describing the place to be searched, and the persons or things to be seized.

Fifth Amendment

No person shall be held to answer for a capital, or otherwise infamous crime, unless on a presentment or indictment of a Grand Jury, except in cases arising in the land or naval forces, or in the Militia, when in actual service in time of War or public danger; nor shall any person be subject for the same offence to be twice put in jeopardy of life or limb; nor shall be compelled in any criminal case to be a witness against himself, nor be deprived of life, liberty, or property, without due process of law; nor shall private property be taken for public use, without just compensation.

Sixth Amendment

In all criminal prosecutions, the accused shall enjoy the right to a speedy and public trial, by an impartial jury of the State and district wherein the crime shall have been committed, which district shall have been previously ascertained by law, and to be informed of the nature and cause of the accusation; to be confronted with the witnesses against him; to have compulsory process for obtaining witnesses in his favor, and to have the Assistance of Counsel for his defence.

Seventh Amendment

In Suits at common law, where the value in controversy shall exceed twenty dollars, the right of trial by jury shall be preserved, and no fact tried by a jury, shall be otherwise re-examined in any Court of the United States, than according to the rules of the common law.

Eighth Amendment

Excessive bail shall not be required, nor excessive fines imposed, nor cruel and unusual punishments inflicted.

Ninth Amendment

The enumeration in the Constitution, of certain rights, shall not be construed to deny or disparage others retained by the people.

Tenth Amendment

The powers not delegated to the United States by the Constitution, nor prohibited by it to the States, are reserved to the States respectively, or to the people.

Study Questions

1. What, if anything, does the First Amendment explicitly state about individual states having a state church?

2. What rights must the federal government protect for a person accused of a crime?

3. Which of the following statements best summarizes how the framers intended the Constitution to function? (Refer especially to the Declaration of Independence, para. 2; the Preamble to the U.S. Constitution; and the Ninth Amendment.)

   A. The Constitution creates rights by declaring that people have specified rights, such as those listed in the first ten amendments (also known as the Bill of Rights).

   B. The Constitution takes power that originates with the people and grants it, in specifically limited ways, to various parts of the government for the service of the people.

4. Explain your answer to question 3.

5. How are the respective authorities of state governments and the federal government related, according to the Constitution and the Ninth and Tenth Amendments?

Eleventh (1798) and Twelfth (1804) Amendments

The Articles of Confederation had been rejected in part because that charter could not be revised except by the unanimous consent of all states. The U.S. Constitution, by contrast, required only a three-fourths majority of the states for an amendment to be ratified. Following the Bill of Rights, the next amendment to be ratified was the Eleventh, addressing the balance between federal and state court jurisdictions. Soon after came the Twelfth, which modified the procedure for electing the president.

Eleventh Amendment

(proposed, 1794; ratified, 1798)

The Judicial power of the United States shall not be construed to extend to any suit in law or equity, commenced or prosecuted against one of the United States by Citizens of another State, or by Citizens or Subjects of any Foreign State.

Twelfth Amendment

(proposed, 1803; ratified, 1804)

The Electors shall meet in their respective states, and vote by ballot for President and Vice-President, one of whom, at least, shall not be an inhabitant of the same state with themselves; they shall name in their ballots the person voted for as President, and in distinct ballots the person voted for as Vice-President, and they shall make distinct lists of all persons voted for as President, and of all persons voted for as Vice-President, and of the number of votes for each, which lists they shall sign and certify, and transmit sealed to the seat of the government of the United States, directed to the President of the Senate;—The President of the Senate shall, in the presence of the Senate and House of Representatives, open all the certificates and the votes shall then be counted;—The person having the greatest number of votes for President, shall be the President, if such number be a majority of the whole number of Electors appointed; and if no person have such majority, then from the persons having the highest numbers not exceeding three on the list of those voted for as President, the House of Representatives shall choose immediately, by ballot, the President. But in choosing the President, the votes shall be taken by states, the representation from each state having one vote; a quorum for this purpose shall consist of a member or members from two-thirds of the states, and a majority of all the states shall be necessary to a choice. And if the House of Representatives shall not choose a President whenever the right of choice shall devolve upon them, before the fourth day of March next following, then the Vice-President shall act as President, as in the case of the death or other constitutional disability of the President.—The person having the greatest number of votes as Vice-President, shall be the Vice-President, if such number be a majority of the whole number of Electors appointed, and if no person have a majority, then from the two highest numbers on the list, the Senate shall choose the Vice-President; a quorum for the purpose shall consist of two-thirds of the whole number of Senators, and a majority of the whole number shall be necessary to a choice. But no person constitutionally ineligible to the office of President shall be eligible to that of Vice-President of the United States.

Study Questions

1. In what way does the Eleventh Amendment strengthen the power of state courts? (Hint: Review the Tenth Amendment and consider its relation to the Eleventh.)

2. In 1896, Federalist Party candidate John Adams received the most votes for president, and Republican Party candidate Thomas Jefferson received the second most; the result was that Adams became president and Jefferson became vice president, despite their partisan differences. In 1800, two Republican candidates—Thomas Jefferson and Aaron Burr—tied, requiring the House of Representatives to determine which one would be president. In what ways does the Twelfth Amendment help presidential elections work more smoothly than they had in 1796 and 1800?

U.S. Congress, Homestead Act (1862)

Prior to the Civil War, the House of Representatives passed several bills attempting to open western lands for settlement. The Senate withheld support from most of these. Even when both houses of Congress agreed to a homestead bill in 1860, President James Buchanan vetoed it. The resistance centered on the slavery question: would the settlement of western territories lead to the formation of more slave states, or more free states? The two factions were delicately balanced, and any change in federal land policy could have far-reaching implications. By 1862, however, the slavery question had a clear answer, at least in the Union: slavery was on its way to extinction. President Lincoln signed the Homestead Act, opening up western lands for settlement.

An Act to Secure Homesteads to Actual Settlers on the Public Domain

SEC. 1. Be it enacted by the Senate and House of Representatives of the United States of America in Congress assembled, That any person who is the head of a family, or who has arrived at the age of twenty-one years, and is a citizen of the United States, or who shall have filed his declaration of intention to become such, as required by the naturalization laws of the United States, and who has never borne arms against the United States Government or given aid and comfort to its enemies, shall, from and after the first January, eighteen hundred and sixty-three, be entitled to enter one quarter section or a less quantity of unappropriated public lands, upon which said person may have filed a preemption claim, or which may at the time the application is made, be subject to preemption at one dollar and twenty-five cents, or less, per acre; or eighty acres or less of such unappropriated lands, at two dollars and fifty cents per acre, to be located in a body, in conformity to the legal subdivisions of the public lands, and after the same shall have been surveyed: Provided, That any person owning and residing on land may, under the provisions of this act, enter other land lying contiguous to his or her said land, which shall not, with the land so already owned and occupied, exceed in the aggregate one hundred and sixty acres.

SEC. 2. And be it further enacted, That the person applying for the benefit of this act shall, upon application to the register of the land office in which he or she is about to make such entry, make affidavit before the said register or receiver that he or she is the head of a family, or is twenty-one years or more of age, or shall have performed service in the army or navy of the United States, and that he has never borne arms against the Government of the United States or is given aid and comfort to its enemies, and that such application is made for his or her exclusive use and benefit, and that said entry is made for the purpose of actual settlement and cultivation, and not either directly or indirectly for the use or benefit of any other person or persons whomsoever; and upon filing the said affidavit with the register or receiver, and on payment of ten dollars, he or she shall thereupon be permitted to enter the quantity of land specified: Provided, however, That no certificate shall be given or patent to issued therefor until the expiration of five years from the date of such entry; and if, at the expiration of such time, or at any time within two years thereafter, the person making such entry; or, if he be dead, his widow; or in case of her death, his heirs or devisee; or in case of a widow making such entry, her heirs or devisee, in case of her death; shall prove by two credible witnesses that he, she, or they have resided upon or cultivated the same for the term of five years immediately succeeding the time of filing the affidavit aforesaid, and shall make affidavit that no part of said land has, been alienated, and that he has borne true allegiance to the Government of the United States; then, in such case, he, she, or they, if at that time a citizen of the United States, shall be entitled to a patent, as in other cases provided for by law. . . .

SEC. 5. And be it further enacted, That if, at any time after the filing of the affidavit, as required in the second section of this act, and before the expiration of the five years aforesaid, it shall be proven, after due notice to the settler, to the satisfaction of the register of the land office, that the person having filed such affidavit shall have actually changed his or her residence, or abandoned the said land for more than six months at any time, then and in that event the land so entered shall revert to the government.

SEC. 6. And be it further enacted, That no individual shall be permitted to acquire title to more than one quarter section under the provisions of this act; . . . [and], further, That no person who has served, or may hereafter serve, for a period of not less than fourteen days in the army or navy of the United States, either regular or volunteer, under the laws thereof, during the existence of an actual war, domestic or foreign, shall be deprived of the benefits of this act on account of not having attained the age of twenty-one years. . . .

APPROVED, May 20, 1862.

Study Questions

1. Who was eligible to claim a homestead, and who was not? Consider what this reveals about the historical context in which this law was enacted.

2. What purpose was served by requiring homesteaders to reside on and cultivate their land for a minimum of five years?

Abraham Lincoln, "Gettysburg Address" (1863)

In July 1863, the Confederacy launched a bold attack into Union territory at Gettysburg, Pennsylvania. The Union repelled the invasion, but not without significant carnage on both sides. In November of that year, the bloody battlefield was transformed into a cemetery for burying fallen soldiers from both armies. At the dedication ceremony, President Lincoln delivered a few brief remarks, which constitute one of the best known speeches in American history.

Fourscore and seven years ago, our fathers brought forth on this continent a new nation, conceived in liberty and dedicated to the proposition that all men are created equal. Now we are engaged in a great civil war, testing whether that nation, or any nation so conceived and so dedicated, can long endure. We are met on a great battle-field of that war. We have come to dedicate a portion of that field as a final resting-place for those who here gave their lives that that nation might live. It is altogether fitting and proper that we should do this. But in a larger sense, we cannot dedicate, we cannot consecrate, we cannot hallow this ground. The brave men, living and dead, who struggled here, have consecrated it far above our poor power to add or detract. The world will little note, nor long remember, what we say here, but it can never forget what they did here. It is for us, the living, rather to be dedicated here to the unfinished work which they who fought here have thus far so nobly advanced. It is rather for us to be here dedicated to the great task remaining before us,—that from these honored dead we take increased devotion to that cause for which they gave the last full measure of devotion,—that we here highly resolve that these dead shall not have died in vain,—that this nation, under God, shall have a new birth of freedom,—and that government of the people, by the people, for the people, shall not perish from the earth.

Study Questions

1. "Score" is an old-fashioned term for the number twenty. To which event was Lincoln referring, when he directed his audience back "fourscore and seven years ago"?

2. What did Lincoln hope would "not perish from the earth"—and why was he so passionate about this?

Reconstruction Amendments (1865, 1868, 1870)

The Constitution of 1787 included several compromises regarding slavery. The Emancipation Proclamation and the Union victory in the Civil War led to three constitutional amendments, known as the Reconstruction Amendments, which ended slavery and provided for civil rights and voting privileges for the recently freed slaves.

Thirteenth Amendment

(proposed, 1865; ratified, 1865)

Section 1. Neither slavery nor involuntary servitude, except as a punishment for crime whereof the party shall have been duly convicted, shall exist within the United States, or any place subject to their jurisdiction.

Section 2. Congress shall have power to enforce this article by appropriate legislation.

Fourteenth Amendment

(proposed, 1866; ratified, 1868)

Section 1. All persons born or naturalized in the United States, and subject to the jurisdiction thereof, are citizens of the United States and of the State wherein they reside. No State shall make or enforce any law which shall abridge the privileges or immunities of citizens of the United States; nor shall any State deprive any person of life, liberty, or property, without due process of law; nor deny to any person within its jurisdiction the equal protection of the laws.

Section 2. Representatives shall be apportioned among the several States according to their respective numbers, counting the whole number of persons in each State, excluding Indians not taxed. But when the right to vote at any election for the choice of electors for President and Vice President of the United States, Representatives in Congress, the Executive and Judicial officers of a State, or the members of the Legislature thereof, is denied to any of the male inhabitants of such State, being twenty-one years of age, and citizens of the United States, or in any way abridged, except for participation in rebellion, or other crime, the basis of representation therein shall be reduced in the proportion which the number of such male citizens shall bear to the whole number of male citizens twenty-one years of age in such State.

Section 3. No person shall be a Senator or Representative in Congress, or elector of President and Vice President, or hold any office, civil or military, under the United States, or under any State, who, having previously taken an oath, as a member of Congress, or as an officer of the United States, or as a member of any State legislature, or as an executive or judicial officer of any State, to support the Constitution of the United States, shall have engaged in insurrection or rebellion against the same, or given aid or comfort to the enemies thereof. But Congress may by a vote of two-thirds of each House, remove such disability.

Section 4. The validity of the public debt of the United States, authorized by law, including debts incurred for payment of pensions and bounties for services in suppressing insurrection or rebellion, shall not be questioned. But neither the United States nor any State shall assume or pay any debt or obligation incurred in aid of insurrection or rebellion against the United States, or any claim for the loss or emancipation of any slave; but all such debts, obligations and claims shall be held illegal and void.

Section 5. The Congress shall have power to enforce, by appropriate legisla-tion, the provisions of this article.

Fifteenth Amendment

(proposed, 1869; ratified, 1870)

Section 1. The right of citizens of the United States to vote shall not be denied or abridged by the United States or by any State on account of race, color, or previous condition of servitude.

Section 2. The Congress shall have power to enforce this article by appropriate legislation.

Study Questions

1. What does the Thirteenth Amendment prohibit?

2. Which rights does the Fourteenth Amendment guarantee in Section 1?

3. Why is it significant that Section 2 of the Fourteenth Amendment apportions congressional representation in terms of "the whole number of persons in each State"? (Hint: Review the U.S. Constitution, Article 1, Section 2, paragraph 3, on pp. 26–27).

4. What does the Fifteenth Amendment guarantee?

5. How did the Thirteenth, Fourteenth, and Fifteenth Amendments (together known as the Reconstruction Amendments) transform American identity?

PART 1:

America in the Gilded Age

1877–1901

The Gilded Age: The Building of Industrial America

In some periods of American history, great political leaders stand out for their ideas and actions that set the course for the nation. Such was the case, for example, with George Washington, John Adams, and Thomas Jefferson—the nation's first three presidents. The decades preceding the Civil War are named "the Jacksonian Era" in honor of President Andrew Jackson, whose strong personality led to a complete realignment of politics during the 1830s. It happened again during the presidency of Abraham Lincoln in the 1860s. After Lincoln, however, a series of less-than-exemplary presidents followed; more precisely stated, the collective American memory has forgotten who those presidents were and what they did.

Politics during the late 1800s centered around controversies that today seem quaintly old-fashioned, if not downright boring: civil service reform, tariff rates, and the coinage of silver. Historians refer to this period as "the Gilded Age," a phrase borrowed from the title of an 1873 novel by Mark Twain and Charles Dudley Warner. Even that book was no *Adventures of Huckleberry Finn*. And yet, Twain and Dudley hit the nail on the head in some respects. American corporations were acquiring unprecedented levels of wealth, and some capitalists were losing their scruples along the way. By the century's end, sociologist Thorstein Veblen identified "conspicuous consumption" as a characteristic of this wealthy class (*Theory of the Leisure Class*, 1899):

> In order to gain and to hold the esteem of men it is not sufficient merely to possess wealth or power. The wealth or power must be put in evidence, for esteem is awarded only on evidence. And not only does the evidence of wealth serve to impress one's importance on others and to keep their sense of his importance alive and alert, but it is of scarcely less use in building up and preserving one's self-complacency.

The Gilded Age, therefore, has often been regarded as not merely a time of wealth-production, but also a time of superfluous wealth-flaunting. "To gild" means "to layer something with gold," but what if gold itself is gilded? William Shakespeare portrayed such ostentatious embellishment in *King John* (1595)—an apt description, in the view of many historians, for America's own Gilded Age:

> Therefore, to be possess'd with double pomp,
> To guard a title that was rich before,
> To gild refined gold, to paint the lily,
> To throw a perfume on the violet,
> To smooth the ice, or add another hue
> Unto the rainbow, or with taper-light
> To seek the beauteous eye of heaven to garnish,
> Is wasteful and ridiculous excess.

But did Americans really become "wasteful and ridiculous" during the Gilded Age? A different way of telling the story would be to emphasize the manner in which captains of industry not only padded their own pocketbooks but also benefited others. As the profits of industrial monopolies grew, wages generally also increased among the working class. As mass-production lowered the per unit cost of manufactured goods, consumer prices fell. Potentially, everyone would benefit. The protective tariff, similarly, offered benefits not only to the investors who received dividends when local producers profited, but also to the wage workers who shared in those same profits. The Gilded Age, therefore, does not fit into neat and tidy categories, as if the wealthy always prospered and the poor always suffered.

Indeed, there is strong evidence that all social classes benefited in times of economic boom. On the other hand, the lower classes tended to suffer disproportionately during economic downturns, experiencing a decline in wages if not unemployment. Those who did have jobs often worked ten to twelve hours per day, six days per week, in factories where they repeated the same arduous—and often dangerous—task minute after minute. Often whole families, including children as young as ten years old, labored in the meat packing plants or coal mines, trying to cover their living costs and escape the seemingly endless cycle of debt.

In 1869, a secret fraternity known as the Knights of Labor began planning ways to improve the lot of laborers. Growing to a membership of 700,000 by 1886, the Knights focused especially on improving working conditions in the railroad industry. Terrence Powderly hoped the Knights could transform capitalism into a cooperative ownership by the workers, but his socialist visions never materialized. The organization fell apart by the end of the century, as members challenged Powderly's leadership and led a haphazard series of strikes, several of which turned violent.

In December 1886, New York cigar maker Samuel Gompers established an alternative organization, the American Federation of Labor, which brought together skilled workers from a variety of trade unions. Unlike the Knights, the AFL did not seek to transform the nation's political economy. Rather, Gompers sought to work within the capitalist system, primarily through the tool of collective bargaining. The AFL attempted to acquire higher wages and shorter working days for its members, while also respecting corporate leadership.

The captains of industry, meanwhile, offered a mixed response. For example, Andrew Carnegie sincerely sought to offer his workers a fair contract. On the other hand, Carnegie did not hesitate to hire the Pinkerton Detectives as a private police force to protect his steel mills from violent protesters. John D. Rockefeller, the founder of Standard Oil, also had a philanthropic spirit, but his endorsement of *laissez-faire* economics was subject to criticism, particularly during the Progressive Era (the early 1900s) when the federal government sought to break up the Standard Oil monopoly. A few academics, such as William Graham Sumner at Yale, unabashedly promoted an extreme *laissez-faire* philosophy, called social Darwinism—the notion that the economy fairs best when competition is fierce enough to promote the survival of only the fittest companies.

For its part, the federal government imposed few regulations on industry during the Gilded Age. First, there was the question of whether the government properly had a role in regulating the economic liberties of private entrepreneurs. Second, there was the question of whether the government had the means to do so. The Gilded Age, therefore, marked a time of puzzling contrasts. During 2008–2009, the federal government appropriated trillions of dollars to bail out failing banks and major industries, whereas in 1895, it was the finance captain J.P. Morgan who bailed out Uncle Sam! Yes, unprecedented economic progress at times was experienced across all social classes, yet monopolies amassed more power than the government and the unions combined. This was America during the Gilded Age.

The last of the Gilded Age presidents, William McKinley, brought America into a new order of world affairs. In part to protect business interests oversees, McKinley led the nation into a war against Spain in 1898. As a result, the old Monroe Doctrine of isolationism gave way to a new interventionism that continues to characterize American foreign policy even today. By the close of the nineteenth century, America had become an industrial giant; in the twentieth century (and beyond), its military power likewise would become a major player in global affairs.

Chronological Overview: The Gilded Age

1877   A railroad strike in Martinsburg, West Virginia, spreads to Philadelphia, Pittsburgh, Louisville, Cincinnati, and Chicago, becoming the first nation-wide labor protest in American history.

1881   John Rockefeller establishes the Standard Oil Trust, a legal device to bypass existing anti-monopoly regulations.

1883   The Pendleton Civil Service Act prohibits political bribes and institutes merit-based procedures for the selection of appointed office-holders.

1886   Immigrant laborers rally in Chicago's Haymarket Square to protest the police for killing a striker the preceding day. A riot results.

        Samuel Gompers founds the American Federation of Labor.

1887   The Interstate Commerce Act requires railroads to charge reasonable rates and forbids discounts to preferred customers.

1890   The Sherman Anti-Trust Act forbids horizontal-combination (industry-wide) monopolies. Corporations adapt by forming highly productive vertical combinations, which internalize the costs of all production stages and result, ironically, in the growth of the very companies targeted by the Act.

        The McKinley Tariff increases import taxes to record levels, justified by the expectation that domestic producers—both capitalists and laborers—will benefit from the protection these taxes provide against the low-priced imports of their foreign competitors.

1891   Western farmers form the Populist Party, challenging the two-party system and seeking federal protection from corporate monopolies, the nationalization of railroads, a graduated income tax, and the coinage of silver (since inflation would ease the burden of debts).

1892   Steelworkers at Carnegie's Homestead, Pennsylvania, plant go on strike in protest of wage reductions. General Manager Henry Frick, unmoved, closes the plant. A battle between strikers and state militia ensues.

        Chicago hosts the World Columbian Exhibition, commemorating the 400th anniversary of Columbus's discovery of America by displaying works of technological progress, including the first ferris wheel.

1894   Pullman Palace Car Company factory workers and United Railway unionists organize a strike in protest of declining wages. President Grover Cleveland intervenes by ordering the U.S. Army to operate the trains.

1898   The United States wages the Spanish-American War to purge Spanish power from the colonies of Cuba and the Philippines, both for the protection of human rights and the advancement of American trade interests.

Presidents of the Gilded Age, 1877–1901

Rutherford B. Hayes (Republican—Ohio), 1877–1881

America stood at a crossroads during the presidential election of 1876. Ulysses S. Grant, the military general to whom Confederate Gen. Robert E. Lee had surrendered at the close of the Civil War in 1865, now was serving as United States president. Southerners of that generation had been twice defeated, first by the Union army and second by congressional Republicans, who imposed reconstruction regulations that appeared to punish the South. Federal troops still were stationed in the South, and federal agents still oversaw the elections taking place there. Neither Grant nor his Republican Party was popular among southern whites. But northerners also had reason to dislike Grant, for he denied or belittled accusations that leading congressional Republicans and members of his Treasury Department had participated in corrupt economic dealings. Many voters, both North and South, settled upon Samuel J. Tilden, a New York Democrat, as the next president. Tilden had reformed state politics, breaking up Boss Tweed's political machine, and promised to do the same in Washington. He also would bring to a close the Republican dynasty of Reconstruction and permit the Democratic South to arise once more from the ashes of the Civil War.

Alas, this was not to be. Although Tilden secured a majority of the popular vote, he failed to win a majority in the electoral college. In fact, neither did his opponent, Rutherford B. Hayes, the Republican governor of Ohio. Election scandals left nineteen votes undetermined, and these votes would break the stalemate between the two candidates. To allot the contested votes, Congress appointed a special electoral commission, consisting of seven Republicans, seven Democrats, and one U.S. Supreme Court justice, a Republican. An 8–7 party-line vote determined the outcome: Hayes would be the nation's next president. But that did not immediately end the matter. Congressional Democrats threatened a filibuster inside the Capitol Building, while rumors of another civil war circulated outside. Somehow—historians are not sure how—a deal was struck giving the victory to Hayes in exchange for the removal of federal troops from the statehouses of South Carolina and Louisiana. Reconstruction was over. A new era, the Gilded Age, was about to begin.

Hayes sought to uphold high principles while in office. His mother had instilled him with religious virtue from childhood. In 1852, Hayes married Lucy Webb, an anti-slavery activist. As a Whig, and later a Republican, Hayes supported the policies of Abraham Lincoln, for whom he campaigned in 1860. After serving in the Civil War, for which he attained the rank of Major General, Hayes was elected to Congress in 1865. He joined the radical wing of the Republican Party, which supported civil rights for the recently freed slaves and punitive measures against the former Confederate states. During his presidency, Hayes repeatedly faced off against congressional Democrats.

Class and ethnicity characterized the partisan divisions of the day, with Hayes exercising the veto and Congress at times over-powering his veto with a two-thirds super-majority. For example, Congress passed the Bland-Allison Act over Hayes's veto in 1878, requiring the Treasury Department to purchase between two and four million dollars' worth of silver each month. Hayes feared this would feed inflation and ruin the economy, so he ordered the Treasury to purchase only the minimum amount. Meanwhile, debtors felt squeezed by the short supply of currency and questioned whether the president cared about their needs. Hayes also lost favor with the working class when he dispatched federal troops to restore order amid labor strikes in West Virginia and Pennsylvania.

As for ethnic tensions, Hayes showed a sensitivity unusual for his day. He promoted civil liberties for African Americans, although he conceded that their exercise of suffrage rights should be preceded by educational improvements. Hayes also admitted, in his first inaugural address, that white Americans had broken their promises to Indians. Moreover, Hayes vetoed an attempt by Congress to ban Chinese immigration, a bill that violated the 1868 Burlingame Treaty.

Despite honorable attempts to uphold what he believed to be sound moral principles, Hayes suffered ridicule from his opponents, who branded him "His Fraudulency" and "Rutherfraud" in reference to the apparent stealing of an election that arguably should have gone to Tilden. Having guided the nation through a delicate time, Hayes sought to do what he believed to be moral and just. In his final month as president, Hayes banned the sale of alcohol at military posts, a move likely suggested by his wife "Lemonade Lucy," a vocal supporter of the temperance movement. Those who today would fault Hayes for being too moralistic should remember that he was, if anything, ahead of his time, for it was President Hayes who signed into law a bill that permitted female attorneys to argue before the U.S. Supreme Court.

James A. Garfield (Republican—Ohio), 1881

President Hayes identified James A. Garfield as "the ideal candidate" to succeed him into office. For Garfield, however, the road to prominence had been long and arduous. Born in a log cabin outside Cleveland, Ohio, in 1831, Garfield spent his youth struggling against poverty after the untimely death of his father. At age sixteen, he began working on the Erie Canal, but proved so clumbsy that he fell into the water at least fourteen times—leaving him seriously infirm with chills and a fever. His mother nursed him back to health and packed him off to an academy, where he supported himself through carpentry and teaching.

In 1850, Garfield converted to the Disciples of Christ, a "no creed but the Bible" denomination which he later served as a lay preacher. The religious fervor he soaked up during those years fostered a strong disapproval of slavery. In 1856, Garfield became a professor, and eventually the president, at Western Reserve College near Cleveland. Election to the Ohio Senate in 1859 brought Garfield into a political career that would enable him to do something about slavery. He supported Abraham Lincoln's candidacy in 1860 and, adjusting his pacifist convictions, endorsed the Union cause in the Civil War as a necessary means for freedom to triumph over slavery. In fact, Garfield was commissioned into the army, achieving the rank of major general by 1863, when he resigned to take office in the U.S. House of Representatives, where he served for the next eighteen years.

By the 1870s, Garfield was recognized as one of the greatest financial minds in the House. He stood firmly for "honest money," by which he meant free trade and hard currency. Garfield believed that inflation, particularly when spawned by the coinage of silver, was nothing less than robbery, since it devalued the coins that people already held. "Paper money," insisted Garfield, "must represent what it professes on its face. I do not wish to hold in my hands the printed lies of the government."

Garfield supported congressional efforts to end the abuses of patronage by adopting civil service reform legislation, but his own election to the presidency in 1880 placed him unwittingly in the position of returning political favors by nominating his supporters for government posts. As Garfield tried to navigate through the confusion, one office-seeker became excessively frustrated and shot him in the back. Doctors treated the wounded president for over two months, never discovering where the bullet had lodged. In September 1881, before completing his first year as president, Garfield died of blood poisoning.

Garfield, the "preacher president," left a legacy that reformers packaged into a recipe for adopting civil service legislation. It was, they could say, a disgruntled office-seeker from a corrupt political machine that had shot the president. The 1883 Pendleton Civil Service Reform Act, enacted as a memorial to Garfield, prohibited political tests for federal offices and instituted instead merit-based exams. Though serving less than a year in the nation's highest office, Garfield left his mark as an unusual president—the only who has been a preacher, the first who was left-handed, and the second to be assassinated in office. Garfield also was an unusually savvy campaigner who courted the people not only in English but also in Spanish.

Chester A. Arthur (Republican—New York), 1881–1885

When the 1880 Republican convention nominated Chester A. Arthur for the vice presidency, reformers had reason to be alarmed; three years later, those same reformers would have reason to celebrate. Arthur had ascended into politics under the tutelage of Senator Roscoe Conkling, master of the New York political machine. His career was checkered with charges of corruption. In 1878, suspicion led President Hayes to depose Arthur from his patronage post in the New York Customs House.

Perhaps the only reason he slipped by as a vice presidential nominee two years later was that everyone knew that the vice president does not exercise much power anyway. At least that was what reformer Edward L. Godkin thought, remarking, "There is no place in which [Arthur's] power of mischief will be so small as in the vice presidency."

When the death of President Garfield elevated Arthur into the presidency, he surprised everyone by championing patronage reform. In 1883, Arthur signed into law the Pendleton Civil Service Act, turning his back on the machines that had given his political career its start. Arthur also vetoed the Rivers and Harbors Act of 1882, a pork-barrel measure designed by certain congressmen to reward their political supporters rather than benefit the nation as a whole. Like Hayes, Arthur also vetoed a restriction of Chinese immigration that would have violated an existing treaty with China.

Arthur was less successful in his aim to lower tariffs, for although Congress passed a tariff reduction, the bill included so many complexities as to be ineffective. This "Mongrel Tariff" of 1883, as critics called it, actually raised tax rates for some imports, while only reducing the average by about 1.5%. With many tariffs remaining at 35% to 40%, protectionism remained the dominant philosophy. President Arthur, however, sought to loosen trade restrictions by another means as well. Bypassing Congress, he instructed the secretary of state to negotiate reciprocal trade agreements with nations that supplied raw materials vital to the American economy.

Arthur worked only six hours per day, from 10 a.m. to 4 p.m. His night life exemplified the new prosperity of the Gilded Age: fine dining while dressed in impeccable fashion. Behind the outward show, however, Arthur's heart ached over the loss of his wife Ellen, who had died in 1880. The president himself also was slowly dying of kidney disease, which took its toll in 1886.

The likes of George Washington, Thomas Jefferson, Andrew Jackson, and Abraham Lincoln had not held the presidency for many years. Nor did any of the Gilded Age presidents foreshadow the dynamism of a Roosevelt, a Kennedy, or a Reagan. As some observers have summarized, presidential elections during the late 1800s were boring contests between "tweedle dee" and "tweedle dum." Fulfilling that pattern, Arthur left office with but a modest legacy: he would be remembered as a politician who owed his career to corruption and yet signed the Pendleton Act to purge federal jobs from corrupt influences.

Grover Cleveland (Democrat—New York), 1885–1889, 1893–1897

Grover Cleveland stands unique among Gilded Ages presidents. He is the only president ever to serve two non-consecutive terms and the only Democrat to be elected between James Buchanan (1856) and Woodrow Wilson (1912). He also excercised the veto an astonishing 584 times, or about once every five days. Arthur, by contrast, had vetoed only 12 bills. In his first term alone, Cleveland vetoed over twice as many bills as all of his predecessors combined. If Mount Rushmore had included a Gilded Age president, it certainly would have been Grover Cleveland, the one man who transformed the office into something that fit a grander vision than what he had inherited from his predecessors.

As sheriff of Erie County, New York, in the early 1870s, Cleveland earned a reputation as a straight shooter who had no toleration for political graft. His political career continued with the mayorship of Buffalo and, in 1882, the governorship of New York. Two years later, Cleveland had a strong reputation as a reformer who cleared the civil service rolls of corrupt appointments and also prevented legislators from wasting public funds on personal pet projects.

As president, Cleveland took seriously his oath to uphold the U.S. Constitution. He rejected paternalistic interpretations of the Constitution, as if the job of the federal government was to care for the people's basic needs, and urged people to find their own solutions to emergencies. For example, Cleveland vetoed an 1887 farm relief bill that supporters argued was necessary assistance in time of a drought. Cleveland also vetoed hundreds of Civil War pension awards because he found them to be fraudulent. (Many of the intended recipients had never even served in the war.) Typically, Cleveland made statements explaining the constitutional basis for his vetoes.

During Cleveland's presidency, tensions between capital and labor escalated. In 1886, a demonstration for the eight-hour work day turned riotous in Chicago's Haymarket Square. In 1894, a Pullman Railroad strike also turned violent. Cleveland was a big business, small government Democrat—a combination that in later decades would almost universally be considered more fitting for the rival Republican Party. When the Pullman strikers did not return to work, a post office car was hitched to the train. Now that the local disturbance had become a federal issue, Cleveland took action. "If it takes the entire army and navy . . . to deliver a postcard in Chicago," he said, "that card will be delivered." On Cleveland's order, the U.S. Army got the trains moving again.

Cleveland worked hard during his first term to reduce tariffs, believing that taxes on imports unfairly favored local producers while passing on costs to consumers. He also objected to the pork-barrel schemes by which congressmen plotted to spend the revenue raised through import taxes. Cleveland envisioned the government as simple, lean, and fair. Republicans, meanwhile, championed high tariffs as a necessary protection for capitalists and laborers alike against foreign competition. In the election of 1888, the Republican message put Cleveland out of office, but Cleveland made a remarkable comeback in 1892, winning election to a delayed second term.

Even the Panic of 1893—the most severe economic downturn the nation had yet experienced—did not prompt Cleveland to compromise his principles. During that singular year, seventy-four railroads failed, together with some six hundred banks. As people rushed to redeem silver certificates for gold at the U.S. Treasury, Cleveland urged Congress to repeal the 1890 Sherman Silver Purchase Act. Even so, the Treasury nearly ran out of gold by 1895, leaving the president with few options but to borrow from a group of bankers led by financier J.P. Morgan. Such was the Gilded Age: corporate America had greater wealth than the U.S. government. Grover Cleveland, a strict constitutionalist, did not see this as a problem. The government had a small but important job to do, and his responsibility as president was to carry out that job without assuming additional projects at additional taxpayer expense.

Benjamin Harrison (Republican—Indiana), 1889–1893

One hundred years after George Washington's inauguration as the first president under the U.S. Constitution, Benjamin Harrison took the same oath of office. His great-grandfather, also named Benjamin, had signed the Declaration of Independence. His grandfather, "Old Tippecanoe" Harrison, served as the nation's ninth president. Benjamin Harrison continued the family tradition of public service. Although losing the popular vote to Grover Cleveland in 1888, he won a majority of the electoral votes, becoming the nation's twenty-third president.

Unlike Chester Arthur, Harrison was not much of a socialite; some thought him as cold as an iceberg. But Harrison had distinguished himself in the debating society at Miami University in Oxford, Ohio. Public speaking was his forté, a skill he applied fruitfully during his career as a lawyer. Although he initially resisted political invitations, Harrison agreed to run for Indiana governor in 1876—the same post his grandfather had held during the War of 1812. Woefully unprepared for campaign mudslinging, the grandson lost. In 1881, however, the Republican majority in the state legislature appointed Harrison to the U.S. Senate. (Senators were not elected by popular vote until after the ratification of the Seventeenth Amendment in 1913.) When the Democrats took control of the legislature, Harrison's chances of re-election evaporated and he returned to private life.

Meanwhile, the Republican Party identified Harrison as a candidate to wrestle the presidency from Grover Cleveland. Harrison launched a campaign from his front-porch, delivering speeches to delegates who visited his home during the 1888 election cycle. Not a physically imposing person (standing only five feet, six inches tall), he relied on his well-honed gifts as a persuasive speaker. Behind the scenes, political strategist Matt Quay secured votes for Harrison by making promises Harrison himself never issued. While Harrison attributed the victory to divine providence, Quay quietly took credit for his own machinations.

Once elected, Harrison pursued the Republican agenda. In 1890, he signed into law the McKinley Tariff, the Sherman Silver Purchase Act, and the Sherman Anti-Trust Act. The McKinley bill increased tariffs to record levels, driving consumer prices sky-high and giving Cleveland leverage for a re-election campaign in 1892. Cleveland also opposed the silver act, persuading Congress to repeal it in 1893. The anti-trust act enjoyed the longest staying power of the three, but it was not effectively implemented until Theodore Roosevelt's administration a decade later.

Harrison, meanwhile, typified the Gilded Age, with his thick sideburns and gentlemanly hobbies—ranging from cigar-smoking to duck-hunting. Even so, Harrison did not always find it easy to live up to that image. For example, he became the subject of a political lampoon when news broke in December 1889 that on his recent racoon-hunting venture he had accidentally shot a pig instead. More substantive criticism came from the Populist Movement, which faulted Washington elites for being out of step with common farmers and laborers. To this, however, Harrison had a ready answer. At an 1898 celebration of George Washington's birthday in Chicago, then ex-President Harrison said:

> The great bulk of our people are lovers of justice. They do not believe that poverty is a virtue or property a crime. They believe in an equality of opportunity and not of dollars. But there must be no handicapping of the dull brother and no chicanery or fraud or shirking. . . . The men who have wealth must not hide it from the tax gatherer, and flaunt it on the street.

Entitled "The Obligations of Wealth," Harrison's message called for proportionate taxing of the wealthy in order to forestall the more radical upheaval of Gilded Age society that populist and socialist reformers envisioned. His speech stands as a monument to remind future generations that the wealthy do not always seek to get ahead at the expense of others, but nor do they wish to fall behind at their own expense; the obligations of wealth must be delicately proportioned in order for the nation to prosper. One of those obligations, said Harrison, was leadership: "The men of wealth in our great communities should lead the movement."

William McKinley (Republican—Ohio), 1897–1901

William McKinley served under Col. Rutherford B. Hayes in the Civil War, being promoted to the rank of Major in 1865. A devout Methodist, McKinley was called by his contemporaries a "Christian gentleman." He cared dearly for his wife Ida, who suffered from epilepsy.

In politics, McKinley was best known for his promotion of American nationalism through a high protective tariff, which he believed would prosper the workingman, the farmer, and the corporation all at once. As U.S. Senator, he sponsored the McKinley Tariff of 1890, setting taxes on imported woolen manufactures, tin plate, barley, and other goods at an average of 48%. His political opponents blamed the Panic of 1893 on the high tariff, leading to the law's repeal in 1894 and furthermore channeling agrarian unrest into the Populist Movement that supported Democrat William Jennings Bryan for the presidency in 1896.

McKinley's opponent Bryan boldly promoted bimetallism, the coinage of both gold and silver, in order to relieve farmers of their debts through inflation. McKinley's campaign manager, Marcus A. Hanna, responded by spinning the gold standard as the only way to protect worker's wages from inflation. Whereas Bryan said, "You shall not crucify mankind upon a cross of gold," the McKinley campaign warned of a devalued "57-cent dollar" if silver coinage were allowed to run wild. Voters responded with the election of McKinley by a generous margin.

The Spanish-American War (1898) transformed McKinley's presidency and set American foreign policy on a new path that would last into both the twentieth and the twenty-first centuries. Although McKinley initially expressed reluctance to become involved in the Cuban independence movement, once he committed the U.S. military to action against Spain he also promised liberation and protection to Cuba and the Philippines. The result was the emergence of an American empire overseas, built on Methodist moralism and Republican nationalism. Similar patterns of U.S. military intervention would be repeated throughout the Cold War of the late twentieth century.

After securing re-election in 1900, McKinley visited the Pan-American Exposition in Buffalo, New York. There he shook hands too readily with the public, allowing Leon Czolgosz, an unemployed mill worker who had been reading anarchist literature, to come close enough to fire two shots at point-blank range. Though McKinley had touted protectionism as an economic promise of prosperity for all Americans, his assassin represented a disgruntled working class that believed McKinley stood for selfish privilege.

American presidents after McKinley would more openly commit the federal government to regulating the economy in the name of benefiting the common worker. McKinley in a way represents the fading of the Gilded Age, an era in which the government had favored domestic producers through a mixture of high tariffs and laissez-faire domestic policies. His presidency marks a transition also in the realm of foreign affairs. By waging war against Spain, America left the isolationist Monroe Doctrine behind to gather dust in the annals of the nineteenth century; the nation henceforth would pursue a path toward becoming the policeman of the entire world. Cuba and the Philippines no longer were colonies of Spain, but instead were "protectorates" of the United States—colonies in a looser sense, receiving the promise of political self-determination while remaining under America's protective arm.

Study Questions

1. How did civil service reform and the tariff shape the presidency during the Gilded Age?

2. In what ways was Grover Cleveland unusual for a Gilded Age president?

3. What legacy would the Spanish-American War have for presidents following McKinley?

Supreme Court Decisions during the Gilded Age

Two major themes characterize the Supreme Court rulings of the Gilded Age. First, the Court applied the Fourteenth Amendment to a situation that had not been foremost on the minds of congressmen when they proposed that amendment. Congress intended the amendment to guarantee the full rights of citizenship to recently freed slaves, but the Court instead utilized the amendment to promote *laissez-faire* economics by protecting the rights of corporations and individuals to contract freely in the market without government interference. Second, when the Court did address the question of African American rights, it limited the Equal Protection clause of the Fourteenth Amendment enough to permit segregation, thus validating the regime of Jim Crow. Meanwhile, a few other cases confirmed that although church and state are distinct, America was founded generally as a Christian nation, with Christian morals shaping public policy.

1878   *Reynolds v. U.S.*: Although the First Amendment's Free Exercise clause permits Mormons to *believe* that polygamy is moral, it does not permit them to *practice* polygamy where it is prohibited by law; laws respecting monogamy serve a state interest consistent with the nation's heritage.

1892   *Holy Trinity Church v. U.S.*: The Court declared that "the United States is a Christian nation," exempting religious organizations from certain labor regulations that apply to secular organizations.

1895   *U.S. v E. C. Knight Co.*: The Sherman Anti-Trust Act applies only to businesses conducting interstate commerce, not to businesses engaged solely in production. Therefore, manufacturers may develop monopolies.

1895   *Income Tax Cases*: The federal income tax is unconstitutional.

1896   *Plessy v. Ferguson*: The Fourteenth Amendment does not restrict states from treating persons differently by race, so long as "separate but equal" facilities (in this instance, train seats) are provided.

1897   *Allgeyer v. Louisiana*: The Due Process clause of the Fourteenth Amendment protects "liberty of contract" between companies and their customers; the government may not regulate such contracts except to serve a compelling state interest.

1898   *Smyth v. Ames*: A state law fixing railroad rates violates the "liberty of contract" guaranteed under the Fourteenth Amendment.

Study Question

Review the Fourteenth Amendment for the phrases "due process" and "equal protection." Note that corporations are "legal persons" before the law. On that basis, explain how the Court reasoned that corporations have a right to *laissez-faire* economics.

Rutherford B. Hayes, Inaugural Address (1877)

In an inaugural address, a president greets both government officials and the American citizenry whom he has been elected to serve. For Rutherford B. Hayes, the task could not be taken lightly, for many Americans thought his election to be illegitimate. Southern whites, in particular, feared the continual control of the federal government by Republicans intent upon punishing the South for the Civil War. Hayes sought carefully to appease this constituency, while at the same time not neglecting the legitimate claims of African Americans, whom the amended U.S. Constitution now regarded as full citizens.

Fellow-Citizens:

We have assembled to repeat the public ceremonial, begun by Washington, observed by all my predecessors, and now a time-honored custom, which marks the commencement of a new term of the Presidential office. Called to the duties of this great trust, I proceed, in compliance with usage, to announce some of the leading principles, on the subjects that now chiefly engage the public attention, by which it is my desire to be guided in the discharge of those duties. I shall not undertake to lay down irrevocably principles or measures of administration, but rather to speak of the motives which should animate us, and to suggest certain important ends to be attained in accordance with our institutions and essential to the welfare of our country.

At the outset of the discussions which preceded the recent Presidential election it seemed to me fitting that I should fully make known my sentiments in regard to several of the important questions which then appeared to demand the consideration of the country. Following the example, and in part adopting the language, of one of my predecessors, I wish now, when every motive for misrepresentation has passed away, to repeat what was said before the election, trusting that my coun- trymen will candidly weigh and under- stand it, and that they will feel assured that the sentiments declared in accepting the nomination for the Presidency will be the standard of my conduct in the path before me, charged, as I now am, with the grave and difficult task of carrying them out in the practical administration of the Government so far as depends, under the Constitution and laws on the Chief Execut- ive of the nation.

The permanent pacification of the country upon such principles and by such measures as will secure the complete pro- tection of all its citizens in the free enjoyment of all their constitutional rights is now the one subject in our public affairs which all thoughtful and patriotic citizens regard as of supreme importance.

Many of the calamitous efforts of the tremendous revolution which has passed over the Southern States still remain. The immeasurable benefits which will surely follow, sooner or later, the hearty and gen- erous acceptance of the legitimate results of that revolution have not yet been real- ized. Difficult and embarrassing questions meet us at the threshold of this subject. The people of those States are still impov- erished, and the inestimable blessing of wise, honest, and peaceful local self-gov- ernment is not fully enjoyed. Whatever difference of opinion may exist as to the cause of this condition of things, the fact is clear that in the progress of events the time has come when such government is the imperative necessity required by all the varied interests, public and private, of those States. But it must not be forgotten that only a local government which recognizes and maintains inviolate the rights of all is a true self-government.

With respect to the two distinct races whose peculiar relations to each other have brought upon us the deplorable complications and perplexities which exist in those States, it must be a government which guards the interests of both races carefully and equally. It must be a government which submits loyally and heartily to the Constitution and the laws—the laws of the nation and the laws of the States themselves—accepting and obeying faithfully the whole Constitution as it is.

Resting upon this sure and substantial foundation, the superstructure of beneficent local governments can be built up, and not otherwise. In furtherance of such obedience to the letter and the spirit of the Constitution, and in behalf of all that its attainment implies, all so-called party interests lose their apparent importance, and party lines may well be permitted to fade into insignificance. The question we have to consider for the immediate welfare of those States of the Union is the question of government or no government; of social order and all the peaceful industries and the happiness that belongs to it, or a return to barbarism. It is a question in which every citizen of the nation is deeply interested, and with respect to which we ought not to be, in a partisan sense, either

Republicans or Democrats, but fellow-citizens and fellowmen, to whom the interests of a common country and a common humanity are dear.

The sweeping revolution of the entire labor system of a large portion of our country and the advance of 4,000,000 people from a condition of servitude to that of citizenship, upon an equal footing with their former masters, could not occur without presenting problems of the gravest moment, to be dealt with by the emancipated race, by their former masters, and by the General Government, the author of the act of emancipation. That it was a wise, just, and providential act, fraught with good for all concerned, is now generally conceded throughout the country. That a moral obligation rests upon the National Government to employ its constitutional power and influence to establish the rights of the people it has emancipated, and to protect them in the enjoyment of those rights when they are infringed or assailed, is also generally admitted.

The evils which afflict the Southern States can only be removed or remedied by the united and harmonious efforts of both races, actuated by motives of mutual sympathy and regard; and while in duty bound and fully determined to protect the rights of all by every constitutional means at the disposal of my Administration, I am sincerely anxious to use every legitimate influence in favor of honest and efficient local 'self'-government as the true resource of those States for the promotion of the contentment and prosperity of their citizens. In the effort I shall make to accomplish this purpose I ask the cordial cooperation of all who cherish an interest in the welfare of the country, trusting that party ties and the prejudice of race will be freely surrendered in behalf of the great purpose to be accomplished. In the important work of restoring the South it is not the political situation alone that merits attention. The material development of that section of the country has been arrested by the social and political revolution through which it has passed, and now needs and deserves the considerate care of the National Government within the just limits prescribed by the Constitution and wise public economy.

But at the basis of all prosperity, for that as well as for every other part of the country, lies the improvement of the intellectual and moral condition of the people. Universal suffrage should rest upon universal education. To this end, liberal and permanent provision should be made for the support of free schools by the State governments, and, if need be, supplemented by legitimate aid from national authority.

Let me assure my countrymen of the Southern States that it is my earnest desire to regard and promote their truest interest —the interests of the white and of the colored people both and equally—and to put forth my best efforts in behalf of a civil policy which will forever wipe out in our political affairs the color line and the distinction between North and South, to the end that we may have not merely a united North or a united South, but a united country.

I ask the attention of the public to the paramount necessity of reform in our civil service—a reform not merely as to certain abuses and practices of so-called official patronage which have come to have the sanction of usage in the several Departments of our Government, but a change in the system of appointment itself; a reform that shall be thorough, radical, and complete; a return to the principles and practices of the founders of the Government. They neither expected nor desired from public officers any partisan service. They meant that public officers should owe their whole service to the Government and to the people. They meant that the officer should be secure in his tenure as long as his personal character remained untarnished and the performance of his duties satisfactory. They held that appointments to office were not to be made nor expected merely as rewards for partisan services, nor merely on the nomination of members of Congress, as being entitled in any respect to the control of such appointments.

The fact that both the great political parties of the country, in declaring their principles prior to the election, gave a prominent place to the subject of reform of our civil service, recognizing and strongly urging its necessity, in terms almost identical in their specific import with those I have here employed, must be accepted as a conclusive argument in behalf of these measures. It must be regarded as the expression of the united voice and will of the whole country upon this subject, and both political parties are virtually pledged to give it their unreserved support.

The President of the United States of necessity owes his election to office to the suffrage and zealous labors of a political party, the members of which cherish with ardor and regard as of essential importance the principles of their party organization; but he should strive to be always mindful of the fact that he serves his party best who serves the country best.

In furtherance of the reform we seek, and in other important respects a change of great importance, I recommend an amendment to the Constitution prescribing a term of six years for the Presidential office and forbidding a reelection.

With respect to the financial condition of the country, I shall not attempt an extended history of the embarrassment and prostration which we have suffered during the past three years. The depression in all our varied commercial and manufacturing interests throughout the country, which began in September, 1873, still continues. It is very gratifying, however, to be able to say that there are indications all around us of a coming change to prosperous times.

Upon the currency question, intimately connected, as it is, with this topic, I may be permitted to repeat here the statement made in my letter of acceptance, that in my judgment the feeling of uncertainty inseparable from an irredeemable paper currency, with its fluctuation of values, is one of the greatest obstacles to a return to prosperous times. The only safe paper currency is one which rests upon a coin basis and is at all times and promptly convertible into coin.

I adhere to the views heretofore expressed by me in favor of Congressional legislation in behalf of an early resumption of specie payments, and I am satisfied not only that this is wise, but that the interests, as well as the public sentiment, of the country imperatively demand it.

Passing from these remarks upon the condition of our own country to consider our relations with other lands, we are reminded by the international complications abroad, threatening the peace of Europe, that our traditional rule of noninterference in the affairs of foreign nations has proved of great value in past times and ought to be strictly observed.

The policy inaugurated by my honored predecessor, President Grant, of submitting to arbitration grave questions in dispute between ourselves and foreign powers points to a new, and incomparably the best, instrumentality for the preservation of peace, and will, as I believe, become a beneficent example of the course to be pursued in similar emergencies by other nations.

If, unhappily, questions of difference should at any time during the period of my Administration arise between the United States and any foreign government, it will certainly be my disposition and my hope to aid in their settlement in the same peaceful and honorable way, thus securing to our country the great blessings of peace and mutual good offices with all the nations of the world.

Fellow-citizens, we have reached the close of a political contest marked by the excitement which usually attends the contests between great political parties whose members espouse and advocate with earnest faith their respective creeds. The circumstances were, perhaps, in no respect extraordinary save in the closeness and the consequent uncertainty of the result.

For the first time in the history of the country it has been deemed best, in view of the peculiar circumstances of the case, that the objections and questions in dispute with reference to the counting of the electoral votes should be referred to the decision of a tribunal appointed for this purpose.

That tribunal—established by law for this sole purpose; its members, all of them, men of long-established reputation for integrity and intelligence, and, with the exception of those who are also members of the supreme judiciary, chosen equally from both political parties; its deliberations enlightened by the research and the arguments of able counsel—was entitled to the fullest confidence of the American people. Its decisions have been patiently waited for, and accepted as legally conclusive by the general judgment of the public. For the present, opinion will widely vary as to the wisdom of the several conclusions announced by that tribunal. This is to be anticipated in every instance where matters of dispute are made the subject of arbitration under the forms of law. Human judgment is never unerring, and is rarely regarded as otherwise than wrong by the unsuccessful party in the contest.

The fact that two great political parties have in this way settled a dispute in regard to which good men differ as to the facts and the law no less than as to the proper course to be pursued in solving the question in controversy is an occasion for general rejoicing.

Upon one point there is entire unanimity in public sentiment—that conflicting claims to the Presidency must be amicably and peaceably adjusted, and that when so adjusted the general acquiescence of the nation ought surely to follow.

It has been reserved for a government of the people, where the right of suffrage is universal, to give to the world the first example in history of a great nation, in the midst of the struggle of opposing parties for power, hushing its party tumults to yield the issue of the contest to adjustment according to the forms of law.

Looking for the guidance of that Divine Hand by which the destinies of nations and individuals are shaped, I call upon you, Senators, Representatives, judges, fellow-citizens, here and everywhere, to unite with me in an earnest effort to secure to our country the blessings, not only of material prosperity, but of justice, peace, and union—a union depending not upon the constraint of force, but upon the loving devotion of a free people; "and that all things may be so ordered and settled upon the best and surest foundations that peace and happiness, truth and justice, religion and piety, may be established among us for all generations."

Study Questions

1. What solution did Hayes outline for the economic, political, and racial problems of the South?

2. Why did Hayes think "reform in our civil service" was necessary, and what did he recommend?

3. How did Hayes seek to calm the concerns of voters who did not regard him as the properly elected president?

William Graham Sumner, Testimony before a Committee of the U.S. House of Representatives (1878)

William Graham Sumner taught economics at Yale College in New Haven, Connecticut. He was America's leading prophet of social Darwinism, a philosophy developed by the British social theorist Herbert Spencer. It was Spencer who coined "survival of the fittest," a phrase that Charles Darwin applied to his theory of biological evolution and that Spencer applied to a parallel theory of social evolution. Cut-throat competition, argued the social Darwinists, was the best recipe for economic progress. Even in a severe economic downturn, the government should not intervene but rather should step out of the way and let the free market correct itself. Social Darwinists thus became staunch supporters of the *laissez-faire* (French for "let it be") economic philosophy, which called for minimal government regulation.

Mr. SUMNER appeared by invitation before a select committee of the U.S. House of Representatives.

The CHAIRMAN: Please to state your occupation.

Mr. SUMNER: I am professor of political and social science in Yale College.

The CHAIRMAN: How long have you held that position?

Mr. SUMNER: I have been in that chair for six years.

The CHAIRMAN: Of course, you have made the relations of capital and labor a study in the performance of your regular duties?

Mr. SUMNER: Yes, sir; that is my professional duty.

The CHAIRMAN: Have you given any special attention to the condition of labor and of business generally at the present time in the United States?

Mr. SUMNER: That is within the range of my professional studies. I have studied it and given all the attention I could to it, and I have availed myself of all the means that I know of for forming ideas about it. I should like to say that the means of forming ideas about it on the part of professional economists are very meager and unsatisfactory. It is exceedingly difficult for any person, however well trained he may be, to embrace this whole subject of the causes of the present depression in the United States; and he would be a very bold man indeed who should claim that he had sounded the whole question. I am certainly not in that position before this committee. I should think that that question ought to be carefully considered in two different points of view. There has been very great industrial reaction over the whole world during the last five or six years, and the United States have, of course, participated in the general state of industry and commerce over the whole world. They have had their share of it. There have been other local and peculiar circumstances in the United States which should be considered by themselves as combining with and intensifying here the effects produced by general causes the world over. Now, I do not know any one in the world who has undertaken to study the whole question of the present commercial crisis over the world in all its bearings, or who has ventured to publish his opinion as to what the cause of this general depression may be, because I am sure that any professional economist would regard that as a subject of enormous magnitude, and would be very timid about any of his conclusions in regard to it. I do not care to enter into that. . . .

Mr. RICE: What is the effect of machinery on those laborers whom for the time being it turns out of employment?

Mr. SUMNER: Of course, a loss of income and a loss of comfort. There are plenty of people in the United States to-day whose fathers were displaced from their labor in some of the old countries by the introduction of machinery, and who suffered very great poverty, and who were forced to emigrate to this country by the pressure of necessity, poverty, and famine. When they came to this country they entered on a new soil and a new system of industry, and their children to-day may look back on the temporary distress through which their parents went as a great family blessing.

Mr. RICE: But the fathers had to suffer from it?

Mr. SUMNER: They had to suffer from it.

Mr. RICE: Is there any way to help it?

Mr. SUMNER: Not at all. There is no way on this earth to help it. The only way is to meet it bravely, go ahead, make the best of circumstances: and if you cannot go on in the way you were going, try another

way, and still another, until you work yourself out as an individual.

The CHAIRMAN: Your idea is that the introduction of machinery has improved the condition of a great many people, although individuals have had hard times in the transition?

Mr. SUMNER: Individuals and classes have had to go through it. What is the reason anybody ever came to America originally? A few came because they had some religious ideas which they wanted to carry out, but they were an insignificant part of the migration to America. The people who came to America came because they were uncomfortable in the old countries, because there was distress and pressure upon them, because they were mostly at the bottom and worst off, and the chance for them was to get to a new soil where it would be easier to get a living and to struggle forward. That is what they all came to this country for. They never abandoned their old homes because they liked to do so. They disliked it very much.

Mr. RICE: Then the pressure of necessity is one of the prime elements in the progress and civilization of mankind?

Mr. SUMNER: Yes; we have been forced to progress, and that is the reason why we have made it. . . .

The CHAIRMAN: You said just now that we had a sparse population on a very productive soil, and therefore that if there is distress here there must be some artificial causes for it. Do you admit that there is what you call distress among the laboring classes of this country?

Mr. SUMNER: No, sir; I do not admit

any such thing. I cannot get any evidence of it. There is only one single fact before the public, so far as I know (and I have been looking for facts), with reference to the number of unemployed persons, and that is the report of Mr. Wright, of Massachusetts, in which he puts down the number of unemployed persons in that State as 28,000, men and women (21,000 men). Whatever may be said in the way of using figures one way or the other, I do not know practically of any evidence that is before the people of the United States to-day except that statement. That statement was carefully made by a trained man who understands his business in that line, and who took all the care he could to collect the data which are given to us. Now the State of Massachusetts is perhaps quite as badly off as any State in the Union, perhaps worse off. When you go into the agricultural communities you find that they are not in any such condition at all. If there is any State worse off than Massachusetts it is Pennsylvania, on account of the coal and iron depression, and I should not wonder if they were worse off there. But there is another thing. A vast number of these people have, of course, family connections, and those people who are supposed to be unemployed are not in a condition bordering either upon starvation or crime. They do not take to the road as tramps, they do not beg, and they do not steal; that is, they do not beg publicly. The chief centers of distress, I should think, from any observation, were the large cities. In all the large cities there are vast numbers of persons who have no regular and steady means of support, who live by irregular occupations and in nondescript ways. These people do not like to leave the cities; they will not leave the cities. In times of slack industry and commerce, of course they find it harder to get a living than at other times; and I suppose that there are in all our cities great numbers of these persons. Furthermore, I should say that this kind of distress where it exists is a great deal deeper and more widespread among clerks, salesmen, bookkeepers, office men, and all that range of occupations than among any other class. . . .

Mr. SUMNER: That brings right on another point which I want to speak about. Up to the time that the crisis of 1873 came, the general opinion of all persons acquainted with business here at that time would be this: that nobody wanted to pay and wind up; nobody wanted to liquidate; everybody wanted to renew his obligations, to extend his operations, because he expected a rise in the market still further. Everybody's confidence in the market was such that he did not want to pay his debt. He thought he was sure to be able to pay his interest on it, and he wanted to make every transaction, as far as possible, the basis for another transaction, so as to extend his operations and get profit on his larger capital. When the crisis of 1873 came, it just shook that confidence, and everybody turned around and began to ask himself whether his inventory figures were good or not—whether the figures at which he had rated his property were correct. He knew that he had debts, and then he had to ask himself whether he was solvent, if he did not pay his debts very soon. He found that prices began to fall, and he found that it was all in vain for him to inventory his property at so much, and then his debts at so much, and his margin at so much. By and by the question was, whether his margin was not wiped out. Everybody, I think, set to work immediately, with the natural good sense of every individual, to discharge his obligations and to reduce his debts, and to pay up and bring his affairs into close order again just as fast and steadily as he could; and the establish and solidify the credit transactions which had been opened up to that time. A great many people found themselves insolvent, and have failed and have gone out of the account. But the natural good sense of every man simply showed him what he ought to do. Every individual had to reduce his expenditures, to economize as much as he could, and to turn in his capital as rapidly as he could to the liquidation of his obligations. In other words, the people of the United States have been, within the last five years, accumulating capital with great rapidity, in order to turn it in to pay their debts. But they have been saving money. Every man has reduced his expenditures, and has contracted his obligations in that way. That, of course, is one great reason for the slackness in trade. When people are not buying goods, if they can possibly help it, of course, trade is dull. That runs through everything. It runs through manufactures and everything else. When people are all avoiding expenses as much as possible, a dullness of trade is produced.

The CHAIRMAN: And all that leads necessarily to a slack demand for labor?

Mr. SUMNER: Of course.

The CHAIRMAN: And the laborer suffers?

Mr. SUMNER: Certainly.

The CHAIRMAN: I do not know whether you are ready to take up the question of remedies. Do you think that there is any remedy that may be applied by legislation or otherwise to relieve labor from the consequences of this speculative era?

Mr. SUMNER: And every one must do the best he can.

The CHAIRMAN: Can legislation do anything toward relieving this accumulation of labor by transferring it to some other place where labor is in request or can be utilized?

Mr. SUMNER: Legislation might do a great deal of mischief, but nothing else. There is one other point which I would like to bring on in this connection because it bears on that point. I have not said as much as I want to yet about the protective tariff.

The CHAIRMAN: Do you want to go on with it at this point?

Mr. SUMNER: Yes. Of course we have had to put up with very heavy taxation since the war. That could not be helped, and taxation is nothing but a burden. We have got to carry it and to make the best of it. It is one of the inevitable hardships of life. But, then, there is the entirely different question of paying in taxes for protection; that is, taxes that are paid by the people, not for the government, but for the protection of manufacturers. In the first place, any taxes of that kind (and we have had frightful ones laid on in this country, unexampled ones) that are laid on for that purpose are a dead burden to the people, coming out of the war with all their other difficulties upon them. In the second place, if you protect anybody, you have got to undertake to decide what things ought to be done in this country. As you [to Mr. Rice] suggested a while ago, some people think it necessary that we should work iron in this country, whether it is profitable or not; that is to say whether it is as profitable as something else that could be done or not (for that is the real question). Now, if the legislature makes up its mind that there are some things that ought to be done here, and sets to work to lay protective duties, in order to force those things to be done, there will be some other consequences which we must take into account. One of them will be, right away, that you will force the industry of the country into disproportionate development.

We have heard a good deal within a few years past about over-production. I do not know what in the world over-production can mean. You cannot give any intelligible definition of it. The only thing that is possible in that direction is not over-production in any sense at all, but disproportionate production. To illustrate that: If you want to build houses, you have got to have wood and brick and lime and nails, &c. (the component materials), to go into the building. If you have wood and nails and lime enough to build 1,000 houses, and you have brick enough to build 2,000 houses, you have a disproportionate production; and the bricks for 1,000 houses have got to lie idle until you can bring up the production of lumber and nails and plaster to the limit of 2,000 houses, in order to fill out the necessary composition with the bricks, and to use them up. That disproportionate production is the only kind of over-production that I know anything about. Now, when you lay on a protective tariff for the purpose of developing certain industries, one great trouble is, that you bring about that disproportionate production. Is such a disproportionate production possible in a natural state of things? Not at all. The law of supply and demand makes it utterly impossible. You cannot produce brick for 2,000 houses when the other materials are only sufficient for 1,000 houses, because the bricks would immediately begin to be reduced in their market price. You would have your warning. But, when you have this protective system in force, the first thing you know is that you have brought out a disproportionate production of commodities in those particular lines.

The next result that you must look out for is that you will draw your population to the particular localities which you have artificially decided on by law. You have invited the population and encouraged them, as it is called, to come to places, and to occupy themselves in occupations into which they would not have gone naturally if things had been left to take their own course. For instance, you can produce a congestion of population in the iron districts (they have got it now in Pennsylvania, and perhaps would like to get rid of it) by deciding that you want to force iron production whether the circumstances of the country call for it or not; but because it is a good thing to have, you gather your population together there where they would not have gone had they been left to distribute themselves just where the greatest profit called them. . . .

Mr. SUMNER: . . . I suppose that the only other question which you want to ask me is the one which you did ask; that is, about the remedies. Of course, I have not any remedy to offer for such a state of things as this. The only answer I can give to a question like that would be the application of simple sound doctrine and sound principles to the case in point. I do not know of anything that the government can do that is at all specific to assist labor—to assist non-capitalists. The only things that the government can do are general things, such as are in the province of a government. The general things that a government can do to assist the non-capitalist in the accumulation of capital (for that is what he wants) are two things. The first thing is to give him the greatest possible measure of liberty in the directing of his own energies for his own development, and the second is to give him the greatest possible security in the possession and use of the products of his own industry. I do not see anything more than that that a government can do in the premises. . . .

The CHAIRMAN: The grievance complained of is that, in the operations of society, certain persons, who are just as deserving as others, find it impossible to get any employment at all. They say that society owes them a living; that, if they cannot get work at private hands, the public should intervene for the time being and provide some place where their labor could be employed, and where they could get a livelihood. They claim that they are just as industrious and meritorious as other citizens; and the proposition is for government to intervene and provide them with employment. What have you got to say to that? Can that be done?

Mr. SUMNER: Sir. The moment that government provided work for one, it would have to provide work for all, and there would be no end whatever possible. Society does not owe any man a living. In all the cases that I have ever known of young men who claimed that society owed them a living, it has turned out that society paid them—in the State prison. I do not see any other result. Society does not owe any man a living. The fact that a man is here is no demand upon other people that they shall keep him alive and sustain him. He has got to fight the battle with nature as every other man has; and if he fights it with the same energy and enterprise and skill and industry as any other man, I cannot imagine his failing—that is, misfortune apart.

Study Questions

1. Why do historians classify Sumner as a "social Darwinist"?

2. Why did Sumner criticize the protective tariff?

James A. Garfield, Inaugural Address (1881)

Two factions vied for control of the Republican Party at the 1880 national convention. Stalwarts, who occured and shared power through the old spoils system under the tutelage of Senator Roscoe Conkling, aimed to re-elect Ulysses S. Grant, who had been upstaged by Hayes in the previous election. A rival group, known as the Half Breeds, rallied around James G. Blaine, a senator from Maine. At last, the Stalwarts and Half Breeds settled upon James A. Garfield as a compromise candidate. Meanwhile, the Democrats put forth war hero Winfield Scott Hancock, who had commanded Union troops in the Battle of Gettysburg. What Hancock enjoyed on his military record, he lacked in statesmanship. The Republicans published a book entitled *Record of the Statesmanship and Achievements of General Winfield Scott Hancock*, consisting entirely of blank pages. Voters took the hint and chose Garfield by 214 electoral votes to 155.

Fellow-Citizens:

We stand to-day upon an eminence which overlooks a hundred years of national life—a century crowded with perils, but crowned with the triumphs of liberty and law. Before continuing the onward march let us pause on this height for a moment to strengthen our faith and renew our hope by a glance at the pathway along which our people have traveled.

It is now three days more than a hundred years since the adoption of the first written constitution of the United States—the Articles of Confederation and Perpetual Union. The new Republic was then beset with danger on every hand. It had not conquered a place in the family of nations. The decisive battle of the war for independence, whose centennial anniversary will soon be gratefully celebrated at Yorktown, had not yet been fought. The colonists were struggling not only against the armies of a great nation, but against the settled opinions of mankind; for the world did not then believe that the supreme authority of government could be safely intrusted to the guardianship of the people themselves.

We can not overestimate the fervent love of liberty, the intelligent courage, and the sum of common sense with which our fathers made the great experiment of self-government. When they found, after a short trial, that the confederacy of States, was too weak to meet the necessities of a vigorous and expanding republic, they boldly set it aside, and in its stead established a National Union, founded directly upon the will of the people, endowed with full power of self-preservation and ample authority for the accomplishment of its great object.

Under this Constitution the boundaries of freedom have been enlarged, the foundations of order and peace have been strengthened, and the growth of our people in all the better elements of national life has indicated the wisdom of the founders and given new hope to their descendants. Under this Constitution our people long ago made themselves safe against danger from without and secured for their mariners and flag equality of rights on all the seas. Under this Constitution twenty-five States have been added to the Union, with constitutions and laws, framed and enforced by their own citizens, to secure the manifold blessings of local self-government.

The jurisdiction of this Constitution now covers an area fifty times greater than that of the original thirteen States and a population twenty times greater than that of 1780.

The supreme trial of the Constitution came at last under the tremendous pressure of civil war. We ourselves are witnesses that the Union emerged from the blood and fire of that conflict purified and made stronger for all the beneficent purposes of good government.

And now, at the close of this first century of growth, with the inspirations of its history in their hearts, our people have lately reviewed the condition of the nation, passed judgment upon the conduct and opinions of political parties, and have registered their will concerning the future administration of the Government. To interpret and to execute that will in accordance with the Constitution is the paramount duty of the Executive.

Even from this brief review it is manifest that the nation is resolutely facing to the front, resolved to employ its best energies in developing the great possibilities of the future. Sacredly preserving whatever has been gained to liberty and good government during the century, our people are determined to leave behind them all those bitter controversies concerning things which have been irrevocably settled, and the further discussion of which can only stir up strife and delay the onward march.

The supremacy of the nation and its

laws should be no longer a subject of debate. That discussion, which for half a century threatened the existence of the Union, was closed at last in the high court of war by a decree from which there is no appeal—that the Constitution and the laws made in pursuance thereof are and shall continue to be the supreme law of the land, binding alike upon the States and the people. This decree does not disturb the autonomy of the States nor interfere with any of their necessary rights of local self-government, but it does fix and establish the permanent supremacy of the Union.

The will of the nation, speaking with the voice of battle and through the amended Constitution, has fulfilled the great promise of 1776 by proclaiming "liberty throughout the land to all the inhabitants thereof."

The elevation of the negro race from slavery to the full rights of citizenship is the most important political change we have known since the adoption of the Constitution of 1787. No thoughtful man can fail to appreciate its beneficent effect upon our institutions and people. It has freed us from the perpetual danger of war and dissolution. It has added immensely to the moral and industrial forces of our people. It has liberated the master as well as the slave from a relation which wronged and enfeebled both. It has surrendered to their own guardianship the manhood of more than 5,000,000 people, and has opened to each one of them a career of freedom and usefulness. It has given new inspiration to the power of self-help in both races by making labor more honorable to the one and more necessary to the other. The influence of this force will grow greater and bear richer fruit with the coming years.

No doubt this great change has caused serious disturbance to our Southern communities. This is to be deplored, though it was perhaps unavoidable. But those who resisted the change should remember that under our institutions there was no middle ground for the negro race between slavery and equal citizenship. There can be no permanent disfranchised peasantry in the United States. Freedom can never yield its fullness of blessings so long as the law or its administration places the smallest obstacle in the pathway of any virtuous citizen.

The emancipated race has already made remarkable progress. With unquestioning devotion to the Union, with a patience and gentleness not born of fear, they have "followed the light as God gave them to see the light." They are rapidly laying the material foundations of self-support, widening their circle of intelligence, and beginning to enjoy the blessings that gather around the homes of the industrious poor. They deserve the generous encouragement of all good men. So far as my authority can lawfully extend they shall enjoy the full and equal protection of the Constitution and the laws.

The free enjoyment of equal suffrage is still in question, and a frank statement of the issue may aid its solution. It is alleged that in many communities citizens are practically denied the freedom of the ballot. In so far as the truth of this allegation is admitted, it is answered that in many places honest local government is impossible if the mass of uneducated negroes are allowed to vote. These are grave allegations. So far as the latter is true, it is the only palliation that can be offered for opposing the freedom of the ballot. Bad local government is certainly a great evil, which ought to be prevented; but to violate the freedom and sanctities of the suffrage is more than an evil. It is a crime which, if persisted in, will destroy the Government itself. Suicide is not a remedy. If in other lands it be high treason to compass the death of the king, it shall be counted no less a crime here to strangle our sovereign power and stifle its voice.

It has been said that unsettled questions have no pity for the repose of nations. It should be said with the utmost emphasis that this question of the suffrage will never give repose or safety to the States or to the nation until each, within its own jurisdiction, makes and keeps the ballot free and pure by the strong sanctions of the law.

But the danger which arises from ignorance in the voter can not be denied. It covers a field far wider than that of negro suffrage and the present condition of the race. It is a danger that lurks and hides in the sources and fountains of power in every state. We have no standard by which to measure the disaster that may be brought upon us by ignorance and vice in the citizens when joined to corruption and fraud in the suffrage.

The voters of the Union, who make and unmake constitutions, and upon whose will hang the destinies of our governments, can transmit their supreme authority to no successors save the coming generation of voters, who are the sole heirs of sovereign power. If that generation comes to its inheritance blinded by ignorance and corrupted by vice, the fall of the Republic will be certain and remediless.

The census has already sounded the alarm in the appalling figures which mark how dangerously high the tide of illiteracy has risen among our voters and their children.

To the South this question is of supreme importance. But the responsibility for the existence of slavery did not rest upon the South alone. The nation itself is responsible for the extension of the suffrage, and is under special obligations to aid in removing the illiteracy which it has added to the voting population. For the North and South alike there is but one remedy. All the constitutional power of the nation and of the States and all the volunteer forces of the people should be surrendered to meet this danger by the savory influence of universal education.

It is the high privilege and sacred duty of those now living to educate their successors and fit them, by intelligence and virtue, for the inheritance which awaits them.

In this beneficent work sections and races should be forgotten and partisanship should be unknown. Let our people find a new meaning in the divine oracle which declares that "a little child shall lead them," for our own little children will soon control the destinies of the Republic.

My countrymen, we do not now differ in our judgment concerning the controversies of past generations, and fifty years hence our children will not be divided in their opinions concerning our controver-

sies. They will surely bless their fathers and their fathers' God that the Union was preserved, that slavery was overthrown, and that both races were made equal before the law. We may hasten or we may retard, but we can not prevent, the final reconciliation. Is it not possible for us now to make a truce with time by anticipating and accepting its inevitable verdict?

Enterprises of the highest importance to our moral and material well-being unite us and offer ample employment of our best powers. Let all our people, leaving behind them the battlefields of dead issues, move forward and in their strength of liberty and the restored Union win the grander victories of peace.

The prosperity which now prevails is without parallel in our history. Fruitful seasons have done much to secure it, but they have not done all. The preservation of the public credit and the resumption of specie payments, so successfully attained by the Administration of my predecessors, have enabled our people to secure the blessings which the seasons brought.

By the experience of commercial nations in all ages it has been found that gold and silver afford the only safe foundation for a monetary system. Confusion has recently been created by variations in the relative value of the two metals, but I confidently believe that arrangements can be made between the leading commercial nations which will secure the general use of both metals. Congress should provide that the compulsory coinage of silver now required by law may not disturb our monetary system by driving either metal out of circulation. If possible, such an adjustment should be made that the purchasing power of every coined dollar will be exactly equal to its debt-paying power in all the markets of the world.

The chief duty of the National Government in connection with the currency of the country is to coin money and declare its value. Grave doubts have been entertained whether Congress is authorized by the Constitution to make any form of paper money legal tender. The present issue of United States notes has been sustained by the necessities of war; but such paper should depend for its value and currency upon its convenience in use and its prompt redemption in coin at the will of the holder, and not upon its compulsory circulation. These notes are not money, but promises to pay money. If the holders demand it, the promise should be kept.

The refunding of the national debt at a lower rate of interest should be accomplished without compelling the withdrawal of the national-bank notes, and thus disturbing the business of the country.

I venture to refer to the position I have occupied on financial questions during a long service in Congress, and to say that time and experience have strengthened the opinions I have so often expressed on these subjects.

The finances of the Government shall suffer no detriment which it may be possible for my Administration to prevent.

The interests of agriculture deserve more attention from the Government than they have yet received. The farms of the United States afford homes and employment for more than one-half our people, and furnish much the largest part of all our exports. As the Government lights our coasts for the protection of mariners and the benefit of commerce, so it should give to the tillers of the soil the best lights of practical science and experience.

Our manufacturers are rapidly making us industrially independent, and are opening to capital and labor new and profitable fields of employment. Their steady and healthy growth should still be matured. Our facilities for transportation should be promoted by the continued improvement of our harbors and great interior waterways and by the increase of our tonnage on the ocean.

The development of the world's commerce has led to an urgent demand for shortening the great sea voyage around Cape Horn by constructing ship canals or railways across the isthmus which unites the continents. Various plans to this end have been suggested and will need consideration, but none of them has been sufficiently matured to warrant the United States in extending pecuniary aid. The subject, however, is one which will immediately engage the attention of the Government with a view to a thorough protection to American interests. We will urge no narrow policy nor seek peculiar or exclusive privileges in any commercial route; but, in the language of my predecessor, I believe it to be the right "and duty of the United States to assert and maintain such supervision and authority over any interoceanic canal across the isthmus that connects North and South America as will protect our national interest."

The Constitution guarantees absolute religious freedom. Congress is prohibited

from making any law respecting an establishment of religion or prohibiting the free
exercise thereof. The Territories of the
United States are subject to the direct
legislative authority of Congress, and
hence the General Government is responsible for any violation of the Constitution in
any of them. It is therefore a reproach to
the Government that in the most populous
of the Territories the constitutional guaranty is not enjoyed by the people and the
authority of Congress is set at naught. The
Mormon Church not only offends the
moral sense of manhood by sanctioning
polygamy, but prevents the administration
of justice through ordinary instrumentalities of law.

In my judgment it is the duty of Congress, while respecting to the uttermost
the conscientious convictions and religious
scruples of every citizen, to prohibit within
its jurisdiction all criminal practices, especially of that class which destroy the family
relations and endanger social order. Nor
can any ecclesiastical organization be
safely permitted to usurp in the smallest
degree the functions and powers of the
National Government.

The civil service can never be placed on
a satisfactory basis until it is regulated by
law. For the good of the service itself, for
the protection of those who are intrusted
with the appointing power against the
waste of time and obstruction to the public
business caused by the inordinate pressure
for place, and for the protection of incumbents against intrigue and wrong, I shall at
the proper time ask Congress to fix the
tenure of the minor offices of the several
Executive Departments and prescribe the
grounds upon which removals shall be
made during the terms for which incumbents have been appointed.

Finally, acting always within the
authority and limitations of the Constitution, invading neither the rights of the
States nor the reserved rights of the
people, it will be the purpose of my
Administration to maintain the authority
of the nation in all places within its jurisdiction; to enforce obedience to all the
laws of the Union in the interests of the
people; to demand rigid economy in all the
expenditures of the Government, and to
require the honest and faithful service of
all executive officers, remembering that
the offices were created, not for the benefit
of incumbents or their supporters, but for
the service of the Government.

And now, fellow-citizens, I am about to
assume the great trust which you have
committed to my hands. I appeal to you
for that earnest and thoughtful support
which makes this Government in fact, as it
is in law, a government of the people.

I shall greatly rely upon the wisdom
and patriotism of Congress and of those
who may share with me the responsibilities and duties of administration, and,
above all, upon our efforts to promote the
welfare of this great people and their Government I reverently invoke the support
and blessings of Almighty God.

Study Questions

1. What connection did Garfield perceive between race and illiteracy with respect to equal suffrage in the South?

2. How did Garfield characterize the economic climate of the United States, and what role did he recommend for the government in developing the economy?

3. Did Garfield think Mormons had a First Amendment right to practice polygamy? Explain his position.

U.S. Congress, Pendleton Civil Service Act (1883)

Attempting to purge corruption from national politics, reformers secured a majority in Congress to pass the Pendleton Civil Service Act, which President Chester A. Arthur—though a product of the spoils system himself—signed into law. Senator George H. Pendleton, a Democrat representing Ohio, sponsored the act. Arthur's endorsement of the law cost him re-election in 1884, since the political machines operated by Republican Stalwarts fell under the scrutiny of the Civil Service Commission.

An act to regulate and improve the civil service of the United States.

Section 1

Be it enacted by the Senate and House of Representatives of the United States of America in Congress assembled, That the President is authorized to appoint, by and with the advice and consent of the Senate, three persons, not more than two of whom shall be adherents of the same party, as Civil Service Commissioners, and said three commissioners shall constitute the United States Civil Service Commission. Said commissioners shall hold no other official place under the United States. . . .

The commissioners shall each receive a salary of three thousand five hundred dollars a year. And each of said commissioners shall be paid his necessary traveling expenses incurred in the discharge of his duty as a commissioner.

Section 2

That it shall be the duty of said commissioners:

FIRST. To aid the President, as he may request, in preparing suitable rules for carrying this act into effect, and when said rules shall have been promulgated it shall be the duty of all officers of the United States in the departments and offices to which any such rules may relate to aid, in all proper ways, in carrying said rules, and any modifications thereof; into effect.

SECOND. And, among other things, said rules shall provide and declare, as nearly as the conditions of good administration will warrant, as follows:

First, for open, competitive examinations for testing the fitness of applicants for the public service now classified or to be classified hereunder. Such examinations shall be practical in their character, and so far as may be shall relate to those matters which will fairly test the relative capacity and fitness of the persons examined to discharge the duties of the service into which they seek to be appointed.

Second, that all the offices, places, and employments so arranged or to be arranged in classes shall be filled by selections according to grade from among those graded highest as the results of such competitive examinations.

Third, appointments to the public service aforesaid in the departments at Washington shall be apportioned among the several States and Territories and the District of Columbia upon the basis of population as ascertained at the last preceding census. Every application for an examination shall contain, among other things, a statement, under oath, setting forth his or her actual bona fide residence at the time of making the application, as well as how long he or she has been a resident of such place.

Fourth, that there shall be a period of probation before any absolute appointment or employment aforesaid.

Fifth, that no person in the public service is for that reason under any obligations to contribute to any political fund, or to render any political service, and that he will not be removed or otherwise prejudiced for refusing to do so.

Sixth, that no person in said service has any right to use his official authority or influence to coerce the political action of any person or body.

Seventh, there shall be non-competitive examinations in all proper cases before the commission, when competent persons do not compete, after notice has been given of the existence of the vacancy, under such rules as may be prescribed by the commissioners as to the manner of giving notice.

Eighth, that notice shall be given in writing by the appointing power to said commission of the persons selected for appointment or employment from among those who have been examined, of the place of residence of such persons, of the rejection of any such persons after probation, of transfers, resignations, and removals and of the date thereof, and a record of the same shall be kept, by said commission. And any necessary exceptions from said eight fundamental provisions of the rules shall be set forth in connection with such rules, and the reasons there-for shall be stated in the annual reports of the commission.

THIRD. Said commission shall, subject to the rules that may be made by the President, make regulations for, and have control of, such examinations, and, through its members or the examiners, it shall supervise and preserve the records of the same; and said commission shall keep minutes of its own proceedings.

FOURTH. Said commission may make investigations concerning the facts, and may report upon all matters touching the enforcement and effects of said rules and regulations, and concerning the action of any examiner or board of examiners hereinafter provided for, and its own subordinates, and those in the public service, in respect to the execution of this act.

FIFTH. Said commission shall make an annual report to the President for transmission to Congress, showing its own action, the rules and regulations and the exceptions thereto in force, the practical effects thereof, and any suggestions it may approve for the more effectual accomplishment of the purposes of this act.

Section 3

That said commission is authorized to employ a chief examiner, a part of whose duty it shall be, under its direction, to act with the examining boards, so far as practicable, whether at Washington or elsewhere, and to secure accuracy, uniformity, and justice in all their proceedings, which shall be at all times open to him. The chief examiner shall be entitled to receive a salary at the rate of three thousand dollars a year, and he shall be paid his necessary traveling expenses incurred in the discharge of his duty. The commission shall have a secretary, to be appointed by the President, who shall receive a salary of one thousand six hundred dollars per annum. It may, when necessary, employ a stenographer, and a messenger, who shall be paid, when employed, the former at the rate of one thousand six hundred dollars a year, and the latter at the rate of six hundred dollars a year. The commission shall, at Washington, and in one or more places in each State and Territory where examinations are to take place, designate and select a suitable number of persons, not less than three, in the official service of the United States, residing in said State or Territory, after consulting the head of the department or office in which such persons serve, to be members of boards of examiners, and may at any time substitute any other person in said service living in such State or Territory in the place of anyone so selected. Such boards of examiners shall be so located as to make it reasonably convenient and inexpensive for applicants to attend before them; and where there are persons to be examined in any State or Territory, examinations shall be held therein at least twice in each year. It shall be the duty of the collector, postmaster, and other officers of the United States at any place outside of the District of Columbia where examinations are directed by the President or by said board to be held, to allow the reasonable use of the public buildings for holding such examinations, and in all proper ways to facilitate the same. . . .

Section 5

That any said commissioner, examiner, copyist, or messenger, or any person in the public service who shall willfully and corruptly, by himself or in co-operation with one or more other persons, defeat, deceive, or obstruct any person in respect of his or her right of examination according to any such rules or regulations, or who shall willfully, corruptly, and falsely mark, grade, estimate, or report upon the examination or proper standing of any person examined hereunder, or aid in so doing, or who shall willfully and corruptly make any false representations concerning the same or concerning the person examined, or who shall willfully and corruptly furnish to any person any special or secret information for the purpose of either improving or injuring the prospects or chances of any person so examined, or to be examined, being appointed, employed, or promoted, shall for each such offense be deemed guilty of a misdemeanor, and upon conviction thereof, shall be punished by a fine of not less than one hundred dollars, nor more than one thousand dollars, or by imprisonment not less than ten days, nor more than one year, or by both such fine and imprisonment. . . .

Section 8

That no person habitually using intoxicating beverages to excess shall be appointed to, or retained in, any office, appointment, or employment to which the provisions of this act are applicable.

Section 9

That whenever there are already two or more members of a family in the public service in the grades covered by this act, no other member of such family shall be eligible to appointment to any of said grades. . . .

Section 11

That no Senator, or Representative, or Territorial Delegate of the Congress, or Senator, Representative, or Delegate elect, or any officer or employee of either of said houses, and no executive, judicial, military, or naval officer of the United States, and no clerk or employee of any department, branch or bureau of the executive, judicial, or military or naval service of the United States, shall, directly or indirectly, solicit or receive, or be in any manner concerned ill soliciting or receiving, any assessment, subscription, or contribution for any political purpose whatever, from any officer, clerk, or employee of the United States, or any department, branch, or bureau thereof, or from any person receiving any salary or compensation from moneys derived from the Treasury of the United States. . . .

Section 13

No officer or employee of the United States mentioned in this act shall discharge, or promote, or degrade, or in manner change the official rank or compensation of any other officer or employee, or promise or threaten so to do, for giving or withholding or neglecting to make any contribution of money or other valuable thing for any political purpose.

Section 14

That no officer, clerk, or other person in the service of the United States shall, directly or indirectly, give or hand over to any other officer, clerk, or person in the service of the United States, or to any Senator or Member of the House of Representatives, or Territorial Delegate, any money or other valuable thing on account of or to be applied to the promotion of any political object whatever.

Section 15

That any person who shall be guilty of violating any provision of the four foregoing sections shall be deemed guilty of a misdemeanor, and shall, on conviction thereof, be punished by a fine not exceeding five thousand dollars, or by imprisonment for a term not exceeding three years, or by such fine and imprisonment both, in the discretion of the court.

Approved, January sixteenth, 1883.

Study Questions

1. Where, precisely, did the Pendleton Act draw the line between who was, and who was not, eligible for appointment to a federal civil service job?

2. Did the Stalwarts oppose this law simply out of self-interest, or might they have had more respectable principles in mind?

Grover Cleveland, First Inaugural Address (1885)

A nineteenth-century Democrat who governed like a twentieth-century Republican, Grover Cleveland occupies a unique place in history among the Gilded Age presidents. His election in 1884 did not come easily. The Republicans endorsed James G. Blaine and criticized the Democrats as the party of "rum, Romanism, and rebellion"—references to the alcohol consumption, Roman Catholicism, and labor protests that stereotypically characterized immigrant voters recruited by Democratic machines. Worse, Blaine's supporters accused Cleveland of fathering a child out of wedlock. Political cartoons lampooned the presidential candidate with the slogan, "Ma, Ma, where's my pa?" Cleveland, although neither admitting nor denying paternity, at least saw to it that the child received adequate care and for his part refused to sling back the same kind of mud on Blaine when documents surfaced implicating the Republican candidate in an extramarital affair. Ultimately, Cleveland secured not only the Democratic vote but also a significant number of Republican votes from "Mugwumps" who bolted from the party of Blaine's machine to support Cleveland's record of political reform.

Fellow-Citizens:

In the presence of this vast assemblage of my countrymen I am about to supplement and seal by the oath which I shall take the manifestation of the will of a great and free people. In the exercise of their power and right of self-government they have committed to one of their fellow-citizens a supreme and sacred trust, and he here consecrates himself to their service.

This impressive ceremony adds little to the solemn sense of responsibility with which I contemplate the duty I owe to all the people of the land. Nothing can relieve me from anxiety lest by any act of mine their interests may suffer, and nothing is needed to strengthen my resolution to engage every faculty and effort in the promotion of their welfare.

Amid the din of party strife the people's choice was made, but its attendant circumstances have demonstrated anew the strength and safety of a government by the people. In each succeeding year it more clearly appears that our democratic principle needs no apology, and that in its fearless and faithful application is to be found the surest guaranty of good government.

But the best results in the operation of a government wherein every citizen has a share largely depend upon a proper limitation of purely partisan zeal and effort and a correct appreciation of the time when the heat of the partisan should be merged in the patriotism of the citizen.

To-day the executive branch of the Government is transferred to new keeping. But this is still the Government of all the people, and it should be none the less an object of their affectionate solicitude. At this hour the animosities of political strife, the bitterness of partisan defeat, and the exultation of partisan triumph should be supplanted by an ungrudging acquiescence in the popular will and a sober, conscientious concern for the general weal. Moreover, if from this hour we cheerfully and honestly abandon all sectional prejudice and distrust, and determine, with manly confidence in one another, to work out harmoniously the achievements of our national destiny, we shall deserve to realize all the benefits which our happy form of government can bestow.

On this auspicious occasion we may well renew the pledge of our devotion to the Constitution, which, launched by the founders of the Republic and consecrated by their prayers and patriotic devotion, has for almost a century borne the hopes and the aspirations of a great people through prosperity and peace and through the shock of foreign conflicts and the perils of domestic strife and vicissitudes.

By the Father of his Country our Constitution was commended for adoption as "the result of a spirit of amity and mutual concession." In that same spirit it should be administered, in order to promote the lasting welfare of the country and to secure the full measure of its priceless benefits to us and to those who will succeed to the blessings of our national life. The large variety of diverse and competing interests subject to Federal control, persistently seeking the recognition of their claims, need give us no fear that "the greatest good to the greatest number" will fail to be accomplished if in the halls of national legislation that spirit of amity and mutual concession shall prevail in which the Constitution had its birth. If this involves the surrender or postponement of private interests and the abandonment of local advantages, compensation will be found in the assurance that the common interest is subserved and the general welfare advanced.

In the discharge of my official duty I shall endeavor to be guided by a just and unstrained construction of the Constitution, a careful observance of the distinction between the powers granted to the Federal Government and those reserved to the States or to the people, and by a cautious appreciation of those functions which by the Constitution and laws have been especially assigned to the executive branch of the Government.

But he who takes the oath today to preserve, protect, and defend the Constitution of the United States only assumes the solemn obligation which every patriotic citizen—on the farm, in the workshop, in the busy marts of trade, and everywhere— should share with him. The Constitution which prescribes his oath, my countrymen, is yours; the Government you have chosen him to administer for a time is yours; the suffrage which executes the will of freemen is yours; the laws and the entire scheme of our civil rule, from the town meeting to the State capitals and the national capital, is yours. Your every voter, as surely as your Chief Magistrate, under the same high sanction, though in a different sphere, exercises a public trust. Nor is this all. Every citizen owes to the country a vigilant watch and close scrutiny of its public servants and a fair and reasonable estimate of their fidelity and usefulness. Thus is the people's will impressed upon the whole framework of our civil polity—municipal, State, and Federal; and this is the price of our liberty and the inspiration of our faith in the Republic.

It is the duty of those serving the people in public place to closely limit public expenditures to the actual needs of the

Government economically administered, because this bounds the right of the Government to exact tribute from the earnings of labor or the property of the citizen, and because public extravagance begets extravagance among the people. We should never be ashamed of the simplicity and prudential economies which are best suited to the operation of a republican form of government and most compatible with the mission of the American people. Those who are selected for a limited time to manage public affairs are still of the people, and may do much by their example to encourage, consistently with the dignity of their official functions, that plain way of life which among their fellow-citizens aids integrity and promotes thrift and prosperity.

The genius of our institutions, the needs of our people in their home life, and the attention which is demanded for the settlement and development of the resources of our vast territory dictate the scrupulous avoidance of any departure from that foreign policy commended by the history, the traditions, and the prosperity of our Republic. It is the policy of independence, favored by our position and defended by our known love of justice and by our power. It is the policy of peace suitable to our interests. It is the policy of neutrality, rejecting any share in foreign broils and ambitions upon other continents and repelling their intrusion here. It is the policy of Monroe and of Washington and Jefferson—"Peace, commerce, and honest friendship with all nations; entangling alliance with none."

A due regard for the interests and prosperity of all the people demands that our finances shall be established upon such a sound and sensible basis as shall secure the safety and confidence of business interests and make the wage of labor sure and steady, and that our system of revenue shall be so adjusted as to relieve the people of unnecessary taxation, having a due regard to the interests of capital invested and workingmen employed in American industries, and preventing the accumulation of a surplus in the Treasury to tempt extravagance and waste.

Care for the property of the nation and for the needs of future settlers requires that the public domain should be protected from purloining schemes and unlawful occupation.

The conscience of the people demands that the Indians within our boundaries shall be fairly and honestly treated as wards of the Government and their education and civilization promoted with a view to their ultimate citizenship, and that polygamy in the Territories, destructive of the family relation and offensive to the moral sense of the civilized world, shall be repressed.

The laws should be rigidly enforced which prohibit the immigration of a servile class to compete with American labor, with no intention of acquiring citizenship, and bringing with them and retaining habits and customs repugnant to our civilization.

The people demand reform in the administration of the Government and the application of business principles to public affairs. As a means to this end, civil-service reform should be in good faith enforced. Our citizens have the right to protection from the incompetency of public employees who hold their places solely as the reward of partisan service, and from the corrupting influence of those who promise and the vicious methods of those who expect such rewards; and those who worthily seek public employment have the right to insist that merit and competency shall be recognized instead of party subserviency or the surrender of honest political belief.

In the administration of a government pledged to do equal and exact justice to all men there should be no pretext for anxiety touching the protection of the freedmen in their rights or their security in the enjoyment of their privileges under the Constitution and its amendments. All discussion as to their fitness for the place accorded to them as American citizens is idle and unprofitable except as it suggests the necessity for their improvement. The fact that they are citizens entitles them to all the rights due to that relation and charges them with all its duties, obligations, and responsibilities.

These topics and the constant and ever-varying wants of an active and enterprising population may well receive the attention and the patriotic endeavor of all who make and execute the Federal law. Our duties are practical and call for industrious application, an intelligent perception of the claims of public office, and, above all, a firm determination, by united action, to secure to all the people of the land the full benefits of the best form of government ever vouchsafed to man. And let us not trust to human effort alone, but humbly acknowledging the power and goodness of Almighty God, who presides over the destiny of nations, and who has at all times been revealed in our country's history, let us invoke His aid and His blessings upon our labors.

Study Questions

1. What did Cleveland mean when he said that he would "be guided by a just and unstrained construction of the Constitution"?

2. What did Cleveland promise regarding government expenditures and taxation?

3. How did Cleveland's commitment to a strict construction of the Constitution apply to the "freedmen" (former slaves) of the American South? Consider, specifically, what he meant when referring to "their rights . . . [and] their privileges under the Constitution and Its amendments."

Chronological Overview: Native American Affairs

1831   In *Cherokee v. Georgia*, the U.S. Supreme Court declares that Indian tribes are "domestic dependent nations." Tribal sovereignty extends far enough for the United States to enter into treaties with Indian tribes, and yet unlike sovereign foreign nations these tribes remain within U.S. territory as protectorates of the federal government.

1862   The Homestead Act encourages American citizens and recent immigrants to settle the West. Each household may purchase 160 acres at a nominal sum and take title to the property after five years of resident farming.

1867   Congress passes the Reservation Act "for establishing peace with certain Indian tribes now at war with the United States."

1869   The Golden Spike connects the Union Pacific and Central Pacific lines at Promontory, Utah, completing the transcontinental railroad and accelerating the westward migration of U.S. citizens and recent immigrants.

1876   Crazy Horse and Sitting Bull lead Sioux and Cheyenne Indians in a victorious show of force against U.S. Gen. George Custer in the Battle of Little Bighorn, thus delaying the removal of these Indians to federally established Indian reservations.

1877   Chief Joseph attempts to lead the Nez Percé into Canada after the U.S. government evicted them from Idaho, but the U.S. catches up to them and relocates the tribe to a reservation in present-day Oklahoma.

1883   William F. Cody launches his "Wild West" show, based on both actual and legendary events. Novelist Ned Buntline published a series of books about "Buffalo Bill," starting in 1869, and also cast Cody himself in an 1872 theatrical performance. Cody later cast Chief Sitting Bull in his own "Wild West" series.

1887   The Dawes Severalty Act individualizes U.S.–Indian relations that previously were tribal. In the decades that follow, nearly two-thirds of tribal lands become privatized.

1889   President Harrison opens 1.9 million acres of Indian territory for settlement by U.S. citizens, beginning at noon on April 22, 1889. In the resulting "Oklahoma Land Rush," over 50,000 people hasten to stake their claims.

1890   When Wovoka, an Indian religious leader, revives the Ghost Dance tradition and promises liberation from the white man, the U.S. Seventh Calvary surrounds 200 Indians at Wounded Knee (present-day South Dakota). In a panic, the U.S. military massacres the Indians.

The U.S. census declares that whites have now settled the entire frontier.

Frederick Jackson Turner, *The Frontier in American History* (1921), ch. 1

Taking his cue from an 1890 census report which claimed the western frontier had vanished, historian Frederick Jackson Turner presented an essay entitled "The Significance of the Frontier in American History" at the 1893 meeting of the American Historical Association. The meeting was held in Chicago—a city that once had been "in the West" but no longer could be considered so. Turner believed that "westward expansion was the most important single process in American history" from colonial times until the late 1800s. Turner expanded his ideas into a book, excerpted below.

Chapter 1—The Significance of the Frontier in American History

In a recent bulletin of the Superintendent of the Census for 1890 appear these significant words:

> Up to and including 1880 the country had a frontier of settlement, but at present the unsettled area has been so broken into by isolated bodies of settlement that there can hardly be said to be a frontier line. In the discussion of its extent, its westward movement, etc., it can not, therefore, any longer have a place in the census reports.

This brief official statement marks the closing of a great historic movement. Up to our own day American history has been in a large degree the history of the colonization of the Great West. The existence of an area of free land, its continuous recession, and the advance of American settlement westward, explain American development.

Behind institutions, behind constitutional forms and modifications, lie the vital forces that call these organs into life and shape them to meet changing conditions. The peculiarity of American institutions is, the fact that they have been compelled to adapt themselves to the changes of an expanding people—to the changes involved in crossing a continent, in winning a wilderness, and in developing at each area of this progress out of the primitive economic and political conditions of the frontier into the complexity of city life. ... Thus American development has exhibited not merely advance along a single line, but a return to primitive conditions on a continually advancing frontier line, and a new development for that area. American social development has been continually beginning over again on the frontier. This perennial rebirth, this fluidity of American life, this expansion westward with its new opportunities, its continuous touch with the simplicity of primitive society, furnish the forces dominating American character. The true point of view in the history of this nation is not the Atlantic coast, it is the Great West. Even the slavery struggle, which is made so exclusive an object of attention by writers like Professor von Holst, occupies its important place in American history because of its relation to westward expansion.

... The legislation which most developed the powers of the national government, and played the largest part in its activity, was conditioned on the frontier.

Writers have discussed the subjects of tariff, land, and internal improvement, as subsidiary to the slavery question. But when American history comes to be rightly viewed it will be seen that the slavery question is an incident. In the period from the end of the first half of the present century to the close of the Civil War slavery rose to primary, but far from exclusive, importance. But this does not justify Dr. von Holst (to take an example) in treating our constitutional history in its formative period down to 1828 in a single volume, giving six volumes chiefly to the history of slavery from 1828 to 1861, under the title "Constitutional History of the United States." The growth of nationalism and the evolution of American political institutions were dependent on the advance of the frontier. Even so recent a writer as Rhodes, in his "History of the United States since the Compromise of 1850," has treated the legislation called out by the western advance as incidental to the slavery struggle.

This is a wrong perspective. The pioneer needed the goods of the coast, and so the grand series of internal improvement and railroad legislation began, with potent nationalizing effects. Over internal improvements occurred great debates, in which grave constitutional questions were discussed. Sectional groupings appear in the votes, profoundly significant for the historian. Loose construction increased as the nation marched westward. But the West was not content with bringing the farm to the factory. Under the lead of Clay —"Harry of the West"—protective tariffs were passed, with the cry of bringing the factory to the farm. The disposition of the public lands was a third important subject of national legislation influenced by the frontier.

The public domain has been a force of profound importance in the nationalization and development of the government. The effects of the struggle of the landed and the landless States, and of the Ordinance of 1787, need no discussion. Administratively the frontier called out some of the highest and most vitalizing activities of the general government. The purchase of Louisiana was perhaps the constitutional turning point in the history of the Republic, inasmuch as it afforded both a new area for national legislation and the occasion of the downfall of the policy of strict construction. But the purchase of Louisiana was called out by frontier needs and demands. As frontier States accrued to the Union the national power grew. In a speech on the dedication of the Calhoun monument Mr. Lamar explained: "In 1789 the States were the creators of the Federal Government; in 1861 the Federal Government was the creator of a large majority of the States."

. . . It was this nationalizing tendency of the West that transformed the democracy of Jefferson into the national republicanism of Monroe and the democracy of Andrew Jackson. The West of the War of 1812, the West of Clay, and Benton and Harrison, and Andrew Jackson, shut off by the Middle States and the mountains from the coast sections, had a solidarity of its own with national tendencies. On the tide of the Father of Waters, North and South met and mingled into a nation. Interstate migration went steadily on—a process of crossfertilization of ideas and institutions.

The fierce struggle of the sections over slavery on the western frontier does not diminish the truth of this statement; it proves the truth of it. Slavery was a sectional trait that would not down, but in the West it could not remain sectional. It was the greatest of frontiersmen [Abraham Lincoln] who declared: "I believe this Government can not endure permanently half slave and half free. It will become all of one thing or all of the other." Nothing works for nationalism like intercourse within the nation. Mobility of population is death to localism, and the western frontier worked irresistibly in unsettling population. The effect reached back from the frontier and affected profoundly the Atlantic coast and even the Old World.

But the most important effect of the frontier has been in the promotion of democracy here and in Europe. As has been indicated, the frontier is productive of individualism. Complex society is precipitated by the wilderness into a kind of primitive organization based on the family. The tendency is anti-social. It produces antipathy to control, and particularly to any direct control. The tax-gatherer is viewed as a representative of oppression. Prof. Osgood, in an able article, has pointed out that the frontier conditions prevalent in the colonies are important factors in the explanation of the American Revolution, where individual liberty was sometimes confused with absence of all effective government. The same conditions aid in explaining the difficulty of instituting a strong government in the period of the confederacy [i.e., government under the Articles of Confederation]. The frontier individualism has from the beginning pro-

moted democracy. The frontier States that came into the Union in the first quarter of a century of its existence came in with democratic suffrage provisions, and had reactive effects of the highest importance upon the older States whose peoples were being attracted there. An extension of the franchise became essential. It was western New York that forced an extension of suffrage in the constitutional convention of that State in 1821; and it was western Virginia that compelled the tide-water region to put a more liberal suffrage provision in the constitution framed in 1830, and to give to the frontier region a more nearly proportionate representation with the tide-water aristocracy. The rise of democracy as an effective force in the nation came in with western preponderance under Jackson and William Henry Harrison, and it meant the triumph of the frontier—with all of its good and with all of its evil elements. An interesting illustration of the tone of frontier democracy in 1830 comes from the same debates in the Virginia convention already referred to. A representative from western Virginia declared:

> But, sir, it is not the increase of population in the West which this gentleman ought to fear. It is the energy which the mountain breeze and western habits impart to those emigrants. They are regenerated, politically I mean, sir. They soon become working politicians, and the difference, sir, between a talking and a working politician is immense. The Old Dominion has long been celebrated for producing great orators; the ablest metaphysicians in policy; men that can split hairs in all abstruse questions of political economy. But at home, or when they return from Congress, they have

negroes to fan them asleep. But a Pennsylvania, a New York, an Ohio, or a western Virginia statesman, though far inferior in logic, metaphysics, and rhetoric to an old Virginia statesman, has this advantage, that when he returns home he takes off his coat and takes hold of the plow. This gives him bone and muscle, sir, and preserves his republican principles pure and uncontaminated.

So long as free land exists, the opportunity for a competency exists, and economic power secures political power. But the democracy born of free land, strong in selfishness and individualism, intolerant of administrative experience and education, and pressing individual liberty beyond its proper bounds, has its dangers as well as its benefits. Individualism in America has allowed a laxity in regard to governmental affairs which has rendered possible the spoils system and all the manifest evils that follow from the lack of a highly developed civic spirit. In this connection may be noted also the influence of frontier conditions in permitting lax business honor, inflated paper currency and wild-cat banking. . . .

From the conditions of frontier life came intellectual traits of profound importance. The works of travelers along each frontier from colonial days onward describe certain common traits, and these traits have, while softening down, still persisted as survivals in the place of their origin, even when a higher social organization succeeded. The result is that to the frontier the American intellect owes its striking characteristics. That coarseness and strength combined with acuteness and inquisitiveness; that practical, inventive turn of mind, quick to find expedients; that masterful grasp of material things, lacking in the artistic but powerful to effect great ends; that restless, nervous energy; that dominant individualism, working for good and for evil, and withal that buoyancy and exuberance which comes with freedom-these are traits of the frontier, or traits called out elsewhere because of the existence of the frontier. Since the days when the fleet of Columbus sailed into the waters of the New World, America has been another name for opportunity, and the people of the United States have taken their tone from the incessant expansion which has not only been open but has even been forced upon them. He would be a rash prophet who should assert that the expansive character of American life has now entirely ceased. Movement has been its dominant fact, and, unless this training has no effect upon a people, the American energy will continually demand a wider field for its exercise. But never again will such gifts of free land offer themselves. For a moment, at the frontier, the bonds of custom are broken and unrestraint is triumphant. There is no *tabula rasa*. The stubborn American environment is there with its imperious summons to accept its conditions; the inherited ways of doing things are also there; and yet, in spite of environment, and in spite of custom, each frontier did indeed furnish a new field of opportunity, a gate of escape from the bondage of the past; and freshness, and confidence, and scorn of older society, impatience of its restraints and its ideas, and indifference to its lessons, have accompanied the frontier. What the Mediterranean Sea was to the Greeks, breaking the bond of custom, offering new experiences, calling out new institutions and activities, that, and more, the ever retreating frontier has been to the United States directly, and to the nations of Europe more remotely. And now, four centuries from the discovery of America, at the end of a hundred years of life under the Constitution, the frontier has gone, and with its going has closed the first period of American history....

Study Questions

1. According to Turner, which factor contributed more significantly to the development of America in the early 1800s—the slavery debate, or the settlement of the frontier? Explain how Turner supported this conclusion.

2. What relationship did Turner perceive between frontier settlement and democracy?

3. With the frontier now settled, what is to become of America in the future?

Chief Joseph, "Selected Speeches by the Nez Percé Chief" (1879)

Chief Joseph led an Indian tribe known as the Nez Percé, a French phrase meaning "pierced nose." Capt. Meriwether Lewis and Lt. William Clark had encountered this tribe during their 1804–1806 exploration of the Louisiana Purchase. Their translator, Toussaint Charbonneau, named the tribe, although not all members actually pierced their noses. Whereas relations between the Nez Percé and the Lewis and Clark expedition were friendly, by the late 1800s white settlers were competing against the Indians for a territory in present-day Idaho. In 1877, the U.S. Army pursued Chief Joseph and his tribe for some 1,200 miles, finally capturing the Indians and relocating them to a reservation in Oklahoma. Two years later, Chief Joseph appealed to President Rutherford B. Hayes in an effort to regain his homeland; his request was denied.

I. The first white men of your people who came to our country were named Lewis and Clark. They brought many things which our people had never seen. They talked straight and our people gave them a great feast as proof that their hearts were friendly. They made presents to our chiefs and our people made presents to them. We had a great many horses of which we gave them what they needed, and they gave us guns and tobacco in return. All the Nez Percé made friends with Lewis and Clark and agreed to let them pass through their country and never to make war on white men. This promise the Nez Percé have never broken.

II. For a short time we lived quietly. But this could not last. White men had found gold in the mountains around the land of the Winding Water. They stole a great many horses from us and we could not get them back because we were Indians. The white men told lies for each other. They drove off a great many of our cattle. Some white men branded our young cattle so they could claim them. We had no friends who would plead our cause before the law councils. It seemed to me that some of the white men in Wallowa were doing these things on purpose to get up a war. They knew we were not strong enough to fight them. I labored hard to avoid trouble and bloodshed. We gave up some of our country to the white men, thinking that then we could have peace. We were mistaken. The white men would not let us alone. We could have avenged our wrongs many times, but we did not. Whenever the Government has asked for help against other Indians we have never refused. When the white men were few and we were strong we could have killed them off, but the Nez Percé wishes to live at peace.

On account of the treaty made by the other bands of the Nez Percé the white man claimed my lands. We were troubled with white men crowding over the line. Some of them were good men, and we lived on peaceful terms with them, but they were not all good. Nearly every year the agent came over from Lapwai and ordered us to the reservation. We always replied that we were satisfied to live in Wallowa. We were careful to refuse the presents or annuities which he offered.

Through all the years since the white man came to Wallowa we have been threatened and taunted by them and the treaty Nez Percé. They have given us no rest. We have had a few good friends among the white men, and they have always advised my people to bear these taunts without fighting. Our young men are quick tempered and I have had great trouble in keeping them from doing rash things. I have carried a heavy load on my back ever since I was a boy. I learned then that we were but few while the white men were many, and that we could not hold our own with them. We were like deer. They were like grizzly bears. We had a small country. Their country was large. We were contented to let things remain as the Great Spirit Chief made them. They were not; and would change the mountains and rivers if they did not suit them.

III. [At his surrender in the Bear Paw Mountains, 1877] Tell General Howard that I know his heart. What he told me before I have in my heart. I am tired of fighting. Our chiefs are killed. Looking Glass is dead, Tu-hul-hil-sote is dead. The old men are all dead. It is the young men who now say yes or no. He who led the young men [Joseph's brother Alikut] is dead. It is cold and we have no blankets. The little children are freezing to death. My people—some of them have run away to the hills and have no blankets and no food. No one knows where they are—perhaps freezing to death. I want to have time to look for my children and see how many of them I can find. Maybe I shall find them among the dead. Hear me, my chiefs, my heart is sick and sad. From where the sun now stands I will fight no more against the white man.

IV. [On a visit to Washington, D.C., 1879] At last I was granted permission to come to Washington and bring my friend Yellow Bull and our interpreter with me. I am glad I came. I have shaken hands with a good many friends, but there are some things I want to know which no one seems able to explain. I cannot understand how the Government sends a man out to fight us, as it did General Miles, and then breaks his word. Such a government has something wrong about it. I cannot understand why so many chiefs are allowed to talk so many different ways, and promise so many different things. I have seen the Great Father Chief [President Hayes]; the Next Great Chief [Secretary of the Interior]; the Commissioner Chief; the Law Chief; and many other law chiefs [Congressmen] and they all say they are my friends, and that I shall have justice, but while all their mouths talk right I do not understand why nothing is done for my people. I have heard talk and talk but nothing is done. Good words do not last long unless they amount to something. Words do not pay for my dead people. They do not pay for my country now over-run by white men. They do not protect my father's grave. They do not pay for my horses and cattle. Good words do not give me back my children. Good words will not make good the promise of your war chief, General Miles. Good words will not give my people a home where they can live in peace and take care of themselves. I am tired of talk that comes to nothing. It makes my heart sick when I remember all the good words and all the broken promises. There has been too much talking by men who had no right to talk. Too many misinterpretations have been made; too many misunderstandings have come up between the white men and the Indians. If the white man wants to live in peace with the Indian he can live in peace. There need be no trouble. Treat all men alike. Give them the same laws. Give them all an even chance to live and grow. All men were made by the same Great Spirit Chief. They are all brothers. The earth is the mother of all people, and all people should have equal rights upon it. You might as well expect all rivers to run backward as that any man who was born a free man should be contented penned up and denied liberty to go where he pleases. If you tie a horse to a stake, do you expect he will grow fat? If you pen an Indian up on a small spot of earth and compel him to stay there, he will not be contented nor will he grow and prosper. I have asked some of the Great White Chiefs where they get their authority to say to the Indian that he shall stay in one place, while he sees white men going where they please. They cannot tell me.

I only ask of the Government to be treated as all other men are treated. If I cannot go to my own home, let me have a home in a country where my people will not die so fast. I would like to go to Bitter Root Valley. There my people would be happy; where they are now they are dying. Three have died since I left my camp to come to Washington.

When I think of our condition, my heart is heavy. I see men of my own race treated as outlaws and driven from country to country, or shot down like animals.

I know that my race must change. We cannot hold our own with the white men as we are. We only ask an even chance to live as other men live. We ask to be recognized as men. We ask that the same law shall work alike on all men. If an Indian breaks the law, punish him by the law. If a white man breaks the law, punish him also.

Let me be a free man, free to travel, free to stop, free to work, free to trade where I choose, free to choose my own teachers, free to follow the religion of my fathers, free to talk, think and act for myself—and I will obey every law or submit to the penalty.

Whenever the white man treats the Indian as they treat each other then we shall have no more wars. We shall be all alike—brothers of one father and mother, with one sky above us and one country around us and one government for all. Then the Great Spirit Chief who rules above will smile upon this land and send rain to wash out the bloody spots made by brothers' hands upon the face of the earth. For this time the Indian race is waiting and praying. I hope no more groans of wounded men and women will ever go to the ear of the Great Spirit Chief above, and that all people may be one people.

Hin-mah-too-yah-lat-kekht has spoken for his people.

Study Questions

1. What specific complaints does Chief Joseph make concerning the white people's relation to his tribe?

2. What solution does Chief Joseph envision for his people?

Chief Red Horse, "The Battle of the Little Bighorn, an Eyewitness Account" (1881)

The Battle of the Little Big Horn marked the highpoint of Native American resistance to the U.S. government. Lt. Col. George Custer, commanding the Seventh Calvary, sought to round up Indians and force them onto a reservation. Instead, the Indians stood their ground and Custer was fatally wounded. Known as "Custer's last stand," the Battle of the Little Big Horn also marked the last significant success that Native American would have in resisting the power of the U.S. Army.

Recorded in pictographs and text at the Cheyenne River Reservation, 1881.

Five springs ago I, with many Sioux Indians, took down and packed up our tipis and moved from Cheyenne river to the Rosebud river, where we camped a few days; then took down and packed up our lodges and moved to the Little Bighorn river and pitched our lodges with the large camp of Sioux.

The Sioux were camped on the Little Bighorn river as follows: The lodges of the Uncpapas were pitched highest up the river under a bluff. The Santee lodges were pitched next. The Oglala's lodges were pitched next. The Brule lodges were pitched next. The Minneconjou lodges were pitched next. The Sans Arcs' lodges were pitched next. The Blackfeet lodges were pitched next. The Cheyenne lodges were pitched next. A few Arikara Indians were among the Sioux (being without lodges of their own). Two-Kettles, among the other Sioux (without lodges).

I was a Sioux chief in the council lodge. My lodge was pitched in the center of the camp. The day of the attack I and four women were a short distance from the camp digging wild turnips. Suddenly one of the women attracted my attention to a cloud of dust rising a short distance from camp. I soon saw that the soldiers were charging the camp. To the camp I and the women ran. When I arrived a person told me to hurry to the council lodge. The soldiers charged so quickly we could not talk (council). We came out of the council lodge and talked in all directions. The Sioux mount horses, take guns, and go fight the soldiers. Women and children mount horses and go, meaning to get out of the way.

Among the soldiers was an officer who rode a horse with four white feet. [This officer was evidently Capt. French, Seventh Cavalry.] The Sioux have for a long time fought many brave men of different people, but the Sioux say this officer was the bravest man they had ever fought. I don't know whether this was Gen. Custer or not. Many of the Sioux men that I hear talking tell me it was. I saw this officer in the fight many times, but did not see his body. It has been told me that he was killed by a Santee Indian, who took his horse. This officer wore a large-brimmed hat and a deerskin coat. This officer saved the lives of many soldiers by turning his horse and covering the retreat. Sioux say this officer was the bravest man they ever fought. I saw two officers looking alike, both having long yellowish hair.

Before the attack the Sioux were camped on the Rosebud River. Sioux moved down a river running into the Little Bighorn river, crossed the Little Bighorn river, and camped on its west bank.

This day [day of attack] a Sioux man started to go to Red Cloud agency, but when he had gone a short distance from camp he saw a cloud of dust rising and turned back and said he thought a herd of buffalo was coming near the village.

The day was hot. In a short time the soldiers charged the camp. [This was Maj. Reno's battalion of the Seventh Cavalry.] The soldiers came on the trail made by the Sioux camp in moving, and crossed the Little Bighorn river above where the Sioux crossed, and attacked the lodges of the Uncpapas, farthest up the river. The women and children ran down the Little Bighorn River a short distance into a ravine. The soldiers set fire to the lodges. All the Sioux now charged the soldiers and drove them in confusion across the Little Bighorn River, which was very rapid, and several soldiers were drowned in it. On a hill the soldiers stopped and the Sioux surrounded them. A Sioux man came and said that a different party of Soldiers had all the women and children prisoners. Like a whirlwind the word went around, and the Sioux all heard it and left the soldiers on the hill and went quickly to save the women and children.

From the hill that the soldiers were on to the place where the different soldiers [by this term Red-Horse always means the battalion immediately commanded by General Custer, his mode of distinction being that they were a different body from

that first encountered] were seen was level ground with the exception of a creek. Sioux thought the soldiers on the hill [i e., Reno's battalion] would charge them in rear, but when they did not the Sioux thought the soldiers on the hill were out of cartridges. As soon as we had killed all the different soldiers the Sioux all went back to kill the soldiers on the hill. All the Sioux watched around the hill on which were the soldiers until a Sioux man came and said many walking soldiers were coming near. The coming of the walking soldiers was the saving of the soldiers on the hill. Sioux can not fight the walking soldiers [infantry], being afraid of them, so the Sioux hurriedly left.

The soldiers charged the Sioux camp about noon. The soldiers were divided, one party charging right into the camp. After driving these soldiers across the river, the Sioux charged the different soldiers [i.e., Custer's] below, and drive them in confusion; these soldiers became foolish, many throwing away their guns and raising their hands, saying, "Sioux, pity us; take us prisoners." The Sioux did not take a single soldier prisoner, but killed all of them; none were left alive for even a few minutes. These different soldiers discharged their guns but little. I took a gun and two belts off two dead soldiers; out of one belt two cartridges were gone, out of the other five.

The Sioux took the guns and cartridges off the dead soldiers and went to the hill on which the soldiers were, surrounded and fought them with the guns and cartridges of the dead soldiers. Had the soldiers not divided I think they would have killed many Sioux. The different soldiers [i.e., Custer's battalion] that the Sioux killed made five brave stands. Once the Sioux charged right in the midst of the different soldiers and scattered them all, fighting among the soldiers hand to hand.

One band of soldiers was in rear of the Sioux. When this band of soldiers charged, the Sioux fell back, and the Sioux and the soldiers stood facing each other. Then all the Sioux became brave and charged the soldiers. The Sioux went but a short distance before they separated and surrounded the soldiers. I could see the officers riding in front of the soldiers and hear them shooting. Now the Sioux had many killed. The soldiers killed 136 and wounded 160 Sioux. The Sioux killed all these different soldiers in the ravine.

The soldiers charged the Sioux camp farthest up the river. A short time after the different soldiers charged the village below. While the different soldiers and Sioux were fighting together the Sioux chief said, "Sioux men, go watch soldiers on the hill and prevent their joining the different soldiers." The Sioux men took the clothing off the dead and dressed themselves in it. Among the soldiers were white men who were not soldiers. The Sioux dressed in the soldiers' and white men's clothing fought the soldiers on the hill.

The banks of the Little Bighorn river were high, and the Sioux killed many of the soldiers while crossing. The soldiers on the hill dug up the ground [i.e., made earth-works], and the soldiers and Sioux fought at long range, sometimes the Sioux charging close up. The fight continued at long range until a Sioux man saw the walking soldiers coming. When the walking soldiers came near the Sioux became afraid and ran away.

Study Questions

1. Chief Red Horse provided this account in 1881. From internal evidence, determine the year in which the battle that he describes took place.

2. What happened at Little Bighorn?

Congress, Dawes Severalty Act (1887)

In the 1880s, Senator Henry Laurens Dawes of Massachusetts sponsored an "Act to Provide for the Allotment of Lands in Severally to Indians on the Various Reservations, and to Extend the Protection of the Laws of the United States and the Territories over the Indians." Rather than relocate Indian tribes to reservations, the nation's new policy would offer land ownership and citizenship to Indians as individuals—thus "severing" their tribal landholdings into private allotments.

Be it enacted by the Senate and House of Representatives of the United States of America in Congress assembled,

SEC. 1. That in all cases where any tribe or band of Indians has been, or shall hereafter be, located upon any reservation created for their use, either by treaty stipulation or by virtue of an act of Congress or executive order setting apart the same for their use, the President of the United States be, and he hereby is, authorized, whenever in his opinion any reservation or any part thereof of such Indians is advantageous for agricultural and grazing purposes, to cause said reservation, or any part thereof, to be surveyed, or resurveyed if necessary, and to allot the lands in said reservation in severalty to any Indian located thereon in quantities as follows: To each head of a family, one-quarter of a section; To each single person over eighteen years of age, one-eighth of a section; To each orphan child under eighteen years of age, one-eighth of a section; and To each other single person under eighteen years now living, or who may be born prior to the date of the order of the President directing an allotment of the lands embraced in any reservation, one-sixteenth of a section. . . .

SEC. 2. That all allotments set apart under the provisions of this act shall be selected by the Indians, heads of families selecting for their minor children, and the agents shall select for each orphan child, and in such manner as to embrace the improvements of the Indians making the selection. . . .

SEC. 3. That the allotments provided for in this act shall be made by special agents appointed by the President for such purpose, and the agents in charge of the respective reservations on which the allotments are directed to be made, under such rules and regulations as the Secretary of the Interior may from time to time prescribe, and shall be certified by such agents to the Commissioner of Indian Affairs, in duplicate, one copy to be retained in the Indian Office and the other to be transmitted to the Secretary of the Interior for his action, and to be deposited in the General Land Office.

SEC. 4. That where any Indian not residing upon a reservation, or for whose tribe no reservation has been provided by treaty, act of Congress, or executive order, shall make settlement upon any surveyed or unsurveyed lands of the United States not otherwise appropriated, he or she shall be entitled, upon application to the local land-office for the district in which the lands arc located, to have the same allotted to him or her, and to his or her children, in quantities and manner as provided in this act for Indians residing upon reservations. . . .

SEC. 5. That upon the approval of the allotments provided for in this act by the Secretary of the Interior, he shall cause patents to issue therefor in the name of the allottees, which patents shall be of the legal effect, and declare that the United States does and will hold the land thus allotted, for the period of twenty-five years, in trust for the sole use and benefit of the Indian to whom such allotment shall have been made, or, in case of his decease, of his heirs according to the laws of the State or Territory where such land is located, and that at the expiration of said period the United States will convey the same by patent to said Indian, or his heirs as aforesaid, in fee, discharged of said trust and free of all charge or encumbrance whatsoever: Provided, That the President of the United States may in any case in his discretion extend the period. . . .

SEC. 6. That upon the completion of said allotments and the patenting of the lands to said allottees, each and every number of the respective bands or tribes of Indians to whom allotments have been made shall have the benefit of and be subject to the laws, both civil and criminal, of the State or Territory in which they may reside; and no Territory shall pass or enforce any law denying any such Indian within its jurisdiction the equal protection of the law. And every Indian born within the territorial limits of the United States to whom allotments shall have been made under the provisions of this act, or under any law or treaty, and every Indian born within the territorial limits of the United States who has voluntarily taken up, within said limits, his residence separate and apart from any tribe of Indians therein, and has adopted the habits of civilized life, is hereby declared to be a citizen of the United States, and is entitled to all the rights, privileges, and immunities of such citizens, whether said Indian has been or not, by birth or otherwise, a member of any tribe of Indians within the territorial limits of the United States without in any manner affecting the right of any such Indian to tribal or other property.

. . . Approved, February, 8, 1887.

Study Questions

1. Compare the Dawes Act to the Homestead Act of 1862: What were the chief similarities and differences?

2. What motivated the adoption of the Dawes Act?

Edward Bellamy, *Looking Backwards from 2000 to 1887* (1888)

In the science-fiction classic *Looking Backwards*, Julian West (the narrator and viewpoint character) falls asleep in America during the Gilded Age and is discovered in the year 2000 by Dr. Leete. America has changed greatly during the 113 intervening years. As West and Leete converse to discuss the differences, West comes to recognize the inhumane tendencies of Gilded Age capitalism and to appreciate the progress that a century of socialist reform has produced for Dr. Leete and his contemporaries. Edward Bellamy, the author of *Looking Backwards*, received training as a lawyer but ultimately settled upon a career in journalism, initially writing for the *New York Evening Post*. In 1891, Bellamy founded the *New Nation*, a Boston newspaper dedicated to socialist reform. *Looking Backwards* ranked as a national best-seller, inspiring a cadre of reform activists to organize "Bellamy Clubs" in promotion of socialist ideals.

Chapter 5

... [Dr. Leete:] "What should you name as the most prominent feature of the labor troubles of your day."

"Why, the strikes, of course," I replied.

"Exactly; but what made the strikes so formidable."

"The great labor organizations."

"And what was the motive of these great organizations."

"The workmen claimed they had to organize to get their rights from the big corporations," I replied.

"That is just it," said Dr. Leete; "the organization of labor and the strikes were an effect, merely, of the concentration of capital in greater masses than had ever been known before. Before this concentration began, while as yet commerce and industry were conducted by innumerable petty concerns with small capital, instead of a small number of great concerns with vast capital, the individual workman was relatively important and independent in his relations to the employer. Moreover, when a little capital or a new idea was enough to start a man in business for himself, workingmen were constantly becoming employers and there was no hard and fast line between the two classes. Labor unions were needless then, and general strikes out of the question. But when the era of small concerns with small capital was succeeded by that of the great aggregations of capital, all this was changed. The individual laborer, who had been relatively important to the small employer, was reduced to insignificance and powerlessness over against the great corporation, while at the same time the way upward to the grade of employer was closed to him. Self-defense drove him to union with his fellows.

"The records of the period show that the outcry against the concentration of capital was furious. Men believed that it threatened society with a form of tyranny more abhorrent than it had ever endured. They believed that the great corporations were preparing for them the yoke of a baser servitude than had ever been imposed on the race, servitude not to men but to soulless machines incapable of any motive but insatiable greed. Looking back, we cannot wonder at their desperation, for certainly humanity was never confronted with a fate more sordid and hideous than would have been the era of corporate tyranny which they anticipated.

"Meanwhile, without being in the smallest degree checked by the clamor against it, the absorption of business by ever larger monopolies continued. In the United States there was not, after the beginning of the last quarter of the century, any opportunity whatever for individual enterprise in any important field of industry, unless backed by a great capital. During the last decade of the century, such small businesses as still remained were fast-failing survivals of a past epoch, or mere parasites on the great corporations, or else existed in fields too small to attract the great capitalists. Small businesses, as far as they still remained, were reduced to the condition of rats and mice, living in holes and corners, and counting on evading notice for the enjoyment of existence. The railroads had gone on combining till a few great syndicates controlled every rail in the land. In manufactories, every important staple was controlled by a syndicate. These syndicates, pools, trusts, or whatever their name, fixed prices and crushed all competition except when combinations as vast as themselves arose. Then a struggle, resulting in a still greater consolidation, ensued. The great city bazar crushed its country rivals with branch stores, and in the city itself absorbed its smaller rivals till the business of a whole quarter was concentrated under one roof, with a hundred

former proprietors of shops serving as clerks. Having no business of his own to put his money in, the small capitalist, at the same time that he took service under the corporation, found no other investment for his money but its stocks and bonds, thus becoming doubly dependent upon it.

"The fact that the desperate popular opposition to the consolidation of business in a few powerful hands had no effect to check it proves that there must have been a strong economical reason for it. The small capitalists, with their innumerable petty concerns, had in fact yielded the field to the great aggregations of capital, because they belonged to a day of small things and were totally incompetent to the demands of an age of steam and telegraphs and the gigantic scale of its enterprises. To restore the former order of things, even if possible, would have involved returning to the day of stagecoaches. Oppressive and intolerable as was the regime of the great consolidations of capital, even its victims, while they cursed it, were forced to admit the prodigious increase of efficiency which had been imparted to the national industries, the vast economies effected by concentration of management and unity of organization, and to confess that since the new system had taken the place of the old the wealth of the world had increased at a rate before undreamed of. To be sure this vast increase had gone chiefly to make the rich richer, increasing the gap between them and the poor; but the fact remained that, as a means merely of producing wealth, capital had been proved efficient in proportion to its consolidation. The restoration of the old system with the subdivision of capital, if it were possible, might indeed bring back a greater equality of conditions, with more individual dignity and freedom, but it would be at the price of general poverty and the arrest of material progress.

"Was there, then, no way of commanding the services of the mighty wealth-producing principle of consolidated capital without bowing down to a plutocracy like that of Carthage? As soon as men began to ask themselves these questions, they found the answer ready for them. The movement toward the conduct of business by larger and larger aggregations of capital, the tendency toward monopolies, which had been so desperately and vainly resisted, was recognized at last, in its true significance, as a process which only needed to complete its logical evolution to open a golden future to humanity.

"Early in the last century [i.e., the early 1900s] the evolution was completed by the final consolidation of the entire capital of the nation. The industry and commerce of the country, ceasing to be conducted by a set of irresponsible corporations and syndicates of private persons at their caprice and for their profit, were intrusted to a single syndicate representing the people, to be conducted in the common interest for the common profit. The nation, that is to say, organized as the one great business corporation in which all other corporations were absorbed; it became the one capitalist in the place of all other capitalists, the sole employer, the final monopoly in which all previous and lesser monopolies were swallowed up, a monopoly in the profits and economies of which all citizens shared. The epoch of trusts had ended in

The Great Trust. In a word, the people of the United States concluded to assume the conduct of their own business, just as one hundred odd years before they had assumed the conduct of their own government, organizing now for industrial purposes on precisely the same grounds that they had then organized for political purposes. At last, strangely late in the world's history, the obvious fact was perceived that no business is so essentially the public business as the industry and commerce on which the people's livelihood depends, and that to entrust it to private persons to be managed for private profit is a folly similar in kind, though vastly greater in magnitude, to that of surrendering the functions of political government to kings and nobles to be conducted for their personal glorification."

"Such a stupendous change as you describe," said I, "did not, of course, take place without great bloodshed and terrible convulsions."

"On the contrary," replied Dr. Leete, "there was absolutely no violence. The change had been long foreseen. Public opinion had become fully ripe for it, and the whole mass of the people was behind it. There was no more possibility of opposing it by force than by argument. On the other hand the popular sentiment toward the great corporations and those identified with them had ceased to be one of bitterness, as they came to realize their necessity as a link, a transition phase, in the evolution of the true industrial system. The most violent foes of the great private monopolies were now forced to recognize how invaluable and indispensable had been their office in educating the people up to the point of assuming control of their own business. Fifty years before, the consolidation of the industries of the country under national control would have seemed a very daring experiment to the most sanguine. But by a series of object lessons, seen and studied by all men, the great corporations had taught the people an entirely new set of ideas on this subject. They had seen for many years syndicates handling revenues greater than those of states, and directing the labors of hundreds of thousands of men with an efficiency and economy unattainable in smaller operations. It had come to be recognized as an axiom that the larger the business the simpler the principles that can be applied to it; that, as the machine is truer than the hand, so the system, which in a great concern does the work of the master's eye in a small business, turns out more accurate results. Thus it came about that, thanks to the corporations themselves, when it was proposed that the nation should assume their functions, the suggestion implied nothing which seemed impracticable even to the timid. To be sure it was a step beyond any yet taken, a broader generalization, but the very fact that the nation would be the sole corporation in the field would, it was seen, relieve the undertaking of many difficulties with which the partial monopolies had contended."

Chapter 6

Dr. Leete ceased speaking, and I remained silent, endeavoring to form some general conception of the changes in the arrangements of society implied in the tremendous revolution which he had described.

Finally I said, "The idea of such an extension of the functions of government is, to say the least, rather overwhelming."

"Extension," he repeated, "where is the extension?"

"In my day," I replied, "it was considered that the proper functions of government, strictly speaking, were limited to keeping the peace and defending the people against the public enemy, that is, to the military and police powers."

"And, in heaven's name, who are the public enemies?" exclaimed Dr. Leete. "Are they France, England, Germany, or hunger, cold, and nakedness? In your day governments were accustomed, on the slightest international misunderstanding, to seize upon the bodies of citizens and deliver them over by hundreds of thousands to death and mutilation, wasting their treasures the while like water; and all this oftenest for no imaginable profit to the victims. We have no wars now, and our governments no war powers, but in order to protect every citizen against hunger, cold, and nakedness, and provide for all his physical and mental needs, the function is assumed of directing his industry for a term of years. No, Mr. West, I am sure on reflection you will perceive that it was in your age, not in ours, that the extension of the functions of governments was extraordinary. Not even for the best ends would men now allow their governments such powers as were then used for the most maleficent."

"Leaving comparisons aside," I said, "the demagoguery and corruption of our public men would have been considered, in my day, insuperable objections to any assumption by government of the charge of the national industries. We should have thought that no arrangement could be worse than to entrust the politicians with control of the wealth-producing machinery of the country. Its material interests were quite too much the football of parties as it was."

"No doubt you were right," rejoined Dr. Leete, "but all that is changed now. We have no parties or politicians, and as for demagoguery and corruption, they are words having only an historical significance."

"Human nature itself must have changed very much," I said.

"Not at all," was Dr. Leete's reply, "but the conditions of human life have changed, and with them the motives of human action. The organization of society with you was such that officials were under a constant temptation to misuse their power for the private profit of themselves or others. Under such circumstances it seems almost strange that you dared entrust them with any of your affairs. Nowadays, on the contrary, society is so constituted that there is absolutely no way in which an official, however ill-disposed, could possibly make any profit for himself or any one else by a misuse of his power. Let him be as bad an official as you please, he cannot be a corrupt one. There is no motive to be. The social system no longer offers a premium on dishonesty. But these are matters which you can only understand as you come, with time, to know us better."

"But you have not yet told me how you have settled the labor problem. It is the problem of capital which we have been discussing," I said. "After the nation had assumed conduct of the mills, machinery, railroads, farms, mines, and capital in general of the country, the labor question still remained. In assuming the responsibilities of capital the nation had assumed the difficulties of the capitalist's position."

"The moment the nation assumed the responsibilities of capital those difficulties vanished," replied Dr. Leete. "The national organization of labor under one direction was the complete solution of what was, in your day and under your system, justly regarded as the insoluble labor problem. When the nation became the sole employer, all the citizens, by virtue of their citizenship, became employees, to be distributed according to the needs of industry."

"That is," I suggested, "you have simply applied the principle of universal military service, as it was understood in our day, to the labor question."

"Yes," said Dr. Leete, "that was something which followed as a matter of course as soon as the nation had become the sole capitalist. The people were already accustomed to the idea that the obligation of every citizen, not physically disabled, to contribute his military services to the defense of the nation was equal and absolute. That it was equally the duty of every citizen to contribute his quota of industrial or intellectual services to the maintenance of the nation was equally evident, though it was not until the nation became the employer of labor that citizens were able to render this sort of service with any pretense either of universality or equity. No organization of labor was possible when the employing power was divided among hundreds or thousands of individuals and corporations, between which concert of any kind was neither desired, nor indeed feasible. It constantly happened then that vast numbers who desired to labor could find no opportunity, and on the other hand, those who desired to evade a part or all of their debt could easily do so."

"Service, now, I suppose, is compulsory upon all," I suggested.

"It is rather a matter of course than of compulsion," replied Dr. Leete. "It is regarded as so absolutely natural and reasonable that the idea of its being compulsory has ceased to be thought of. He would be thought to be an incredibly contemptible person who should need compulsion in such a case. Nevertheless, to speak of service being compulsory would be a weak way to state its absolute inevitableness. Our entire social order is so wholly based upon and deduced from it that if it were conceivable that a man could escape it, he would be left with no possible way to provide for his existence. He would have excluded himself from the world, cut himself off from his kind, in a word, committed suicide."

"Is the term of service in this industrial army for life?"

"Oh, no; it both begins later and ends earlier than the average working period in your day. Your workshops were filled with children and old men, but we hold the period of youth sacred to education, and the period of maturity, when the physical forces begin to flag, equally sacred to ease and agreeable relaxation. The period of

industrial service is twenty-four years, beginning at the close of the course of education at twenty-one and terminating at forty-five. After forty-five, while discharged from labor, the citizen still remains liable to special calls, in case of emergencies causing a sudden great increase in the demand for labor, till he reaches the age of fifty-five, but such calls are rarely, in fact almost never, made. The fifteenth day of October of every year is what we call Muster Day, because those who have reached the age of twenty-one are then mustered into the industrial service, and at the same time those who, after twenty-four years' service, have reached the age of forty-five, are honorably mustered out. It is the great day of the year with us, whence we reckon all other events, our Olympiad, save that it is annual." . . .

Chapter 9

"But what inducement," I asked, "can a man have to put forth his best endeavors when, however much or little he accomplishes, his income remains the same? High characters may be moved by devotion to the common welfare under such a system, but does not the average man tend to rest back on his oar, reasoning that it is of no use to make a special effort, since the effort will not increase his income, nor its withholding diminish it."

"Does it then really seem to you," answered my companion, "that human nature is insensible to any motives save fear of want and love of luxury, that you should expect security and equality of livelihood to leave them without possible incentives to effort? Your contemporaries did not really think so, though they might fancy they did. When it was a question of the grandest class of efforts, the most absolute self-devotion, they depended on quite other incentives. Not higher wages, but honor and the hope of men's gratitude, patriotism and the inspiration of duty, were the motives which they set before their soldiers when it was a question of dying for the nation, and never was there an age of the world when those motives did not call out what is best and noblest in men. And not only this, but when you come to analyze the love of money which was the general impulse to effort in your day, you find that the dread of want and desire of luxury was but one of several motives which the pursuit of money represented; the others, and with many the more influential, being desire of power, of social position, and reputation for ability and success. So you see that though we have abolished poverty and the fear of it, and inordinate luxury with the hope of it, we have not touched the greater part of the motives which underlay the love of money in former times, or any of those which prompted the supremer sorts of effort. The coarser motives, which no longer move us, have been replaced by higher motives wholly unknown to the mere wage earners of your age. Now that industry of whatever sort is no longer self-service, but service of the nation, patriotism, passion for humanity, impel the worker as in your day they did the soldier. The army of industry is an army, not alone by virtue of its perfect organization, but by reason also of the ardor of self-devotion which animates its members.

"But as you used to supplement the motives of patriotism with the love of glory, in order to stimulate the valor of your soldiers, so do we. Based as our industrial system is on the principle of requiring the same unit of effort from every man, that is, the best he can do, you will see that the means by which we spur the workers to do their best must be a very essential part of our scheme. With us, diligence in the national service is the sole and certain way to public repute, social distinction, and official power. The value of a man's services to society fixes his rank in it. Compared with the effect of our social arrangements in impelling men to be zealous in business, we deem the object-lessons of biting poverty and wanton luxury on which you depended a device as weak and uncertain as it was barbaric. The lust of honor even in your sordid day notoriously impelled men to more desperate effort than the love of money could."

Study Questions

1. How, according to Dr. Leete, has the socialist restructuring of society prevented corruption—a problem the Gilded Age failed to solve?

2. How did Dr. Leete and Julian West differ in their perceptions of what motivates human nature?

Andrew Carnegie, "The Gospel of Wealth" (1889)

Andrew Carnegie exemplified the American dream. Arriving in American in 1848 as an impoverished immigrant from Scotland, he worked his way up from sweeping the floors and running telegraph messages to establishing Carnegie Steel, one of the most productive and profitable companies of the Gilded Age. Carnegie's genius lay in his ability to streamline processes for efficiency while also respecting the contributions that each worker made. Critics have faulted Carnegie for getting rich at the expense of others, but in this article, originally published in the *North American Review*, Carnegie explains that the proper use of wealth is for improving the lives of others, not amassing riches for oneself.

We accept and welcome ... as conditions to which we must accommodate ourselves great inequality of environment, the concentration of business—industrial and commercial—in the hands of a few, and the law of competition between these as being not only beneficial but essential for the future progress of the race. Having accepted these, it follows that there must be great scope for the exercise of special ability in the merchant and in the manufacturer who has to conduct affairs upon a great scale. That this talent for organization and management is rare among men is proved by the fact that it invariably secures for its possessor enormous rewards, no matter where or under what laws or conditions. The experienced in affairs always rate the man whose services can be obtained as a partner as not only the first consideration but such as to render the question of his capital scarcely worth considering, for such men soon create capital; while, without the special talent required, capital soon takes wings.

Such men become interested in firms or corporations using millions; and estimating only simple interest to be made upon the capital invested, it is inevitable that their income must exceed their expenditures and that they must accumulate wealth. Nor is there any middle ground which such men can occupy, because the great manufacturing or commercial concern which does not earn at least interest upon its capital soon becomes bankrupt. It must either go forward or fall behind: to stand still is impossible. It is a condition essential for its successful operation that it should be thus far profitable, and even that, in addition to interest on capital, it should make profit. It is a law, as certain as any of the others named, that men possessed of this peculiar talent for affairs, under the free play of economic forces, must, of necessity, soon be in receipt of more revenue than can be judiciously expended upon themselves; and this law is as beneficial for the race as the others.

Objections to the foundations upon which society is based are not in order because the condition of the race is better with these than it has been with any others which have been tried. Of the effect of any new substitutes proposed, we cannot be sure. The socialist or anarchist who seeks to overturn present conditions is to be regarded as attacking the foundation upon which civilization itself rests, for civilization took its start from the day that the capable, industrious workman said to his incompetent and lazy fellow, "If thou dost not sow, thou shalt not reap," and thus ended primitive Communism by separating the drones from the bees. One who studies this subject will soon be brought face to face with the conclusion that upon the sacredness of property civilization itself depends—the right of the laborer to his $100 in the savings bank, and equally the legal right of the millionaire to his millions.

To those who propose to substitute Communism for this intense individualism the answer, therefore, is: The race has tried that. All progress from that barbarous day to the present time has resulted from its displacement. Not evil, but good, has come to the race from the accumulation of wealth by those who have the ability and energy that produce it. But even if we admit for a moment that it might be better for the race to discard its present foundation, individualism—that it is a nobler ideal that man should labor, not for himself alone but in and for a brotherhood of his fellows and share with them all in common, realizing Swedenborg's idea of heaven, where, as he says, the angels derive their happiness, not from laboring for self but for each other—even admit all this, and a sufficient answer is: This is not evolution, but revolution.

It necessitates the changing of human nature itself—a work of aeons, even if it were good to change it, which we cannot know. It is not practicable in our day or in our age. Even if desirable theoretically, it belongs to another and long-succeeding sociological stratum. Our duty is with what is practicable now; with the next step possible in our day and generation. It is criminal to waste our energies in endeavoring to uproot, when all we can profitably or possibly accomplish is to bend the universal tree of humanity a little in the direction most favorable to the production of good fruit under existing circumstances.

We might as well urge the destruction of the highest existing type of man because he failed to reach our ideal as to favor the destruction of individualism, private property, the law of accumulation of wealth, and the law of competition; for these are the highest results of human experience, the soil in which society so far has produced the best fruit. Unequally or unjustly, perhaps, as these laws sometimes operate, and imperfect as they appear to the idealist, they are, nevertheless, like the highest type of man, the best and most valuable of all that humanity has yet accomplished.

We start, then, with a condition of affairs under which the best interests of the race are promoted, but which inevitably gives wealth to the few. Thus far, accepting conditions as they exist, the situation can be surveyed and pronounced good. The question then arises—and, if the foregoing be correct, it is the only question with which we have to deal—What is the proper mode of administering wealth after the laws upon which civilization is founded have thrown it into the hands of the few? And it is of this great question that I believe I offer the true solution. It will be understood that fortunes are here spoken of, not moderate sums saved by many years of effort, the returns from which are required for the comfortable maintenance and education of families. This is not wealth but only competence, which it should be the aim of all to acquire.

There are but three modes in which surplus wealth can be disposed of. It can be left to the families of the decedents; or it can be bequeathed for public purposes; or, finally, it can be administered during their lives by its possessors. Under the first and second modes most of the wealth of the world that has reached the few has hitherto been applied. Let us in turn consider each of these modes.

The first is the most injudicious. In monarchical countries, the estates and the greatest portion of the wealth are left to the first son that the vanity of the parent may be gratified by the thought that his name and title are to descend to succeeding generations unimpaired. The condition of this class in Europe today teaches the futility of such hopes or ambitions. The successors have become impoverished through their follies or from the fall in the value of land. Even in Great Britain the strict law of entail has been found inadequate to maintain the status of an hereditary class. Its soil is rapidly passing into the hands of the stranger. Under republican institutions the division of property among the children is much fairer, but the question which forces itself upon thoughtful men in all lands is: Why should men leave great fortunes to their children? If this is done from affection, is it not misguided affection? Observation teaches that, generally speaking, it is not well for the children that they should be so burdened. Neither is it well for the state. Beyond providing for the wife and daughters moderate sources of income, and very moderate allowances indeed, if any, for the sons, men may well hesitate, for it is no

longer questionable that great sums bequeathed oftener work more for the injury than for the good of the recipients. Wise men will soon conclude that, for the best interests of the members of their families and of the state, such bequests are an improper use of their means.

It is not suggested that men who have failed to educate their sons to earn a livelihood shall cast them adrift in poverty. If any man has seen fit to rear his sons with a view to their living idle lives, or, what is highly commendable, has instilled in them the sentiment that they are in a position to labor for public ends without reference to pecuniary considerations, then, of course, the duty of the parent is to see that such are provided for in moderation. There are instances of millionaires' sons unspoiled by wealth, who, being rich, still perform great services in the community. Such are the very salt of the earth, as valuable as, unfortunately, they are rare; still it is not the exception but the rule that men must regard, and, looking at the usual result of enormous sums conferred upon legatees, the thoughtful man must shortly say, "I would as soon leave to my son a curse as the almighty dollar," and admit to himself that it is not the welfare of the children but family pride which inspires these enormous legacies.

As to the second mode, that of leaving wealth at death for public uses, it may be said that this is only a means for the disposal of wealth, provided a man is content to wait until he is dead before it becomes of much good in the world. Knowledge of the results of legacies bequeathed is not calculated to inspire the brightest hopes of much posthumous good being accomplished. The cases are not few in which the real object sought by the testator is not attained, nor are they few in which his real wishes are thwarted. In many cases the bequests are so used as to become only monuments of his folly.

It is well to remember that it requires the exercise of not less ability than that which acquired the wealth to use it so as to be really beneficial to the community. Besides this, it may fairly be said that no man is to be extolled for doing what he cannot help doing, nor is he to be thanked by the community to which he only leaves wealth at death. Men who leave vast sums in this way may fairly be thought men who would not have left it at all had they been able to take it with them. The memories of such cannot be held in grateful remembrance, for there is no grace in their gifts. It is not to be wondered at that such bequests seem so generally to lack the blessing.

The growing disposition to tax more and more heavily large estates left at death is a cheering indication of the growth of a salutary change in public opinion. The state of Pennsylvania now takes—subject to some exceptions—one-tenth of the property left by its citizens. The budget presented in the British Parliament the other day proposes to increase the death duties; and, most significant of all, the new tax is to be a graduated one. Of all forms of taxation, this seems the wisest. Men who continue hoarding great sums all their lives, the proper use of which for public ends would work good to the community, should be made to feel that the community, in the form of the state, cannot thus be deprived of its proper share. By taxing estates heavily at death the state marks its condemnation of the selfish millionaire's unworthy life.

It is desirable that nations should go much further in this direction. Indeed, it is difficult to set bounds to the share of a rich man's estate which should go at his death to the public through the agency of the state, and by all means such taxes should be graduated, beginning at nothing upon moderate sums to dependents and increasing rapidly as the amounts swell, until, of the millionaire's hoard as of Shylock's, at least—The other half comes to the privy coffer of the state.

This policy would work powerfully to induce the rich man to attend to the administration of wealth during his life, which is the end that society should always have in view, as being that by far most fruitful for the people. Nor need it be feared that this policy would sap the root of enterprise and render men less anxious to accumulate, for to the class whose ambition it is to leave great fortunes and be talked about after their death, it will attract even more attention, and, indeed, be a somewhat nobler ambition to have enormous sums paid over to the state from their fortunes.

There remains, then, only one mode of using great fortunes; but in this we have the true antidote for the temporary unequal distribution of wealth, the reconciliation of the rich and the poor—a reign of harmony—another ideal, differing, indeed, from that of the Communist in requiring only the further evolution of existing conditions, not the total overthrow of our civilization. It is founded

upon the present most intense individualism, and the race is prepared to put it in
practice by degrees whenever it pleases.
Under its sway we shall have an ideal state
in which the surplus wealth of the few will
become, in the best sense, the property of
the many, because administered for the
common good; and this wealth, passing
through the hands of the few, can be made
a much more potent force for the elevation
of our race than if it had been distributed
in small sums to the people themselves.
Even the poorest can be made to see this
and to agree that great sums gathered by
some of their fellow citizens and spent for
public purposes, from which the masses
reap the principal benefit, are more valuable to them than if scattered among them
through the course of many years in tri-
fling amounts.

Poor and restricted are our opportunities in this life; narrow our horizon; our
best work most imperfect; but rich men
should be thankful for one inestimable
boon. They have it in their power during
their lives to busy themselves in organizing
benefactions from which the masses of
their fellows will derive lasting advantage,
and thus dignify their own lives. The
highest life is probably to be reached, not
by such imitation of the life of Christ as
Count Tolstoi gives us but, while animated
by Christ's spirit, by recognizing the
changed conditions of this age and adopting modes of expressing this spirit suitable
to the changed conditions under which we
live; still laboring for the good of our fellows, which was the essence of his life and
teaching, but laboring in a different manner.

This, then, is held to be the duty of the
man of wealth: first, to set an example of
modest, unostentatious living, shunning
display or extravagance; to provide moder-
ately for the legitimate wants of those
dependent upon him; and after doing so to
consider all surplus revenues which come
to him simply as trust funds which he is
called upon to administer, and strictly
bound as a matter of duty to administer in
the manner which, in his judgment, is best
calculated to produce the most beneficial
results for the community—the man of
wealth thus becoming the mere agent and
trustee for his poorer brethren, bringing to
their service his superior wisdom, experience, and ability to administer, doing for
them better than they would or could do
for themselves. . . .

In bestowing charity, the main consideration should be to help those who will
help themselves; to provide part of the
means by which those who desire to
improve may do so; to give those who
desire to rise the aids by which they may
rise; to assist, but rarely or never to do all.
Neither the individual nor the race is
improved by almsgiving. Those worthy of
assistance, except in rare cases, seldom
require assistance. The really valuable men
of the race never do, except in cases of
accident or sudden change. Everyone has,
of course, cases of individuals brought to
his own knowledge where temporary
assistance can do genuine good, and these
he will not overlook. But the amount
which can be wisely given by the individual
for individuals is necessarily limited by his
lack of knowledge of the circumstances
connected with each. He is the only true
reformer who is as careful and as anxious
not to aid the unworthy as he is to aid the

worthy, and, perhaps, even more so, for in almsgiving more injury is probably done by rewarding vice than by relieving virtue. . . .

Thus is the problem of rich and poor to be solved. The laws of accumulation will be left free; the laws of distribution free. Individualism will continue, but the millionaire will be but a trustee for the poor; entrusted for a season with a great part of the increased wealth of the community, but administering it for the community far better than it could or would have done for itself. The best minds will thus have reached a stage in the development of the race in which it is clearly seen that there is no mode of disposing of surplus wealth creditable to thoughtful and earnest men into whose hands it flows save by using it year by year for the general good.

This day already dawns. But a little while, and although, without incurring the pity of their fellows, men may die sharers in great business enterprises from which their capital cannot be or has not been withdrawn, and is left chiefly at death for public uses, yet the man who dies leaving behind him millions of available wealth, which was his to administer during life, will pass away "unwept, unhonored, and unsung," no matter to what uses he leaves the dross which he cannot take with him. Of such as these the public verdict will then be: "The man who dies thus rich dies disgraced."

Such, in my opinion, is the true gospel concerning wealth, obedience to which is destined some day to solve the problem of the rich and the poor, and to bring "Peace on earth, among men goodwill."

Study Questions

1. What distinction did Carnegie identify between communism and individualism, and which of these philosophies did he favor?

2. What duty did Carnegie assign to the wealthy?

3. Why is Carnegie's economic philosophy called the "gospel of wealth"?

Benjamin Harrison, Inaugural Address (1889)

Although Grover Cleveland won the popular vote in the election of 1888, Benjamin Harrison secured a majority of the electoral votes. His "front-porch campaign" had attracted over 300,000 people to his home, where he spoke primarily in defense of the tariff. Cleveland, meanwhile, had alienated even some members of his own Democratic Party by criticizing the tariff as "an indefensible extortion and a culpable betrayal of American fairness" in his December 1887 message to Congress. As the political pendulum continued to swing, Harrison would find himself losing out to Cleveland four years later, in the 1892 election, after the McKinley Tariff (1890) raised import taxes to astronomical levels and the economy fell into a deep slump.

Fellow-Citizens:

There is no constitutional or legal requirement that the President shall take the oath of office in the presence of the people, but there is so manifest an appropriateness in the public induction to office of the chief executive officer of the nation that from the beginning of the Government the people, to whose service the official oath consecrates the officer, have been called to witness the solemn ceremonial. The oath taken in the presence of the people becomes a mutual covenant. The officer covenants to serve the whole body of the people by a faithful execution of the laws, so that they may be the unfailing defense and security of those who respect and observe them, and that neither wealth, station, nor the power of combinations shall be able to evade their just penalties or to wrest them from a beneficent public purpose to serve the ends of cruelty or selfishness.

My promise is spoken; yours unspoken, but not the less real and solemn. The people of every State have here their representatives. Surely I do not misinterpret the spirit of the occasion when I assume that the whole body of the people covenant with me and with each other to-day to support and defend the Constitution and the Union of the States, to yield willing obedience to all the laws and each to every other citizen his equal civil and political rights. Entering thus solemnly into covenant with each other, we may reverently invoke and confidently expect the favor and help of Almighty God—that He will give to me wisdom, strength, and fidelity, and to our people a spirit of fraternity and a love of righteousness and peace.

This occasion derives peculiar interest from the fact that the Presidential term which begins this day is the twenty-sixth under our Constitution. The first inauguration of President Washington took place in New York, where Congress was then sitting, on the 30th day of April, 1789, having been deferred by reason of delays attending the organization of the Congress and the canvass of the electoral vote. Our people have already worthily observed the centennials of the Declaration of Independence, of the battle of Yorktown, and of the adoption of the Constitution, and will shortly celebrate in New York the institution of the second great department of our constitutional scheme of government. When the centennial of the institution of the judicial department, by the organization of the Supreme Court, shall have been suitably observed, as I trust it will be, our nation will have fully entered its second century.

I will not attempt to note the marvelous and in great part happy contrasts between our country as it steps over the threshold into its second century of organized existence under the Constitution and that weak but wisely ordered young nation that looked undauntedly down the first century, when all its years stretched out before it.

Our people will not fail at this time to recall the incidents which accompanied the institution of government under the Constitution, or to find inspiration and guidance in the teachings and example of Washington and his great associates, and hope and courage in the contrast which thirty-eight populous and prosperous States offer to the thirteen States, weak in everything except courage and the love of liberty, that then fringed our Atlantic seaboard.

The Territory of Dakota has now a population greater than any of the original States (except Virginia) and greater than the aggregate of five of the smaller States in 1790. The center of population when our national capital was located was east of Baltimore, and it was argued by many well-informed persons that it would move eastward rather than westward; yet in 1880 it was found to be near Cincinnati, and the new census about to be taken will show another stride to the westward. That which was the body has come to be only the rich fringe of the nation's robe. But our growth has not been limited to territory, population and aggregate wealth, marvelous as it has been in each of those directions. The masses of our people are better fed, clothed, and housed than their fathers were. The facilities for popular education have been vastly enlarged and more generally diffused.

The virtues of courage and patriotism have given recent proof of their continued presence and increasing power in the hearts and over the lives of our people. The influences of religion have been multiplied and strengthened. The sweet offices of charity have greatly increased. The virtue of temperance is held in higher estimation. We have not attained an ideal condition. Not all of our people are happy and prosperous; not all of them are virtuous and law-abiding. But on the whole the opportunities offered to the individual to secure the comforts of life are better than are found elsewhere and largely better than they were here one hundred years ago.

The surrender of a large measure of sovereignty to the General Government, effected by the adoption of the Constitution, was not accomplished until the suggestions of reason were strongly reenforced by the more imperative voice of experience. The divergent interests of peace speedily demanded a "more perfect union." The merchant, the shipmaster, and the manufacturer discovered and disclosed to our statesmen and to the people that commercial emancipation must be added to the political freedom which had been so bravely won. The commercial policy of the mother country had not relaxed any of its hard and oppressive features. To hold in check the development of our commercial marine, to prevent or retard the establishment and growth of manufactures in the States, and so to secure the American market for their shops and the carrying trade for their ships, was the policy of European statesmen, and was pursued with the most selfish vigor.

Petitions poured in upon Congress urging the imposition of discriminating duties that should encourage the production of needed things at home. The patriotism of the people, which no longer found afield of exercise in war, was energetically directed to the duty of equipping the young Republic for the defense of its independence by making its people self-dependent. Societies for the promotion of home manufactures and for encouraging the use of domestics in the dress of the people were organized in many of the States. The revival at the end of the century of the same patriotic interest in the preservation and development of domestic industries and the defense of our working people against injurious foreign competition is an incident worthy of attention. It is not a departure but a return that we have witnessed. The protective policy had then its opponents. The argument was made, as now, that its benefits inured to particular classes or sections.

If the question became in any sense or at any time sectional, it was only because slavery existed in some of the States. But for this there was no reason why the cotton-producing States should not have led or walked abreast with the New England States in the production of cotton fabrics. There was this reason only why the States that divide with Pennsylvania the mineral treasures of the great southeastern and central mountain ranges should have been

so tardy in bringing to the smelting furnace and to the mill the coal and iron from their near opposing hillsides. Mill fires were lighted at the funeral pile of slavery. The emancipation proclamation was heard in the depths of the earth as well as in the sky; men were made free, and material things became our better servants.

The sectional element has happily been eliminated from the tariff discussion. We have no longer States that are necessarily only planting States. None are excluded from achieving that diversification of pursuits among the people which brings wealth and contentment. The cotton plantation will not be less valuable when the product is spun in the country town by operatives whose necessities call for diversified crops and create a home demand for garden and agricultural products. Every new mine, furnace, and factory is an extension of the productive capacity of the State more real and valuable than added territory.

Shall the prejudices and paralysis of slavery continue to hang upon the skirts of progress? How long will those who rejoice that slavery no longer exists cherish or tolerate the incapacities it put upon their communities? I look hopefully to the continuance of our protective system and to the consequent development of manufacturing and mining enterprises in the States hitherto wholly given to agriculture as a potent influence in the perfect unification of our people. The men who have invested their capital in these enterprises, the farmers who have felt the benefit of their neighborhood, and the men who work in shop or field will not fail to find and to defend a community of interest.

Is it not quite possible that the farmers and the promoters of the great mining and manufacturing enterprises which have recently been established in the South may yet find that the free ballot of the working-man, without distinction of race, is needed for their defense as well as for his own? I do not doubt that if those men in the South who now accept the tariff views of Clay and the constitutional expositions of Webster would courageously avow and defend their real convictions they would not find it difficult, by friendly instruction and cooperation, to make the black man their efficient and safe ally, not only in establishing correct principles in our national administration, but in preserving for their local communities the benefits of social order and economical and honest government. At least until the good offices of kindness and education have been fairly tried the contrary conclusion can not be plausibly urged.

I have altogether rejected the suggestion of a special Executive policy for any section of our country. It is the duty of the Executive to administer and enforce in the methods and by the instrumentalities pointed out and provided by the Constitution all the laws enacted by Congress. These laws are general and their administration should be uniform and equal. As a citizen may not elect what laws he will obey, neither may the Executive elect which he will enforce. The duty to obey and to execute embraces the Constitution in its entirety and the whole code of laws enacted under it. The evil example of permitting individuals, corporations, or communities to nullify the laws because they cross some selfish or local interest or

prejudices is full of danger, not only to the nation at large, but much more to those who use this pernicious expedient to escape their just obligations or to obtain an unjust advantage over others. They will presently themselves be compelled to appeal to the law for protection, and those who would use the law as a defense must not deny that use of it to others.

If our great corporations would more scrupulously observe their legal limitations and duties, they would have less cause to complain of the unlawful limitations of their rights or of violent interference with their operations. The community that by concert, open or secret, among its citizens denies to a portion of its members their plain rights under the law has severed the only safe bond of social order and prosperity. The evil works from a bad center both ways. It demoralizes those who practice it and destroys the faith of those who suffer by it in the efficiency of the law as a safe protector. The man in whose breast that faith has been darkened is naturally the subject of dangerous and uncanny suggestions. Those who use unlawful methods, if moved by no higher motive than the selfishness that prompted them, may well stop and inquire what is to be the end of this.

An unlawful expedient can not become a permanent condition of government. If the educated and influential classes in a community either practice or connive at the systematic violation of laws that seem to them to cross their convenience, what can they expect when the lesson that convenience or a supposed class interest is a sufficient cause for lawlessness has been well learned by the ignorant classes? A community where law is the rule of conduct and where courts, not mobs, execute its penalties is the only attractive field for business investments and honest labor.

Our naturalization laws should be so amended as to make the inquiry into the character and good disposition of persons applying for citizenship more careful and searching. Our existing laws have been in their administration an unimpressive and often an unintelligible form. We accept the man as a citizen without any knowledge of his fitness, and he assumes the duties of citizenship without any knowledge as to what they are. The privileges of American citizenship are so great and its duties so grave that we may well insist upon a good knowledge of every person applying for citizenship and a good knowledge by him of our institutions. We should not cease to be hospitable to immigration, but we should cease to be careless as to the character of it. There are men of all races, even the best, whose coming is necessarily a burden upon our public revenues or a threat to social order. These should be identified and excluded.

We have happily maintained a policy of avoiding all interference with European affairs. We have been only interested spectators of their contentions in diplomacy and in war, ready to use our friendly offices to promote peace, but never obtruding our advice and never attempting unfairly to coin the distresses of other powers into commercial advantage to ourselves. We have a just right to expect that our European policy will be the American policy of European courts.

It is so manifestly incompatible with those precautions for our peace and safety which all the great powers habitually observe and enforce in matters affecting them that a shorter waterway between our eastern and western seaboards should be dominated by any European Government that we may confidently expect that such a purpose will not be entertained by any friendly power.

We shall in the future, as in the past, use every endeavor to maintain and enlarge our friendly relations with all the great powers, but they will not expect us to look kindly upon any project that would leave us subject to the dangers of a hostile observation or environment. We have not sought to dominate or to absorb any of our weaker neighbors, but rather to aid and encourage them to establish free and stable governments resting upon the consent of their own people. We have a clear right to expect, therefore, that no European Government will seek to establish colonial dependencies upon the territory of these independent American States. That which a sense of justice restrains us from seeking they may be reasonably expected willingly to forego.

It must not be assumed, however, that our interests are so exclusively American that our entire inattention to any events that may transpire elsewhere can be taken for granted. Our citizens domiciled for purposes of trade in all countries and in many of the islands of the sea demand and will have our adequate care in their personal and commercial rights. The necessities of our Navy require convenient coaling stations and dock and harbor privileges. These and other trading privileges we will feel free to obtain only by means that do not in any degree partake of coercion, however feeble the government from which we ask such concessions. But having fairly obtained them by methods and for purposes entirely consistent with the most friendly disposition toward all other powers, our consent will be necessary to any modification or impairment of the concession.

We shall neither fail to respect the flag of any friendly nation or the just rights of its citizens, nor to exact the like treatment for our own. Calmness, justice, and consideration should characterize our diplomacy. The offices of an intelligent diplomacy or of friendly arbitration in proper cases should be adequate to the peaceful adjustment of all international difficulties. By such methods we will make our contribution to the world's peace, which no nation values more highly, and avoid the opprobrium which must fall upon the nation that ruthlessly breaks it.

The duty devolved by law upon the President to nominate and, by and with the advice and consent of the Senate, to appoint all public officers whose appointment is not otherwise provided for in the Constitution or by act of Congress has become very burdensome and its wise and efficient discharge full of difficulty. The civil list is so large that a personal knowledge of any large number of the applicants is impossible. The President must rely upon the representations of others, and these are often made inconsiderately and without any just sense of responsibility. I have a right, I think, to insist that those who volunteer or are invited to give advice as to appointments shall exercise consideration and fidelity. A high sense of duty and an ambition to improve the service should characterize all public officers.

There are many ways in which the convenience and comfort of those who have business with our public offices may be promoted by a thoughtful and obliging officer, and I shall expect those whom I may appoint to justify their selection by a conspicuous efficiency in the discharge of their duties. Honorable party service will certainly not be esteemed by me a disqualification for public office, but it will in no case be allowed to serve as a shield of official negligence, incompetency, or delinquency. It is entirely creditable to seek public office by proper methods and with proper motives, and all applicants will be treated with consideration; but I shall need, and the heads of Departments will need, time for inquiry and deliberation. Persistent importunity will not, therefore, be the best support of an application for office. Heads of Departments, bureaus, and all other public officers having any duty connected therewith will be expected to enforce the civil-service law fully and without evasion. Beyond this obvious duty I hope to do something more to advance the reform of the civil service. The ideal, or even my own ideal, I shall probably not attain. Retrospect will be a safer basis of judgment than promises. We shall not, however, I am sure, be able to put our civil service upon a nonpartisan basis until we have secured an incumbency that fair-minded men of the opposition will approve for impartiality and integrity. As the number of such in the civil list is increased removals from office will diminish.

While a Treasury surplus is not the greatest evil, it is a serious evil. Our revenue should be ample to meet the ordinary annual demands upon our Treasury, with a sufficient margin for those extraordinary but scarcely less imperative demands which arise now and then. Expenditure should always be made with economy and only upon public necessity. Wastefulness, profligacy, or favoritism in public expenditures is criminal. But there is nothing in the condition of our country or of our people to suggest that anything presently necessary to the public prosperity, security, or honor should be unduly postponed.

It will be the duty of Congress wisely to forecast and estimate these extraordinary demands, and, having added them to our ordinary expenditures, to so adjust our revenue laws that no considerable annual surplus will remain. We will fortunately be able to apply to the redemption of the public debt any small and unforeseen excess of revenue. This is better than to reduce our income below our necessary expenditures, with the resulting choice between another change of our revenue laws and an increase of the public debt. It is quite possible, I am sure, to effect the necessary reduction in our revenues without breaking down our protective tariff or seriously injuring any domestic industry.

The construction of a sufficient number of modern war ships and of their necessary armament should progress as rapidly as is consistent with care and perfection in plans and workmanship. The spirit, courage, and skill of our naval officers and seamen have many times in our history given to weak ships and inefficient guns a rating greatly beyond that of the naval list. That they will again do so upon occasion I do not doubt; but they ought not, by premeditation or neglect, to be left to the risks and exigencies of an unequal combat. We should encourage the establishment of American steamship lines. The exchanges of commerce demand stated, reliable, and rapid means of communication, and until these are provided the development of our trade with the States lying south of us is impossible.

Our pension laws should give more adequate and discriminating relief to the Union soldiers and sailors and to their widows and orphans. Such occasions as this should remind us that we owe everything to their valor and sacrifice.

It is a subject of congratulation that there is a near prospect of the admission into the Union of the Dakotas and Montana and Washington Territories. This act of justice has been unreasonably delayed in the case of some of them. The people who have settled these Territories are intelligent, enterprising, and patriotic, and the accession these new States will add strength to the nation. It is due to the settlers in the Territories who have availed themselves of the invitations of our land laws to make homes upon the public domain that their titles should be speedily adjusted and their honest entries confirmed by patent.

It is very gratifying to observe the general interest now being manifested in the reform of our election laws. Those who have been for years calling attention to the pressing necessity of throwing about the ballot box and about the elector further safeguards, in order that our elections might not only be free and pure, but might clearly appear to be so, will welcome the accession of any who did not so soon discover the need of reform. The National Congress has not as yet taken control of elections in that case over which the Constitution gives it jurisdiction, but has accepted and adopted the election laws of the several States, provided penalties for their violation and a method of supervision. Only the inefficiency of the State laws or an unfair partisan administration of them could suggest a departure from this policy.

It was clearly, however, in the contemplation of the framers of the Constitution that such an exigency might arise, and provision was wisely made for it. The freedom of the ballot is a condition of our national life, and no power vested in Congress or in the Executive to secure or perpetuate it should remain unused upon occasion. The people of all the Congressional districts have an equal interest that the election in each shall truly express the views and wishes of a majority of the qualified electors residing within it. The results of such elections are not local, and the insistence of electors residing in other districts that they shall be pure and free does not savor at all of impertinence.

If in any of the States the public security is thought to be threatened by ignorance among the electors, the obvious remedy is education. The sympathy and help of our people will not be withheld from any community struggling with special embarrassments or difficulties connected with the suffrage if the remedies proposed proceed upon lawful lines and are promoted by just and honorable methods. How shall those who practice election frauds recover that respect for the sanctity of the ballot which is the first condition and obligation of good citizenship? The man who has come to regard the ballot box as a juggler's hat has renounced his allegiance.

Let us exalt patriotism and moderate our party contentions. Let those who would die for the flag on the field of battle give a better proof of their patriotism and a higher glory to their country by promoting fraternity and justice. A party success that is achieved by unfair methods or by practices that partake of revolution is hurtful and evanescent even from a party standpoint. We should hold our differing opinions in mutual respect, and, having submitted them to the arbitrament of the ballot, should accept an adverse judgment with the same respect that we would have demanded of our opponents if the decision had been in our favor.

No other people have a government more worthy of their respect and love or a land so magnificent in extent, so pleasant to look upon, and so full of generous suggestion to enterprise and labor. God has placed upon our head a diadem and has laid at our feet power and wealth beyond definition or calculation. But we must not forget that we take these gifts upon the condition that justice and mercy shall hold the reins of power and that the upward avenues of hope shall be free to all the people.

I do not mistrust the future. Dangers have been in frequent ambush along our path, but we have uncovered and vanquished them all. Passion has swept some of our communities, but only to give us a new demonstration that the great body of our people are stable, patriotic, and law-abiding. No political party can long pursue advantage at the expense of public honor or by rude and indecent methods without protest and fatal disaffection in its own body. The peaceful agencies of commerce are more fully revealing the necessary unity of all our communities, and the increasing intercourse of our people is promoting mutual respect. We shall find unalloyed pleasure in the revelation which our next census will make of the swift development of the great resources of some of the States. Each State will bring its generous contribution to the great aggregate of the nation's increase. And when the harvests from the fields, the cattle from the hills, and the ores of the earth shall have been weighed, counted, and valued, we will turn from them all to crown with the highest honor the State that has most promoted education, virtue, justice, and patriotism among its people.

Study Questions

1. Which two groups did the protective tariff benefit, according to its supporters?

2. What relationship did Harrison envision between the United States and European nations?

3. Why did Harrison say that "a treasury surplus" is "a serious evil"?

Jacob Riis, *How the Other Half Lives: Studies among the Tenements of New York* (1890)

Immigrating from Holland in 1870, Jacob Riis struggled in poverty before finding work as a police reporter for the *New York Tribune* in 1877. His work, like his life, exposed him to the hardships of America's impoverished immigrants. Through documentary photographs and vivid prose, *How the Other Half Lives* (1890) communicated to a middle-class audience the plight of the nation's urban poor, awakening consciences for the social reform that would characterize the Progressive Era (early twentieth century).

Introduction

1. Long ago it was said that "one half of the world does not know how the other half lives." That was true then. It did not know because it did not care. The half that was on top cared little for the struggles, and less for the fate of those who were underneath, so long as it was able to hold them there and keep its own seat. There came a time when the discomfort and crowding below were so great, and the consequent upheavals so violent, that it was no longer an easy thing to do, and then the upper half fell to inquiring what was the matter. Information on the subject has been accumulating rapidly since, and the whole world has had its hands full answering for its old ignorance.

2. In New York, the youngest of the world's great cities, that time came later than elsewhere, because the crowding had not been so great. There were those who believed that it would never come; but their hopes were vain. Greed and reckless selfishness wrought like results here as in the cities of older lands. "When the great riot occurred in 1863," so reads the testimony of the Secretary of the Prison Association of New York before a legislative committee appointed to investigate causes of the increase of crime in the State twenty-five years ago, "every hiding-place and nursery of crime discovered itself by immediate and active participation in the operations of the mob. Those very places and domiciles, and all that are like them, are to-day nurseries of crime, and of the vices and disorderly courses which lead to crime. By far the largest part—eighty per cent at least—of crimes against properly and against the person are perpetrated by individuals who have either lost connection with home life, or never had any, or whose homes had ceased to be sufficiently separate, decent, and desirable to afford what ate regarded as ordinary wholesome influences of home and family. ... The younger criminals seem to come almost exclusively from the worst tenement house districts, that is, when traced back to the very places where they had their homes in the city here." Of one thing New York made sure at that early stage of the inquiry: the boundary line of the Other Half lies through the tenements.

3. It is ten years and over, now, since that line divided New York's population evenly. To-day three-fourths of its people live in the tenements, and the nineteenth century drift of the population to the cities

is sending ever-increasing multitudes to crowd them. The fifteen thousand tenant houses that were the despair of the sanitarian in the past generation have swelled into thirty-seven thousand, and more than twelve hundred thousand persons call them home. The one way out he saw—rapid transit to the suburbs—has brought no relief. We know now that these is no way out; that the "system" that was the evil offspring of public neglect and private greed has come to stay, a storm-centre forever of our civilization. Nothing is left but to make the best of a bad bargain.

4. What the tenements are and how they grow to what they are, we shall see hereafter. The story is dark enough, drawn from the plain public records, to send a chill to any heart. If it shall appear that the sufferings and the sins of the "other half," and the evil they breed, are but as a just punishment upon the community that gave it no other choice, it will be because that is the truth. The boundary line lies there because, while the forces for good on one side vastly outweigh the bad—it were not well otherwise—in the tenements all the influences make for evil; because they are the hot-beds of the epidemics that carry death to rich and poor alike; the nurseries of pauperism and crime that fill our jails and police courts; that throw off a scum of forty thousand human wrecks to the island asylums and workhouses year by year; that turned out in the last eight years a round half million beggars to prey upon our charities; that maintain a standing army of ten thousand tramps with all that that implies; because, above all, they touch the family life with deadly moral contagion. This is their worst crime, insep-

arable from the system. That we have to own it the child of our own wrong does not excuse it, even though it gives it claim upon our utmost patience and tenderest charity.

5. What are you going to do about it? is the question of to-day. It was asked once of our city in taunting defiance by a band of political cutthroats, the legitimate outgrowth of life on the tenement-house level.[1] Law and order found the answer then and prevailed. With our enormously swelling population held in this galling bondage, will that answer always be given? It will depend on how fully the situation that prompted the challenge is grasped. Forty per cent of the distress among the poor, said a recent official report, is due to drunkenness. But the first legislative committee ever appointed to probe this sore went deeper down and uncovered its roots. The "conclusion forced itself upon it that certain conditions and associations of human life and habitation are the prolific parents of corresponding habits and morals," and it recommended "the prevention of drunkenness by providing for every man a clean and comfortable home. Years after, a sanitary inquiry brought to light the fact that "more than one-half of the tenements with two-thirds of their population were held by owners veto trade the keeping of them a business, generally a speculation. The owner was seeking a certain percentage on his outlay, and that percentage very rarely fell below fifteen per cent, and frequently exceeded thirty.[2] . . .

---

[1] Tweed was born and bred in a Fourth Ward tenement.

[2] Forty per cent was declared by witnesses before a Senate Committee to be a fair average

The complaint was universal among the tenants that they were entirely smeared for, and that the only answer to their requests to have the place put in order by repairs and necessary improvements was that they must pay their rent or leave. The agent's instructions were simple but emphatic: 'Collect the rent in advance, or, failing, eject the occupants.'" Upon such a stock grew this upas-tree. Small wonder the fruit is bitter. The remedy that shall be an effective answer to the coming appeal for justice must proceed from the public conscience. Neither legislation nor charity can cover the ground. The greed of capital that wrought the evil must itself undo it, as far as it can now be undone. Homes must be built for the working masses by those who employ their labor; but tenements must cease to be "good property" in the old, heartless sense. "Philanthropy and five per cent" is the penance exacted.

6. If this is true from a purely economic point of view, what then of the outlook from the Christian standpoint? Not long ago a great meeting was held in this city, of all denominations of religious faith, to discuss the question how to lay hold of these teeming masses in the tenements with Christian influences, to which they are now too often strangers. Might not the conference have found in the warning of one Brooklyn builder, who has invested his capital on this plan and made it pay more than a money interest, a hint worth heeding: "How shall the love of God be understood by those who have been nurtured in sight only of the greed of man?"

---

interest on tenement property. Instances were given of its being one hundred percent and over.

Chapter 3: The Mixed Crowd

When once I asked the agent of a notorious Fourth Ward alley how many people might be living in it I was told: One hundred and forty families, one hundred Irish, thirty-eight Italian, and two that spoke the German tongue. Barring the agent herself, there was not a native-born individual in the court. The answer was characteristic of the cosmopolitan character of lower New York, very nearly so of the whole of it, wherever it runs to alleys and courts. One may find for the asking an Italian, a German, a French, African, Spanish, Bohemian, Russian, Scandinavian, Jewish, and Chinese colony. Even the Arab, who peddles "holy earth" from the Battery as a direct importation from Jerusalem, has his exclusive preserves at the lower end of Washington Street. The one thing you shall vainly ask for in the chief city of America is a distinctively American community. There is none; certainly not among the tenements. Where have they gone to, the old inhabitants? I put the question to one who might fairly be presumed to be of the number, since I had found him sighing for the "good old days" when the legend "no Irish need apply" was familiar in the advertising columns of the newspapers. He looked at me with a puzzled air. "I don't know," he said. "I wish I did. Some went to California in '49, some to the war and never came back. The rest, I expect, have gone to heaven, or somewhere. I don't see them 'round here."

Whatever the merit of the good man's conjectures, his eyes did not deceive him. They are not here. In their place has come this queer conglomerate mass of heterogeneous elements, ever striving and working like whiskey and water in one glass, and with the like result: final union and a prevailing taint of whiskey. The once unwelcome Irishman has been followed in his turn by the Italian, the Russian Jew, and the Chinaman, and has himself taken a hand at opposition, quite as bitter and quite as ineffectual, against these later hordes. Wherever these have gone they have crowded him out, possessing the block, the street, the ward with their denser swarms. . . .

Chapter 18: The Reign of Rum

Where God builds a church the devil builds next door—a saloon, is an old saying that has lost its point in New York. Either the devil was on the ground first, or he has been doing a good deal more in the way of building. I tried once to find out how the account stood, and counted to 111 Protestant churches, chapels, and places of worship of every kind below Fourteenth Street, 4,065 saloons. The worst half of the tenement population lives down there, and it has to this day the worst half of the saloons. Uptown the account stands a little better, but there are easily ten saloons to every church to-day. I am afraid, too, that the congregations are larger by a good deal; certainly the attendance is steadier and the contributions more liberal the week round, Sunday included. Turn and twist it as we may, over against every bulwark for decency and morality which society erects, the saloon projects its colossal shadow, omen of evil wherever it falls into the lives of the poor. Nowhere is its mark so broad or so black. To their misery it sticketh closer than a brother,

persuading them that within its doors only is refuge, relief. It has the best of the argument, too, for it is true, worse pity, that in many a tenement-house block the saloon is the one bright and cheery and humanly decent spot to be found. It is a sorry admission to make, that to bring the rest of the neighborhood up to the level of the saloon would be one way of squelching it; but it is so. Wherever the tenements thicken, it multiplies. Upon the direst poverty of their crowds it grows fat and prosperous, levying upon it a tax heavier than all the rest of its grievous burdens combined. It is not yet two years since the Excise Board made the rule that no three corners of any street-crossing, not already so occupied, should thenceforward be licensed for rum-selling. And the tardy prohibition was intended for the tenement districts. Nowhere else is there need of it. One may walk many miles through the homes of the poor searching vainly for an open reading-room, a cheerful coffee-house, a decent club that is not a cloak for the traffic in rum. The dramshop yawns at every step, the poor man's club, his forum and his haven of rest when weary and disgusted with the crowding, the quarreling, and the wretchedness at home. With the poison dealt out there he takes his politics, in quality not far apart. As the source, so the stream. The rumshop turns the political crank in New York. The natural yield is rum politics. Of what that means, successive Boards of Aldermen, composed in a measure, if not of a majority, of dive-keepers, have given New York a taste. The disgrace of the infamous "Boodle Board" will be remembered until some corruption even fouler crops out and throws it into the shade.

Study Questions

1. Which two parties were responsible, in Riis's view, for the origin of tenements?

2. What appeal did Riis make to the moral sensibilities of his readers?

3. Describe the political corruption that Riis identified in tenement wards.

Andrew Carnegie, *Autobiography* (1920), chs. 17–18

In 1892, the Amalgamated Association of Iron and Steel Workers organized a strike against a Carnegie steel plant in Homestead, Pennsylvania. The workers objected to a cut in wages, but as Carnegie himself tells the story, their wages actually had increased. Henry Frick, who was managing the plant in Carnegie's absence, decided to keep the operations running despite the strikers by calling for strikebreakers under the protection of Pinkerton agents. This only angered the unionists more. They took up arms and tried to seize control of the facility. Finally, the state militia intervened to restore peace.

Chapter 17: The Homestead Strike

While upon the subject of our manufacturing interests, I may record that on July 1, 1892, during my absence in the Highlands of Scotland, there occurred the one really serious quarrel with our workmen in our whole history. For twenty-six years I had been actively in charge of the relations between ourselves and our men, and it was the pride of my life to think how delightfully satisfactory these had been and were. I hope I fully deserved what my chief partner, Mr. Phipps, said in his letter to the *New York Herald*, January 30, 1904, in reply to one who had declared I had remained abroad during the Homestead strike, instead of flying back to support my partners. It was to the effect that "I was always disposed to yield to the demands of the men, however unreasonable"; hence one or two of my partners did not wish me to return. Taking no account of the reward that comes from feeling that you and your employees are friends and judging only from economical results, I believe that higher wages to men who respect their employers and are happy and contented are a good investment, yielding, indeed, big dividends.

The manufacture of steel was revolutionized by the Bessemer open-hearth and basic inventions. The machinery hitherto employed had become obsolete, and our firm, recognizing this, spent several millions at Homestead reconstructing and enlarging the works. The new machinery made about sixty per cent more steel than the old. Two hundred and eighteen tonnage men (that is, men who were paid by the ton of steel produced) were working under a three years' contract, part of the last year being with the new machinery. Thus their earnings had increased almost sixty per cent before the end of the contract.

The firm offered to divide this sixty per cent with them in the new scale to be made thereafter. That is to say, the earnings of the men would have been thirty per cent greater than under the old scale and the other thirty per cent would have gone to the firm to recompense it for its outlay. The work of the men would not have been much harder than it had been hitherto, as the improved machinery did the work.

This was not only fair and liberal, it was generous, and under ordinary circumstances would have been accepted by the men with thanks. But the firm was then engaged in making armor for the United States Government, which we had declined twice to manufacture and which was urgently needed. It had also the contract to furnish material for the Chicago Exhibition. Some of the leaders of the men, knowing these conditions, insisted upon demanding the whole sixty per cent, thinking the firm would be compelled to give it. The firm could not agree, nor should it have agreed to such an attempt as this to take it by the throat and say, "Stand and deliver." It very rightly declined. Had I been at home nothing would have induced me to yield to this unfair attempt to extort.

Up to this point all had been right enough. The policy I had pursued in cases of difference with our men was that of patiently waiting, reasoning with them, and showing them that their demands were unfair; but never attempting to employ new men in their places—never. The superintendent of Homestead, however, was assured by the three thousand men who were not concerned in the dispute that they could run the works, and were anxious to rid themselves of the two hundred and eighteen men who had banded themselves into a union and into which they had hitherto refused to admit those in other departments—only the "heaters" and "rollers" of steel being eligible.

My partners were misled by this superintendent, who was himself misled. He had not had great experience in such affairs, having recently been promoted from a subordinate position. The unjust demands of the few union men, and the opinion of the three thousand non-union men that they were unjust, very naturally led him into thinking there would be no trouble and that the workmen would do as they had promised. There were many men among the three thousand who could take, and wished to take, the places of the two hundred and eighteen—at least so it was reported to me.

It is easy to look back and say that the vital step of opening the works should never have been taken. All the firm had to do was to say to the men: "There is a labor dispute here and you must settle it between yourselves. The firm has made you a most liberal offer. The works will run when the dispute is adjusted, and not till then. Meanwhile your places remain open to you." Or, it might have been well if the superintendent had said to the three thousand men, "All right, if you will come and run the works without protection," thus throwing upon them the responsibility of protecting themselves—three thousand men as against two hundred and eighteen. Instead of this it was thought advisable (as an additional precaution by the state officials, I understand) to have the sheriff with guards to protect the thousands against the hundreds. The leaders of the latter were violent and aggressive men; they had guns and pistols, and, as was soon proved, were able to intimidate the thousands.

I quote what I once laid down in writing as our rule: "My idea is that the Company should be known as determined to let the men at any works stop work; that it will confer freely with them and wait patiently until they decide to return to work, never thinking of trying new men—never." The best men as men, and the best workmen, are not walking the streets looking for work. Only the inferior class as a rule is idle. The kind of men we desired are rarely allowed to lose their jobs, even in dull times. It is impossible to get new men to run successfully the complicated machinery of a modern steel plant. The attempt to put in new men converted the thousands of old men who desired to work, into lukewarm supporters of our policy, for workmen can always be relied upon to resent the employment of new men. Who can blame them?

If I had been at home, however, I might have been persuaded to open the works, as the superintendent desired, to test whether our old men would go to work as they had promised. But it should be noted that the works were not opened at first by my partners for new men. On the contrary, it was, as I was informed upon my return, at the wish of the thousands of our old men that they were opened. This is a vital point. My partners were in no way blamable for making the trial so recommended by the superintendent. Our rule never to employ new men, but to wait for the old to return, had not been violated so far. In regard to the second opening of the works, after the strikers had shot the sheriff's officers, it is also easy to look back and say, "How much better had the works been closed until the old men voted to return"; but the Governor of Pennsylvania, with eight thousand troops, had meanwhile taken charge of the situation.

I was traveling in the Highlands of Scotland when the trouble arose, and did not hear of it until two days after. Nothing I have ever had to meet in all my life, before or since, wounded me so deeply. No pangs remain of any wound received in my business career save that of Homestead. It was so unnecessary. The men were outrageously wrong. The strikers, with the

new machinery, would have made from four to nine dollars a day under the new scale—thirty per cent more than they were making with the old machinery. While in Scotland I received the following cable from the officers of the union of our workmen:

"Kind master, tell us what you wish us to do and we shall do it for you."

This was most touching, but, alas, too late. The mischief was done, the works were in the hands of the Governor; it was too late. . . .

Chapter 18: Problems of Labor

I should like to record here some of the labor disputes I have had to deal with, as these may point a moral to both capital and labor.

Employers can do so many desirable things for their men at little cost. At one meeting when I asked what we could do for them, I remember this same Billy Edwards rose and said that most of the men had to run in debt to the storekeepers because they were paid monthly. Well I remember his words:

"I have a good woman for wife who manages well. We go into Pittsburgh every fourth Saturday afternoon and buy our supplies wholesale for the next month and save one third. Not many of your men can do this. Shopkeepers here charge so much. And another thing, they charge very high for coal. If you paid your men every two weeks, instead of monthly, it would be as good for the careful men as a raise in wages of ten per cent or more."

"Mr. Edwards, that shall be done," I replied.

It involved increased labor and a few more clerks, but that was a small matter. The remark about high prices charged set me to thinking why the men could not open a cooeperative store. This was also arranged—the firm agreeing to pay the rent of the building, but insisting that the men themselves take the stock and manage it. Out of that came the Braddock's Cooperative Society, a valuable institution for many reasons, not the least of them that it taught the men that business had its difficulties.

The coal trouble was cured effectively by our agreeing that the company sell all its men coal at the net cost price to us (about half of what had been charged by coal dealers, so I was told) and arranging to deliver it at the men's houses—the buyer paying only actual cost of cartage.

There was another matter. We found that the men's savings caused them anxiety, for little faith have the prudent, saving men in banks and, unfortunately, our Government at that time did not follow the British in having post-office deposit banks. We offered to take the actual savings of each workman, up to two thousand dollars, and pay six per cent interest upon them, to encourage thrift. Their money was kept separate from the business, in a trust fund, and lent to such as wished to build homes for themselves. I consider this one of the best things that can be done for the saving workman.

It was such concessions as these that proved the most profitable investments ever made by the company, even from an economical standpoint. It pays to go beyond the letter of the bond with your men. Two of my partners, as Mr. Phipps has put it, "knew my extreme disposition to always grant the demands of labor, however unreasonable," but looking back upon my failing in this respect, I wish it had been greater—much greater. No expenditure returned such dividends as the friendship of our workmen.

We soon had a body of workmen, I truly believe, wholly unequaled—the best workmen and the best men ever drawn together. Quarrels and strikes became things of the past. Had the Homestead men been our own old men, instead of men we had to pick up, it is scarcely possible that the trouble there in 1892 could have arisen. The scale at the steel-rail mills, introduced in 1889, has been running up to the present time (1914), and I think there never has been a labor grievance at the works since. The men, as I have already stated, dissolved their old union because there was no use paying dues to a union when the men themselves had a three years' contract. Although their labor union is dissolved another and a better one has taken its place—a cordial union between the employers and their men, the best union of all for both parties.

It is for the interest of the employer that his men shall make good earnings and have steady work. The sliding scale enables the company to meet the market; and sometimes to take orders and keep the works running, which is the main thing for the working-men. High wages are well enough, but they are not to be compared with steady employment.

Study Questions

1. Who was in the wrong—Frick or the strikers? Explain.

2. With what examples did Carnegie illustrate his point that "Employers can do so many desirable things for their men at little cost"?

Chronological Overview: The Populist Movement

1880s   Farmers organize Farmers Alliances as political action groups for economic security.

1889   Western farmers and urban union workers form the National Farmers Alliance and Industrial Union to mobilize against their common foes: eastern capitalists and financiers.

1890   Alliance members vote third-party candidates into many local and state offices.

1891   A sharp decline in cotton prices prompts the Texas Alliance to propose the subtreasury plan (as described on the following page); the Democratic Party rejects the plan, alienating the Alliance members.

1892   Alliance members form the Populist Party, nominating James B. Weaver for U.S. president. The Omaha Platform calls for nationalized railroads, telegraphs, and telephones; protection of the land from monopoly ownership; postal savings banks; the subtreasury plan; a graduated income tax; and, "the free and unlimited coinage of silver." Weaver carries a majority in several western states, and has a significant following in others, but is defeated by Grover Cleveland (Democrat).

1893   The stock market crashes, banks fail, and unemployment soars to over 20%. President Cleveland persuades Congress to abolish the Sherman Silver Purchase Act, returning the U.S. to gold-only.

1894   Republicans gain congressional seats, Populists win local elections, and Democrats decline.

1896   Silver Democrats nominate William Jennings Bryan for U.S. president, who charismatically proclaims, "You shall not crucify mankind on a cross of gold." Populists likewise nominate Bryan for president, creating a "fusion" ticket, but Bryan loses to the Republican candidate, William McKinley. Fusion and defeat together result in the demise of Populism as a viable third party, but some of its goals would be realized in the Progressive Era (early twentieth century).

Basic Economics for Understanding the Populist Movement

Economic Concept	Who Benefits	Who Loses Out
Tariff: a tax on imported goods, either for "protectionism" (see the next two columns) or for generating revenue.	**Local producers:** the tax forces foreign producers to charge more, which protects the ability of local producers to sell their product at a good profit, and to pay higher wages to workers.	**Local consumers:** the tax drives prices up. **Example:** Farmers oppose tariffs on manufactured goods.
Inflation: a decline in the value of the dollar; also experienced as a rise in prices—if something cost $10 a year ago, but now costs $11, that would be 10% annual inflation.	**Borrowers (Debtors):** each dollar is now worth less, so it is easier to get dollars, and then repay a loan. Example: Many farmers were in debt; inflation made their debts feel lighter, since they could be repaid more easily.	**Lenders (Creditors):** by the time the loan is repaid, each dollar is worth less, so it cannot purchase as much as when it was first lent. This is one reason why lenders charge interest, to make up for inflationary losses.
Currency expansion: the minting of more coins or printing of more bills to increase the amount of currency in circulation.	**Borrowers:** currency expansion leads to inflation. Greenbacks (green-colored dollar bills) were one form of currency expansion. Coining silver was another.	**Lenders:** again, it leads to inflation. Strict adherence to a gold standard keeps the money supply tight (i.e., slows currency expansion), favoring lenders.
Grain Prices: how much people pay, e.g., for a bushel of wheat.	**Farmers** prefer higher prices, since this is income to them.	**Consumers** prefer lower prices, since this is an expense for them.
Subtreasury Plan: the federal government would lend farmers money while they wait for grain prices to rise; the government would lend 80% of the current market value, and charge 1% to 2% annual interest, while storing the crops as collateral.	**Poor Farmers:** rather than selling early (at lower prices, since supply is high at harvest), or borrowing money from lenders who charge high interest rates, they receive a cash advance from the subtreasury and sell their crops later at a higher price.	**Lenders:** their interest rates must drop in order to compete with subtreasury loans, but that decreases the lenders' profits. **Poor Farmers:** if crop prices do not increase, then repaying the subtreasury loan will be difficult.

Frederick Jackson Turner, *The Frontier in American History* (1921), ch. 11

As homesteaders filled the prairies in the mid 1800s, the frontier moved steadily westward until, by century's end, it vanished. Was the nation now rich with settled communities coast to coast? Hardly. Many farms in the Great Plains failed, challenged by droughts, pestilence, debt, and the embarrassing fact that some homesteaders never had a clue how to work the land in the first place; they had been all too easily enticed by the federal government's offer of cheap land. Disgruntled, these farmers began to organize politically, demanding that the government redistribute the nation's wealth in their favor. Known as the Populist Revolt, their movement marked not only the closing of the frontier but also the waning of American individualism. As western radicals took their cue from socialist literature, new expectations for government regulation shattered the *laissez-faire* mold that had crafted the Gilded Age economy.

Chapter 11—The West and American Ideals[3]

True to American traditions that each succeeding generation ought to find in the Republic a better home, once in every year the colleges and universities summon the nation to lift its eyes from the routine of work, in order to take stock of the country's purposes and achievements, to examine its past and consider its future.

This attitude of self-examination is hardly characteristic of the people as a whole. Particularly it is not characteristic of the historic American. He has been an opportunist rather than a dealer in general ideas. Destiny set him in a current which bore him swiftly along through such a wealth of opportunity that reflection and well-considered planning seemed wasted time. He knew not where he was going, but he was on his way, cheerful, optimistic, busy and buoyant. . . .

American democracy was born of no theorist's dream; it was not carried in the *Sarah Constant* to Virginia, nor in the *Mayflower* to Plymouth. It came out of the American forest, and it gained new strength each time it touched a new frontier. Not the constitution, but free land and an abundance of natural resources open to a fit people, made the democratic type of society in America for three centuries while it occupied its empire.

To-day we are looking with a shock upon a changed world. The national problem is no longer how to cut and burn away the vast screen of the dense and daunting forest; it is how to save and wisely use the remaining timber. It is no longer how to get the great spaces of fertile prairie land in humid zones out of the hands of the government into the hands of the pioneer; these lands have already passed into private possession. No longer is it a question of how to avoid or cross the Great Plains and the arid desert. It is a question of how to conquer those rejected lands by new method of farming and by cultivating

---

[3]Commencement Address, University of Washington, June 17, 1914.

new crops from seed collected by the government and by scientists from the cold, dry steppes of Siberia, the burning sands of Egypt, and the remote interior of China. . . .

If we look about the periphery of the nation, everywhere we see the indications that our world is changing. On the streets of Northeastern cities like New York and Boston, the faces which we meet are to a surprising extent those of Southeastern Europe. Puritan New England, which turned its capital into factories and mills and drew to its shores an army of cheap labor, governed these people for a time by a ruling class like an upper stratum between which and the lower strata there was no assimilation. There was no such evolution into an assimilated commonwealth as is seen in Middle Western agricultural States, where immigrant and old native stock came in together and built up a homogeneous society on the principle of give and take. But now the Northeastern coast finds its destiny, politically and economically, passing away from the descendants of the Puritans. It is the little Jewish boy, the Greek or the Sicilian, who takes the traveler through historic streets, now the home of these newer people to the Old North Church or to Paul Revere's house, or to Tea Wharf, and tells you in his strange *patois* the story of revolution against oppression.

Along the Southern Atlantic and the Gulf coast, in spite of the preservative influence of the negro, whose presence has always called out resistance to change on the part of the whites, the forces of social and industrial transformation are at work. The old tidewater aristocracy has surrendered to the up-country democrats. . . .

Turning to view the interior, we see the same picture of change. When the Superintendent of the Census in 1890 declared the frontier line no longer traceable, the beginning of the rush into Oklahoma had just occurred. Here where the broken fragments of Indian nations from the East had been gathered and where the wilder tribes of the Southwest were being settled, came the rush of the land-hungry pioneer. Almost at a blow the old Indian territory passed away, populous cities came into being and it was not long before gushing oil wells made a new era of sudden wealth. The farm lands of the Middle West taken as free homesteads or bought for a mere pittance, have risen so in value that the original owners have in an increasing degree either sold them in order to reinvest in the newer cheap lands of the West, or have moved into the town and have left the tillage to tenant farmers. . . .

Across the Great Plains where buffalo and Indian held sway successive industrial waves are passing. The old free range gave place to the ranch, the ranch to the homestead and now in places in the arid lands the homestead is replaced by the ten or twenty acre irrigated fruit farm. The age of cheap land, cheap corn and wheat, and cheap cattle has gone forever. The federal government has undertaken vast paternal enterprises of reclamation of the desert.

. . . Side by side with this westward marching army of individualistic liberty-loving democratic backwoodsmen, went a more northern stream of pioneers, who cherished similar ideas, but added to them the desire to create new industrial centers, to build up factories, to build railroads, and to develop the country by founding cities and extending prosperity. They were ready to call upon legislatures to aid in this, by subscriptions to stock, grants of franchises, promotion of banking and internal improvements. These were the Whig followers of that other Western leader, Henry Clay, and their early strength lay in the Ohio Valley, and particularly among the well-to-do. In the South their strength was found among the aristocracy of the Cotton Kingdom.

Both of these Western groups, Whigs and Democrats alike, had one common ideal: the desire to leave their children a better heritage than they themselves had received, and both were fired with devotion to the ideal of creating in this New World a home more worthy of mankind. Both were ready to break with the past, to boldly strike out new lines of social endeavor, and both believed in American expansion.

Before these tendencies had worked themselves out, three new forces entered. In the sudden extension of our boundaries to the Pacific Coast, which took place in the forties, the nation won so vast a domain that its resources seemed illimitable and its society seemed able to throw off all its maladies by the very presence of these vast new spaces. At the same period the great activity of railroad building to the Mississippi Valley occurred, making these lands available and diverting attention to the task of economic construction. The third influence was the slavery question which, becoming acute, shaped the American ideals and public discussion for nearly a generation. Viewed from one angle, this struggle involved the great question of national unity. From another it involved the question of the relations of labor and capital, democracy and aristocracy. It was not without significance that Abraham Lincoln became the very type of American pioneer democracy, the first adequate and elemental demonstration to the world that that democracy could produce a man who belonged to the ages.

After the war, new national energies were set loose, and new construction and development engaged the attention of the Westerners as they occupied prairies and Great Plains and mountains. Democracy and capitalistic development did not seem antagonistic.

With the passing of the frontier, Western social and political ideals took new form. Capital began to consolidate in even greater masses, and increasingly attempted to reduce to system and control the processes of industrial development. Labor with equal step organized its forces to destroy the old competitive system. It is not strange that the Western pioneers took alarm for their ideals of democracy as the outcome of the free struggle for the national resources became apparent. They espoused the cause of governmental activity.

It was a new gospel, for the Western radical became convinced that he must sacrifice his ideal of individualism and free competition in order to maintain his ideal of democracy. Under this conviction the Populist revised the pioneer conception of government. He saw in government no longer something outside of him, but the people themselves shaping their own affairs. He demanded therefore an extension of the powers of governments in the interest of his historic ideal of democratic society. He demanded not only free silver, but the ownership of the agencies of communication and transportation, the income tax, the postal savings bank, the provision of means of credit for agriculture, the construction of more effective devices to express the will of the people, primary nominations, direct elections, initiative, referendum and recall. In a word, capital, labor, and the Western pioneer, all deserted the ideal of competitive individualism in order to organize their interests in more effective combinations. The disappearance of the frontier, the closing of the era which was marked by the influence of the West as a form of society, brings with it new problems of social adjustment, new demands for considering our past ideals and our present needs.

Let us recall the conditions of the foreign relations along our borders, the dangers that wait us if we fail to unite in the solution of our domestic problems. Let us recall those internal evidences of the destruction of our old social order. If we take to heart this warning, we shall do well also to recount our historic ideals, to take stock of those purposes, and fundamental assumptions that have gone to make the American spirit and the meaning of America in world history.

First of all, there was the ideal of discovery, the courageous determination to break new paths, indifference to the dogma that because an institution or a condition exists, it must remain. All American experience has gone to the making of the spirit of innovation; it is in the blood and will not be repressed.

Then, there was the ideal of democracy, the ideal of a free self-directing people, responsive to leadership in the forming of programs and their execution, but insistent that the procedure should be that of free choice, not of compulsion.

But there was also the ideal of individualism. This democratic society was not a disciplined army, where all must keep step and where the collective interests destroyed individual will and work. Rather it was a mobile mass of freely circulating atoms, each seeking its own place and finding play for its own powers and for its own original initiative. We cannot lay too much stress upon this point, for it was at the very heart of the whole American movement. The world was to be made a better world by the example of a democracy in which there was freedom of the individual, in which there was the vitality and mobility productive of originality and variety.

Bearing in mind the far-reaching influence of the disappearance of unlimited resources open to all men for the taking, and considering the recoil of the common man when he saw the outcome of the competitive struggle for these resources as the supply came to its end over most of the nation, we can understand the reaction against individualism and in favor of drastic assertion of the powers of government. Legislation is taking the place of the free lands as the means of preserving the ideal of democracy. But at the same time it is endangering the other pioneer ideal of creative and competitive individualism. Both were essential and constituted what was best in America's contribution to history and to progress. Both must be preserved if the nation would be true to its past, and would fulfill its highest destiny. It would be a grave misfortune if these people so rich in experience, in self-confidence and aspiration, in creative genius, should turn to some Old World discipline of socialism or plutocracy, or despotic rule, whether by class or by dictator. Nor shall we be driven to these alternatives. Our ancient hopes, our courageous faith, our underlying good humor and love of fair play will triumph in the end. There will be give and take in all directions. There will be disinterested leadership, under loyalty to the best American ideals. Nowhere is this leadership more likely to arise than among the men trained in the Universities, aware of the promise of the past and the possibilities of the future. The times call for new ambitions and new motives.

In a most suggestive essay on the Problems of Modern Democracy, Mr. Godkin has said:

M. de Tocqueville and all his followers take it for granted that the great incentive to excellence, in all countries in which excellence is found, is the patronage and encouragement of an aristocracy; that democracy is generally content with mediocrity. But where is the proof of this? The incentive to exertion which is widest, most constant, and most powerful in its operations in all civilized countries, is the desire of distinction; and this may be composed either of love of fame or love of wealth or of both. In literary and artistic and scientific pursuits, sometimes the strongest influence is exerted by a love of the subject. But it may safely be said that no man has ever labored in any of the higher colleges to whom the applause and appreciation of his fellows was not one of the sweetest rewards of his exertions.

What is there we would ask, in the nature of democratic institutions, that should render this great spring of action powerless, that should deprive glory of all radiance, and put ambition to sleep? Is it not notorious, on the contrary, that one of the most marked peculiarities of democratic society, or of a society drifting toward democracy, is the fire of competition which rages in it, the fevered anxiety which possesses all its members to rise above the dead level to which the law is ever seeking to confine them, and by some brilliant stroke become something higher and more remarkable than their fellows? The secret of that great restlessness which is one of the most disagreeable accompaniments of life in democratic countries, is in fact due to the eagerness of everybody to grasp the prizes of which in aristocratic countries, only the few have much chance. And in no other society is success more worshiped, is distinction of any kind more widely flattered and caressed.

In democratic societies, in fact, excellence is the first title to distinction; in aristocratic ones there are two or three others which are far stronger and which must be stronger or aristocracy could not exist. The moment you acknowledge that the highest social position ought to be the reward of the man who has the most talent, you make aristocratic institutions impossible.

All that was buoyant and creative in American life would be lost if we gave up the respect for distinct personality, and variety in genius, and came to the dead level of common standards. To be "socialized into an average" and placed "under the tutelage of the mass of us," as a recent writer has put it, would be an irreparable loss. Nor is it necessary in a democracy, as these words of Godkin well disclose. What is needed is the multiplication of motives for ambition and the opening of new lines of achievement for the strongest. As we turn from the task of the first rough conquest of the continent there lies before us a whole wealth of unexploited resources in the realm of the spirit. Arts and letters, science and better social creation, loyalty and political service to the commonweal,— these and a thousand other directions of activity are open to the men, who formerly under the incentive of attaining distinction by amassing extraordinary wealth, saw success only in material display. Newer and finer careers will open to the ambitious when once public opinion shall award the laurels to those who rise above their fellows in these new fields of labor. It has not been the gold, but the getting of the gold, that has caught the imaginations of our captains of industry. Their real enjoyment lay not in the luxuries which wealth brought, but in the work of construction and in the place which society awarded them. A new era will come if schools and universities can only widen the intellectual horizon of the people, help to lay the foundations of a better industrial life, show them new goals for endeavor, inspire them with more varied and higher ideals.

The Western spirit must be invoked for new and nobler achievements. Of that matured Western spirit, Tennyson's *Ulysses* is a symbol.

> I am become a name
> For always roaming with an hungry
>   heart,
> Much have I seen and known . . .
> I am a part of all that I have met;
> Yet all experience is an arch, where thro'
> Gleams that untravelled world, whose
>   margin fades
> Forever and forever when I move.
> How dull it is to pause, to make an end.
> To rust unburnished, not to shine in use!
>
> . . . And this gray spirit yearning in
>   desire
> To follow knowledge like a shining star
> Beyond the utmost bound of human
>   thought.
> . . . Come my friends,
> 'Tis not too late to seek a newer world.
> Push off, and sitting well in order smite
> The sounding furrows; for my purpose
>   holds
> To sail beyond the sunset, and the paths
> Of all the Western stars until I die.
>
> . . . To strike, to seek, to find and not to
>   yield.

Study Questions

1. For what purpose, according to Turner, did both eastern factory workers and western farmers abandon the traditional ideals of American individualism?

2. A socialist critique of the Gilded Age economy might focus on the disparity of wealth between rich and poor. Turner, however, wrote, "It has not been the gold, but the getting of the gold, that has caught the imaginations of our captains of industry." Explain what he meant.

People's Party, *Omaha Platform* (1892)

The Populist Party, also known as the People's Party, drew support from farmers in the West and South together with western miners amid ranchers as well as a small number of eastern industrial laborers. Growing out of the Grange movement (1867) and the Greenbacker Party (1876), Populists urged the government to coin more silver in order to offer inflationary relief to indebted farmers. They also sought to replace the corrupt alliance between federally subsidized railroad owners and Congress with a railway system that would be owned and operated by the government on behalf of farmers. Several of their proposals appear to fall in line with socialism, but socialists within the Western Federation of Miners (1893) and Industrial Workers of the World (1905), or "Wobblies," thought the Populist Party had not been radical enough.

Assembled upon the 116th anniversary of the Declaration of Independence, the People's Party of America, in their first national convention, invoking upon their action the blessing of Almighty God, puts forth in the name and on behalf of the people of this country, the following preamble and declaration of principles:

Preamble

The conditions which surround us best justify out co-operation; we meet in the midst of a nation brought to the verge of moral, political, and material ruin. Corruption dominates the ballot-box, the Legislatures, the Congress, and touches even the ermine of the bench. The people are demoralized; most of the States have been compelled to isolate the voters at the polling places to prevent universal intimidation and bribery. The newspapers are largely subsidized or muzzled, public opinion silenced, business prostrated, homes covered with mortgages, labor impoverished, and the land concentrating in the hands of the capitalists. The urban workmen are denied the right to organize for self-protection, imported pauperized labor beats down their wages, a hireling standing army, unrecognized by out laws, is established to shoot them down, and they are rapidly degenerating into European conditions. The fruits of the toil of millions are boldly stolen to build up the fortunes for a few, unprecedented in the history of mankind; and the possessors of these, in turn, despise the Republic and endanger liberty. From the same prolific womb of governmental injustice we breed the two great classes–tramps and millionaires.

The national power to create money is appropriated to enrich bondholders; a vast public debt, payable in legal tender currency, has been funded into gold-bearing bonds, thereby adding millions to the burdens of the people. Silver, which has been accepted as coin since the dawn of history, has been demonetized to add to the purchasing power of gold by decreasing the value of all forms of property as well as human labor, and the supply of currency is purposely abridged to fatten usurers, bankrupt enterprise, and enslave industry. A vast conspiracy against mankind has been organized on two continents, and it is rapidly taking possession of the world. If not met and overthrown at once it forebodes terrible social convulsions, the destruction of civilization, or the establishment of an absolute despotism.

We have witnessed for more than a quarter of a century the struggles of the two great political parties for power and plunder, while grievous wrongs have been inflicted upon the suffering people. We charge that the controlling influences dominating both these parties have permitted the existing dreadful conditions to develop without serious effort to prevent or restrain them. Neither do they now promise us any substantial reform. They have agreed together to ignore in the coming campaign every issue but one. They propose to drown the outcries of a plundered people with the uproar of a sham battle over the tariff, so that capitalist, corporations, national banks, rings, trust, watered stock, the demonetization of silver, and the oppressions of the usurers may all be lost sight of. They propose to sacrifice our homes, lives, and children on the altar of mammon; to destroy the multitude in order to secure corruption funds from the millionaires.

Assembled on the anniversary of the birthday of the nation, and filled with the spirit of the grand general and chief who established our independence, we seek to restore the government of the Republic to the hands of "the plain people," with which class it originated. We assert or purposed to be identical with the purposes of the National Constitution, "to form a more perfect union and establish justice, insure domestic tranquility, provide for the common defense, promote the general welfare, and secure the blessings of liberty for ourselves and our posterity." We declare that this Republic can only endure as a free government while built upon the love of the whole people for each other and for the nation; that it cannot be pinned together by bayonets; that the civil war is over, and that every passion and resentment which grew out of it must die with it, and that we must be in fact, as we are in name, one united brotherhood of free men.

Our country finds itself confronted by conditions for which there is no precedent in the history of the world; our annual agricultural productions amount to billions of dollars in value, which must, within a few weeks or months, be exchanged for billions of dollars of commodities consumed in their production; the existing currency supply is wholly inadequate to make this exchange; the results are falling prices, the formation of combines and rings, the impoverishment of the producing class. We pledge ourselves, if given power, we will labor to correct these evils by wise and reasonable legislation, in accordance with the terms of our platform. We believe that the power of government—in other words, of the people—should be expanded (as in the case of the postal service) as rapidly and as far as the good sense of an intelligent people and the teaching of experience shall justify, to the end that oppression, injustice, and poverty shall eventually cease in the land.

While our sympathies as a party of reform are naturally upon the side of every proposition which will tend to make men intelligent, virtuous, and temperate, we nevertheless regard these questions—important as they are—as secondary the great issues now pressing for solution, and upon which not only our individual prosperity but the very existence of free institutions depend; and we ask all men to first help us to determine whether we are to have a republic to administer before we differ as to the conditions upon which it is to be administered, believing that the forces of reform this day organized will never cease to move forward until every wrong is remedied, and equal rights and equal privileges securely established for all the men and women of this country.

Platform

We declare, therefore—

First—That the union of the labor forces of the United States this day consummated shall be permanent and perpetual; may its spirit enter into all hearts for the salvation of the Republic and the uplifting of mankind!

Second—Wealth belongs to him who creates it, and every dollar taken from industry without an equivalent is robbery. "If any will not work, neither shall he eat." The interests of rural and civic labor are the same; their enemies are identical.

Third—We believe that the time has come when the railroad corporations will either own the people or the people must own the railroads; and, should the government enter upon the work of owning and managing all railroads, we should favor an amendment to the Constitution by which all person engaged in the government service shall be placed under a civil-service regulation of the most rigid character, so as to prevent the increase of the power of the national administration by the use of such additional government employees.

FINANCE.—We demand a national currency, safe, sound, and flexible, issued by the general government only, a full legal tender for all debts, public and private, and that without the use of banking corporations, a just, equitable, and efficient means of distribution direct to the people, a tax not to exceed two per cent per annum, to be provided as set forth in the sub-treasury plan of the Farmers' Alliance, or a better system; also by payments in discharge of its obligations for public improvements.

1. We demand free and unlimited coinage of silver and gold at the present legal ratio of 16 to 1.

2. We demand that the amount of circulating medium be speedily increased to not less than $50 per capita.

3. We demand a graduated income tax.

4. We believe that the money of the country should be kept as much as possible in the hands of the people, and hence we demand that all State and national revenues shall be limited to the necessary expenses of the government, economically and honestly administered.

5. We demand that postal savings banks be established by the government for the safe deposit of the earnings of the people and to facilitate exchange.

TRANSPORTATION.—Transportation being a means of exchange and a public necessity, the government should own and operate the railroads in the interest of the people. The telegraph, telephone, like the post-office system, being a necessity for the transmission of news, should be owned and operated by the government in the interest of the people.

LAND.—The land, including all the natural sources of wealth, is the heritage of the people, and should not be monopolized for speculative purposes, and alien ownership of land should be prohibited. All land now held by railroads and other corporations in excess of their actual needs, and all lands now owned by aliens should be reclaimed by the government and held for actual settlers only.

Expression of Sentiments

Your committee on Platform and Resolutions beg leave unanimously to report the following:

Whereas, Other questions have been presented for our consideration, we hereby submit the following, not as a part of the Platform of the People's Party, but as resolutions expressive of the sentiment of this Convention:

1. Resolved, That we demand a free ballot and a fair count in all elections, and pledge ourselves to secure it to every legal voter without federal intervention, through the adoption by the States of the unperverted Australian or secret ballot system.

2. Resolved, That the revenue derived from a graduated income tax should be applied to the reduction for the burden of taxation now levied upon the domestic industries of this country.

3. Resolved, That we pledge our support to fair and liberal pensions to ex-Union soldiers and sailors.

4. Resolved, That we condemn the fallacy of protecting American labor under the present system, which opens our ports to the pauper and criminal classes of the world, and crowds out our wage-earners; and we denounce the present ineffective laws against contract labor, and demand the further restriction of undesirable emigration.

5. Resolved, that we cordially sympathize with the efforts of organized workingmen to shorten the hours of labor, and demand a rigid enforcement of the existing eight-hour law on Government work, and ask that a penalty clause be added to the said law.

6. Resolved, That we regard the maintenance of a large standing army of mercenaries, known as the Pinkerton system, as a menace to our liberties, and we demand its abolition; and we condemn the recent invasion of the Territory of Wyoming by the hired assassins of plutocracy, assisted by federal officers.

7. Resolved, That we commend to the favorable consideration of the people and the reform press the legislative system known as the initiative and referendum.

8. Resolved, That we favor a constitutional provision limiting the office of President and Vice-President to one term, and providing for the election of Senators of the United States by a direct vote of the people.

9. Resolved, That we oppose any subsidy or national aid to any private corporation for any purpose.

10. Resolved, That this convention sympathizes with the Knights of Labor and

their righteous contest with the tyrannical combine of clothing manufacturers of Rochester, and declare it to be the duty of all who hate tyranny and oppression to refuse to purchase the goods made by the said manufacturers, or to patronize any merchants who sell such goods.

Study Questions

1. In what manner did the Populists think that the "sham battle over the tariff" had "sacrifice[d] our homes, lives and children on the altar of mammon"?

2. In what sense did the Omaha Platform flow from the spirit of the Declaration of Independence?

3. What aspects of America's heritage did the Omaha Platform reject?

Francis Bellamy, Pledge of Allegiance (1892)

Francis Bellamy was a cousin of Edward Bellamy, who wrote the socialist utopian novel *Looking Backward* (p. 109). Like Edward, Francis also sought to unite Americans with a common sense of brotherhood. Francis especially celebrated the three ideals of the French Revolution: liberty, fraternity, and equality. As a Baptist minister in Boston, he had seen firsthand the plight of the poor. Francis Bellamy regarded covetousness as the greatest sin of the Gilded Age, a covetousness that deprived one's neighbor of what was necessary for his life. Bellamy's associations with socialist organizations put a rift between him and the Boston businessmen who hitherto had supported his church. In 1891, Bellamy resigned from the ministry to accept a position with *The Youth's Companion*, a magazine that soon took a central role in promoting the 400th anniversary of Columbus's arrival in America.

For Bellamy, Columbus Day was an opportunity to unite Americans into a universal brotherhood regardless of their diverse immigrant ethnicities. Cooperating with the National Education Association, and winning over the support of President Harrison and former President Cleveland, Bellamy orchestrated the National Public School Celebration in conjunction with the commemoration of Columbus. The American flag and public schools were the one thing all Americans had in common, argued Bellamy. Therefore, they should play a central role in honoring Columbus. President Harrison proclaimed October 21, 1892, as Columbus Day, calling upon schools to celebrate American heritage by raising up the national flag for salute.

Bellamy wrote a pledge for children to recite while saluting the flag. Initially, he intended to include the words "fraternity" and "equality," but had to leave those terms out because the socialist implications were unpopular with many Americans. He did, however, further his own nationalist agenda by employing the word "allegiance" in his title. Oaths of allegiance had been required during the Civil War and Reconstruction, as the Union sought to eliminate rebels from public office. In a similar spirit, Bellamy wanted schoolchildren to commit themselves to the common good by pledging their allegiance to the nation which they shared. Despite his own socialist leanings, the pledge of allegiance came to signify American patriotism against the national socialism of Germany during World War II, when Congress first adopted the Pledge of Allegiance, and also against Soviet communism during the Cold War, when Congress amended the pledge to commemorate also America's religious heritage.

Originally Published, 1892	*Revised, 1924*
I pledge allegiance to my flag and to the Republic for which it stands; one Nation, indivisible, with liberty and justice for all.	I pledge allegiance to the flag of the United States of America, and to the Republic for which it stands; one Nation, indivisible, with liberty and justice for all.

Adopted by Congress, 1942

That the pledge of allegiance to the flag, "I pledge allegiance to the flag of the United States of America and to the Republic for which it stands, one Nation indivisible, with liberty and justice for all," be rendered by standing with the right hand over the heart; extending the right hand, palm upward, toward the flag at the words "to the flag" and holding this position until the end, when the hand drops to the side. However, civilians will always show full respect to the flag when the pledge is given by merely standing at attention, men removing the headdress. Persons in uniform shall render the military salute.

Amended by Congress, 1954

I pledge allegiance to the flag of the United States of America, and to the Republic for which it stands; one Nation, under God, indivisible, with liberty and justice for all.

Study Questions

1. Why do you suppose the National Flag Conference revised the pledge in the 1920s? How, specifically, did the revision differ from Bellamy's formulation in 1892?

2. What changes did Congress make to the pledge, and why are those changes significant? How, too, did the historical context of the 1940s and the 1950s reshape the meaning of the pledge into something different than Bellamy may have intended?

3. In *Elk Grove Unified School District v. Newdow* (2003), the U.S. Supreme Court ruled to retain the phrasing "under God" in the Pledge of Allegiance against the objections of an atheist father who did not want his child to recite those words in school. How would you have decided the case, and why? Does your opinion change in view of the facts that the child's mother was a Christian who had no objection to the pledge, and that she, rather than the father, had legal custody of the child?

Grover Cleveland, Second Inaugural Address (1893)

A summer of discontent simmered in 1892. At Carnegie's Homestead, Pennsylvania, steelworks, labor went on strike only to face first the Pinkertons and eventually the state militia. Another violent strike occurred in the far western state of Idaho. Southerners and westerners were disgruntled over the McKinley Tariff Act, while debtors did not feel the inflationary relief they had sought under the Sherman Silver Coinage Act. In foreign affairs, President Harrison's efforts at annexing Hawaii proved unsuccessful. The nation offered Grover Cleveland a second chance in the White House.

My Fellow-Citizens:

In obedience of the mandate of my countrymen I am about to dedicate myself to their service under the sanction of a solemn oath. Deeply moved by the expression of confidence and personal attachment which has called me to this service, I am sure my gratitude can make no better return than the pledge I now give before God and these witnesses of unreserved and complete devotion to the interests and welfare of those who have honored me.

I deem it fitting on this occasion, while indicating the opinion I hold concerning public questions of present importance, to also briefly refer to the existence of certain conditions and tendencies among our people which seem to menace the integrity and usefulness of their Government.

While every American citizen must contemplate with the utmost pride and enthusiasm the growth and expansion of our country, the sufficiency of our institutions to stand against the rudest shocks of violence, the wonderful thrift and enterprise of our people, and the demonstrated superiority of our free government, it behooves us to constantly watch for every symptom of insidious infirmity that threatens our national vigor.

The strong man who in the confidence of sturdy health courts the sternest activities of life and rejoices in the hardihood of constant labor may still have lurking near his vitals the unheeded disease that dooms him to sudden collapse.

It can not be doubted that our stupendous achievements as a people and our country's robust strength have given rise to heedlessness of those laws governing our national health which we can no more evade than human life can escape the laws of God and nature.

Manifestly nothing is more vital to our supremacy as a nation and to the beneficent purposes of our Government than a sound and stable currency. Its exposure to degradation should at once arouse to activity the most enlightened statesmanship, and the danger of depreciation in the purchasing power of the wages paid to toil should furnish the strongest incentive to prompt and conservative precaution.

In dealing with our present embarrassing situation as related to this subject we will be wise if we temper our confidence and faith in our national strength and resources with the frank concession that even these will not permit us to defy with impunity the inexorable laws of finance and trade. At the same time, in our efforts to adjust differences of opinion we should be free from intolerance or passion, and our judgments should be unmoved by alluring phrases and unvexed by selfish interests.

I am confident that such an approach to the subject will result in prudent and effective remedial legislation. In the meantime, so far as the executive branch of the Government can intervene, none of the powers with which it is invested will be withheld when their exercise is deemed necessary to maintain our national credit or avert financial disaster.

Closely related to the exaggerated confidence in our country's greatness which tends to a disregard of the rules of national safety, another danger confronts us not less serious. I refer to the prevalence of a popular disposition to expect from the operation of the Government especial and direct individual advantages.

The verdict of our voters which condemned the injustice of maintaining protection for protection's sake enjoins upon the people's servants the duty of exposing and destroying the brood of kindred evils which are the unwholesome progeny of paternalism. This is the bane of republican institutions and the constant peril of our government by the people. It degrades to the purposes of wily craft the plan of rule our fathers established and bequeathed to us as an object of our love and veneration. It perverts the patriotic sentiments of our countrymen and tempts them to pitiful calculation of the sordid gain to be derived from their Government's maintenance. It undermines the self-reliance of our people and substitutes in its place dependence upon govern-

mental favoritism. It stifles the spirit of true Americanism and stupefies every ennobling trait of American citizenship.

The lessons of paternalism ought to be unlearned and the better lesson taught that while the people should patriotically and cheerfully support their Government its functions do not include the support of the people.

The acceptance of this principle leads to a refusal of bounties and subsidies, which burden the labor and thrift of a portion of our citizens to aid ill-advised or languishing enterprises in which they have no concern. It leads also to a challenge of wild and reckless pension expenditure, which overleaps the bounds of grateful recognition of patriotic service and prostitutes to vicious uses the people's prompt and generous impulse to aid those disabled in their country's defense.

Every thoughtful American must realize the importance of checking at its beginning any tendency in public or private station to regard frugality and economy as virtues which we may safely outgrow. The toleration of this idea results in the waste of the people's money by their chosen servants and encourages prodigality and extravagance in the home life of our countrymen.

Under our scheme of government the waste of public money is a crime against the citizen, and the contempt of our people for economy and frugality in their personal affairs deplorably saps the strength and sturdiness of our national character.

It is a plain dictate of honesty and good government that public expenditures should be limited by public necessity, and that this should be measured by the rules of strict economy; and it is equally clear that frugality among the people is the best guaranty of a contented and strong support of free institutions.

One mode of the misappropriation of public funds is avoided when appointments to office, instead of being the rewards of partisan activity, are awarded to those whose efficiency promises a fair return of work for the compensation paid to them. To secure the fitness and competency of appointees to office and remove from political action the demoralizing madness for spoils, civil-service reform has found a place in our public policy and laws. The benefits already gained through this instrumentality and the further usefulness it promises entitle it to the hearty support and encouragement of all who desire to see our public service well performed or who hope for the elevation of political sentiment and the purification of political methods.

The existence of immense aggregations of kindred enterprises and combinations of business interests formed for the purpose of limiting production and fixing prices is inconsistent with the fair field which ought to be open to every independent activity. Legitimate strife in business should not be superseded by an enforced concession to the demands of combinations that have the power to destroy, nor should the people to be served lose the benefit of cheapness which usually results from wholesome competition. These aggregations and combinations frequently constitute conspiracies against the interests of the people, and in all their phases they are unnatural and opposed to

our American sense of fairness. To the extent that they can be reached and restrained by Federal power the General Government should relieve our citizens from their interference and exactions.

Loyalty to the principles upon which our Government rests positively demands that the equality before the law which it guarantees to every citizen should be justly and in good faith conceded in all parts of the land. The enjoyment of this right follows the badge of citizenship wherever found, and, unimpaired by race or color, it appeals for recognition to American manliness and fairness.

Our relations with the Indians located within our border impose upon us responsibilities we can not escape. Humanity and consistency require us to treat them with forbearance and in our dealings with them to honestly and considerately regard their rights and interests. Every effort should be made to lead them, through the paths of civilization and education, to self-supporting and independent citizenship. In the meantime, as the nation's wards, they should be promptly defended against the cupidity of designing men and shielded from every influence or temptation that retards their advancement.

The people of the United States have decreed that on this day the control of their Government in its legislative and executive branches shall be given to a political party pledged in the most positive terms to the accomplishment of tariff reform. They have thus determined in favor of a more just and equitable system of Federal taxation. The agents they have chosen to carry out their purposes are bound by their promises not less than by the command of their masters to devote themselves unremittingly to this service.

While there should be no surrender of principle, our task must be undertaken wisely and without heedless vindictiveness. Our mission is not punishment, but the rectification of wrong. If in lifting burdens from the daily life of our people we reduce inordinate and unequal advantages too long enjoyed, this is but a necessary incident of our return to right and justice. If we exact from unwilling minds acquiescence in the theory of an honest distribution of the fund of the governmental beneficence treasured up for all, we but insist upon a principle which underlies our free institutions. When we tear aside the delusions and misconceptions which have blinded our countrymen to their condition under vicious tariff laws, we but show them how far they have been led away from the paths of contentment and prosperity. When we proclaim that the necessity for revenue to support the Government furnishes the only justification for taxing the people, we announce a truth so plain that its denial would seem to indicate the extent to which judgment may be influenced by familiarity with perversions of the taxing power. And when we seek to reinstate the self-confidence and business enterprise of our citizens by discrediting an abject dependence upon governmental favor, we strive to stimulate those elements of American character which support the hope of American achievement.

Anxiety for the redemption of the pledges which my party has made and solicitude for the complete justification of the trust the people have reposed in us constrain me to remind those with whom I am to cooperate that we can succeed in doing the work which has been especially set before us only by the most sincere, harmonious, and disinterested effort. Even if insuperable obstacles and opposition prevent the consummation of our task, we shall hardly be excused; and if failure can be traced to our fault or neglect we may be sure the people will hold us to a swift and exacting accountability.

The oath I now take to preserve, protect, and defend the Constitution of the United States not only impressively defines the great responsibility I assume, but suggests obedience to constitutional commands as the rule by which my official conduct must be guided. I shall to the best of my ability and within my sphere of duty preserve the Constitution by loyally protecting every grant of Federal power it contains, by defending all its restraints when attacked by impatience and restlessness, and by enforcing its limitations and reservations in favor of the States and the people.

Fully impressed with the gravity of the duties that confront me and mindful of my weakness, I should be appalled if it were my lot to bear unaided the responsibilities which await me. I am, however, saved from discouragement when I remember that I shall have the support and the counsel and cooperation of wise and patriotic men who will stand at my side in Cabinet places or will represent the people in their legislative halls.

I find also much comfort in remembering that my countrymen are just and generous and in the assurance that they will not condemn those who by sincere devotion to their service deserve their forbearance and approval.

Above all, I know there is a Supreme Being who rules the affairs of men and whose goodness and mercy have always followed the American people, and I know He will not turn from us now if we humbly and reverently seek His powerful aid.

Study Questions

1. Cleveland warned that prosperity can lead to carelessness. Explain his specific concerns about "depreciation in the purchasing power of the wages," "maintaining protection for protection's sake," and the "wild and reckless pension expenditure."

2. How did Cleveland apply the principle of "equality before the law" to African Americans?

3. What responsibilities did Cleveland think the federal government had toward American Indians?

William Jennings Bryan, "Cross of Gold Speech" (1896)

After President Cleveland called upon Congress to repeal the Sherman Silver Purchase Act in 1893, South Carolina Governor Ben Tillman, known as the "Pitchfork," called the president "an old bag of beef" and furthermore likened him to Judas, who had betrayed Christ. In 1894, Tillman won election to the U.S. Senate, where he lambasted Cleveland as a "besotted tyrant." Meanwhile, Congressman William Jennings Bryan of Nebraska joined the contest over America's monetary policy. Though being defeated in his 1894 bid for the Senate, Bryan did not lose heart. Both Bryan and Tillman were Democrats, committed to wrestling their party from Cleveland's influence. They challenged Cleveland relentlessly, drawing a mixture of support from silverite Democrats and Populists. In 1896, Bryan won the hearts of the national convention, where he delivered the following speech. So commanding was his charisma that not only the Democrats, but also the Populist Party, nominated Bryan for the presidency.

Here is the line of battle. We care not upon which issue they force the fight. We are prepared to meet them on either issue or on both. If they tell us that the gold standard is the standard of civilization, we reply to them that this, the most enlightened of all nations of the earth, has never declared for a gold standard, and both the parties this year are declaring against it. If the gold standard is the standard of civilization, why, my friends, should we not have it? So if they come to meet us on that, we can present the history of our nation. More than that, we can tell them this, that they will search the pages of history in vain to find a single instance in which the common people of any land ever declared themselves in favor of a gold standard. They can find where the holders of fixed investments have.

Mr. Carlisle said in 1878 that this was a struggle between the idle holders of idle capital and the struggling masses who produce the wealth and pay the taxes of the country; and my friends, it is simply a question that we shall decide upon which side shall the Democratic Party fight.

Upon the side of the idle holders of idle capital, or upon the side of the struggling masses? That is the question that the party must answer first; and then it must be answered by each individual hereafter. The sympathies of the Democratic Party, as described by the platform, are on the side of the struggling masses, who have ever been the foundation of the Democratic Party.

There are two ideas of government. There are those who believe that if you just legislate to make the well-to-do prosperous, that their prosperity will leak through on those below. The Democratic idea has been that if you legislate to make the masses prosperous their prosperity will find its way up and through every class that rests upon it.

You come to us and tell us that the great cities are in favor of the gold standard. I tell you that the great cities rest upon these broad and fertile prairies. Burn down your cities and leave our farms, and your cities will spring up again as if by magic. But destroy our farms and the grass will grow in the streets of every city in the country.

My friends, we shall declare that this nation is able to legislate for its own people on every question without waiting for the aid or consent of any other nation on earth, and upon that issue we expect to carry every single state in the Union.

I shall not slander the fair state of Massachusetts nor the state of New York by saying that when citizens are confronted with the proposition, "Is this nation able to attend to its own business?"—I will not slander either one by saying that the people of those states will declare our helpless impotency as a nation to attend to our own business. It is the issue of 1776 over again. Our ancestors, when but 3 million, had the courage to declare their political independence of every other nation upon earth. Shall we, their descendants, when we have grown to 70 million, declare that we are less independent than our forefathers? No, my friends, it will never be the judgment of this people. Therefore, we care not upon what lines the battle is fought. If they say bimetallism is good but we cannot have it till some nation helps us, we reply that, instead of having a gold standard because England has, we shall restore bimetallism, and then let England have bimetallism because the United States have.

If they dare to come out in the open field and defend the gold standard as a good thing, we shall fight them to the uttermost, having behind us the producing masses of the nation and the world. Having behind us the commercial interests and the laboring interests and all the toiling masses, we shall answer their demands for a gold standard by saying to them, you shall not press down upon the brow of labor this crown of thorns. You shall not crucify mankind upon a cross of gold.

Study Questions

1. What roles in the economy did Bryan think farms and factories each should play?

2. Which of those economic sectors should government favor, according to Bryan?

3. What did Bryan mean in saying, "You shall not crucify mankind upon a cross of gold"?

William McKinley, First Inaugural Address (1897)

As a Congressman, William McKinley had staked his political career on the protective tariff—specifically, not merely a tariff for generating revenue but also for protecting domestic producers. In 1896, political strategist Marcus A. Hannah organized McKinley's campaign for the presidency. Like Benjamin Harrison, McKinley attracted a large crowd to his front porch—over 750,000 people from thirty states. His electoral victories in the North and West established a Republican bloc that expanded in 1900, when McKinley won additional western states, and continued well into the twentieth century. As a result, the Populist Party soon faded into oblivion, and even the Democrats would not marshal a presidential victory until the three-party race of 1912.

Fellow-Citizens:

In obedience to the will of the people, and in their presence, by the authority vested in me by this oath, I assume the arduous and responsible duties of President of the United States, relying upon the support of my countrymen and invoking the guidance of Almighty God. Our faith teaches that there is no safer reliance than upon the God of our fathers, who has so singularly favored the American people in every national trial, and who will not forsake us so long as we obey His commandments and walk humbly in His footsteps.

The responsibilities of the high trust to which I have been called—always of grave importance—are augmented by the prevailing business conditions entailing idleness upon willing labor and loss to useful enterprises. The country is suffering from industrial disturbances from which speedy relief must be had. Our financial system needs some revision; our money is all good now, but its value must not further be threatened. It should all be put upon an enduring basis, not subject to easy attack, nor its stability to doubt or dispute. Our currency should continue under the supervision of the Government.

The several forms of our paper money offer, in my judgment, a constant embarrassment to the Government and a safe balance in the Treasury. Therefore I believe it necessary to devise a system which, without diminishing the circulating medium or offering a premium for its contraction, will present a remedy for those arrangements which, temporary in their nature, might well in the years of our prosperity have been displaced by wiser provisions. With adequate revenue secured, but not until then, we can enter upon such changes in our fiscal laws as will, while insuring safety and volume to our money, no longer impose upon the Government the necessity of maintaining so large a gold reserve, with its attendant and inevitable temptations to speculation. Most of our financial laws are the outgrowth of experience and trial, and should not be amended without investigation and demonstration of the wisdom of the proposed changes. We must be both "sure we are right" and "make haste slowly." If, therefore, Congress, in its wisdom, shall deem it expedient to create a commission to take under early consideration the revision of our coinage, banking and currency laws, and give them that exhaustive, careful and dispassionate examination that their importance demands, I shall cordially concur in such action. If such power is vested in the President, it is my purpose to appoint a commission of prominent, well-informed citizens of different parties, who will command public confidence, both on account of their ability and special fitness for the work. Business experience and public training may thus be combined, and the patriotic zeal of the friends of the country be so directed that such a report will be made as to receive the support of all parties, and our finances cease to be the subject of mere partisan contention. The experiment is, at all events, worth a trial, and, in my opinion, it can but prove beneficial to the entire country.

The question of international bimetallism will have early and earnest attention. It will be my constant endeavor to secure it by co-operation with the other great commercial powers of the world. Until that condition is realized when the parity between our gold and silver money springs from and is supported by the relative value of the two metals, the value of the silver already coined and of that which may hereafter be coined, must be kept constantly at par with gold by every resource at our command. The credit of the Government, the integrity of its currency, and the inviolability of its obligations must be preserved. This was the commanding verdict of the people, and it will not be unheeded.

Economy is demanded in every branch of the Government at all times, but especially in periods, like the present, of depression in business and distress among the people. The severest economy must be observed in all public expenditures, and

extravagance stopped wherever it is found, and prevented wherever in the future it may be developed. If the revenues are to remain as now, the only relief that can come must be from decreased expenditures. But the present must not become the permanent condition of the Government. It has been our uniform practice to retire, not increase our outstanding obligations, and this policy must again be resumed and vigorously enforced. Our revenues should always be large enough to meet with ease and promptness not only our current needs and the principal and interest of the public debt, but to make proper and liberal provision for that most deserving body of public creditors, the soldiers and sailors and the widows and orphans who are the pensioners of the United States.

The Government should not be permitted to run behind or increase its debt in times like the present. Suitably to provide against this is the mandate of duty—the certain and easy remedy for most of our financial difficulties. A deficiency is inevitable so long as the expenditures of the Government exceed its receipts. It can only be met by loans or an increased revenue. While a large annual surplus of revenue may invite waste and extravagance, inadequate revenue creates distrust and undermines public and private credit. Neither should be encouraged. Between more loans and more revenue there ought to be but one opinion. We should have more revenue, and that without delay, hindrance, or postponement. A surplus in the Treasury created by loans is not a permanent or safe reliance. It will suffice while it lasts, but it can not last long while the outlays of the Government are greater than its receipts, as has been the case during the past two years. Nor must it be forgotten that however much such loans may temporarily relieve the situation, the Government is still indebted for the amount of the surplus thus accrued, which it must ultimately pay, while its ability to pay is not strengthened, but weakened by a continued deficit. Loans are imperative in great emergencies to preserve the Government or its credit, but a failure to supply needed revenue in time of peace for the maintenance of either has no justification.

The best way for the Government to maintain its credit is to pay as it goes—not by resorting to loans, but by keeping out of debt—through an adequate income secured by a system of taxation, external or internal, or both. It is the settled policy of the Government, pursued from the beginning and practiced by all parties and Administrations, to raise the bulk of our revenue from taxes upon foreign productions entering the United States for sale and consumption, and avoiding, for the most part, every form of direct taxation, except in time of war. The country is clearly opposed to any needless additions to the subject of internal taxation, and is committed by its latest popular utterance to the system of tariff taxation. There can be no misunderstanding, either, about the principle upon which this tariff taxation shall be levied. Nothing has ever been made plainer at a general election than that the controlling principle in the raising of revenue from duties on imports is zealous care for American interests and American labor. The people have declared that such legislation should be had as will give ample protection and encouragement to the industries and the development of our country. It is, therefore, earnestly hoped and expected that Congress will, at the earliest practicable moment, enact revenue legislation that shall be fair, reasonable, conservative, and just, and which, while supplying sufficient revenue for public purposes, will still be signally beneficial and helpful to every section and every enterprise of the people. To this policy we are all, of whatever party, firmly bound by the voice of the people—a power vastly more potential than the expression of any political platform. The paramount duty of Congress is to stop deficiencies by the restoration of that protective legislation which has always been the firmest prop of the Treasury. The passage of such a law or laws would strengthen the credit of the Government both at home and abroad, and go far toward stopping the drain upon the gold reserve held for the redemption of our currency, which has been heavy and well-nigh constant for several years.

In the revision of the tariff especial attention should be given to the re-enactment and extension of the reciprocity principle of the law of 1890, under which so great a stimulus was given to our foreign trade in new and advantageous markets for our surplus agricultural and manufactured products. The brief trial given this legislation amply justifies a further experiment and additional discretionary power in the making of commercial treaties, the end in view always to be the opening up of new markets for the products of our country, by granting concessions to the products of other lands that we need and cannot produce ourselves, and which do not involve any loss of labor to our own people, but tend to increase their employment.

The depression of the past four years has fallen with especial severity upon the great body of toilers of the country, and upon none more than the holders of small farms. Agriculture has languished and labor suffered. The revival of manufacturing will be a relief to both. No portion of our population is more devoted to the institution of free government nor more loyal in their support, while none bears more cheerfully or fully its proper share in the maintenance of the Government or is better entitled to its wise and liberal care and protection. Legislation helpful to producers is beneficial to all. The depressed condition of industry on the farm and in the mine and factory has lessened the ability of the people to meet the demands upon them, and they rightfully expect that not only a system of revenue shall be established that will secure the largest income with the least burden, but that every means will be taken to decrease, rather than increase, our public expenditures. Business conditions are not the most promising. It will take time to restore the prosperity of former years. If we cannot promptly attain it, we can resolutely turn our faces in that direction and aid its return by friendly legislation. However troublesome the situation may appear, Congress will not, I am sure, be found lacking in disposition or ability to relieve it as far as legislation can do so. The restoration of confidence and the revival of business, which men of all parties so much desire, depend more largely upon the prompt, energetic, and intelligent action of Congress than upon any other single agency affecting the situation.

It is inspiring, too, to remember that no great emergency in the one hundred and eight years of our eventful national life has ever arisen that has not been met with wisdom and courage by the American people, with fidelity to their best interests and highest destiny, and to the honor of the American name. These years of glorious history have exalted mankind and advanced the cause of freedom throughout the world, and immeasurably strengthened the precious free institutions which we enjoy. The people love and will sustain these institutions. The great essential to our happiness and prosperity is that we adhere to the principles upon which the Government was established and insist upon their faithful observance. Equality of rights must prevail, and our laws be always and everywhere respected and obeyed. We may have failed in the discharge of our full duty as citizens of the great Republic, but it is consoling and encouraging to realize that free speech, a free press, free thought, free schools, the free and unmolested right of religious liberty and worship, and free and fair elections are dearer and more universally enjoyed to-day than ever before. These guaranties must be sacredly preserved and wisely strengthened. The constituted authorities must be cheerfully and vigorously upheld. Lynchings must not be tolerated in a great and civilized country like the United States; courts, not mobs, must execute the penalties of the law. The preservation of public order, the right of discussion, the integrity of courts, and the orderly administration of justice must continue forever the rock of safety upon which our Government securely rests.

One of the lessons taught by the late election, which all can rejoice in, is that the citizens of the United States are both law-respecting and law-abiding people, not easily swerved from the path of patriotism and honor. This is in entire accord with the genius of our institutions, and but emphasizes the advantages of inculcating even a greater love for law and order in the future. Immunity should be granted to none who violate the laws, whether individuals, corporations, or communities; and as the Constitution imposes upon the President the duty of both its own execution, and of the statutes enacted in pursuance of its provisions, I shall endeavor carefully to carry them into effect. The declaration of the party now restored to power has been in the past that of "opposition to all combinations of capital organized in trusts, or otherwise, to control arbitrarily the condition of trade among our citizens," and it has supported "such legislation as will prevent the execution of all schemes to oppress the people by undue charges on their supplies, or by unjust rates for the transportation of their products to the market." This purpose will be steadily pursued, both by the enforcement of the laws now in existence and the recommendation and support of such new statutes as may be necessary to carry it into effect.

Our naturalization and immigration laws should be further improved to the constant promotion of a safer, a better, and a higher citizenship. A grave peril to the Republic would be a citizenship too ignorant to understand or too vicious to appreciate the great value and beneficence of our institutions and laws, and against all who come here to make war upon them our gates must be promptly and tightly closed. Nor must we be unmindful of the need of improvement among our own citizens, but with the zeal of our forefathers encourage the spread of knowledge and free education. Illiteracy must be banished from the land if we shall attain that high destiny as the foremost of the enlightened nations of the world which, under Providence, we ought to achieve.

Reforms in the civil service must go on; but the changes should be real and genuine, not perfunctory, or prompted by a zeal in behalf of any party simply because it happens to be in power. As a member of Congress I voted and spoke in favor of the present law, and I shall attempt its enforcement in the spirit in which it was enacted. The purpose in view was to secure the most efficient service of the best men who would accept appointment under the Government, retaining faithful and devoted public servants in office, but shielding none, under the authority of any rule or custom, who are inefficient, incompetent, or unworthy. The best interests of the country demand this, and the people heartily approve the law wherever and whenever it has been thus administered.

Congress should give prompt attention to the restoration of our American merchant marine, once the pride of the seas in all the great ocean highways of commerce. To my mind, few more important subjects so imperatively demand its intelligent consideration. The United States has progressed with marvelous rapidity in every field of enterprise and endeavor until we have become foremost in nearly all the great lines of inland trade, commerce, and industry. Yet, while this is true, our American merchant marine has been steadily declining until it is now lower, both in the percentage of tonnage and the number of vessels employed, than it was prior to the Civil War. Commendable progress has been made of late years in the upbuilding of the American Navy, but we must supplement these efforts by providing as a proper consort for it a merchant marine amply sufficient for our own carrying trade to foreign countries. The question is one that appeals both to our business necessities and the patriotic aspirations of a great people.

It has been the policy of the United States since the foundation of the Government to cultivate relations of peace and amity with all the nations of the world, and this accords with my conception of our duty now. We have cherished the policy of non-interference with affairs of foreign governments wisely inaugurated by Washington, keeping ourselves free from entanglement, either as allies or foes, content to leave undisturbed with them the settlement of their own domestic concerns. It will be our aim to pursue a firm and dignified foreign policy, which shall be just, impartial, ever watchful of our national honor, and always insisting upon the enforcement of the lawful rights of American citizens everywhere. Our diplomacy should seek nothing more and accept nothing less than is due us. We want no wars of conquest; we must avoid the temptation of territorial aggression. War should never be entered upon until every

agency of peace has failed; peace is preferable to war in almost every contingency. Arbitration is the true method of settlement of international as well as local or individual differences. It was recognized as the best means of adjustment of differences between employers and employees by the Forty-ninth Congress, in 1886, and its application was extended to our diplomatic relations by the unanimous concurrence of the Senate and House of the Fifty-first Congress in 1890. The latter resolution was accepted as the basis of negotiations with us by the British House of Commons in 1893, and upon our invitation a treaty of arbitration between the United States and Great Britain was signed at Washington and transmitted to the Senate for its ratification in January last. Since this treaty is clearly the result of our own initiative; since it has been recognized as the leading feature of our foreign policy throughout our entire national history— the adjustment of difficulties by judicial methods rather than force of arms—and since it presents to the world the glorious example of reason and peace, not passion and war, controlling the relations between two of the greatest nations in the world, an example certain to be followed by others, I respectfully urge the early action of the Senate thereon, not merely as a matter of policy, but as a duty to mankind. The importance and moral influence of the ratification of such a treaty can hardly be overestimated in the cause of advancing civilization. It may well engage the best thought of the statesmen and people of every country, and I cannot but consider it fortunate that it was reserved to the United States to have the leadership in so grand a work.

It has been the uniform practice of each President to avoid, as far as possible, the convening of Congress in extraordinary session. It is an example which, under ordinary circumstances and in the absence of a public necessity, is to be commended. But a failure to convene the representatives of the people in Congress in extra session when it involves neglect of a public duty places the responsibility of such neglect upon the Executive himself. The condition of the public Treasury, as has been indicated, demands the immediate consideration of Congress. It alone has the power to provide revenues for the Government. Not to convene it under such circumstances I can view in no other sense than the neglect of a plain duty. I do not sympathize with the sentiment that Congress in session is dangerous to our general business interests. Its members are the agents of the people, and their presence at the seat of Government in the execution of the sovereign will should not operate as an injury, but a benefit. There could be no better time to put the Government upon a sound financial and economic basis than now. The people have only recently voted that this should be done, and nothing is more binding upon the agents of their will than the obligation of immediate action. It has always seemed to me that the postponement of the meeting of Congress until more than a year after it has been chosen deprived Congress too often of the inspiration of the popular will and the country of the corresponding benefits. It is evident, therefore, that to postpone action in the presence of so great a necessity would be unwise on the part of the Executive because unjust to the interests of the people. Our action now will

be freer from mere partisan consideration than if the question of tariff revision was postponed until the regular session of Congress. We are nearly two years from a Congressional election, and politics cannot so greatly distract us as if such contest was immediately pending. We can approach the problem calmly and patriotically, without fearing its effect upon an early election.

Our fellow-citizens who may disagree with us upon the character of this legislation prefer to have the question settled now, even against their preconceived views, and perhaps settled so reasonably, as I trust and believe it will be, as to insure great permanence, than to have further uncertainty menacing the vast and varied business interests of the United States. Again, whatever action Congress may take will be given a fair opportunity for trial before the people are called to pass judgment upon it, and this I consider a great essential to the rightful and lasting settlement of the question. In view of these considerations, I shall deem it my duty as President to convene Congress in extraordinary session on Monday, the 15th day of March, 1897.

In conclusion, I congratulate the country upon the fraternal spirit of the people and the manifestations of good will everywhere so apparent. The recent election not only most fortunately demonstrated the obliteration of sectional or geographical lines, but to some extent also the prejudices which for years have distracted our councils and marred our true greatness as a nation. The triumph of the people, whose verdict is carried into effect today, is not the triumph of one section, nor wholly of one party, but of all sections and all the people. The North and the South no longer divide on the old lines, but upon principles and policies; and in this fact surely every lover of the country can find cause for true felicitation. Let us rejoice in and cultivate this spirit; it is ennobling and will be both a gain and a blessing to our beloved country. It will be my constant aim to do nothing, and permit nothing to be done, that will arrest or disturb this growing sentiment of unity and cooperation, this revival of esteem and affiliation which now animates so many thousands in both the old antagonistic sections, but I shall cheerfully do everything possible to promote and increase it.

Let me again repeat the words of the oath administered by the Chief Justice which, in their respective spheres, so far as applicable, I would have all my countrymen observe: "I will faithfully execute the office of President of the United States, and will, to the best of my ability, preserve, protect, and defend the Constitution of the United States." This is the obligation I have reverently taken before the Lord Most High. To keep it will be my single purpose, my constant prayer; and I shall confidently rely upon the forbearance and assistance of all the people in the discharge of my solemn responsibilities.

Study Questions

1. Why did McKinley propose that the tariff be restored?

2. What problem was so critical that McKinley felt duty-bound to bring Congress into a special, early session?

3. What role did McKinley envision "wars of conquest" having in America's future?

The Spanish-American War, 1898

Under the Monroe Doctrine (1823), the United States had limited its involvement in foreign affairs, avoiding the use of military force overseas until almost the close of the century. In 1898, America waged war against Spain, establishing a new pattern of foreign relations that would characterize much of the following century.

Motives:

1. **Secure free markets.** Westward expansion had fed the American economy for a century, but as Frederick Jackson Turner noted in 1893, the frontier had vanished. Americans accordingly sought to increase their trade abroad, and Havana was a key port—but it was tangled in a revolutionary war, as Cubans rebelled against Spain.

2. **Keep pace with Europe.** Britain, France, Belgium, Italy, and Japan were colonizing Africa and the Pacific Islands.

3. **Retaliate for the sinking of the *U.S.S. Maine* (15 Feb. 1898).** Contemporaries blamed Spain. Scholars today conclude the explosion had resulted from an accident within the ship. Perception matters more than reality, and in 1898 it was perceived to be Spain's fault.

4. **"Yellow Journalism"** by William Hearst's *New York Journal* and other American periodicals spun the stories in favor of American war hawks. The newspapers raised the Spirit of 1776 to sympathize with Cubans oppressed by Spain's imperial rule, and urged retaliation for the sinking of the *Maine*.

5. **Manifest Destiny.** Christianity, politics, economics, and cultural paternalism fused together to justify American liberation and even possession of Spanish colonies. Social Darwinism added to this tradition: America is the fittest, so it should survive.

Battles:

1. **Manila:** A U.S. fleet commanded by George Dewey defeated the Spanish ships stationed at Manila Harbor in the Philippines on 1 May 1898.

2. **San Juan Hill:** Theodore Roosevelt daringly—foolishly, thought some—led his volunteer "Rough Riders" in an uphill battle (both geographically and militarily) in effort to overpower a Spanish garrison on 1 July 1898. The American attack proved amazingly successful.

Legacies:

1. **The U.S. acquired Cuba, Puerto Rico, Hawaii, Guam, and the Philippines**, and soon after sought more control over China. Cuba became independent in 1901, but the Philippines not until 1946. In general, the U.S. policy was of "protectorates": not independent nations, nor states within the U.S.

2. **Theodore Roosevelt became a war hero, then spring-boarded into politics as Vice President (1900) and President (1901, after McKinley's assassination).** Roosevelt's administration was a crucial development of the Progressive Era (early 1900s).

3. **The United States set a precedent of invading other nations** when political instability in those nations threatened its economic and political security. This strategy would be central to U.S. foreign policy during the Cold War (1946–1991) and also applied to the the more recent wars in Iraq (1991 and again starting in 2003).

4. **President McKinley set a precedent of deploying U.S. troops overseas prior to a formal war declaration passed by Congress.** Consider the Vietnam "war," which never was actually declared as a war by Congress.

5. **Anti-imperialists (William Jennings Bryan, Jane Addams, Mark Twain, and "Mugwump" Republicans) were disturbed by the irony that America cherishes liberty at home and yet imperializes abroad.** A similar debate surfaced a century later. Was America justified in invading Iraq in 2003? Has the U.S. forced Iraq into adopting a U.S.-style government?

Study Questions

1. What were the principal causes of the Spanish-American War?

2. What was the lasting significance of the Spanish-American War?

William McKinley, Second Inaugural Address (1901)

For the election of 1900, the Democrats again nominated William Jennings Bryan, but with a military victory abroad and a growing economy at home William McKinley had plenty of momentum to keep him in the White House. Selecting war hero Theodore Roosevelt as the vice presidential candidate made the McKinley ticket unbeatable. The president adopted a "full dinner pail" as his slogan, celebrating the revival of Gilded Age prosperity, which he believed was spreading to all classes.

My Fellow-Citizens:

When we assembled here on the 4th of March, 1897, there was great anxiety with regard to our currency and credit. None exists now. Then our Treasury receipts were inadequate to meet the current obligations of the Government. Now they are sufficient for all public needs, and we have a surplus instead of a deficit. Then I felt constrained to convene the Congress in extraordinary session to devise revenues to pay the ordinary expenses of the Government. Now I have the satisfaction to announce that the Congress just closed has reduced taxation in the sum of $41,000,000. Then there was deep solicitude because of the long depression in our manufacturing, mining, agricultural, and mercantile industries and the consequent distress of our laboring population. Now every avenue of production is crowded with activity, labor is well employed, and American products find good markets at home and abroad.

Our diversified productions, however, are increasing in such unprecedented volume as to admonish us of the necessity of still further enlarging our foreign markets by broader commercial relations. For this purpose reciprocal trade arrangements with other nations should in liberal spirit be carefully cultivated and promoted.

The national verdict of 1896 has for the most part been executed. Whatever remains unfulfilled is a continuing obligation resting with undiminished force upon the Executive and the Congress. But fortunate as our condition is, its permanence can only be assured by sound business methods and strict economy in national administration and legislation. We should not permit our great prosperity to lead us to reckless ventures in business or profligacy in public expenditures. While the Congress determines the objects and the sum of appropriations, the officials of the executive departments are responsible for honest and faithful disbursement, and it should be their constant care to avoid waste and extravagance.

Honesty, capacity, and industry are nowhere more indispensable than in public employment. These should be fundamental requisites to original appointment and the surest guaranties against removal.

Four years ago we stood on the brink of war without the people knowing it and without any preparation or effort at preparation for the impending peril. I did all that in honor could be done to avert the war, but without avail. It became inevitable; and the Congress at its first regular session, without party division, provided money in anticipation of the crisis and in preparation to meet it. It came. The result was signally favorable to American arms and in the highest degree honorable to the Government. It imposed upon us obligations from which we cannot escape and from which it would be dishonorable to seek escape. We are now at peace with the world, and it is my fervent prayer that if differences arise between us and other powers they may be settled by peaceful arbitration and that hereafter we may be spared the horrors of war.

Intrusted by the people for a second time with the office of President, I enter upon its administration appreciating the great responsibilities which attach to this renewed honor and commission, promising unreserved devotion on my part to their faithful discharge and reverently invoking for my guidance the direction and favor of Almighty God. I should shrink from the duties this day assumed if I did not feel that in their performance I should have the co-operation of the wise and patriotic men of all parties. It encourages me for the great task which I now undertake to believe that those who voluntarily committed to me the trust imposed upon the Chief Executive of the Republic will give to me generous support in my duties to "preserve, protect, and defend, the Constitution of the United States" and to "care that the laws be faithfully executed." The national purpose is indicated through a national election. It is the constitutional method of ascertaining the public will. When once it is registered it is a law to us all, and faithful observance should follow its decrees.

Strong hearts and helpful hands are needed, and, fortunately, we have them in every part of our beloved country. We are reunited. Sectionalism has disappeared. Division on public questions can no longer be traced by the war maps of 1861. These old differences less and less disturb the judgment. Existing problems demand the thought and quicken the conscience of the country, and the responsibility for their presence, as well as for their righteous settlement, rests upon us all—no more upon me than upon you. There are some national questions in the solution of which patriotism should exclude partisanship. Magnifying their difficulties will not take them off our hands nor facilitate their adjustment. Distrust of the capacity, integrity, and high purposes of the American people will not be an inspiring theme for future political contests. Dark pictures and gloomy forebodings are worse than useless. These only becloud, they do not help to point the way of safety and honor. "Hope maketh not ashamed." The prophets of evil were not the builders of the Republic, nor in its crises since have they saved or served it. The faith of the fathers was a mighty force in its creation, and the faith of their descendants has wrought its progress and furnished its defenders. They are obstructionists who despair, and who would destroy confidence in the ability of our people to solve wisely and for civilization the mighty problems resting upon them. The American people, intrenched in freedom at home, take their love for it with them wherever they go, and they reject as mistaken and unworthy the doctrine that we lose our own liberties by securing the enduring foundations of liberty to others. Our institutions will not deteriorate by extension, and our sense of justice will not abate under tropic suns in distant seas. As heretofore, so hereafter will the nation demonstrate its fitness to administer any new estate which events devolve upon it, and in the fear of God will "take occasion by the hand and make the bounds of freedom wider yet." If there are those among us who would make our way more difficult, we must not be disheartened, but the more earnestly dedicate ourselves to the task upon which we have rightly entered. The path of progress is seldom smooth. New things are often found hard to do. Our fathers found them so. We find them so. They are inconvenient. They cost us something. But are we not made better for the effort and sacrifice, and are not those we serve lifted up and blessed?

We will be consoled, too, with the fact that opposition has confronted every onward movement of the Republic from its opening hour until now, but without success. The Republic has marched on and on, and its step has exalted freedom and humanity. We are undergoing the same ordeal as did our predecessors nearly a century ago. We are following the course they blazed. They triumphed. Will their successors falter and plead organic impotency in the nation? Surely after 125 years of achievement for mankind we will not now surrender our equality with other powers on matters fundamental and essential to nationality. With no such purpose was the nation created. In no such spirit has it developed its full and independent sovereignty. We adhere to the principle of equality among ourselves, and by no act of ours will we assign to ourselves a subordinate rank in the family of nations.

My fellow-citizens, the public events of the past four years have gone into history. They are too near to justify recital. Some of them were unforeseen; many of them momentous and far-reaching in their consequences to ourselves and our relations with the rest of the world. The part which the United States bore so honorably in the thrilling scenes in China, while new to American life, has been in harmony with its true spirit and best traditions, and in dealing with the results its policy will be that of moderation and fairness.

We face at this moment a most important question that of the future relations of the United States and Cuba. With our near neighbors we must remain close friends. The declaration of the purposes of this Government in the resolution of April 20, 1898, must be made good. Ever since the evacuation of the island by the army of Spain, the Executive, with all practicable speed, has been assisting its people in the successive steps necessary to the establishment of a free and independent government prepared to assume and perform the obligations of international law which now rest upon the United States under the treaty of Paris. The convention elected by the people to frame a constitution is approaching the completion of its labors. The transfer of American control to the new government is of such great importance, involving an obligation resulting from our intervention and the treaty of peace, that I am glad to be advised by the recent act of Congress of the policy which the legislative branch of the Government deems essential to the best interests of Cuba and the United States. The principles which led to our intervention require that the fundamental law upon which the new government rests should be adapted to secure a government capable of performing the duties and discharging the functions of a separate nation, of observing its international obligations of protecting life and property, insuring order, safety, and liberty, and conforming to the established and historical policy of the United States in its relation to Cuba.

The peace which we are pledged to leave to the Cuban people must carry with it the guaranties of permanence. We became sponsors for the pacification of the island, and we remain accountable to the Cubans, no less than to our own country and people, for the reconstruction of Cuba as a free commonwealth on abiding foundations of right, justice, liberty, and assured order. Our enfranchisement of the people will not be completed until free Cuba shall "be a reality, not a name; a perfect entity, not a hasty experiment bearing within itself the elements of failure."

While the treaty of peace with Spain was ratified on the 6th of February, 1899, and ratifications were exchanged nearly two years ago, the Congress has indicated no form of government for the Philippine Islands. It has, however, provided an army to enable the Executive to suppress insurrection, restore peace, give security to the inhabitants, and establish the authority of the United States throughout the archipelago. It has authorized the organization of native troops as auxiliary to the regular force. It has been advised from time to time of the acts of the military and naval officers in the islands, of my action in appointing civil commissions, of the instructions with which they were charged, of their duties and powers, of their recom-

mendations, and of their several acts under executive commission, together with the very complete general information they have submitted. These reports fully set forth the conditions, past and present, in the islands, and the instructions clearly show the principles which will guide the Executive until the Congress shall, as it is required to do by the treaty, determine "the civil rights and political status of the native inhabitants." The Congress having added the sanction of its authority to the powers already possessed and exercised by the Executive under the Constitution, thereby leaving with the Executive the responsibility for the government of the Philippines, I shall continue the efforts already begun until order shall be restored throughout the islands, and as fast as conditions permit will establish local governments, in the formation of which the full co-operation of the people has been already invited, and when established will encourage the people to administer them. The settled purpose, long ago proclaimed, to afford the inhabitants of the islands self-government as fast as they were ready for it will be pursued with earnestness and fidelity. Already something has been accomplished in this direction. The Government's representatives, civil and military, are doing faithful and noble work in their mission of emancipation and merit the approval and support of their countrymen. The most liberal terms of amnesty have already been communicated to the insurgents, and the way is still open for those who have raised their arms against the Government for honorable submission to its authority. Our countrymen should not be deceived. We are not waging war against the inhabitants of the Philippine Islands. A portion of them are making war against the United States. By far the greater part of the inhabitants recognize American sovereignty and welcome it as a guaranty of order and of security for life, property, liberty, freedom of conscience, and the pursuit of happiness. To them full protection will be given. They shall not be abandoned. We will not leave the destiny of the loyal millions the islands to the disloyal thousands who are in rebellion against the United States. Order under civil institutions will come as soon as those who now break the peace shall keep it. Force will not be needed or used when those who make war against us shall make it no more. May it end without further bloodshed, and there be ushered in the reign of peace to be made permanent by a government of liberty under law!

Study Questions

1. Four years earlier America suffered "great anxiety with regard to our currency and credit." How did McKinley summarize the situation for 1901?

2. Four years earlier, McKinley had vowed to avoid "wars of conquest." On what basis did he now justify America's military involvement in Cuba and the Philippines?

PART 2:

Progressive Reform and Human Nature

1901–1929

Progressivism: The Political Ideology of the New Century

"Progressivism" refers to a set of political ideas dominant in America during the early decades of the twentieth century. Key planks of the progressive platform included: government regulations on corporations, especially monopolies; popular representation in politics; scientific management of immigration, urbanization, and industrialization; and the curbing of political corruption—all in the name of "the common good."

Every major political party of the time endorsed progressivism, including both Democrats and Republicans as well as the short-lived Populist Party of the 1890s. Even when Theodore Roosevelt failed to win the 1912 presidential election as a candidate for the Progressive Party, progressivism still triumphed, since the victorious Woodrow Wilson shared many of Roosevelt's ideas about using government as a tool for social and economic reform.

Progressive reformers argued for an expansion of democracy that would curb corrupt legislatures. Amendments to state constitutions allowed for **referenda** (laws proposed by the state legislature but voted on by the people before becoming final), **initiatives** (laws that were both originated and enacted by the people, without any legislative review), and **recall** (popular elections for voting people *out* of office, followed by an emergency election to replace ousted office holders). At the federal level, the Seventeenth Amendment (1913) disenfranchised the state legislatures, which formerly had elected U.S. Senators; henceforth, senators would be elected by statewide popular vote, allegedly to bypass corruption in the state legislatures. Meanwhile, city governments began to mirror corporations, with city councils functioning like boards of directors and mayors becoming responsible not simply to the people, but to the council.

More than anything, the Progressive Era marked the expansion of the government's regulatory reach into the economy. Presidents Theodore Roosevelt and William Howard Taft busted up the trusts. Congress imposed regulations on food packaging and labeling, and on interstate commerce generally. States experimented with minimum wage and maximum hour laws. All of these reforms shared in common the professions that such policies served the public good and that responsibility for distributing resources equitably fell properly to the government.

The Progressive Era (roughly, 1890–1920) redefined the expectations that the American people had for their government. Increasingly, policymakers saw the market as a source of problems and government regulation as the solution. Indeed, much of the twentieth century may be read as a contest between *laissez-faire* liberalism (which came to be renamed "conservatism") and a new brand of liberalism—progressive reform.

"Progress," of course, came at a price. In transitioning to a new kind of social order, American entrepreneurs lost a significant degree of individual liberty. In the twenty-first century, the debate concerning liberty and reform remains as lively as ever.

Chronological Overview: The Progressive Era

1890   Journalist Jacob Riis publishes *How the Other Half Lives*, a series of photo essays depicting the living conditions of impoverished urban immigrants.

1906   The Pure Food and Drug Act regulates food production facilities.

   The Hepburn Act regulates railroad rates, prohibiting free passes for favored customers.

1908   In *Muller v. Oregon*, the Supreme Court validates a state law regulating the working conditions of women, finding it to serve the public health.

1911   In *Standard Oil v. U.S.*, the Court orders Standard Oil Company to be divided into smaller units, finding that the company had restricted free trade by the "monopolistic symptoms" of higher prices, reduced production, and reduced quality.

1913   Three crowning achievements of progressive reform transform the political economy: the Sixteenth Amendment grants Congress the power to tax personal incomes; the Seventeenth Amendment re-characterizes U.S. Senators as representatives of the people rather than of state legislatures; the Federal Reserve Board expands the federal government's role in shaping the nation's money supply.

1914   The Federal Trade Commission regulates corporate deal-making; the Clayton Anti-Trust Act prohibits distinct companies from having interlocking boards of directors.

1917–1918   The United States enters World War I as an ally of Britain, France, Russia, and Italy against Germany and Austria-Hungary. The War Industries Board coordinates industrial production for military applications; the War Labor Policies Board sets minimum wage and maximum hour standards; the Food Administration channels food production for military consumption; and, the Committee on Public Information launches a "100% Americanism" campaign to promote wartime patriotism.

1919   The Eighteenth Amendment prohibits liquor sales, a restriction motivated by the hope of eliminating the social problems associated with alcoholism.

   The Treaty of Versailles incorporates many of Wilson's "Fourteen Points," but the U.S. Senate refuses to ratify it for fear of forfeiting national sovereignty.

1920   The Nineteenth Amendment grants women the right to vote nationally.

Presidents of the Progressive Era, 1901–1921

Theodore Roosevelt (Republican—New York), 1901–1909

Theodore Roosevelt was elected as Vice President in 1900 under William McKinley, who had appointed him Assistant Secretary of the Navy during the Spanish-American War. During the same war, Col. Roosevelt volunteered to lead a U.S. Army cavalry division—the "Rough Riders"—in a daring and stunningly victorious uphill battle at San Juan Hill (near Santiago, Cuba). Roosevelt, more than any other statesman of the time, embodied masculine leadership: confident and courageous action mixed with a gentle and caring spirit. Or, as Roosevelt once described the art of foreign policy, "Speak softly and carry a big stick."

Having served as police commissioner of New York City and later governor of the state, Roosevelt brought to the White House a vision of reform. In his first message to Congress, 1901, the president urged that "corporations engaged in interstate commerce should be regulated if they are found to exercise a license working to the public injury." In 1903, Congress responded by creating a new executive agency, the Department of Commerce and Labor, which would monitor large corporations. The following year, the Roosevelt administration scored a victory in the U.S. Supreme Court, forcing a railroad conglomerate, the Northern Securities Company, to be broken into smaller units that would allow for broader economic competition. Anti-trust suits against other corporations soon followed, including Rockefeller's Standard Oil, the American Tobacco Company, and Du Pont.

Elected in 1904 by a wider popular margin than any previous presidential candidate, Roosevelt continued his course of progressive reform, using government regulation as a tool for promoting his conception of the common good. A 1906 novel by socialist Upton Sinclair helped. Entitled *The Jungle*, the book detailed horrors from within the American meatpacking industry. Congress responded later that year with the Pure Food and Drug Act, which continues to regulate food production and package labeling to this day.

Roosevelt regulated Latin American affairs with an impulse similar to his progressive agenda at home. In 1903 he dispatched a warship to protect Panamanian revolutionaries, who soon signed a hundred-year lease agreement with the United States that the predecessor government of Colombia had recently refused. Thus America was able to build a canal connecting the Atlantic and Pacific Oceans. With U.S. interests tied so closely to Panama, Roosevelt now considered himself the policemen of Latin America. His Roosevelt Corollary to the Monroe Doctrine held that "chronic wrongdoing" by other nations "may force the United States, however reluctantly, in flagrant cases of such wrongdoing or impotence, to the exercise of an international police force," particularly when such wrongdoing impacts the western hemisphere.

In an era of rapid industrialization and urbanization, Roosevelt enjoyed the great American wilderness. In 1902, he embarked on a bear hunting expedition in Mississippi, but finding only one small cub he chose to spare the animal. A *Washington Post* cartoonist memorialized the escapade, and a Brooklyn toy store owner placed the cartoon next to a stuffed animal, which he labeled "Teddy's bear." Henceforth, American children grew up cuddling their teddy bears.

William Howard Taft (Republican—Ohio), 1909–1913

William Taft was Theodore Roosevelt's hand-picked successor. Like Roosevelt, Taft had served in President McKinley's administration, being appointed chief civil administrator in the Philippines in 1900. Roosevelt, in turn, appointed Taft as Secretary of War. By 1907, Roosevelt had is eye on Taft for the 1908 Republican nomination to the presidency, and so it played out.

Taft, however, was not as committed as Roosevelt to expanding presidential power for progressive causes. His four years in the White House represent a delicate balancing act between the progressive and conservative wings within his party. During the 1908 election cycle, William Jennings Bryan (who once again was seeking the high office), saw it all coming: Bryan mused that he was forced to campaign against a western progressive Taft and an eastern conservative Taft simultaneously.

On the one hand, Taft proved his progressivism by initiating some eighty anti-trust suits, busting more trusts than even Roosevelt. But Taft also supported the Payne-Aldrich Act of 1909, which perpetuated high protective tariffs in some areas, even while opening a free trade arrangement between the United States and the Philippines. Progressives turned against Taft because he had supported a tariff compromise that appeared to favor eastern industrialists over western raw material producers.

Meanwhile, a scandal arose in the Department of Interior, driving a wedge between Taft and his former mentor Roosevelt. Gifford Pinchot, who headed the U.S. Forestry Service, promoted Roosevelt's conservation policy, whereas Secretary of the Interior Richard Ballinger desired to reopen lands for settlement, thinking it illegal to have reserved so much federal land from development. Accusations of corruption brought either Ballinger or Pinchot into disrepute, depending whose side one took. Significantly, Taft favored Ballinger over Roosevelt's long-term friend Pinchot. The Ballinger-Pinchot controversy thus left a permanent rift between the Roosevelt and Taft, and distanced Taft from the progressive movement that celebrated Roosevelt's policies.

As for foreign policy, Taft continued to use America as a regulatory force in Latin America, but not necessarily through military deployment. Instead, Taft utilized the U.S. treasury to prop up interested parties. Known as "dollar diplomacy," Taft's program supported a regime change in Nicaragua and sought ways to inject U.S. private capital into foreign markets, hoping to stabilize those markets for future U.S. earnings.

By the 1912 election, a conservative faction was regaining control of the Republican Party, ready to put forth Taft for reelection. Roosevelt felt betrayed, so he entered the race under the banner of the new Progressive Party. When criticized for being too old, he claimed to be as fit as a bull moose, for which reason his movement also was known as the Bull Moose Party. Both Taft and Roosevelt lost that year to Democrat Woodrow Wilson.

Perhaps for Taft it was just as well. He had always preferred law to politics anyway. Stepping down from the presidency, he became a law professor at Yale University. Having served previously as a federal circuit judge, he at last was appointed as Chief Justice to the U.S. Supreme Court by President Warren Harding in 1921.

Woodrow Wilson (Democrat—New Jersey), 1913–1921

The ideology of progressivism culminated in the two-term presidency of Woodrow Wilson. Grover Cleveland had been the last of the small-government Democrats. Wilson's administration, by contrast, continued the progressive course of shifting power from the legislative to the executive branch and of stretching the reach of the federal regulatory hand into the affairs of states and private corporations. Wilson populated his cabinet with progressives, including two champions of populism: William Gibbs McAdoo, as Secretary of the Treasury, and William Jennings Bryan, as Secretary of State.

The only president thus far to earn a Ph.D., Wilson was no intellectual slouch. His book *Congressional Government* (1885) argued that the scheme of checks and balances envisioned by the founding fathers had become obsolete; the federal government had grown, the power of the states had diminished, and Congress in particular had claimed increasing authority. During the Progressive Era, Congress delegated much of that power to new executive agencies, a practice that resumed during the New Deal of the 1930s and the Great Society of the 1960s.

In Wilson's first two years as president, Congress passed four monumental laws for progressivism. The Underwood-Simmons Act reduced tariffs and instituted a graduated income tax, a move made possible by the Sixteenth Amendment that was ratified the same year. The creation of the Federal Trade Commission expanded the government's regulatory reach into Wall Street. Most significant of all, the Federal Reserve Act established a public-private banking partnership, whereby a nationwide network of twelve reserve banks governed by the president's appointees in the Federal Reserve Board would seek to stabilize the financial sector against the risk of economic panics and depressions that characterized the past. In time, "the Fed" would become a central player in the American economy through its ability to modulate the money supply by adjusting interest rates. Meanwhile, in 1914, the Clayton Anti-Trust Act bolstered the Sherman Act of 1890 and solidified the federal government's role in regulating large corporations. Progressivism was at its zenith.

As for foreign policy, Wilson appeared to turn his back on the imperialistic thrust of McKinley and Roosevelt. He vowed that America would "never again seek one additional foot of territory by conquest." Meanwhile, U.S.-Mexican relations proved tenuous. For decades, U.S. citizens had owned nearly forty percent of the real estate in Mexico. Political turbulence in that country therefore threatened American financial interests. While Wilson wavered as to how strictly to intervene, Mexico made plans with Germany for an invasion into the United States that was to culminate in a reconquest of the American southwest—territory that Mexico had lost to the United States in the Mexican War of 1846–1848. In February 1917, British intelligence intercepted a telegram from German foreign minister Arthur Zimmermann to the Mexican foreign office proposing a military alliance. Wilson took this information to Congress in April, urging a declaration of war against Germany. Even so, Wilson avowed himself against imperialism, claiming simply that "the world must be made safe for democracy."

In January 1918, Wilson articulated a vision for postwar peace in "Fourteen Points." He emphasized mutual respect among nations and self-determination for each government. He also proposed a League of Nations for settling disputes without going to war. The 1919 Treaty of Versailles followed Wilson's proposals closely, but the U.S. Senate refused to ratify it. Senator Henry Cabot Lodge objected particularly to the displacement of authority from Congress to the League of Nations, a move that stripped Congress of its constitutional powers. Wilson strove to rally the American people behind the treaty, but he fell ill and never fully recovered. As the president became weak, the nation began to realize that if central planning cannot prevent global war, then perhaps progressivism is not the savior of civilization that people once thought it could be.

Study Questions

1. What do all of the Progressive Era presidents have in common?

2. In what sense does Wilson's presidency mark the high point of progressivism?

Supreme Court Decisions during the Progressive Era

Recall that during the Gilded Age, several Supreme Court decisions promoted *laissez-faire* economics under the Fourteenth Amendment. During the Progressive Era, the Court reversed this trend, as can be seen most clearly in the transition from the *Lockner* (1905) to *Muller* (1908) rulings. The Court also upheld federal laws aimed at restricting monopolistic practices. This time, not even John D. Rockefeller's Standard Oil could escape the government's regulatory power. In general, the Court reinforced the major trend of the Progressive Era: to regulate in the name of the common good. This new approach to jurisprudence drew support from the writings of Oliver Wendell Holmes, Jr., who joined the Court in 1902. The spirit of nationalism associated with America's participation in World War I further solidified the Court's consensus that the Constitution must be interpreted in a manner serving the nation's best interest. The question then became: Who defines "the common good"? The answer: The majority of justices serving on the United States Supreme Court.

1904   *McCray v. U.S.*: Congress has the authority to levy prohibitive taxes that suppress the production of a specified good (in this case, margarine).

1905   *Lockner v. New York*: The Court ruled that a bakery and its employees have a Fourteenth Amendment guarantee of "liberty of contract" that forbids the state from regulating how many hours an employee works.

1905   *Swift and Co. v. U.S.*: Stockyards and meat-packing plants participate in a "stream of commerce," thereby subjecting them to federal regulations under the interstate commerce authority of Congress.

1908   *Muller v. Oregon*: The Court upheld a state law limiting the number of hours that a woman may work in a laundry, based on medical science

1911   *Standard Oil Co. v. U.S.*: The Court upheld the Sherman Anti-Trust Act and, finding Standard Oil Co. in violation, ordered that the corporation be dissolved.

1913   *Hoke v. U.S.*: Congress has the authority under the Interstate Commerce clause to prohibit the interstate transportation of prostitutes.

1918   *Selective Draft Law Cases*: Congress has the authority to draft men for compulsory military service.

1919   *Schenck v. U.S.*: Because of the "clear and present danger" occasioned by World War I, socialists may not claim protection under the First Amendment when circulating anti-war propaganda.

Study Question

How had the Court's perspective on economic regulation changed since the Gilded Age, and why?

Oliver Wendell Holmes, Jr., *The Common Law* (1881), Lecture 1

Oliver Wendell Holmes, Jr., received his legal education from Harvard University. He pioneered a judicial philosophy known as "sociological jurisprudence," or "legal realism." This approach differs from "strict construction" or "originalism" because it does not concern itself so much with the original intention of the lawmaker, but rather with the effects of the law as experienced in society. Judges, in this view, can and should reconstrue the law in a manner that best serves their perceptions of the common good. Holmes served on the Massachusetts Supreme Judicial Court from 1899 to 1902 and the U.S. Supreme Court from 1902 until 1932.

The object of this book is to present a general view of the Common Law. To accomplish the task, other tools are needed besides logic. It is something to show that the consistency of a system requires a particular result, but it is not all. The life of the law has not been logic: it has been experience. The felt necessities of the time, the prevalent moral and political theories, intuitions of public policy, avowed or unconscious, even the prejudices which judges share with their fellow-men, have had a good deal more to do than the syllogism in determining the rules by which men should be governed. The law embodies the story of a nation's development through many centuries, and it cannot be dealt with as if it contained only the axioms and corollaries of a book of mathematics. In order to know what it is, we must know what it has been, and what it tends to become. We must alternately consult history and existing theories of legislation. But the most difficult labor will be to understand the combination of the two into new products at every stage. The substance of the law at any given time pretty nearly corresponds, so far as it goes, with what is then understood to be convenient; but its form and machinery, and the degree to which it is able to work out desired results, depend very much upon its past. . . .

Study Questions

1. What are the advantages and disadvantages to regarding the "life of the law" as one of "logic"?

2. What are the benefits, and the risks, of judges drawing upon "the prejudices which [they] share with their fellow-men" when deciding cases?

Theodore Roosevelt, "The Trusts and the Tariffs" (1902)

President Theodore Roosevelt became known as the "TR the trust buster" for the reforms he advocated that limited the power of trusts. In his own words, he sought "not to destroy corporations, but . . . to make them subserve the public good." Just as corporations had become more powerful through conglomeration into holding companies and trusts, so also TR desired that the government would become more powerful, by conglomerating the states into the federal authority, in order to protect the people's interests from abusive trusts. He delivered the following address in Cincinnati, Ohio.

. . . I intend to make to you an argument from the standpoint simply of one American talking to his fellow-Americans upon one of the great subjects of interest to all alike; and that subject is what are commonly known as trusts. The word is used very loosely and almost always with technical inaccuracy. The average man, however, when he speaks of the trusts means rather vaguely all of the very big corporations, the growth of which has been so signal a feature of our modern civilization, and especially those big corporations which, though organized in one State, do business in several States, and often have a tendency to monopoly.

The whole subject of the trusts is of vital concern to us, because it presents one, and perhaps the most conspicuous, of the many problems forced upon our attention by the tremendous industrial development which has taken place during the last century, a development which is occurring in all civilized countries, notably in our own. There have been many factors responsible for bringing about these changed conditions. Of these, steam and electricity are the chief. The extraordinary changes in the methods of transportation of merchandise and of transmission of news have rendered not only possible, but inevitable, the immense increase in the rate of growth of our great industrial centres that is, of our great cities. I want you to bring home to yourselves that fact. When Cincinnati was founded news could be transmitted and merchandise carried exactly as has been the case in the days of the Roman Empire. . . . It matters very little whether we like these new conditions or whether we dislike them; whether we like the creation of these new opportunities or not. Many admirable qualities which were developed in the older, simpler, less progressive life have tended to atrophy under our rather feverish, high-pressure, complex life of to-day.

But our likes and dislikes have nothing to do with the matter. The new conditions are here. You can't bring back the old days of the canal boat and stagecoach if you wish. The steamboat and the railroad are here. The new forces have produced both good and evil. We can not get rid of them even if it were not undesirable to get rid of them; and our instant duty is to try to accommodate our social, economic and legislative life to them, and to frame a system of law and conduct under which we shall get out of them the utmost possible benefit and the least possible amount of harm. It is foolish to pride ourselves upon our progress and prosperity, upon our commanding position in the international industrial world, and at the same time have nothing but denunciation for the men to whose commanding position we in part owe this very progress and prosperity, this commanding position.

Whenever great social or industrial changes take place, no matter how much good there may be to them, there is sure to be some evil; and it usually takes mankind a number of years and a good deal of experimenting before they find the right ways in which so far as possible to control the new evil, without at the same time nullifying the new good. . . .

The evils attendant upon over-capitalization alone are, in my judgment, sufficient to warrant a far closer supervision and control than now exists over the great corporations. Wherever a substantial monopoly can be shown to exist we should certainly try our utmost to devise an expedient by which it can be controlled. Doubtless some of the evils existing in or because of the great corporations can not be cured by any legislation which has yet been proposed, and doubt less others, which have really been incident to the sudden development in the formation of corporations of all kinds, will in the end cure themselves. But there will remain a certain number which can be cured if we decide that by the power of the Government they are to be cured. The surest way to prevent the possibility of curing any of them is to approach the subject in a spirit of violent rancor, complicated with total ignorance of business interests and fundamental incapacity or unwillingness to understand the limitations upon all lawmaking bodies. No problem, and least of all so difficult a problem as this, can be

solved if the qualities brought to its solution are panic, fear, envy, hatred, and ignorance.

There can exist in a free republic no man more wicked, no man more dangerous to the people, than he who would arouse these feelings in the hope that they would redound to his own political advantage. Corporations that are handled honestly and fairly, so far from being an evil, are a natural business evolution and make for the general prosperity of our land. We do not wish to destroy corporations, but we do wish to make them subserve the public good. All individuals, rich or poor, private or corporate, must be subject to the law of the land; and the government will hold them to a rigid obedience thereof. The biggest corporation, like the humblest private citizen, must be held to strict compliance with the will of the people as expressed in the fundamental law. The rich man who does not see that this is in his interest is indeed short-sighted. When we make him obey the law we ensure for him the absolute protection of the law. . . .

Before speaking, however, of what can be done by way of remedy let me say a word or two as to certain proposed remedies which, in my judgment, would be ineffective or mischievous. . . . A remedy much advocated at the moment is to take off the tariff from all articles which are made by trusts. To do this it will be necessary first to define trusts. The language commonly used by the advocates of the method implies that they mean all articles made by large corporations, and that the changes in tariff are to be made with punitive intent toward these large corporations. Of course if the tariff is to be changed in order to punish them, it should be changed so as to punish those that do ill, not merely those that are prosperous. It would be neither just nor expedient to punish the big corporations as big corporations; what we wish to do is to protect the people from any evil that may grow out of their existence or maladministration. Some of those corporations do well and others do ill. If in any case the tariff is found to foster a monopoly which does ill, of course no protectionist would object to a modification of the tariff sufficient to remedy the evil. But in very few cases does the so-called trust really monopolize the market. Take any very big corporation (I could mention them by the score) which controls, say, something in the neighborhood of half of the products of a given industry. It is the kind of corporation that is always spoken of as a trust. Surely in rearranging the schedules affecting such a corporation it would be necessary to consider the interests of its smaller competitors which control the remaining part, and which, being weaker, would suffer most from any tariff designed to punish all the producers; for, of course, the tariff must be made light or heavy for big and little producers alike. Moreover, such a corporation necessarily employs very many thousands, often very many tens of thousands of work men, and the minute we proceeded from denunciation to action it would be necessary to consider the interests of these workmen. Furthermore, the products of many trusts are unprotected, and would be entirely unaffected by any change in the tariff, or at most very slightly so. The Standard Oil Company offers a case in point; and the corporations which control the anthracite coal output offer another for there is no duty whatever on anthracite coal.

I am not now discussing the question of the tariff as such; whether from the standpoint of the fundamental difference between those who believe in a protective tariff and those who believe in free trade; or from the standpoint of those who, while they believe in a protective tariff, feel that there could be a rearrangement of our schedules, either by direct legislation or by reciprocity treaties, which would result in enlarging our markets; nor yet from the standpoint of those who feel that stability of economic policy is at the moment our prime economic need, and that the benefits to be derived from any change in schedules would not compensate for the damage to business caused by the widespread agitation which would follow any attempted general revision of the tariff at this moment. Without regard to the wisdom of any one of those three positions it remains true that the real evils connected with the trusts can not be remedied by any change in the tariff laws. The trusts can be damaged by depriving them of the benefits of a protective tariff, only on condition of damaging all their smaller competitors, and all the wage-workers employed in the industry.

This point is very important, and it is desirable to avoid any misunderstanding concerning it. I am not now considering whether or not, on grounds totally unconnected with the trusts, it would be well to lower the duties on various schedules, either by direct legislation or by legislation or treaties designed to secure as an offset reciprocal advantages from the nations with which we trade. My point is that changes in the tariff would have little appreciable effect on the trusts save as they shared in the general harm or good proceeding from such changes. . . .

You must face the fact that only harm will come from a proposition to attack the so-called trusts in a vindictive spirit by measures conceived solely with a desire of hurting them, without regard as to whether or not discrimination should be made between the good and evil in them, and without even any regard as to whether a necessary sequence of the action would be the hurting of other interests. The adoption of such a policy would mean temporary damage to the trusts, because it would mean temporary damage to all of our business interests; but the effect would be only temporary, for exactly as the damage affected all alike, good and bad, so the reaction would affect all alike, good and bad. The necessary supervision and control, in which I firmly believe as the only method of eliminating the real evils of the trusts, must come through wisely and cautiously framed legislation, which shall aim in the first place to give definite control to some sovereign over the great corporations, and which shall be followed, when once this power has been conferred, by a system giving to the Government the full knowledge which is the essential for satisfactory action. Then when this knowledge one of the essential features of which is proper publicity has been gained, what further steps of any kind are necessary can be taken with the confidence born of the possession of power to deal with the subject, and of a thorough knowledge of what should and can be done in the matter.

We need additional power; and we need knowledge. Our Constitution was framed when the economic conditions were so different that each State could wisely be left to handle the corporations within its limits as it saw fit. Nowadays all the corporations which I am considering do what is really an interstate business, and as the States have proceeded on very different lines in regulating them, at present a corporation will be organized in one State, not because it intends to do business in that State, but because it does not, and therefore that State can give it better privileges, and then it will do business in some other States, and will claim not to be under the control of the States in which it does business; and of course it is not the object of the State creating it to exercise any control over it, as it does not do any business in that State. Such a system can not obtain. There must be some sovereign. It might be better if all the States could agree along the same lines in dealing with these corporations, but I see not the slightest prospect of such an agreement. Therefore, I personally feel that ultimately the nation will have to assume the responsibility of regulating these very large corporations which do an interstate business. The States must combine to meet the way in which capital has combined; and the way in which the States can combine is through the National Government. But I firmly believe that all these obstacles can be met if only we face them, both with the determination to overcome them, and with the further determination to overcome them in ways which shall not do damage to the country as a whole; which on the contrary shall further our industrial development, and shall help instead of hindering all corporations which work out their success by means that are just and fair toward all men.

Without the adoption of a constitutional amendment, my belief is that a good deal can be done by law. It is difficult to say exactly how much, because experience has taught us that in dealing with these subjects, where the lines dividing the rights and duties of the States and of the Nation are in doubt, it has sometimes been difficult for Congress to forecast the action of the courts upon its legislation. Such legislation (whether obtainable now, or obtainable only after a constitutional amendment) should provide for a reasonable supervision, the most prominent feature of which at first should be publicity; that is, the making public, both to the governmental authorities and to the people at large, the essential facts in which the public is concerned.

This would give us exact knowledge of many points which are now not only in doubt, but the subject of fierce controversy. Moreover, the mere fact of the publication would cure some very grave evils, for the light of day is a deterrent to wrong-doing. It would doubtless disclose other evils with which, for the time being, we could devise no way to grapple. Finally, it would disclose others which could be grappled with and cured by further legislative action.

Remember, I advocate the action which the President can only advise, and which he has no power himself to take. Under our present legislative and constitutional limitations the national executive can work only between narrow lines in the field of action concerning great corporations.

Between those lines, I assure you that exact and even-handed justice will be dealt, and is being dealt, to all men, without regard to persons.

I wish to repeat with all emphasis that desirable though it is that the nation should have the power I suggest, it is equally desirable that it should be used with wisdom and self-restraint. The mechanism of modern business is tremendous in its size and complexity, and ignorant intermeddling with it would be disastrous. We should not be made timid or daunted by the size of the problem; we should not fear to undertake it; but we should undertake it with ever present in our minds dread of the sinister spirits of rancor, ignorance, and vanity.

We need to keep steadily in mind the fact that besides the tangible property in each corporation there lies behind the spirit which brings it success, and in the case of each very successful corporation this is usually the spirit of some one man or set of men. Under exactly similar conditions one corporation will make a stupendous success where another makes a stupendous failure, simply because one is well managed and the other is not. While making it clear that we do not intend to allow wrong-doing by one of the captains of industry any more than by the humblest private in the industrial ranks, we must also in the interests of all of us avoid cramping a strength which, if beneficently used, will be for the good of all of us.

The marvelous prosperity we have been enjoying for the past few years has been due primarily to the high average of honesty, thrift, and business capacity among our people as a whole; but some of it has also been due to the ability of the men who are the industrial leaders of the nation. In securing just and fair dealing by these men let us remember to do them justice in return, and this not only because it is our duty, but because it is our interest; not only for their sakes, but for ours. We are neither the friend of the rich man as such, nor the friend of the poor man as such; we are the friend of the honest man, rich or poor; and we in tend that all men, rich and poor alike, shall obey the law alike and receive its protection alike.

Study Question

1. Define "trust" in the context of the American economy in Theodore Roosevelt's time.

2. Did Roosevelt regard big corporations as inherently evil? Explain.

3. What solutions did Roosevelt propose to the problems he associated with trusts?

Theodore Roosevelt, "Preservation of the Forests" (1903)

Theodore Roosevelt loved breathing fresh air and testing his fortitude in nature excursions. He desired that nature be conserved, but not for itself; rather, he desired that nature be utilized and enjoyed by people. He delivered the following address at Leland Stanford Junior University in Palo Alto, California. David Starr Jordan, a biologist, served as the university's president. He shared with Roosevelt a passion for the great outdoors.

President Jordan, and you, my Fellow-Citizens, and especially you, my Fellow-college Men and Women:

. . . America, the Republic of the United States, is of course in a peculiar sense typical of the present age. We represent the fullest development of the democratic spirit acting on the extraordinary and highly complex industrial growth of the last half century. It behooves us to justify by our acts the claims made for that political and economic progress.

We will never justify the existence of the Republic by merely talking each Fourth of July about what the Republic has done. If our homage is lip loyalty merely, the great deeds of those who went before us, the great deeds of the times of Washington and of the times of Lincoln, the great deeds of the men who won the Revolution and founded the Nation, and of the men who preserved it, who made it a Union and a free Republic, will simply arise to shame us.

We can honor our fathers and our father's fathers only by ourselves striving to rise level to their standard. There are plenty of tendencies for evil in what we see round about us. Thank heaven, there are an even greater number of tendencies for good, and one of the things, Mr. Jordan, which it seems to me give this Nation cause for hope is the national standard of

ambition which makes it possible to recognize with admiration and regard such work as the founding of a university of this character. It speaks well for our Nation that men and women should desire during their lives to devote the fortunes which they were able to acquire or to inherit because of our system of government, because of our social system, to objects so entirely worthy and so entirely admirable as the foundation of a great seat of learning such as this. All that we outsiders can do is to pay our tribute of respect to the dead and to the living who have done such good, and at least to make it evident that we appreciate to the full what has been done.

I have spoken of scholarship; I want to go back to the question of citizenship, a question affecting not merely the scholars among you, not merely those who are hereafter to lead lives devoted to science, to art, to productivity in literature. . . . I want to-day, here in California, to make a special appeal to all of you, and to California as a whole, for work along a certain line the line of preserving your great natural advantages alike from the standpoint of use and from the standpoint of beauty. If the students of this institution have not by the mere fact of their surroundings learned to appreciate beauty, then the fault is in you and not in the surroundings. Here in California you have some of the great wonders of the world. You have a singularly beautiful landscape, singularly beautiful and singularly majestic scenery, and it should certainly be your aim to try to preserve for those who are to come after you that beauty, to try to keep unmarred that majesty.

Closely entwined with keeping unmarred the beauty of your scenery, of your great natural attractions, is the question of making use of, not for the moment merely, but for future time, of your great natural products. Yesterday I saw for the first time a grove of your great trees, a grove which it has taken the ages several thousands of years to build up; and I feel most emphatically that we should not turn into shingles a tree which was old when the first Egyptian conqueror penetrated to the valley of the Euphrates, which it has taken so many thousands of years to build up, and which can be put to better use.

That, you may say, is not looking at the matter from the practical standpoint. There is nothing more practical in the end than the preservation of beauty, than the preservation of anything that appeals to the higher emotions in mankind. But, furthermore, I appeal to you from the standpoint of use. A few big trees, of unusual size and beauty, should be preserved for their own sake; but the forests as a whole should be used for business purposes, only they should be used in a way that will preserve them as permanent sources of national wealth. In many parts of California the whole future welfare of the State depends upon the way in which you are able to use your water supply; and the preservation of the forests and the preservation of the use of the water are inseparably connected.

I believe we are past the stage of national existence when we could look on complacently at the individual who skinned the land and was content for the sake of three years profit for himself to leave a desert for the children of those who were to inherit the soil. I think we have passed that stage. We should handle, and I think we now do handle, all problems such as those of forestry and of the preservation and use of our waters from the standpoint of the permanent interests of the homemaker in any region—the man who comes in not to take what he can out of the soil and leave, having exploited the country, but who comes to dwell therein, to bring up his children, and to leave them a heritage in the country not merely unimpaired, but if possible even improved. That is the sensible view of civic obligation, and the policy of the State and of the Nation should be shaped in that direction. It should be shaped in the interest of the home-maker, the actual resident, the man who is not only to be benefited himself, but whose children and children's children are to be benefited by what he has done. . . .

I appeal to you, as I say, to protect these mighty trees, these wonderful monuments of beauty. I appeal to you to protect them for the sake of their beauty, but I also make the appeal just as strongly on economic grounds; as I am well aware that in dealing with such questions a farsighted economic policy must be that to which alone in the long run one can safely appeal. The interests of California in forests depend directly of course upon the handling of her wood and water supplies and the supply of material from the lumber woods and the production of agricultural products on irrigated farms. The great valleys which stretch through the State between the Sierra Nevada and Coast Ranges must owe their future development as they owe their present prosperity to irrigation. Whatever tends to destroy the water supply of the Sacramento, the San Gabriel, and the other valleys strikes vitally at the welfare of California. The welfare of California depends in no small measure upon the preservation of water for the purposes of irrigation in those beautiful and fertile valleys which can not grow crops by rainfall alone. The forest cover upon the drainage basins of streams used for irrigation purposes is of prime importance to the interests of the entire State.

Now keep in mind that the whole object of forest protection is, as I have said again and again, the making and maintaining of prosperous homes. I am not advocating forest protection from the aesthetic standpoint only. I do advocate the keeping of big trees, the great monarchs of the woods, for the sake of their beauty, but I advocate the preservation and wise use of the forests because I feel it essential to the interests of the actual settlers. I am asking that the forests be used wisely for the sake of the successors of the pioneers, for the sake of the settlers who dwell on the land and by doing so extend the borders of our civilization. I ask it for the sake of the man who makes his farm in the woods, or lower down along the sides of the streams which have their rise in the mountains.

Every phase of the land policy of the United States is, as it by right ought to be,

directed to the upbuilding of the home-maker. The one sure test of all public land legislation should be: does it help to make and to keep prosperous homes? If it does, the legislation is good. If it does not, the legislation is bad. Any legislation which has a tendency to give land in large tracts to people who will lease it out to tenants is undesirable. We do not want ever to let our land policy be shaped so as to create a big class of proprietors who rent to others. We want to make the smaller men who, under such conditions would rent, actual proprietors. We must shape our policy so that these men themselves shall be the land owners, the makers of homes, the keepers of homes.

Certain of our land laws, however beneficent their purposes, have been twisted into an improper use, so that there have grown up abuses under them by which they tend to create a class of men who, under one color and another, obtain large tracts of soil for speculative purposes, or to rent out to others; and there should be now a thorough scrutiny of our land laws with the object of so amending them as to do away with the possibility of such abuses. If it was not for the national irrigation act we would be about past the time when Uncle Sam could give every man a farm. Comparatively little of our land is left which is adapted to farming without irrigation. The home-maker on the public land must hereafter, in the great majority of cases, have water for irrigation, or the making of his home will fail. Let us keep that fact before our minds. Do not misunderstand me when I have spoken of the defects of our land laws. Our land laws have served a noble purpose in the past and have become the models for other governments. The homestead law has been a notable instrument for good. To establish a family permanently upon a quarter section of land, or of course upon a less quantity if it is irrigated land, is the best use to which it can be put. The first need of any nation is intelligent and honest citizens. Such can come only from honest and intelligent homes, and to get the good citizenship we must get the good homes. It is absolutely necessary that the remainder of our public land should be reserved for the homemaker, and it is necessary in my judgment that there should be a revision of the land laws and a cutting out of such provisions from them as in actual practice under present conditions tend to make possible the acquisition of large tracts for speculative purposes or for the purpose of leasing to others.

Citizenship is the prime test in the welfare of the Nation; but we need good laws; and above all we need good land laws throughout the West. We want to see the free farmer own his home. The best of the public lands are already in private hands, and yet the rate of their disposal is steadily increasing. More than six million acres were patented during the first three months of the present year. It is time for us to see that our remaining public lands are saved for the home-maker to the utmost limit of his possible use. I say this to you of this university because we have a right to expect that the best trained, the best educated men on the Pacific Slope, the Rocky Mountains and great plains States will take the lead in the preservation and right use of the forests, in securing the right use of the waters, and in seeing to it that our land policy is not twisted from its original purpose, but is perpetuated by amendment, by change when such change is necessary in the line of that purpose, the purpose being to turn the public domain into farms each to be the property of the man who actually tills it and makes his home on it.

Infinite are the possibilities for usefulness that lie before such a body as that I am addressing. Work? Of course you will have to work. I should be sorry for you if you did not have to work. Of course you will have to work, and I envy you the fact that before you, before the graduates of this university, lies the chance of lives to be spent in hard labor for great and glorious and useful causes, hard labor for the uplifting of your States of the Union, of all mankind.

Study Question

1. What relationship did Roosevelt perceive between "the permanent interests of the home-maker" and the preservation of America's forests?

2. What did Roosevelt hope that new land policies could accomplish?

3. What was Roosevelt's "one sure test of all public lands legislation"?

Booker T. Washington, "The Atlanta Exposition Speech" (1895)

By 1900, "Jim Crow" laws had thoroughly segregated the American South. Blacks and whites had to use separate train cars, separate schools, separate bathrooms—even separate Bibles when swearing in as a witness in court. Despite the Fifteenth Amendment (see p. 48), southern states revised their constitutions and laws with technicalities that prohibited African Americans from voting. The Ku Klux Klan intimidated blacks to stay in the social spaces assigned to them by whites; dissenters were lynched, their bodies displayed publicly as a warning for others not to cross the color line. During this "Jim Crow" era of segregation, African Americans looked especially to Booker T. Washington for leadership. In 1881, Washington founded the Tuskeegee Institute in Alabama as an industrial school for preparing blacks for agricultural and manual labor. He promoted thrift, hard work, and property ownership. Both northern and southern progressives lent their support to his cause. In time, promised Washington, blacks would prove their social worth, but for the present they must patiently accommodate southern white rule.

Mr. President and Gentlemen of the Board of Directors and Citizens:

One-third of the population of the South is of the Negro race. No enterprise seeking the material, civil, or moral welfare of this section can disregard this element of our population and reach the highest success. I but convey to you, Mr. President and Directors, the sentiment of the masses of my race when I say that in no way have the value and manhood of the American Negro been more fittingly and generously recognized than by the managers of this magnificent Exposition at every stage of its progress. It is a recognition that will do more to cement the friendship of the two races than any occurrence since the dawn of our freedom.

Not only this, but the opportunity here afforded will awaken among us a new era of industrial progress. Ignorant and inexperienced, it is not strange that in the first years of our new life we began at the top instead of at the bottom; that a seat in Congress or the state legislature was more sought than real estate or industrial skill; that the political convention or stump speaking had more attractions than starting a dairy farm or truck garden.

A ship lost at sea for many days suddenly sighted a friendly vessel. From the mast of the unfortunate vessel was seen a signal, "Water, water; we die of thirst!" The answer from the friendly vessel at once came back, "Cast down your bucket where you are." A second time the signal, "Water, water; send us water!" ran up from the distressed vessel, and was answered, "Cast down your bucket where you are." And a third and fourth signal for water was answered, "Cast down your bucket where you are." The captain of the distressed vessel, at last heeding the injunction, cast down his bucket, and it came up full of fresh, sparkling water from the mouth of the Amazon River. To those of my race who depend on bettering their condition in a foreign land or who underestimate the importance of cultivating friendly relations with the Southern white man, who is their next-door neighbor, I would say: "Cast down your bucket where you are"—cast it down in making friends in every manly way of the people of all races by whom we are surrounded.

Cast it down in agriculture, mechanics, in commerce, in domestic service, and in the professions. And in this connection it is well to bear in mind that whatever other sins the South may be called to bear, when it comes to business, pure and simple, it is in the South that the Negro is given a man's chance in the commercial world, and in nothing is this Exposition more eloquent than in emphasizing this chance. Our greatest danger is that in the great leap from slavery to freedom we may overlook the fact that the masses of us are to live by the productions of our hands, and fail to keep in mind that we shall prosper in proportion as we learn to dignify and glorify common labour, and put brains and skill into the common occupations of life; shall prosper in proportion as we learn to draw the line between the superficial and the substantial, the ornamental gewgaws of life and the useful. No race can prosper till it learns that there is as much dignity in tilling a field as in writing a poem. It is at the bottom of life we must begin, and not at the top. Nor should we permit our grievances to overshadow our opportunities.

To those of the white race who look to the incoming of those of foreign birth and strange tongue and habits for the prosperity of the South, were I permitted I would repeat what I say to my own race, "Cast down your bucket where you are." Cast it down among the eight millions of Negroes whose habits you know, whose fidelity and

love you have tested in days when to have proved treacherous meant the ruin of your firesides. Cast down your bucket among these people who have, without strikes and labour wars, tilled your fields, cleared your forests, builded your railroads and cities, and brought forth treasures from the bowels of the earth, and helped make possible this magnificent representation of the progress of the South. Casting down your bucket among my people, helping and encouraging them as you are doing on these grounds, and to education of head, hand, and heart, you will find that they will buy your surplus land, make blossom the waste places in your fields, and run your factories. While doing this, you can be sure in the future, as in the past, that you and your families will be surrounded by the most patient, faithful, law-abiding, and unresentful people that the world has seen. As we have proved our loyalty to you in the past, in nursing your children, watching by the sick-bed of your mothers and fathers, and often following them with tear-dimmed eyes to their graves, so in the future, in our humble way, we shall stand by you with a devotion that no foreigner can approach, ready to lay down our lives, if need be, in defense of yours, interlacing our industrial, commercial, civil, and religious life with yours in a way that shall make the interests of both races one. In all things that are purely social we can be as separate as the fingers, yet one as the hand in all things essential to mutual progress.

There is no defense or security for any of us except in the highest intelligence and development of all. If anywhere there are efforts tending to curtail the fullest growth of the Negro, let these efforts be turned into stimulating, encouraging, and making him the most useful and intelligent citizen. Effort or means so invested will pay a thousand per cent interest. These efforts will be twice blessed—blessing him that gives and him that takes. There is no escape through law of man or God from the inevitable:

> The laws of changeless justice bind
> Oppressor with oppressed;
> And close as sin and suffering joined
> We march to fate abreast.

Nearly sixteen millions of hands will aid you in pulling the load upward, or they will pull against you the load downward. We shall constitute one-third and more of the ignorance and crime of the South, or one-third [of] its intelligence and progress; we shall contribute one-third to the business and industrial prosperity of the South, or we shall prove a veritable body of death, stagnating, depressing, retarding every effort to advance the body politic.

Gentlemen of the Exposition, as we present to you our humble effort at an exhibition of our progress, you must not expect overmuch. Starting thirty years ago with ownership here and there in a few quilts and pumpkins and chickens (gathered from miscellaneous sources), remember the path that has led from these to the inventions and production of agricultural implements, buggies, steam-engines, newspapers, books, statuary, carving, paintings, the management of drug stores and banks, has not been trodden without contact with thorns and thistles. While we take pride in what we exhibit as a result of our independent efforts, we do not for a moment forget that

our part in this exhibition would fall far short of your expectations but for the constant help that has come to our educational life, not only from the Southern states, but especially from Northern philanthropists, who have made their gifts a constant stream of blessing and encouragement.

The wisest among my race understand that the agitation of questions of social equality is the extremist folly, and that progress in the enjoyment of all the privileges that will come to us must be the result of severe and constant struggle rather than of artificial forcing. No race that has anything to contribute to the markets of the world is long in any degree ostracized. It is important and right that all privileges of the law be ours, but it is vastly more important that we be prepared for the exercise of these privileges. The opportunity to earn a dollar in a factory just now is worth infinitely more than the opportunity to spend a dollar in an opera-house.

In conclusion, may I repeat that nothing in thirty years has given us more hope and encouragement, and drawn us so near to you of the white race, as this opportunity offered by the Exposition; and here bending, as it were, over the altar that represents the results of the struggles of your race and mine, both starting practically empty-handed three decades ago, I pledge that in your effort to work out the great and intricate problem which God has laid at the doors of the South, you shall have at all times the patient, sympathetic help of my race; only let this he constantly in mind, that, while from representations in these buildings of the product of field, of forest, of mine, of factory, letters, and art, much good will come, yet far above and beyond material benefits will be that higher good, that, let us pray God, will come, in a blotting out of sectional differences and racial animosities and suspicions, in a determination to administer absolute justice, in a willing obedience among all classes to the mandates of law. This, coupled with our material prosperity, will bring into our beloved South a new heaven and a new earth.

Study Question

What did Washington mean when he said, "In all things that are purely social we can be as separate as the fingers, yet one as the hand in all things essential to mutual progress"? (Be sure to identify who is included in "we.")

W.E.B. DuBois, *The Souls of Black Folk* (1903)

The first African American to earn a Ph.D. from Harvard University, W.E.B. DuBois offered a bolder vision for African Americans than Booker T. Washington. In 1909, DuBois founded the National Association for the Advancement of Colored People (NAACP), where he served for twenty-four years as publicist and research director. The NAACP advocated for social and political reform, not patient accommodation as Washington had suggested. DuBois himself was convinced that patience would get African Americans nowhere so long as public policy continued to tolerate lynching. An accomplished scholar, DuBois chaired the Sociology Department at Atlanta University from 1933 to 1944. Eventually he gave up on the American creed of capitalism and representative government, becoming convinced that communism offered better promise for racial equality. Of course, before one can offer viable solutions to a problem, one first must understand the problem, and that was DuBois's task in *The Souls of Black Folk*.

The Forthright

Between me and the other world there is ever an unasked question: unasked by some through feelings of delicacy; by others through the difficulty of rightly framing it. All, nevertheless, flutter round it. They approach me in a half-hesitant sort of way, eye me curiously or compassionately, and then, instead of saying directly, How does it feel to be a problem? . . .

The Negro is a sort of seventh son, born with a veil, and gifted with second-sight in this American world,—a world which yields him no true self-consciousness, but only lets him see himself through the revelation of the other world. It is a peculiar sensation, this double-consciousness, this sense of always looking at one's self through the eyes of others, measuring one's soul by the tape of a world that looks on in amused contempt and pity. One ever feels his two-ness,—an American, a Negro; two souls, two thoughts, two unreconciled strivings; two warring ideals in one dark body, whose dogged strength alone keeps it from being torn asunder.

The history of the American Negro is the history of this strife,—this longing to attain self-conscious manhood, to merge his double self into a better and truer self. In this merging he wishes neither of the older selves to be lost. He would not Africanize America, for America has too much to teach the world and Africa. He would not bleach his Negro soul in a flood of white Americanism, for he knows that Negro blood has a message for the world. He simply wishes to make it possible for a man to be both a Negro and an American, without being cursed and spit upon by his fellows, without having the doors of Opportunity closed roughly in his face. . . .

Chapter 2—Of the Dawn of Freedom

The problem of the twentieth century is the problem of the color-line,—the relation of the darker to the lighter races of men in Asia and Africa, in America and the islands of the sea. It was a phase of this problem that caused the Civil War; and however much they who marched South and North in 1861 may have fixed on the technical points, of union and local autonomy as a shibboleth, all nevertheless knew, as we know, that the question of Negro slavery was the real cause of the conflict. Curious it was, too, how this deeper question ever forced itself to the surface despite effort and disclaimer. No sooner had Northern armies touched Southern soil than this old question, newly guised, sprang from the earth,—What shall be done with Negroes? Peremptory military commands this way and that, could not answer the query; the Emancipation Proclamation seemed but to broaden and intensify the difficulties; and the War Amendments made the Negro problems of to-day. . . .

They that walked in darkness sang songs in the olden days—Sorrow Songs—for they were weary at heart. And so before each thought that I have written in this book I have set a phrase, a haunting echo of these weird old songs in which the soul of the black slave spoke to men. Ever since I was a child these songs have stirred me strangely. They came out of the South unknown to me, one by one, and yet at once I knew them as of me and of mine. Then in after years when I came to Nashville I saw the great temple builded of these songs towering over the pale city. To me Jubilee Hall seemed ever made of the songs themselves, and its bricks were red with the blood and dust of toil. Out of them rose for me morning, noon, and night, bursts of wonderful melody, full of the voices of my brothers and sisters, full of the voices of the past.

Little of beauty has America given the world save the rude grandeur God himself stamped on her bosom; the human spirit in this new world has expressed itself in vigor and ingenuity rather than in beauty. And so by fateful chance the Negro folk-song—the rhythmic cry of the slave—stands to-day not simply as the sole American music, but as the most beautiful expression of human experience born this side the seas. It has been neglected, it has been, and is, half despised, and above all it has been persistently mistaken and misunderstood; but notwithstanding, it still remains as the singular spiritual heritage of the nation and the greatest gift of the Negro people. . . .

Chapter 14—Of the Sorrow Songs

Yet the soul-hunger is there, the restlessness of the savage, the wail of the wanderer, and the plaint is put in one little phrase:

My soul wants something that's new, that's new

Over the inner thoughts of the slaves and their relations one with another the shadow of fear ever hung, so that we get but glimpses here and there, and also with them, eloquent omissions and silences. Mother and child are sung, but seldom father; fugitive and weary wanderer call for pity and affection, but there is little of wooing and wedding; the rocks and the mountains are well known, but home is unknown. Strange blending of love and helplessness sings through the refrain:

Yonder's my ole mudder,

> Been waggin' at de hill so long;
> 'Bout time she cross over,
> Git home bime-by."

Elsewhere comes the cry of the "motherless" and the "Fare-well, farewell, my only child." . . .

Through all the sorrow of the Sorrow Songs there breathes a hope—a faith in the ultimate justice of things. The minor cadences of despair change often to triumph and calm confidence. Sometimes it is faith in life, sometimes a faith in death, sometimes assurance of boundless justice in some fair world beyond. But whichever it is, the meaning is always clear: that sometime, somewhere, men will judge men by their souls and not by their skins. Is such a hope justified? Do the Sorrow Songs sing true?

The silently growing assumption of this age is that the probation of races is past, and that the backward races of to-day are of proven inefficiency and not worth the saving. Such an assumption is the arrogance of peoples irreverent toward Time and ignorant of the deeds of men. A thousand years ago such an assumption, easily possible, would have made it difficult for the Teuton to prove his right to life. Two thousand years ago such dogmatism, readily welcome, would have scouted the idea of blond races ever leading civilization. So woefully unorganized is sociological knowledge that the meaning of progress, the meaning of "swift" and "slow" in human doing, and the limits of human perfectibility, are veiled, unanswered sphinxes on the shores of science. Why should AEschylus have sung two thousand years before Shakespeare was born? Why has civiliza-

tion flourished in Europe, and flickered, flamed, and died in Africa? So long as the world stands meekly dumb before such questions, shall this nation proclaim its ignorance and unhallowed prejudices by denying freedom of opportunity to those who brought the Sorrow Songs to the Seats of the Mighty?

Your country? How came it yours? Before the Pilgrims landed we were here. Here we have brought our three gifts and mingled them with yours: a gift of story and song—soft, stirring melody in an ill-harmonized and unmelodious land; the gift of sweat and brawn to beat back the wilderness, conquer the soil, and lay the foundations of this vast economic empire two hundred years earlier than your weak hands could have done it; the third, a gift of the Spirit. Around us the history of the land has centered for thrice a hundred years; out of the nation's heart we have called all that was best to throttle and subdue all that was worst; fire and blood, prayer and sacrifice, have billowed over this people, and they have found peace only in the altars of the God of Right. Nor has our gift of the Spirit been merely passive. Actively we have woven ourselves with the very warp and woof of this nation,—we fought their battles, shared their sorrow, mingled our blood with theirs, and generation after generation have pleaded with a headstrong, careless people to despise not Justice, Mercy, and Truth, lest the nation be smitten with a curse. Our song, our toil, our cheer, and warning have been given to this nation in blood-brotherhood. Are not these gifts worth the giving? Is not this work and striving? Would America have been America without her Negro people?

Study Questions

1. What did DuBois mean by "double-consciousness," or "two-ness"?

2. Explain what DuBois meant when he asked, "Your country? How came it yours?" (Be sure to identify who is meant by "your.")

3. Why did W.E.B. DuBois think that Washington's strategy of accommodation was wrong-headed?

Theodore Roosevelt, Inaugural Address (1905)

In a private letter dated 1900, Theodore Roosevelt quoted a West African proverb, "speak softly and carry a big stick." In time this statement became associated with his own foreign policy as president. In 1903, Roosevelt accepted the invitation of Philippe Banau-Varilla to secure the Panama Canal Zone from Colombia as Banau-Varilla's revolutionary party established Panama as an independent nation. Thereafter Latin American affairs would be closely intertwined with American interests. In his December 1904 message to Congress, Roosevelt announced a corollary to the Monroe Doctrine, establishing the United States as the policeman of Latin America:

> Chronic wrongdoing, or an impotence which results in a general loosening of the ties of civilized society, may in America, as elsewhere, ultimately require intervention by some civilized nation, and in the Western Hemisphere the adherence of the United States to the Monroe Doctrine may force the United States, however reluctantly, in flagrant cases of such wrongdoing or impotence, to the exercise of an international police power.

Upon his inauguration to a new term as president in 1905, Roosevelt spoke confidently of America's potential to fulfill solemn responsibilities, to its own people and to the world.

My fellow-citizens:

No people on earth have more cause to be thankful than ours, and this is said reverently, in no spirit of boastfulness in our own strength, but with gratitude to the Giver of Good who has blessed us with the conditions which have enabled us to achieve so large a measure of well-being and of happiness. To us as a people it has been granted to lay the foundations of our national life in a new continent. We are the heirs of the ages, and yet we have had to pay few of the penalties which in old countries are exacted by the dead hand of a bygone civilization. We have not been obliged to fight for our existence against any alien race; and yet our life has called for the vigor and effort without which the manlier and hardier virtues wither away. Under such conditions it would be our own fault if we failed; and the success which we have had in the past, the success which we confidently believe the future will bring, should cause in us no feeling of vainglory, but rather a deep and abiding realization of all which life has offered us; a full acknowledgment of the responsibility which is ours; and a fixed determination to show that under a free government a mighty people can thrive best, alike as regards the things of the body and the things of the soul.

Much has been given us, and much will rightfully be expected from us. We have duties to others and duties to ourselves; and we can shirk neither. We have become a great nation, forced by the fact of its greatness into relations with the other nations of the earth, and we must behave as beseems a people with such responsibilities. Toward all other nations, large and small, our attitude must be one of cordial and sincere friendship. We must show not only in our words, but in our deeds, that we are earnestly desirous of securing their good will by acting toward them in a spirit of just and generous recognition of all their rights. But justice and generosity in a nation, as in an individual, count most when shown not by the weak but by the strong. While ever careful to refrain from wrongdoing others, we must be no less insistent that we are not wronged ourselves. We wish peace, but we wish the peace of justice, the peace of righteousness. We wish it because we think it is right and not because we are afraid. No weak nation that acts manfully and justly should ever have cause to fear us, and no strong power should ever be able to single us out as a subject for insolent aggression.

Our relations with the other powers of the world are important; but still more important are our relations among ourselves. Such growth in wealth, in population, and in power as this nation has seen during the century and a quarter of its national life is inevitably accompanied by a like growth in the problems which are ever before every nation that rises to greatness. Power invariably means both responsibility and danger. Our forefathers faced certain perils which we have outgrown. We now face other perils, the very existence of which it was impossible that they should foresee. Modern life is both complex and intense, and the tremendous changes wrought by the extraordinary industrial development of the last half century are felt in every fiber of our social and political being. Never before have men tried so vast and formidable an experiment as that of administering the affairs of a

continent under the forms of a Democratic republic. The conditions which have told for our marvelous material well-being, which have developed to a very high degree our energy, self-reliance, and individual initiative, have also brought the care and anxiety inseparable from the accumulation of great wealth in industrial centers. Upon the success of our experiment much depends, not only as regards our own welfare, but as regards the welfare of mankind. If we fail, the cause of free self-government throughout the world will rock to its foundations, and therefore our responsibility is heavy, to ourselves, to the world as it is to-day, and to the generations yet unborn. There is no good reason why we should fear the future, but there is every reason why we should face it seriously, neither hiding from ourselves the gravity of the problems before us nor fearing to approach these problems with the unbending, unflinching purpose to solve them aright.

Yet, after all, though the problems are new, though the tasks set before us differ from the tasks set before our fathers who founded and preserved this Republic, the spirit in which these tasks must be undertaken and these problems faced, if our duty is to be well done, remains essentially unchanged. We know that self-government is difficult. We know that no people needs such high traits of character as that people which seeks to govern its affairs aright through the freely expressed will of the freemen who compose it. But we have faith that we shall not prove false to the memories of the men of the mighty past. They did their work, they left us the splendid heritage we now enjoy. We in our turn have an assured confidence that we shall be able to leave this heritage unwasted and enlarged to our children and our children's children. To do so we must show, not merely in great crises, but in the everyday affairs of life, the qualities of practical intelligence, of courage, of hardihood, and endurance, and above all the power of devotion to a lofty ideal, which made great the men who founded this Republic in the days of Washington, which made great the men who preserved this Republic in the days of Abraham Lincoln.

Study Questions

1. What are the "manlier and hardier virtues" that Roosevelt considered essential to American progress?

2. What challenges did America's system of self-government face, given that "modern life is both complex and intense"?

3. How did Roosevelt envision America's place in world leadership?

Upton Sinclair, *The Jungle* (1906)

Just as Harriet Beecher Stowe's *Uncle Tom's Cabin* (1852) awakened the consciences of northerners against the horrors of southern slavery, so also Upton Sinclair's *The Jungle* (1906) awakened the consciences of the middle class against the horrors of factory labor endured by the working class. More specifically, Sinclair revealed—albeit through the tool of fiction—that the food consumed by the middle class was produced under inhumane conditions jeopardizing the safety of workers and consumers alike. The moral outrage that Sinclair and his contemporary "muckraker" journalists produced motivated President Roosevelt and the U.S. Congress to take action. In 1906, Congress enacted the Pure Food and Drug Act, which prohibited the sale of contaminated or spoiled food and required that product labeling accurately report the ingredients and weight of the food being sold. For example, Section 7 of the Act forbade the sale of any food that "consists in whole or in part of a filthy, decomposed, or putrid animal or vegetable substance, or any portion of an animal unfit for food, whether manufactured or not, or if it is the product of a diseased animal, or one that has died otherwise than by slaughter."

Chapter 4

Promptly at seven the next morning Jurgis reported for work. He came to the door that had been pointed out to him, and there he waited for nearly two hours. The boss had meant for him to enter, but had not said this, and so it was only when on his way out to hire another man that he came upon Jurgis. He gave him a good cursing, but as Jurgis did not understand a word of it he did not object. He followed the boss, who showed him where to put his street clothes, and waited while he donned the working clothes he had bought in a secondhand shop and brought with him in a bundle; then he led him to the "killing beds." The work which Jurgis was to do here was very simple, and it took him but a few minutes to learn it. He was provided with a stiff besom, such as is used by street sweepers, and it was his place to follow down the line the man who drew out the smoking entrails from the carcass of the steer; this mass was to be swept into a trap, which was then closed, so that no one might slip into it. As Jurgis came in, the first cattle of the morning were just making their appearance; and so, with scarcely time to look about him, and none to speak to any one, he fell to work. It was a sweltering day in July, and the place ran with steaming hot blood—one waded in it on the floor. The stench was almost overpowering, but to Jurgis it was nothing. His whole soul was dancing with joy—he was at work at last! He was at work and earning money! All day long he was figuring to himself. He was paid the fabulous sum of seventeen and a half cents an hour; and as it proved a rush day and he worked until nearly seven o'clock in the evening, he went home to the family with the tidings that he had earned more than a dollar and a half in a single day! . . .

Chapter 5

. . . One of the first problems that Jurgis ran upon was that of the unions. He had had no experience with unions, and he had to have it explained to him that the men were banded together for the purpose of fighting for their rights. Jurgis asked them what they meant by their rights, a question in which he was quite sincere, for he had not any idea of any rights that he had, except the right to hunt for a job, and do as he was told when he got it. Generally, however, this harmless question would only make his fellow workingmen lose their tempers and call him a fool. There was a delegate of the butcher-helpers' union who came to see Jurgis to enroll him; and when Jurgis found that this meant that he would have to part with some of his money, he froze up directly, and the delegate, who was an Irishman and only knew a few words of Lithuanian, lost his temper and began to threaten him. In the end Jurgis got into a fine rage, and made it sufficiently plain that it would take more than one Irishman to scare him into a union. Little by little he gathered that the main thing the men wanted was to put a stop to the habit of "speeding-up"; they were trying their best to force a lessening of the pace, for there were some, they said, who could not keep up with it, whom it was killing. But Jurgis had no sympathy with such ideas as this—he could do the work himself, and so could the rest of them, he declared, if they were good for anything. If they couldn't do it, let them go somewhere else. Jurgis had not studied the books, and he would not have known how to pronounce "*laissez faire*"; but he had been round the world enough to know that a man has to shift for himself in it, and that if he gets the worst of it, there is nobody to listen to him holler.

Yet there have been known to be philosophers and plain men who swore by Malthus in the books, and would, nevertheless, subscribe to a relief fund in time of a famine. It was the same with Jurgis, who consigned the unfit to destruction, while going about all day sick at heart because of his poor old father, who was wandering somewhere in the yards begging for a chance to earn his bread. Old Antanas had been a worker ever since he was a child; he had run away from home when he was twelve, because his father beat him for trying to learn to read. And he was a faithful man, too; he was a man you might leave alone for a month, if only you had made him understand what you wanted him to do in the meantime. And now here he was, worn out in soul and body, and with no more place in the world than a sick dog. He had his home, as it happened, and some one who would care for him if he never got a job; but his son could not help thinking, suppose this had not been the case. Antanas Rudkus had been into every building in Packingtown by this time, and into nearly every room; he had stood mornings among the crowd of applicants till the very policemen had come to know his face and to tell him to go home and give it up. He had been likewise to all the stores and saloons for a mile about, begging for some little thing to do; and everywhere they had ordered him out, sometimes with curses, and not once even stopping to ask him a question.

So, after all, there was a crack in the fine structure of Jurgis' faith in things as they are. The crack was wide while Dede Antanas was hunting a job—and it was yet wider when he finally got it. For one evening the old man came home in a great state of excitement, with the tale that he had been approached by a man in one of the corridors of the pickle rooms of Durham's, and asked what he would pay to get a job. He had not known what to make of this at first; but the man had gone on with matter-of-fact frankness to say that he could get him a job, provided that he were willing to pay one-third of his wages for it. Was he a boss? Antanas had asked; to which the man had replied that that was nobody's business, but that he could do what he said.

Jurgis had made some friends by this time, and he sought one of them and asked what this meant. The friend, who was named Tamoszius Kuszleika, was a sharp little man who folded hides on the killing beds, and he listened to what Jurgis had to say without seeming at all surprised. They were common enough, he said, such cases of petty graft. It was simply some boss who proposed to add a little to his income. After Jurgis had been there awhile he would know that the plants were simply honeycombed with rottenness of that sort —the bosses grafted off the men, and they grafted off each other; and some day the superintendent would find out about the boss, and then he would graft off the boss. Warming to the subject, Tamoszius went on to explain the situation. Here was Durham's, for instance, owned by a man who was trying to make as much money out of it as he could, and did not care in the least how he did it; and underneath him, ranged in ranks and grades like an

army, were managers and superintendents and foremen, each one driving the man next below him and trying to squeeze out of him as much work as possible. And all the men of the same rank were pitted against each other; the accounts of each were kept separately, and every man lived in terror of losing his job, if another made a better record than he. So from top to bottom the place was simply a seething caldron of jealousies and hatreds; there was no loyalty or decency anywhere about it, there was no place in it where a man counted for anything against a dollar. And worse than there being no decency, there was not even any honesty. The reason for that? Who could say? It must have been old Durham in the beginning; it was a heritage which the self-made merchant had left to his son, along with his millions.

Jurgis would find out these things for himself, if he stayed there long enough; it was the men who had to do all the dirty jobs, and so there was no deceiving them; and they caught the spirit of the place, and did like all the rest. Jurgis had come there, and thought he was going to make himself useful, and rise and become a skilled man; but he would soon find out his error—for nobody rose in Packingtown by doing good work. You could lay that down for a rule— if you met a man who was rising in Packingtown, you met a knave. That man who had been sent to Jurgis' father by the boss, he would rise; the man who told tales and spied upon his fellows would rise; but the man who minded his own business and did his work—why, they would "speed him up" till they had worn him out, and then they would throw him into the gutter.

Jurgis went home with his head buzzing. Yet he could not bring himself to believe such things—no, it could not be so. Tamoszius was simply another of the grumblers. He was a man who spent all his time fiddling; and he would go to parties at night and not get home till sunrise, and so of course he did not feel like work. Then, too, he was a puny little chap; and so he had been left behind in the race, and that was why he was sore. And yet so many strange things kept coming to Jurgis' notice every day! . . .

Now Antanas Rudkus was the meekest man that God ever put on earth; and so Jurgis found it a striking confirmation of what the men all said, that his father had been at work only two days before he came home as bitter as any of them, and cursing Durham's with all the power of his soul. For they had set him to cleaning out the traps; and the family sat round and listened in wonder while he told them what that meant. It seemed that he was working in the room where the men prepared the beef for canning, and the beef had lain in vats full of chemicals, and men with great forks speared it out and dumped it into trucks, to be taken to the cooking room. When they had speared out all they could reach, they emptied the vat on the floor, and then with shovels scraped up the balance and dumped it into the truck. This floor was filthy, yet they set Antanas with his mop slopping the "pickle" into a hole that connected with a sink, where it was caught and used over again forever; and if that were not enough, there was a trap in the pipe, where all the scraps of meat and odds and ends of refuse were caught, and every few days it was the old man's task to clean these out, and shovel their contents into one of the trucks with the rest of the meat! . . .

Chapter 7

All summer long the family toiled, and in the fall they had money enough for Jurgis and Ona to be married according to home traditions of decency. In the latter part of November they hired a hall, and invited all their new acquaintances, who came and left them over a hundred dollars in debt.

It was a bitter and cruel experience, and it plunged them into an agony of despair. . . .

He had to protect her, to do battle for her against the horror he saw about them. He was all that she had to look to, and if he failed she would be lost; he would wrap his arms about her, and try to hide her from the world. He had learned the ways of things about him now. It was a war of each against all, and the devil take the hindmost. You did not give feasts to other people, you waited for them to give feasts to you. You went about with your soul full of suspicion and hatred; you understood that you were environed by hostile powers that were trying to get your money, and who used all the virtues to bait their traps with. The store-keepers plastered up their windows with all sorts of lies to entice you; the very fences by the wayside, the lamp-posts and telegraph poles, were pasted over with lies. The great corporation which employed you lied to you, and lied to the whole country—from top to bottom it was nothing but one gigantic lie. . . .

There were many such dangers, in

which the odds were all against them. Their children were not as well as they had been at home; but how could they know that there was no sewer to their house, and that the drainage of fifteen years was in a cesspool under it? How could they know that the pale-blue milk that they bought around the corner was watered, and doctored with formaldehyde besides? When the children were not well at home, Teta Elzbieta would gather herbs and cure them; now she was obliged to go to the drugstore and buy extracts—and how was she to know that they were all adulterated? How could they find out that their tea and coffee, their sugar and flour, had been doctored; that their canned peas had been colored with copper salts, and their fruit jams with aniline dyes? And even if they had known it, what good would it have done them, since there was no place within miles of them where any other sort was to be had? The bitter winter was coming, and they had to save money to get more clothing and bedding; but it would not matter in the least how much they saved, they could not get anything to keep them warm. All the clothing that was to be had in the stores was made of cotton and shoddy, which is made by tearing old clothes to pieces and weaving the fiber again. If they paid higher prices, they might get frills and fanciness, or be cheated; but genuine quality they could not obtain for love nor money.

Chapter 9

. . . Then one Sunday evening, Jurgis sat puffing his pipe by the kitchen stove, and talking with an old fellow whom Jonas had introduced, and who worked in the can-

ning rooms at Durham's; and so Jurgis learned a few things about the great and only Durham canned goods, which had become a national institution. They were regular alchemists at Durham's; they advertised a mushroom-catsup, and the men who made it did not know what a mushroom looked like. They advertised "potted chicken,"—and it was like the boardinghouse soup of the comic papers, through which a chicken had walked with rubbers on. Perhaps they had a secret process for making chickens chemically—who knows? said Jurgis' friend; the things that went into the mixture were tripe, and the fat of pork, and beef suet, and hearts of beef, and finally the waste ends of veal, when they had any. They put these up in several grades, and sold them at several prices; but the contents of the cans all came out of the same hopper. And then there was "potted game" and "potted grouse," "potted ham," and "deviled ham"—de-vyled, as the men called it. "De-vyled" ham was made out of the waste ends of smoked beef that were too small to be sliced by the machines; and also tripe, dyed with chemicals so that it would not show white; and trimmings of hams and corned beef; and potatoes, skins and all; and finally the hard cartilaginous gullets of beef, after the tongues had been cut out. All this ingenious mixture was ground up and flavored with spices to make it taste like something. Anybody who could invent a new imitation had been sure of a fortune from old Durham, said Jurgis' informant; but it was hard to think of anything new in a place where so many sharp wits had been at work for so long; where men welcomed tuberculosis in the cattle they were feeding, because it made them fatten more quickly; and where they bought up all the old rancid butter left over in the grocery stores of a continent, and "oxidized" it by a forced-air process, to take away the odor, rechurned it with skim milk, and sold it in bricks in the cities! Up to a year or two ago it had been the custom to kill horses in the yards—ostensibly for fertilizer; but after long agitation the newspapers had been able to make the public realize that the horses were being canned. Now it was against the law to kill horses in Packing-town, and the law was really complied with —for the present, at any rate. Any day, however, one might see sharp-horned and shaggy-haired creatures running with the sheep and yet what a job you would have to get the public to believe that a good part of what it buys for lamb and mutton is really goat's flesh!

There was another interesting set of statistics that a person might have gathered in Packingtown—those of the various afflictions of the workers. When Jurgis had first inspected the packing plants with Szedvilas, he had marveled while he listened to the tale of all the things that were made out of the carcasses of animals, and of all the lesser industries that were maintained there; now he found that each one of these lesser industries was a separate little inferno, in its way as horrible as the killing beds, the source and fountain of them all. The workers in each of them had their own peculiar diseases. And the wandering visitor might be skeptical about all the swindles, but he could not be skeptical about these, for the worker bore the evidence of them about on his own person—generally he had only to hold out his hand.

There were the men in the pickle rooms, for instance, where old Antanas had gotten his death; scarce a one of these that had not some spot of horror on his person. Let a man so much as scrape his finger pushing a truck in the pickle rooms, and he might have a sore that would put him out of the world; all the joints in his fingers might be eaten by the acid, one by one. Of the butchers and floorsmen, the beef-boners and trimmers, and all those who used knives, you could scarcely find a person who had the use of his thumb; time and time again the base of it had been slashed, till it was a mere lump of flesh against which the man pressed the knife to hold it. The hands of these men would be criss-crossed with cuts, until you could no longer pretend to count them or to trace them. They would have no nails,—they had worn them off pulling hides; their knuckles were swollen so that their fingers spread out like a fan. There were men who worked in the cooking rooms, in the midst of steam and sickening odors, by artificial light; in these rooms the germs of tuberculosis might live for two years, but the supply was renewed every hour. There were the beef-luggers, who carried two-hundred-pound quarters into the refriger-ator-cars; a fearful kind of work, that began at four o'clock in the morning, and that wore out the most powerful men in a few years. There were those who worked in the chilling rooms, and whose special disease was rheumatism; the time limit that a man could work in the chilling rooms was said to be five years. There were the wool-pluckers, whose hands went to pieces even sooner than the hands of the pickle men; for the pelts of the sheep had to be painted with acid to loosen the wool, and then the pluckers had to pull out this wool with their bare hands, till the acid had eaten their fingers off. There were those who made the tins for the canned meat; and their hands, too, were a maze of cuts, and each cut represented a chance for blood poisoning. Some worked at the stamping machines, and it was very seldom that one could work long there at the pace that was set, and not give out and forget himself and have a part of his hand chopped off. There were the "hoisters," as they were called, whose task it was to press the lever which lifted the dead cattle off the floor. They ran along upon a rafter, peering down through the damp and the steam; and as old Durham's architects had not built the killing room for the convenience of the hoisters, at every few feet they would have to stoop under a beam, say four feet above the one they ran on; which got them into the habit of stooping, so that in a few years they would be walking like chimpanzees. Worst of any, however, were the fertilizer men, and those who served in the cooking rooms. These people could not be shown to the visitor,—for the odor of a fertilizer man would scare any ordinary visitor at a hundred yards, and as for the other men, who worked in tank rooms full of steam, and in some of which there were open vats near the level of the floor, their peculiar trouble was that they fell into the vats; and when they were fished out, there was never enough of them left to be worth exhibiting,—sometimes they would be overlooked for days, till all but the bones of them had gone out to the world as Durham's Pure Leaf Lard!

Chapter 11

... Ona was now making about thirty dollars a month, and Stanislovas about thirteen. To add to this there was the board of Jonas and Marija, about forty-five dollars. Deducting from this the rent, interest, and installments on the furniture, they had left sixty dollars, and deducting the coal, they had fifty. They did without everything that human beings could do without; they went in old and ragged clothing, that left them at the mercy of the cold, and when the children's shoes wore out, they tied them up with string. Half invalid as she was, Ona would do herself harm by walking in the rain and cold when she ought to have ridden; they bought literally nothing but food—and still they could not keep alive on fifty dollars a month. They might have done it, if only they could have gotten pure food, and at fair prices; or if only they had known what to get—if they had not been so pitifully ignorant! But they had come to a new country, where everything was different, including the food. They had always been accustomed to eat a great deal of smoked sausage, and how could they know that what they bought in America was not the same—that its color was made by chemicals, and its smoky flavor by more chemicals, and that it was full of "potato flour" besides? Potato flour is the waste of potato after the starch and alcohol have been extracted; it has no more food value than so much wood, and as its use as a food adulterant is a penal offense in Europe, thousands of tons of it are shipped to America every year. It was amazing what quantities of food such as this were needed every day, by eleven hungry persons. A dollar sixty-five a day was simply not enough to feed them, and there was no use trying; and so each week they made an inroad upon the pitiful little bank account that Ona had begun. . . .

Chapter 13

. . . The sausage-room was an interesting place to visit, for two or three minutes, and provided that you did not look at the people; the machines were perhaps the most wonderful things in the entire plant. Presumably sausages were once chopped and stuffed by hand, and if so it would be interesting to know how many workers had been displaced by these inventions. On one side of the room were the hoppers, into which men shoveled loads of meat and wheelbarrows full of spices; in these great bowls were whirling knives that made two thousand revolutions a minute, and when the meat was ground fine and adulterated with potato flour, and well mixed with water, it was forced to the stuffing machines on the other side of the room. The latter were tended by women; there was a sort of spout, like the nozzle of a hose, and one of the women would take a long string of "casing" and put the end over the nozzle and then work the whole thing on, as one works on the finger of a tight glove. This string would be twenty or thirty feet long, but the woman would have it all on in a jiffy; and when she had several on, she would press a lever, and a stream of sausage meat would be shot out, taking the casing with it as it came. Thus one might stand and see appear, miraculously born from the machine, a wriggling snake of sausage of incredible length. In front was a big pan which caught these

creatures, and two more women who seized them as fast as they appeared and twisted them into links. This was for the uninitiated the most perplexing work of all; for all that the woman had to give was a single turn of the wrist; and in some way she contrived to give it so that instead of an endless chain of sausages, one after another, there grew under her hands a bunch of strings, all dangling from a single center. It was quite like the feat of a prestidigitator—for the woman worked so fast that the eye could literally not follow her, and there was only a mist of motion, and tangle after tangle of sausages appearing. In the midst of the mist, however, the visitor would suddenly notice the tense set face, with the two wrinkles graven in the forehead, and the ghastly pallor of the cheeks; and then he would suddenly recollect that it was time he was going on. The woman did not go on; she stayed right there—hour after hour, day after day, year after year, twisting sausage links and racing with death. It was piecework, and she was apt to have a family to keep alive; and stern and ruthless economic laws had arranged it that she could only do this by working just as she did, with all her soul upon her work, and with never an instant for a glance at the well-dressed ladies and gentlemen who came to stare at her, as at some wild beast in a menagerie. . . .

Chapter 14

With one member trimming beef in a cannery, and another working in a sausage factory, the family had a first-hand knowledge of the great majority of Packingtown swindles. For it was the custom, as they found, whenever meat was so spoiled that it could not be used for anything else, either to can it or else to chop it up into sausage. With what had been told them by Jonas, who had worked in the pickle rooms, they could now study the whole of the spoiled-meat industry on the inside, and read a new and grim meaning into that old Packingtown jest—that they use everything of the pig except the squeal. . . .

It was only when the whole ham was spoiled that it came into the department of Elzbieta. Cut up by the two-thousand-revolutions-a-minute flyers, and mixed with half a ton of other meat, no odor that ever was in a ham could make any difference. There was never the least attention paid to what was cut up for sausage; there would come all the way back from Europe old sausage that had been rejected, and that was moldy and white—it would be dosed with borax and glycerine, and dumped into the hoppers, and made over again for home consumption. There would be meat that had tumbled out on the floor, in the dirt and sawdust, where the workers had tramped and spit uncounted billions of consumption germs. There would be meat stored in great piles in rooms; and the water from leaky roofs would drip over it, and thousands of rats would race about on it. It was too dark in these storage places to see well, but a man could run his hand over these piles of meat and sweep off handfuls of the dried dung of rats. These rats were nuisances, and the packers would put poisoned bread out for them; they would die, and then rats, bread, and meat would go into the hoppers together. This is no fairy story and no joke; the meat would be shoveled into carts, and the man who did the shoveling would not trouble to

lift out a rat even when he saw one—there were things that went into the sausage in comparison with which a poisoned rat was a tidbit. There was no place for the men to wash their hands before they ate their dinner, and so they made a practice of washing them in the water that was to be ladled into the sausage. There were the butt-ends of smoked meat, and the scraps of corned beef, and all the odds and ends of the waste of the plants, that would be dumped into old barrels in the cellar and left there. Under the system of rigid economy which the packers enforced, there were some jobs that it only paid to do once in a long time, and among these was the cleaning out of the waste barrels. Every spring they did it; and in the barrels would be dirt and rust and old nails and stale water—and cartload after cartload of it would be taken up and dumped into the hoppers with fresh meat, and sent out to the public's breakfast. Some of it they would make into "smoked" sausage—but as the smoking took time, and was therefore expensive, they would call upon their chemistry department, and preserve it with borax and color it with gelatine to make it brown. All of their sausage came out of the same bowl, but when they came to wrap it they would stamp some of it "special," and for this they would charge two cents more a pound. . . .

Chapter 23

. . . The evangelist was preaching "sin and redemption," the infinite grace of God and His pardon for human frailty. He was very much in earnest, and he meant well, but Jurgis, as he listened, found his soul filled with hatred. What did he know about sin and suffering—with his smooth, black coat and his neatly starched collar, his body warm, and his belly full, and money in his pocket—and lecturing men who were struggling for their lives, men at the death grapple with the demon powers of hunger and cold!—This, of course, was unfair; but Jurgis felt that these men were out of touch with the life they discussed, that they were unfitted to solve its problems; nay, they themselves were part of the problem—they were part of the order established that was crushing men down and beating them! They were of the triumphant and insolent possessors; they had a hall, and a fire, and food and clothing and money, and so they might preach to hungry men, and the hungry men must be humble and listen! They were trying to save their souls—and who but a fool could fail to see that all that was the matter with their souls was that they had not been able to get a decent existence for their bodies?

Study Questions

1. Initially, Jurgis had a joyous outlook concerning his new job. Why did he later become disappointed, even despondent, as he discovered more about the packing house?

2. Explain how Jurgis and his family suffered at multiple levels: as tenants, as laborers, and as consumers.

3. What was the root cause of the struggles that Jurgis and his family encountered?

4. Why did the evangelist's message not seem comforting to Jurgis? How might this part of the story suggest a context for the emergence of the Social Gospel Movement (see p. 221)?

Washington Gladden, *The Church and Modern Life* (1908), ch. 4

During the early twentieth century, American Christians became increasingly concerned about the plight of the poor. They observed the challenges that immigrants and industrial laborers faced in the rapidly growing cities. Recalling that Jesus had taught, "Love your neighbor as yourself," Walter Rauschenbusch, Washington Gladden, and other pastors began to promote a "social gospel": living a Christian life of service to one's neighbor. Focusing more on earth than on heaven, and not permitting doctrinal differences to impede interdenominational cooperation, these ministers sought to reorganize the church as a tool for social progress. In doing so, they gave the progressive movement a theological impetus. Rauschenbusch's *Theology of the Social Gospel* (1917) urged the church to think less about forgiveness for personal sins and more about cooperative solutions to social problems. The church, to be relevant in the Progressive Era, would have to lend a hand—or even take a leading role—in building a better civilization. In *The Church and Modern Life* (1908), excerpted below, Gladden argued that the reconciliation that Christ provides between the individual and God the Father serves a broader purpose: the reconciliation of individuals to each other.

Chapter 4—The Business of the Church

That wonderful passage in the eighth chapter of the Romans shows how strongly Paul had grasped the old prophetic idea; he beholds the whole creation humiliated and disfigured by its share in man's degeneration, and waiting to be delivered with man from the bondage of corruption into the liberty of the glory of the children of God. That expectation is yet to be realized. It is an essential part of the Christian expectation. It is part of what redemption means. . . .

The redemption of the physical order will be the result of the socialization of mankind. It is an integral part of the work that Christ came into the world to do. It is part of what he meant when he said that he came to save the world. When we realize this, we get some idea of the scope of the redemption which he proclaims. It is not a superficial or a sentimental thing that he proposes; it takes hold of life with the most comprehensive grasp; it proposes to redeem not only man but his environment.

It is not, however, the redemption of the physical order to which Christ primarily addresses himself. He begins in the spiritual realm. He begins with the individual. His first concern is to reveal to every child of God the great fact of the divine Fatherhood, and to bring him into filial relations. His whole programme for humanity rests on this simple possibility of realizing the Fatherhood of God. If this can be realized, everything else will follow. If any man is in the right filial relations with his Father in heaven, he cannot be in wrong social relations with his brother on the earth. If he is in harmony with God in thought and feeling, he must think God's thoughts about his neighbor, and the law of love will be the law of all his conduct.

No man can love the God and Father of our Lord Jesus Christ with heart and soul and mind without loving his neighbor as himself. Heartily to believe what Jesus has told us about the Father, and fully to enter into fellowship with him, is to put ourselves into such relations with our fellow men that every duty we owe them will be spontaneously performed. In a society composed of men who were thus in harmony with God the only social question for each man would be, "How can I best befriend and serve my neighbor?"

That the religion of Jesus begins here, in the heart of the individual, cannot be questioned. And it must never be forgotten that there can be no sound social construction which does not build on this foundation. But it is well to remember also that here, as everywhere, a foundation calls for a building, and is useless and unsightly and obstructive without it. The foundation of Christianity is the reconciliation of individual souls to God, and the establishment of friendship between these individual souls and God; but what is the structure for which this foundation is laid? It is the establishment of the same divine friendship among men. That is the building for which the foundation calls. If the building does not go up, the foundation is worthless. If the building does not go up, the foundation itself will crumble and decay. The only way to save a foundation is to cover it with a building. . . .

It is evident, therefore, that a religion which has no room in it for social questions cannot be the Christian religion. The social question is the one question which Christianity—genuine Christianity—never ceases to ask. The first thing it wishes to know about your religious experience is, how it affects your relations with your fellow men. It insists that your relations must first be right with God, but in the same breath it declares that there is no way of knowing whether or not your relations are right with God except by observing how you behave among your fellow men. Faith is the root, but faith without works is dead, being alone; and works concern your human relations.

These principles enable us to determine what is the business of the church. Its business is to foster and propagate Christianity, and Christianity exists to establish in this world the kingdom of heaven. The church is not, therefore, an end in itself; it is an instrument; it is a means employed by God for the promotion, in the world, of the kingdom of heaven. The kingdom of heaven is not an ecclesiastical establishment; it includes the whole of life,— business, politics, art, education, philanthropy, society in the narrow sense, the family: when all these shall be pervaded and controlled by the law of love, then the kingdom of heaven will have fully come. And the business of the church in the world is to bring all these departments of life under Christ's law of love. If it seeks to convert men, it is that they may be filled with the spirit of Christ and may govern their conduct among men by Christ's law. If it gathers them together for instruction or for inspiration, it is that they may be taught Christ's way of life and sent out into the world to live as he lived among their fellow men. Its function is to fill the world with the knowledge of Christ, the love of Christ, the life of Christ. That is what Christ meant by saving the world. The world is saved when this is true of it, and it is never saved till then. The work of the church is successful just to the extent to which it succeeds in Christianizing the social order in the midst of which it stands . . .

Even though it be true that large numbers are added to its membership, that its congregations are crowded, its revenues abundant, its missionary contributions liberal, and its social prestige high; yet if the standards of social morality in its neighborhood are sinking rather than rising, and the general social drift and tendency is toward animalism and greed and luxury and strife, the church must be pronounced a failure: nay, even if it be believed that the church is succeeding in getting a great many people safely to heaven when they die; yet if the social tendencies in the world about it are all downward, its work, on the whole, must be regarded as a fail-

ure. Its main business is not saving people out of the world, it is saving the world. When it is evident that the world, under its ministration, is growing no better but rather worse, no matter what other good things it may have the credit of doing, the verdict is against it. . . .

The point on which attention must be fixed is simply this, that the test of the efficiency of the church must be found in the social conditions of the community to which it ministers. Its business is to Christianize that community. There is no question but that the resources are placed within its reach by which this business may be done. If it is done, the church may hope to hear the commendation, "Well done, good and faithful servant!" If it is not done, no matter how many other gains are made, the church must expect the condemnation of its Master.

Study Questions

1. What did Gladden claim should be "the business of the church"?

2. How, according to the social gospel movement, is an effective congregation to be distinguished from a failing congregation?

William Howard Taft, Inaugural Address (1909)

William Howard Taft had close ties to both the McKinley and Roosvelt administrations. McKinley appointed him Governor-General of the Philippines in 1901. In 1904, Roosevelt appointed Taft to serve as the Secretary of War. Simultaneously, Taft also functioned as the provisional governor of Cuba for several months during 1906. By 1908, Roosevelt was convinced that Taft would be the nation's best pick as the next president. At his inauguration in 1909, Taft promised to maintain the course that his predecessor had set, for both foreign and domestic policy.

My Fellow-Citizens:

Anyone who has taken the oath I have just taken must feel a heavy weight of responsibility. If not, he has no conception of the powers and duties of the office upon which he is about to enter, or he is lacking in a proper sense of the obligation which the oath imposes.

The office of an inaugural address is to give a summary outline of the main policies of the new administration, so far as they can be anticipated. I have had the honor to be one of the advisers of my distinguished predecessor, and, as such, to hold up his hands in the reforms he has initiated. I should be untrue to myself, to my promises, and to the declarations of the party platform upon which I was elected to office, if I did not make the maintenance and enforcement of those reforms a most important feature of my administration. They were directed to the suppression of the lawlessness and abuses of power of the great combinations of capital invested in railroads and in industrial enterprises carrying on interstate commerce. The steps which my predecessor took and the legislation passed on his recommendation have accomplished much, have caused a general halt in the vicious policies which created popular alarm, and have brought about in the busi-

ness affected a much higher regard for existing law.

To render the reforms lasting, however, and to secure at the same time freedom from alarm on the part of those pursuing proper and progressive business methods, further legislative and executive action are needed. Relief of the railroads from certain restrictions of the antitrust law have been urged by my predecessor and will be urged by me. On the other hand, the administration is pledged to legislation looking to a proper federal supervision and restriction to prevent excessive issues of bonds and stock by companies owning and operating interstate commerce railroads.

Then, too, a reorganization of the Department of Justice, of the Bureau of Corporations in the Department of Commerce and Labor, and of the Interstate Commerce Commission, looking to effective cooperation of these agencies, is needed to secure a more rapid and certain enforcement of the laws affecting interstate railroads and industrial combinations.

I hope to be able to submit at the first regular session of the incoming Congress, in December next, definite suggestions in respect to the needed amendments to the antitrust and the interstate commerce law and the changes required in the executive departments concerned in their enforcement.

It is believed that with the changes to be recommended American business can be assured of that measure of stability and certainty in respect to those things that may be done and those that are prohibited which is essential to the life and growth of all business. Such a plan must include the right of the people to avail themselves of those methods of combining capital and effort deemed necessary to reach the highest degree of economic efficiency, at the same time differentiating between combinations based upon legitimate economic reasons and those formed with the intent of creating monopolies and artificially controlling prices.

The work of formulating into practical shape such changes is creative word of the highest order, and requires all the deliberation possible in the interval. I believe that the amendments to be proposed are just as necessary in the protection of legitimate business as in the clinching of the reforms which properly bear the name of my predecessor.

A matter of most pressing importance is the revision of the tariff. In accordance with the promises of the platform upon which I was elected, I shall call Congress into extra session to meet on the 15th day of March, in order that consideration may be at once given to a bill revising the Dingley Act. This should secure an adequate revenue and adjust the duties in such a manner as to afford to labor and to all industries in this country, whether of the farm, mine or factory, protection by tariff equal to the difference between the cost of production abroad and the cost of production here, and have a provision which shall put into force, upon executive determination of certain facts, a higher or maximum tariff against those countries whose trade policy toward us equitably requires such discrimination. It is thought that there has been such a change in conditions since the enactment of the Dingley Act, drafted on a similarly protective principle, that the measure of the tariff above stated will permit the reduction of rates in certain schedules and will require the advancement of few, if any.

The proposal to revise the tariff made in such an authoritative way as to lead the business community to count upon it necessarily halts all those branches of business directly affected; and as these are most important, it disturbs the whole business of the country. It is imperatively necessary, therefore, that a tariff bill be drawn in good faith in accordance with promises made before the election by the party in power, and as promptly passed as due consideration will permit. It is not that the tariff is more important in the long run than the perfecting of the reforms in respect to antitrust legislation and interstate commerce regulation, but the need for action when the revision of the tariff has been determined upon is more immediate to avoid embarrassment of business. To secure the needed speed in the passage of the tariff bill, it would seem wise to attempt no other legislation at the extra session. I venture this as a suggestion only, for the course to be taken by Congress, upon the call of the Executive, is wholly within its discretion.

In the mailing of a tariff bill the prime motive is taxation and the securing thereby of a revenue. Due largely to the business depression which followed the financial panic of 1907, the revenue from customs and other sources has decreased to such an extent that the expenditures for the current fiscal year will exceed the receipts by $100,000,000. It is imperative that such a deficit shall not continue, and the framers of the tariff bill must, of course, have in mind the total revenues likely to be produced by it and so arrange the duties as to secure an adequate income. Should it be impossible to do so by import duties, new kinds of taxation must be adopted, and among these I recommend a graduated inheritance tax as correct in principle and as certain and easy of collection.

The obligation on the part of those responsible for the expenditures made to carry on the Government, to be as economical as possible, and to make the burden of taxation as light as possible, is plain, and should be affirmed in every declaration of government policy. This is especially true when we are face to face with a heavy deficit. But when the desire to win the popular approval leads to the cutting off of expenditures really needed to make the Government effective and to enable it to accomplish its proper objects, the result is as much to be condemned as the waste of government funds in unnecessary expenditure. The scope of a modern government in what it can and ought to accomplish for its people has been widened far beyond the principles laid down by the old "*laissez-faire*" school of political writers, and this widening has met popular approval.

In the Department of Agriculture the use of scientific experiments on a large scale and the spread of information derived from them for the improvement of general agriculture must go on.

The importance of supervising business of great railways and industrial combinations and the necessary investigation and prosecution of unlawful business methods are another necessary tax upon Government which did not exist half a century ago.

The putting into force of laws which shall secure the conservation of our resources, so far as they may be within the jurisdiction of the Federal Government, including the most important work of saving and restoring our forests and the great improvement of waterways, are all proper government functions which must involve large expenditure if properly performed. While some of them, like the reclamation of arid lands, are made to pay for themselves, others are of such an indirect benefit that this cannot be expected of them. A permanent improvement, like the Panama Canal, should be treated as a distinct enterprise, and should be paid for by the proceeds of bonds, the issue of which will distribute its cost between the present and future generations in accordance with the benefits derived. It may well be submitted to the serious consideration of Congress whether the deepening and control of the channel of a great river system, like that of the Ohio or of the Mississippi, when definite and practical plans for the enterprise have been approved and determined upon, should not be provided for in the same way.

Then, too, there are expenditures of Government absolutely necessary if our country is to maintain its proper place among the nations of the world, and is to exercise its proper influence in defense of its own trade interests in the maintenance of traditional American policy against the colonization of European monarchies in this hemisphere, and in the promotion of peace and international morality. I refer to the cost of maintaining a proper army, a proper navy, and suitable fortifications upon the mainland of the United States and in its dependencies.

We should have an army so organized and so officered as to be capable in time of emergency, in cooperation with the national militia and under the provisions of a proper national volunteer law, rapidly to expand into a force sufficient to resist all probable invasion from abroad and to furnish a respectable expeditionary force if necessary in the maintenance of our traditional American policy which bears the name of President Monroe.

Our fortifications are yet in a state of only partial completeness, and the number of men to man them is insufficient. In a few years however, the usual annual appropriations for our coast defenses, both on the mainland and in the dependencies, will make them sufficient to resist all direct attack, and by that time we may hope that the men to man them will be provided as a necessary adjunct. The distance of our shores from Europe and Asia of course reduces the necessity for maintaining under arms a great army, but it does not take away the requirement of mere prudence—that we should have an army sufficiently large and so constituted as to form a nucleus out of which a suitable force can quickly grow.

What has been said of the army may be affirmed in even a more emphatic way of the navy. A modern navy can not be improvised. It must be built and in existence when the emergency arises which calls for its use and operation. My distinguished predecessor has in many speeches and messages set out with great force and striking language the necessity for maintaining a strong navy commensurate with the coast line, the governmental resources, and the foreign trade of our Nation; and I wish to reiterate all the reasons which he has presented in favor of the policy of maintaining a strong navy as the best conservator of our peace with other nations, and the best means of securing respect for the assertion of our rights, the defense of our interests, and the exercise of our influence in international matters.

Our international policy is always to promote peace. We shall enter into any war with a full consciousness of the awful consequences that it always entails, whether successful or not, and we, of course, shall make every effort consistent with national honor and the highest national interest to avoid a resort to arms. We favor every instrumentality, like that of the Hague Tribunal and arbitration treaties made with a view to its use in all international controversies, in order to maintain peace and to avoid war. But we should be blind to existing conditions and should allow ourselves to become foolish idealists if we did not realize that, with all the nations of the world armed and prepared for war, we must be ourselves in a similar condition, in order to prevent other nations from taking advantage of us and of our inability to defend our interests and assert our rights with a strong hand.

In the international controversies that are likely to arise in the Orient growing out of the question of the open door and other issues the United States can maintain her interests intact and can secure respect for her just demands. She will not be able to do so, however, if it is understood that she never intends to back up her assertion of right and her defense of her interest by anything but mere verbal protest and diplomatic note. For these reasons the expenses of the army and navy and of coast defenses should always be considered as something which the Government must pay for, and they should not be cut off through mere consideration of economy. Our Government is able to afford a suitable army and a suitable navy. It may maintain them without the slightest danger to the Republic or the cause of free institutions, and fear of additional taxation ought not to change a proper policy in this regard.

The policy of the United States in the Spanish war and since has given it a position of influence among the nations that it never had before, and should be constantly exerted to securing to its *bona fide* citizens, whether native or naturalized, respect for them as such in foreign countries. We should make every effort to prevent humiliating and degrading prohibition against any of our citizens wishing temporarily to sojourn in foreign countries because of race or religion.

The admission of Asiatic immigrants who cannot be amalgamated with our population has been made the subject either of prohibitory clauses in our treaties and statutes or of strict administrative regulation secured by diplomatic negotiation. I sincerely hope that we may continue to minimize the evils likely to arise from such immigration without unnecessary friction and by mutual concessions between self-respecting governments. Meantime we must take every precaution to prevent, or failing that, to punish outbursts of race feeling among our people against foreigners of whatever nationality who have by our grant a treaty right to pursue lawful business here and to be protected against lawless assault or injury.

This leads me to point out a serious defect in the present federal jurisdiction, which ought to be remedied at once. Having assured to other countries by treaty the protection of our laws for such of their subjects or citizens as we permit to come within our jurisdiction, we now leave to a state or a city, not under the control of the Federal Government, the duty of performing our international obligations in this respect. By proper legislation we may, and ought to, place in the hands of the Federal Executive the means of enforcing the treaty rights of such aliens in the courts of the Federal Government. It puts our Government in a pusillanimous position to make definite engagements to protect aliens and then to excuse the failure to perform those engagements by an explanation that the duty to keep them is in States or cities, not within our control. If we would promise we must put ourselves in a position to perform our promise. We cannot permit the possible failure of justice, due to local prejudice in any State or municipal government, to expose us to the risk of a war which might be avoided if federal jurisdiction was asserted by suitable legislation by Congress and carried out by proper proceedings instituted by the Executive in the courts of the National Government.

One of the reforms to be carried out during the incoming administration is a change of our monetary and banking laws, so as to secure greater elasticity in the forms of currency available for trade and to prevent the limitations of law from operating to increase the embarrassment of a financial panic. The monetary commission, lately appointed, is giving full consideration to existing conditions and to all proposed remedies, and will doubtless suggest one that will meet the requirements of business and of public interest.

We may hope that the report will embody neither the narrow dew of those who believe that the sole purpose of the new system should be to secure a large return on banking capital or of those who would have greater expansion of currency with little regard to provisions for its immediate redemption or ultimate security. There is no subject of economic discussion so intricate and so likely to evoke differing views and dogmatic statements as this one. The commission, in studying the general influence of currency on business and of business on currency, have wisely extended their investigations in European banking and monetary methods. The information that they have derived from such experts as they have found abroad will undoubtedly be found helpful in the solution of the difficult problem they have in hand.

The incoming Congress should promptly fulfill the promise of the Republican platform and pass a proper postal savings bank bill. It will not be unwise or excessive paternalism. The promise to repay by the Government will furnish an inducement to savings deposits which private enterprise can not supply and at such a low rate of interest as not to withdraw custom from existing banks. It will substantially increase the funds available for investment as capital in useful enterprises. It will furnish absolute security which makes the proposed scheme of government guaranty of deposits so alluring, without its pernicious results.

I sincerely hope that the incoming Congress will be alive, as it should be, to the importance of our foreign trade and of encouraging it in every way feasible. The possibility of increasing this trade in the Orient, in the Philippines, and in South America are known to everyone who has given the matter attention. The direct effect of free trade between this country and the Philippines will be marked upon our sales of cottons, agricultural machinery, and other manufactures. The necessity of the establishment of direct lines of steamers between North and South America has been brought to the attention of Congress by my predecessor and by Mr. Root before and after his noteworthy visit to that continent, and I sincerely hope that Congress may be induced to see the wisdom of a tentative effort to establish such lines by the use of mail subsidies.

The importance of the part which the Departments of Agriculture and of Commerce and Labor may play in ridding the markets of Europe of prohibitions and discriminations against the importation of our products is fully understood, and it is hoped that the use of the maximum and minimum feature of our tariff law to be soon passed will be effective to remove many of those restrictions.

The Panama Canal will have a most important bearing upon the trade between the eastern and far western sections of our country, and will greatly increase the facilities for transportation between the eastern and the western seaboard, and may possibly revolutionize the transcontinental rates with respect to bulky merchandise. It will also have a most beneficial effect to increase the trade between the eastern seaboard of the United States and the western coast of South America, and, indeed, with some of the important ports on the east coast of South America reached by rail from the west coast.

The work on the canal is making most satisfactory progress. The type of the canal as a lock canal was fixed by Congress after a full consideration of the conflicting reports of the majority and minority of the consulting board, and after the recommendation of the War Department and the Executive upon those reports. Recent suggestion that something had occurred on the Isthmus to make the lock type of the canal less feasible than it was supposed to be when the reports were made and the policy determined on led to a visit to the Isthmus of a board of competent engineers to examine the Gatun dam and locks, which are the key of the lock type. The report of that board shows nothing has occurred in the nature of newly revealed evidence which should change the views once formed in the original discussion. The construction will go on under a most effective organization controlled by Colonel Goethals and his fellow army engineers associated with him, and will certainly be completed early in the next administration, if not before.

Some type of canal must be constructed. The lock type has been selected. We are all in favor of having it built as promptly as possible. We must not now, therefore, keep up a fire in the rear of the agents whom we have authorized to do our work on the Isthmus. We must hold up their hands, and speaking for the incoming administration I wish to say that I propose to devote all the energy possible and under my control to pushing of this work on the plans which have been adopted, and to stand behind the men who are doing faithful, hard work to bring about the early completion of this, the greatest constructive enterprise of modern times.

The governments of our dependencies in Puerto Rico and the Philippines are progressing as favorably as could be desired. The prosperity of Puerto Rico continues unabated. The business conditions in the Philippines are not all that we could wish them to be, but with the passage of the new tariff bill permitting free trade between the United States and the archipelago, with such limitations on sugar and tobacco as shall prevent injury to domestic interests in those products, we can count on an improvement in business conditions in the Philippines and the development of a mutually profitable trade between this country and the islands. Meantime our Government in each dependency is upholding the traditions of civil liberty and increasing popular control which might be expected under American auspices. The work which we are doing there redounds to our credit as a nation.

I look forward with hope to increasing the already good feeling between the South and the other sections of the country. My chief purpose is not to effect a change in the electoral vote of the Southern States. That is a secondary consideration. What I look forward to is an increase in the tolerance of political views of all kinds and

their advocacy throughout the South, and the existence of a respectable political opposition in every State; even more than this, to an increased feeling on the part of all the people in the South that this Government is their Government, and that its officers in their states are their officers.

The consideration of this question can not, however, be complete and full without reference to the negro race, its progress and its present condition. The thirteenth amendment secured them freedom; the fourteenth amendment due process of law, protection of property, and the pursuit of happiness; and the fifteenth amendment attempted to secure the negro against any deprivation of the privilege to vote because he was a negro. The thirteenth and fourteenth amendments have been generally enforced and have secured the objects for which they are intended. While the fifteenth amendment has not been generally observed in the past, it ought to be observed, and the tendency of Southern legislation today is toward the enactment of electoral qualifications which shall square with that amendment. Of course, the mere adoption of a constitutional law is only one step in the right direction. It must be fairly and justly enforced as well. In time both will come. Hence it is clear to all that the domination of an ignorant, irresponsible element can be prevented by constitutional laws which shall exclude from voting both negroes and whites not having education or other qualifications thought to be necessary for a proper electorate. The danger of the control of an ignorant electorate has therefore passed. With this change, the interest which many of the Southern white citizens take in the welfare of the negroes has increased. The colored men must base their hope on the results of their own industry, self-restraint, thrift, and business success, as well as upon the aid and comfort and sympathy which they may receive from their white neighbors of the South.

There was a time when Northerners who sympathized with the negro in his necessary struggle for better conditions sought to give him the suffrage as a protection to enforce its exercise against the prevailing sentiment of the South. The movement proved to be a failure. What remains is the fifteenth amendment to the Constitution and the right to have statutes of States specifying qualifications for electors subjected to the test of compliance with that amendment. This is a great protection to the negro. It never will be repealed, and it never ought to be repealed. If it had not passed, it might be difficult now to adopt it; but with it in our fundamental law, the policy of Southern legislation must and will tend to obey it, and so long as the statutes of the States meet the test of this amendment and are not otherwise in conflict with the Constitution and laws of the United States, it is not the disposition or within the province of the Federal Government to interfere with the regulation by Southern States of their domestic affairs. There is in the South a stronger feeling than ever among the intelligent well-to-do, and influential element in favor of the industrial education of the negro and the encouragement of the race to make themselves useful members of the community. The progress which the negro has made in the last fifty years, from slavery, when its statistics are reviewed, is

marvelous, and it furnishes every reason to hope that in the next twenty-five years a still greater improvement in his condition as a productive member of society, on the farm, and in the shop, and in other occupations may come.

The negroes are now Americans. Their ancestors came here years ago against their will, and this is their only country and their only flag. They have shown themselves anxious to live for it and to die for it. Encountering the race feeling against them, subjected at times to cruel injustice growing out of it, they may well have our profound sympathy and aid in the struggle they are making. We are charged with the sacred duty of making their path as smooth and easy as we can. Any recognition of their distinguished men, any appointment to office from among their number, is properly taken as an encouragement and an appreciation of their progress, and this just policy should be pursued when suitable occasion offers.

But it may well admit of doubt whether, in the case of any race, an appointment of one of their number to a local office in a community in which the race feeling is so widespread and acute as to interfere with the ease and facility with which the local government business can be done by the appointee is of sufficient benefit by way of encouragement to the race to outweigh the recurrence and increase of race feeling which such an appointment is likely to engender. Therefore the Executive, in recognizing the negro race by appointments, must exercise a careful discretion not thereby to do it more harm than good. On the other hand, we must be careful not to encourage the mere pretense of race feeling manufactured in the interest of individual political ambition.

Personally, I have not the slightest race prejudice or feeling, and recognition of its existence only awakens in my heart a deeper sympathy for those who have to bear it or suffer from it, and I question the wisdom of a policy which is likely to increase it. Meantime, if nothing is done to prevent it, a better feeling between the negroes and the whites in the South will continue to grow, and more and more of the white people will come to realize that the future of the South is to be much benefited by the industrial and intellectual progress of the negro. The exercise of political franchises by those of this race who are intelligent and well to do will be acquiesced in, and the right to vote will be withheld only from the ignorant and irresponsible of both races.

There is one other matter to which I shall refer. It was made the subject of great controversy during the election and calls for at least a passing reference now. My distinguished predecessor has given much attention to the cause of labor, with whose struggle for better things he has shown the sincerest sympathy. At his instance Congress has passed the bill fixing the liability of interstate carriers to their employees for injury sustained in the course of employment, abolishing the rule of fellow-servant and the common-law rule as to contributory negligence, and substituting therefor the so-called rule of "comparative negligence." It has also passed a law fixing the compensation of government employees for injuries sustained in the employ of the Government through the negligence of the superior. It has also passed a model child-labor law for the District of Columbia. In previous administrations an arbitration law for interstate commerce railroads and their employees, and laws for the application of safety devices to save the lives and limbs of employees of interstate railroads had been passed. Additional legislation of this kind was passed by the outgoing Congress.

I wish to say that insofar as I can I hope to promote the enactment of further legislation of this character. I am strongly convinced that the Government should make itself as responsible to employees injured in its employ as an interstate-railway corporation is made responsible by federal law to its employees; and I shall be glad, whenever any additional reasonable safety device can be invented to reduce the loss of life and limb among railway employees, to urge Congress to require its adoption by interstate railways.

Another labor question has arisen which has awakened the most excited discussion. That is in respect to the power of the federal courts to issue injunctions in industrial disputes. As to that, my convictions are fixed. Take away from the courts, if it could be taken away, the power to issue injunctions in labor disputes, and it would create a privileged class among the laborers and save the lawless among their number from a most needful remedy available to all men for the protection of their business against lawless invasion. The proposition that business is not a property or pecuniary right which can be protected by equitable injunction is utterly without foundation in precedent or reason. The proposition is usually linked with one to make the secondary boycott lawful. Such a proposition is at variance with the American instinct, and will find no support, in my judgment, when submitted to the American people. The secondary boycott is an instrument of tyranny, and ought not to be made legitimate.

The issue of a temporary restraining order without notice has in several instances been abused by its inconsiderate exercise, and to remedy this the platform upon which I was elected recommends the formulation in a statute of the conditions under which such a temporary restraining order ought to issue. A statute can and ought to be framed to embody the best modern practice, and can bring the subject so closely to the attention of the court as to make abuses of the process unlikely in the future. The American people, if I understand them, insist that the authority of the courts shall be sustained, and are opposed to any change in the procedure by which the powers of a court may be weakened and the fearless and effective administration of justice be interfered with.

Having thus reviewed the questions likely to recur during my administration, and having expressed in a summary way the position which I expect to take in recommendations to Congress and in my conduct as an Executive, I invoke the considerate sympathy and support of my fellow-citizens and the aid of the Almighty God in the discharge of my responsible duties.

Study Questions

1. "The scope of a modern government," said Taft, "has been widened far beyond the principles laid down by the old '*laissez-faire*' school of political writers." Did Taft approve of this change? Give examples with respect to: agriculture, railroads, "industrial combinations" (monopolies), banking, and "the cause of labor."

2. What did Taft recommend about the enforcement of the Fifteenth Amendment in the South?

Jane Addams, *Twenty Years at Hull House* (1910), ch. 6

In 1889, Jane Addams opened Hull House to assist impoverished and uneducated immigrants in Chicago. Relying on sociological research from the University of Chicago, Addams sought to help immigrants assimilate to American culture. She enlisted the help of a growing number of college-educated, unmarried women whose maternal aspirations had yet to be fulfilled. They became, as it were, adoptive mothers to immigrant families. Numerous other settlement homes copied this model in the years that followed.

Chapter 6—Subjective Necessity for Social Settlements

The Ethical Culture Societies held a summer school at Plymouth, Massachusetts, in 1892, to which they invited several people representing the then new Settlement movement, that they might discuss with others the general theme of Philanthropy and Social Progress.

I venture to produce here parts of a lecture I delivered in Plymouth, both because I have found it impossible to formulate with the same freshness those early motives and strivings, and because, when published with other papers given that summer, it was received by the Settlement people themselves as a satisfactory statement.

I remember one golden summer afternoon during the sessions of the summer school that several of us met on the shores of a pond in a pine wood a few miles from Plymouth, to discuss our new movement. The natural leader of the group was Robert A. Woods. He had recently returned from a residence in Toynbee Hall, London, to open Andover House in Boston, and had just issued a book, *English Social Movements*, in which he had gathered together and focused the many forms of social endeavor preceding and contemporaneous

with the English Settlements. There were Miss Vida D. Scudder and Miss Helena Dudley from the College Settlement Association, Miss Julia C. Lathrop and myself from Hull-House. Some of us had numbered our years as far as thirty, and we all carefully avoided the extravagance of statement which characterizes youth, and yet I doubt if anywhere on the continent that summer could have been found a group of people more genuinely interested in social development or more sincerely convinced that they had found a clue by which the conditions in crowded cities might be understood and the agencies for social betterment developed.

We were all careful to avoid saying that we had found a "life work," perhaps with an instinctive dread of expending all our energy in vows of constancy, as so often happens; and yet it is interesting to note that of all the people whom I have recalled as the enthusiasts at that little conference have remained attached to Settlements in actual residence for longer or shorter periods each year during the eighteen years that have elapsed since then, although they have also been closely identified as publicists or governmental officials with movements outside. It is as if they had discovered that the Settlement was too valuable as a method as a way of approach to the social question to abandoned, although they had long since discovered it was not a "social movement" in itself. This, however, is anticipating the future, whereas the following paper on "The Subjective Necessity for Social Settlements" should have a chance to speak for itself. It is perhaps too late in the day to express regret for its stilted title.

This paper is an attempt to analyze the motives which underlie a movement based, not only upon conviction, but upon genuine emotion, wherever educated young people are seeking an outlet for that sentiment for universal brotherhood, which the best spirit of our times is forcing from an emotion into a motive. These young people accomplish little toward the solution of this social problem, and bear the brunt of being cultivated into unnourished, oversensitive lives. They have been shut off from the common labor by which they live which is a great source of moral and physical health. They feel a fatal want of harmony between their theory and their lives, a lack of coordination between thought and action. I think it is hard for us to realize how seriously many of them are taking to the notion of human brotherhood, how eagerly they long to give tangible expression to the democratic ideal. These young men and women, longing to socialize their democracy, are animated by certain hopes which may be thus loosely formulated; that if in a democratic country nothing can be permanently achieved save through the masses of the people, it will be impossible to establish a higher political life than the people themselves crave; that it is difficult to see how the notion of a higher civic life can be fostered save through common intercourse; that the blessings which we associate with a life of refinement and cultivation can be made universal and must be made universal if they are to be permanent; that the good we secure for ourselves is precarious and uncertain, is floating in mid-air, until it is secured for all of us and incorporated into our common life. It is easier to state these hopes than to formulate the line of motives, which I believe to constitute the trend of the subjective pressure toward the Settlement. There is something primordial about these motives, but I am perhaps overbold in designating them as a great desire to share the race life. We all bear traces of the starvation struggle which for so long made up the life of the race. Our very organism holds memories and glimpses of that long life of our ancestors, which still goes on among so many of our contemporaries. Nothing so deadens the sympathies and shrivels the power of enjoyment as the persistent keeping away from the great opportunities for helpfulness and a continual ignoring of the starvation struggle which makes up the life of at least half the race. To shut one's self away from that half of the race life is to shut one's self away from the most vital part of it; it is to live out but half the humanity to which we have been born heir and to use but half our faculties. We have all had longings for a fuller life which should include the use of these faculties. These longings are the physical complement of the "Intimations of Immortality," on which no ode has yet been written. To portray these would be the work of a poet, and it is hazardous for any but a poet to attempt it.

You may remember the forlorn feeling which occasionally seizes you when you arrive early in the morning a stranger in a great city: the stream of laboring people goes past you as you gaze through the plate-glass window of your hotel; you see hard working men lifting great burdens; you hear the driving and jostling of huge carts and your heart sinks with a sudden sense of futility. The door opens behind you and you turn to the man who brings you in your breakfast with a quick sense of human fellowship. You find yourself praying that you may never lose your hold on it all. A more poetic prayer would be that the great mother breasts of our common humanity, with its labor and suffering and its homely comforts, may never be withheld from you. You turn helplessly to the waiter and feel that it would be almost grotesque to claim from him the sympathy you crave because civilization has placed you apart, but you resent your position with a sudden sense of snobbery. Literature is full of portrayals of these glimpses: they come to shipwrecked men on rafts; they overcome the differences of an incongruous multitude when in the presence of a great danger or when moved by a common enthusiasm. They are not, however, confined to such moments, and if we were in the habit of telling them to each other, the recital would be as long as the tales of children are, when they sit down on the green grass and confide to each other how many times they have remembered that they lived once before. If these childish tales are the stirring of inherited impressions, just so surely is the other the striving of inherited powers.

"It is true that there is nothing after disease, indigence and a sense of guilt, so fatal to health and to life itself as the want of a proper outlet for active faculties." I have seen young girls suffer and grow sensibly lowered in vitality in the first years after they leave school. In our attempt then to give a girl pleasure and freedom from care we succeed, for the most part, in making her pitifully miserable. She finds "life" so different from what she expected it to be. She is besotted with innocent little ambitions, and does not understand this apparent waste of herself, this elaborate preparation, if no work is provided for her. There is a heritage of noble obligation which young people accept and long to perpetuate. The desire for action, the wish to right wrong and alleviate suffering haunts them daily. Society smiles at it indulgently instead of making it of value to itself. The wrong to them begins even farther back, when we restrain the first childish desires for "doing good," and tell them that they must wait until they are older and better fitted. We intimate that social obligation begins at a fixed date, forgetting that it begins at birth itself. We treat them as children who, with strong-growing limbs, are allowed to use their legs but not their arms, or whose legs are daily carefully exercised that after a while their arms may be put to high use. We do this in spite of the protest of the best educators, Locke and Pestalozzi. We are fortunate in the meantime if their unused members do not weaken and disappear. They do sometimes. There are a few girls who, by the time they are "educated," forget their old childish desires to help the world and to play with poor little girls "who haven't playthings." Parents are often inconsistent: they deliberately expose their daughters to knowledge of the distress in the world; they send them to hear missionary addresses on famines in India and China; they accompany them to lectures on the suffering in Siberia; they agitate together over the forgotten region of East London. In addition to this, from babyhood the altruistic tendencies of these daughters are persistently cultivated. They are taught to be self-forgetting and self-sacrificing, to consider the good of the whole before the good of the ego. But when all this information and culture show results, when the daughter comes back from college and begins to recognize her social claim to the "submerged tenth," and to evince a disposition to fulfill it, the family claim is strenuously asserted; she is told that she is unjustified, ill-advised in her efforts. If she persists, the family too often are injured and unhappy unless the efforts are called missionary and the religious zeal of the family carry them over their sense of abuse. When this zeal does not exist, the result is perplexing. It is a curious violation of what we would fain believe a fundamental law—that the final return of the deed is upon the head of the doer. The deed is that of exclusiveness and caution, but the return, instead of falling upon the head of the exclusive and cautious, falls upon a young head full of generous and unselfish plans. The girl loses something vital out of her life to which she is entitled. She is restricted and unhappy; her elders meanwhile, are unconscious of the situation and we have all the elements of a tragedy.

We have in America a fast-growing number of cultivated young people who have no recognized outlet for their active faculties. They hear constantly of the great social maladjustment, but no way is provided for them to change it, and their uselessness hangs about them heavily. Huxley declares that the sense of uselessness is the severest shock which the human system can sustain, and that if persistently sustained, it results in atrophy of function. These young people have had advantages of college, of European travel, and of economic study, but they are sustaining this shock of inaction. They have pet phrases, and they tell you that the things that make us all alike are stronger than the things that make us different. They say that all men are united by needs and sympathies far more permanent and radical than anything that temporarily divides them and sets them in opposition to each other. If they affect art, they say that the decay in artistic expression is due to the decay in ethics, that art when shut away from the human interests and from the great mass of humanity is self-destructive. They tell their elders with all the bitterness of youth that if they expect success from them in business or politics or in whatever lines their ambition for them has run, they must let them consult all of humanity; that they must let them find out what the people want and how they want it. It is only the stronger young people, however, who formulate this. Many of them dissipate their energies in so-called enjoyment. Others not content with that, go on studying and go back to college for their second degrees; not that they are especially fond of study, but because they want something definite to do, and their powers have been trained in the direction of mental accumulation. Many are buried beneath this mental accumulation with lowered vitality and discontent. Walter Besant says they have had the vision that Peter had when he saw the great sheet let down from heaven, wherein was neither clean nor unclean. He calls it the sense of humanity. It is not philanthropy nor benevolence, but a thing fuller and wider than either of these.

This young life, so sincere in its emotion and good phrases and yet so undirected, seems to me as pitiful as the other great mass of destitute lives. One is supplementary to the other, and some method of communication can surely be devised. Mr. Barnett, who urged the first Settlement,—Toynbee Hall, in East London,—recognized this need of outlet for the young men of Oxford and Cambridge, and hoped that the Settlement would supply the communication. It is easy to see why the Settlement movement originated in England, where the years of education are more constrained and definite than they are here, where class distinctions are more rigid. The necessity of it was greater there, but we are fast feeling the pressure of the need and meeting the necessity for Settlements in America. Our young people feel nervously the need of putting theory into action, and respond quickly to the Settlement form of activity.

Other motives which I believe make toward the Settlement are the result of a certain renaissance going forward in Christianity. The impulse to share the lives of the poor, the desire to make social service, irrespective of propaganda, express the spirit of Christ, is as old as Christianity itself. We have no proof from the records themselves that the early Roman Christians, who strained their simple art to the

point of grotesqueness in their eagerness to record a "good news" on the walls of the catacombs, considered this good news a religion. Jesus had no set of truths labeled Religious. On the contrary, his doctrine was that all truth is one, that the appropriation of it is freedom. His teaching had no dogma to mark it off from truth and action in general. He himself called it a revelation —a life. These early Roman Christians received the Gospel message, a command to love all men, with a certain joyous simplicity. The image of the Good Shepherd is blithe and gay beyond the gentlest shepherd of Greek mythology; the hart no longer pants, but rushes to the water brooks. The Christians looked for the continuous revelation, but believed what Jesus said, that this revelation, to be retained and made manifest, must be put into terms of action; that action is the only medium man has for receiving and appropriating truth; that the doctrine must be known through the will.

That Christianity has to be revealed and embodied in the line of social progress is a corollary to the simple proposition, that man's action is found in his social relationships in the way in which he connects with his fellows; that his motives for action are the zeal and affection with which he regards his fellows. By this simple process was created a deep enthusiasm for humanity; which regarded man as at once the organ and the object of revelation; and by this process came about the wonderful fellowship, the true democracy of the early Church, that so captivates the imagination. The early Christians were preeminently nonresistant. They believed in love as a cosmic force. There was no iconoclasm during the minor peace of the Church. They did not yet denounce nor tear down temples, nor preach the end of the world. They grew to a mighty number, but it never occurred to them, either in their weakness or in their strength, to regard other men for an instant as their foes or as aliens. The spectacle of the Christians loving all men was the most astounding Rome had ever seen. They were eager to sacrifice themselves for the weak, for children, and for the aged; they identified themselves with slaves and did not avoid the plague; they longed to share the common lot that they might receive the constant revelation. It was a new treasure which the early Christians added to the sum of all treasures, a joy hitherto unknown in the world —the joy of finding the Christ which lieth in each man, but which no man can unfold save in fellowship. A happiness ranging from the heroic to the pastoral enveloped them. They were to possess a revelation as long as life had new meaning to unfold, new action to propose.

I believe that there is a distinct turning among many young men and women toward this simple acceptance of Christ's message. They resent the assumption that Christianity is a set of ideas which belong to the religious consciousness, whatever that may be. They insist that it cannot be proclaimed and instituted apart from the social life of the community and that it must seek a simple and natural expression in the social organism itself. The Settlement movement is only one manifestation of that wider humanitarian movement which throughout Christendom, but preeminently in England, is endeavoring to embody itself, not in a sect, but in society itself.

I believe that this turning, this renaissance of the early Christian humanitarianism, is going on in America, in Chicago, if you please, without leaders who write or philosophize, without much speaking, but with a bent to express in social service and in terms of action the spirit of Christ. Certain it is that spiritual force is found in the Settlement movement, and it is also true that this force must be evoked and must be called into play before the success of any Settlement is assured. There must be the overmastering belief that all that is noblest in life is common to men as men, in order to accentuate the likenesses and ignore the differences which are found among the people whom the Settlement constantly brings into juxtaposition. It may be true, as the Positivists insist, that the very religious fervor of man can be turned into love for his race, and his desire for a future life into content to live in the echo of his deeds; Paul's formula of seeking for the Christ which lieth in each man and founding our likenesses on him, seems a simpler formula to many of us.

In a thousand voices singing the Hallelujah Chorus in Handel's "Messiah," it is possible to distinguish the leading voices, but the differences of training and cultivation between them and the voices in the chorus, are lost in the unity of purpose and in the fact that they are all human voices lifted by a high motive. This is a weak illustration of what a Settlement attempts to do. It aims, in a measure, to develop whatever of social life its neighborhood may afford, to focus and give form to that life, to bring to bear upon it the results of cultivation and training; but it receives in exchange for the music of isolated voices the volume and strength of the chorus. It is quite impossible for me to say in what proportion or degree the subjective necessity which led to the opening of Hull-House combined the three trends: first, the desire to interpret democracy in social terms; secondly, the impulse beating at the very source of our lives, urging us to aid in the race progress; and, thirdly, the Christian movement toward humanitarianism. It is difficult to analyze a living thing; the analysis is at best imperfect. Many more motives may blend with the three trends; possibly the desire for a new form of social success due to the nicety of imagination, which refuses worldly pleasures unmixed with the joys of self-sacrifice; possibly a love of approbation, so vast that it is not content with the treble clapping of delicate hands, but wishes also to hear the bass notes from toughened palms, may mingle with these.

The Settlement then, is an experimental effort to aid in the solution of the social and industrial problems which are engendered by the modern conditions of life in a great city. It insists that these problems are not confined to any one portion of a city. It is an attempt to relieve, at the same time, the over accumulation at one end of society and the destitution at the other; but it assumes that this over accumulation and destitution is most sorely felt in the things that pertain to social and educational privileges. From its very nature it can stand for no political or social propaganda. It must, in a sense, give the warm welcome of an inn to all such propaganda, if perchance one of them be found an angel. The only thing to be dreaded in the Settlement is that it lose its flexibility, its power of quick adaptation, its readiness to change its methods as its environment may demand. It must be open to conviction and must have a deep and abiding sense of tolerance. It must be hospitable and ready for experiment. It should demand from its residents a scientific patience in the accumulation of facts and the steady holding of their sympathies as one of the best instruments for that accumulation. It must be grounded in a philosophy whose foundation is on the solidarity of the human race, a philosophy which will not waver when the race happens to be represented by a drunken woman or an idiot boy. Its residents must be emptied of all conceit of opinion and all self-assertion, and ready to arouse and interpret the public opinion of their neighborhood. They must be content to live quietly side by side with their neighbors, until they grow into a sense of relationship and mutual interests. Their neighbors are held apart by differences of race and language which the residents can more easily overcome. They are bound to see the needs of their neighborhood as a whole, to furnish data for legislation, and to use their influence to secure it. In short, residents are pledged to devote themselves to the duties of good citizenship and to the arousing of the social energies which too largely lie dormant in every neighborhood given over to industrialism. They are bound to regard the entire life of their city as organic, to make an effort to unify it, and to protest against its over-differentiation.

It is always easy to make all philosophy

point one particular moral and all history adorn one particular tale; but I may be forgiven the reminder that the best speculative philosophy sets forth the solidarity of the human race; that the highest moralists have taught that without the advance and improvement of the whole, no man can hope for any lasting improvement in his own moral or material individual condition; and that the subjective necessity for Social Settlements is therefore identical with that necessity, which urges us on toward social and individual salvation.

Study Questions

1. Define "settlement house."

2. What specific motivations behind the Settlement Movement did Addams identify?

3. Addams spoke of a "renaissance [rebirth] going forward in Christianity." What can be inferred about her definition of Christianity by the way in which she discussed religion and social reform? (*Hint*: historians often associate the settlement house movement with the Social Gospel movement of the early twentieth century.)

The Progressive Party Platform (1912)

Although progressive visions for economic reform held great influence in American politics during the opening decade of the twentieth century, some progressive leaders doubted that either the Democrats or the Republicans would carry the vision far enough. Within the Republican Party, the progressives and conservatives struggled against each other, each trying to steer President Taft a different direction. But even when Taft moved against U.S. Steel, he failed to satisfy Roosevelt's sense of progressivism, for Roosevelt had identified that company as a good trust that should be preserved, not a malicious one that should be dissolved by government intervention. Taft, however, held considerable influence over the 1912 Republican National Convention, leaving Roosevelt's supporters with little room to maneuver. Therefore, the Roosevelt faction left the party to form a new one, the Progressive Party.

The conscience of the people, in a time of grave national problems, has called into being a new party, born of the nation's sense of justice. We of the Progressive party here dedicate ourselves to the fulfillment of the duty laid upon us by our fathers to maintain the government of the people, by the people and for the people whose foundations they laid.

We hold with Thomas Jefferson and Abraham Lincoln that the people are the masters of their Constitution, to fulfill its purposes and to safeguard it from those who, by perversion of its intent, would convert it into an instrument of injustice. In accordance with the needs of each generation the people must use their sovereign powers to establish and maintain equal opportunity and industrial justice, to secure which this Government was founded and without which no republic can endure.

This country belongs to the people who inhabit it. Its resources, its business, its institutions and its laws should be utilized, maintained or altered in whatever manner will best promote the general interest.

It is time to set the public welfare in the first place.

The Old Parties

Political parties exist to secure responsible government and to execute the will of the people.

From these great tasks both of the old parties have turned aside. Instead of instruments to promote the general welfare, they have become the tools of corrupt interests which use them impartially to serve their selfish purposes. Behind the ostensible government sits enthroned an invisible government owing no allegiance and acknowledging no responsibility to the people.

To destroy this invisible government, to dissolve the unholy alliance between corrupt business and corrupt politics is the first task of the statesmanship of the day.

The deliberate betrayal of its trust by the Republican party, the fatal incapacity of the Democratic party to deal with the new issues of the new time, have compelled the people to forge a new instrument of government through which to give effect to their will in laws and institutions.

Unhampered by tradition, uncorrupted by power, undismayed by the magnitude of the task, the new party offers itself as the instrument of the people to sweep away old abuses, to build a new and nobler commonwealth.

A Covenant with the People

This declaration is our covenant with the people, and we hereby bind the party and its candidates in State and Nation to the pledges made herein.

The Rule of the People

The National Progressive party, committed to the principles of government by a self-controlled democracy expressing its will through representatives of the people, pledges itself to secure such alterations in the fundamental law of the several States and of the United States as shall insure the representative character of the government.

In particular, the party declares for direct primaries for the nomination of State and National officers, for nation-wide preferential primaries for candidates for the presidency; for the direct election of United States Senators by the people; and we urge on the States the policy of the short ballot, with responsibility to the people secured by the initiative, referendum and recall.

Amendment of Constitution

The Progressive party, believing that a free people should have the power from time to time to amend their fundamental law so as to adapt it progressively to the changing needs of the people, pledges itself to provide a more easy and expeditious method of amending the Federal Constitution.

Nation and State

Up to the limit of the Constitution, and later by amendment of the Constitution, if found necessary, we advocate bringing under effective national jurisdiction those problems which have expanded beyond reach of the individual States.

It is as grotesque as it is intolerable that the several States should by unequal laws in matter of common concern become competing commercial agencies, barter the lives of their children, the health of their women and the safety and well being of their working people for the benefit of their financial interests.

The extreme insistence on States' rights by the Democratic party in the Baltimore platform demonstrates anew its inability to understand the world into which it has survived or to administer the affairs of a union of States which have in all essential respects become one people.

Equal Suffrage

The Progressive party, believing that no people can justly claim to be a true democracy which denies political rights on account of sex, pledges itself to the task of securing equal suffrage to men and women alike.

Corrupt Practices

We pledge our party to legislation that will compel strict limitation of all campaign contributions and expenditures, and detailed publicity of both before as well as after primaries and elections.

Publicity and Public Service

We pledge our party to legislation compelling the registration of lobbyists; publicity of committee hearings except on foreign affairs, and recording of all votes in committee; and forbidding federal appointees from holding office in State or National political organizations, or taking part as officers or delegates in political conventions for the nomination of elective State or National officials.

The Courts

The Progressive party demands such restriction of the power of the courts as shall leave to the people the ultimate authority to determine fundamental questions of social welfare and public policy. To secure this end, it pledges itself to provide:

1. That when an Act, passed under the police power of the State, is held unconstitutional under the State Constitution, by the courts, the people, after an ample interval for deliberation, shall have an opportunity to vote on the question whether they desire the Act to become law, notwithstanding such decision.

2. That every decision of the highest appellate court of a State declaring an Act of the Legislature unconstitutional on the ground of its violation of the Federal Constitution shall be subject to the same review by the Supreme Court of the United States as is now accorded to decisions sustaining such legislation.

Administration of Justice

The Progressive party, in order to secure to the people a better administration of justice and by that means to bring about a more general respect for the law and the courts, pledges itself to work unceasingly for the reform of legal procedure and judicial methods.

We believe that the issuance of injunctions in cases arising out of labor disputes should be prohibited when such injunctions would not apply when no labor disputes existed.

We also believe that a person cited for contempt in labor disputes, except when such contempt was committed in the actual presence of the court or so near thereto as to interfere with the proper administration of justice, should have a right to trial by jury.

Social and Industrial Justice

The supreme duty of the Nation is the conservation of human resources through an enlightened measure of social and industrial justice. We pledge ourselves to work unceasingly in State and Nation for:

Effective legislation looking to the prevention of industrial accidents, occupational diseases, overwork, involuntary unemployment, and other injurous effects incident to modern industry;

The fixing of minimum safety and health standards for the various occupations, and the exercise of the public authority of State and Nation, including the Federal Control over interstate commerce, and the taxing power, to maintain such standards;

The prohibition of child labor;

Minimum wage standards for working women, to provide a "living wage" in all industrial occupations;

The general prohibition of night work for women and the establishment of an eight hour day for women and young persons;

One day's rest in seven for all wage workers;

The eight hour day in continuous twenty-four hour industries;

The abolition of the convict contract labor system; substituting a system of prison production for governmental consumption only; and the application of prisoners' earnings to the support of their dependent families;

Publicity as to wages, hours and conditions of labor; full reports upon industrial accidents and diseases, and the opening to public inspection of all tallies, weights, measures and check systems on labor products;

Standards of compensation for death by industrial accident and injury and trade disease which will transfer the burden of lost earnings from the families of working people to the industry, and thus to the community;

The protection of home life against the hazards of sickness, irregular employment and old age through the adoption of a system of social insurance adapted to American use;

The development of the creative labor power of America by lifting the last load of illiteracy from American youth and establishing continuation schools for industrial education under public control and encouraging agricultural education and demonstration in rural schools;

The establishment of industrial research laboratories to put the methods and discoveries of science at the service of American producers;

We favor the organization of the workers, men and women, as a means of protecting their interests and of promoting their progress.

Department of Labor

We pledge our party to establish a department of labor with a seat in the cabinet, and with wide jurisdiction over matters affecting the conditions of labor and living.

Country Life

The development and prosperity of country life are as important to the people who live in the cities as they are to the farmers. Increase of prosperity on the farm will favorably affect the cost of living, and promote the interests of all who dwell in the country, and all who depend upon its products for clothing, shelter and food.

We pledge our party to foster the development of agricultural credit and co-operation, the teaching of agriculture in schools, agricultural college extension, the use of mechanical power on the farm, and to re-establish the Country Life Commission, thus directly promoting the welfare of the farmers, and bringing the benefits of better farming, better business and better living within their reach. . . .

Health

We favor the union of all the existing agencies of the Federal Government dealing with the public health into a single national health service without discrimination against or for any one set of therapeutic methods, school of medicine, or school of healing with such additional powers as may be necessary to enable it to perform efficiently such duties in the protection of the public from preventable diseases as may be properly undertaken by the Federal authorities, including the executing of existing laws regarding pure food, quarantine and cognate subjects, the promotion of vital statistics and the extension of the registration area of such statistics, and co-operation with the health activities of the various States and cities of the Nation.

Business

We believe that true popular government, justice and prosperity go hand in hand, and, so believing, it is our purpose to secure that large measure of general prosperity which is the fruit of legitimate and honest business, fostered by equal justice and by sound progressive laws.

We demand that the test of true prosperity shall be the benefits conferred thereby on all the citizens, not confined to individuals or classes, and that the test of corporate efficiency shall be the ability better to serve the public; that those who profit by control of business affairs shall justify that profit and that control by sharing with the public the fruits thereof.

We therefore demand a strong National regulation of inter-State corporations. The corporation is an essential part of modern business. The concentration of modern business, in some degree, is both inevitable and necessary for national and international business efficiency. But the existing concentration of vast wealth under a corporate system, unguarded and uncontrolled by the Nation, has placed in the hands of a few men enormous, secret, irresponsible power over the daily life of the citizen—a power insufferable in a free Government and certain of abuse.

This power has been abused, in monopoly of National resources, in stock watering, in unfair competition and unfair privileges, and finally in sinister influences on the public agencies of State and Nation. We do not fear commercial power, but we insist that it shall be exercised openly, under publicity, supervision and regulation of the most efficient sort, which will preserve its good while eradicating and preventing its ill.

To that end we urge the establishment of a strong Federal administrative commission of high standing, which shall maintain permanent active supervision over industrial corporations engaged in inter-State commerce, or such of them as are of public importance, doing for them what the Government now does for the National banks, and what is now done for the railroads by the Inter-State Commerce Commission.

Such a commission must enforce the complete publicity of those corporation transactions which are of public interest; must attack unfair competition, false capitalization and special privilege, and by continuous trained watchfulness guard and keep open equally all the highways of American commerce.

Thus the business man will have certain knowledge of the law, and will be able to conduct his business easily in conformity therewith; the investor will find security for his capital; dividends will be rendered more certain, and the savings of the people will be drawn naturally and safely into the channels of trade.

Under such a system of constructive regulation, legitimate business, freed from confusion, uncertainty and fruitless litigation, will develop normally in response to the energy and enterprise of the American business man.

We favor strengthening the Sherman Law by prohibiting agreement to divide territory or limit output; refusing to sell to customers who buy from business rivals; to sell below cost in certain areas while maintaining higher prices in other places; using the power of transportation to aid or injure special business concerns; and other unfair trade practices. . . .

Conservation

The natural resources of the Nation must be promptly developed and generously used to supply the people's needs, but we cannot safely allow them to be wasted, exploited, monopolized or controlled against the general good. We heartily favor the policy of conservation, and we pledge our party to protect the National forests without hindering their legitimate use for the benefit of all the people.

Agricultural lands in the National forests are, and should remain, open to the genuine settler. Conservation will not retard legitimate development. The honest settler must receive his patent promptly, without hindrance, rules or delays.

We believe that the remaining forests, coal and oil lands, water powers and other natural resources still in State or National control (except agricultural lands) are more likely to be wisely conserved and utilized for the general welfare if held in the public hands.

In order that consumers and producers, managers and workmen, now and hereafter, need not pay toll to private monopolies of power and raw material, we demand that such resources shall be retained by the State or Nation, and opened to immediate use under laws which will encourage development and make to the people a moderate return for benefits conferred.

In particular we pledge our party to require reasonable compensation to the public for water power rights hereafter granted by the public.

We pledge legislation to lease the public grazing lands under equitable provisions now pending which will increase the production of food for the people and thoroughly safeguard the rights of the actual homemaker. Natural resources, whose conservation is necessary for the National welfare, should be owned or controlled by the Nation.

Good Roads

We recognize the vital importance of good roads and we pledge our party to foster their extension in every proper way, and we favor the early construction of National highways. We also favor the extension of the rural free delivery service. . . .

Panama Canal

The Panama Canal, built and paid for by the American people, must be used primarily for their benefit.

We demand that the canal shall be so operated as to break the transportation monopoly now held and misused by the transcontinental railroads by maintaining sea competition with them; that ships directly or indirectly owned or controlled by American railroad corporations shall not be permitted to use the canal, and that American ships engaged in coastwise trade shall pay no tolls.

The Progressive party will favor legislation having for its aim the development of friendship and commerce between the United States and Latin-American nations.

Tariff

We believe in a protective tariff which shall equalize conditions of competition between the United States and foreign countries, both for the farmer and the manufacturer, and which shall maintain for labor an adequate standard of living.

Primarily the benefit of any tariff should be disclosed in the pay envelope of the laborer. We declare that no industry deserves protection which is unfair to labor or which is operating in violation of Federal law. We believe that the presumption is always in favor of the consuming public.

We demand tariff revision because the present tariff is unjust to the people of the United States. Fair dealing toward the people requires an immediate downward revision of those schedules wherein duties are shown to be unjust or excessive.

We pledge ourselves to the establishment of a non-partisan scientific tariff commission, reporting both to the President and to either branch of Congress, which shall report, first, as to the costs of production, efficiency of labor, capitalization, industrial organization and efficiency and the general competitive position in this country and abroad of industries seeking protection from Congress; second, as to the revenue producing power of the tariff and its relation to the resources of Government; and, third, as to the effect of the tariff on prices, operations of middlemen, and on the purchasing power of the consumer.

We believe that this commission should have plenary power to elicit information, and for this purpose to prescribe a uniform system of accounting for the great protected industries. The work of the commission should not prevent the immediate adoption of acts reducing these schedules generally recognized as excessive.

We condemn the Payne-Aldrich bill as unjust to the people. The Republican organization is in the hands of those who have broken, and cannot again be trusted to keep, the promise of necessary downward revision.

The Democratic party is committed to the destruction of the protective system through a tariff for revenue only–a policy which would inevitably produce widespread industrial and commercial disaster.

We demand the immediate repeal of the Canadian Reciprocity Act.

Inheritance and Income Tax

We believe in a graduated inheritance tax as a National means of equalizing the obligations of holders of property to Government, and we hereby pledge our party to enact such a Federal law as will tax large inheritances, returning to the States an equitable percentage of all amounts collected.

We favor the ratification of the pending amendment to the Constitution giving the Government power to levy an income tax.

Peace and National Defense

The Progressive party deplores the survival in our civilization of the barbaric system of warfare among nations with its enormous waste of resources even in time of peace, and the consequent impoverishment of the life of the toiling masses. We pledge the party to use its best endeavors to substitute judicial and other peaceful means of settling international differences.

We favor an international agreement for the limitation of naval forces. Pending such an agreement, and as the best means of preserving peace, we pledge ourselves to maintain for the present the policy of building two battleships a year.

Treaty Rights

We pledge our party to protect the rights of American citizenship at home and abroad. No treaty should receive the sanction of our Government which discriminates between American citizens because of birthplace, race, or religion, or that does not recognize the absolute right of expatriation.

The Immigrant

Through the establishment of industrial standards we propose to secure to the able-bodied immigrant and to his native fellow workers a larger share of American opportunity.

We denounce the fatal policy of indifference and neglect which has left our enormous immigrant population to become the prey of chance and cupidity.

We favor Governmental action to encourage the distribution of immigrants away from the congested cities, to rigidly supervise all private agencies dealing with them and to promote their assimilation, education and advancement.

Pensions

We pledge ourselves to a wise and just policy of pensioning American soldiers and sailors and their widows and children by the Federal Government. And we approve the policy of the southern States in granting pensions to the ex-Confederate soldiers and sailors and their widows and children. . . .

Government Supervision Over Investments

The people of the United States are swindled out of many millions of dollars every year, through worthless investments. The plain people, the wage earner and the men and women with small savings, have no way of knowing the merit of concerns sending out highly colored prospectuses offering stock for sale, prospectuses that make big returns seem certain and fortunes easily within grasp.

We hold it to be the duty of the Government to protect its people from this kind of piracy. We, therefore, demand wise, carefully thought out legislation that will give us such Governmental supervision over this matter as will furnish to the people of the United States this much-needed protection, and we pledge ourselves thereto.

Conclusion

On these principles and on the recognized desirability of uniting the Progressive forces of the Nation into an organization which shall unequivocally represent the Progressive spirit and policy we appeal for the support of all American citizens, without regard to previous political affiliations.

Study Questions

1. What fault did the Progressive Party identify in the two major existing parties?

2. What changes did the Progressive Party propose to the federal and state constitutions, and why?

3. What reforms did the Progressive Party recommend for "Industrial Justice"?

4. Compare the Progressive Party's attitude toward the tariff with those of the Republican and Democratic parties.

Theodore Roosevelt, "The Right of the People to Rule" (1912)

Campaigning as the Progressive Party candidate for the U.S. presidency, Theodore Roosevelt delivered the following address, which was broadcast by radio, from Carnegie Hall, New York. He defended four key progressive reforms that had been introduced in various states: the initiative, the referendum, the recall, and the direct primary. Roosevelt also championed a progressive reinterpretation of the U.S. Constitution, thinking the amendment process to be cumbersome and unnecessary for the aims he envisioned.

The great fundamental issue now before the Republican party and before our people can be stated briefly. It is: Are the American people fit to govern themselves, to rule themselves, to control themselves? I believe they are. My opponents do not. I believe in the right of the people to rule. I believe the majority of the plain people of the United States will, day in and day out, make fewer mistakes in governing themselves than any smaller class or body of men, no matter what their training, will make in trying to govern them. I believe, again, that the American people are, as a whole, capable of self-control and of learning by their mistakes. Our opponents pay lip-loyalty to this doctrine; but they show their real beliefs by the way in which they champion every device to make the nominal rule of the people a sham.

I have scant patience with this talk of the tyranny of the majority. Wherever there is tyranny of the majority, I shall protest against it with all my heart and soul. But we are today suffering from the tyranny of minorities. It is a small minority that is grabbing our coal-deposits, our water-powers, and our harbor fronts. A small minority is battening on the sale of adulterated foods and drugs. It is a small minority that lies behind monopolies and trusts. It is a small minority that stands behind the present law of master and servant, the sweat-shops, and the whole calendar of social and industrial injustice. It is a small minority that is today using our convention system to defeat the will of a majority of the people in the choice of delegates to the Chicago Convention. The only tyrannies from which men, women, and children are suffering in real life are the tyrannies of minorities.

If the majority of the American people were in fact tyrannous over the minority, if democracy had no greater self-control than empire, then indeed no written words which our forefathers put into the Constitution could stay that tyranny.

No sane man who has been familiar with the government of this country for the last twenty years will complain that we have had too much of the rule of the majority. The trouble has been a far different one that, at many times and in many localities, there have held public office in the States and in the nation men who have, in fact, served not the whole people, but some special class or special interest. I am not thinking only of those special interests which by grosser methods, by bribery and crime, have stolen from the people. I am thinking as much of their respectable allies and figureheads, who have ruled and legislated and decided as if in some way the vested rights of privilege had a first mortgage on the whole United States, while the rights of all the people were merely an unsecured debt. Am I overstating the case? Have our political leaders always, or generally, recognized their duty to the people as anything more than a duty to disperse the mob, see that the ashes are taken away, and distribute patronage? Have our leaders always, or generally, worked for the benefit of human beings, to increase the prosperity of all the people, to give each some opportunity of living decently and bringing up his children well? The questions need no answer.

Now there has sprung up a feeling deep in the hearts of the people not of the bosses and professional politicians, not of the beneficiaries of special privilege—a pervading belief of thinking men that when the majority of the people do in fact, as well as theory, rule, then the servants of the people will come more quickly to answer and obey, not the commands of the special interests, but those of the whole people. To reach toward that end the Progressives of the Republican party in certain States have formulated certain proposals for change in the form of the State government—certain new "checks and balances" which may check and balance the special interests and their allies. That is their purpose. Now turn for a moment to their proposed methods.

First, there are the "initiative and referendum," which are so framed that if the legislatures obey the command of some special interest, and obstinately refuse the will of the majority, the majority may step in and legislate directly. No man would say that it was best to conduct all legislation by direct vote of the people—it would mean the loss of deliberation, of patient consideration but, on the other hand, no one whose mental arteries have not long since hardened can doubt that the proposed changes are needed when the legislatures refuse to carry out the will of the people. The proposal is a method to reach an undeniable evil. Then there is the recall of public officers the principle that an officer chosen by the people who is unfaithful may be recalled by vote of the majority before he finishes his term. I will speak of the recall of judges in a moment—leave that aside—but as to the other officers, I have heard no argument advanced against the proposition, save that it will make the public officer timid and always currying favor with the mob. That argument means that you can fool all the people all the time, and is an avowal of disbelief in democracy. If it be true (and I believe it is not) it is less important than to stop those public officers from currying favor with the interests. Certain States may need the recall, others may not; where the term of elective office is short it may be quite needless; but there are occasions when it meets a real evil, and provides a needed check and balance against the special interests.

Then there is the direct primary—the real one, not the New York one and that, too, the Progressives offer as a check on the special interests. Most clearly of all does it seem to me that this change is wholly good for every State. The system of party government is not written in our constitutions, but it is none the less a vital and essential part of our form of government. In that system the party leaders should serve and carry out the will of their own party. There is no need to show how far that theory is from the facts, or to rehearse the vulgar thieving partnerships of the corporations and the bosses, or to show how many times the real government lies in the hands of the boss, protected from the commands and the revenge of the voters by his puppets in office and the power of patronage. We need not be told how he is thus intrenched nor how hard he is to overthrow. The facts stand out in the history of nearly every State in the Union. They are blots on our political system. The direct primary will give the voters a method ever ready to use, by which the party leader shall be made to obey their command. The direct primary, if accompanied by a stringent corrupt-practices act, will help break up the corrupt partnership of corporations and politicians.

My opponents charge that two things in my programme are wrong because they intrude into the sanctuary of the judiciary. The first is the recall of judges; and the second, the review by the people of judicial decisions on certain constitutional questions. I have said again and again that I do not advocate the recall of judges in all States and in all communities. In my own State I do not advocate it or believe it to be needed, for in this State our trouble lies not with corruption on the bench, but with the effort by the honest but wrong-headed judges to thwart the people in their struggle for social justice and fair dealing. The integrity of our judges from Marshall to White and Holmes and to Cullen and many others in our own State is a fine page of American history. But I say it soberly: democracy has a right to approach the sanctuary of the courts when a special interest has corruptly found sanctuary there; and this is exactly what has happened in some of the States where the recall of the judges is a living issue. I would far more willingly trust the whole people to judge such a case than some special tribunal—perhaps appointed by the same power that chose the judge if that tribunal is not itself really responsible to the people and is hampered and clogged by the technicalities of impeachment proceedings.

I have stated that the courts of the several States—not always but often—have construed the "due process" clause of the State constitutions as if it prohibited the whole people of the State from adopting methods of regulating the use of property so that human life, particularly the lives of the working men, shall be safer, freer, and happier. No one can successfully impeach this statement. I have insisted that the true construction of "due process" is that pronounced by Justice Holmes in delivering the unanimous opinion of the Supreme Court of the United States, when he said: "The police power extends to all the great public need. It may be put forth in aid of what is sanctioned by usage, or held by the prevailing morality or strong and preponderant opinion to be greatly and immediately necessary to the public welfare."

I insist that the decision of the New York court of appeals in the Ives case, which set aside the will of the majority of the people as to the compensation of injured workmen in dangerous trades, was intolerable and based on a wrong political philosophy. I urge that in such cases where the courts construe the due process clause as if property rights, to the exclusion of human rights, had a first mortgage on the Constitution, the people may, after sober deliberation, vote, and finally determine whether the law which the court set aside shall be valid or not. By this method can be clearly and finally ascertained the preponderant opinion of the people which Justice Holmes makes the test of due process in the case of laws enacted in the exercise of the police power. The ordinary methods now in vogue of amending the Constitution have in actual practice proved wholly inadequate to secure justice in such cases with reasonable speed, and cause intolerable delay and injustice, and those who stand against the changes I propose are champions of wrong and injustice, and of tyranny by the wealthy and the strong over the weak and the helpless.

So that no man may misunderstand me, let me recapitulate:

(1) I am not proposing anything in connection with the Supreme Court of the United States, or with the Federal Constitution.

(2) I am not proposing anything having any connection with ordinary suits, civil or criminal, as between individuals.

(3) I am not speaking of the recall of judges.

(4) I am proposing merely that in a certain class of cases involving police power, when a State court has set aside as unconstitutional a law passed by the legislature for the general welfare, the question of the validity of the law, which should depend, as Justice Holmes so well phrases it, upon the prevailing morality or preponderant opinion be submitted for final determination to a vote of the people, taken after due time for consideration.

And I contend that the people, in the nature of things, must be better judges of what is the preponderant opinion than the courts, and that the courts should not be allowed to reverse the political philosophy of the people. My point is well illustrated by a recent decision of the Supreme Court, holding that the court would not take jurisdiction of a case involving the constitutionality of the initiative and referendum laws of Oregon. The ground of the decision was that such a question was not judicial in its nature, but should be left for determination to the other coordinate departments of the government. Is it not equally plain that the question whether a given social policy is for the public good is not of a judicial nature, but should be settled by the legislature, or in the final instance by the people themselves?

The President of the United States, Mr. Taft, devoted most of a recent speech to criticism of this proposition. He says that it "is utterly without merit or utility, and, instead of being in the interest of all the people, and of the stability of popular government, is sowing the seeds of confusion and tyranny." (By this he, of course, means the tyranny of the majority, that is, the tyranny of the American people as a whole.) He also says that my proposal (which, as he rightly sees, is merely a proposal to give the people a real, instead of only a nominal, chance to construe and amend a State constitution with reasonable rapidity) would make such amendment and interpretation "depend on the feverish, uncertain, and unstable determination of successive votes on different laws by temporary and changing majorities"; and that "it lays the axe at the root of the tree of well-ordered freedom, and subjects the guaranties of life, liberty, and property without remedy to the fitful impulse of a temporary majority of an electorate."

This criticism is really less a criticism of my proposal than a criticism of all popular government. It is wholly unfounded, unless it is founded on the belief that the people are fundamentally untrustworthy. If the Supreme Court's definition of due process in relation to the police power is sound, then an act of the legislature to promote the collective interests of the community must be valid, if it embodies a policy held by the prevailing morality or a preponderant opinion to be necessary to the public welfare.

This is the question that I propose to submit to the people. How can the prevailing morality or a preponderant opinion be better and more exactly ascertained than by a vote of the people? The people must know better than the court what their own morality and their own opinion is. I ask that you, here, you and the others like you, you the people, be given the chance to state your own views of justice and public morality, and not sit meekly by and have your views announced for you by well-meaning adherents of outworn philosophies, who exalt the pedantry of formulas above the vital needs of human life.

The object I have in view could probably be accomplished by an amendment of the State constitutions taking away from the courts the power to review the legislature's determination of a policy of social justice, by defining due process of law in accordance with the views expressed by Justice Holmes of the Supreme Court. But my proposal seems to me more democratic and, I may add, less radical. For under the method I suggest the people may sustain the court as against the legislature, whereas, if due process were defined in the Constitution, the decision of the legislature would be final. . . .

Study Questions

1. Define "initiative" and "referendum" and explain why Roosevelt endorsed them.

2. Define "direct primary" and explain why Roosevelt thought it was important.

3. Why did Roosevelt think it necessary for the people to be able to exercise a collective veto power over the courts?

Woodrow Wilson, "What Is Progress?" (1912)

With the Republican vote split between reelecting President Taft or reverting back to Theodore Roosevelt, now under the banner of the Progressive Party, the Democrats united to support Woodrow Wilson. For his part, Wilson showed that if Americans wanted progress, they did not have to settle for the Taft and Roosevelt varieties. Woodrow Wilson delivered the following speech when campaigning for the presidency in 1912. It was published the next year in his book, *The New Freedom*.

In that sage and veracious chronicle, "Alice Through the Looking-Glass," it is recounted how, on a noteworthy occasion, the little heroine is seized by the Red Chess Queen, who races her off at a terrific pace. They run until both of them are out of breath; then they stop, and Alice looks around her and says, "Why, we are just where we were when we started!" "Oh, yes," says the Red Queen; "you have to run twice as fast as that to get anywhere else."

That is a parable of progress. The laws of this country have not kept up with the change of economic circumstances in this country; they have not kept up with the change of political circumstances; and, therefore, we are not even where we were when we started. We shall have to run, not until we are out of breath, but until we have caught up with our own conditions, before we shall be where we were when we started; when we started this great experiment which has been the hope and the beacon of the world. And we should have to run twice as fast as any rational program I have seen in order to get anywhere else.

I am, therefore, forced to be a progressive, if for no other reason, because we have not kept up with our changes of conditions, either in the economic field or in the political field. We have not kept up as well as other nations have. We have not kept our practices adjusted to the facts of the case, and until we do, and unless we do, the facts of the case will always have the better of the argument; because if you do not adjust your laws to the facts, so much the worse for the laws, not for the facts, because law trails along after the facts. Only that law is unsafe which runs ahead of the facts and beckons to it and makes it follow the will-o'-the-wisps of imaginative projects.

Business is in a situation in America which it was never in before; it is in a situation to which we have not adjusted our laws. Our laws are still meant for business done by individuals; they have not been satisfactorily adjusted to business done by great combinations, and we have got to adjust them. I do not say we may or may not; I say we must; there is no choice. If your laws do not fit your facts, the facts are not injured, the law is damaged; because the law, unless I have studied it amiss, is the expression of the facts in legal relationships. Laws have never altered the facts; laws have always necessarily expressed the facts; adjusted interests as they have arisen and have changed toward one another.

Politics in America is in a case which sadly requires attention. The system set up by our law and our usage doesn't work,—or at least it can't be depended on; it is made to work only by a most unreasonable expenditure of labor and pains. The government, which was designed for the people, has got into the hands of bosses and their employers, the special interests. An invisible empire has been set up above the forms of democracy.

There are serious things to do. Does any man doubt the great discontent in this country? Does any man doubt that there are grounds and justifications for discontent? Do we dare stand still? Within the past few months we have witnessed (along with other strange political phenomena, eloquently significant of popular uneasiness) on one side a doubling of the Socialist vote and on the other the posting on dead walls and hoardings all over the country of certain very attractive and diverting bills warning citizens that it was "better to be safe than sorry" and advising them to "let well enough alone." Apparently a good many citizens doubted whether the situation they were advised to let alone was really well enough, and concluded that they would take a chance of being sorry. To me, these counsels of do-nothingism, these counsels of sitting still for fear something would happen, these counsels addressed to the hopeful, energetic people of the United States, telling them that they are not wise enough to touch their own affairs without marring them, constitute the most extraordinary argument of fatuous ignorance I ever heard. Americans are not yet cowards. True, their self-reliance has been sapped by years of submission to the doctrine that prosperity is something that benevolent magnates provide for them with the aid of the government; their self-reliance has

been weakened, but not so utterly destroyed that you can twit them about it. The American people are not naturally stand-patters. Progress is the word that charms their ears and stirs their hearts.

There are, of course, Americans who have not yet heard that anything is going on. The circus might come to town, have the big parade and go, without their catching a sight of the camels or a note of the calliope. There are people, even Americans, who never move themselves or know that anything else is moving.

A friend of mine who had heard of the Florida "cracker," as they call a certain ne'er-do-well portion of the population down there, when passing through the State in a train, asked some one to point out a "cracker" to him. The man asked replied, "Well, if you see something off in the woods that looks brown, like a stump, you will know it is either a stump or a cracker; if it moves, it is a stump."

Now, movement has no virtue in itself. Change is not worth while for its own sake. I am not one of those who love variety for its own sake. If a thing is good today, I should like to have it stay that way tomorrow. Most of our calculations in life are dependent upon things staying the way they are. For example, if, when you got up this morning, you had forgotten how to dress, if you had forgotten all about those ordinary things which you do almost automatically, which you can almost do half awake, you would have to find out what you did yesterday. I am told by the psychologists that if I did not remember who I was yesterday, I should not know who I am today, and that, therefore, my very identity depends upon my being able to tally today with yesterday. If they do not tally, then I am confused; I do not know who I am, and I have to go around and ask somebody to tell me my name and where I came from.

I am not one of those who wish to break connection with the past; I am not one of those who wish to change for the mere sake of variety. The only men who do that are the men who want to forget something, the men who filled yesterday with something they would rather not recollect today, and so go about seeking diversion, seeking abstraction in something that will blot out recollection, or seeking to put something into them which will blot out all recollection. Change is not worth while unless it is improvement. If I move out of my present house because I do not like it, then I have got to choose a better house, or build a better house, to justify the change.

It would seem a waste of time to point out that ancient distinction—between mere change and improvement. Yet there is a class of mind that is prone to confuse them. We have had political leaders whose conception of greatness was to be forever frantically doing something—it mattered little what; restless, vociferous men, without sense of the energy of concentration, knowing only the energy of succession. Now, life does not consist of eternally running to a fire. There is no virtue in going anywhere unless you will gain something by being there. The direction is just as important as the impetus of motion.

All progress depends on how fast you are going, and where you are going, and I fear there has been too much of this thing of knowing neither how fast we were going or where we were going. I have my private belief that we have been doing most of our progressiveness after the fashion of those things that in my boyhood days we called "treadmills," a treadmill being a moving platform, with cleats on it, on which some poor devil of a mule was forced to walk forever without getting anywhere. Elephants and even other animals have been known to turn treadmills, making a good deal of noise, and causing certain wheels to go round, and I daresay grinding out some sort of product for somebody, but without achieving much progress. Lately, in an effort to persuade the elephant to move, really, his friends tried dynamite. It moved—in separate and scattered parts, but it moved.

A cynical but witty Englishman said, in a book, not long ago, that it was a mistake to say of a conspicuously successful man, eminent in his line of business, that you could not bribe a man like that, because, he said, the point about such men is that they have been bribed—not in the ordinary meaning of that word, not in any gross, corrupt sense, but they have achieved their great success by means of the existing order of things and therefore they have been put under bonds to see that that existing order of things is not changed; they are bribed to maintain the *status quo*.

It was for that reason that I used to say, when I had to do with the administration of an educational institution, that I should like to make the young gentlemen of the rising generation as unlike their fathers as possible. Not because their fathers lacked character or intelligence or knowledge or patriotism, but because their fathers, by reason of their advancing years and their established position in society, had lost touch with the processes of life; they had forgotten what it was to begin; they had forgotten what it was to rise; they had forgotten what it was to be dominated by the circumstances of their life on their way up from the bottom to the top, and, therefore, they were out of sympathy with the creative, formative and progressive forces of society.

Progress! Did you ever reflect that that word is almost a new one? No word comes more often or more naturally to the lips of modern man, as if the thing it stands for were almost synonymous with life itself, and yet men through many thousand years never talked or thought of progress. They thought in the other direction. Their stories of heroisms and glory were tales of the past. The ancestor wore the heavier armor and carried the larger spear. "There were giants in those days." Now all that has altered. We think of the future, not the past, as the more glorious time in comparison with which the present is nothing. Progress, development—those are modern words. The modern idea is to leave the past and press onward to something new.

But what is progress going to do with the past, and with the present? How is it going to treat them? With ignominy, or respect? Should it break with them altogether, or rise out of them, with its roots still deep in the older time? What attitude shall progressives take toward the existing order, toward those institutions of conservatism, the Constitution, the laws, and the courts?

Are those thoughtful men who fear that we are now about to disturb the ancient foundations of our institutions justified in their fear? If they are, we ought to go very slowly about the processes of change. If it is indeed true that we have grown tired of the institutions which we have so carefully and sedulously built up, then we ought to go very slowly and very carefully about the very dangerous task of altering them. We ought, therefore, to ask ourselves, first of all, whether thought in this country is tending to do anything by which we shall retrace our steps, or by which we shall change the whole direction of our development?

I believe, for one, that you cannot tear up ancient rootages and safely plant the tree of liberty in soil which is not native to it. I believe that the ancient traditions of a people are its ballast; you cannot make a tabula rasa upon which to write a political program. You cannot take a new sheet of paper and determine what your life shall be tomorrow. You must knit the new into the old. You cannot put a new patch on an old garment without ruining it; it must be not a patch, but something woven into the old fabric, of practically the same pattern, of the same texture and intention. If I did not believe that to be progressive was to preserve the essentials of our institutions, I for one could not be a progressive.

One of the chief benefits I used to derive from being president of a university was that I had the pleasure of entertaining thoughtful men from all over the world. I cannot tell you how much has dropped into my granary by their presence. I had been casting around in my mind for something by which to draw several parts of my political thought together when it was my good fortune to entertain a very interesting Scotsman who had been devoting himself to the philosophical thought of the seventeenth century. His talk was so engaging that it was delightful to hear him speak of anything, and presently there came out of the unexpected region of his thought the thing I had been waiting for. He called my attention to the fact that in every generation all sorts of speculation and thinking tend to fall under the formula of the dominant thought of the age. For example, after the Newtonian Theory of the universe had been developed, almost all thinking tended to express itself in the analogies of the Newtonian Theory, and since the Darwinian Theory has reigned amongst us, everybody is likely to express whatever he wishes to expound in terms of development and accommodation to environment.

Now, it came to me, as this interesting man talked, that the Constitution of the United States had been made under the dominion of the Newtonian Theory. You have only to read the papers of The Federalist to see that fact written on every page. They speak of the "checks and balances" of the Constitution, and use to express their idea the simile of the organization of the universe, and particularly of the solar system,—how by the attraction of gravitation the various parts are held in their orbits; and then they proceed to represent Congress, the Judiciary, and the President as a sort of imitation of the solar system.

They were only following the English Whigs, who gave Great Britain its modern constitution. Not that those Englishmen analyzed the matter, or had any theory about it; Englishmen care little for theories. It was a Frenchman, Montesquieu, who pointed out to them how faithfully they had copied Newton's description of the mechanism of the heavens.

The makers of our Federal Constitution read Montesquieu with true scientific enthusiasm. They were scientists in their way—the best way of their age—those fathers of the nation. Jefferson wrote of "the laws of Nature"—and then by way of afterthought—"and of Nature's God." And they constructed a government as they would have constructed an orrery—to display the laws of nature. Politics in their thought was a variety of mechanics. The Constitution was founded on the law of gravitation. The government was to exist and move by virtue of the efficacy of "checks and balances."

The trouble with the theory is that government is not a machine, but a living thing. It falls, not under the theory of the universe, but under the theory of organic life. It is accountable to Darwin, not to Newton. It is modified by its environment, necessitated by its tasks, shaped to its functions by the sheer pressure of life. No living thing can have its organs offset against each other, as checks, and live. On the contrary, its life is dependent upon their quick co-operation, their ready response to the commands of instinct or intelligence, their amicable community of purpose. Government is not a body of blind forces; it is a body of men, with highly differentiated functions, no doubt, in our modern day, of specialization, with a common task and purpose. Their co-operation is indispensable, their warfare fatal. There can be no successful government without the intimate, instinctive coordination of the organs of life and action.

This is not theory, but fact, and displays its force as fact, whatever theories may be thrown across its track. Living political constitutions must be Darwinian in structure and in practice. Society is a living organism and must obey the laws of life, not of mechanics; it must develop.

All that progressives ask or desire is permission—in an era when "development," "evolution," is the scientific word—to interpret the Constitution according to the Darwinian principle; all they ask is recognition of the fact that a nation is a living thing and not a machine.

Some citizens of this country have never got beyond the Declaration of Independence, signed in Philadelphia, July 4th, 1776. Their bosoms swell against George III, but they have no consciousness of the war for freedom that is going on today.

The Declaration of Independence did not mention the questions of our day. It is of no consequence to us unless we can translate its general terms into examples of the present day and substitute them in some vital way for the examples it itself gives, so concrete, so intimately involved in the circumstances of the day in which it was conceived and written. It is an eminently practical document, meant for the use of practical men; not a thesis for philosophers, but a whip for tyrants; not a theory of government, but a program of action. Unless we can translate it into the questions of our own day, we are not worthy of it, we are not the sons of the sires who acted in response to its challenge.

What form does the contest between tyranny and freedom take today? What is the special form of tyranny we now fight? How does it endanger the rights of the people, and what do we mean to do in order to make our contest against it effectual? What are to be the items of our new declaration of independence?

By tyranny, as we now fight it, we mean control of the law, of legislation and adjudication, by organizations which do not represent the people, by means which are private and selfish. We mean, specifically, the conduct of our affairs and the shaping of our legislation in the interest of special bodies of capital and those who organize their use. We mean the alliance, for this purpose, of political machines with selfish business. We mean the exploitation of the people by legal and political means. We have seen many of our governments under these influences cease to be representative governments, cease to be governments representative of the people, and become governments representative of special interests, controlled by machines, which in their turn are not controlled by the people.

Sometimes, when I think of the growth of our economic system, it seems to me as if, leaving our law just about where it was before any of the modern inventions or developments took place, we had simply at haphazard extended the family residence, added an office here and a workroom there, and a new set of sleeping rooms there, built up higher on our foundations, and put out little lean-tos on the side, until we have a structure that has no character whatever. Now, the problem is to continue to live in the house and yet change it.

Well, we are architects in our time, and our architects are also engineers. We don't have to stop using a railroad terminal because a new station is being built. We don't have to stop any of the processes of our lives because we are rearranging the structures in which we conduct those processes. What we have to undertake is to systematize the foundations of the house, then to thread all the old parts of the structure with the steel which will be laced together in modern fashion, accommodated to all the modern knowledge of structural strength and elasticity, and then slowly change the partitions, relay the walls, let in the light through new apertures, improve the ventilation; until finally, a generation or two from now, the scaffolding will be taken away, and there will be the family in a great building whose noble architecture will at last be disclosed, where men can live as a single community, co-operative as in a perfected, coordinated beehive, not afraid of any storm of nature, not afraid of any artificial storm, any imitation of thunder and lightning, knowing that the foundations go down to the bedrock of principle, and knowing that whenever they please they can change that plan again and accommodate it as they please to the altering necessities of their lives.

But there are a great many men who don't like the idea. Some wit recently said, in view of the fact that most of our American architects are trained in a certain École in Paris, that all American architecture in recent years was either bizarre or "Beaux Arts." I think that our economic architecture is decidedly bizarre; and I am afraid that there is a good deal to learn about matters other than architecture from the same source from which our

architects have learned a great many things. I don't mean the School of Fine Arts at Paris, but the experience of France; for from the other side of the water, men can now hold up against us the reproach that we have not adjusted our lives to modern conditions to the same extent that they have adjusted theirs. I was very much interested in some of the reasons given by our friends across the Canadian border for being very shy about the reciprocity arrangements. They said: "We are not sure whither these arrangements will lead, and we don't care to associate too closely with the economic conditions of the United States until those conditions are as modern as ours." And when I resented it, and asked for particulars, I had, in regard to many matters, to retire from the debate. Because I found that they had adjusted their regulations of economic development to conditions we had not yet found a way to meet in the United States.

Well, we have started now at all events. The procession is under way. The standpatter doesn't know there is a procession. He is asleep in the back part of his house. He doesn't know that the road is resounding with the tramp of men going to the front. And when he wakes up, the country will be empty. He will be deserted, and he will wonder what has happened. Nothing has happened. The world has been going on. The world has a habit of going on. The world has a habit of leaving those behind who won't go with it. The world has always neglected stand-patters. And, therefore, the stand-patter does not excite my indignation; he excites my sympathy. He is going to be so lonely before it is all over. And we are good fellows, we are good company; why doesn't he come along? We are not going to do him any harm. We are going to show him a good time. We are going to climb the slow road until it reaches some upland where the air is fresher, where the whole talk of mere politicians is stilled, where men can look in each other's faces and see that there is nothing to conceal, that all they have to talk about they are willing to talk about in the open and talk about with each other; and whence, looking back over the road, we shall see at last that we have fulfilled our promise to mankind. We had said to all the world, "America was created to break every kind of monopoly, and to set men free, upon a footing of equality, upon a footing of opportunity, to match their brains and their energies." And now we have proved that we meant it.

Study Questions

1. In what sense did the founding fathers have a "Newtonian" view of the U.S. Constitution, and why did Wilson promote a "Darwinian" vision in its place?

2. What was the connection that Wilson offered between the Declaration of Independence and the use of the federal government to break up monopolies? Do you agree? Explain.

Woodrow Wilson, First Inaugural Address (1913)

Ever since the Civil War, the Democratic Party had struggled to rebuild itself as a viable national party. Only one of the Gilded Age presidents—Grover Cleveland—was a Democrat. Although Democrats held the majority in southern states, the Republicans had the upper hand in national affairs. Would the election of Woodrow Wilson signal a change? And was that change about more than just a party name—was it about a fundamental shift in the way Americans would define ordered liberty?

There has been a change of government. It began two years ago, when the House of Representatives became Democratic by a decisive majority. It has now been completed. The Senate about to assemble will also be Democratic. The offices of President and Vice-President have been put into the hands of Democrats. What does the change mean? That is the question that is uppermost in our minds to-day. That is the question I am going to try to answer, in order, if I may, to interpret the occasion.

It means much more than the mere success of a party. The success of a party means little except when the Nation is using that party for a large and definite purpose. No one can mistake the purpose for which the Nation now seeks to use the Democratic Party. It seeks to use it to interpret a change in its own plans and point of view. Some old things with which we had grown familiar, and which had begun to creep into the very habit of our thought and of our lives, have altered their aspect as we have latterly looked critically upon them, with fresh, awakened eyes; have dropped their disguises and shown themselves alien and sinister. Some new things, as we look frankly upon them, willing to comprehend their real character, have come to assume the aspect of things long believed in and familiar, stuff of our own convictions. We have been refreshed by a new insight into our own life.

We see that in many things that life is very great. It is incomparably great in its material aspects, in its body of wealth, in the diversity and sweep of its energy, in the industries which have been conceived and built up by the genius of individual men and the limitless enterprise of groups of men. It is great, also, very great, in its moral force. Nowhere else in the world have noble men and women exhibited in more striking forms the beauty and the energy of sympathy and helpfulness and counsel in their efforts to rectify wrong, alleviate suffering, and set the weak in the way of strength and hope. We have built up, moreover, a great system of government, which has stood through a long age as in many respects a model for those who seek to set liberty upon foundations that will endure against fortuitous change, against storm and accident. Our life contains every great thing, and contains it in rich abundance.

But the evil has come with the good, and much fine gold has been corroded. With riches has come inexcusable waste. We have squandered a great part of what we might have used, and have not stopped to conserve the exceeding bounty of nature, without which our genius for enterprise would have been worthless and impotent, scorning to be careful, shamefully prodigal as well as admirably efficient. We have been proud of our industrial achievements, but we have not hitherto stopped thoughtfully enough to count the human cost, the cost of lives snuffed out, of energies overtaxed and broken, the fearful physical and spiritual cost to the men and women and children upon whom the dead weight and burden of it all has fallen pitilessly the years through. The groans and agony of it all had not yet reached our ears, the solemn, moving undertone of our life, coming up out of the mines and factories, and out of every home where the struggle had its intimate and familiar seat. With the great Government went many deep secret things which we too long delayed to look into and scrutinize with candid, fearless eyes. The great Government we loved has too often been made use of for private and selfish purposes, and those who used it had forgotten the people.

At last a vision has been vouchsafed us of our life as a whole. We see the bad with the good, the debased and decadent with the sound and vital. With this vision we approach new affairs. Our duty is to cleanse, to reconsider, to restore, to correct the evil without impairing the good, to purify and humanize every process of our common life without weakening or sentimentalizing it. There has been something crude and heartless and unfeeling in our haste to succeed and be great. Our thought has been "Let every man look out for himself, let every generation look out for itself," while we reared giant machinery which made it impossible that any but those who stood at the levers of control should have a chance to look out for themselves. We had not forgotten our morals. We remembered well enough that we had set up a policy which was meant to serve the humblest as well as the most powerful, with an eye single to the standards of justice and fair play, and remembered it with pride. But we were very heedless and in a hurry to be great.

We have come now to the sober second thought. The scales of heedlessness have fallen from our eyes. We have made up our minds to square every process of our national life again with the standards we so proudly set up at the beginning and have always carried at our hearts. Our work is a work of restoration.

We have itemized with some degree of particularity the things that ought to be altered and here are some of the chief items: A tariff which cuts us off from our proper part in the commerce of the world, violates the just principles of taxation, and makes the Government a facile instrument in the hand of private interests; a banking and currency system based upon the necessity of the Government to sell its bonds fifty years ago and perfectly adapted to concentrating cash and restricting credits; an industrial system which, take it on all its sides, financial as well as administrative, holds capital in leading strings, restricts the liberties and limits the opportunities of labor, and exploits without renewing or conserving the natural resources of the country; a body of agricultural activities never yet given the efficiency of great business undertakings or served as it should be through the instrumentality of science taken directly to the farm, or afforded the facilities of credit best suited to its practical needs; water-courses undeveloped, waste places unreclaimed, forests untended, fast disappearing without plan or prospect of renewal, unregarded waste heaps at every mine. We have studied as perhaps no other nation has the most effective means of production, but we have not studied cost or economy as we should either as organizers of industry, as statesmen, or as individuals.

Nor have we studied and perfected the means by which government may be put at the service of humanity, in safeguarding the health of the Nation, the health of its men and its women and its children, as well as their rights in the struggle for existence. This is no sentimental duty. The firm basis of government is justice, not pity. These are matters of justice. There can be no equality or opportunity, the first essential of justice in the body politic, if men and women and children be not shielded in their lives, their very vitality, from the consequences of great industrial and social processes which they can not alter, control, or singly cope with. Society must see to it that it does not itself crush or weaken or damage its own constituent parts. The first duty of law is to keep sound the society it serves. Sanitary laws, pure food laws, and laws determining conditions of labor which individuals are powerless to determine for themselves are intimate parts of the very business of justice and legal efficiency.

These are some of the things we ought to do, and not leave the others undone, the old-fashioned, never-to-be-neglected, fundamental safeguarding of property and of individual right. This is the high enterprise of the new day: To lift everything that concerns our life as a Nation to the light that shines from the hearthfire of every man's conscience and vision of the right. It is inconceivable that we should do this as partisans; it is inconceivable we should do it in ignorance of the facts as they are or in blind haste. We shall restore, not destroy. We shall deal with our economic system as it is and as it may be modified, not as it might be if we had a clean sheet of paper to write upon; and step by step we shall make it what it should be, in the spirit of those who question their own wisdom and seek counsel and knowledge, not shallow self-satisfaction or the excitement of excursions whither they can not tell. Justice, and only justice, shall always be our motto.

And yet it will be no cool process of mere science. The Nation has been deeply stirred, stirred by a solemn passion, stirred by the knowledge of wrong, of ideals lost, of government too often debauched and made an instrument of evil. The feelings with which we face this new age of right and opportunity sweep across our heartstrings like some air out of God's own presence, where justice and mercy are reconciled and the judge and the brother are one. We know our task to be no mere task of politics but a task which shall search us through and through, whether we be able to understand our time and the need of our people, whether we be indeed their spokesmen and interpreters, whether we have the pure heart to comprehend and the rectified will to choose our high course of action.

This is not a day of triumph; it is a day of dedication. Here muster, not the forces of party, but the forces of humanity. Men's hearts wait upon us; men's lives hang in the balance; men's hopes call upon us to say what we will do. Who shall live up to the great trust? Who dares fail to try? I summon all honest men, all patriotic, all forward-looking men, to my side. God helping me, I will not fail them, if they will but counsel and sustain me!

Study Questions

1. What "evils" did Wilson associate with *laissez-faire* economics?

2. What did Wilson mean when he said, "the firm basis of government is justice, not pity"?

Herbert Croly, *Progressive Democracy* (1914), ch. 12

Many Progressives abandoned the natural law and natural rights philosophies of America's founding fathers in favor of an evolutionary view of human history that saw modern science as the best tool for social progress. Having studied the atheistic, evolutionary sociology of August Comte as a student at Harvard University, Herbert Croly cast a vision of social reform that assumed the perfectibility of human civilization. Along the way, he abandoned the founders' vision for the American Republic as a representative government protective of natural rights and replaced it with a vision for social democracy, in which all the people would learn to speak and act as one. He advocated this new spirit of progressivism in *The New Republic*, a journal founded in 1914, as well as in his book, published that same year, *Progressive Democracy*.

The Advent of Direct Government

The Federal Constitution is in many other respects besides its amending clause a most unsatisfactory instrument for a courageous and thoroughgoing democracy. In the not very remote future it will have to be modified in certain essential matters both by amendment and by interpretation. In the present connection, however, the discussion of the detailed character of these amendments need not detain us. As soon as public opinion is aroused to the plain fact that the amending clause is the most formidable legal obstacle to the democratizing of the American political system, that article of the Constitution will become the centre of attack. Conservatives of all classes will rally to its defence, and for a good many years the issue will dominate American politics and work havoc among existing partisan alignments. But until the fight is on and some of the intervening years have elapsed, it is scarcely worth while to discuss the specific use to which the democracy will put its newly won freedom of action. The controversy itself will help to develop a specific program of revision, the nature of which cannot be at the present time plausibly or profitably denned.

Very different, however, is the situation with respect to the state constitutions and governments. They offer to the American people a unique and priceless opportunity for collective experimentation, which seeks to accomplish social purposes by means of democratic political agencies. Many American states are already using their legal powers with courage and with success in the interest of some kind of a social program. Almost as many have exhibited a similar intention to modify their political organizations according to what are considered to be thoroughly democratic political principles. In carrying out these social and political programs the people of the states are not hampered usually by the difficulty of amending their constitutions. A majority of the citizens voting at an election can, in a majority of the states, ratify constitutional amendments. They have used the machinery of amendment freely in the past. They are by way of using it at the present time more freely than ever. When using it, their action is generally dictated by the interest, or the supposed interest, of progressive democracy. The alterations which progressive democracy may or should make in state political organization become, consequently, a matter of immediately profitable political discussion. . . .

That the American democracy has consumed over one hundred years in finding out that it cannot wholly delegate the active exercise of its responsibilities is not surprising. The preliminary attempts to create a democratic political system necessarily involve serious difficulties of adjustment with the varied and alien stock of living political institutions and traditions. These institutions originated during a period in which public opinion was sluggish, ignorant and incompetent, in which social development had frequently to be subordinated to social conservation, in which the popular will had no effective means of expression except in local riots, and in which the national will necessarily escaped popular control. Yet alien as they were to the policy and methods of a democracy, the prevailing political institutions were so deeply rooted in contemporary human nature that the new democratic system had to make use of them. A similar difficulty confronted the European democracies in an even more acute and difficult form. The contrivances which have been invented as instruments of democratic purposes and policy have varied widely in different countries; but they have all tended to have a common defect. They have all tended to impose upon certain traditional representative agencies duties which a thoroughgoing democracy needed, but was not sufficiently prepared, to accomplish for itself.

On the continent of Europe, for instance, where during the seventeenth and eighteenth centuries monarchy had become national without the assistance or check of a general representative body, the democracy, when it came, found it difficult either to get along without the monarchy or to get along with the monarchy. It was alternately too dependent on the executive and too suspicious of him. In Great Britain the nation had become united under parliamentary rather than under royal leadership, and when democracy came, it confided its responsibility to Parliament and was for long apparently well satisfied with the result. But of late years the tendency has been to subordinate Parliament to the executive and for the executive to rest directly on popular public opinion. To an outsider it looks as if the necessary practical result of such a tendency would be an increase of direct popular control over the government. It is just beginning to be understood that representative government of any type becomes, in actual practice, a species of class government. It cannot succeed except by virtue of a ruling class which has earned the privilege of leadership and which has deserved and retained popular support. But it does not work so well in the case of a nation like France, which has lost confidence in its hereditary leaders, without having altogether rid itself of the political characteristics with which that hereditary leadership was associated. Neither does it or would it work well in a country like the United States, which has and can have no ruling class, and which, from the beginning, has been feeling its way towards the development of some kind of leadership adapted to ultimate popular political responsibility. It remains to be seen whether a representative system can be wrought for the benefit of a people who seek wholly to dispense with class leadership, and who have exhibited a consistent desire to democratize all their institutions.

If economic, social, political and technical conditions had remained very much as they were at the end of the eighteenth century, the purely democratic political aspirations might never have obtained the chance of expression. Some form of essentially representative government was at that time apparently the only dependable kind of liberal political organization. It was imposed by the physical and technical conditions under which government had to be conducted. Direct government did not seem to be possible outside of city or tribal states, whose population and area was sufficiently small to permit the actual assemblage of the body politic at some particular place, either at regular intervals or in case of an emergency. But in the case of states chiefly devoted to agriculture, whose free citizens were distributed over a wide area, and were, in any event, too numerous for actual assemblage in any one spot, it seemed necessary for the people to delegate to a body of representatives the power required not merely for public administration, but for the discussion of public questions, the adoption of public policies and the supervising of the administration itself. Some form of a responsible representative government, that is, was prescribed by fundamental economic and social conditions. The function was performed in the several states

according to the method best adapted to local traditions and by the class which had proved itself capable of leadership.

In the twentieth century, however, these practical conditions of political association have again changed, and have changed in a manner which enables the mass of the people to assume some immediate control of their political destinies. While it is more impossible than ever for the citizens of a modern industrial and agricultural state actually to assemble after the manner of a New England town-meeting, it is no longer necessary for them so to assemble. They have abundant opportunities of communication and consultation without any actual meeting at one time and place. They are kept in constant touch with one another by means of the complicated agencies of publicity and intercourse which are afforded by the magazines, the press and the like. The active citizenship of the country meets every morning and evening and discusses the affairs of the nation with the newspaper as an impersonal interlocutor. Public opinion has a thousand methods of seeking information and obtaining definite and effective expression which it did not have four generations ago. The community is broken up into innumerable smaller communities, each of which is united by common interests and ideas and each of which is seeking to bring a larger number of people under the influence of its interests and ideas. Under such conditions the discussions which take place in a Congress or a Parliament no longer possess their former function. They no longer create and guide what public opinion there is. Their purpose rather is to provide a mirror for public opinion, to advertise and illuminate its constituent ideas and purposes, and to confront the advocates of those ideas with the discipline of effective resistance and, perhaps, with the responsibilities of power. Phases of public opinion form, develop, gather to a head, assert their power and find their place chiefly by the activity of other more popular unofficial agencies. Thus the democracy has at its disposal a mechanism of developing and exchanging opinions, and of reaching decisions, which is independent of representative assemblies, and which is, or may become, superior to that which it formerly obtained by virtue of occasional popular assemblages.

The adoption of the machinery of direct government is a legitimate expression of this change. After centuries of political development, in which certain forms of representation were imposed upon progressive nations by conditions of practical efficiency, and in which these representative forms grew continually in variety and complexity, underlying conditions have again shifted. Pure democracy has again become not merely possible, but natural and appropriate. The attempt to return to it is no more retrogressive than was the attempt to recover classic humanism after its eclipse during the Middle Ages. Society has been passing through a period of prodigious fertility, during which new social aspirations, purposes, instruments and activities have multiplied with unprecedented rapidity. If these new interests and activities are to be assimilated, they must be recognized and incorporated into the system of government. As a consequence of the attempt to incorporate them into the system of government, society may seem to be yielding to the power of disintegrating economic and social forces. This appears to be the beginning of a reverse process of denationalization which will be equivalent to dissolution. Those who place any such interpretation upon the facts of modern social development and the corresponding political changes fail to understand their meaning. Increasing direct popular political action is coming to have a function in the political organization of a modern society, because only in this way can the nation again become a master in its own house. Its very fecundity, and the enormous power which many of its offspring obtain, have compelled a democratic nation to adopt a more thoroughgoing method of promoting its integrity. As yet it is not making very much headway. It is distracted and disconcerted by its own fertility. It is terrified in particular by the capitalist and labor organizations to which it has given birth. But it will not continue to be disconcerted and terrified. It is adopting the very political instruments which are necessary for the purpose of keeping control of the increasingly numerous and increasingly powerful agencies of its own life. The attempt, far from being a reactionary reversion to an earlier political and social type, prepares the way, it may be hoped, for an advance towards a better and deeper social and political union, associated with direct popular political action and responsibility.

Study Questions

1. What criticisms did Croly have of the constitutional amendment process?

2. What, in Croly's opinion, had replaced the town-hall meeting as the method for solidifying public opinion?

3. Do you agree with Croly's suggestion that a direct popular democracy should replace the representative republic? Explain why or why not.

Margaret Sanger, *The Woman Rebel* (1914)

Few women influenced twentieth-century American culture as much as Margaret Sanger. An outspoken radical, she endorsed socialism and atheism and attacked Christianity, especially Roman Catholicism. She particularly objected to the Christian vision for marriage, with its high emphasis on motherhood. In 1914, she founded a journal entitled *The Woman Rebel*, with "NO GODS! NO MASTERS!" appearing on the masthead. In article after article, she defied the 1873 Comstock Law, which forbade the distribution of both contraceptives and information concerning them. It was Sanger who coined "birth control," founded Planned Parenthood, and provided the research funding for developing the most frequently prescribed drug worldwide—a drug so common that it goes simply by the name "the Pill." Sanger's crusades for birth control and abortion also had a decisively racist tilt: as an advocate of eugenics, she sought to limit the population of "inferior" races in order to spur on social evolution among the "favored" races.

This paper will not be the champion of any "ism."

All rebel women are invited to contribute to its columns.

The majority of papers usually adjust themselves to the ideas of their readers but the WOMAN REBEL will obstinately refuse to be adjusted.

The aim of this paper will be to stimulate working women to think for themselves and to build up a conscious fighting character.

An early feature will be a series of articles written by the editor for girls from fourteen to eighteen years of age. In this present chaos of sex atmosphere it is difficult for the girl of this uncertain age to know just what to do or really what constitutes clean living without prudishness. All this slushy talk about white slavery, the man painted and described as a hideous vulture pouncing down upon the young, pure and innocent girl, drugging her through the medium of grape juice and lemonade and then dragging her off to his foul den for other men equally as vicious to feed and fatten on her enforced slavery—surely this picture is enough to sicken and disgust every thinking woman and man, who has lived even a few years past the adolescent age. Could any more repulsive and foul conception of sex be given to adolescent girls as a preparation for life than this picture that is being perpetuated by the stupidly ignorant in the name of "sex education"!

If it were possible to get the truth from girls who work in prostitution to-day, I believe most of them would tell you that the first sex experience was with a sweetheart or through the desire for a sweetheart or something impelling within themselves, the nature of which they knew not, neither could they control. Society does not forgive this act when it is based upon the natural impulses and feelings of a young girl. It prefers the other story of the grape juice procurer which makes it easy to shift the blame from its own shoulders, to cast the stone and to evade the unpleasant facts that it alone is responsible for. It sheds sympathetic tears over white slavery, holds the often mythical procurer up as a target, while in reality it is supported by the misery it engenders.

If, as reported, there are approximately 35,000 women working as prostitutes in New York City alone, is it not sane to conclude that some force, some living, powerful, social force is at play to compel these women to work at a trade which involves police persecution, social ostracism and the constant danger of exposure to venereal diseases. From my own knowledge of adolescent girls and from sincere expressions of women working as prostitutes inspired by mutual understanding and confidence I claim that the first sexual act of these so-called wayward girls is partly given, partly desired yet reluctantly so because of the fear of the consequences together with the dread of lost respect of the man. These fears interfere with mutuality of expression—the man becomes conscious of the responsibility of the set and often refuses to see her again, sometimes leaving the town and usually denouncing her as having been with "other fellows." His sole aim is to throw off responsibility. The same uncertainty in these emotions is experienced by girls in marriage in as great a proportion as in the unmarried. After the first experience the life of a girl varies. All these girls do not necessarily go into prostitution. They have had an experience which has not "ruined" them, but rather given them a larger vision of life, stronger feelings and a broader understanding of human nature. The adolescent girl does not understand herself. She is full of contradictions, whims, emotions. For her emotional nature longs for caresses, to touch, to kiss. She is often as well satisfied to hold hands or to go arm in arm with a girl as in the companionship of a boy.

It is these and kindred facts upon which the WOMAN REBEL will dwell from time to time and from which it is hoped the young girl will derive some knowledge of her nature, and conduct her life upon such knowledge.

It will also be the aim of the WOMAN REBEL to advocate the prevention of conception and to impart such knowledge in the columns of this paper.

Other subjects, including the slavery through motherhood; through things, the home, public opinion and so forth, will be dealt with.

It is also the aim of this paper to circulate among those women who work in prostitution; to voice their wrongs; to expose the police persecution which hovers over them and to give free expression to their thoughts, hopes and opinions.

And at all times the WOMAN REBEL will strenuously advocate economic emancipation.

The Prevention of Conception

Is there any reason why women should not receive clean, harmless, scientific knowledge on how to prevent conception? Everybody is aware that the old, stupid fallacy that such knowledge will cause a girl to enter into prostitution has long been shattered. Seldom does a prostitute become pregnant. Seldom does the girl practicing promiscuity become pregnant. The woman of the upper middle class have all available knowledge and implements to prevent conception. The woman of the lower middle class is struggling for this knowledge. She tries various methods of prevention, and after a few years of experience plus medical advice succeeds in discovering some method suitable to her individual self. The woman of the people is the only one left in ignorance of this information. Her neighbors, relatives and friends tell her stories of special devices and the success of them all. They tell her also of the blood-sucking men with M.D. after their names who perform operations for the price of so-and-so. But the working woman's purse is thin. Its far cheaper to have a baby, "though God knows what it will do after it gets here." Then, too, all other classes of women live in places where there is at least a semblance of privacy and sanitation. It is easier for them to care for themselves whereas the large majority of the women of the people have no bathing or sanitary conveniences. This accounts too for the fact that the higher the standard of living, the more care can be taken and fewer children result. No plagues, famine or wars could ever frighten the capitalist class so much as the universal practice of the prevention of conception. On the other hand no better method could be utilized for increasing the wages of the workers.

As is well known, a law exists forbidding the imparting of information on this subject, the penalty being several years' imprisonment. Is it not time to defy this law! And what fitter place could be found than in the pages of the WOMAN REBEL!

Marriage

Marriage, which is a personal agreement between a man and a woman, should be no concern of the State or of the Church. Never have either of these institutions interested themselves in the happiness or health of the individual. Never have they concerned themselves that children be born in healthy and clean surroundings, which might insure their highest development. The Church has been and is anxious only if a child be trained Catholic, Baptist, Methodist and so forth. The State and the Church are concerned only in maintaining and perpetuating themselves even to the detriment and sacrifice of the human race. In the willingness to accept without protest or question the indignities imposed through the barbarities of the Law, together with the stupid superstitions of the Church, can be traced a great proportion of the world's misery.

That there exists in all Nature an attraction which takes place between particles of bodies and unites to form a chemical compound is not doubted. This same attraction exists in men and women and will, unconsciously perhaps, cause them to seek a mate just as other organisms do.

Priests and marriage laws have no power or control over this attraction nor can they make desirable a union where this attraction does not exist.

Marriage laws abrogate the freedom of woman by enforcing upon her a continuous sexual slavery and a compulsory motherhood.

Marriage laws have been dictated and

dominated by the Church always and ever upon the unquestionable grounds of the wisdom of the Bible.

A man and woman who under a natural condition avow their love for each other should be immediately qualified by this to give expression to their love or to perpetuate the race without the necessity of a public declaration.

A reciprocal, spontaneous voluntary declaration of love and mutual feelings by a man and woman is the expression of Nature's desires. Were it not natural it would not be so and being natural it is right.

The marriage institution viewed from the light of human experience and the demands of the individual has proven a failure. Statistical reports show that one out of every twelve marriages in the United States has resulted in a divorce—which does not include the thousands of women who want divorces—but on account of the Church and conventions are restrained from obtaining them. Nor does it mention the thousands of women too poor to obtain the price to set in motion the ponderous machinery of the divorce courts. The divorce courts give us only a hint of the dissatisfaction and unhappiness underlying the institution of marriage.

Superstition; blind following; unthinking obedience on the part of working women; together with the pretence, hypocrisy and sham morality of the women of the middle class have been the greatest obstacles in the obtaining of woman's freedom.

Every change in social life is accomplished only by a struggle. Rebel women of the world must fight for the freedom to harmonize their actions with the natural desires of their being, for their deeds are but the concrete expressions of their thoughts.

The Post Office Ban

The woman rebel feels proud the post office authorities did not approve of her.

She shall blush with shame if ever she be approved of by officialism of "comstockism."

Rebel Women Wanted

Who deny the right of the State to deprive women of such knowledge as would enable them to take upon themselves voluntary motherhood.

Who deny the right of the State to prohibit such knowledge which would add to the freedom and happiness of the people.

Who demand that those desiring to live together in love shall be provided with such knowledge and experience as Science has developed, which would prevent conception.

Who will assist in the work of increasing the demand for this information.

Who have the courage and backbone to fight with "THE WOMAN REBEL" against this outrageous suppression, whereby a woman has no control of the function of motherhood.

Who are willing to enter this fight, and continue to the end.

Study Questions

1. Who likely would sympathize with Sanger? Explain.

2. Who would likely see Sanger as a threat to America? Explain.

Progressive Era Amendments (1913–1920)

Amendments to the U.S. Constitution have tended to come in waves. The states ratified the first ten amendments as a group, known as the Bill of Rights, in 1791 (p. 39). In the years following the Civil War, three Reconstruction Amendments were ratified (p. 47). Then forty-three years passed with no amendments, until 1913 when the Sixteenth and Seventeenth Amendments were ratified. Two more amendments soon followed. Historians refer to the Sixteenth through Nineteenth Amendments collectively as "Progressive Era Amendments" in view of both the time and the spirit of their adoption.

The Sixteenth Amendment was preceded by decades of debate, and court battles, over attempts by Congress to tax individual incomes. A strict reading of the Constitution limited Congress to indirect taxation of states in proportion to population, disallowing the direct taxation of individuals on their incomes. The Sixteenth Amendment inserted language into the Constitution stating plainly that henceforth Congress may tax individual incomes. In the years that followed, personal and corporate income tax became the chief sources of federal revenue, rather than tariffs. Income taxation also provided progressive reformers with a tool for redistributing wealth in American society.

The Seventeenth Amendment served another progressive aim: in bypassing the state legislatures' choice of U.S. senators, it linked the electorate more tightly to the federal government. Individuals thereafter became accustomed to direct federal entitlements.

The Eighteenth Amendment exemplifies the progressives' vision of using government to scientifically regulate the economy in the name of the common good. In this case, medical science identified health risks from liquor consumption, and social science identified a link from alcoholism to poverty and crime. However, in the 1920s Americans would recognize how difficult it was to enforce the ban on liquor.

The Nineteenth Amendment expanded voting rights in federal elections to women, a practice that already had become widespread among the states. Some women opposed this amendment on the grounds that they trusted their fathers and husbands to vote on behalf of the entire household and that they feared voting rights would come with a cost, such as having to serve as jurors in cases involving grotesque crimes. Other women endorsed the amendment as an extension of women's caretaking role from the home into the community, even as progressives such as Florence Kelley (National Consumers League) and Jane Addams (the Hull House settlement) had assumed public roles in the preceding decades.

Sixteenth Amendment

(proposed, 1909; ratified, 1913)

The Congress shall have power to lay and collect taxes on incomes, from whatever source derived, without apportionment among the several States, and without regard to any census or enumeration.

Seventeenth Amendment

(proposed, 1912; ratified, 1913)

The Senate of the United States shall be composed of two Senators from each State, elected by the people thereof, for six years; and each Senator shall have one vote. The electors in each State shall have the qualifications requisite for electors of the most numerous branch of the State legislatures.

When vacancies happen in the representation of any State in the Senate, the executive authority of such State shall issue writs of election to fill such vacancies: Provided, That the legislature of any State may empower the executive thereof to make temporary appointments until the people fill the vacancies by election as the legislature may direct.

This amendment shall not be so construed as to affect the election or term of any Senator chosen before it becomes valid as part of the Constitution.

Eighteenth Amendment

(proposed, 1917; ratified, 1919)

1. After one year from the ratification of this article the manufacture, sale, or transportation of intoxicating liquors within, the importation thereof into, or the exportation thereof from the United States and all territory subject to the jurisdiction thereof for beverage purposes is hereby prohibited.

2. The Congress and the several States shall have concurrent power to enforce this article by appropriate legislation.

3. This article shall be inoperative unless it shall have been ratified as an amendment to the Constitution by the legislatures of the several States, as provided in the Constitution, within seven years from the date of the submission hereof to the States by the Congress.

Nineteenth Amendment

(proposed, 1919; ratified, 1920)

The right of citizens of the United States to vote shall not be denied or abridged by the United States or by any State on account of sex.

Congress shall have power to enforce this article by appropriate legislation.

Study Questions

1. Identify some characteristics of progressivism that were reflected in the Sixteenth through Nineteenth Amendments.

2. Explain how the Sixteenth and Seventeenth Amendments transformed voters into a new kind of stakeholder in the arena of national politics.

World War I (1914–1918)

Preceding Conditions

1. **Nationalism:** With the decline of the Ottoman Empire, distinct ethnic groups desired to have their own nations in the Balkan peninsula. Meanwhile, Germany had been recently unified by Otto von Bismarck under a nationalist spirit that celebrated German culture.

2. **Standing Armies:** European nations were developing larger and more powerful armies, even in times of peace. In 1905, Alfred von Schlieffen formulated a strategy anticipating Germany's need to defend itself to both the east and the west should war ever come. The Schlieffen Plan called for quick and decisive action against France to the west, followed by a second attack against Russia to the east.

3. **Imperial Ambitions:** European nations desired both to protect and to expand their colonies throughout the world.

4. **Entangling Alliances:** Although intending to pledge mutual protection, a series of alliances also entailed coordinated aggression against outside parties that displayed belligerence. Thus, one nation quickly could become entangled in the conflict between two other nations, in a domino effect that might soon involve many other nations.

    A. **The Triple Alliance (1882):** Austria-Hungary, Germany, and Italy pledged to defend each other against other European nations.
    B. **The *Entente Cordiale*, or "Friendly Agreement" (1904):** France and Britain pledged to defend each other against other European nations.
    C. **The *Triple Entente*, or "Three-way Agreement" (1907):** Russia joined with France and Britain, expanding the *Entente Cordiale*.

5. **Tense Borderlands:** Because existing political boundaries did not always follow the ethnic and religious dimensions of human geography, several European national borders were tense. For example, Austria seized Bosnia and Herzegovina in 1908. Then Serbia, supported by Russia, incited Bosnians to revolt against Austria.

The Outbreak of War

On June 28, 1914 in Sarajevo, Bosnia, a nineteen-year-old student named Gavrilo Princip shot Archduke Franz Ferdinand, the heir to the Austro-Hungarian throne, and his wife Sophie, Duchess of Hohenberg. The assassin had been sponsored by Serbian military officers intending to establish a unified Serbian nation, free of Austro-Hungarian influences. His gunshot acted like a match tossed into a powder keg, igniting war throughout the Balkans and across Europe; eventually, even the United States would enter the conflict.

First, Austria declared war against Serbia. Then Russia, being linked by a secret treaty to Serbia, mobilized for war against Austria. Germany, implementing the Schlieffen Plan, declared war against France and Russia. Great Britain, being pledged to assist those nations, declared war against Germany. Italy, however did not fulfill the expectation of the Triple Alliance. Faulting Austria-Hungary for aggression in the Balkans and lured by the opportunity to gain some territory, Italy joined the Allies—France, Britain, and Russia—in 1915. Battles were waged not only in Europe, but throughout the world, as the belligerents competed for each other's colonies in a global conflagration.

American Involvement

The United States remained officially neutral, although lending more financial support to the Allies than to the Central Powers. In May 1915, a German torpedo sunk the British passenger ship *Lusitania*, killing 128 U.S. civilians. Even so, President Woodrow Wilson pledged the nation to a course of neutrality. Wilson hoped especially to position the United States as a peacemaker which could arbitrate among the European nations at the close of the conflict.

In early 1917, however, British intelligence intercepted a telegraph message from German foreign secretary Arthur Zimmermann designed to entice Mexico to join the Central Powers. Mexico had lost about one third of its territory to the United States at the conclusion of the Mexican War in 1848. More recently, Theodore Roosevelt had established the United States as a policeman of Latin America—a move that from the Mexican perspective interfered with their domestic affairs. Wilson therefore judged the Zimmermann telegram as a clear and immediate threat to American security. On April 2, he urged Congress to declare war against Germany, seeking to make the world "safe for democracy."

An overwhelming majority of the votes in both the House and the Senate responded in favor of war on April 6. In May, Congress passed the Selective Service Act, drafting civilians, ages 21 to 30, into military service. In June, 15,000 U.S. troops entered the European theater; many others were in training to follow them. In May 1918, 60,000 members of the American Expeditionary Force supported British efforts to hold the Germans back from Paris. By summer's end, Gen. John J. Pershing had one million American troops positioned against a declining, weakened Germany army.

The western front—the line between Germany and France—filled with atrocities. Both sides dug themselves into trenches, where a bloody stalemate had persisted for years. In 1915 alone, 1.4 million French soldiers died on the front. On a single day in 1916, 60,000 British soldiers died. In 1917, 400,000 French soldiers gave their lives so the army could advance a mere four miles. By 1918, the western battle had become a war of attrition: which side would run out of troops first? The Germans staged a final push in July, but the Allies now had strong reinforcements from America. By November 11—today commemorated as Veterans Day—Germany had no choice but armistice.

The Impact of the War upon the Home Front

World War I transformed America at home. On the one hand, the war mobilization effort witnessed progressivism at its finest; on the other hand, the bleak reality of war itself testified to the human limitations of progressive reform.

The Sixteenth Amendment, ratified in 1913, had authorized Congress to tax personal and corporate incomes. Initially, Congress set the highest tax rate at 7%. During the war, this was raised to 70%. Consistent with the progressive movement's desire to redistribute wealth, income taxes focused on the wealthiest corporations and individuals. Taxes generated about one third the revenue required to fund the war, with "liberty bonds"—loans from investors—covering the rest.

In July 1917, Congress established the War Industries Board, headed by Bernard Baruch, to coordinate industrial production around the war effort. The WIB gathered data and made recommendations for quantities and costs of production. Baruch urged voluntary compliance, rather than coercion, hoping that industries would cooperate with the government in the name of the common good.

In August 1917, Congress established the Food Administration, directed by Herbert Hoover. Here again the goal was to draw private individuals into a public effort to supply food for the Allies in Europe. Americans developed the habits of abstaining from meat on Mondays and from wheat on Wednesdays, while subsisting as much as possible on mere potatoes so that more food would be available to fill the needs in Europe. "If U fast, U beat U boats," so went the slogan, but "if U feast, U boats beat U."

In April 1918, Congress established a third major agency, the War Labor Policies Board. Cooperating with the American Federation of Labor, the WLPB limited work days to eight-hour shifts, with time-and-half paid for any overtime hours. The eight-hour day had been proposed a generation earlier, but lacked national support during the Gilded Age. The exigencies of World War I, however, lent progressivism a boost. The government now would be more involved than ever before in regulating the economy for the common good.

Meanwhile, the Wilson administration also deployed propaganda to rally support for America's entrance into the war. The Committee on Public Information, established in April 1917, sought to educate Americans, especially immigrants, about the virtues of democracy and the vices of German imperialism. Led by George Creel, the CPI used literature, film clips, stump speeches, and posters to promote "100% Americanism": no longer would immigrants identify as Italian-Americans or German-Americans, especially not at a time when the nation was at war with the German fatherland. All Americans must be, simply, Americans—100% and no less. Even food had to change its name. Sauerkraut became "liberty cabbage"; and hamburgers, "liberty sandwiches."

But even in America, liberty was not universal. The Espionage Act (1917) banned the sending of treasonous publications in the U.S. mail. The Sedition Act (1918) prohibited anyone from speaking disloyally about the government or military. Eugene V. Debs, a socialist politician, was imprisoned in 1919, but nonetheless ran for president from his jail cell in 1920. Charles T. Schenck, the secretary of the Socialist Party, was convicted for distributing treasonous pamphlets. In the quest for ordered liberty, Americans agreed to sacrifice a degree of freedom of speech in order to guarantee national security.

Meanwhile, progressive reformers began to lose heart. Many of them, including Jane Addams and William Jennings Bryan, had been pacifists. They felt betrayed by Wilson's call for war, and yet their visions for scientifically managing society also proved inept in the face of human nature's recalcitrant belligerence. As the anti-war progressive Randolph Bourne wrote to the pro-war progressive John Dewey, "If the war is too strong for you to prevent, how is it going to be weak enough for you to control and mold to your liberal purposes?"

The Treaty of Versailles

In January 1918, President Wilson delivered a message to Congress, outlining fourteen points for a postwar peace. The Treaty of Versailles (1919) incorporated many of his suggestions. However, the U.S. Congress refused to ratify the treaty. Peace thus was established in Europe without America giving its full assent. Republican Senators, led by Henry Cabot Lodge, objected particularly to the proposed League of Nations, which risked surrendering U.S. sovereignty to an international body.

Study Questions

1. Debate: The outbreak of World War I came inevitably; even if Gavrilo Princip had not fired a single shot, a global war would have erupted sooner or later.

2. What prompted the United States to enter World War I?

3. How did America's involvement in World War I transform domestic affairs?

Woodrow Wilson, Second Inaugural Address (1917)

As Woodrow Wilson recited the oath of the presidential office for the second time, Europe was at war but the United States remained, thus far, officially neutral. Even so, Wilson hinted that Americans sympathized more with Britain and the Allies than with Germany and the Central Powers. The United States, for the time being, would hold the course of neutrality—not apathetically, but "stand[ing] firm in armed neutrality."

The four years which have elapsed since last I stood in this place have been crowded with counsel and action of the most vital interest and consequence. Perhaps no equal period in our history has been so fruitful of important reforms in our economic and industrial life or so full of significant changes in the spirit and purpose of our political action. We have sought very thoughtfully to set our house in order, correct the grosser errors and abuses of our industrial life, liberate and quicken the processes of our national genius and energy, and lift our politics to a broader view of the people's essential interests.

It is a record of singular variety and singular distinction. But I shall not attempt to review it. It speaks for itself and will be of increasing influence as the years go by. This is not the time for retrospect. It is time rather to speak our thoughts and purposes concerning the present and the immediate future.

Although we have centered counsel and action with such unusual concentration and success upon the great problems of domestic legislation to which we addressed ourselves four years ago, other matters have more and more forced themselves upon our attention—matters lying outside our own life as a nation and over which we had no control, but which, despite our wish to keep free of them, have drawn us more and more irresistibly into their own current and influence.

It has been impossible to avoid them. They have affected the life of the whole world. They have shaken men everywhere with a passion and an apprehension they never knew before. It has been hard to preserve calm counsel while the thought of our own people swayed this way and that under their influence. We are a composite and cosmopolitan people. We are of the blood of all the nations that are at war. The currents of our thoughts as well as the currents of our trade run quick at all seasons back and forth between us and them. The war inevitably set its mark from the first alike upon our minds, our industries, our commerce, our politics and our social action. To be indifferent to it, or independent of it, was out of the question.

And yet all the while we have been conscious that we were not part of it. In that consciousness, despite many divisions, we have drawn closer together. We have been deeply wronged upon the seas, but we have not wished to wrong or injure in return; have retained throughout the consciousness of standing in some sort apart, intent upon an interest that transcended the immediate issues of the war itself.

As some of the injuries done us have become intolerable we have still been clear that we wished nothing for ourselves that we were not ready to demand for all mankind—fair dealing, justice, the freedom to live and to be at ease against organized wrong.

It is in this spirit and with this thought that we have grown more and more aware, more and more certain that the part we wished to play was the part of those who mean to vindicate and fortify peace. We have been obliged to arm ourselves to make good our claim to a certain minimum of right and of freedom of action. We stand firm in armed neutrality since it seems that in no other way we can demonstrate what it is we insist upon and cannot forget. We may even be drawn on, by circumstances, not by our own purpose or desire, to a more active assertion of our rights as we see them and a more immediate association with the great struggle itself. But nothing will alter our thought or our purpose. They are too clear to be obscured. They are too deeply rooted in the principles of our national life to be altered. We desire neither conquest nor advantage. We wish nothing that can be had only at the cost of another people. We always professed unselfish purpose and we covet the opportunity to prove our professions are sincere.

There are many things still to be done at home, to clarify our own politics and add new vitality to the industrial processes of our own life, and we shall do them as time and opportunity serve, but we realize that the greatest things that remain to be done must be done with the whole world for stage and in cooperation with the wide and universal forces of mankind, and we are making our spirits ready for those things.

We are provincials no longer. The tragic events of the thirty months of vital turmoil through which we have just passed have made us citizens of the world. There can be no turning back. Our own fortunes as a nation are involved whether we would have it so or not.

And yet we are not the less Americans on that account. We shall be the more American if we but remain true to the principles in which we have been bred. They are not the principles of a province or of a single continent. We have known and boasted all along that they were the principles of a liberated mankind. These, therefore, are the things we shall stand for, whether in war or in peace:

That all nations are equally interested in the peace of the world and in the political stability of free peoples, and equally responsible for their maintenance; that the essential principle of peace is the actual equality of nations in all matters of right or privilege; that peace cannot securely or justly rest upon an armed balance of power; that governments derive all their just powers from the consent of the governed and that no other powers should be supported by the common thought, purpose or power of the family of nations; that the seas should be equally free and safe for the use of all peoples, under rules set up by common agreement and consent, and that, so far as practicable, they should be accessible to all upon equal terms; that national armaments shall be limited to the necessities of national order and domestic safety; that the community of interest and of power upon which peace must henceforth depend imposes upon each nation the duty of seeing to it that all influences proceeding from its own citizens meant to encourage or assist revolution in other states should be sternly and effectually suppressed and prevented.

I need not argue these principles to you, my fellow countrymen; they are your own part and parcel of your own thinking and your own motives in affairs. They spring up native amongst us. Upon this as a platform of purpose and of action we can stand together. And it is imperative that we should stand together. We are being forged into a new unity amidst the fires that now blaze throughout the world. In their ardent heat we shall, in God's Providence, let us hope, be purged of faction and division, purified of the errant humors of party and of private interest, and shall stand forth in the days to come with a new dignity of national pride and spirit. Let each man see to it that the dedication is in his own heart, the high purpose of the nation in his own mind, ruler of his own will and desire.

I stand here and have taken the high and solemn oath to which you have been audience because the people of the United States have chosen me for this august delegation of power and have by their gracious judgment named me their leader in affairs.

I know now what the task means. I real-ize to the full the responsibility which it involves. I pray God I may be given the wisdom and the prudence to do my duty in the true spirit of this great people. I am their servant and can succeed only as they sustain and guide me by their confidence and their counsel. The thing I shall count upon, the thing without which neither counsel nor action will avail, is the unity of America—an America united in feeling, in purpose and in its vision of duty, of opportunity and of service.

We are to beware of all men who would turn the tasks and the necessities of the nation to their own private profit or use them for the building up of private power.

United alike in the conception of our duty and in the high resolve to perform it in the face of all men, let us dedicate ourselves to the great task to which we must now set our hand. For myself I beg your tolerance, your countenance and your united aid.

The shadows that now lie dark upon our path will soon be dispelled, and we shall walk with the light all about us if we be but true to ourselves—to ourselves as we have wished to be known in the counsels of the world and in the thought of all those who love liberty and justice and the right exalted.

Study Questions

1. "Perhaps no equal period in our history has been so fruitful of important reforms," said Wilson concerning the accomplishments of his first term as president. Although Wilson did not summarize those reforms in this speech, list a few examples drawn from elsewhere in this book that illustrate Wilson's role as a progressive reformer.

2. What did Wilson mean when he said, "We stand firm in armed neutrality?"

3. For what principles would Wilson's America take its stand "whether in war or in peace"?

Woodrow Wilson, "War Message" (1917)

Less than one month after his second inaugural address, pledging "armed neutrality," President Woodrow Wilson called upon Congress to declare war against Germany, a nation he claimed had embarked on a "warfare against mankind . . . a war against all nations." American lives already had been lost, and recent intelligence reports indicated new threats on the horizon. What else did America's duty require, but to enter the war for the aid of the Allies and the defense of the United States? "The world," asserted Wilson, "must be made safe for democracy."

Gentlemen of the Congress:

I have called the Congress into extraordinary session because there are serious, very serious, choices of policy to be made, and made immediately, which it was neither right nor constitutionally permissible that I should assume the responsibility of making.

On the 3d of February last I officially laid before you the extraordinary announcement of the Imperial German Government that on and after the 1st day of February it was its purpose to put aside all restraints of law or of humanity and use its submarines to sink every vessel that sought to approach either the ports of Great Britain and Ireland or the western coasts of Europe or any of the ports controlled by the enemies of Germany within the Mediterranean.

That had seemed to be the object of the German submarine warfare earlier in the war, but since April of last year the Imperial Government had somewhat restrained the commanders of its undersea craft in conformity with its promise then given to us that passenger boats should not be sunk and that due warning would be given to all other vessels which its submarines might seek to destroy, when no resistance was offered or escape attempted, and care

taken that their crews were given at least a fair chance to save their lives in their open boats. The precautions taken were meagre and haphazard enough, as was proved in distressing instance after instance in the progress of the cruel and unmanly business, but a certain degree of restraint was observed.

The new policy has swept every restriction aside. Vessels of every kind, whatever their flag, their character, their cargo, their destination, their errand, have been ruthlessly sent to the bottom without warning and without thought of help or mercy for those on board, the vessels of friendly neutrals along with those of belligerents. Even hospital ships and ships carrying relief to the sorely bereaved and stricken people of Belgium, though the latter were provided with safe-conduct through the proscribed areas by the German Government itself and were distinguished by unmistakable marks of identity, have been sunk with the same reckless lack of compassion or of principle.

I was for a little while unable to believe that such things would in fact be done by any government that had hitherto subscribed to the humane practices of civilized nations. International law had its origin in the attempt to set up some law which would be respected and observed upon the seas, where no nation had right of dominion and where lay the free highways of the world. By painful stage after stage has that law been built up, with meagre enough results, indeed, after all was accomplished that could be accomplished, but always with a clear view, at least, of what the heart and conscience of mankind demanded.

This minimum of right the German Government has swept aside under the plea of retaliation and necessity and because it had no weapons which it could use at sea except these which it is impossible to employ as it is employing them without throwing to the winds all scruples of humanity or of respect for the understandings that were supposed to underlie the intercourse of the world. I am not now thinking of the loss of property involved, immense and serious as that is, but only of the wanton and wholesale destruction of the lives of noncombatants, men, women, and children, engaged in pursuits which have always, even in the darkest periods of modern history, been deemed innocent and legitimate. Property can be paid for; the lives of peaceful and innocent people can not be. The present German submarine warfare against commerce is a warfare against mankind.

It is a war against all nations. American ships have been sunk, American lives taken, in ways which it has stirred us very deeply to learn of, but the ships and people of other neutral and friendly nations have been sunk and overwhelmed in the waters in the same way. There has been no discrimination. The challenge is to all mankind. Each nation must decide for itself how it will meet it. The choice we make for ourselves must be made with a moderation of counsel and a temperateness of judgment befitting our character and our motives as a nation. We must put excited feeling away. Our motive will not be revenge or the victorious assertion of the physical might of the nation, but only the vindication of right, of human right, of which we are only a single champion.

When I addressed the Congress on the 26th of February last, I thought that it would suffice to assert our neutral rights with arms, our right to use the seas against unlawful interference, our right to keep our people safe against unlawful violence. But armed neutrality, it now appears, is impracticable. Because submarines are in effect outlaws when used as the German submarines have been used against merchant shipping, it is impossible to defend ships against their attacks as the law of nations has assumed that merchantmen would defend themselves against privateers or cruisers, visible craft giving chase upon the open sea. It is common prudence in such circumstances, grim necessity indeed, to endeavour to destroy them before they have shown their own intention. They must be dealt with upon sight, if dealt with at all. The German Government denies the right of neutrals to use arms at all within the areas of the sea which it has proscribed, even in the defense of rights which no modern publicist has ever before questioned their right to defend. The intimation is conveyed that the armed guards which we have placed on our merchant ships will be treated as beyond the pale of law and subject to be dealt with as pirates would be. Armed neutrality is ineffectual enough at best; in such circumstances and in the face of such pretensions it is worse than ineffectual; it is likely only to produce what it was meant to prevent; it is practically certain to draw us into the war without either the rights or the effectiveness of belligerents. There is one choice we can not make, we are incapable of making: we will not choose the path of submission and suffer the most sacred rights of our nation and our people to be ignored or violated. The wrongs against which we now array ourselves are no common wrongs; they cut to the very roots of human life.

With a profound sense of the solemn and even tragical character of the step I am taking and of the grave responsibilities which it involves, but in unhesitating obedience to what I deem my constitutional duty, I advise that the Congress declare the recent course of the Imperial German Government to be in fact nothing less than war against the Government and people of the United States; that it formally accept the status of belligerent which has thus been thrust upon it, and that it take immediate steps not only to put the country in a more thorough state of defense but also to exert all its power and employ all its resources to bring the Government of the German Empire to terms and end the war.

What this will involve is clear. It will involve the utmost practicable cooperation in counsel and action with the governments now at war with Germany, and, as incident to that, the extension to those governments of the most liberal financial credits, in order that our resources may so far as possible be added to theirs. It will involve the organization and mobilization of all the material resources of the country to supply the materials of war and serve the incidental needs of the nation in the most abundant and yet the most economical and efficient way possible. It will involve the immediate full equipment of the Navy in all respects but particularly in supplying it with the best means of dealing with the enemy's submarines. It will involve the immediate addition to the armed forces of the United States already provided for by law in case of war at least 500,000 men, who should, in my opinion, be chosen upon the principle of universal liability to service, and also the authorization of subsequent additional increments of equal force so soon as they may be needed and can be handled in training. It will involve also, of course, the granting of adequate credits to the Government, sustained, I hope, so far as they can equitably be sustained by the present generation, by well conceived taxation. . . .

We have no quarrel with the German people. We have no feeling towards them but one of sympathy and friendship. It was not upon their impulse that their Government acted in entering this war. It was not with their previous knowledge or approval. It was a war determined upon as wars used to be determined upon in the old, unhappy days when peoples were nowhere consulted by their rulers and wars were provoked and waged in the interest of dynasties or of little groups of ambitious men who were accustomed to use their fellow men as pawns and tools. Self-governed nations do not fill their neighbour states with spies or set the course of intrigue to bring about some critical posture of affairs which will give them an opportunity to strike and make conquest. Such designs can be successfully worked out only under cover and where no one has the right to ask questions. Cunningly contrived plans of deception or aggression, carried, it may be, from generation to generation, can be worked out and kept from the light only within the privacy of courts or behind the carefully guarded confidences of a narrow and privileged class. They are happily impossible where public opinion commands and insists upon full information concerning all the nation's affairs.

A steadfast concert for peace can never be maintained except by a partnership of democratic nations. No autocratic government could be trusted to keep faith within it or observe its covenants. It must be a league of honour, a partnership of opinion. Intrigue would eat its vitals away; the plottings of inner circles who could plan what they would and render account to no one would be a corruption seated at its very heart. Only free peoples can hold their purpose and their honour steady to a common end and prefer the interests of mankind to any narrow interest of their own.

Does not every American feel that assurance has been added to our hope for the future peace of the world by the wonderful and heartening things that have been happening within the last few weeks in Russia? Russia was known by those who knew it best to have been always in fact democratic at heart, in all the vital habits of her thought, in all the intimate relationships of her people that spoke their natural instinct, their habitual attitude towards life. The autocracy that crowned the summit of her political structure, long as it had

stood and terrible as was the reality of its power, was not in fact Russian in origin, character, or purpose; and now it has been shaken off and the great, generous Russian people have been added in all their naive majesty and might to the forces that are fighting for freedom in the world, for justice, and for peace. Here is a fit partner for a league of honour.

One of the things that has served to convince us that the Prussian autocracy was not and could never be our friend is that from the very outset of the present war it has filled our unsuspecting communities and even our offices of government with spies and set criminal intrigues everywhere afoot against our national unity of counsel, our peace within and without our industries and our commerce. Indeed it is now evident that its spies were here even before the war began; and it is unhappily not a matter of conjecture but a fact proved in our courts of justice that the intrigues which have more than once come perilously near to disturbing the peace and dislocating the industries of the country have been carried on at the instigation, with the support, and even under the personal direction of official agents of the Imperial Government accredited to the Government of the United States. Even in checking these things and trying to extirpate them we have sought to put the most generous interpretation possible upon them because we knew that their source lay, not in any hostile feeling or purpose of the German people towards us (who were, no doubt, as ignorant of them as we ourselves were), but only in the selfish designs of a Government that did what it pleased and told its people nothing. But they have played their part in serving to convince us at last that that Government entertains no real friendship for us and means to act against our peace and security at its convenience. That it means to stir up enemies against us at our very doors the intercepted note to the German Minister at Mexico City is eloquent evidence.

We are accepting this challenge of hostile purpose because we know that in such a government, following such methods, we can never have a friend; and that in the presence of its organized power, always lying in wait to accomplish we know not what purpose, there can be no assured security for the democratic governments of the world. We are now about to accept gauge of battle with this natural foe to liberty and shall, if necessary, spend the whole force of the nation to check and nullify its pretensions and its power. We are glad, now that we see the facts with no veil of false pretense about them, to fight thus for the ultimate peace of the world and for the liberation of its peoples, the German peoples included: for the rights of nations great and small and the privilege of men everywhere to choose their way of life and of obedience. The world must be made safe for democracy. Its peace must be planted upon the tested foundations of political liberty. We have no selfish ends to serve. We desire no conquest, no dominion. We seek no indemnities for ourselves, no material compensation for the sacrifices we shall freely make. We are but one of the champions of the rights of mankind. We shall be satisfied when those rights have been made as secure as the faith and the freedom of nations can make them.

Just because we fight without rancour and without selfish object, seeking nothing for ourselves but what we shall wish to share with all free peoples, we shall, I feel confident, conduct our operations as belligerents without passion and ourselves observe with proud punctilio the principles of right and of fair play we profess to be fighting for.

I have said nothing of the governments allied with the Imperial Government of Germany because they have not made war upon us or challenged us to defend our right and our honour. The Austro-Hungarian Government has, indeed, avowed its unqualified endorsement and acceptance of the reckless and lawless submarine warfare adopted now without disguise by the Imperial German Government, and it has therefore not been possible for this Government to receive Count Tarnowski, the Ambassador recently accredited to this Government by the Imperial and Royal Government of Austria-Hungary; but that Government has not actually engaged in warfare against citizens of the United States on the seas, and I take the liberty, for the present at least, of postponing a discussion of our relations with the authorities at Vienna. We enter this war only where we are clearly forced into it because there are no other means of defending our rights.

It will be all the easier for us to conduct ourselves as belligerents in a high spirit of right and fairness because we act without animus, not in enmity towards a people or with the desire to bring any injury or disadvantage upon them, but only in armed opposition to an irresponsible government which has thrown aside all considerations of humanity and of right and is running amuck. We are, let me say again, the sincere friends of the German people, and shall desire nothing so much as the early reestablishment of intimate relations of mutual advantage between us—however hard it may be for them, for the time being, to believe that this is spoken from our hearts. We have borne with their present government through all these bitter months because of that friendship—exercising a patience and forbearance which would otherwise have been impossible. We shall, happily, still have an opportunity to prove that friendship in our daily attitude and actions towards the millions of men and women of German birth and native sympathy, who live amongst us and share our life, and we shall be proud to prove it towards all who are in fact loyal to their neighbours and to the Government in the hour of test. They are, most of them, as true and loyal Americans as if they had never known any other fealty or allegiance. They will be prompt to stand with us in rebuking and restraining the few who may be of a different mind and purpose. If there should be disloyalty, it will be dealt with with a firm hand of stern repression; but, if it lifts its head at all, it will lift it only here and there and without countenance except from a lawless and malignant few.

It is a distressing and oppressive duty, gentlemen of the Congress, which I have performed in thus addressing you. There are, it may be, many months of fiery trial and sacrifice ahead of us. It is a fearful thing to lead this great peaceful people into war, into the most terrible and disastrous of all wars, civilization itself seeming to be in the balance. But the right is more precious than peace, and we shall fight for the things which we have always carried nearest our hearts—for democracy, for the right of those who submit to authority to have a voice in their own governments, for the rights and liberties of small nations, for a universal dominion of right by such a concert of free peoples as shall bring peace and safety to all nations and make the world itself at last free. To such a task we can dedicate our lives and our fortunes, everything that we are and everything that we have, with the pride of those who know that the day has come when America is privileged to spend her blood and her might for the principles that gave her birth and happiness and the peace which she has treasured. God helping her, she can do no other.

Study Question

1. Wilson said, "We have no quarrel with the German people." Why, then, did he urge Congress to declare that a state of war existed between Germany and the United States?

2. How, exactly, did Wilson think warfare could make the world "safe for democracy"?

Woodrow Wilson, "Fourteen Points" (1918)

Woodrow Wilson remained an idealist his entire life. Amid the turmoil of World War I, he envisioned a peaceful order in which nations would have self-determination, would pursue the American values of capitalism and democracy, and would cooperate with one another under the League of Nations. For Wilson, there was no contradiction among these three points. But would self-determination necessarily lead a nation to embrace American values? And would America herself agree to be subordinate to the League of Nations? Indeed, history would demonstrate that Wilson's greatest hope also was his greatest tragedy.

Delivered by President Woodrow Wilson to a Joint Session of Congress, January 8, 1918.

Gentlemen of the Congress:

Once more, as repeatedly before, the spokesmen of the Central Empires have indicated their desire to discuss the objects of the war and the possible basis of a general peace. Parleys have been in progress at Brest-Litovsk between Russian representatives and representatives of the Central Powers to which the attention of all the belligerents have been invited for the purpose of ascertaining whether it may be possible to extend these parleys into a general conference with regard to terms of peace and settlement.

The Russian representatives presented not only a perfectly definite statement of the principles upon which they would be willing to conclude peace but also an equally definite program of the concrete application of those principles. The representatives of the Central Powers, on their part, presented an outline of settlement which, if much less definite, seemed susceptible of liberal interpretation until their specific program of practical terms was added. That program proposed no concessions at all either to the sovereignty of Russia or to the preferences of the populations with whose fortunes it dealt, but meant, in a word, that the Central Empires were to keep every foot of territory their armed forces had occupied—every province, every city, every point of vantage —as a permanent addition to their territories and their power.

It is a reasonable conjecture that the general principles of settlement which they at first suggested originated with the more liberal statesmen of Germany and Austria, the men who have begun to feel the force of their own people's thought and purpose, while the concrete terms of actual settlement came from the military leaders who have no thought but to keep what they have got. The negotiations have been broken off. The Russian representatives were sincere and in earnest. They cannot entertain such proposals of conquest and domination.

The whole incident is full of significances. It is also full of perplexity. With whom are the Russian representatives dealing? For whom are the representatives of the Central Empires speaking? Are they speaking for the majorities of their respective parliaments or for the minority parties, that military and imperialistic minority which has so far dominated their whole policy and controlled the affairs of Turkey and of the Balkan states which have felt obliged to become their associates in this war?

The Russian representatives have insisted, very justly, very wisely, and in the true spirit of modern democracy, that the conferences they have been holding with the Teutonic and Turkish statesmen should be held within open not closed, doors, and all the world has been audience, as was desired. To whom have we been listening, then? To those who speak the spirit and intention of the resolutions of the German Reichstag of the 9th of July last, the spirit and intention of the Liberal leaders and parties of Germany, or to those who resist and defy that spirit and intention and insist upon conquest and subjugation? Or are we listening, in fact, to both, unreconciled and in open and hopeless contradiction? These are very serious and pregnant questions. Upon the answer to them depends the peace of the world.

But, whatever the results of the parleys at Brest-Litovsk, whatever the confusions of counsel and of purpose in the utterances of the spokesmen of the Central Empires, they have again attempted to acquaint the world with their objects in the war and have again challenged their adversaries to say what their objects are and what sort of settlement they would deem just and satisfactory. There is no good reason why that challenge should not be responded to, and responded to with the utmost candor. We did not wait for it. Not once, but again and again, we have laid our whole thought and purpose before the world, not in general terms only, but each time with sufficient definition to make it clear what sort of def-

inite terms of settlement must necessarily spring out of them. Within the last week Mr. Lloyd George has spoken with admirable candor and in admirable spirit for the people and Government of Great Britain.

There is no confusion of counsel among the adversaries of the Central Powers, no uncertainty of principle, no vagueness of detail. The only secrecy of counsel, the only lack of fearless frankness, the only failure to make definite statement of the objects of the war, lies with Germany and her allies. The issues of life and death hang upon these definitions. No statesman who has the least conception of his responsibility ought for a moment to permit himself to continue this tragical and appalling outpouring of blood and treasure unless he is sure beyond a peradventure that the objects of the vital sacrifice are part and parcel of the very life of Society and that the people for whom he speaks think them right and imperative as he does.

There is, moreover, a voice calling for these definitions of principle and of purpose which is, it seems to me, more thrilling and more compelling than any of the many moving voices with which the troubled air of the world is filled. It is the voice of the Russian people. They are prostrate and all but hopeless, it would seem, before the grim power of Germany, which has hitherto known no relenting and no pity. Their power, apparently, is shattered. And yet their soul is not subservient. They will not yield either in principle or in action. Their conception of what is right, of what is humane and honorable for them to accept, has been stated with a frankness, a largeness of view, a generosity of spirit, and a universal human sympathy which must challenge the admiration of every friend of mankind; and they have refused to compound their ideals or desert others that they themselves may be safe.

They call to us to say what it is that we desire, in what, if in anything, our purpose and our spirit differ from theirs; and I believe that the people of the United States would wish me to respond, with utter simplicity and frankness. Whether their present leaders believe it or not, it is our heartfelt desire and hope that some way may be opened whereby we may be privileged to assist the people of Russia to attain their utmost hope of liberty and ordered peace.

It will be our wish and purpose that the processes of peace, when they are begun, shall be absolutely open and that they shall involve and permit henceforth no secret understandings of any kind. The day of conquest and aggrandizement is gone by; so is also the day of secret covenants entered into in the interest of particular governments and likely at some unlooked-for moment to upset the peace of the world. It is this happy fact, now clear to the view of every public man whose thoughts do not still linger in an age that is dead and gone, which makes it possible for every nation whose purposes are consistent with justice and the peace of the world to avow now or at any other time the objects it has in view.

We entered this war because violations of right had occurred which touched us to the quick and made the life of our own people impossible unless they were corrected and the world secure once for all against their recurrence. What we demand

in this war, therefore, is nothing peculiar to ourselves. It is that the world be made fit and safe to live in; and particularly that it be made safe for every peace-loving nation which, like our own, wishes to live its own life, determine its own institutions, be assured of justice and fair dealing by the other peoples of the world as against force and selfish aggression. All the peoples of the world are in effect partners in this interest, and for our own part we see very clearly that unless justice be done to others it will not be done to us. The program of the world's peace, therefore, is our program; and that program, the only possible program, as we see it, is this:

I. Open covenants of peace, openly arrived at, after which there shall be no private international understandings of any kind but diplomacy shall proceed always frankly and in the public view.

II. Absolute freedom of navigation upon the seas, outside territorial waters, alike in peace and in war, except as the seas may be closed in whole or in part by international action for the enforcement of international covenants.

III. The removal, so far as possible, of all economic barriers and the establishment of an equality of trade conditions among all the nations consenting to the peace and associating themselves for its maintenance.

IV. Adequate guarantees given and taken that national armaments will be reduced to the lowest point consistent with domestic safety.

V. A free, open-minded, and absolutely impartial adjustment of all colonial claims, based upon a strict observance of the principle that in determining all such questions of sovereignty the interests of the populations concerned must have equal weight with the equitable claims of the government whose title is to be determined.

VI. The evacuation of all Russian territory and such a settlement of all questions affecting Russia as will secure the best and freest cooperation of the other nations of the world in obtaining for her an unhampered and unembarrassed opportunity for the independent determination of her own political development and national policy and assure her of a sincere welcome into the society of free nations under institutions of her own choosing; and, more than a welcome, assistance also of every kind that she may need and may herself desire. The treatment accorded Russia by her sister nations in the months to come will be the acid test of their good will, of their comprehension of her needs as distinguished from their own interests, and of their intelligent and unselfish sympathy.

VII. Belgium, the whole world will agree, must be evacuated and restored, without any attempt to limit the sovereignty which she enjoys in common with all other free nations. No other single act will serve as this will serve to restore confidence among the nations in the laws which they have themselves set and determined for the government of their relations with one another. Without this healing act the whole structure and validity of international law is forever impaired.

VIII. All French territory should be freed and the invaded portions restored, and the wrong done to France by Prussia in 1871 in the matter of Alsace-Lorraine, which has unsettled the peace of the world for nearly fifty years, should be righted, in order that peace may once more be made secure in the interest of all.

IX. A readjustment of the frontiers of Italy should be effected along clearly recognizable lines of nationality.

X. The peoples of Austria-Hungary, whose place among the nations we wish to see safeguarded and assured, should be accorded the freest opportunity to autonomous development.

XI. Rumania, Serbia, and Montenegro should be evacuated; occupied territories restored; Serbia accorded free and secure access to the sea; and the relations of the several Balkan states to one another determined by friendly counsel along historically established lines of allegiance and nationality; and international guarantees of the political and economic independence and territorial integrity of the several Balkan states should be entered into.

XII. The Turkish portion of the present Ottoman Empire should be assured a secure sovereignty, but the other nationalities which are now under Turkish rule should be assured an undoubted security of life and an absolutely unmolested opportunity of autonomous development, and the Dardanelles should be permanently opened as a free passage to the ships and commerce of all nations under international guarantees.

XIII. An independent Polish state should be erected which should include the territories inhabited by indisputably Polish populations, which should be assured a free and secure access to the sea, and whose political and economic independence and territorial integrity should be guaranteed by international covenant.

XIV. A general association of nations must be formed under specific covenants for the purpose of affording mutual guarantees of political independence and territorial integrity to great and small states alike.

In regard to these essential rectifications of wrong and assertions of right we feel ourselves to be intimate partners of all the governments and peoples associated together against the Imperialists. We cannot be separated in interest or divided in purpose. We stand together until the end. For such arrangements and covenants we are willing to fight and to continue to fight until they are achieved; but only because we wish the right to prevail and desire a just and stable peace such as can be secured only by removing the chief provocations to war, which this program does remove. We have no jealousy of German greatness, and there is nothing in this program that impairs it. We grudge her no achievement or distinction of learning or of pacific enterprise such as have made her record very bright and very enviable. We do not wish to injure her or to block in any way her legitimate influence or power. We do not wish to fight her either with arms or with hostile arrangements of trade if she is willing to associate herself with us and the other peace-loving nations of the world in covenants of justice and law and fair dealing. We wish her only to accept a place of equality among the peoples of the world,— the new world in which we now live,— instead of a place of mastery.

Neither do we presume to suggest to her any alteration or modification of her institutions. But it is necessary, we must frankly say, and necessary as a preliminary to any intelligent dealings with her on our part, that we should know whom her spokesmen speak for when they speak to us, whether for the Reichstag majority or for the military party and the men whose creed is imperial domination.

We have spoken now, surely, in terms too concrete to admit of any further doubt or question. An evident principle runs through the whole program I have outlined. It is the principle of justice to all peoples and nationalities, and their right to live on equal terms of liberty and safety with one another, whether they be strong or weak.

Unless this principle be made its foundation no part of the structure of international justice can stand. The people of the United States could act upon no other principle; and to the vindication of this principle they are ready to devote their lives, their honor, and everything they possess. The moral climax of this the culminating and final war for human liberty has come, and they are ready to put their own strength, their own highest purpose, their own integrity and devotion to the test.

Study Question

Distill Wilson's fourteen points into about four or five summary points. Do you agree with his approach to postwar foreign policy? Why or why not?

U.S. Supreme Court, *Schenck v. U.S.* (1919)

Charles Schenck, as secretary of the Socialist Party of America, managed the printing and distribution of some 15,000 pamphlets criticizing the military draft that Congress imposed during World War I. The pamphlets compared compulsory military service to slavery—which the Thirteenth Amendment had abolished—and urged citizens to resist the draft. A federal court convicted Schenck of violating the Espionage Act (1917), which forbade the mailing of treasonous materials. Schenck's lawyer, however, maintained that the First Amendment guarantees all citizens, even socialists, the rights to free speech and freedom of the press. What would the Supreme Court decide?

Mr. Justice HOLMES delivered the opinion of the Court.

This is an indictment in three counts. The first charges a conspiracy to violate the Espionage Act of June 15, 1917, by causing and attempting to cause insubordination, &c., in the military and naval forces of the United States, and to obstruct the recruiting and enlistment service of the United States, when the United States was at war with the German Empire, to-wit, that the defendant willfully conspired to have printed and circulated to men who had been called and accepted for military service under the Act of May 18, 1917, a document set forth and alleged to be calculated to cause such insubordination and obstruction. The count alleges overt acts in pursuance of the conspiracy, ending in the distribution of the document set forth. The second count alleges a conspiracy to commit an offense against the United States, to-wit, to use the mails for the transmission of matter declared to be non-mailable by title 12, 2, of the Act of June 15, 1917, to-wit, the above mentioned document, with an averment of the same overt acts. The third count charges an unlawful use of the mails for the transmission of the same matter and otherwise as above. The defendants were found guilty on all the counts. They set up the First Amendment to the Constitution forbidding Congress to make any law abridging the freedom of speech, or of the press, and bringing the case here on that ground have argued some other points also of which we must dispose.

It is argued that the evidence, if admissible, was not sufficient to prove that the defendant Schenck was concerned in sending the documents. According to the testimony Schenck said he was general secretary of the Socialist party and had charge of the Socialist headquarters from which the documents were sent. He identified a book found there as the minutes of the Executive Committee of the party. The book showed a resolution of August 13, 1917, that 15,000 leaflets should be printed on the other side of one of them in use, to be mailed to men who had passed exemption boards, and for distribution. Schenck personally attended to the printing. On August 20 the general secretary's report said 'Obtained new leaflets from printer and started work addressing envelopes' &c.; and there was a resolve that Comrade Schenck be allowed $125 for sending leaflets through the mail. He said that he had about fifteen or sixteen thousand printed. There were files of the circular in question in the inner office which he said were printed on the other side of the one sided circular and were there for distribution. Other copies were proved to have been sent through the mails to drafted men. Without going into confirmatory details that were proved, no reasonable man could doubt that the defendant Schenck was largely instrumental in sending the circulars about. As to the defendant Baer there was evidence that she was a member of the Executive Board and that the minutes of its transactions were hers. The argument as to the sufficiency of the evidence that the defendants conspired to send the documents only impairs the seriousness of the real defence.

It is objected that the documentary evidence was not admissible because obtained upon a search warrant, valid so far as appears. The contrary is established. *Adams v. New York*; *Weeks v. United States*. The search warrant did not issue against the defendant but against the Socialist headquarters at 1326 Arch street and it would seem that the documents technically were not even in the defendants' possession. See *Johnson v. United States*. Notwithstanding some protest in argument the notion that evidence even directly proceeding from the defendant in a criminal proceeding is excluded in all cases by the Fifth Amendment is plainly unsound. *Holt v. United States*.

The document in question upon its first printed side recited the first section of the Thirteenth Amendment, said that the idea embodied in it was violated by the conscription act and that a conscript is little better than a convict. In impassioned language it intimated that conscription was despotism in its worst form and a monstrous wrong against humanity in the interest of Wall Street's chosen few. It said, 'Do not submit to intimidation,' but in form at least confined itself to peaceful measures such as a petition for the repeal of the act. The other and later printed side of the sheet was headed 'Assert Your Rights.' It stated reasons for alleging that any one violated the Constitution when he refused to recognize 'your right to assert your opposition to the draft,' and went on, 'If you do not assert and support your rights, you are helping to deny or disparage rights which it is the solemn duty of all citizens and residents of the United States to retain.' It described the arguments on the other side as coming from cunning politicians and a mercenary capitalist press, and even silent consent to the conscription law as helping to support an infamous conspiracy. It denied the power to send our citizens away to foreign shores to shoot up the people of other lands, and added that words could not express the condemnation such cold-blooded ruthlessness deserves, &c., &c., winding up, 'You must do your share to maintain, support and uphold the rights of the people of this country.' Of course the document would not have been sent unless it had been intended to have some effect, and we do not see what effect it could be expected to have upon persons subject to the draft except to influence them to obstruct the carrying of it out. The defendants do not deny that the jury might find against them on this point.

But it is said, suppose that that was the tendency of this circular, it is protected by the First Amendment to the Constitution.

Two of the strongest expressions are said to be quoted respectively from well-known public men. It well may be that the prohibition of laws abridging the freedom of speech is not confined to previous restraints, although to prevent them may have been the main purpose, as intimated in *Patterson v. Colorado*. We admit that in many places and in ordinary times the defendants in saying all that was said in the circular would have been within their constitutional rights. But the character of every act depends upon the circumstances in which it is done. *Aikens v. Wisconsin*. The most stringent protection of free speech would not protect a man in falsely shouting fire in a theatre and causing a panic. It does not even protect a man from an injunction against uttering words that may have all the effect of force. *Gompers v. Buck's Stove & Range Co.* The question in every case is whether the words used are used in such circumstances and are of such a nature as to create a clear and present danger that they will bring about the substantive evils that Congress has a right to prevent. It is a question of proximity and degree. When a nation is at war many things that might be said in time of peace are such a hindrance to its effort that their utterance will not be endured so long as men fight and that no Court could regard them as protected by any constitutional right. It seems to be admitted that if an actual obstruction of the recruiting service were proved, liability for words that produced that effect might be enforced. The statute of 1917 in section 4 punishes conspiracies to obstruct as well as actual obstruction. If the act, (speaking, or circulating a paper,) its tendency and the intent with which it is done are the same, we perceive no ground for saying that success alone warrants making the act a crime. *Goldman v. United States*. Indeed that case might be said to dispose of the present contention if the precedent covers all media concludendi. But as the right to free speech was not referred to specially, we have thought fit to add a few words.

It was not argued that a conspiracy to obstruct the draft was not within the words of the Act of 1917. The words are 'obstruct the recruiting or enlistment service,' and it might be suggested that they refer only to making it hard to get volunteers. Recruiting heretofore usually having been accomplished by getting volunteers the word is apt to call up that method only in our minds. But recruiting is gaining fresh supplies for the forces, as well by draft as otherwise. It is put as an alternative to enlistment or voluntary enrollment in this act. The fact that the Act of 1917 was enlarged by the amending Act of May 16, 1918, of course, does not affect the present indictment and would not, even if the former act had been repealed.

Judgments affirmed.

Study Question

How did the Supreme Court's ruling in *Schenck* square with the First Amendment? (Refer to the First Amendment, p. 39.) Do you think the Supreme Court made the right decision, given that the nation was at war? Why or why not?

Presidents of the Roaring Twenties, 1921–1929

In *Only Yesterday: An Informal History of the 1920s* (1931), Frederick Lewis Allen observed that "the eleven years between the end of the war with Germany (November 11, 1918) and the stock market-panic which culminated on November 13, 1929 . . . may be considered as a distinct era in American history." President Warren Harding urged a return to "normalcy" at the beginning of the new decade, as will be explained below. Others have called those years "the roaring twenties," whether for the "Coolidge Prosperity" associated with a long bull market on Wall Street or for the rowdy nightlife at the speakeasies. In any case, the 1920s do not quite fit the mold of the Progressive Era, nor do those years predict the pattern of the Great Depression and New Deal of the 1930s. The presidents of the 1920s therefore will be treated as a stand-alone unit.

Warren G. Harding (Republican—Ohio), 1921–1923

While progressive reformers focused on the problems associated with urbanization, the early career of Warren G. Harding demonstrated that the American Republic remained vibrant in the small towns. Growing up in Marion, Ohio, he tried his skill at both teaching and law before settling into the editorship of the *Marion Star*, a small-town weekly newspaper. Deepening his local relationships and broadening his connections into state politics, Harding spring-boarded from journalism into the state senate in 1899. In 1910, he ran for Ohio governor. Though unsuccessful in that election, his stature in the Republican party grew as he served as a delegate at the 1912 national convention, nominating William Howard Taft for the presidency. Two years later, Harding himself was elected to the U.S. Senate in the first senatorial election based on popular vote, now that the Seventeenth Amendment had been ratified.

As Harding's term in the Senate neared its end, Theodore Roosevelt contemplated running again for the presidency in 1920 with Harding as his vice-presidential candidate. When Roosevelt fell ill and died of a heart attack in 1919, several of TR's supporters competed for the Republican endorsement. None, however, received the requisite majority at the national convention. Then Harding's nomination came forth as a compromise measure, since several of the party's factions had shared Harding in common as their second-choice candidate.

The nation could plainly see that Harding was no Woodrow Wilson, and in 1920 that sat favorably with many of them. Wilson, the former president of Princeton University, outshone the semi-schooled Harding intellectually, but Wilson's health was failing and his political support dwindling as controversy brewed over the League of Nations. The economy, meanwhile, buckled under the postwar pressures of unemployment and inflation, even as the protests of foreign-born radical labor leaders aroused public fears of a communist revolution. Though not particularly gifted for oratory,

Harding struck the right chord with the American people when he promised in a May 1920 speech, "not heroics, but healing; not nostrums, but normalcy."

Following his election, Harding assembled a powerful cabinet. Charles Evan Hughes, who later would become Supreme Court Chief Justice, served as Secretary of State. Herbert Hoover, who had been head of the Food Administration, became Secretary of Commerce. Andrew Mellon, the third richest American (after John D. Rockefeller and Henry Ford), served as Secretary of the Treasury. With Hughes, Harding worked toward international disarmament. With Mellon, Harding persuaded Congress to reduce taxes and reform the federal budgeting process. Hoover, meanwhile, introduced a federal blueprint for local zoning regulations. In *Village of Euclid v. Ambler Realty* (1926), the Supreme Court upheld municipal zoning, reasoning that "a nuisance may be merely a right thing in the wrong place—like a pig in the parlor instead of the barnyard."

In a departure from Wilson's firm policy against dissenters, Harding pardoned socialist Eugene V. Debs of his conviction under the 1917 Espionage Act for his agitation against U.S. involvement in World War I. Many Americans, even if disapproving of socialism, felt Debs should not have been imprisoned merely for speaking his mind. The First Amendment, if taken at face value, guarantees freedom of speech for everyone.

In the summer of 1923, it seemed all but inevitable that the Republican Party would nominate Harding for reelection the following year. But the pressures of the presidency had taken a toll on Harding's health. As he traveled throughout the West on a "voyage of understanding" campaign tour, Harding became progressively weaker. An infection of his lungs and irregularities with his heart briefly reversed for the better, and then suddenly he died in the middle of a conversation, likely from a stroke.

Unfortunately for Harding's widow, Florence King DeWolfe, a series of posthumous scandals swallowed up any fame that would have remained for her husband's name. Bribes within the cabinet, sexual infidelity in the White House, and suicides among his fellow-accused dragged the name Warren G. Harding deep into the mud. Generations of schoolchildren would learn a simpler, more sanitized tale: that Harding had called the nation back to "normalcy," whatever that means. Lacking the eloquence of a Roosevelt or a Wilson, Harding easily became upstaged in the annals of the American presidents. Even his relatively silent successor, Calvin Coolidge, is better known today.

Calvin Coolidge (Republican—Massachusetts), 1923–1929

At five feet, nine inches tall and never speaking more than necessary, Coolidge easily could escape notice. Worse, his critics claimed he slept his way through five and half years of the presidency. Upon the announcement of his death, the running joke was, "How can you tell?" Popularity ratings often have placed him at the bottom of the heap of

American leaders. The best that can be said for Coolidge is that he was behind the times —and yet, in a way, that statement extends a very great compliment.

Coolidge conscientiously rejected the legacy of the Progressive Era. He believed in a small government for a free people. He belonged to the nineteenth century, not the twentieth, and that was both his greatest strength and his greatest liability. Born on the Fourth of July, 1872, Coolidge was raised in Vermont and settled, after attending Amherst College, in Massachusetts. Repeatedly running for office in the small town of Northampton, he progressed from city council to mayor. Of twenty attempts, he only lost one political race—for school board—and that was due to the fact that he and his bride took their honeymoon right in the middle of the campaign. No matter, Coolidge still managed to climb to the very top of the Massachusetts political ladder, being elected lieutenant governor in 1915 and governor in 1918.

In September 1919, Boston police officers, organized under the American Federation of Labor, went on strike to protest low wages. When the police commissioner dismissed the union leaders, the majority of the police force walked out. Governor Coolidge did not waste any time in reacting. He summoned the Massachusetts militia to keep the peace, declaring to AFL president Samuel Gompers, "There is no right to strike against public safety by anybody, anywhere, any time." Although such a decisive stance risked political alienation by those concerned for workers' rights, Coolidge instead became a national celebrity for his bold preservation of law and order. The following summer, the Republican National Convention paired Coolidge with Warren G. Harding. The duo won by the greatest popular margin up to that time, bringing Coolidge into the nation's second highest office.

The vice presidency, however, has a reputation for being a rather thankless job. By virtue of the Constitution, the vice president serves as the presiding officer of the Senate, but few senators took a liking to Coolidge. In the senate restaurant, he frequently ate lunch alone, in the corner. It seemed all but certain that Harding would choose a different running mate for the 1924 election.

Following Harding's untimely death, however, Coolidge assumed the presidency with firm leadership. When evidence of corruption surfaced within the cabinet he had inherited from Harding, Coolidge cleaned house, restoring a respectability to his office. By November 1924, Coolidge's demonstration of character had paid off; he won election by a landslide. Whereas other presidents have seized upon the popular vote as a mandate for innovative action, Coolidge sought to slow the course and clean up the ship. For productivity, Coolidge directed Americans to business; for ordered liberty at as low a cost to the taxpayers as possible, he directed Americans to a minimalist federal government. Consequently, he proposed little to Congress, and vetoed much. No matter their popular appeal, this *laissez-faire* president would tolerate nothing of wage hikes for postal workers, bonuses for World War I veterans, or price fixing to support farmers amid an agricultural depression. Presciently he remarked, "Government price fixing, once started, has alike no justice and no end."

Coolidge retained from the Harding administration Andrew Mellon as Secretary of the Treasury and Herbert Hoover as Commerce Secretary. Mellon in particular espoused with Coolidge the nineteenth-century doctrine of *laissez faire*. Mellon also had a practical view: by lowering tax rates, the government could stimulate economic growth, which would result in higher tax revenues because incomes would be larger. The plan worked. The stock market surged, unemployment evaporated down to 2%, and production efficiency brought consumer costs into the affordable reach of the common family. Americans achieved this unparalleled decade of economic improvement not through government intervention but through welfare capitalism, such as Henry Ford's "family wage" policy of paying each autoworker enough to support an entire household. The prosperity of the 1920s became known as the "Coolidge boom" not because of what the president did, but because of what he refused to have the government do.

Content that he had done enough by doing little, Coolidge announced in 1927, "I do not choose to run for president in 1928." This statement surprised even his own wife, Grace, but that was Silent Cal's style. The couple retired to their Northampton home, where he sketched out an autobiography and got into the habit of writing a nationally syndicated newspaper column. When he quietly died of a heart attack in January 1933, American prosperity had been swallowed up by the Great Depression and all eyes were fixed on president-elect Franklin Delano Roosevelt and Coolidge's immediate successor, the scapegoated Herbert Hoover.

Study Questions

1. For what contributions to American political life does President Warren G. Harding best deserve to be remembered?

2. Identify the fundamental similarities between the political philosophies of Grover Cleveland and Calvin Coolidge.

3. In what ways can the economic prosperity of the 1920s be attributed to Coolidge's *in*action as president? How does this demonstrate the limitations of progressivism?

Supreme Court Decisions during the Twenties

During the first two decades of the twentieth century—a time known as the Progressive Era—both federal and state governments increasingly regulated economic activities. It seemed as though the nineteenth-century doctrine of *laissez faire* would never return. In the 1920s, however, *laissez faire* experienced a revival. Republican lawmakers at the federal and state levels put the breaks on progressive reform, as did the U.S. Supreme Court. Even an institution as popular as public schools could not take priority over individual choice. Nevertheless, the Court thought it appropriate that some behaviors should still be regulated, particularly free speech when such speech threatened to undermine the American Republic. With the Russian Revolution (1917) fresh in people's memories, communists and socialists were particularly suspect amid America's own "Red Scare" that began with labor uprisings in 1919 and persisted into the 1920s.

1923   *Adkins v. Children's Hospital*: A federal law mandating a minimum wage for women and children employed in the District of Columbia was found unconstitutional. The Court ruled that the Due Process clause of the Fifth Amendment guarantees liberty of contract.

1923   *Wolff Packing Co. v. Kansas Court of Industrial Relations*: The Court found a Kansas law, which regulated wages in the meat packing industry, to be null in view of the liberty of contract guaranteed by the Due Process clause of the Fourteenth Amendment.

1925   *Gitlow v. New York*: The Court ruled that the Free Speech clause of the First Amendment does not protect socialists who participate in organizations subversive to the United States government.

1925   *Pierce v. Society of Sisters*: The Court held that parents have a right, protected by the Fourteenth Amendment, to determine their children's education; a state may not require parents to enroll their children in a public school against the parents' religious convictions.

1927   *Whitney v. California*: The Court ruled that the First Amendment does not guarantee an absolute right to free speech; state laws may prohibit persons from engaging in communist propaganda that endangers the foundations of American government.

1927   *Tyson v. Banton*: A New York law regulating the prices at which theater tickets may be resold was found unconstitutional. Ticket sales fall under the liberty of contract protected by the Fourteenth Amendment.

Study Question

Why did the Court expand individual liberty in matters of economics, while constraining individual liberty in matters of free speech during the 1920s?

Warren G. Harding, Inaugural Address (1921)

To historians who place their favor upon action-oriented presidents who swell the ranks of the federal government in order to regulate the national economy for the service of some grand vision of progress, Warren G. Harding is best forgotten—and the sooner the better. His most memorable expression is "return to normalcy," the keynote of his 1920 presidential campaign. In his inaugural address of the following year, Harding again urged Americans to "strive for normalcy," that is, to return to the lifestyle that preceded World War I. Only then, he believed, would America be ready to continue "onward" in a "normal way." His contemporaries, meanwhile, must have wondered what "normal" meant after two decades of progressive reform.

When one surveys the world about him after the great storm, noting the marks of destruction and yet rejoicing in the ruggedness of the things which withstood it, if he is an American he breathes the clarified atmosphere with a strange mingling of regret and new hope. We have seen a world passion spend its fury, but we contemplate our Republic unshaken, and hold our civilization secure. Liberty—liberty within the law—and civilization are inseparable, and though both were threatened we find them now secure; and there comes to Americans the profound assurance that our representative government is the highest expression and surest guaranty of both.

Standing in this presence, mindful of the solemnity of this occasion, feeling the emotions which no one may know until he senses the great weight of responsibility for himself, I must utter my belief in the divine inspiration of the founding fathers. Surely there must have been God's intent in the making of this new-world Republic. Ours is an organic law which had but one ambiguity, and we saw that effaced in a baptism of sacrifice and blood, with union maintained, the Nation supreme, and its concord inspiring. We have seen the world rivet its hopeful gaze on the great truths on which the founders wrought. We have seen civil, human, and religious liberty verified and glorified. In the beginning the Old World scoffed at our experiment; today our foundations of political and social belief stand unshaken, a precious inheritance to ourselves, an inspiring example of freedom and civilization to all mankind. Let us express renewed and strengthened devotion, in grateful reverence for the immortal beginning, and utter our confidence in the supreme fulfillment.

The recorded progress of our Republic, materially and spiritually, in itself proves the wisdom of the inherited policy of non-involvement in Old World affairs. Confident of our ability to work out our own destiny, and jealously guarding our right to do so, we seek no part in directing the destinies of the Old World. We do not mean to be entangled. We will accept no responsibility except as our own conscience and judgment, in each instance, may determine.

Our eyes never will be blind to a developing menace, our ears never deaf to the call of civilization. We recognize the new order in the world, with the closer contacts which progress has wrought. We sense the call of the human heart for fellowship, fraternity, and cooperation. We crave friendship and harbor no hate. But America, our America, the America builded on the foundation laid by the inspired fathers, can be a party to no permanent military alliance. It can enter into no political commitments, nor assume any economic obligations which will subject our decisions to any other than our own authority.

I am sure our own people will not misunderstand, nor will the world misconstrue. We have no thought to impede the paths to closer relationship. We wish to promote understanding. We want to do our part in making offensive warfare so hateful that Governments and peoples who resort to it must prove the righteousness of their cause or stand as outlaws before the bar of civilization.

We are ready to associate ourselves with the nations of the world, great and small, for conference, for counsel; to seek the expressed views of world opinion; to recommend a way to approximate disarmament and relieve the crushing burdens of military and naval establishments. We elect to participate in suggesting plans for mediation, conciliation, and arbitration, and would gladly join in that expressed conscience of progress, which seeks to clarify and write the laws of international relationship, and establish a world court for the disposition of such justiciable questions as nations are agreed to submit thereto. In expressing aspirations, in seeking practical plans, in translating humanity's new concept of righteousness and justice and its hatred of war into recommended action we are ready most

heartily to unite, but every commitment must be made in the exercise of our national sovereignty. Since freedom impelled, and independence inspired, and nationality exalted, a world supergovernment is contrary to everything we cherish and can have no sanction by our Republic. This is not selfishness, it is sanctity. It is not aloofness, it is security. It is not suspicion of others, it is patriotic adherence to the things which made us what we are.

Today, better than ever before, we know the aspirations of humankind, and share them. We have come to a new realization of our place in the world and a new appraisal of our Nation by the world. The unselfishness of these United States is a thing proven; our devotion to peace for ourselves and for the world is well established; our concern for preserved civilization has had its impassioned and heroic expression. There was no American failure to resist the attempted reversion of civilization; there will be no failure today or tomorrow.

The success of our popular government rests wholly upon the correct interpretation of the deliberate, intelligent, dependable popular will of America. In a deliberate questioning of a suggested change of national policy, where internationality was to supersede nationality, we turned to a referendum, to the American people. There was ample discussion, and there is a public mandate in manifest understanding.

America is ready to encourage, eager to initiate, anxious to participate in any seemly program likely to lessen the probability of war, and promote that brotherhood of mankind which must be God's highest conception of human relationship. Because we cherish ideals of justice and peace, because we appraise international comity and helpful relationship no less highly than any people of the world, we aspire to a high place in the moral leadership of civilization, and we hold a maintained America, the proven Republic, the unshaken temple of representative democracy, to be not only an inspiration and example, but the highest agency of strengthening good will and promoting accord on both continents.

Mankind needs a world-wide benediction of understanding. It is needed among individuals, among peoples, among governments, and it will inaugurate an era of good feeling to make the birth of a new order. In such understanding men will strive confidently for the promotion of their better relationships and nations will promote the comities so essential to peace.

We must understand that ties of trade bind nations in closest intimacy, and none may receive except as he gives. We have not strengthened ours in accordance with our resources or our genius, notably on our own continent, where a galaxy of Republics reflects the glory of new-world democracy, but in the new order of finance and trade we mean to promote enlarged activities and seek expanded confidence.

Perhaps we can make no more helpful contribution by example than prove a Republic's capacity to emerge from the wreckage of war. While the world's embittered travail did not leave us devastated lands nor desolated cities, left no gaping wounds, no breast with hate, it did involve us in the delirium of expenditure, in expanded currency and credits, in unbalanced industry, in unspeakable waste, and disturbed relationships. While it uncovered our portion of hateful selfishness at home, it also revealed the heart of America as sound and fearless, and beating in confidence unfailing.

Amid it all we have riveted the gaze of all civilization to the unselfishness and the righteousness of representative democracy, where our freedom never has made offensive warfare, never has sought territorial aggrandizement through force, never has turned to the arbitrament of arms until reason has been exhausted. When the Governments of the earth shall have established a freedom like our own and shall have sanctioned the pursuit of peace as we have practiced it, I believe the last sorrow and the final sacrifice of international warfare will have been written.

Let me speak to the maimed and wounded soldiers who are present today, and through them convey to their comrades the gratitude of the Republic for their sacrifices in its defense. A generous country will never forget the services you rendered, and you may hope for a policy under Government that will relieve any maimed successors from taking your places on another such occasion as this.

Our supreme task is the resumption of our onward, normal way. Reconstruction, readjustment, restoration all these must follow. I would like to hasten them. If it will lighten the spirit and add to the resolution with which we take up the task, let me repeat for our Nation, we shall give no people just cause to make war upon us; we hold no national prejudices; we entertain no spirit of revenge; we do not hate; we do not covet; we dream of no conquest, nor boast of armed prowess.

If, despite this attitude, war is again forced upon us, I earnestly hope a way may be found which will unify our individual and collective strength and consecrate all America, materially and spiritually, body and soul, to national defense. I can vision the ideal republic, where every man and woman is called under the flag for assignment to duty for whatever service, military or civic, the individual is best fitted; where we may call to universal service every plant, agency, or facility, all in the sublime sacrifice for country, and not one penny of war profit shall inure to the benefit of private individual, corporation, or combination, but all above the normal shall flow into the defense chest of the Nation. There is something inherently wrong, something out of accord with the ideals of representative democracy, when one portion of our citizenship turns its activities to private gain amid defensive war while another is fighting, sacrificing, or dying for national preservation.

Out of such universal service will come a new unity of spirit and purpose, a new confidence and consecration, which would make our defense impregnable, our triumph assured. Then we should have little or no disorganization of our economic, industrial, and commercial systems at home, no staggering war debts, no swollen fortunes to flout the sacrifices of our soldiers, no excuse for sedition, no pitiable slackerism, no outrage of treason. Envy and jealousy would have no soil for their menacing development, and revolution would be without the passion which engenders it.

A regret for the mistakes of yesterday must not, however, blind us to the tasks of today. War never left such an aftermath. There has been staggering loss of life and measureless wastage of materials. Nations are still groping for return to stable ways. Discouraging indebtedness confronts us like all the war-torn nations, and these obligations must be provided for. No civilization can survive repudiation.

We can reduce the abnormal expenditures, and we will. We can strike at war taxation, and we must. We must face the grim necessity, with full knowledge that the task is to be solved, and we must proceed with a full realization that no statute enacted by man can repeal the inexorable laws of nature. Our most dangerous tendency is to expect too much of government, and at the same time do for it too little. We contemplate the immediate task of putting our public household in order. We need a rigid and yet sane economy, combined with fiscal justice, and it must be attended by individual prudence and thrift, which are so essential to this trying hour and reassuring for the future.

The business world reflects the disturbance of war's reaction. Herein flows the lifeblood of material existence. The economic mechanism is intricate and its parts interdependent, and has suffered the shocks and jars incident to abnormal demands, credit inflations, and price upheavals. The normal balances have been impaired, the channels of distribution have been clogged, the relations of labor and management have been strained. We must seek the readjustment with care and courage. Our people must give and take. Prices must reflect the receding fever of war activities. Perhaps we never shall know the old levels of wages again, because war invariably readjusts compensations, and the necessaries of life will show their inseparable relationship, but we must strive for normalcy to reach stability. All the penalties will not be light, nor evenly distributed. There is no way of making them so. There is no instant step from disorder to order. We must face a condition of grim reality, charge off our losses and start afresh. It is the oldest lesson of civilization. I would like government to do all it can to mitigate; then, in understanding, in mutuality of interest, in concern for the common good, our tasks will be solved. No altered system will work a miracle. Any wild experiment will only add to the confusion. Our best assurance lies in efficient administration of our proven system.

The forward course of the business cycle is unmistakable. Peoples are turning from destruction to production. Industry has sensed the changed order and our own people are turning to resume their normal, onward way. The call is for productive America to go on. I know that Congress and the Administration will favor every wise Government policy to aid the resumption and encourage continued progress.

I speak for administrative efficiency, for lightened tax burdens, for sound commercial practices, for adequate credit facilities, for sympathetic concern for all agricultural problems, for the omission of unnecessary interference of Government with business, for an end to Government's experiment in business, and for more efficient business in Government administration. With all of this must attend a mindfulness of the human side of all activities, so that social, industrial, and economic justice will be squared with the purposes of a righteous people.

With the nation-wide induction of womanhood into our political life, we may count upon her intuitions, her refinements, her intelligence, and her influence to exalt the social order. We count upon her exercise of the full privileges and the performance of the duties of citizenship to speed the attainment of the highest state.

I wish for an America no less alert in guarding against dangers from within than it is watchful against enemies from without. Our fundamental law recognizes no class, no group, no section; there must be none in legislation or administration. The supreme inspiration is the common weal. Humanity hungers for international peace, and we crave it with all mankind. My most reverent prayer for America is for industrial peace, with its rewards, widely and generally distributed, amid the inspirations of equal opportunity. No one justly may deny the equality of opportunity which made us what we are. We have mistaken unpreparedness to embrace it to be a challenge of the reality, and due concern for making all citizens fit for participation will give added strength of citizenship and magnify our achievement.

If revolution insists upon overturning established order, let other peoples make the tragic experiment. There is no place for it in America. When World War threatened civilization we pledged our resources and our lives to its preservation, and when revolution threatens we unfurl the flag of law and order and renew our consecration. Ours is a constitutional freedom where the popular will is the law supreme and minorities are sacredly protected. Our revisions, reformations, and evolutions reflect a deliberate judgment and an orderly progress, and we mean to cure our ills, but never destroy or permit destruction by force.

I had rather submit our industrial controversies to the conference table in advance than to a settlement table after conflict and suffering. The earth is thirsting for the cup of good will, understanding is its fountain source. I would like to acclaim an era of good feeling amid dependable prosperity and all the blessings which attend.

It has been proved again and again that we cannot, while throwing our markets open to the world, maintain American standards of living and opportunity, and hold our industrial eminence in such unequal competition. There is a luring fallacy in the theory of banished barriers of trade, but preserved American standards require our higher production costs to be reflected in our tariffs on imports. Today, as never before, when peoples are seeking trade restoration and expansion, we must adjust our tariffs to the new order. We seek participation in the world's exchanges, because therein lies our way to widened influence and the triumphs of peace. We know full well we cannot sell where we do not buy, and we cannot sell successfully where we do not carry. Opportunity is calling not alone for the restoration, but for a new era in production, transportation and trade. We shall answer it best by meeting the demand of a surpassing home market, by promoting self-reliance in production, and by bidding enterprise, genius, and efficiency to carry our cargoes in American bottoms to the marts of the world.

We would not have an America living within and for herself alone, but we would have her self-reliant, independent, and ever nobler, stronger, and richer. Believing in our higher standards, reared through constitutional liberty and maintained opportunity, we invite the world to the same heights. But pride in things wrought is no reflex of a completed task. Common welfare is the goal of our national endeavor. Wealth is not inimical to welfare; it ought to be its friendliest agency. There never can be equality of rewards or possessions so long as the human plan contains varied talents and differing degrees of industry and thrift, but ours ought to be a country free from the great blotches of distressed poverty. We ought to find a way to guard against the perils and penalties of unemployment. We want an America of homes, illumined with hope and happiness, where mothers, freed from the necessity for long hours of toil beyond their own doors, may preside as befits the hearthstone of American citizenship. We want the cradle of American childhood rocked under conditions so wholesome and so hopeful that no blight may touch it in its development, and we want to provide that no selfish interest, no material necessity, no lack of opportunity shall prevent the gaining of that education so essential to best citizenship.

There is no short cut to the making of these ideals into glad realities. The world has witnessed again and again the futility and the mischief of ill-considered remedies for social and economic disorders. But we are mindful today as never before of the friction of modern industrialism, and we must learn its causes and reduce its evil consequences by sober and tested methods. Where genius has made for great possibilities, justice and happiness must be reflected in a greater common welfare.

Service is the supreme commitment of life. I would rejoice to acclaim the era of the Golden Rule and crown it with the autocracy of service. I pledge an administration wherein all the agencies of Government are called to serve, and ever promote an understanding of Government purely as an expression of the popular will.

One cannot stand in this presence and be unmindful of the tremendous responsibility. The world upheaval has added heavily to our tasks. But with the realization comes the surge of high resolve, and there is reassurance in belief in the God-given destiny of our Republic. If I felt that there is to be sole responsibility in the Executive for the America of tomorrow I should shrink from the burden. But here are a hundred millions, with common concern and shared responsibility, answerable to God and country. The Republic summons them to their duty, and I invite co-operation.

I accept my part with single-mindedness of purpose and humility of spirit, and implore the favor and guidance of God in His Heaven. With these I am unafraid, and confidently face the future.

I have taken the solemn oath of office on that passage of Holy Writ wherein it is asked: "What doth the Lord require of thee but to do justly, and to love mercy, and to walk humbly with thy God" [Micah 6:8]. This I plight to God and country.

Study Questions

1. Why was "liberty within the law" so important, and why did Harding insist that America should make "no permanent military alliance"?

2. What objections did Harding state to establishing a "world supergovernment" (a reference to the League of Nations)?

3. What proposals did Harding present for "putting our public household in order"?

4. What relationship did Harding identify between "wealth" and "welfare"?

5. Upon which Bible passage did Harding place his hand while taking the presidential oath? Why was this significant?

Herbert Hoover, *American Individualism* (1922)

Herbert Hoover, a Quaker by upbringing, contributed to numerous humanitarian causes during the early twentieth century. Long before the United States entered World War I, Hoover was at work in Belgium distributing food and clothing, train tickets and cash, and assisting the evacuation of over one hundred thousand Americans from Europe. In 1917, President Woodrow Wilson appointed Hoover as the head of the U.S. Food Administration. Claiming "Food will win the war," Hoover encouraged Americans to reduce consumption in order to send more food to Europe. In 1921, President Warren Harding appointed Hoover to serve as Secretary of Commerce, a post he utilized for promoting zoning regulations that would separate residential from commercial neighborhoods in America's growing cities. Whether during war or peace, Hoover sought cooperation between government and business in a manner that he thought would promote progressive reform while still preserving the individualism that Americans treasured.

Five or six great social philosophies are at struggle in the world for ascendancy. There is the Individualism of America. There is the Individualism of the more democratic states of Europe with its careful reservations of castes and classes. There are Communism, Socialism, Syndicalism, Capitalism, and finally there is Autocracy—whether by birth, by possessions, militarism, or divine right of kings. Even the Divine Right still lingers on although our lifetime has seen fully two-thirds of the earth's population, including Germany, Austria, Russia, and China, arrive at a state of angry disgust with this type of social motive power and throw it on the scrap heap.

All these thoughts are in ferment today in every country in the world. They fluctuate in ascendancy with times and places. They compromise with each other in daily reaction on governments and peoples. Some of these ideas are perhaps more adapted to one race than another. Some are false, some are true. What we are interested in is their challenge to the physical and spiritual forces of America.

The partisans of some of these other brands of social schemes challenge us to comparison; and some of their partisans even among our own people are increasing in their agitation that we adopt one or another or parts of their devices in place of our tried individualism. They insist that our social foundations are exhausted, that like feudalism and autocracy America's plan has served its purpose—that it must be abandoned.

There are those who have been left in sober doubt of our institutions or are confounded by bewildering catchwords of vivid phrases. For in this welter of discussions there is much attempt to glorify or defame social and economic forces with phrases. Nor indeed should we disregard the potency of some of these phrases in their stir to action.—"The dictatorship of the Proletariat," "Capitalistic nations," "Germany over all," and a score of others. We need only to review those that have jumped to horseback during the last ten years in order that we may be properly awed by the great social and political havoc that can be worked where the bestial instincts of hate, murder, and destruction are clothed by the demagogue in the fine terms of political idealism.

For myself, let me say at the very outset that my faith in the essential truth, strength, and vitality of the developing creed by which we have hitherto lived in this country of ours has been confirmed and deepened by the searching experiences of seven years of service in the backwash and misery of war. Seven years of contending with economic degeneration, with social disintegration, with incessant political dislocation, with all of its seething and ferment of individual and class conflict, could but impress me with the primary motivation of social forces, and the necessity for broader thought upon their great issues to humanity. And from it all I emerge an individualist—an unashamed individualist. But let me say also that I am an American individualist. For America has been steadily developing the ideals that constitute progressive individualism.

No doubt, individualism run riot, with no tempering principle, would provide a long category of inequalities, of tyrannies, dominations, and injustices. America, however, has tempered the whole conception of individualism by the injection of a definite principle, and from this principle it follows that attempts at domination, whether in government or in the processes of industry and commerce, are under an insistent curb. If we would have the values of individualism, their stimulation to initiative, to the development of hand and intellect, to the high development of thought and spirituality, they must be tempered with that firm and fixed ideal of American individualism—*an equality of opportunity*. If we would have these values we must soften its hardness and stimulate progress through that sense of service that lies in our people.

Therefore, it is not the individualism of other countries for which I would speak, but the individualism of America. Our individualism differs from all others because it embraces these great ideals: *that while we build our society upon the attainment of the individual, we shall safeguard to every individual an equality of opportunity to take that position in the community to which his intelligence, character, ability, and ambition entitle him; that we keep the social solution free from frozen strata of classes; that we shall stimulate effort of each individual to achievement; that through an enlarging sense of responsibility and understanding we shall assist him to this attainment; while he in turn must stand up to the emery wheel of competition.*

Individualism cannot be maintained as the foundation of a society if it looks to only legalistic justice based upon contracts, property, and political equality. Such legalistic safeguards are themselves not enough. In our individualism we have long since abandoned the *laissez faire* of the 18th Century—the notion that it is "every man for himself and the devil take the hindmost." We abandoned that when we adopted the ideal of equality of opportunity—the fair chance of Abraham Lincoln. We have confirmed its abandonment in terms of legislation, of social and economic justice,—in part because we have learned that it is the hindmost who throws the bricks at our social edifice, in part because we have learned that the foremost are not always the best nor the hindmost the worst—and in part because we have learned that social injustice is the destruction of justice itself. We have learned that the impulse to production can only be maintained at a high pitch if there is a fair division of the product. We have also learned that fair division can only be obtained by certain restrictions on the strong and the dominant. . . .

The will-o'-the wisp of all breeds of socialism is that they contemplate a motivation of human animals by altruism alone. It necessitates a bureaucracy of the entire population, in which, having obliterated the economic stimulation of each member, the fine gradations of character and ability are to be arranged in relative authority by ballot of more likely by a Tammany Hall or a Bolshevist party, or some other form of tyranny. The proof of the futility of these ideas as a stimulation to the development and activity of the individual does not lie alone in the ghastly failure of Russia, but also lies in our own failure in attempts at nationalized industry.

Likewise the basic foundations of autocracy, whether it be class government or capitalism in the sense that a few men through unrestrained control of property determine the welfare of great numbers, is as far apart from the rightful expression of American individualism as the two poles. The will-o'-the-wisp of autocracy in any form is that it supposes that the good Lord endowed a special few with all the divine attributes. It contemplates one human animal dealing to the other human animals his just share of earth, of glory, and of immortality. The proof of the futility of these ideas in the development of the world does not lie alone in the grim failure of Germany, but it lies in the damage to our moral and social fabric from those who have sought economic domination in America, whether employer or employee.

We in America, have had too much experience of life to fool ourselves into pretending that all men are equal in ability, in character, in intelligence, in ambition. That was part of the claptrap of the French Revolution. We have grown to understand that all we can all hope to assure to the individual through government is liberty, justice, intellectual welfare, equality of opportunity, and stimulation to service.

It is in maintenance of a society fluid to these human qualities that our individualism departs from the individualism of Europe. There can be no rise for the individual through the frozen strata of classes, or of castes, and no stratification can take place in a mass livened by the free stir of its particles. This guarding of our individualism against stratification insists not only in preserving in the social solution an equal opportunity for the able and ambitious to rise from the bottom; it also insists that the sons of the successful shall not by any mere right of birth or favor continue to occupy their fathers' places of power against the rise of a new generation in process of coming up from the bottom. The pioneers of our American individualism had the good sense not to reward Washington and Jefferson and Hamilton with hereditary dukedoms and fixtures in landed estates, as Great Britain rewarded

Marlborough and Nelson. Otherwise our American fields of opportunity would have been clogged with long generations inheriting their fathers' privileges without their fathers' capacity for service.

That high and increasing standards of living and comfort should be the first of considerations in public mind and in government needs no apology. We have long since realized that the basis of an advancing civilization must be a high and growing standard of living for all the people, not for a single class; that education, food, clothing, housing, and the spreading use of what we so often term non-essentials, are the real fertilizers of the soil from which spring the finer flowers of life. The economic development of the past fifty years has lifted the general standard of comfort far beyond the dreams of our forefathers. The only road to further advance in the standard of living is by greater invention, greater elimination of waste, greater production and better distribution of commodities and services, for by increasing their ratio to our numbers and dividing them justly we each will have more of them.

Study Questions

1. How did Hoover's brand of "American individualism" differ from the alternative philosophies that were prevalent in his day?

2. What specific lessons did Hoover draw from the experiences of Germany, Russia, and France?

3. It may be tempting to equate individualism with *laissez-faire* economics. Hoover, however, rejected *laissez faire* and endorsed a peculiar form of individualism. Trace the influence of the Progressive Era upon Hoover's "individualism."

Immigration and Reform, 1890–1924

Prior to 1890, most immigrants to the United States came from northwestern Europe, principally Germany and Ireland, as well as a large number from Scandinavian countries. From 1890 to 1920, however, immigrants came increasingly from southern and eastern European nations, including Italy, Hungary, and Russia. In 1914, the peak year of immigration, nearly three out of every four immigrants came from southeastern Europe. These new immigrants differed from the old immigrants not only as to their ethnicity but also as to their numbers. For example, in the 1850s—the decade following the potato famine in Ireland—about 1.7 million people immigrated to the United States, whereas over 8 million people immigrated to America during the first decade of the twentieth century. Moreover, the proportion of population increase attributable to immigration also rose dramatically. In the 1850s, immigration accounted for 28% of the nation's population growth, with the remaining 72% resulting from natural increase (the excess of births over deaths), whereas during 1900–1909, 51% of the population increase was attributable to immigration.

Most immigrants settled in cities. Consequently, New York City mushroomed from 3.4 million people in 1900 to 4.8 million in 1910. Philadelphia and Chicago experienced similar growth. Progressive reformers struggled to keep up with the new demands placed upon cities: would their be sufficient housing, jobs, roads, and sewage treatment to handle the growing population? Settlement homes, such as Jane Addams's Hull House in Chicago, offered to acclimate immigrants to American culture. Meanwhile, some reformers questioned whether America could continue to absorb the growing number of immigrants, and whether the ethnic diversity of those immigrants would undermine the Anglo-American political traditions upon which the American Republic was founded.

Congress revised immigration procedures several times, most notably in 1924. The Immigration Act of 1924 reduced the total number of immigrants permitted per year from about 360,000 (1922–1923) to about 160,000 (1923–1924). More notably, the law also imposed a quota system based on the 1890 census: the number of immigrants from any particular nation could not exceed 2% of the number of persons with similar ancestry who lived in the United States in 1890. Since most immigrants prior to 1890 had come from northern and western Europe, this policy skewed future immigration toward those same nations while significantly reducing the number of eligible immigrants from southern and eastern European nations. As a result, Italian immigration fell by more than 90% in the years immediately following this act.

The 1924 Immigration Act received support from multiple distinct factions. Several scientists, schooled in the new field of eugenics, advised Congress that privileging the immigration of northwest European "stock" would promote the healthy evolution of the American race. Other eugenic measures included state laws that mandated sterilization of criminals, the "feeble-minded," and paupers, under the conviction that these conditions were heritable and needed to be weeded out of the gene pool so that civilization could progress. Meanwhile, Samuel Gompers of the American Federation of Labor supported the immigration law for a different reason: his constituents did not want an influx of new immigrants competing for jobs against current citizens, since that would weaken the effectiveness of collective bargaining and strikes. More broadly, the quota system reaffirmed a traditional Anglo-American ancestry, promoting a nationalist identity in the wake of World War I. To that end, the 1924 act barred Asians from immigrating altogether.

Study Questions

1. Contrast the "old" versus the "new" immigrants in terms of their respective time periods, ethnic heritage, and numbers.

2. Explain three distinct rationales supporting the 1924 Immigration Act.

Jazz, the Harlem Renaissance, Flappers, and Bootleggers

In the final weeks of 1923, George Gershwin began feverishly composing a new jazz piece commissioned by Paul Whiteman for a New York concert to be held the following February. Entitling the song *Rhapsody in Blue*, Gershwin described his work as a "sort of musical kaleidoscope of America—of our vast melting pot, of our unduplicated national pep, of our metropolitan madness." Jazz surely was the music of a new age, an age of ethnic diversity forged by mass immigration, as well as an age of young, unmarried persons challenging social norms through music and dance. Jazz clubs, at times meeting secretly in basements, provided the working class with a sense of freedom from their long, dull days of servitude in the factories.

Jazz also provided African Americans an entrance into the arts. In Harlem, a black neighborhood of New York City, music, literature, and the visual arts experienced a revival during the 1920s known as the Harlem Renaissance. Going against the grain of Jim Crow, African Americans expressed pride in their race and fostered the culture of "the New Negro"—a young generation no longer content to remain second-class. Although not a significant political force at this time, the African American community was growing stronger and would arise in the 1950s to claim an equal share of civil rights.

White women, meanwhile, also challenged the prevailing social conventions. Painting their lips and faces with makeup, smoking cigarettes, drinking liquor, and exposing more flesh than their Victorian mothers, the "flappers" of the 1920s frequented jazz clubs and speakeasies as they pursued independent pleasures without thought of marriage, children, or chastity. They were precisely the "rebel women" whom the birth-control fanatic Margaret Sanger celebrated in her campaign to "emancipate" women from the "slavery" of Christian morality. So far, her plan was working: the divorce rate reached record levels and the birth rate fell to an historic low.

For their part, progressive reformers could not figure out where they had gone wrong. The Eighteenth Amendment (1919), by prohibiting the sale of intoxicating liquors, had been scientifically calculated to rid society of vice. Instead, the suppression of vice only pushed it underground, as bootleggers supplied speakeasies with alcohol and gangsters established their own version of law and order in back alleys. Far from re-engineering society for the public good, progressive reform had merely exposed the corruption of the human heart and diverted the power of entrepreneurship into a lucrative black market.

Study Question

Sometimes historians speak of the 1920s in terms of "social decadence." Is that characterization justified? Explain.

Calvin Coolidge, Inaugural Address (1925)

When President Warren G. Harding died suddenly in August 1923, Vice President Calvin Coolidge was visiting his childhood home in Vermont, a farmhouse with neither running water nor electricity. When messengers knocked on the door in the middle of the night, his father answered the door in his nightshirt and the called upstairs to his son; being a notary public, John Coolidge swore his son Calvin into the office of the presidency using the family Bible under the light of a kerosine lamp. Although both his contemporaries as well as historians of later generations have questioned whether Calvin Coolidge was up to the task, the American people elected him to continue in office in 1924. His inaugural address the following year revealed that Coolidge, more than most presidents, understood the powers of the federal government as defined and limited by the U.S. Constitution.

My Countrymen:

No one can contemplate current conditions without finding much that is satisfying and still more that is encouraging. Our own country is leading the world in the general readjustment to the results of the great conflict. Many of its burdens will bear heavily upon us for years, and the secondary and indirect effects we must expect to experience for some time. But we are beginning to comprehend more definitely what course should be pursued, what remedies ought to be applied, what actions should be taken for our deliverance, and are clearly manifesting a determined will faithfully and conscientiously to adopt these methods of relief. Already we have sufficiently rearranged our domestic affairs so that confidence has returned, business has revived, and we appear to be entering an era of prosperity which is gradually reaching into every part of the Nation. Realizing that we can not live unto ourselves alone, we have contributed of our resources and our counsel to the relief of the suffering and the settlement of the disputes among the European nations. Because of what America is and what America has done, a firmer courage, a higher hope, inspires the heart of all humanity.

These results have not occurred by mere chance. They have been secured by a constant and enlightened effort marked by many sacrifices and extending over many generations. We can not continue these brilliant successes in the future, unless we continue to learn from the past. It is necessary to keep the former experiences of our country both at home and abroad continually before us, if we are to have any science of government. If we wish to erect new structures, we must have a definite knowledge of the old foundations. We must realize that human nature is about the most constant thing in the universe and that the essentials of human relationship do not change. We must frequently take our bearings from these fixed stars of our political firmament if we expect to hold a true course. If we examine carefully what we have done, we can determine the more accurately what we can do.

We stand at the opening of the one hundred and fiftieth year since our national consciousness first asserted itself [in 1776] by unmistakable action with an array of force. The old sentiment of detached and dependent colonies disappeared in the new sentiment of a united and independent Nation. Men began to discard the narrow confines of a local charter for the broader opportunities of a national constitution. Under the eternal urge of freedom we became an independent Nation. A little less than 50 years later that freedom and independence were reasserted in the face of all the world, and guarded, supported, and secured by the Monroe doctrine [of 1823]. The narrow fringe of States along the Atlantic seaboard advanced its frontiers across the hills and plains of an intervening continent until it passed down the golden slope to the Pacific. We made freedom a birthright. We extended our domain over distant islands in order to safeguard our own interests and accepted the consequent obligation to bestow justice and liberty upon less favored peoples [in the Spanish-American War]. In the defense of our own ideals and in the general cause of liberty we entered the Great War [i.e., World War I]. When victory had been fully secured, we withdrew to our own shores unrecompensed save in the consciousness of duty done.

Throughout all these experiences we have enlarged our freedom, we have strengthened our independence. We have been, and propose to be, more and more American. We believe that we can best serve our own country and most successfully discharge our obligations to humanity by continuing to be openly and candidly, intensely and scrupulously, American. If we have any heritage, it has been that. If we have any destiny, we have found it in that direction.

But if we wish to continue to be distinctively American, we must continue to make that term comprehensive enough to embrace the legitimate desires of a civilized and enlightened people determined in all their relations to pursue a conscientious and religious life. We can not permit ourselves to be narrowed and dwarfed by slogans and phrases. It is not the adjective, but the substantive, which is of real importance. It is not the name of the action, but the result of the action, which is the chief concern. It will be well not to be too much disturbed by the thought of either isolation or entanglement of pacifists and militarists. The physical configuration of the earth has separated us from all of the Old World, but the common brotherhood of man, the highest law of all our being, has united us by inseparable bonds with all humanity. Our country represents nothing but peaceful intentions toward all the earth, but it ought not to fail to maintain such a military force as comports with the dignity and security of a great people. It ought to be a balanced force, intensely modern, capable of defense by sea and land, beneath the surface and in the air. But it should be so conducted that all the world may see in it, not a menace, but an instrument of security and peace.

This Nation believes thoroughly in an honorable peace under which the rights of its citizens are to be everywhere protected. It has never found that the necessary enjoyment of such a peace could be maintained only by a great and threatening array of arms. In common with other nations, it is now more determined than ever to promote peace through friendliness and good will, through mutual understandings and mutual forbearance. We have never practiced the policy of competitive armaments. We have recently committed ourselves by covenants with the other great nations to a limitation of our sea power. As one result of this, our Navy ranks larger, in comparison, than it ever did before. Removing the burden of expense and jealousy, which must always accrue from a keen rivalry, is one of the most effective methods of diminishing that unreasonable hysteria and misunderstanding which are the most potent means of fomenting war. This policy represents a new departure in the world. It is a thought, an ideal, which has led to an entirely new line of action. It will not be easy to maintain. Some never moved from their old positions, some are constantly slipping back to the old ways of thought and the old action of seizing a musket and relying on force. America has taken the lead in this new direction, and that lead America must continue to hold. If we expect others to rely on our fairness and justice we must show that we rely on their fairness and justice.

If we are to judge by past experience, there is much to be hoped for in international relations from frequent conferences and consultations. We have before us the beneficial results of the Washington conference and the various consultations recently held upon European affairs, some of which were in response to our suggestions and in some of which we were active participants. Even the failures can not but be accounted useful and an immeasurable advance over threatened or actual warfare.

I am strongly in favor of continuation of this policy, whenever conditions are such that there is even a promise that practical and favorable results might be secured.

In conformity with the principle that a display of reason rather than a threat of force should be the determining factor in the intercourse among nations, we have long advocated the peaceful settlement of disputes by methods of arbitration and have negotiated many treaties to secure that result. The same considerations should lead to our adherence to the Permanent Court of International Justice. Where great principles are involved, where great movements are under way which promise much for the welfare of humanity by reason of the very fact that many other nations have given such movements their actual support, we ought not to withhold our own sanction because of any small and inessential difference, but only upon the ground of the most important and compelling fundamental reasons. We can not barter away our independence or our sovereignty, but we ought to engage in no refinements of logic, no sophistries, and no subterfuges, to argue away the undoubted duty of this country by reason of the might of its numbers, the power of its resources, and its position of leadership in the world, actively and comprehensively to signify its approval and to bear its full share of the responsibility of a candid and disinterested attempt at the establishment of a tribunal for the administration of even-handed justice between nation and nation. The weight of our enormous influence must be cast upon the side of a reign not of force but of law and trial, not by battle but by reason.

We have never any wish to interfere in the political conditions of any other countries. Especially are we determined not to become implicated in the political controversies of the Old World. With a great deal of hesitation, we have responded to appeals for help to maintain order, protect life and property, and establish responsible government in some of the small countries of the Western Hemisphere. Our private citizens have advanced large sums of money to assist in the necessary financing and relief of the Old World. We have not failed, nor shall we fail to respond, whenever necessary to mitigate human suffering and assist in the rehabilitation of distressed nations. These, too, are requirements which must be met by reason of our vast powers and the place we hold in the world.

Some of the best thought of mankind has long been seeking for a formula for permanent peace. Undoubtedly the clarification of the principles of international law would be helpful, and the efforts of scholars to prepare such a work for adoption by the various nations should have our sympathy and support. Much may be hoped for from the earnest studies of those who advocate the outlawing of aggressive war. But all these plans and preparations, these treaties and covenants, will not of themselves be adequate. One of the greatest dangers to peace lies in the economic pressure to which people find themselves subjected. One of the most practical things to be done in the world is to seek arrangements under which such pressure may be removed, so that opportunity may be renewed and hope may be revived. There must be some assurance

that effort and endeavor will be followed by success and prosperity. In the making and financing of such adjustments there is not only an opportunity, but a real duty, for America to respond with her counsel and her resources. Conditions must be provided under which people can make a living and work out of their difficulties. But there is another element, more important than all, without which there can not be the slightest hope of a permanent peace. That element lies in the heart of humanity. Unless the desire for peace be cherished there, unless this fundamental and only natural source of brotherly love be cultivated to its highest degree, all artificial efforts will be in vain. Peace will come when there is realization that only under a reign of law, based on righteousness and supported by the religious conviction of the brotherhood of man, can there be any hope of a complete and satisfying life. Parchment will fail, the sword will fail, it is only the spiritual nature of man that can be triumphant.

It seems altogether probable that we can contribute most to these important objects by maintaining our position of political detachment and independence. We are not identified with any Old World interests. This position should be made more and more clear in our relations with all foreign countries. We are at peace with all of them. Our program is never to oppress, but always to assist. But while we do justice to others, we must require that justice be done to us. With us a treaty of peace means peace, and a treaty of amity means amity. We have made great contributions to the settlement of contentious differences in both Europe and Asia. But there is a very definite point beyond which we can not go. We can only help those who help themselves. Mindful of these limitations, the one great duty that stands out requires us to use our enormous powers to trim the balance of the world.

While we can look with a great deal of pleasure upon what we have done abroad, we must remember that our continued success in that direction depends upon what we do at home. Since its very outset, it has been found necessary to conduct our Government by means of political parties. That system would not have survived from generation to generation if it had not been fundamentally sound and provided the best instrumentalities for the most complete expression of the popular will. It is not necessary to claim that it has always worked perfectly. It is enough to know that nothing better has been devised. No one would deny that there should be full and free expression and an opportunity for independence of action within the party. There is no salvation in a narrow and bigoted partisanship. But if there is to be responsible party government, the party label must be something more than a mere device for securing office. Unless those who are elected under the same party designation are willing to assume sufficient responsibility and exhibit sufficient loyalty and coherence, so that they can cooperate with each other in the support of the broad general principles, of the party platform, the election is merely a mockery, no decision is made at the polls, and there is no representation of the popular will. Common honesty and good faith with the people who support a party at the polls require that party, when it enters office, to

assume the control of that portion of the Government to which it has been elected. Any other course is bad faith and a violation of the party pledges.

When the country has bestowed its confidence upon a party by making it a majority in the Congress, it has a right to expect such unity of action as will make the party majority an effective instrument of government. This Administration has come into power with a very clear and definite mandate from the people. The expression of the popular will in favor of maintaining our constitutional guarantees was overwhelming and decisive. There was a manifestation of such faith in the integrity of the courts that we can consider that issue rejected for some time to come. Likewise, the policy of public ownership of railroads and certain electric utilities met with unmistakable defeat. The people declared that they wanted their rights to have not a political but a judicial determination, and their independence and freedom continued and supported by having the ownership and control of their property, not in the Government, but in their own hands. As they always do when they have a fair chance, the people demonstrated that they are sound and are determined to have a sound government.

When we turn from what was rejected to inquire what was accepted, the policy that stands out with the greatest clearness is that of economy in public expenditure with reduction and reform of taxation. The principle involved in this effort is that of conservation. The resources of this country are almost beyond computation. No mind can comprehend them. But the cost of our combined governments is likewise almost beyond definition. Not only those who are now making their tax returns, but those who meet the enhanced cost of existence in their monthly bills, know by hard experience what this great burden is and what it does. No matter what others may want, these people want a drastic economy. They are opposed to waste. They know that extravagance lengthens the hours and diminishes the rewards of their labor. I favor the policy of economy, not because I wish to save money, but because I wish to save people. The men and women of this country who toil are the ones who bear the cost of the Government. Every dollar that we carelessly waste means that their life will be so much the more meager. Every dollar that we prudently save means that their life will be so much the more abundant. Economy is idealism in its most practical form.

If extravagance were not reflected in taxation, and through taxation both directly and indirectly injuriously affecting the people, it would not be of so much consequence. The wisest and soundest method of solving our tax problem is through economy. Fortunately, of all the great nations this country is best in a position to adopt that simple remedy. We do not any longer need wartime revenues. The collection of any taxes which are not absolutely required, which do not beyond reasonable doubt contribute to the public welfare, is only a species of legalized larceny. Under this republic the rewards of industry belong to those who earn them. The only constitutional tax is the tax which ministers to public necessity. The property of the country belongs to the people of the country. Their title is absolute. They do

not support any privileged class; they do not need to maintain great military forces; they ought not to be burdened with a great array of public employees. They are not required to make any contribution to Government expenditures except that which they voluntarily assess upon themselves through the action of their own representatives. Whenever taxes become burdensome a remedy can be applied by the people; but if they do not act for themselves, no one can be very successful in acting for them.

The time is arriving when we can have further tax reduction, when, unless we wish to hamper the people in their right to earn a living, we must have tax reform. The method of raising revenue ought not to impede the transaction of business; it ought to encourage it. I am opposed to extremely high rates, because they produce little or no revenue, because they are bad for the country, and, finally, because they are wrong. We can not finance the country, we can not improve social conditions, through any system of injustice, even if we attempt to inflict it upon the rich. Those who suffer the most harm will be the poor. This country believes in prosperity. It is absurd to suppose that it is envious of those who are already prosperous. The wise and correct course to follow in taxation and all other economic legislation is not to destroy those who have already secured success but to create conditions under which every one will have a better chance to be successful. The verdict of the country has been given on this question. That verdict stands. We shall do well to heed it.

These questions involve moral issues.

We need not concern ourselves much about the rights of property if we will faithfully observe the rights of persons. Under our institutions their rights are supreme. It is not property but the right to hold property, both great and small, which our Constitution guarantees. All owners of property are charged with a service. These rights and duties have been revealed, through the conscience of society, to have a divine sanction. The very stability of our society rests upon production and conservation. For individuals or for governments to waste and squander their resources is to deny these rights and disregard these obligations. The result of economic dissipation to a nation is always moral decay.

These policies of better international understandings, greater economy, and lower taxes have contributed largely to peaceful and prosperous industrial relations. Under the helpful influences of restrictive immigration and a protective tariff, employment is plentiful, the rate of pay is high, and wage earners are in a state of contentment seldom before seen. Our transportation systems have been gradually recovering and have been able to meet all the requirements of the service. Agriculture has been very slow in reviving, but the price of cereals at last indicates that the day of its deliverance is at hand.

We are not without our problems, but our most important problem is not to secure new advantages but to maintain those which we already possess. Our system of government made up of three separate and independent departments, our divided sovereignty composed of Nation and State, the matchless wisdom that is enshrined in our Constitution, all

these need constant effort and tireless vigilance for their protection and support.

In a republic the first rule for the guidance of the citizen is obedience to law. Under a despotism the law may be imposed upon the subject. He has no voice in its making, no influence in its administration, it does not represent him. Under a free government the citizen makes his own laws, chooses his own administrators, which do represent him. Those who want their rights respected under the Constitution and the law ought to set the example themselves of observing the Constitution and the law. While there may be those of high intelligence who violate the law at times, the barbarian and the defective always violate it. Those who disregard the rules of society are not exhibiting a superior intelligence, are not promoting freedom and independence, are not following the path of civilization, but are displaying the traits of ignorance, of servitude, of savagery, and treading the way that leads back to the jungle.

The essence of a republic is representative government. Our Congress represents the people and the States. In all legislative affairs it is the natural collaborator with the President. In spite of all the criticism which often falls to its lot, I do not hesitate to say that there is no more independent and effective legislative body in the world. It is, and should be, jealous of its prerogative. I welcome its cooperation, and expect to share with it not only the responsibility, but the credit, for our common effort to secure beneficial legislation.

These are some of the principles which America represents. We have not by any means put them fully into practice, but we have strongly signified our belief in them. The encouraging feature of our country is not that it has reached its destination, but that it has overwhelmingly expressed its determination to proceed in the right direction. It is true that we could, with profit, be less sectional and more national in our thought. It would be well if we could replace much that is only a false and ignorant prejudice with a true and enlightened pride of race. But the last election showed that appeals to class and nationality had little effect. We were all found loyal to a common citizenship. The fundamental precept of liberty is toleration. We can not permit any inquisition either within or without the law or apply any religious test to the holding of office. The mind of America must be forever free.

It is in such contemplations, my fellow countrymen, which are not exhaustive but only representative, that I find ample warrant for satisfaction and encouragement. We should not let the much that is to do obscure the much which has been done. The past and present show faith and hope and courage fully justified. Here stands our country, an example of tranquility at home, a patron of tranquility abroad. Here stands its Government, aware of its might but obedient to its conscience. Here it will continue to stand, seeking peace and prosperity, solicitous for the welfare of the wage earner, promoting enterprise, developing waterways and natural resources, attentive to the intuitive counsel of womanhood, encouraging education, desiring the advancement of religion, supporting the cause of justice and honor among the nations. America seeks no earthly empire built on blood and force. No ambition, no temptation, lures her to thought of foreign dominions. The legions which she sends forth are armed, not with the sword, but with the cross. The higher state to which she seeks the allegiance of all mankind is not of human, but of divine origin. She cherishes no purpose save to merit the favor of Almighty God.

Study Questions

1. What was Coolidge's conception of human nature, and how did this shape his political philosophy?

2. What role did Coolidge want America to play in international affairs?

3. What guiding principles did Coolidge offer for tax policy?

4. What main features of the constitutional republic did Coolidge cherish?

Fundamentalism and Modernism

During the early twentieth century, American Protestants split into two major camps: fundamentalists and modernists. The modernists championed the social gospel—an application of Christian ethics for social reforms that ameliorate poverty—while also finding allies among secular thinkers. Fundamentalists, for their part, sought to preserve traditional religious teachings. The two groups shared some common roots, but had different values—and different fears.

	Fundamentalism (Religious)	Modernism (Religious and Secular)
Roots	• nineteenth-century Protestant establishment • premillennialism (expecting society to decay until Christ returns to earth to restore it) • popular revivalism	• nineteenth-century Protestant establishment • postmillennialism (confident that people can improve society in preparation for Christ's return) • secular elitism
Values	• salvation of souls for heaven • preserve a remnant for the millennium • Bible as foundation for society	• make heaven on earth • transform society into the millennium • practical religion • experimental science
Fears	• higher criticism • communism (1919 "Red Scare") • evolutionism	• anti-intellectualism • out-dated traditionalism • biblical literalism
People	• William Riley (evangelist) • Charles Schofield (study Bible) • J. Gresham Machen (theologian) • Wm. Jennings Bryan (politician)	• Walter Rauschenbusch (social gospel) • Margaret Sanger (birth control) • John Dewey (education reformer) • Clarence Darrow (attorney)
Movements	• late 1800s: Moody Bible Institute • 1910: Presbyterian General Assembly • 1912–1915: *The Fundamentals* • 1919: World Christian Fundamentals Association	• late 1800s: higher criticism • *ca.* 1900: social gospel movement • *ca.* 1900–1920: Progressive Era (scientific planning; government regulation)
Big Divide	The Scopes "Monkey" Trial (see next page)	

State of Tennessee v. Scopes (1925)

The *Scopes* trial marked the growing rift between modernists and fundamentalists. After the Tennessee legislature outlawed the teaching of evolution in public schools, the American Civil Liberties Union (ACLU) asked high school teacher John Scopes to teach it anyway. The ACLU intended for Scopes to get caught, and then the law could be challenged in the courts.

Scopes went to trial with Clarence Darrow as his defense attorney. Darrow had a national reputation for taking on controversial cases. For example, he had recently defended a pair of murder suspects by blaming their genes and negative social influences. Personally an agnostic, if not an atheist, Darrow favored evolutionism. William Jennings Bryan was the prosecutor, the same man who had campaigned for "free silver" in 1896 and served as the Secretary of State under President Wilson. In the midst of World War I, Bryan became a crusader for fundamentalist America by stump-speaking against communism and evolutionism while advocating for the prohibition Amendment.

The *Scopes* trial quickly became a circus show, as vendors filled the town of Dayton, Tennessee, to sell monkey souvenirs and journalists from out of state gathered to write up the story. Darrow managed to divert attention away from his client Scopes toward the Book of Genesis, including the prosecutor's own religious interpretations of that book. In an unusual turn of events, Bryan agreed to Darrow's plan that each attorney would take the witness stand to be examined by the other. Darrow cross-examined Bryan first, revealing that Bryan did not take the entire creation account literally. For example, Bryan suggested that the "days" referenced in Genesis chapter 1 might refer to long eons of time, allowing for a slow creation process. Having demonstrated that not all "fundamentalists" share a common young-earth creationist viewpoint, Darrow surrendered his case—meaning that now Bryan would not have any opportunity to cross-examine him.

The court found Scopes guilty as charged, but the fundamentalists could hardly consider themselves winners in this case. Bryan, exhausted by the whole ordeal, died a few days later from heart failure. The media, especially the celebrated columnist H. L. Mencken, lampooned Bryan's trial tactics and painted fundamentalists as hinterland imbeciles. Scopes, celebrated as a martyr for science and progress, was later excused on appeal due to a technicality.

Study Questions

1. Who "won" the Scopes trial, and in what sense?

2. What does the Scopes trial reveal about the division in American religion during the early twentieth century?

PART 3:

The Emergence of
the American Superpower

1929–1953

The Great Depression, World War II, and the Cold War

Between 1929 and 1953 America changed profoundly. During the 1920s, America had risen to new heights of economic prosperity while also remaining aloof from international conflicts. By the end of that decade, however, the stock market was tail-spinning into the Great Depression. Before her economic troubles could be overcome, America would find herself fighting a war on three continents. Military success and economic productivity during World War II (1939–1945) transformed America into a world leader, but the world, meanwhile, also was being transformed. Soon after Fascist Italy, Nazi Germany, and Imperial Japan surrendered to the Allies, a new kind of conflict —the Cold War—followed, this time pitting the Western nations against Soviet communists. As the Great Depression and World War II faded into the past, the United States emerged as a leading world superpower—a new identity, with new responsibilities. When the Cold War turned hot in the Korean Conflict (1950–1953), Americans discovered that stalemate, rather than victory, was becoming the new normal.

The Great Depression

Every school child knows that the Great Depression began when the stock market crashed in October 1929. After peaking at 381.17 on September 3, the Dow Jones Industrial Average dropped to 230.07 on "Black Tuesday," October 29. On April 17, 1930, the Dow Jones closed at 294.07, suggesting the potential for economic recovery, but then the market resumed its decline, bottoming out on July 8, 1932 at 41.22, or 89% below its historic peak. Not until November 23, 1954 did the Dow Jones again exceed 381 to reclaim the losses of the preceding twenty-five years.

Why did stock values decline so severely? Why did economic struggles persist for a decade or more? A standard answer to these questions identifies speculation as the main culprit. According to this telling of the story, investors irrationally expected to become rich by buying more and more shares of stocks. The demand for stocks drove up prices, but by late 1929 people began to realize that prices no longer reflected the profitability of the companies issuing the stock, but only the emotional whims of the stock purchasers. Like in the game "musical chairs," the music stopped and quite a number of people realized they did not have any place to sit down. They were holding shares of stocks that nobody else wanted to buy, and the market registered that drop in demand as a decline in prices.

An alternative explanation points not to greed on Wall Street but incompetence in Washington, DC. In 1929, Congress was debating the Smoot-Hawley Tariff. On Black Tuesday, rumors circulated that President Herbert Hoover would not veto the act if Congress passed it. In May 1929, the House had passed its version of the bill, proposing to increase taxes on agricultural imports in an effort to protect local farmers from foreign competitors. But while tariffs offer protection to some producers, they also present higher costs to consumers. Moreover, too strong a tariff on imports to America could prompt other nations to retaliate by imposing counter tariffs on American exports to their own economies. The result would be a decline in world trade, which ultimately would hurt American producers—ironically, the very group that the original tariff was supposed to help. Predicting such devastation, over one thousand economists signed a petition urging the government not to adopt Smoot-Hawley. Investors, meanwhile, became nervous about the future profitability of the companies they owned, and so a great sell-off on Wall Street began. After President Hoover signed the act on June 17, 1930, the market declined steadily over the next twenty-five months. Fears of what might happen then blended into a new reality of what was in fact becoming the Great Depression.

Just as the causes of the Depression remain a subject of debate among economic historians, so also the sources of economic recovery escape easy identification. Once again, a standard story blames private investors for the downfall and credits government intervention for rebuilding the economy. Specifically, this version of history demonizes Hoover for not doing enough and celebrates his successor, Franklin D. Roosevelt, for ushering in the New Deal—FDR's catchall title for an avalanche of legislation that promised relief, recovery, and reform.

On the other hand, evidence also suggests that the New Deal accomplished next to nothing in terms of economic stimulus and merely bloated the federal government with bureaucratic nightmares that would haunt private business owners for decades to come. According to this interpretation, recovery came not from government intervention in the domestic economy, but rather from U.S. intervention abroad—the mobilization of economic resources to support the allied military engagements against Germany, Italy, and Japan from 1939 through 1945.

World War II

Curiously, war had been declared illegal about a decade before World War II began. The preamble to the Kellogg-Briand Pact of 1928 announced "a frank renunciation of war as an instrument of national policy." Specifically, the participating nations agreed to "condemn recourse to war for the solution of international controversies, and renounce it, as an instrument of national policy in their relations with one another." They promised that "settlement or solution of all disputes or conflicts of whatever nature or of whatever origin they may be, which may arise among them, shall never be sought except by pacific means." U.S. Secretary of State Frank Kellogg led the international effort to establish this lasting peace among nations. Germany, Italy, and Japan all agreed to the Kellogg-Briand Pact, as did France, Britain, and Russia.

Nevertheless, Japan invaded Manchuria, Italy invaded Ethiopia, and Germany invaded Czechoslovakia before the supposedly perpetual peace agreement had matured ten years. Britain, the Soviet Union, and the United States soon found themselves joined against those Axis Powers in World War II. How had peace given way to war so soon? Did the war arise from the imperialistic ambitions of Japan? Or the desire of Germany to resurrect an Aryan Reich from the ash heap of World War I? Was it cultural supremacy that left Italians supposing they could revive the old empire centered at Rome? What about the racial supremacy that prompted the Germany Nazis to cast Jews into labor camps, use their barely living bodies for medical experiments, and then gas them to death and incinerate them? Whether one looks at the Jewish Holocaust or the willingness of Japanese pilots to perform suicidal crash-landings on enemy targets, the answer must go deeper than economic, cultural, or racial motivations. Something was fundamentally wrong with human nature itself. World War II revealed that the progressive reformers had made a mistake; human nature is not perfectible by human means.

Even so, World War II also brought out the finest in human nature. America, in particular, recommitted itself to the ideals of ordered liberty that respect the inalienable rights of each person to life, liberty, and property. As American Christians and Jews cooperated in national life, the notion of "Judeo-Christian values" became central to civic identity. This moral foundation set Americans apart from the totalitarian regimes of Europe and the Pacific. America and her allies could not in good conscience leave German Nazism, Italian fascism, or Japanese imperialism unchecked. Nor did Americans after the war ignore another movement which threatened to undermine the moral code according to which human nature had been designed. That threat came, ironically, from one of the powers that assisted the western Allies in defeating Nazism: Soviet communism.

The Emergence of the Cold War

Even as American veterans returned home to pursue higher education under the G.I. Bill, a new concern occupied President Harry S. Truman's national security advisors. The Soviet Union appeared to be embarking along a predetermined path toward world domination. Eastern Europe, northern Korea, and the entirety of China fell under communist influence. Other nations soon might follow. The former allies, now becoming foes, divided postwar Germany into two sections: Soviet communists claimed the east while the western Allies—Britain, France, and the United States—supported the west.

With Europe split down the middle, French demographer Alfred Sauvy introduced the expression "third world" to describe other nations that were neither communist nor capitalist, but neutral outsiders to the Soviet-American tension. Soon such nations as Greece, Cuba, and Vietnam became pawns in the global chess match between the Soviet Union and the United States. By 1950, American policymakers concluded that the United States had no choice but to stand up as a world superpower on the side of freedom against communist oppression. Little did they know, this commitment would stretch some forty years into the future.

Chronological Overview: The Great Depression

1929   The New York Stock Exchange crashes, and the national economy falls into depression.

1930   Congress enacts the Smoot-Hawley Tariff, increasing taxes on imports to the highest level in a century—nearly as high as the "Tariff of Abomination" enacted in 1828. By putting the brakes on foreign trade, this tariff intensifies and prolongs the Great Depression.

1932   Congress establishes the Reconstruction Finance Corporation in an attempt to stabilize the economy by infusing $2 billion in federal aid.

1933   President Franklin D. Roosevelt's Congress launches the New Deal for economic recovery: federal public works create jobs; agricultural producers and industries cooperate with government price-fixing; nevertheless, the depression persists.

1935   FDR proposes a second New Deal, this time focusing on relief for the poor rather than cooperation between government and big corporations. The economy, however, is slow to recover.

The Social Security Act promises aid to retirees and the disabled, fundamentally changing people's relation to the federal government.

The National Labor Relations Act positions the federal government as a broker for labor unions' disputes with corporations.

1937   President Roosevelt attempts to persuade Congress to adopt a judicial reform bill that would enable him immediately to appoint New Deal–friendly judges to the U.S. Supreme Court. Critics blast the effort as a "court packing" scheme, and even congressional Democrats reject it.

1937–1938   The economy slumps again, in what some observers dub "the Roosevelt Recession." Manufacturing falls back to 1934 levels as unemployment jumps from 14% to 19%.

1939   As the Great Depression extends into its tenth year in America, a second world war breaks out in Europe.

Presidents from the Great Depression to the Early Cold War, 1929–1953

Herbert Hoover (Republican—California), 1929–1933

Through his service in the cabinets of Presidents Warren G. Harding and Calvin Coolidge, plus his prior position as Food Administrator under President Woodrow Wilson, Herbert Hoover had become one of the most respected men in American politics by 1928. Facing off against New York Governor Alfred E. Smith, the first Catholic candidate for the presidency, Hoover won by a strong margin. His winning campaign slogan promised an expansion of Coolidge prosperity: "a chicken in every pot and a car in every garage." Hoover's optimism, however, would soon appear naive, and his popularity would plummet as the national economy fell into the abyss of the deepest depression Americans have ever known.

To understand Hoover's leadership style during the onset of the Great Depression, one must look back at his own career as a mining engineer and international businessman, as well as at the political philosophy that he promoted while serving, as one contemporary phrased it, "as Secretary of Commerce and undersecretary of everything else." Orphaned in early childhood, Hoover rose to join the first graduating class at Stanford University (1895) and became a millionaire by age 40 through his mining projects in Australia and China. He believed in capitalism, but also recognized that not all capitalists exercise social responsibility as they should. He hoped that with some encouragement, most Americans would voluntarily agree to the aims of progressive reform without need of coercive government regulations. In this manner, Hoover thought that individualism and social responsibility were two sides of the same coin. This philosophy shaped the humanitarian work he directed as head of the Food Administration during World War I and as coordinator of a famine relief effort in Russia soon after the war. Hoover believed in helping people who genuinely needed help, without forcing charity through excessive regulation and without perpetuating a dependency upon welfare handouts.

When the stock market fell in October 1929, Hoover initially remained optimistic. Ups and downs form the natural rhythm of the business cycle, with the market tending to correct itself over time. "Prosperity is right around the corner," he assured Americans. As a gentle stimulus to the economy, Hoover agreed to a $19 million appropriation for highways, waterways, hospitals, and military bases, but economic recovery still remained around the corner—how far around the corner, no one could know. In 1932, Hoover signed legislation establishing the Reconstruction Finance Corporation, a government agency that would spend $2 billion per year for the next few years to extend aid to state and local governments and to provide loans for banks, railroads, and agricultural cooperatives. By stabilizing the financial sector, the RFC sought to give capitalists a second chance to pull the nation out of the depression.

Despite his good intentions, positive results did not materialize during Hoover's administration. Unemployment, homelessness, and hunger plagued a growing number of Americans, many of whom blamed the president. His critics called the burgeoning Shantytowns "Hoovervilles." Defeated in the 1932 election by Franklin Delano Roosevelt, Hoover left office as a very unpopular man. But Hoover's service to the nation did not end with his presidency. He lived another thirty-one years, remaining active in humanitarian causes well into his eighties. During World War II, for example, Hoover assisted in food relief efforts reminiscent of his earlier projects during World War I and following the Russian Revolution.

Franklin D. Roosevelt (Democrat—New York), 1933–1945

As unemployment exceeded 20% in 1932, with no end to the Great Depression in sight, Franklin Delano Roosevelt promised Americans an opportunity to reshuffle their cards and enjoy a "new deal" in the complex game of life. Voters seized the opportunity, ousting Hoover and electing Roosevelt by a landslide margin of 472 electoral votes to 59. Henceforth "FDR" and "New Deal" would be synonyms in the American lexicon as Roosevelt's winsome persona permanently transformed people's expectations of their government. The laissez-faire Coolidge years faded from memory while Franklin Roosevelt revived the Progressive Era that his cousin Theodore had launched a generation earlier. In the wake of the New Deal, few Americans would be able to imagine economic stability apart from an interventionist economic policy.

Roosevelt achieved what no other American president had accomplished before him (and none would accomplish after him): he won election to the nation's highest office four times in a row. He owed his success to personal determination, the encouragement of his wife Eleanor—an able policymaker in her own right—and the media. Ever since 1921, Roosevelt had been crippled as a result of a polio infection, but few American voters knew that he could not walk without wearing leg braces and holding the arm of the person next to him. Photojournalists selected favorable camera angles and reporters never mentioned the president's debility. His confident voice assured Americans that they had "nothing to fear but fear itself." More privately, Roosevelt acknowledged that his greatest weakness had become his greatest strength: "If you had spent two years in bed trying to wiggle your toe, after that anything would seem easy."

Roosevelt came from a long lineage of military heroes and political leaders, stretching back to an ancestor who fought in the American Revolution and including, more recently, his cousin TR. During World War I, Franklin D. Roosevelt served as Assistant Secretary of the Navy. In 1929, he was elected governor of New York. As U.S. president, he tackled not only the Great Depression but also a second world war.

Roosevelt began the presidency with a running start, pushing a series of bills through Congress during the famous "first hundred days." An alphabet soup of new federal agencies emerged: the AAA (Agricultural Adjustment Administration), the CAA (Civil Aeronautics Administration), the CCC (Civilian Conservation Corps), another CCC (Commodity Credit Corporation), the CWA (Civil Works Administration)—on and on went the list to include, most notably, the FDIC (Federal Deposit Insurance Corporation), the NRA (National Recovery Administration), the PWA (Public Works Administration), and the TVA (Tennessee Valley Authority). These New Deal agencies did not, however, arise from a systematic plan for economic recovery, but rather emerged piecemeal as one political experiment after another. The projects had two common aims: relieve people's greatest fears and build their confidence in the Roosevelt administration. It was not the success of the first hundred days, but rather the inadequacy of those reforms, that occasioned a new wave of legislation, sometimes called the Second New Deal, begun in 1935: the Works Progress Administration (WPA), the National Labor Relations (Wagner) Act (NLBA), and the Social Security Act (SSA).

When the U.S. Supreme Court declared aspects of the AAA and the NRA to be unconstitutional, Roosevelt did not get discouraged. Determined as ever, he planned for Congress to expand the number of justices on the Court and to force retirements by existing justices so that Roosevelt would have the opportunity to appoint New Deal supporters in their place. This "court packing" scheme raised the eyebrows even of congressional Democrats, who refused to support the president's plan.

Nevertheless, Roosevelt retained popularity with the common man. His portrait hung in American living rooms, where people listened to his grandfatherly "fireside chats" on the radio. "He gave me a job," thought many Americans, and they repaid the favor every four years at the polls. Whether the New Deal actually generated a national economic recovery remains a topic of dispute among economists. Compounded by a "Roosevelt Recession" in 1938, the Great Depression lingered into the 1940s. By that time, however, the domestic economy began to take second chair to a more pressing matter: World War II.

FDR adeptly walked just one short pace ahead of public opinion, pledging neutrality through the late 1930s, supporting the quasi-neutral Lend-Lease Act in 1941, but not urging Congress to declare war until it became a defensive response to the Pearl Harbor invasion of December 7, 1941. Once America entered the war, FDR assumed an active role in administering the strategy. With England's Winston Churchill, he agreed that the defeat of Nazi Germany would be the first priority, a plan to which Joseph Stalin of the Soviet Union also could agree. However, delays in targeting Germany itself left the Soviets bearing the brunt of Nazi aggression, thus alienating Stalin from the western Allies.

As FDR's health declined during the war, he longed to return to the solitude of a private home, yet he also insisted that the American people needed continuity in leadership in 1944. After being elected for a fourth term, he sought to bring the war to a peaceful conclusion and urged the establishment of the United Nations. His wife Eleanor, who had received thousands of personal letters from impoverished American families during the Depression, would herself play a crucial role in crafting the U.N. Universal Declaration on Human Rights (1948). FDR would not survive to see that day nor would he witness the surrender of Germany; he died of cerebral hemorrhage on April 14, 1945, two weeks before Adolph Hitler committed suicide and three weeks before the Third Reich surrendered.

Harry S. Truman (Democrat—Missouri), 1945–1953

Harry Truman was a humble farmer, a failed businessman, and a gullible politician who—though honest himself—unwittingly got elected to local office by a corrupt machine. Whereas Woodrow Wilson had a Ph.D., Truman never even went to college. Whereas FDR was famous for his initials, Truman did not even have a middle name—although he added the "S" just to have something. Nevertheless, Truman won the confidence of the American people and eventually occupied the most powerful office in the world, the U.S. presidency. It was at Truman's command that the first atomic bomb was dropped on an enemy nation. Truman also set the course for the duration of the Cold War (1946–1991) by identifying the containment of communism as the nation's top priority for foreign policy.

Harry Truman grew up on the family farm in Independence, Missouri. After a joint venture for a men's clothing shop left him holding his partner's debt, Truman made every necessary effort to pay off the loans himself—an ordeal that lasted fifteen years. Meanwhile, Thomas Pendergast, a Kansas City Democratic boss, channeled Truman into local politics, launching a career that would usher him onto the world stage. In 1934, and again in 1940, Truman won election to the U.S. Senate. As a member of the Senate Appropriations Committee, Truman facilitated the administration of the New Deal, a policy he enthusiastically supported. Distancing himself from the corrupt Pendergast machine, Truman chaired a special Senate committee during his second term to investigate waste and fraud, particularly in the National Defense Program.

In 1944, the Democratic National Convention paired Truman with Franklin Roosevelt, transforming the senator from Missouri into the nation's vice president. Only twice during Truman's vice presidency did the two men actually have a person-to-person meeting. When Roosevelt died in April 1945, Truman faced a steep learning curve as he succeeded to the presidency and learned of the Manhattan Project—a secret plan for developing an atomic weapon. Whereas Roosevelt had charmed both Winston Churchill and Joseph Stalin into a grand alliance, Truman—less than two weeks into the presidency—frankly spoke his mind, criticizing Soviet foreign minister Vyacheslav

Molotov to his face because the Soviets had failed to meet their commitment for fostering free elections in Poland.

By July 1945, when leaders of the United States, Great Britain, and the Soviet Union met at Potsdam, Germany, Truman was becoming increasingly suspicious of Soviet intentions. Would communism spread through eastern to central Europe? Why were the Soviets sponsoring a revolution in Greece? What would happen in Iran and Turkey? For the moment, however, the Empire of Japan still occupied Truman's mind more than anything else. While at Potsdam, he learned that the atomic bomb had been successfully tested at Los Alamos, Mexico. The following month, he authorized its use against two Japanese cities, Hiroshima and Nagasaki—a controversial tactic that quickly brought World War II to a close.

No sooner had that war ended than a new one began—and a new kind of war, too. It was the "Cold War." In March 1946, President Truman hosted former British Prime Minister Winston Churchill for a visit to Missouri. Churchill solemnly proclaimed to college students in the town of Fulton that "an iron curtain has descended across the continent" of Europe, for the Soviet empire was spreading the menace of communism into Poland, Czechoslovakia, Hungary, Romania, and Bulgaria. Twelve months later, the president adopted the "Truman Doctrine," committing the United States to assist free peoples throughout the world in resisting the spread of communism. The National Security Administration prepared a strategy of "containment," aimed at preventing the Soviet empire from encroaching upon third-world nations. In 1950, the containment policy necessitated military deployment to Korea, where the Cold War turned hot for the next few years.

After being elected to a full term in 1948, Truman offered a domestic agenda called the Fair Deal. He sought to expand upon the New Deal. Congress agreed only partly: raising minimum wage, expanding Social Security, and subsidizing housing for low-income families, while stopping short of Truman's pleas for national health insurance and nationalized education. Truman thus showed his colors as a progressive reformer in the tradition of Wilson and FDR, but the Republican opposition held his most ambitious plans in check.

Despite partisan squabbles over policy, Truman's character never was at issue. A wooden sign propped on his desk read: "The buck stops here!" Truman forthrightly accepted responsibility for all of his decisions, never regretting the use of atomic weapons to shorten the war and save millions of lives, both American and Japanese. Faithfully married to Elizabeth "Bess" Wallace, he had come from small-town America, where a man's word still meant something. Unlike Eleanor Roosevelt, Bess preferred the quiet life to the spotlight of Washington, DC, so the Trumans gracefully retired to their Independence, Missouri, home after the inauguration of Dwight D. Eisenhower in 1953.

Study Questions

1. Explain why Herbert Hoover appeared progressive when compared to Calvin Coolidge, but conservative when compared to Franklin Roosevelt.

2. Evaluate the long-term impact that Franklin Roosevelt has had on America's sense of ordered liberty.

3. What early career experiences shaped Harry Truman for the presidency?

4. When Hoover left office, America was in the depths of depression; when Truman left office, the nation had become the world's leading military and industrial power. What accounts for that transformation?

Herbert Hoover, Inaugural Address (1929)

Chief Justice William Howard Taft, who had served as president from 1909 to 1913, administered the oath of office at the inauguration of President Herbert Hoover in March 1929. Listeners around the world heard the new president's message via radio. In classic Hoover style, he praised both capitalism and government reform in the same breath, calling for mutual cooperation in the name of national progress. Inheriting the prosperity Americans enjoyed under Calvin Coolidge, Hoover maintained his composure despite the heavy downpour of rain. In the coming years, no matter the season, no matter the weather, President Hoover would play "Hooverball" on the White House lawn every morning before breakfast. It was a game of his own invention, like volleyball but with a heavy-weight medicine ball sure to keep anyone in top physical condition.

My countrymen:

This occasion is not alone the administration of the most sacred oath which can be assumed by an American citizen. It is a dedication and consecration under God to the highest office in service of our people. I assume this trust in the humility of knowledge that only through the guidance of Almighty Providence can I hope to discharge its ever-increasing burdens.

It is in keeping with tradition throughout our history that I should express simply and directly the opinions which I hold concerning some of the matters of present importance.

Our Progress

If we survey the situation of our Nation both at home and abroad, we find many satisfactions; we find some causes for concern. We have emerged from the losses of the Great War and the reconstruction following it with increased virility and strength. From this strength we have contributed to the recovery and progress of the world. What America has done has given renewed hope and courage to all who have faith in government by the people. In the large view, we have reached a higher degree of comfort and security than ever existed before in the history of the world. Through liberation from widespread poverty we have reached a higher degree of individual freedom than ever before. The devotion to and concern for our institutions are deep and sincere. We are steadily building a new race—a new civilization great in its own attainments. The influence and high purposes of our Nation are respected among the peoples of the world. We aspire to distinction in the world, but to a distinction based upon confidence in our sense of justice as well as our accomplishments within our own borders and in our own lives. For wise guidance in this great period of recovery the Nation is deeply indebted to Calvin Coolidge.

But all this majestic advance should not obscure the constant dangers from which self-government must be safeguarded. The strong man must at all times be alert to the attack of insidious disease.

The Failure of Our System of Criminal Justice

The most malign of all these dangers today is disregard and disobedience of law. Crime is increasing. Confidence in rigid and speedy justice is decreasing. I am not prepared to believe that this indicates any decay in the moral fibre of the American people. I am not prepared to believe that it indicates an impotence of the Federal Government to enforce its laws.

It is only in part due to the additional burdens imposed upon our judicial system by the 18th amendment. The problem is much wider than that. Many influences had increasingly complicated and weakened our law enforcement organization long before the adoption of the 18th amendment.

To reestablish the vigor and effectiveness of law enforcement we must critically consider the entire Federal machinery of justice, the redistribution of its functions, the simplification of its procedure, the provision of additional special tribunals, the better selection of juries, and the more effective organization of our agencies of investigation and prosecution that justice may be sure and that it may be swift. While the authority of the Federal Government extends to but part of our vast system of national, State, and local justice, yet the standards which the Federal Government establishes have the most profound influence upon the whole structure.

We are fortunate in the ability and integrity of our Federal judges and attorneys. But the system which these officers are called upon to administer is in many respects ill adapted to present-day conditions. Its intricate and involved rules of procedure have become the refuge of both big and little criminals. There is a belief abroad that by invoking technicalities, subterfuge, and delay, the ends of justice may be thwarted by those who can pay the cost.

Reform, reorganization, and strengthening of our whole judicial and enforcement system, both in civil and criminal sides, have been advocated for years by statesmen, judges, and bar associations. First steps toward that end should not longer be delayed. Rigid and expeditious justice is the first safeguard of freedom, the basis of all ordered liberty, the vital force of progress. It must not come to be in our Republic that it can be defeated by the indifference of the citizens, by exploitation of the delays and entanglements of the law, or by combinations of criminals. Justice must not fail because the agencies of enforcement are either delinquent or inefficiently organized. To consider these evils, to find their remedy, is the most sore necessity of our times.

Enforcement of the 18th Amendment

Of the undoubted abuses which have grown up under the 18th amendment, part are due to the causes I have just mentioned; but part are due to the failure of some States to accept their share of responsibility for concurrent enforcement and to the failure of many State and local officials to accept the obligation under their oath of office zealously to enforce the laws. With the failures from these many causes has come a dangerous expansion in the criminal elements who have found enlarged opportunities in dealing in illegal liquor.

But a large responsibility rests directly upon our citizens. There would be little traffic in illegal liquor if only criminals patronized it. We must awake to the fact that this patronage from large numbers of law-abiding citizens is supplying the rewards and stimulating crime.

I have been selected by you to execute and enforce the laws of the country. I propose to do so to the extent of my own abilities, but the measure of success that the Government shall attain will depend upon the moral support which you, as citizens, extend. The duty of citizens to support the laws of the land is coequal with the duty of their Government to enforce the laws which exist. No greater national service can be given by men and women of good will—who, I know, are not unmindful of the responsibilities of citizenship—than that they should, by their example, assist in stamping out crime and outlawry by refusing participation in and condemning all transactions with illegal liquor. Our whole system of self-government will crumble either if officials elect what laws they will enforce or citizens elect what laws they will support. The worst evil of disregard for some law is that it destroys respect for all law. For our citizens to patronize the violation of a particular law on the ground that they are opposed to it is destructive of the very basis of all that protection of life, of homes and property which they rightly claim under other laws. If citizens do not like a law, their duty as honest men and women is to discourage its

violation; their right is openly to work for its repeal.

To those of criminal mind there can be no appeal but vigorous enforcement of the law. Fortunately they are but a small percentage of our people. Their activities must be stopped.

A National Investigation

I propose to appoint a national commission for a searching investigation of the whole structure of our Federal system of jurisprudence, to include the method of enforcement of the 18th amendment and the causes of abuse under it. Its purpose will be to make such recommendations for reorganization of the administration of Federal laws and court procedure as may be found desirable. In the meantime it is essential that a large part of the enforcement activities be transferred from the Treasury Department to the Department of Justice as a beginning of more effective organization.

The Relation of Government to Business

The election has again confirmed the determination of the American people that regulation of private enterprise and not Government ownership or operation is the course rightly to be pursued in our relation to business. In recent years we have established a differentiation in the whole method of business regulation between the industries which produce and distribute commodities on the one hand and public utilities on the other. In the former, our laws insist upon effective competition; in the latter, because we substantially confer a monopoly by limiting competition, we must regulate their services and rates. The rigid enforcement of the laws applicable to both groups is the very base of equal opportunity and freedom from domination for all our people, and it is just as essential for the stability and prosperity of business itself as for the protection of the public at large. Such regulation should be extended by the Federal Government within the limitations of the Constitution and only when the individual States are without power to protect their citizens through their own authority. On the other hand, we should be fearless when the authority rests only in the Federal Government.

Cooperation by the Government

The larger purpose of our economic thought should be to establish more firmly stability and security of business and employment and thereby remove poverty still further from our borders. Our people have in recent years developed a new-found capacity for cooperation among themselves to effect high purposes in public welfare. It is an advance toward the highest conception of self-government. Self-government does not and should not imply the use of political agencies alone. Progress is born of cooperation in the community—not from governmental restraints. The Government should assist and encourage these movements of collective self-help by itself cooperating with them. Business has by cooperation made great progress in the advancement of service, in stability, in regularity of employment, and in the correction of its own abuses. Such progress, however, can

continue only so long as business manifests its respect for law.

There is an equally important field of cooperation by the Federal Government with the multitude of agencies, State, municipal, and private, in the systematic development of those processes which directly affect public health, recreation, education, and the home. We have need further to perfect the means by which Government can be adapted to human service.

Education

Although education is primarily a responsibility of the States and local communities, and rightly so, yet the Nation as a whole is vitally concerned in its development everywhere to the highest standards and to complete universality. Self-government can succeed only through an instructed electorate. Our objective is not simply to overcome illiteracy. The Nation has marched far beyond that. The more complex the problems of the Nation become, the greater is the need for more and more advanced instruction. Moreover, as our numbers increase and as our life expands with science and invention, we must discover more and more leaders for every walk of life. We cannot hope to succeed in directing this increasingly complex civilization unless we can draw all the talent of leadership from the whole people. One civilization after another has been wrecked upon the attempt to secure sufficient leadership from a single group or class. If we would prevent the growth of class distinctions and would constantly refresh our leadership with the ideals of our people, we must draw constantly from the general mass. The full opportunity for every boy and girl to rise through the selective processes of education can alone secure to us this leadership.

Public Health

In public health the discoveries of science have opened a new era. Many sections of our country and many groups of our citizens suffer from diseases the eradication of which are mere matters of administration and moderate expenditure. Public health service should be as fully organized and as universally incorporated into our governmental system as is public education. The returns are a thousandfold in economic benefits, and infinitely more in reduction of suffering and promotion of human happiness.

World Peace

The United States fully accepts the profound truth that our own progress, prosperity, and peace are interlocked with the progress, prosperity, and peace of all humanity. The whole world is at peace. The dangers to a continuation of this peace today are largely the fear and suspicion which still haunt the world. No suspicion or fear can be rightly directed toward our country.

Those who have a true understanding of America know that we have no desire for territorial expansion, for economic or other domination of other peoples. Such purposes are repugnant to our ideals of human freedom. Our form of government is ill adapted to the responsibilities which inevitably follow permanent limitation of the independence of other peoples. Superficial observers seem to find no destiny for our abounding increase in population, in wealth and power except that of imperialism. They fail to see that the American people are engrossed in the building for themselves of a new economic system, a new social system, a new political system— all of which are characterized by aspirations of freedom of opportunity and thereby are the negation of imperialism. They fail to realize that because of our abounding prosperity our youth are pressing more and more into our institutions of learning; that our people are seeking a larger vision through art, literature, science, and travel; that they are moving toward stronger moral and spiritual life—that from these things our sympathies are broadening beyond the bounds of our Nation and race toward their true expression in a real brotherhood of man. They fail to see that the idealism of America will lead it to no narrow or selfish channel, but inspire it to do its full share as a Nation toward the advancement of civilization. It will do that not by mere declaration but by taking a practical part in supporting all useful international undertakings. We not only desire peace with the world, but to see peace maintained throughout the world. We wish to advance the reign of justice and reason toward the extinction of force.

The recent treaty for the renunciation of war as an instrument of national policy sets an advanced standard in our conception of the relations of nations. Its acceptance should pave the way to greater limitation of armament, the offer of which we sincerely extend to the world. But its full realization also implies a greater and greater perfection in the instrumentalities for pacific settlement of controversies between nations. In the creation and use of these instrumentalities we should support every sound method of conciliation, arbitration, and judicial settlement. American statesmen were among the first to propose, and they have constantly urged upon the world, the establishment of a tribunal for the settlement of controversies of a justiciable character. The Permanent Court of International Justice in its major purpose is thus peculiarly identified with American ideals and with American statesmanship. No more potent instrumentality for this purpose has ever been conceived and no other is practicable of establishment. The reservations placed upon our adherence should not be misinterpreted. The United States seeks by these reservations no special privilege or advantage but only to clarify our relation to advisory opinions and other matters which are subsidiary to the major purpose of the Court. The way should, and I believe will, be found by which we may take our proper place in a movement so fundamental to the progress of peace.

Our people have determined that we should make no political engagements such as membership in the League of Nations, which may commit us in advance as a nation to become involved in the settlements of controversies between other countries. They adhere to the belief that the independence of America from such obligations increases its ability and availability for service in all fields of human progress.

I have lately returned from a journey among our sister Republics of the Western Hemisphere. I have received unbounded hospitality and courtesy as their expression of friendliness to our country. We are held by particular bonds of sympathy and common interest with them. They are each of them building a racial character and a culture which is an impressive contribution to human progress. We wish only for the maintenance of their independence, the growth of their stability and their prosperity. While we have had wars in the Western Hemisphere, yet on the whole the record is in encouraging contrast with that of other parts of the world. Fortunately the New World is largely free from the inheritances of fear and distrust which have so troubled the Old World. We should keep it so.

It is impossible, my countrymen, to speak of peace without profound emotion. In thousands of homes in America, in millions of homes around the world, there are vacant chairs. It would be a shameful confession of our unworthiness if it should develop that we have abandoned the hope for which all these men died. Surely civilization is old enough, surely mankind is mature enough so that we ought in our own lifetime to find a way to permanent peace. Abroad, to west and east, are nations whose sons mingled their blood with the blood of our sons on the battlefields. Most of these nations have contributed to our race, to our culture, our knowledge, and our progress. From one of them we derive our very language and from many of them much of the genius of our institutions. Their desire for peace is as deep and sincere as our own.

Peace can be contributed to by respect for our ability in defense. Peace can be promoted by the limitation of arms and by the creation of the instrumentalities for peaceful settlement of controversies. But it will become a reality only through self-restraint and active effort in friendliness and helpfulness. I covet for this administration a record of having further contributed to advance the cause of peace.

Party Responsibilities

In our form of democracy the expression of the popular will can be effected only through the instrumentality of political parties. We maintain party government not to promote intolerant partisanship but because opportunity must be given for expression of the popular will, and organization provided for the execution of its mandates and for accountability of government to the people. It follows that the government both in the executive and the legislative branches must carry out in good faith the platforms upon which the party was entrusted with power. But the government is that of the whole people; the party is the instrument through which policies are determined and men chosen to bring them into being. The animosities of elections should have no place in our Government for government must concern itself alone with the common weal.

Special Session of the Congress

Action upon some of the proposals upon which the Republican Party was returned to power, particularly further agricultural relief and limited changes in the tariff, cannot in justice to our farmers, our labor, and our manufacturers be postponed. I shall therefore request a special session of Congress for the consideration of these two questions. I shall deal with each of them upon the assembly of the Congress.

Other Mandates from the Election

It appears to me that the more important further mandates from the recent election were the maintenance of the integrity of the Constitution; the vigorous enforcement of the laws; the continuance of economy in public expenditure; the continued regulation of business to prevent domination in the community; the denial of ownership or operation of business by the Government in competition with its citizens; the avoidance of policies which would involve us in the controversies of foreign nations; the more effective reorganization of the departments of the Federal Government; the expansion of public works; and the promotion of welfare activities affecting education and the home.

These were the more tangible determinations of the election, but beyond them was the confidence and belief of the people that we would not neglect the support of the embedded ideals and aspirations of America. These ideals and aspirations are the touchstones upon which the day-today administration and legislative acts of government must be tested. More than this, the Government must, so far as lies within its proper powers, give leadership to the realization of these ideals and to the fruition of these aspirations. No one can adequately reduce these things of the spirit to phrases or to a catalogue of definitions. We do know what the attainments of these ideals should be: the preservation of self-government and its full foundations in local government; the perfection of justice whether in economic or in social fields; the maintenance of ordered liberty; the denial of domination by any group or class; the building up and preservation of equality of opportunity; the stimulation of initiative and individuality; absolute integrity in public affairs; the choice of officials for fitness to office; the direction of economic progress toward prosperity and the further lessening of poverty; the freedom of public opinion; the sustaining of education and of the advancement of knowledge; the growth of religious spirit and the tolerance of all faiths; the strengthening of the home; the advancement of peace.

There is no short road to the realization of these aspirations. Ours is a progressive people, but with a determination that progress must be based upon the foundation of experience. Ill-considered remedies for our faults bring only penalties after them. But if we hold the faith of the men in our mighty past who created these ideals, we shall leave them heightened and strengthened for our children.

Conclusion

This is not the time and place for exten-ded discussion. The questions before our country are problems of progress to higher standards; they are not the problems of degeneration. They demand thought and they serve to quicken the conscience and enlist our sense of responsibility for their settlement. And that responsibility rests upon you, my countrymen, as much as upon those of us who have been selected for office.

Ours is a land rich in resources, stimulating in its glorious beauty, filled with millions of happy homes, blessed with comfort and opportunity. In no nation are the institutions of progress more advanced. In no nation are the fruits of accomplishment more secure. In no nation is the government more worthy of respect. No country is more loved by its people. I have an abiding faith in their capacity, integrity, and high purpose. I have no fears for the future of our country. It is bright with hope.

In the presence of my countrymen, mindful of the solemnity of this occasion, knowing what the task means and the responsibility which it involves, I beg your tolerance, your aid, and your cooperation. I ask the help of Almighty God in this service to my country to which you have called me.

Study Questions

1. For what improvements to American life did Hoover credit Coolidge?

2. Did Hoover promote progressive reform, *laissez faire*, or some third form of economic policy? Provide examples that illustrate his position.

Franklin D. Roosevelt, First Inaugural Address (1933)

Campaigning for the presidency in April 1932, Franklin D. Roosevelt criticized Herbert Hoover with this charge:

> It is said that Napoleon lost the battle of Waterloo because he forgot his infantry—he staked too much upon the more spectacular but less substantial cavalry. The present administration in Washington provides a close parallel. It has either forgotten or it does not want to remember the infantry of our economic army.

Roosevelt's "Forgotten Man" speech also faulted Congress for the Smoot-Hawley Tariff of 1930, which he believed crippled the foreign trade upon which American economic recovery depended. Although Hoover had adopted some reforms for the financial sector, Roosevelt believed that the federal government should provide more direct forms of relief, and he would not be shy to demand authorization from Congress to build new government agencies in response to the economic crisis. Accepting the nomination of the Democratic Party in July 1932, Roosevelt promised: "I pledge you, I pledge myself, to a new deal for the American people." The people responded with warm applause at the convention and an electoral victory that November.

I am certain that my fellow Americans expect that on my induction into the Presidency I will address them with a candor and a decision which the present situation of our Nation impels. This is preeminently the time to speak the truth, the whole truth, frankly and boldly. Nor need we shrink from honestly facing conditions in our country today. This great Nation will endure as it has endured, will revive and will prosper. So, first of all, let me assert my firm belief that the only thing we have to fear is fear itself—nameless, unreasoning, unjustified terror which paralyzes needed efforts to convert retreat into advance. In every dark hour of our national life a leadership of frankness and vigor has met with that understanding and support of the people themselves which is essential to victory. I am convinced that you will again give that support to leadership in these critical days.

In such a spirit on my part and on yours we face our common difficulties. They concern, thank God, only material things. Values have shrunken to fantastic levels; taxes have risen; our ability to pay has fallen; government of all kinds is faced by serious curtailment of income; the means of exchange are frozen in the currents of trade; the withered leaves of industrial enterprise lie on every side; farmers find no markets for their produce; the savings of many years in thousands of families are gone.

More important, a host of unemployed citizens face the grim problem of existence, and an equally great number toil with little return. Only a foolish optimist can deny the dark realities of the moment.

Yet our distress comes from no failure of substance. We are stricken by no plague of locusts. Compared with the perils which our forefathers conquered because they believed and were not afraid, we have still much to be thankful for. Nature still offers her bounty and human efforts have multiplied it. Plenty is at our doorstep, but a generous use of it languishes in the very sight of the supply. Primarily this is because rulers of the exchange of mankind's goods have failed through their own stubbornness and their own incompetence, have admitted their failure, and have abdicated. Practices of the unscrupulous money changers stand indicted in the court of public opinion, rejected by the hearts and minds of men.

True they have tried, but their efforts have been cast in the pattern of an outworn tradition. Faced by failure of credit they have proposed only the lending of more money. Stripped of the lure of profit by which to induce our people to follow their false leadership, they have resorted to exhortations, pleading tearfully for restored confidence. They know only the rules of a generation of self-seekers. They have no vision, and when there is no vision the people perish.

The money changers have fled from their high seats in the temple of our civilization. We may now restore that temple to the ancient truths. The measure of the restoration lies in the extent to which we apply social values more noble than mere monetary profit.

Happiness lies not in the mere possession of money; it lies in the joy of achievement, in the thrill of creative effort. The joy and moral stimulation of work no longer must be forgotten in the mad chase of evanescent profits. These dark days will be worth all they cost us if they teach us that our true destiny is not to be ministered unto but to minister to ourselves and to our fellow men.

Recognition of the falsity of material wealth as the standard of success goes hand in hand with the abandonment of the false belief that public office and high political position are to be valued only by the standards of pride of place and personal profit; and there must be an end to a conduct in banking and in business which too often has given to a sacred trust the likeness of callous and selfish wrongdoing. Small wonder that confidence languishes, for it thrives only on honesty, on honor, on the sacredness of obligations, on faithful protection, on unselfish performance; without them it cannot live. Restoration calls, however, not for changes in ethics alone. This Nation asks for action, and action now.

Our greatest primary task is to put people to work. This is no unsolvable problem if we face it wisely and courageously. It can be accomplished in part by direct recruiting by the Government itself, treating the task as we would treat the emergency of a war, but at the same time, through this employment, accomplishing greatly needed projects to stimulate and reorganize the use of our natural resources.

Hand in hand with this we must frankly recognize the overbalance of population in our industrial centers and, by engaging on a national scale in a redistribution, endeavor to provide a better use of the land for those best fitted for the land. The task can be helped by definite efforts to raise the values of agricultural products and with this the power to purchase the output of our cities. It can be helped by preventing realistically the tragedy of the growing loss through foreclosure of our small homes and our farms. It can be helped by insistence that the Federal, State, and local governments act forthwith on the demand that their cost be drastically reduced. It can be helped by the unifying of relief activities which today are often scattered, uneconomical, and unequal. It can be helped by national planning for and supervision of all forms of transportation and of communications and other utilities which have a definitely public character. There are many ways in which it can be helped, but it can never be helped merely by talking about it. We must act and act quickly.

Finally, in our progress toward a resumption of work we require two safeguards against a return of the evils of the old order: there must be a strict supervision of all banking and credits and investments, so that there will be an end to speculation with other people's money; and there must be provision for an adequate but sound currency.

These are the lines of attack. I shall presently urge upon a new Congress, in special session, detailed measures for their fulfillment, and I shall seek the immediate assistance of the several States.

Through this program of action we address ourselves to putting our own national house in order and making income balance outgo. Our international trade relations, though vastly important, are in point of time and necessity secondary to the establishment of a sound national economy. I favor as a practical policy the putting of first things first. I shall spare no effort to restore world trade by international economic readjustment, but the emergency at home cannot wait on that accomplishment.

The basic thought that guides these specific means of national recovery is not narrowly nationalistic. It is the insistence, as a first considerations, upon the interdependence of the various elements in and parts of the United States—a recognition of the old and permanently important manifestation of the American spirit of the pioneer. It is the way to recovery. It is the immediate way. It is the strongest assurance that the recovery will endure.

In the field of world policy I would dedicate this Nation to the policy of the good neighbor—the neighbor who resolutely respects himself and, because he does so, respects the rights of others—the neighbor who respects his obligations and respects the sanctity of his agreements in and with a world of neighbors.

If I read the temper of our people correctly, we now realize as we have never realized before our interdependence on each other; that we cannot merely take but we must give as well; that if we are to go forward, we must move as a trained and loyal army willing to sacrifice for the good of a common discipline, because without such discipline no progress is made, no leadership becomes effective. We are, I know, ready and willing to submit our lives and property to such discipline, because it makes possible a leadership which aims at a larger good. This I propose to offer, pledging that the larger purposes will bind upon us all as a sacred obligation with a unity of duty hitherto evoked only in time of armed strife.

With this pledge taken, I assume unhesitatingly the leadership of this great army of our people dedicated to a disciplined attack upon our common problems.

Action in this image and to this end is feasible under the form of government which we have inherited from our ancestors. Our Constitution is so simple and practical that it is possible always to meet extraordinary needs by changes in emphasis and arrangement without loss of essential form. That is why our constitutional system has proved itself the most superbly enduring political mechanism the modern world has produced. It has met every stress of vast expansion of territory, of foreign wars, of bitter internal strife, of world relations.

It is to be hoped that the normal balance of Executive and legislative authority may be wholly adequate to meet the unprecedented task before us. But it may be that an unprecedented demand and need for undelayed action may call for temporary departure from that normal balance of public procedure.

I am prepared under my constitutional duty to recommend the measures that a stricken Nation in the midst of a stricken world may require. These measures, or such other measures as the Congress may build out of its experience and wisdom, I shall seek, within my constitutional authority, to bring to speedy adoption.

But in the event that the Congress shall fail to take one of these two courses, and in the event that the national emergency is still critical, I shall not evade the clear course of duty that will then confront me. I shall ask the Congress for the one remaining instrument to meet the crisis—broad Executive power to wage a war against the emergency, as great as the power that would be given to me if we were in fact invaded by a foreign foe.

For the trust reposed in me I will return the courage and the devotion that befit the time. I can do no less.

We face the arduous days that lie before us in the warm courage of national unity; with the clear consciousness of seeking old and precious moral values; with the clean satisfaction that comes from the stern performance of duty by old and young alike. We aim at the assurance of a rounded and permanent national life.

We do not distrust the future of essential democracy. The people of the United States have not failed. In their need they have registered a mandate that they want direct, vigorous action. They have asked for discipline and direction under leadership. They have made me the present instrument of their wishes. In the spirit of the gift I take it.

In this dedication of a Nation we humbly ask the blessing of God. May He protect each and every one of us. May He guide me in the days to come.

Study Questions

1. What did Roosevelt mean when he said, "the only thing we have to fear is fear itself"?

2. Identify two "lines of attack" that Roosevelt proposed for dealing with the economic depression.

3. In what sense did Roosevelt desire America to follow "the policy of the Good Neighbor" among other nations?

4. Could Roosevelt hope to implement his economic programs without abandoning the U.S. Constitution? Explain.

The First New Deal (1933–1934)

During the first hundred days (March to June 1933) of Franklin Roosevelt's administration, Congress enacted numerous laws aimed at stimulating economic recovery. Banking reforms sought to stabilize the financial sector; federal public works programs created jobs; new agencies brought farms and factories into price-fixing arrangements. The New Deal had come in with a roar. Nevertheless, the depression persisted. Was the New Deal an ill-conceived plan? Or would it simply take more time before its benefits could be realized?

Banking and Investment

Program	Description
Emergency Banking Act	Following an executive "bank holiday" order that had closed all banks, this act established guidelines for re-opening healthy banks and salvaging failing banks.
Glass-Steagall Banking Act	This banking reform established the Federal Deposit Insurance Corporation (FDIC) to stabilize banks and protect consumers and also prohibited the commingling of funds between investment banks and commercial banks.
Federal Securities Act	This act boosted the authority of the Federal Trade Commission to supervise Wall Street so that investor confidence would rebound. In 1934, an extension of this act established the Securities and Exchange Commission for regulating publicly traded companies.

Employment

Program	Description
Civilian Conservation Corps (CCC)	The federal government employed 3 million youth in forest preservation and park maintenance jobs, aiming to boost the economy and conserve natural resources.
National Industrial Recovery Act (NIRA)	The Public Works Administration (PWA) created jobs for adults, while other provisions of the NIRA supported collective bargaining rights for unions.
	As a result, union workers joined the Democratic coalition.

| Tennessee Valley Authority (TVA) | Many analysts regard this program as the most successful part of the New Deal; it created about 30,000 jobs and brought electricity to rural areas. |

Business Cooperation

Program	Description
Agricultural Adjustment Administration (AAA)	The AAA subsidized farmers who cut livestock and grain production. This government-induced reduction in supply was intended to drive up prices to keep farmers in business, but Americans were alarmed to see food wasted while people starved.
National Recovery Administration (NRA)	"Blue Eagle" codes encouraged industries to establish fair prices, wages, working conditions, and production regulations. Participation was voluntary, but business owners thought they could attract more customers by displaying the "Blue Eagle" in their store windows.

After the first hundred days, Roosevelt continued to add components to his ever-evolving New Deal. For example, the Gold Reserve Act (1934) reset the nominal price for gold from $20.67 per troy ounce to $35, which effectively authorized the Federal Reserve Bank to increase the amount of money in circulation. This reform followed on the heels of an even more controversial policy: the suspension of the gold standard in 1933 and the requirement that Americans surrender their private gold holdings to the U.S. Department of the Treasury. On the one hand, a manipulation of currency valuation increased the amount of money in circulation, thus lubricating the economy; on the other hand, these inflationary programs decreased the spending power of each individual dollar, effectively robbing Americans of what little wealth they still had.

Study Questions

1. What was the most beneficial accomplishment of the First New Deal? Explain.

2. What was the most damaging result of the First New Deal? Explain.

Economic Indicators during the Great Depression

Statistics that measure economic activity are known as economic indicators. Leading indicators precede major economic changes and thus offer economists a hint of what is to come. Coincident indicators occur simultaneously with major economic changes. Lagging indicators happen after the economy as a whole has changed.

Economists consider the stock market to be a leading economic indicator, since major changes in stock prices tend to foreshadow future economic conditions. Unemployment, by contrast, is a lagging economic indicator, since shifts in the unemployment rate happen after the economy as a whole changes. For example, the decline of the stock market from 1929 to 1932 signaled the start of the Great Depression, with unemployment rates peaking in 1933 and remaining higher than normal for the remainder of the decade, despite an upward trend in the stock market.

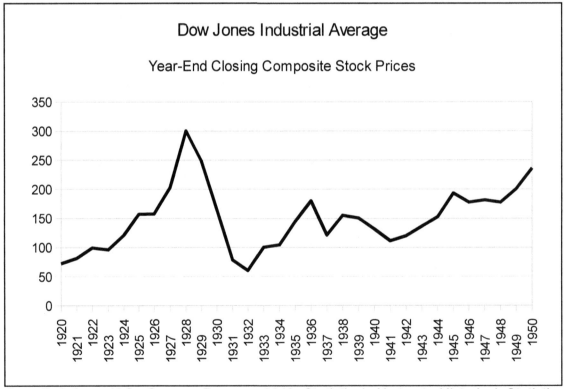

Compiled from U.S. Census Bureau, *2012 Statistical Abstract: Historical Statistics* (2013).

Unemployment

As a Percentage of Civilian Labor Force

Historical estimates of unemployment during the early twentieth-century vary considerably. The chart above was compiled from *The Measurement and Behavior of Unemployment* (1957), Table 1.

The gross domestic product (GDP) measures the nation's total economic output. Because the GDP is measured in dollars, it is sensitive to inflation. Therefore, economists sometimes recalculate the GDP in inflation-adjusted dollars. The GDP also is dependent to some degree upon the total population, since the productive capacity of a nation generally increases in proportion to population. To account for both inflation and population growth, the following chart expresses the inflation-adjusted per capita dollar value of America's 1929 GDP as 100%, a benchmark against which later years may be compared.

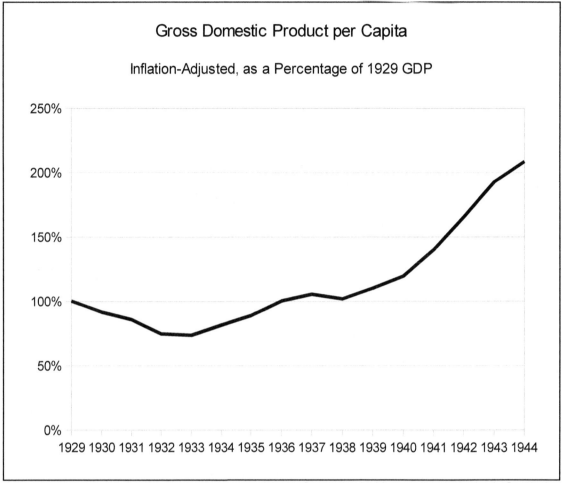

Compiled from U.S. Census Bureau, *2012 Statistical Abstract: Historical Statistics* (2013).

Study Questions

1. At what point in time did the stock market begin a steady recovery following the 1929 crash? Offer an explanation of why this recovery occurred when it did.

2. At what point in time did the unemployment level return to its pre-Depression range? Offer an explanation of why this recovery occurred when it did.

3. As measured by GDP, the American economy apparently had recovered from the Great Depression by 1936. However, a major surge in productive output occurred starting in 1939 and accelerating in 1941. What historical factors account for the nation's economic growth leading into the 1940s?

4. Which hypothesis do you consider more reasonable—that the New Deal rescued America from the Great Depression, or that demand for production occasioned by World War II rescued America from the Great Depression? Explain.

Twentieth and Twenty-First Amendments (1933)

The states ratified two amendments to the U.S. Constitution in 1933, one adjusting the starting date for newly elected officials and the other rescinding the prohibition amendment. The Twentieth Amendment shifted the term of office for U.S. presidents to commence on January 20, rather than March 4, of years immediately following a presidential election. This amendment also made provisions for who would succeed the president elect in the case of death. The Twenty-First Amendment repealed the Eighteenth Amendment, a progressive reform that had outlawed liquor. After over a decade of failed enforcement, prohibition seemed not only impractical but also dangerous, for the demand for liquor on the black market led to other vices as well.

Twentieth Amendment

(proposed, 1932; ratified, 1933)

Section 1. The terms of the President and Vice President shall end at noon on the 20th day of January, and the terms of Senators and Representatives at noon on the 3d day of January, of the years in which such terms would have ended if this article had not been ratified; and the terms of their successors shall then begin.

Section 2. The Congress shall assemble at least once in every year, and such meeting shall begin at noon on the 3d day of January, unless they shall by law appoint a different day.

Section 3. If, at the time fixed for the beginning of the term of the President, the President elect shall have died, the Vice President elect shall become President. If a President shall not have been chosen before the time fixed for the beginning of his term, or if the President elect shall have failed to qualify, then the Vice President elect shall act as President until a President shall have qualified; and the Congress may by law provide for the case wherein neither a President elect nor a Vice President elect shall have qualified, declaring who shall then act as President, or the manner in which one who is to act shall be selected, and such person shall act accordingly until a President or Vice President shall have qualified.

Section 4. The Congress may by law provide for the case of the death of any of the persons from whom the House of Representatives may choose a President whenever the right of choice shall have devolved upon them, and for the case of the death of any of the persons from whom the Senate may choose a Vice President whenever the right of choice shall have devolved upon them.

Section 5. Sections 1 and 2 shall take effect on the 15th day of October following the ratification of this article.

Section 6. This article shall be inoperative unless it shall have been ratified as an amendment to the Constitution by the legislatures of three-fourths of the several States within seven years from the date of its submission.

Twenty-First Amendment

(proposed, 1933; ratified 1933)

Section 1. The eighteenth article of amendment to the Constitution of the United States is hereby repealed.

Section 2. The transportation or importation into any State, Territory, or possession of the United States for delivery or use therein of intoxicating liquors, in violation of the laws thereof, is hereby prohibited.

Section 3. This article shall be inoperative unless it shall have been ratified as an amendment to the Constitution by conventions in the several States, as provided in the Constitution, within seven years from the date of the submission hereof to the States by the Congress.

Study Questions

1. Why did the founding fathers not draft and ratify the Twentieth Amendment themselves? Consider how the world changed during the 150 years between the American Revolution and the Great Depression.

2. What can be inferred about human nature, and the prospects for ordered liberty, from the history of the Eighteenth and Twenty-First Amendments?

The Second New Deal (1935–1938)

Reactions to the First New Deal

Despite the simple tale often told today—that the New Deal brought America out of the Great Depression—economic hardship in fact persisted and in some cases worsened after Roosevelt's first hundred days. The president faced criticisms from many sides:

1. **Keynesian Economics:** In December 1933, British economist John Maynard Keynes published an open letter to President Roosevelt in the *New York Times*, advising him to adopt a demand-side economic theory. Known as Keynesian Economics, this theory calls for the government to lower interest rates and also to take on debt in order to put more cash in the hands of consumers, with the hope that as consumers spend more, production will increase to meet the new demand, and as production increases, employment should rise, too.

2. **The Supreme Court** invalidated aspects of the Agricultural Adjustment Act and the National Industrial Recovery Act—two of the core components of Roosevelt's effort to relieve the depression through economic reform. In *Butler* (1936), the Supreme Court struck down the AAA wheat milling tax as unconstitutional. In *Schechter* (1935), the Supreme Court struck down NIRA's *intra*state commerce regulations as an unconstitutional stretch of Congress' *inter*state commerce authority.

3. **Conservatives in Congress** accused Roosevelt of permitting socialism to creep into the nation through the newly established federal agencies.

4. **Critics from the far left** blamed Roosevelt for not being progressive enough.

   a. **Father Charles Coughlin**, a popular radio speaker who headed the National Union for Social Justice, proposed nationalization of the banks to stabilize the economy. He claimed that Roosevelt had betrayed America by not pursuing such nationalization plans.

   b. **Dr. Francis Townsend**, a physician who suddenly attracted a huge political following, suggested that the government should encourage senior citizens to retire by paying them $200 per month (or about $3,500 in 2013 dollars) on the condition that they spend it within thirty days. Townsend hoped thereby to open jobs for younger workers while also stimulating production through the subsidization of elderly consumers.

   c. **Senator Huey Long** of Louisiana launched the "Share Our Wealth" campaign, proposing a 100% tax on incomes over $1 million and estates valued over $5 million; these tax revenues would fund a guaranteed minimum income of $2,000 per year (or about $35,000 in 2013 dollars) for every family.

The Second New Deal: A Move to the Left

Roosevelt sought to become more aggressive in what historians call the "Second New Deal," a wave of progressive reform begun in 1935. The Second New Deal set a new benchmark for American liberalism—no longer would "liberal" carry the nineteenth-century connotation of *laissez faire* but rather it would represent a government commitment to providing relief for the poor through structural economic reform.

New Deal Legislation of 1935

Program	Description
Social Security Administration (SSA)	Designed by Grace Abbott (Children's Bureau) and Frances Perkins (Secretary of Labor), the act established Old-Age and Disability Insurance (OADI) funded by payroll taxes.
	Unlike welfare reforms in the 1960s and later, the Social Security Act presumed that married households were foundational to economic stability. Thus, for example, a widow could receive a retirement benefit based on her husband's earnings rather than only receiving a benefit based on her own earnings—which generally would have been lower than his earnings.
National Labor Relations Act (NLRA), or Wagner Act	The NLRA required employers to recognize designated labor representatives for collective bargaining arrangements and prohibited employers from discriminating against unionized employees.
	The U.S. Supreme Court upheld this law in 1937.
Works Progress Administration (WPA)	The WPA provided federally funded jobs, including the Federal Writers' Project, the Federal Theatre Project, the Federal Arts Project, and several construction projects for bridges and tunnels.
	The approach was similar to the PWA of the First New Deal, but this time with a significantly larger budget.
Revenue Act of 1935	Derided by critics as a "soak the rich" tax, this reform increased the highest tax bracket to 75%, but also allowed for loopholes.

The New Democratic Coalition (1936)

Roosevelt won reelection in 1936 by a landslide. His immense popularity united diverse groups of Americans into a new Democratic coalition that would continue faithfully to support that party for decades to come. Southern whites, small western farmers, urban ethnic laborers, union workers, African Americans, and women all supported the party of Roosevelt, despite the fact that several of these groups had been strong Republicans and others had been more evenly balanced prior to the New Deal.

The Roosevelt Recession (1937–1938)

Due in part to the Social Security and Revenue Acts of 1935, both of which took money out of consumers' hands, consumption staggered and the economy slipped once more. Critics of the president seized upon the opportunity to call this the "Roosevelt Recession."

The Peak of Progressive Reform (1938)

In the **Fair Labor Standards Act (1938)**, Congress outlawed child labor and established a 40-cent minimum wage and 40-hour maximum work week. Similar reforms had been effected at the state level during the Progressive Era; now progressivism had become a national policy.

Study Questions

1. If you had been president during the 1930s, whose advice would you have followed and why—Keynes's, Coughlin's, Townsend's, or Long's? Or the Republicans'?

2. How did the so-called Second New Deal differ from the First New Deal?

3. Describe the political realignment that resulted from Roosevelt's policies.

Supreme Court Decisions during the Great Depression

During the early years of the New Deal, the U.S. Supreme Court wavered between a continuation of the more *laissez-faire* spirit of the 1920s and acceptance of progressive reform for the sake of economic recovery. At times, the Court challenged Roosevelt's vision by nullifying key planks of the New Deal as unconstitutional. However, the Court's posture shifted in 1937, when a majority of the justices upheld minimum wage and other labor regulations. This progressive trend continued, reaching an absurd conclusion in 1942, when the Court held that a man could be prosecuted under federal law for growing food for family consumption rather than purchasing it from a federally regulated market.

1934   In *Home Building and Loan Association v. Blaisdell*, the Court upheld a Minnesota law that permitted borrowers to pay back their mortgage debts more slowly without incurring penalties. In *Nebbia v. New York*, the Court upheld a price-fixing law on milk sales within New York.

1935   The Court ruled the National Industrial Recovery Act unconstitutional in *Schechter Poultry Corp. v. U.S.* because the act violated the separation of powers and exceeded Congress's interstate commerce power.

1936   In *U.S. v. Butler*, the Court struck down the Agricultural Adjustment Act as an unconstitutional invasion of state rights and an abuse of federal tax power. In *Morehead v. N.Y. ex rel. Tipaldo*, the Court rejected a state-imposed minimum wage as a violation of liberty of contract.

1937   Overruling *Adkins v. Children's Hospital* (1923) and saying that "liberty of contract" appears nowhere in the Constitution, the Court upheld a minimum wage law protecting women in *West Coast Hotel v. Parrish*. In *National Labor Relations Board v. Jones and Laughlin Steel Co.*, the Court upheld the constitutionality of the National Labor Relations Act.

1941   Overruling *Hammer v. Dagenhart* (1918), the court sustained the Fair Labor Standards Act in *U.S. v. Darby Lumber Co.*

1942   In *Wickard v. Filburn*, the Court interpreted Congress's "interstate commerce" power broadly to encompass any intrastate activity that might plausibly impact the interstate commerce of other parties; in this instance, a man was prosecuted for growing too much wheat on his own property for feeding his own family and his own livestock, since this made him less likely to purchase from interstate wheat sources.

Study Question

Between 1930 and 1941, eight of the nine justices serving on the Supreme Court were replaced—seven of the new appointments being made by President Roosevelt. How might these facts explain the trend in rulings during the New Deal era?

Franklin D. Roosevelt, Second Inaugural Address (1937)

"The true conservative," proclaimed FDR in the 1936 presidential campaign, "seeks to protect the system of private property and free enterprise by correcting such injustices and inequalities as arise from it." Republicans in Congress tried to pull back the reigns on Roosevelt's New Deal, as did some of the justices in the U.S. Supreme Court. Critics from the far left, however, thought FDR had not done enough. Tacking carefully to the left while avoiding blatant socialism, Roosevelt had persuaded Congress to approve the Social Security Act (1935) as a pay-as-you-go plan for working Americans, not a government handout for the unemployed. He was the most progressive president the nation had yet seen, and yet he styled himself a "true conservative" for saving capitalism from itself, as he explained the nature of Great Depression. Whether his analysis was correct or not, American voters responded overwhelmingly with favor; only Vermont and Maine turned out for the Republican challenger, Alf Landon. This left 523 of the nation's 531 electoral votes for Roosevelt.

When four years ago we met to inaugurate a President, the Republic, single-minded in anxiety, stood in spirit here. We dedicated ourselves to the fulfillment of a vision—to speed the time when there would be for all the people that security and peace essential to the pursuit of happiness. We of the Republic pledged ourselves to drive from the temple of our ancient faith those who had profaned it; to end by action, tireless and unafraid, the stagnation and despair of that day. We did those first things first.

Our covenant with ourselves did not stop there. Instinctively we recognized a deeper need—the need to find through government the instrument of our united purpose to solve for the individual the ever-rising problems of a complex civilization. Repeated attempts at their solution without the aid of government had left us baffled and bewildered. For, without that aid, we had been unable to create those moral controls over the services of science which are necessary to make science a useful servant instead of a ruthless master of mankind. To do this we knew that we must find practical controls over blind economic forces and blindly selfish men.

We of the Republic sensed the truth that democratic government has innate capacity to protect its people against disasters once considered inevitable, to solve problems once considered unsolvable. We would not admit that we could not find a way to master economic epidemics just as, after centuries of fatalistic suffering, we had found a way to master epidemics of disease. We refused to leave the problems of our common welfare to be solved by the winds of chance and the hurricanes of disaster.

In this we Americans were discovering no wholly new truth; we were writing a new chapter in our book of self-government.

This year marks the one hundred and fiftieth anniversary of the Constitutional Convention which made us a nation. At that Convention our forefathers found the way out of the chaos which followed the

Revolutionary War; they created a strong government with powers of united action sufficient then and now to solve problems utterly beyond individual or local solution. A century and a half ago they established the Federal Government in order to promote the general welfare and secure the blessings of liberty to the American people.

Today we invoke those same powers of government to achieve the same objectives.

Four years of new experience have not belied our historic instinct. They hold out the clear hope that government within communities, government within the separate States, and government of the United States can do the things the times require, without yielding its democracy. Our tasks in the last four years did not force democracy to take a holiday.

Nearly all of us recognize that as intricacies of human relationships increase, so power to govern them also must increase power to stop evil; power to do good. The essential democracy of our Nation and the safety of our people depend not upon the absence of power, but upon lodging it with those whom the people can change or continue at stated intervals through an honest and free system of elections. The Constitution of 1787 did not make our democracy impotent.

In fact, in these last four years, we have made the exercise of all power more democratic; for we have begun to bring private autocratic powers into their proper subordination to the public's government. The legend that they were invincible above and beyond the processes of a democracy—has

been shattered. They have been challenged and beaten.

Our progress out of the depression is obvious. But that is not all that you and I mean by the new order of things. Our pledge was not merely to do a patchwork job with second-hand materials. By using the new materials of social justice we have undertaken to erect on the old foundations a more enduring structure for the better use of future generations.

In that purpose we have been helped by achievements of mind and spirit. Old truths have been relearned; untruths have been unlearned. We have always known that heedless self-interest was bad morals; we know now that it is bad economics. Out of the collapse of a prosperity whose builders boasted their practicality has come the conviction that in the long run economic morality pays. We are beginning to wipe out the line that divides the practical from the ideal; and in so doing we are fashioning an instrument of unimagined power for the establishment of a morally better world.

This new understanding undermines the old admiration of worldly success as such. We are beginning to abandon our tolerance of the abuse of power by those who betray for profit the elementary decencies of life.

In this process evil things formerly accepted will not be so easily condoned. Hard-headedness will not so easily excuse hardheartedness. We are moving toward an era of good feeling. But we realize that there can be no era of good feeling save among men of good will.

For these reasons I am justified in

believing that the greatest change we have witnessed has been the change in the moral climate of America.

Among men of good will, science and democracy together offer an ever-richer life and ever-larger satisfaction to the individual. With this change in our moral climate and our rediscovered ability to improve our economic order, we have set our feet upon the road of enduring progress.

Shall we pause now and turn our back upon the road that lies ahead? Shall we call this the promised land? Or, shall we continue on our way? For "each age is a dream that is dying, or one that is coming to birth."

Many voices are heard as we face a great decision. Comfort says, "Tarry a while." Opportunism says, "This is a good spot." Timidity asks, "How difficult is the road ahead."

True, we have come far from the days of stagnation and despair. Vitality has been preserved. Courage and confidence have been restored. Mental and moral horizons have been extended.

But our present gains were won under the pressure of more than ordinary circumstance. Advance became imperative under the goad of fear and suffering. The times were on the side of progress.

To hold to progress today, however, is more difficult. Dulled conscience, irresponsibility, and ruthless self-interest already reappear. Such symptoms of prosperity may become portents of disaster! Prosperity already tests the persistence of our progressive purpose.

Let us ask again: Have we reached the goal of our vision of that fourth day of March, 1933? Have we found our happy valley?

I see a great nation, upon a great continent, blessed with a great wealth of natural resources. Its hundred and thirty million people are at peace among themselves; they are making their country a good neighbor among the nations. I see a United States which can demonstrate that, under democratic methods of government, national wealth can be translated into a spreading volume of human comforts hitherto unknown, and the lowest standard of living can be raised far above the level of mere subsistence.

But here is the challenge to our democracy: In this nation I see tens of millions of its citizens—a substantial part of its whole population—who at this very moment are denied the greater part of what the very lowest standards of today call the necessities of life.

I see millions of families trying to live on incomes so meager that the pall of family disaster hangs over them day by day.

I see millions whose daily lives in city and on farm continue under conditions labeled indecent by a so-called polite society half a century ago.

I see millions denied education, recreation, and the opportunity to better their lot and the lot of their children.

I see millions lacking the means to buy the products of farm and factory and by their poverty denying work and productiveness to many other millions.

I see one-third of a nation ill-housed,

ill-clad, ill-nourished.

It is not in despair that I paint you that picture. I paint it for you in hope—because the Nation, seeing and understanding the injustice in it, proposes to paint it out. We are determined to make every American citizen the subject of his country's interest and concern; and we will never regard any faithful, law-abiding group within our borders as superfluous. The test of our progress is not whether we add more to the abundance of those who have much; it is whether we provide enough for those who have too little.

If I know aught of the spirit and purpose of our Nation, we will not listen to Comfort, Opportunism, and Timidity. We will carry on.

Overwhelmingly, we of the Republic are men and women of good will; men and women who have more than warm hearts of dedication; men and women who have cool heads and willing hands of practical purpose as well. They will insist that every agency of popular government use effective instruments to carry out their will.

Government is competent when all who compose it work as trustees for the whole people. It can make constant progress when it keeps abreast of all the facts. It can obtain justified support and legitimate criticism when the people receive true information of all that government does.

If I know aught of the will of our people, they will demand that these conditions of effective government shall be created and maintained. They will demand a nation uncorrupted by cancers of injustice and, therefore, strong among the nations in its example of the will to peace.

Today we reconsecrate our country to long-cherished ideals in a suddenly changed civilization. In every land there are always at work forces that drive men apart and forces that draw men together. In our personal ambitions we are individualists. But in our seeking for economic and political progress as a nation, we all go up, or else we all go down, as one people.

To maintain a democracy of effort requires a vast amount of patience in dealing with differing methods, a vast amount of humility. But out of the confusion of many voices rises an understanding of dominant public need. Then political leadership can voice common ideals, and aid in their realization.

In taking again the oath of office as President of the United States, I assume the solemn obligation of leading the American people forward along the road over which they have chosen to advance.

While this duty rests upon me I shall do my utmost to speak their purpose and to do their will, seeking Divine guidance to help us each and every one to give light to them that sit in darkness and to guide our feet into the way of peace.

Study Questions

1. What role did Roosevelt envision for the government amid the economic struggles of the Great Depression?

2. The most well-known sentence in this address is: "I see one-third of a nation ill-housed, ill-clad, ill-nourished." How, then, could Roosevelt claim to be saying this "not in despair" but "in hope"?

Chronological Overview: World War II and the Emergence of the Cold War

1931   Japan invades Manchuria, with plans of spreading further into Asia.

1933   In his First Inaugural Address, Franklin D. Roosevelt pledges America to the "Good Neighbor Policy," announcing a non-interventionist posture toward Latin America.

1936   Nazi Germany occupies the Rhineland.

       Italian armies conquer Ethiopia.

       A civil war begins in Spain.

1937   Congress passes a Neutrality Act, prohibiting U.S. arms sales to nations at war and requiring that belligerent nations pay cash for any nonmilitary goods as well as provide their own ships for transporting them.

       Japan invades Nanking, killing over 200,000 civilians, even by conservative estimates.

1938   Germany annexes Austria and reclaims the Sudetenland, a portion of Czechoslovakia that Germany had lost following World War I.

       At a meeting in Munich, British Prime Minister Neville Chamberlain attempts to appease Hitler by allowing Germany to retain possession of the Sudetenland so long as Hitler agrees not to claim any more of Czechoslovakia.

1939   Hitler breaks the Munich Agreement and invades not only the rest of Czechoslovakia but also Poland. Within days of the invasion of Poland, France and Britain declare war against Germany.

       The U.S. Congress amends its neutrality acts to allow a cash-and-carry policy for selling arms to belligerents. Although neutral on its face, the policy favors the British, and to some extent the Soviets, against the Germans.

       Albert Einstein, a German physicist who immigrated to the United States in 1933, sends a letter to President Roosevelt advising him to support research on developing an atomic weapon.

1941   Congress adopts the Lend-Lease Act, which authorizes the lending and leasing of weapons to any nation whose defense pertains to U.S. national security, thus replacing cash-and-carry with a more open endorsement of the Allied Powers.

       Japan attacks Pearl Harbor, prompting the United States to enter World War II allied with Britain, France, and the Soviet Union against Germany, Italy, and Japan.

1944   The Allied Forces storm the beaches of Normandy and advance into Germany to stop the Germans' last great offensive in what becomes known as the Battle of the Bulge.

1945   Germany surrenders, marking the end of World War II in Europe.

The United Nations is formed, with the U.S. as a charter member, establishing a global federation for preserving world peace.

After the U.S. drops two atomic bombs on Japan, Japan surrenders, ending history's deadliest war.

1946   Winston Churchill speaks of the Soviet expansionism as an "iron curtain" and calls for cooperation between England and America to stop further expansion of communism.

1946–1989   Tensions between the United States and the Soviet Union persist in the "Cold War," largely a standoff between two nations with nuclear weapons, but at times erupting into battles as the two powers compete for alliances in Korea, Cuba, Vietnam, and other nations.

1947   President Truman pledges U.S. aid to Greece and to any other nation where free people struggle against outside oppressors—a policy that becomes known as the Truman Doctrine.

1949   The United States joins with western Allies in the North Atlantic Treaty Organization, promising mutual support against the Soviet Union.

1950   The National Security Council recommends to President Truman that the containment policy be strictly followed, based on the conclusions that the Soviet and American systems are mutually incompatible, that the Soviets intend to expand the reach of communism across the globe, and that American resistance to that expansion is the world's only hope for preserving freedom.

1951–1953   The United States commits troops to a U.N. coalition supporting South Korea in the Korean Conflict.

Franklin D. Roosevelt, "The Four Freedoms" (1941)

In his January 1941 State of the Union Address, Roosevelt articulated America's priorities, both domestic and foreign. Like many presidents before him, he spoke of "freedom." How he parsed the term differed from the past. Henceforth, the government would provide not merely a freedom for individual opportunity, but also a substantive guarantee of basic socioeconomic goods—what Roosevelt called "freedom from want" and "freedom from fear." Following over a decade of economic depression, with European warfare on one horizon and Asian warfare on the other, Roosevelt's words struck a chord. In 1943, the *Saturday Evening Post* published a series of oil paintings, produced by Norman Rockwell, that depicted Roosevelt's "Four Freedoms." The United Nations later codified Roosevelt's vision in the Universal Declaration on Human Rights (1948).

To The Congress of the United States:

I address you, the Members of the Seventy-Seventh Congress, at a moment unprecedented in the history of the Union. I use the word "unprecedented," because at no previous time has American security been as seriously threatened from without as it is today.

Since the permanent formation of our government under the Constitution in 1789, most of the periods of crisis in our history have related to our domestic affairs. And, fortunately, only one of these —the four-year war between the States— ever threatened our national unity. Today, thank God, 130,000,000 Americans in forty-eight States have forgotten points of the compass in our national unity.

It is true that prior to 1914 the United States often had been disturbed by events in other Continents. We had even engaged in two wars with European nations and in a number of undeclared wars in the West Indies, in the Mediterranean and in the Pacific for the maintenance of American rights and for the principles of peaceful commerce. In no case, however, had a serious threat been raised against our national safety or our independence.

What I seek to convey is the historic truth that the United States as a nation has at all times maintained opposition to any attempt to lock us behind an ancient Chinese wall while the procession of civilization went past. Today, thinking of our children and their children, we oppose enforced isolation for ourselves or for any part of the Americas.

Even when the World War broke our in 1914, it seemed to contain only a small threat of danger to our own American future. But, as time went on, the American people began to visualize what the downfall of democratic nations might mean to our own democracy.

We need not over-emphasize imperfections in the Peace of Versailles. We need not harp on failure of the democracies to deal with problems of world deconstruction. We should remember that the Peace of 1919 was far less unjust than the kind of "pacification" which began even before Munich, and which is being carried on under the new order of tyranny that seeks to spread over every continent today. The American people have unalterably set their faces against that tyranny.

Every realist knows that the democratic way of life is at this moment being directly assailed in every part of the world—assailed either by arms, or by secret spreading of poisonous propaganda by those who seek to destroy unity and promote discord in nations still at peace. During sixteen months this assault has blotted out the whole pattern of democratic life in an appalling number of independent nations, great and small. The assailants are still on the march, threatening other nations, great and small.

Therefore, as your president, performing my constitutional duty to "give to the Congress information of the state of the Union," I find it necessary to report that the future and safety of our country and of our democracy are overwhelmingly involved in events far beyond our borders.

Armed defense of democratic existence is now being gallantly waged on four continents. If that defense fails, all the population and all the resources of Europe, Asia, Africa, and Australasia will be dominated by the conquerors. The total of those populations and their resources greatly exceeds the sum total of the population and resources of the whole of the Western Hemisphere—many times over.

In times like these it is immature—and incidentally untrue—for anybody to brag that an unprepared America, single-handed, and with one hand tied behind its back, can hold off the whole world.

No realistic American can expect from a dictator's peace international generosity, or return of true independence, or world disarmament, or freedom of expression, or freedom of religion—or even good business. Such a peace would bring no security for us or for our neighbors. "Those, who would give up essential liberty to purchase the little temporary safety, deserve neither liberty nor safety." As a nation we may take pride in the fact that we are soft-hearted; but we cannot afford to be soft-hearted. We must always be wary of those who with sounding brass and the tinkling cymbal preach the "ism" of appeasement. We must especially beware of that small group of selfish men who would clip the wings of the American eagle in order to feather their own nests.

I have recently pointed out how quickly the tempo of modern warfare could bring into our very midst the physical attack which we must expect if the dictator nations win this war.

There is much loose talk of our immunity from immediate and direct invasion from across the seas. Obviously, as long as the British Navy retains its power, no such danger exists. Even if there were no British Navy, it is not probable that any enemy would be stupid enough to attack by landing troops in the United States from across thousands of miles of ocean, until it had acquired strategic bases from which to operate. But we learn much from the lessons of the past years in Europe—particularly the lesson of Norway, whose essential seaports were captured by treachery and surprise built up over a series of years. The first phase of the invasion of this Hemisphere would not be the landing of regular troops. The necessary strategic points would be occupied by secret agents and their dupes—great numbers of them are already here, and in Latin America.

As long as the aggressor nations maintain the offensive, they—not we—will choose the time and the place and the method of their attack. That is why the future of all American Republics is today in serious danger. That is why this Annual Message to the Congress is unique in our history. That is why every member of the Executive Branch of the government and every member of Congress face great responsibility—and great accountability.

The need of the moment is that our actions and our policy should be devoted primarily—almost exclusively—to meeting the foreign peril. For all our domestic problems are now a part of the great emergency. Just as our national policy in internal affairs has been based upon a decent respect for the rights and dignity of all our fellowmen within our gates, so our national policy in foreign affairs has been based on a decent respect for the rights and dignity of all nations, large and small. And the justice of morality must and will win in the end.

Our national policy is this.

First, by an impressive expression of the public will and without regard to partisanship, we are committed to all-inclusive national defense.

Second, by an impressive expression of the public will and without regard to partisanship, we are committed to full support of all those resolute peoples, everywhere, who are resisting aggression and are thereby keeping war away from our Hemisphere. By this support, we express our determination that the democratic cause shall prevail; and we strengthen the defense and security of our own nation.

Third, by an impressive expression of the public will and without regard to partisanship, we are committed to the proposition that principles of morality and considerations for our own security will never permit us to acquiesce in a peace dictated by aggressors and sponsored by appeasers. We know that enduring peace cannot be bought at the cost of other people's freedom.

In recent national elections there was no substantial difference between the two great parties in respect to that national policy. No issue was fought out on this line before the American electorate. Today, it is abundantly evident that American citizens everywhere are demanding and supporting speedy and complete action in recognition of obvious danger. Therefore, the immediate need is a swift and driving increase in our armament production. Leaders of industry and labor have responded to our summons. Goals of speed have been set. In some cases these goals are being reached ahead of time. In some cases we are on schedule; in other cases there are slight but not serious delays. And in some cases —and, I am sorry to say, very important cases—we are all concerned by the slowness of the accomplishment of our plans. The Army and Navy, however, have made substantial progress during the past year. Actual experience is improving and speeding up our methods of production with every passing day. And today's best is not good enough for tomorrow.

I am not satisfied with the progress

thus far made. The men in charge of the program represent the best in training, in ability and in patriotism. They are not satisfied with the progress thus far made. None of us will be satisfied until the job is done. No matter whether the original goal was set too high or too low, our objective is quicker and better results. To give you two illustrations: We are behind schedule in turning out finished airplanes. We are working day and night to solve the innumerable problems and to catch up.

We are ahead of schedule in building warships, but we are working to get even further ahead of that schedule. To change a whole nation from a basis of peacetime production of implements of peace to a basis of wartime production of implements of war is no small task. The greatest difficulty comes at the beginning of the program, when new tools, new plant facilities, new assembly lines, new shipways must first be constructed before the actual material begins to flow steadily and speedily from them.

The Congress of course, must rightly keep itself informed at all times of the progress of the program. However, there is certain information, as the Congress itself will readily recognize, which, in the interests of our own security and those of the nations that we are supporting, must of needs be kept in confidence. New circumstances are constantly begetting new needs for our safety. I shall ask this Congress for greatly increased new appropriations and authorizations to carry on what we have begun.

I also ask this Congress for authority and for funds sufficient to manufacture additional munitions and war supplies of many kinds, to be turned over to those nations which are now in actual war with aggressor nations. Our most useful and immediate role is to act as an arsenal for them as well as for ourselves. They do not need man power. They do need billions of dollars worth of the weapons of defense. Taking counsel of expert military and naval authorities, considering what is best for our own security, we are free to decide how much should be kept here and how much should be sent abroad to our friends who, by their determined and heroic resistance, are giving us time in which to make ready our own defense.

For what we send abroad we shall be repaid, repaid within a reasonable time following the close of hostilities, repaid in similar materials, or at our option in other goods of many kinds which they can produce and which we need. Let us say to the democracies: "we Americans are vitally concerned in your defense of freedom. We are putting forth our energies, our resources and our organizing powers to give you the strength to regain and maintain a free world. We shall send you, in ever increasing numbers, ships, planes, tanks, guns. This is our purpose and our pledge."

In fulfillment of this purpose we will not be intimidated by the threats of dictators that they will regard as a breach of international law and as an act of war our aid to the democracies which dare resist their aggression. Such aid is not an act of war, even if a dictator should unilaterally proclaim it so to be. When the dictators are ready to make war upon us, they will not wait for an act of war on our part. They did not wait for Norway or Belgium or the Netherlands to commit an act of war. Their only interest is in a new one-way international law, which lacks mutuality in its observance, and, therefore, becomes an instrument of oppression.

The happiness of future generations of Americans may well depend upon how effective and how immediate we can make our aid felt. No one can tell the exact character of the emergency situations that we may be called upon to meet. The Nation's hands must not be tied when the Nation's life is in danger. We must prepare to make the sacrifices that the emergency—as serious as war itself—demands. Whatever stands in the way of speed and efficiency in defense preparations must give way to the national need.

A free nation has the right to expect full cooperation from all groups. A free nation has the right to look to the leaders of business, of labor, and of agriculture to take the lead in stimulating effort, not among other groups but within their own groups. The best way of dealing with the few slackers or trouble makers in our midst is, first, to shame them by patriotic example, and if that fails, to use the sovereignty of government to save government.

As men do not live by bread alone, they do not fight by armaments alone. Those who man our defenses, and those behind them who build our defenses, must have the stamina and courage which come from an unshakable belief in the manner of life which they are defending. The mighty action which we are calling for cannot be based on a disregard of all things worth fighting for.

The Nation takes great satisfaction and much strength from the things which have been done to make its people conscious of their individual stake in the preservation of democratic life in America. Those things have toughened the fibre of our people, have renewed their faith and strengthened their devotion to the institutions we make ready to protect. Certainly this is no time to stop thinking about the social and economic problems which are the root cause of the social revolution which is today a supreme factor in the world.

There is nothing mysterious about the foundations of a healthy and strong democracy. The basic things expected by our people of their political and economic systems are simple. They are: equality of opportunity for youth and for others; jobs for those who can work; security for those who need it; the ending of special privilege for the few; the preservation of civil liberties for all; the enjoyment of the fruits of scientific progress in a wider and constantly rising standard of living.

These are the simple and basic things that must never be lost sight of in the turmoil and unbelievable complexity of our modern world. The inner and abiding strength of our economic and political systems is dependent upon the degree to which they fulfill these expectations.

Many subjects connected with our social economy call for immediate improvement. As examples: We should bring more citizens under the coverage of old age pensions and unemployment insurance. We should widen the opportunities for adequate medical care. We should plan a better system by which person deserving or needing gainful employment may obtain it.

I have called for personal sacrifice. I am assured of the willingness of almost all Americans to respond to that call. . . .

In the future days, which we seek to make secure, we look forward to a world founded upon four essential human freedoms.

The first is freedom of speech and expression—everywhere in the world.

The second is freedom of every person to worship God in his own way—everywhere in the world.

The third is freedom from want—which, translated into world terms, means economic understandings which will secure to every nation a healthy peace time life for its inhabitants—everywhere in the world.

The fourth is freedom from fear—which, translated into world terms, means a world-wide reduction of armaments to such a point and in such a thorough fashion that no nation will be in a position to commit an act of physical aggression against any neighbor—anywhere in the world.

That is no vision of a distant millennium. It is a definite basis for a kind of world attainable in our own time and generation. That kind of world is the very antithesis of the so-called new order of tyranny which the dictators seek to create with the crash of a bomb.

To that new order we oppose the greater conception—the moral order. A good society is able to face schemes of world domination and foreign revolutions alike without fear.

Since the beginning of our American history we have been engaged in change—in a perpetual peaceful revolution—a revolution which goes on steadily, quietly adjusting itself to changing conditions—without the concentration camp or the quick-lime in the ditch. The world order which we seek is the cooperation of free countries, working together in a friendly, civilized society.

This nation has placed its destiny in the hands and heads and hearts of its million of free men and women; and its faith in freedom under the guidance of God. Freedom means the supremacy of human rights everywhere. Our support goes to those who struggle to gain those rights or keep them. Our strength is in our unity of purpose.

To that high concept there can be no end save victory.

Study Questions

1. Identify and explain each of the "four freedoms" that Roosevelt highlighted in his address. Why did each of them matter at that particular time?

2. Which of these freedoms fit most readily with the *laissez-faire* theory of government?

3. Which of these freedoms fit most readily with progressive reform?

Supreme Court Decisions during World War II

During and immediately following World War II, the U.S. Supreme Court grappled with several controversies concerning the relationship between national security and individual liberty. Can a school require all students to salute the American flag? Does the president have the authority to detain citizens who have an ancestral relation to a nation against which America has declared war? Do individuals have the right to support the Communist Party, which seeks to undermine the government?

1940   In *Minersville School District v. Gobitis* the Court upheld disciplinary action against Jehovah's Witness students who refused to salute the flag in school. Although the children claimed a First Amendment right to religious liberty, and showed that saluting the flag violated their religion, the Court determined that local school boards have discretion to set policies promoting patriotism, especially since patriotism serves national security.

1943   Overruling the *Minersville* case, the Court decided in *West Virginia Board of Education v. Barnette* that a law requiring students to salute the U.S. flag violates the First Amendment. Writing for the majority, Justice Robert H. Jackson reasoned: "If there is any fixed star in our constitutional constellation, it is that no official, high or petty, can prescribe what shall be orthodox in politics, nationalism, religion, or other matters of opinion or force citizens to confess by word or act their faith therein."

1944   In *Korematsu v. U.S.*, the Court upheld an executive order commanding the internment of Japanese-American citizens as a constitutional means for preserving national security while the nation was at war with Japan.

1947   The Court ruled in *Adamson v. California* that the Fifth Amendment applies only at the federal level, not against state courts that may require a defendant to testify against himself. However, the justices did not conclude unanimously and in fact had a spirited debate over the question of "incorporation": which rights listed in the Bill of Rights apply only at the federal level, and which rights are "incorporated" under the Fourteenth Amendment to apply also at the state level? This question would prove to be highly significant in future cases.

1951   In *Dennis v. U.S.*, the Court upheld the conviction of Communist Party leaders under the Smith Act, denying First Amendment protection to persons who conspire and teach others to overthrow the government.

Study Question

How did the Court seek to preserve ordered liberty under the Constitution during World War II? Explain whether you agree or disagree with the Court's decisions.

Franklin D. Roosevelt, Third Inaugural Address (1941)

In 1940, President Roosevelt broke from the tradition, established a century and half earlier by George Washington, of not seeking election to more than two terms in the nation's highest office. With America recovering from the Depression at home, and other nations embroiled in World War II abroad, FDR sought to preserve his coalition of labor-union voters while also assuring the nation that he would keep America at peace. Republican candidate Wendell Wilkie garnered support from business leaders and challenged the president by asking whether he had done enough to prepare the nation for possible war. In a December 1940 radio address, the victorious Franklin Roosevelt channeled such criticisms back into a support for his own administration. Although not calling for war, he insisted:

> We must be the great arsenal of democracy. For us this is an emergency as serious as war itself. We must apply ourselves to our task with the same resolution, the same sense of urgency, the same spirit of patriotism and sacrifice as we would show were we at war.

A few weeks later, he delivered the following inaugural address.

On each national day of Inauguration since 1789, the people have renewed their sense of dedication to the United States.

In Washington's day the task of the people was to create and weld together a Nation.

In Lincoln's day the task of the people was to preserve that Nation from disruption from within.

In this day the task of the people is to save that Nation and its institutions from disruption from without.

To us there has come a time, in the midst of swift happenings, to pause for a moment and take stock—to recall what our place in history has been, and to rediscover what we are and what we may be. If we do not, we risk the real peril of isolation, the real peril of inaction.

Lives of Nations are determined not by the count of years, but by the lifetime of the human spirit. The life of a man is threescore years and ten: a little more, a little less. The life of a Nation is the fullness of the measure of its will to live.

There are men who doubt this. There are men who believe that democracy, as a form of government and a frame of life, is limited or measured by a kind of mystical and artificial fate that, for some unexplained reason, tyranny and slavery have become the surging wave of the future—and that freedom is an ebbing tide.

But we Americans know that this is not true.

Eight years ago, when the life of this Republic seemed frozen by a fatalistic terror, we proved that this is not true. We were in the midst of shock—but we acted. We acted quickly, boldly, decisively.

These later years have been living years—fruitful years for the people of this democracy. For they have brought to us greater security and, I hope, a better understanding that life's ideals are to be measured in other than material things.

Most vital to our present and to our future is this experience of a democracy which successfully survived crisis at home; put away many evil things; built new structures on enduring lines; and, through it all, maintained the fact of its democracy.

For action has been taken within the three-way framework of the Constitution of the United States. The coordinate branches of the Government continue freely to function. The Bill of Rights remains inviolate. The freedom of elections is wholly maintained. Prophets of the downfall of American democracy have seen their dire predictions come to naught.

No, democracy is not dying.

We know it because we have seen it revive—and grow.

We know it cannot die—because it is built on the unhampered initiative of individual men and women joined together in a common enterprise—an enterprise undertaken and carried through by the free expression of a free majority.

We know it because democracy alone, of all forms of government, enlists the full force of men's enlightened will.

We know it because democracy alone has constructed an unlimited civilization capable of infinite progress in the improvement of human life.

We know it because, if we look below the surface, we sense it still spreading on every continent—for it is the most humane, the most advanced, and in the end the most unconquerable of all forms of human society.

A Nation, like a person, has a body—a body that must be fed and clothed and housed, invigorated and rested, in a manner that measures up to the standards of our time.

A Nation, like a person, has a mind—a mind that must be kept informed and alert, that must know itself, that understands the hopes and the needs of its neighbors—all the other Nations that live within the narrowing circle of the world.

A Nation, like a person, has something deeper, something more permanent, something larger than the sum of all its parts. It is that something which matters most to its future—which calls forth the most sacred guarding of its present.

It is a thing for which we find it difficult —even impossible to hit upon a single, simple word.

And yet, we all understand what it is— the spirit—the faith of America. It is the product of centuries. It was born in the multitudes of those who came from many lands—some of high degree, but mostly plain people—who sought here, early and late, to find freedom more freely.

The democratic aspiration is no mere recent phase in human history. It is human history. It permeated the ancient life of early peoples. It blazed anew in the Middle Ages. It was written in Magna Charta.

In the Americas its impact has been irresistible. America has been the New World in all tongues, and to all peoples, not because this continent was a new-found land, but because all those who came here believed they could create upon this continent a new life—a life that should be new in freedom.

Its vitality was written into our own Mayflower Compact, into the Declaration of Independence, into the Constitution of the United States, into the Gettysburg Address.

Those who first came here to carry out the longings of their spirit, and the millions who followed, and the stock that sprang from them—all have moved forward constantly and consistently toward an ideal which in itself has gained stature and clarity with each generation.

The hopes of the Republic cannot forever tolerate either undeserved poverty or self-serving wealth.

We know that we still have far to go; that we must more greatly build the security and the opportunity and the knowledge of every citizen, in the measure justified by the resources and the capacity of the land.

But it is not enough to achieve these purposes alone. It is not enough to clothe and feed the body of this Nation, to instruct, and inform its mind. For there is also the spirit. And of the three, the greatest is the spirit.

Without the body and the mind, as all men know, the Nation could not live.

But if the spirit of America were killed, even though the Nation's body and mind, constricted in an alien world, lived on, the America we know would have perished.

That spirit—that faith—speaks to us in our daily lives in ways often unnoticed, because they seem so obvious. It speaks to us here in the Capital of the Nation. It speaks to us through the processes of governing in the sovereignties of 48 States. It speaks to us in our counties, in our cities, in our towns, and in our villages. It speaks to us from the other Nations of the hemisphere, and from those across the seas—the enslaved, as well as the free. Sometimes we fail to hear or heed these voices of freedom because to us the privilege of our freedom is such an old, old story.

The destiny of America was proclaimed in words of prophecy spoken by our first President in his first Inaugural in 1789-words almost directed, it would seem, to this year of 1941: "The preservation of the sacred fire of liberty and the destiny of the republican model of government are justly considered. . . deeply, . . . finally, staked on the experiment intrusted to the hands of the American people."

If you and I in this later day lose that sacred fire—if we let it be smothered with doubt and fear—then we shall reject the destiny which Washington strove so valiantly and so triumphantly to establish. The preservation of the spirit and faith of the Nation does, and will, furnish the highest justification for every sacrifice that we may make in the cause of national defense.

In the face of great perils never before encountered, our strong purpose is to protect and to perpetuate the integrity of democracy.

For this we muster the spirit of America, and the faith of America.

We do not retreat. We are not content to stand still. As Americans, we go forward, in the service of our country, by the will of God.

Study Questions

1. How did Roosevelt see America's needs shifting from the time of Washington's presidency, to that of Lincoln, and finally to his own?

2. Roosevelt said, "The democratic aspiration is no mere recent phase in human history. It *is* human history." Do you agree? Is it significant that he spoke of democratic, rather than republican, government?

3. What did Roosevelt have in mind when speaking of America as "an arsenal of democracy"?

Franklin D. Roosevelt and Winston S. Churchill, Atlantic Charter (1941)

The U.S. Department of State issued a press release summarizing an August 1941 agreement between U.S. President Franklin D. Roosevelt and British Prime Minister Winston S. Churchill concerning their hopes for peace amid the turmoil of the Second World War. Although this declaration did not have the full legal force of a properly ratified treaty, nonetheless it was encouraging for Britain and her allies to know that the American president sympathized with their cause. In September 1941, representatives of ten allied nations, including the Soviet Union, convened in London, adding their signatures to a declaration of solidarity around the principles expressed in the Atlantic Charter.

The following statement signed by the President of the United States and the Prime Minister of Great Britain is released for the information of the Press:

The President of the United States and the Prime Minister, Mr. Churchill, representing His Majesty's Government in the United Kingdom, have met at sea.

They have been accompanied by officials of their two Governments, including high ranking officers of the Military, Naval and Air Services

The whole problem of the supply of munitions of war, as provided by the Lease-Lend Act, for the armed forces of the United States and for those countries actively engaged in resisting aggression has been further examined.

Lord Beaverbrook, the Minister of Supply of the British Government, has joined in these conferences. He is going to proceed to Washington to discuss further details with appropriate officials of the United States Government. These conferences will also cover the supply problems of the Soviet Union.

The President and the Prime Minister have had several conferences. They have considered the dangers to world civilization arising from the policies of military domination by conquest upon which the Hitlerite government of Germany and other governments associated therewith have embarked, and have made clear the stress which their countries are respectively taking for their safety in the face of these dangers.

They have agreed upon the following joint declaration:

Joint declaration of the President of the United States of America and the Prime Minister, Mr. Churchill, representing His Majesty's Government in the United Kingdom, being met together, deem it right to make known certain common principles in the national policies of their respective countries on which they base their hopes for a better future for the world.

First, their countries seek no aggrandizement, territorial or other;

Second, they desire to see no territorial changes that do not accord with the freely expressed wishes of the peoples concerned;

Third, they respect the right of all peoples to choose the form of government under which they will live; and they wish to see sovereign rights and self government restored to those who have been forcibly deprived of them;

Fourth, they will endeavor, with due respect for their existing obligations, to further the enjoyment by all States, great or small, victor or vanquished, of access, on equal terms, to the trade and to the raw materials of the world which are needed for their economic prosperity;

Fifth, they desire to bring about the fullest collaboration between all nations in the economic field with the objector securing, for all, improved labor standards, economic advancement and social security;

Sixth, after the final destruction of the Nazi tyranny, they hope to see established a peace which will afford to all nations the means of dwelling in safety within their own boundaries, and which will afford assurance that all the men in all the lands may live out their lives in freedom from fear and want;

Seventh, such a peace should enable all men to traverse the high seas and oceans without hindrance;

Eighth, they believe that all of the nations of the world, for realistic as well as spiritual reasons must come to the abandonment of the use of force. Since no future peace can be maintained if land, sea or air armaments continue to be employed by nations which threaten, or may threaten, aggression outside of their frontiers, they believe, pending the establishment of a wider and permanent system of general security, that the disarmament of such nations is essential. They will likewise aid and encourage all other practicable measures which will lighten for peace-loving peoples the crushing burden of armaments.

FRANKLIN D. ROOSEVELT

WINSTON S. CHURCHILL

Study Questions

1. The third principle of the Atlantic Charter reflects a long-standing American ideal. How might the alliance with the Soviet Union lead to disputes over the meaning of this principle?

2. How did the sixth principle incorporate some aspirations from Roosevelt's "Four Freedoms" address (p. 387)?

Franklin D. Roosevelt, "Pearl Harbor Address" (1941)

Only rarely has an American president addressed the United State Congress to call for a war resolution. December 8, 1941 was one of those occasions. An early draft of Franklin Roosevelt's message began with a reference to "December 7, 1941, a date which will live in world history," but then Roosevelt struck those last two words and replaced them with "infamy." Japan had rapidly expanded an empire encompassing large portions of the Pacific islands and Asian mainland, but such militarism left her starved for oil. The United States sought to halt further Japanese aggression by instituting an oil embargo against Japan. In the fall of 1941, Japan's new prime minister, Gen. Hideki Tojo, issued an ultimatum in reply: supply oil, or be attacked. However, the Japanese attack at Pearl Harbor was not a new plan; Japan had been preparing to attack not only Pearl Harbor but also the Philippines and Malaysia for some time. Who would have guessed that Tokyo would be so bold as to attempt all three simultaneously?

Mr. Vice President, and Mr. Speaker, and Members of the Senate and House of Representatives:

Yesterday, December 7, 1941—a date which will live in infamy—the United States of America was suddenly and deliberately attacked by naval and air forces of the Empire of Japan.

The United States was at peace with that Nation and, at the solicitation of Japan, was still in conversation with its Government and its Emperor looking toward the maintenance of peace in the Pacific. Indeed, one hour after Japanese air squadrons had commenced bombing in the American Island of Oahu, the Japanese Ambassador to the United States and his colleague delivered to our Secretary of State a formal reply to a recent American message. And while this reply stated that it seemed useless to continue the existing diplomatic negotiations, it contained no threat or hint of war or of armed attack.

It will be recorded that the distance of Hawaii from Japan makes it obvious that the attack was deliberately planned many days or even weeks ago. During the intervening time the Japanese Government has deliberately sought to deceive the United States by false statements and expressions of hope for continued peace.

The attack yesterday on the Hawaiian Islands has caused severe damage to American naval and military forces. I regret to tell you that very many American lives have been lost. In addition American ships have been reported torpedoed on the high seas between San Francisco and Honolulu.

Yesterday the Japanese Government also launched an attack against Malaya.

Last night Japanese forces attacked Hong Kong.

Last night Japanese forces attacked Guam.

Last night Japanese forces attacked the Philippine Islands.

Last night the Japanese attacked Wake Island. And this morning the Japanese attacked Midway Island.

Japan has, therefore, undertaken a surprise offensive extending throughout the Pacific area. The facts of yesterday and today speak for themselves. The people of the United States have already formed their opinions and well understand the implications to the very life and safety of our Nation.

As Commander in Chief of the Army and Navy I have directed that all measures be taken for our defense.

But always will our whole Nation remember the character of the onslaught against us.

No matter how long it may take us to overcome this premeditated invasion, the American people in their righteous might will win through to absolute victory. I believe that I interpret the will of the Congress and of the people when I assert that we will not only defend ourselves to the uttermost but will make it very certain that this form of treachery shall never again endanger us.

Hostilities exist. There is no blinking at the fact that our people, our territory, and our interests are in grave danger.

With confidence in our armed forces—with the unbounding determination of our people—we will gain the inevitable triumph—so help us God.

I ask that the Congress declare that since the unprovoked and dastardly attack by Japan on Sunday, December 7, 1941, a state of war has existed between the United States and the Japanese Empire.

Study Question

1. How extensive was the Japanese military campaign of December 7, 1941?

2. What did Roosevelt recommend to Congress in response to the Japanese attack?

American Military Engagements in World War II

Prior to America's entrance into World War II, Germany had defeated French and British forces in northwestern Europe and gained control of both France and Norway, as well as spreading the Third Reich eastward past Poland into Soviet territory. Both Italy and Germany also had established strong footholds in North Africa. Meanwhile, Japan, which joined the Axis Powers in 1940, had ambitions for a vast Asian-Pacific empire. Beginning in 1942, the United States made a series of decisive military contributions to the Allied efforts in World War II, ultimately achieving victory in North Africa, Europe, and the Pacific islands.

The North African Campaign

1942   **Egypt** (October–November): British Gen. Bernard Montgomery defeated the Afrika Korps of Gen. Erwin Rommel at El Alamein, Egypt, but allowed Rommel to escape into Tunisia.

Morocco and Algieria (November): The Allied Forces, under Gen. George Patton, launched a major invasion into North Africa, moving from the west to meet Montgomery's forces that were pushing from the east.

1943   **Cassablanca Meeting** (January): Roosevelt and Churchill agreed to accept nothing less than "unconditional surrender" from the Axis Powers.

Kesserine Pass (February): Rommel's forces repelled an American corps in their first experience against German soldiers, but British allies blocked Rommel's further offensive plans in Tunisia. The American setback prompted Gen. Patton to personally recondition the troops into world-class soldiers—which he firmly accomplished in quick order.

Axis Surrender (May): Over 250,000 German and Italian soldiers surrendered North Africa to the Allies.

The European Theater

1943   **Bombing of Wilhelmshaven** (January): U.S. bombers commenced their first attack against Germany.

Invasion of Sicily (July): Allied Forces quickly conquered Sicily.

Italy's Surrender (September): Soon after the Allies invaded mainland Italy, the government of Pietro Badoglio—Mussolini's successor—surrendered.

1944   **Battle of Leningrad** (January): The Soviets defeated German forces in the eastern front; thereafter, the Red Army would push the Nazis in a westward retreat toward Berlin.

D-Day (June 6): U.S. Gen. Dwight D. Eisenhower, as Supreme Commander of the Allied Forces, led an amphibious invasion of Normandy, resulting in the liberation of Paris by August. Thus opened the western front, as Churchill and Roosevelt had promised Stalin at a meeting in Tehran in 1943.

Battle of the Bulge (December): Germany attempted one last offensive, ripping a 45-mile-wide hole into the western front. By January 1945, Eisenhower's troops managed to repel the Nazi advance.

1945 **Race to Berlin** (April): Patton and Montgomery had each crossed the Rhine in March. The Soviets attacked Berlin on April 16, with U.S. and Soviet forces converging upon the Elbe River on April 25.

V-E Day (May 8): Germany, having been thoroughly compressed between the eastern and western fronts, surrendered—an occasion that the Allies celebrated as "Victory in Europe Day."

The Pacific Theater

1940 **Axis Alliance** (September): Japan joined the European Axis Powers.

1941 **Pearl Harbor** (December 7): Japan attacked the U.S. naval fleet in Hawaii, prompting Congress to declare war. Every ship except for the *U.S.S. Arizona* was repaired and redeployed later in the war. Moreover, three U.S. aircraft carriers escaped entirely unharmed, since they were out on maneuvers at the time of attack.

Philippines, Wake Islands, Guam, Thailand, Malaya, Hong Kong (December 8): Declaring war on the United States and Great Britain, Japan bombed several Pacific islands and invaded the Asian mainland.

1942 **Bombing of Tokyo** (April): Admiral Jimmy Doolittle led a bombing campaign against Japan's capital city.

Bataan Death March (April): U.S. troops surrendered to the Japanese invasion force in the Philippines. Japanese soldiers forced thousands of Filipino and American prisoners of war to march, without food or water, through the Bataan peninsula; many died along the way.

Battle of Midway (June): U.S. Admiral Chester W. Nimitz surprised a Japanese fleet with the power of naval carriers and airplanes. This American victory marked a turning point in the war against Japan.

1943 **Guadalcanal** (February): After months of battle, U.S. troops at last secured Guadalcanal, in the Solomon Islands, foiling the efforts of Japan to establish an airbase there.

1944 **Invasion of the Philippines** (October): From an amphibious landing at

Leyte, U.S. forces led by Gen. Douglas MacArthur began the liberation of the Philippines.

1945   **Iwo Jima** (February): 7,000 U.S. Marines gave their lives, while nearly 20,000 others suffered injuries, to capture a five-square-mile island from 21,000 Japanese troops. Only 200 Japanese surrendered, the remainder fighting to their deaths. The U.S. strategy of "island hopping" toward mainland Japan proved slow and costly.

Okinawa (April–May): Another 12,000 U.S. soldiers lost their lives, with 40,000 more suffering battle wounds, yielding a casualty rate more severe than the invasion of Normandy. Nearly 2,000 Japanese kamikaze pilots went on suicide rampages against the Allies while thousands of Japanese infantry killed themselves with grenades rather than surrendering.

Hiroshima (August 6): After neither diplomatic efforts nor the recent wave of American victories brought Japan to surrender, the United States warned the civilian population to evacuate and then dropped the first atomic bomb, named "Little Boy."

Nagasaki (August 9): The United States dropped a second atomic bomb, "Fat Man."

V-J Day (August 14): The Empire of Japan surrendered.

Study Questions

1. The Sultan of Morocco presented Gen. Patton with a military award labeled, "*Les Lions dans leurs tanières tremblent en le voyant approcher* [The lions in their dens tremble at his approach]." Why was this inscription appropriate?

2. What marked the decisive turning point in the European theater?

3. What events preceding the dropping of two atomic bombs led the Americans to recognize the necessity of sudden and decisive force against Japan in order to avoid the continuation of innumerable casualties?

Franklin D. Roosevelt, "A Second Bill of Rights" (1944)

On January 11, 1944, President Roosevelt delivered his annual State of the Union address to Congress. Reflecting on both the Great Depression and World War II, Roosevelt urged Congress to adopt a "second Bill of Rights." He spoke in the past tense concerning the original Bill of Rights, which guaranteed U.S. citizens the rights to religious liberty, free speech, and trial by jury. Suggesting that these rights no longer sufficed, he proposed a new set of rights for economic security, including employment, housing, and education. In other words, Roosevelt called for a repudiation of *laissez faire* and an expansion of the progressive reforms begun during the New Deal.

This Nation in the past two years has become an active partner in the world's greatest war against human slavery.

We have joined with like-minded people in order to defend ourselves in a world that has been gravely threatened with gangster rule.

But I do not think that any of us Americans can be content with mere survival. Sacrifices that we and our allies are making impose upon us all a sacred obligation to see to it that out of this war we and our children will gain something better than mere survival.

We are united in determination that this war shall not be followed by another interim which leads to new disaster—that we shall not repeat the tragic errors of ostrich isolationism—that we shall not repeat the excesses of the wild twenties when this Nation went for a joy ride on a roller coaster which ended in a tragic crash.

When Mr. Hull went to Moscow in October, and when I went to Cairo and Teheran in November, we knew that we were in agreement with our allies in our common determination to fight and win this war. But there were many vital questions concerning the future peace, and they were discussed in an atmosphere of complete candor and harmony.

In the last war such discussions, such meetings, did not even begin until the shooting had stopped and the delegates began to assemble at the peace table. There had been no previous opportunities for man-to-man discussions which lead to meetings of minds. The result was a peace which was not a peace.

That was a mistake which we are not repeating in this war.

And right here I want to address a word or two to some suspicious souls who are fearful that Mr. Hull or I have made "commitments" for the future which might pledge this Nation to secret treaties, or to enacting the role of Santa Claus.

To such suspicious souls—using a polite terminology—I wish to say that Mr. Churchill, and Marshal Stalin, and Generalissimo Chiang Kai-shek are all thoroughly conversant with the provisions of our Constitution. And so is Mr. Hull. And so am I.

Of course we made some commitments. We most certainly committed ourselves to very large and very specific military plans which require the use of all Allied forces to bring about the defeat of our enemies at the earliest possible time.

But there were no secret treaties or political or financial commitments.

The one supreme objective for the future, which we discussed for each Nation individually, and for all the United Nations, can be summed up in one word: Security.

And that means not only physical security which provides safety from attacks by aggressors. It means also economic security, social security, moral security—in a family of Nations.

In the plain down-to-earth talks that I had with the Generalissimo and Marshal Stalin and Prime Minister Churchill, it was abundantly clear that they are all most deeply interested in the resumption of peaceful progress by their own peoples—progress toward a better life. All our allies want freedom to develop their lands and resources, to build up industry, to increase education and individual opportunity, and to raise standards of living.

All our allies have learned by bitter experience that real development will not be possible if they are to be diverted from their purpose by repeated wars—or even threats of war.

China and Russia are truly united with Britain and America in recognition of this essential fact:

The best interests of each Nation, large and small, demand that all freedom-loving Nations shall join together in a just and durable system of peace. In the present world situation, evidenced by the actions of Germany, Italy, and Japan, unques-

tioned military control over disturbers of the peace is as necessary among Nations as it is among citizens in a community. And an equally basic essential to peace is a decent standard of living for all individual men and women and children in all Nations. Freedom from fear is eternally linked with freedom from want.

There are people who burrow through our Nation like unseeing moles, and attempt to spread the suspicion that if other Nations are encouraged to raise their standards of living, our own American standard of living must of necessity be depressed.

The fact is the very contrary. It has been shown time and again that if the standard of living of any country goes up, so does its purchasing power—and that such a rise encourages a better standard of living in neighboring countries with whom it trades. That is just plain common sense—and it is the kind of plain common sense that provided the basis for our discussions at Moscow, Cairo, and Teheran.

Returning from my journeyings, I must confess to a sense of "let-down" when I found many evidences of faulty perspective here in Washington. The faulty perspective consists in overemphasizing lesser problems and thereby under-emphasizing the first and greatest problem.

The overwhelming majority of our people have met the demands of this war with magnificent courage and understanding. They have accepted inconveniences; they have accepted hardships; they have accepted tragic sacrifices. And they are ready and eager to make whatever further contributions are needed to win the war as quickly as possible—if only they are given the chance to know what is required of them.

However, while the majority goes on about its great work without complaint, a noisy minority maintains an uproar of demands for special favors for special groups. There are pests who swarm through the lobbies of the Congress and the cocktail bars of Washington, representing these special groups as opposed to the basic interests of the Nation as a whole. They have come to look upon the war primarily as a chance to make profits for themselves at the expense of their neighbors—profits in money or in terms of political or social preferment.

Such selfish agitation can be highly dangerous in wartime. It creates confusion. It damages morale. It hampers our national effort. It muddies the waters and therefore prolongs the war.

If we analyze American history impartially, we cannot escape the fact that in our past we have not always forgotten individual and selfish and partisan interests in time of war—we have not always been united in purpose and direction. We cannot overlook the serious dissensions and the lack of unity in our war of the Revolution, in our War of 1812, or in our War Between the States, when the survival of the Union itself was at stake.

In the first World War we came closer to national unity than in any previous war. But that war lasted only a year and a half, and increasing signs of disunity began to appear during the final months of the conflict.

In this war, we have been compelled to learn how interdependent upon each other are all groups and sections of the population of America.

Increased food costs, for example, will bring new demands for wage increases from all war workers, which will in turn raise all prices of all things including those things which the farmers themselves have to buy. Increased wages or prices will each in turn produce the same results. They all have a particularly disastrous result on all fixed income groups.

And I hope you will remember that all of us in this Government represent the fixed income group just as much as we represent business owners, workers, and farmers. This group of fixed income people includes: teachers, clergy, policemen, firemen, widows and minors on fixed incomes, wives and dependents of our soldiers and sailors, and old-age pensioners. They and their families add up to one-quarter of our one hundred and thirty million people. They have few or no high pressure representatives at the Capitol. In a period of gross inflation they would be the worst sufferers.

If ever there was a time to subordinate individual or group selfishness to the national good, that time is now. Disunity at home—bickerings, self-seeking partisanship, stoppages of work, inflation, business as usual, politics as usual, luxury as usual—these are the influences which can undermine the morale of the brave men ready to die at the front for us here.

Those who are doing most of the complaining are not deliberately striving to sabotage the national war effort. They are laboring under the delusion that the time is past when we must make prodigious sacrifices—that the war is already won and we can begin to slacken off. But the dangerous folly of that point of view can be measured by the distance that separates our troops from their ultimate objectives in Berlin and Tokyo—and by the sum of all the perils that lie along the way.

Overconfidence and complacency are among our deadliest enemies. Last spring —after notable victories at Stalingrad and in Tunisia and against the U-boats on the high seas—overconfidence became so pronounced that war production fell off. In two months, June and July, 1943, more than a thousand airplanes that could have been made and should have been made were not made. Those who failed to make them were not on strike. They were merely saying, "The war's in the bag—so let's relax."

That attitude on the part of anyone— Government or management or labor—can lengthen this war. It can kill American boys.

Let us remember the lessons of 1918. In the summer of that year the tide turned in favor of the allies. But this Government did not relax. In fact, our national effort was stepped up. In August, 1918, the draft age limits were broadened from 21–31 to 18–45. The President called for "force to the utmost," and his call was heeded. And in November, only three months later, Germany surrendered.

That is the way to fight and win a war— all out—and not with half-an-eye on the battlefronts abroad and the other eye-and-a-half on personal, selfish, or political interests here at home.

Therefore, in order to concentrate all our energies and resources on winning the war, and to maintain a fair and stable economy at home, I recommend that the Congress adopt:

(1) A realistic tax law—which will tax all unreasonable profits, both individual and corporate, and reduce the ultimate cost of the war to our sons and daughters. The tax bill now under consideration by the Congress does not begin to meet this test.

(2) A continuation of the law for the renegotiation of war contracts—which will prevent exorbitant profits and assure fair prices to the Government. For two long years I have pleaded with the Congress to take undue profits out of war.

(3) A cost of food law—which will enable the Government (a) to place a reasonable floor under the prices the farmer may expect for his production; and (b) to place a ceiling on the prices a consumer will have to pay for the food he buys. This should apply to necessities only; and will require public funds to carry out. It will cost in appropriations about one percent of the present annual cost of the war.

(4) Early reenactment of the stabilization statute of October, 1942. This expires June 30, 1944, and if it is not extended well in advance, the country might just as well expect price chaos by summer.

We cannot have stabilization by wishful thinking. We must take positive action to maintain the integrity of the American dollar.

(5) A national service law—which, for the duration of the war, will prevent strikes, and, with certain appropriate

exceptions, will make available for war production or for any other essential services every able-bodied adult in this Nation.

These five measures together form a just and equitable whole. I would not recommend a national service law unless the other laws were passed to keep down the cost of living, to share equitably the burdens of taxation, to hold the stabilization line, and to prevent undue profits.

The Federal Government already has the basic power to draft capital and property of all kinds for war purposes on a basis of just compensation.

As you know, I have for three years hesitated to recommend a national service act. Today, however, I am convinced of its necessity. Although I believe that we and our allies can win the war without such a measure, I am certain that nothing less than total mobilization of all our resources of manpower and capital will guarantee an earlier victory, and reduce the toll of suffering and sorrow and blood.

I have received a joint recommendation for this law from the heads of the War Department, the Navy Department, and the Maritime Commission. These are the men who bear responsibility for the procurement of the necessary arms and equipment, and for the successful prosecution of the war in the field. They say:

"When the very life of the Nation is in peril the responsibility for service is common to all men and women. In such a time there can be no discrimination between the men and women who are assigned by the Government to its defense at the battlefront and the men and women assigned to producing the vital materials essential to successful military operations. A prompt enactment of a National Service Law would be merely an expression of the universality of this responsibility."

I believe the country will agree that those statements are the solemn truth.

National service is the most democratic way to wage a war. Like selective service for the armed forces, it rests on the obligation of each citizen to serve his Nation to his utmost where he is best qualified.

It does not mean reduction in wages. It does not mean loss of retirement and seniority rights and benefits. It does not mean that any substantial numbers of war workers will be disturbed in their present jobs. Let these facts be wholly clear.

Experience in other democratic Nations at war—Britain, Canada, Australia, and New Zealand—has shown that the very existence of national service makes unnecessary the widespread use of compulsory power. National service has proven to be a unifying moral force based on an equal and comprehensive legal obligation of all people in a Nation at war.

There are millions of American men and women who are not in this war at all. It is not because they do not want to be in it. But they want to know where they can best do their share. National service provides that direction. It will be a means by which every man and woman can find that inner satisfaction which comes from making the fullest possible contribution to victory.

I know that all civilian war workers will be glad to be able to say many years hence to their grandchildren: "Yes, I, too, was in service in the great war. I was on duty in an airplane factory, and I helped make hundreds of fighting planes. The Government told me that in doing that I was performing my most useful work in the service of my country."

It is argued that we have passed the stage in the war where national service is necessary. But our soldiers and sailors know that this is not true. We are going forward on a long, rough road—and, in all journeys, the last miles are the hardest. And it is for that final effort—for the total defeat of our enemies—that we must mobilize our total resources. The national war program calls for the employment of more people in 1944 than in 1943.

It is my conviction that the American people will welcome this win-the-war measure which is based on the eternally just principle of "fair for one, fair for all."

It will give our people at home the assurance that they are standing four-square behind our soldiers and sailors. And it will give our enemies demoralizing assurance that we mean business -that we, 130,000,000 Americans, are on the march to Rome, Berlin, and Tokyo.

I hope that the Congress will recognize that, although this is a political year, national service is an issue which transcends politics. Great power must be used for great purposes.

As to the machinery for this measure, the Congress itself should determine its nature—but it should be wholly nonpartisan in its make-up.

Our armed forces are valiantly fulfilling their responsibilities to our country and our people. Now the Congress faces the responsibility for taking those measures which are essential to national security in this the most decisive phase of the Nation's greatest war.

Several alleged reasons have prevented the enactment of legislation which would preserve for our soldiers and sailors and marines the fundamental prerogative of citizenship—the right to vote. No amount of legalistic argument can becloud this issue in the eyes of these ten million American citizens. Surely the signers of the Constitution did not intend a document which, even in wartime, would be construed to take away the franchise of any of those who are fighting to preserve the Constitution itself.

Our soldiers and sailors and marines know that the overwhelming majority of them will be deprived of the opportunity to vote, if the voting machinery is left exclusively to the States under existing State laws—and that there is no likelihood of these laws being changed in time to enable them to vote at the next election. The Army and Navy have reported that it will be impossible effectively to administer forty-eight different soldier voting laws. It is the duty of the Congress to remove this unjustifiable discrimination against the men and women in our armed forces—and to do it as quickly as possible.

It is our duty now to begin to lay the plans and determine the strategy for the winning of a lasting peace and the establishment of an American standard of living higher than ever before known. We cannot be content, no matter how high that general standard of living may be, if some fraction of our people—whether it be one-third or one-fifth or one-tenth—is ill-fed, ill-clothed, ill housed, and insecure.

This Republic had its beginning, and grew to its present strength, under the protection of certain inalienable political rights—among them the right of free speech, free press, free worship, trial by jury, freedom from unreasonable searches and seizures. They were our rights to life and liberty.

As our Nation has grown in size and stature, however—as our industrial economy expanded—these political rights proved inadequate to assure us equality in the pursuit of happiness.

We have come to a clear realization of the fact that true individual freedom cannot exist without economic security and independence. "Necessitous men are not free men." People who are hungry and out of a job are the stuff of which dictatorships are made.

In our day these economic truths have become accepted as self-evident. We have accepted, so to speak, a second Bill of Rights under which a new basis of security and prosperity can be established for all regardless of station, race, or creed.

Among these are:

The right to a useful and remunerative job in the industries or shops or farms or mines of the Nation;

The right to earn enough to provide adequate food and clothing and recreation;

The right of every farmer to raise and sell his products at a return which will give him and his family a decent living;

The right of every businessman, large and small, to trade in an atmosphere of freedom from unfair competition and domination by monopolies at home or abroad;

The right of every family to a decent home;

The right to adequate medical care and the opportunity to achieve and enjoy good health;

The right to adequate protection from the economic fears of old age, sickness, accident, and unemployment;

The right to a good education.

All of these rights spell security. And after this war is won we must be prepared to move forward, in the implementation of these rights, to new goals of human happiness and well-being.

America's own rightful place in the world depends in large part upon how fully these and similar rights have been carried into practice for our citizens. For unless there is security here at home there cannot be lasting peace in the world.

One of the great American industrialists of our day—a man who has rendered yeoman service to his country in this crisis-recently emphasized the grave dangers of "rightist reaction" in this Nation. All clear-thinking businessmen share his concern. Indeed, if such reaction should develop—if history were to repeat itself and we were to return to the so-called "normalcy" of the 1920s—then it is certain that even though we shall have conquered our enemies on the battlefields abroad, we shall have yielded to the spirit of Fascism here at home.

I ask the Congress to explore the means for implementing this economic bill of rights—for it is definitely the responsibility of the Congress so to do. Many of these problems are already before committees of the Congress in the form of proposed legislation. I shall from time to time communicate with the Congress with respect to these and further proposals. In the event that no adequate program of progress is evolved, I am certain that the Nation will be conscious of the fact.

Our fighting men abroad—and their families at home—expect such a program and have the right to insist upon it. It is to their demands that this Government should pay heed rather than to the whining demands of selfish pressure groups who seek to feather their nests while young Americans are dying.

The foreign policy that we have been following—the policy that guided us at Moscow, Cairo, and Teheran—is based on the common sense principle which was best expressed by Benjamin Franklin on July 4, 1776: "We must all hang together, or assuredly we shall all hang separately."

I have often said that there are no two fronts for America in this war. There is only one front. There is one line of unity which extends from the hearts of the people at home to the men of our attacking forces in our farthest outposts. When we speak of our total effort, we speak of the factory and the field, and the mine as well as of the battleground—we speak of the soldier and the civilian, the citizen and his Government.

Each and every one of us has a solemn obligation under God to serve this Nation in its most critical hour—to keep this Nation great—to make this Nation greater in a better world.

Study Questions

1. Compare Roosevelt's proposal of a "second Bill of Rights" with the original Bill of Rights. Were the new rights that Roosevelt endorsed natural and inalienable rights in the same manner as the old rights endorsed by the nation's founding fathers?

2. On what basis did Roosevelt claim that the original Bill of Rights no longer was adequate for American life during the 1940s? Do you agree? Explain.

Franklin D. Roosevelt, Fourth Inaugural Address (1945)

In the 1944 presidential campaign, Franklin D. Roosevelt courted the American people with a new running-mate, Senator Harry S. Truman. Republicans accused the Roosevelt administration of too readily cooperating with Soviet communists and of corruptly handling domestic affairs. The choice of Truman, who had led Senate investigations of corruption and inefficiency, no doubt helped Roosevelt win reelection, but even so the margin of victory was far slimmer than in previous years. For the Republicans, New York Governor Thomas E. Dewey won 46% of the popular vote, but carried only twelve out of forty-eight states. The Roosevelt-Truman ticket secured the White House for another four years of Democratic control. FDR hoped more than anything to use his new lease of influence for the establishment of the United Nations.

Mr. Chief Justice, Mr. Vice President, my friends:

You will understand and, I believe, agree with my wish that the form of this inauguration be simple and its words brief.

We Americans of today, together with our allies, are passing through a period of supreme test. It is a test of our courage—of our resolve—of our wisdom—of our essential democracy.

If we meet that test—successfully and honorably—we shall perform a service of historic importance which men and women and children will honor throughout all time.

As I stand here today, having taken the solemn oath of office in the presence of my fellow countrymen—in the presence of our God—I know that it is America's purpose that we shall not fail.

In the days and the years that are to come, we shall work for a just and honorable peace, a durable peace, as today we work and fight for total victory in war.

We can and we will achieve such a peace.

We shall strive for perfection. We shall not achieve it immediately—but we still shall strive. We may make mistakes—but they must never be mistakes which result from faintness of heart or abandonment of moral principle.

I remember that my old schoolmaster, Dr. Peabody, said—in days that seemed to us then to be secure and untroubled, "Things in life will not always run smoothly. Sometimes we will be rising toward the heights—then all will seem to reverse itself and start downward. The great fact to remember is that the trend of civilization itself is forever upward; that a line drawn through the middle of the peaks and the valleys of the centuries always has an upward trend."

Our Constitution of 1787 was not a perfect instrument; it is not perfect yet. But it provided a firm base upon which all manner of men, of all races and colors and creeds, could build our solid structure of democracy.

Today, in this year of war, 1945, we have learned lessons—at a fearful cost—and we shall profit by them.

We have learned that we cannot live

alone, at peace; that our own well-being is dependent on the well-being of other Nations, far away. We have learned that we must live as men and not as ostriches, nor as dogs in the manger.

We have learned to be citizens of the world, members of the human community.

We have learned the simple truth, as Emerson said, that, "The only way to have a friend is to be one."

We can gain no lasting peace if we approach it with suspicion and mistrust—or with fear. We can gain it only if we proceed with the understanding and the confidence and the courage which flow from conviction.

The Almighty God has blessed our land in many ways. He has given our people stout hearts and strong arms with which to strike mighty blows for freedom and truth. He has given to our country a faith which has become the hope of all peoples in an anguished world.

So we pray to Him now for the vision to see our way clearly to see the way that leads to a better life for ourselves and for all our fellow men—and to the achievement of His will to peace on earth.

Study Questions

1. What "supreme test" faced America and her allies in January 1945?

2. What did Roosevelt mean when he said, "We have learned to be citizens of the world"?

Joseph Stalin, Franklin D. Roosevelt, and Winston S. Churchill, Yalta Agreement (1945)

In February 1945, the "Big Three"—Joseph Stalin of the Soviet Union, Franklin D. Roosevelt of the United States, and Winston S. Churchill of Great Britain—convened in Yalta, Crimea, a Ukrainian peninsula in the Black Sea, to plan the resolution of World War II and a postwar peace. The U.S. State Department released a copy of their agreement to the American press on March 24. The agreement included a summons to other nations to convene on April 25, 1945, for the establishment of the United Nations; a declaration of liberation for Europe; war reparations and trials for war criminals; policies regarding the occupation and governance of Poland, Yugoslavia, and other occupied nations; as well as an agreement to open another war front against Japan.

I. World Organization

It was decided:

1. That a United Nations conference on the proposed world organization should be summoned for Wednesday, 25 April, 1945, and should be held in the United States of America. . . .

4. That the text of the invitation to be issued to all the nations which would take part in the United Nations conference should be as follows:

The Government of the United States of America, on behalf of itself and of the Governments of the United Kingdom, the Union of Soviet Socialistic Republics and the Republic of China and of the Provisional Government of the French Republic invite the Government of—to send representatives to a conference to be held on 25 April, 1945, or soon thereafter, at San Francisco, in the United States of America, to prepare a charter for a general international organization for the maintenance of international peace and security. . . .

II. Declaration of Liberated Europe

The following declaration has been approved:

The Premier of the Union of Soviet Socialist Republics, the Prime Minister of the United Kingdom and the President of the United States of America have consulted with each other in the common interests of the people of their countries and those of liberated Europe. They jointly declare their mutual agreement to concert during the temporary period of instability in liberated Europe the policies of their three Governments in assisting the peoples liberated from the domination of Nazi Germany and the peoples of the former Axis satellite states of Europe to solve by democratic means their pressing political and economic problems.

The establishment of order in Europe and the rebuilding of national economic life must be achieved by processes which will enable the liberated peoples to destroy the last vestiges of nazism and fascism and to create democratic institutions of their own choice. This is a principle of the Atlantic Charter—the right of all people to choose the form of government under which they will live—the restoration of sovereign rights and self-government to those peoples who have been forcibly deprived to them by the aggressor nations.

To foster the conditions in which the liberated people may exercise these rights, the three governments will jointly assist the people in any European liberated state or former Axis state in Europe where, in their judgment conditions require,

(a) to establish conditions of internal peace;

(b) to carry out emergency relief measures for the relief of distressed peoples;

(c) to form interim governmental authorities broadly representative of all democratic elements in the population and pledged to the earliest possible establishment through free elections of Governments responsive to the will of the people; and

(d) to facilitate where necessary the holding of such elections.

The three Governments will consult the other United Nations and provisional authorities or other Governments in Europe when matters of direct interest to them are under consideration.

When, in the opinion of the three Governments, conditions in any European liberated state or former Axis satellite in Europe make such action necessary, they will immediately consult together on the measure necessary to discharge the joint responsibilities set forth in this declaration.

By this declaration we reaffirm our faith in the principles of the Atlantic Charter, our pledge in the Declaration by the United Nations and our determination to build in cooperation with other peace-loving nations world order, under law, dedicated to peace, security, freedom and general well-being of all mankind.

In issuing this declaration, the three powers express the hope that the Provisional Government of the French Republic may be associated with them in the procedure suggested.

III. Dismemberment of Germany

It was agreed that Article 12 (a) of the Surrender terms for Germany should be amended to read as follows:

The United Kingdom, the United States of America and the Union of Soviet Socialist Republics shall possess supreme authority with respect to Germany. In the exercise of such authority they will take such steps, including the complete dismemberment of Germany as they deem requisite for future peace and security. . . .

VII. Poland

The following declaration on Poland was agreed by the conference:

A new situation has been created in Poland as a result of her complete liberation by the Red Army. This calls for the establishment of a Polish Provisional Government which can be more broadly based than was possible before the recent liberation of the western part of Poland. The Provisional Government which is now functioning in Poland should therefore be reorganized on a broader democratic basis with the inclusion of democratic leaders from Poland itself and from Poles abroad. This new Government should then be called the Polish Provisional Government of National Unity.

M. Molotov, Mr. Harriman and Sir A. Clark Kerr are authorized as a commission to consult in the first instance in Moscow with members of the present Provisional Government and with other Polish democratic leaders from within Poland and from abroad, with a view to the reorganization of the present Government along the above lines. This Polish Provisional Government of National Unity shall be pledged to the holding of free and unfettered elections as soon as possible on the basis of universal suffrage and secret ballot. In these elections all democratic and anti-Nazi parties shall have the right to take part and to put forward candidates.

When a Polish Provisional of Government National Unity has been properly formed in conformity with the above, the Government of the U.S.S.R., which now maintains diplomatic relations with the present Provisional Government of Poland, and the Government of the United Kingdom and the Government of the United States of America will establish diplomatic relations with the new Polish Provisional Government National Unity, and will exchange Ambassadors by whose reports the respective Governments will be kept informed about the situation in Poland.

The three heads of Government consider that the eastern frontier of Poland should follow the Curzon Line with digressions from it in some regions of five to eight kilometers in favor of Poland. They recognize that Poland must receive substantial accessions in territory in the north and west. They feel that the opinion of the new Polish Provisional Government of National Unity should be sought in due course of the extent of these accessions and that the final delimitation of the western frontier of Poland should thereafter await the peace conference. . . .

Agreement regarding Japan

The leaders of the three great powers—the Soviet Union, the United States of America and Great Britain—have agreed that in two or three months after Germany has surrendered and the war in Europe is terminated, the Soviet Union shall enter into war against Japan on the side of the Allies on condition that:

1. The status quo in Outer Mongolia (the Mongolian People's Republic) shall be preserved.

2. The former rights of Russia violated by the treacherous attack of Japan in 1904 shall be restored, viz.:

(a) The southern part of Sakhalin as well as the islands adjacent to it shall be returned to the Soviet Union;

(b) The commercial port of Dairen shall be internationalized, the pre-eminent interests of the Soviet Union in this port being safeguarded, and the lease of Port Arthur as a naval base of the U.S.S.R. restored;

(c) The Chinese-Eastern Railroad and the South Manchurian Railroad, which provide an outlet to Dairen, shall be jointly operated by the establishment of a joint Soviet-Chinese company, it being understood that the pre-eminent interests of the Soviet Union shall be safeguarded and that China shall retain sovereignty in Manchuria;

3. The Kurile Islands shall be handed over to the Soviet Union.

It is understood that the agreement concerning Outer Mongolia and the ports and railroads referred to above will require concurrence of Generalissimo Chiang Kai-shek. The President will take measures in order to maintain this concurrence on advice from Marshal Stalin.

The heads of the three great powers have agreed that these claims of the Soviet Union shall be unquestionably fulfilled after Japan has been defeated.

For its part, the Soviet Union expresses it readiness to conclude with the National Government of China a pact of friendship and alliance between the U.S.S.R. and China in order to render assistance to China with its armed forces for the purpose of lib- | erating China from the Japanese yoke.

Study Questions

1. What was to be the purpose of the proposed United Nations?

2. The Soviet Union desired to maintain Poland as a buffer zone, protecting the Soviets from the aggression that Germany brought in both world wars. How did the Yalta Conference handle Poland's future?

Harry S. Truman, "Announcement of the Dropping of the Atomic Bomb" (1945)

Secretary of War Henry Stimson released the following statement to the press on August 6, 1945, shortly after the first atomic bomb had been dropped on Japan. President Truman meanwhile was aboard the *U.S.S. Augusta*, returning from the Potsdam Conference. When in Germany, Truman had authorized the use of the bomb and drafted this statement to explain his course of action to the American people. Neither Truman nor Winston Churchill ever regretted the decision to use an atomic weapon against Japan. In *Triumph and Tragedy*, Churchill painted the image starkly: "To avert a vast, indefinite butchery, to bring the war to an end, to give peace to the world, to lay healing upon its tortured peoples by a manifestation of overwhelming power at the cost of a few explosions, seemed, after all our toils and perils, a miracle of deliverance." By Churchill's calculation, failure to use the bomb would have prolonged the war to the loss of an additional one million American lives, plus a likely larger number of Japanese lives, given the unwillingness of the Japanese to surrender.

Sixteen hours ago an American airplane dropped one bomb on Hiroshima, an important Japanese Army base. That bomb had more power than 20,000 tons of T.N.T. It had more than two thousand times the blast power of the British "Grand Slam" which is the largest bomb ever yet used in the history of warfare.

The Japanese began the war from the air at Pearl Harbor. They have been repaid many fold. And the end is not yet. With this bomb we have now added a new and revolutionary increase in destruction to supplement the growing power of our armed forces. In their present form these bombs are now in production and even more powerful forms are in development.

It is an atomic bomb. It is a harnessing of the basic power of the universe. The force from which the sun draws its power has been loosed against those who brought war to the Far East.

Before 1939, it was the accepted belief of scientists that it was theoretically pos-sible to release atomic energy. But no one knew any practical method of doing it. By 1942, however, we knew that the Germans were working feverishly to find a way to add atomic energy to the other engines of war with which they hoped to enslave the world. But they failed. We may be grateful to Providence that the Germans got the V-1's and V-2's late and in limited quantities and even more grateful that they did not get the atomic bomb at all.

The battle of the laboratories held fateful risks for us as well as the battles of the air, land and sea, and we have now won the battle of the laboratories as we have won the other battles.

Beginning in 1940, before Pearl Harbor, scientific knowledge useful in war was pooled between the United States and Great Britain, and many priceless helps to our victories have come from that arrangement. Under that general policy the research on the atomic bomb was begun. With American and British scientists working together we entered the race of discovery against the Germans.

The United States had available the large number of scientists of distinction in the many needed areas of knowledge. It had the tremendous industrial and financial resources necessary for the project and they could be devoted to it without undue impairment of other vital war work. In the United States the laboratory work and the production plants, on which a substantial start had already been made, would be out of reach of enemy bombing, while at that time Britain was exposed to constant air attack and was still threatened with the possibility of invasion. For these reasons Prime Minister Churchill and President Roosevelt agreed that it was wise to carry on the project here.

We now have two great plants and many lesser works devoted to the production of atomic power. Employment during peak construction numbered 125,000 and over 65,000 individuals are even now engaged in operating the plants. Many have worked there for two and a half years. Few know what they have been producing. They see great quantities of material going in and they see nothing coming out of these plants, for the physical size of the explosive charge is exceedingly small. We have spent two billion dollars on the greatest scientific gamble in history—and won.

But the greatest marvel is not the size of the enterprise, its secrecy, nor its cost, but the achievement of scientific brains in putting together infinitely complex pieces of knowledge held by many men in different fields of science into a workable plan. And hardly less marvelous has been the capacity of industry to design, and of labor to operate, the machines and methods to do things never done before so that the brain child of many minds came forth in physical shape and performed as it was supposed to do. Both science and industry worked under the direction of the United States Army, which achieved a unique success in managing so diverse a problem in the advancement of knowledge in an amazingly short time. It is doubtful if such another combination could be got together in the world. What has been done is the greatest achievement of organized science in history. It was done under high pressure and without failure.

We are now prepared to obliterate more rapidly and completely every productive enterprise the Japanese have above ground in any city. We shall destroy their docks, their factories, and their communications. Let there be no mistake; we shall completely destroy Japan's power to make war.

It was to spare the Japanese people from utter destruction that the ultimatum of July 26 was issued at Potsdam. Their leaders promptly rejected that ultimatum. If they do not now accept our terms they may expect a rain of ruin from the air, the like of which has never been seen on this earth. Behind this air attack will follow sea and land forces in such numbers and power as they have not yet seen and with the fighting skill of which they are already well aware.

The Secretary of War, who has kept in personal touch with all phases of the project, will immediately make public a statement giving further details.

His statement will give facts concerning the sites at Oak Ridge near Knoxville, Tennessee, and at Richland near Pasco, Washington, and an installation near Santa Fe, New Mexico. Although the workers at the sites have been making materials to be used in producing the greatest destructive force in history they have not themselves been in danger beyond that of many other occupations, for the utmost care has been taken of their safety.

The fact that we can release atomic energy ushers in a new era in man's understanding of nature's forces. Atomic energy may in the future supplement the power that now comes from coal, oil, and falling water, but at present it cannot be produced on a basis to compete with them commercially. Before that comes there must be a long period of intensive research.

It has never been the habit of the scientists of this country or the policy of this Government to withhold from the world scientific knowledge. Normally, therefore, everything about the work with atomic energy would be made public.

But under present circumstances it is not intended to divulge the technical processes of production or all the military applications, pending further examination of possible methods of protecting us and the rest of the world from the danger of sudden destruction.

I shall recommend that the Congress of the United States consider promptly the establishment of an appropriate commission to control the production and use of atomic power within the United States. I shall give further consideration and make further recommendations to the Congress as to how atomic power can become a powerful and forceful influence towards the maintenance of world peace.

Study Question

1. How did Truman describe the power of the atomic bomb?

2. On what basis did Truman justify using an atomic bomb against Japan?

The Emergence of the Cold War, 1946–1949

Two Incompatible World Systems

The Cold War (1946–1991) developed from fundamental ideological differences between the United States and the Soviet Union, compounded by the suspicions of each side that the other would relentlessly seek world domination. The United States had a long tradition of representative government fostering a capitalist economy. America's founding fathers had identified the preservation of natural rights as the chief purpose of government. Americans regarded rights to life, liberty, and property as inalienable gifts from God. The Soviet Union submitted to a different worldview. Individuals served the state, and the state in turn distributed social goods to the people. The Soviets criticized capitalism because it tolerated inequality; communism promised to relieve poverty in a way that the free market never could.

More than just a conflict of ideas, the Cold War also stemmed from very practical concerns. In both world wars, and especially in the second, the Soviets had suffered the brunt of German aggression. Fearing a third episode, Joseph Stalin desired that Poland and other eastern European states would serve as buffer zones between the Soviet Union and central Europe. Stalin therefore negotiated at Yalta for a sphere of influence in eastern Europe. Similar concerns motivated the Soviet troops to remain in northern Korea after World War II. The United States, meanwhile, worried that the Soviets would not be content to have a buffer zone along their own border, but would expand until a communist empire filled the world. Could Stalin at Yalta be trusted any more than Hitler at Munich—when Hitler had promised not to invade the remainder of Czechoslovakia?

The "Iron Curtain" (1946)

England's Winston Churchill had deep suspicions concerning Stalin's posture in eastern Europe. Speaking at Westminster College in Fulton, Missouri, with his typical oratorical skills, Churchill introduced the term "iron curtain" to describe the division between Western powers and the area controlled by the Soviet Union. Delivered on March 5, 1946, this speech symbolically marked the onset of the Cold War:

> The United States stands at this time at the pinnacle of world power. It is a solemn moment for the American democracy. For with this primacy in power is also joined an awe-inspiring accountability to the future. . . . From Stettin in the Baltic to Trieste in the Adriatic an iron curtain has descended across the Continent. Behind that line lie all the capitals of the ancient states of Central and Eastern Europe. Warsaw, Berlin, Prague, Vienna, Budapest, Belgrade, Bucharest and Sofia; all these famous cities and the populations around them lie in what I must call the Soviet sphere,

and all are subject, in one form or another, not only to Soviet influence but to a very high and in some cases increasing measure of control from Moscow.

Churchill rejected "the old doctrine of a balance of power" as "unsound" and called for a new alliance between America and Great Britain that would establish supremacy around the globe in order to forestall any further expansion by the Soviet Union. He continued:

> If the population of the English-speaking Commonwealth be added to that of the United States, with all that such cooperation implies in the air, on the sea, all over the globe, and in science and in industry, and in moral force, there will be no quivering, precarious balance of power to offer its temptation to ambition or adventure. On the contrary there will be an overwhelming assurance of security.

The Truman Doctrine in Greece and Beyond (1947)

U.S. President Harry S. Truman reinforced Churchill's rhetoric and introduced, in March 1947, the Truman Doctrine of foreign policy: "I believe that it must be the policy of the United States to support free peoples who are resisting attempted subjugation by armed minorities or by outside pressures." Truman especially had in mind Greece, where a parliamentary monarchy had become vulnerable to a populist uprising sponsored by Soviet communists. Previously, British foreign aid had supported the Greek government, but when Britain pulled out due to its own economic struggles, a populist faction threatened revolution. To contain communism from spreading into Greece, as it already had spread into several eastern European nations, Congress answered Truman's summons by appropriating $400 million in foreign aid for Greece and Turkey.

The Truman Doctrine flowed from the scholarly analysis of George Keenan, the Undersecretary of State. Keenan, an expert on the Soviet Union, had concluded that the United States had the capacity to contain communism in southeastern Europe. Keenan warned, however, that if America failed to act then the Soviet Union would prevail over Greece. The choice was simple: contain communism.

In July 1947, Congress approved the National Security Act. This legislation created both the National Security Council and the Central Intelligence Agency, restructured the War Department and the Navy Department into the Department of Defense, and shifted aspects of foreign policy decision-making from the legislative to the executive branch. The president now could implement the containment policy—whether in Greece or elsewhere—with greater administrative efficiency.

In April 1950, the National Security Council delivered a top secret report to Truman, NSC–68, detailing the necessity of preventing communism from spreading into third world nations. This outlook would determine American foreign policy in Korea just a few months later. NSC–68 continued to shape America's interventionist role throughout the Cold War.

The Marshall Plan and the Berlin Airlift (1948)

In 1948, Congress authorized the European Recovery Program, or Marshall Plan, named for Secretary of State George Marshall. The program extended aid for rebuilding war-torn Europe, while requiring that monies be spent on U.S. goods in the process. American critics called it an "international WPA," detecting a socialist agenda for revitalizing American industry through government contracts. The eastern bloc nations of Europe, however, thought the Marshall Plan was a capitalist plot to woo them away from Soviet influence.

While Congress debated the measure, the Soviets staged a brutal *coup d'etat* in Czechoslovakia, overthrowing the U.S.-approved coalition government that had been elected following World War II. Congress now had little choice but to adopt the Marshall Plan and rebuild western Europe before the Iron Curtain smothered the entire continent.

Later that year, the United States, Britain, and France merged the sections of Berlin occupied by their troops and began circulating a common currency. The Soviet Union, which controlled the remaining quarter of the Germany capital, feared the growth of capitalism within its sphere of influence. The Soviets therefore established a blockade against all traffic into West Berlin by highway, rail, or river. In response, the U.S. Air Force filled its bombers with food and supplies. For eleven months—from June 1948 through May 1949—U.S. planes landed daily to sustain West Berliners until Stalin finally lifted the blockade.

The North American Treaty Organization (1949)

Stalin's invasion of Czechoslovakia and the blockade against West Berlin convinced Americans of the need to coordinate their containment policy with western European nations. In April 1949, the United States joined the North Atlantic Treaty Organization (NATO) under a treaty stating that "an armed attack against one or more [of the member nations] in Europe or North America shall be construed as an attack against them all." The same year, the Soviet Union formed the Council of Mutual Economic Assistance (COM-ECON) with eastern Europe, which later evolved into the Warsaw Pact (1955).

In May 1949, the NATO nations recognized the Federal Republic of Germany as the legitimate government for West Germany. In October the Soviets established the

German Democratic Republic (East Germany). Thus, the nation of Germany and the continent of Europe had become severed into two rival factions: one supported by the United States and the other by the Soviet Union.

Study Questions

1. What did Churchill mean by the term "iron curtain," and what actions did he propose in response?

2. What is the Truman Doctrine, and why did the president believe this foreign policy posture was prudent?

3. What motivated the United States and the Soviet Union as each nation took part in events that resulted in the division of Germany?

United Nations, Universal Declaration on Human Rights (1948)

The United Nations, established in April 1945, consists of a General Assembly that includes representatives of all member nations plus a Security Council. The Security Council has five permanent members, each with veto power over any security resolutions: the United States, Great Britain, the Soviet Union, France, and China. Several additional nations are represented as temporary members on a rotating basis. Whereas the Security Council responds with sanctions to aggression among nations, the General Council establishes policies of a more philosophical nature. One of the most influential policy documents adopted by the General Council is the 1948 Universal Declaration on Human Rights. Eleanor Roosevelt served as one of the chief authors of this declaration, which echoed the suggestions that her husband, Franklin D. Roosevelt, had shared with Congress in his 1944 State of the Union Address, when calling for an "economic bill of rights." Although the Universal Declaration has shaped numerous policies adopted within the United States, it does not have the standing of an international treaty and was never ratified by the U.S. Senate. "The Universal Declaration of Human Rights is merely a resolution of the United Nations [like other, similar resolutions]; none is binding on the United States or on this court," *Feng Hsin Chen v. John Ashcroft and Luis Garcia*, U.S. Ct. of Appeals (10th Cir. 2004).

Preamble

[1] Whereas recognition of the inherent dignity and of the equal and inalienable rights of all members of the human family is the foundation of freedom, justice and peace in the world,

[2] Whereas disregard and contempt for human rights have resulted in barbarous acts which have outraged the conscience of mankind, and the advent of a world in which human beings shall enjoy freedom of speech and belief and freedom from fear and want has been proclaimed as the highest aspiration of the common people,

[3] Whereas it is essential, if man is not to be compelled to have recourse, as a last resort, to rebellion against tyranny and oppression, that human rights should be protected by the rule of law,

[4] Whereas it is essential to promote the development of friendly relations between nations,

[5] Whereas the peoples of the United Nations have in the Charter reaffirmed their faith in fundamental human rights, in the dignity and worth of the human person and in the equal rights of men and women and have determined to promote social progress and better standards of life in larger freedom,

[6] Whereas Member States have pledged themselves to achieve, in co-operation with the United Nations, the promotion of universal respect for and observance of human rights and fundamental freedoms,

[7] Whereas a common understanding of these rights and freedoms is of the greatest importance for the full realization

of this pledge,

[8] Now, Therefore THE GENERAL ASSEMBLY proclaims THIS UNIVERSAL DECLARATION OF HUMAN RIGHTS as a common standard of achievement for all peoples and all nations, to the end that every individual and every organ of society, keeping this Declaration constantly in mind, shall strive by teaching and education to promote respect for these rights and freedoms and by progressive measures, national and international, to secure their universal and effective recognition and observance, both among the peoples of Member States themselves and among the peoples of territories under their jurisdiction.

Article 1

All human beings are born free and equal in dignity and rights. They are endowed with reason and conscience and should act towards one another in a spirit of brotherhood.

Article 2

Everyone is entitled to all the rights and freedoms set forth in this Declaration, without distinction of any kind, such as race, colour, sex, language, religion, political or other opinion, national or social origin, property, birth or other status. Furthermore, no distinction shall be made on the basis of the political, jurisdictional or international status of the country or territory to which a person belongs, whether it be independent, trust, non-self-governing or under any other limitation of sovereignty.

Article 3

Everyone has the right to life, liberty and security of person.

Article 4

No one shall be held in slavery or servitude; slavery and the slave trade shall be prohibited in all their forms.

Article 5

No one shall be subjected to torture or to cruel, inhuman or degrading treatment or punishment.

Article 6

Everyone has the right to recognition everywhere as a person before the law.

Article 7

All are equal before the law and are entitled without any discrimination to equal protection of the law. All are entitled to equal protection against any discrimination in violation of this Declaration and against any incitement to such discrimination.

Article 8

Everyone has the right to an effective remedy by the competent national tribunals for acts violating the fundamental rights granted him by the constitution or by law.

Article 9

No one shall be subjected to arbitrary arrest, detention or exilc.

Article 10

Everyone is entitled in full equality to a fair and public hearing by an independent and impartial tribunal, in the determination of his rights and obligations and of any criminal charge against him.

Article 11

(1) Everyone charged with a penal offence has the right to be presumed innocent until proved guilty according to law in a public trial at which he has had all the guarantees necessary for his defence.

(2) No one shall be held guilty of any penal offence on account of any act or omission which did not constitute a penal offence, under national or international law, at the time when it was committed. Nor shall a heavier penalty be imposed than the one that was applicable at the time the penal offence was committed.

Article 12

No one shall be subjected to arbitrary interference with his privacy, family, home or correspondence, nor to attacks upon his honour and reputation. Everyone has the right to the protection of the law against such interference or attacks.

Article 13

(1) Everyone has the right to freedom of movement and residence within the borders of each state.

(2) Everyone has the right to leave any country, including his own, and to return to his country.

Article 14

(1) Everyone has the right to seek and to enjoy in other countries asylum from persecution.

(2) This right may not be invoked in the case of prosecutions genuinely arising from non-political crimes or from acts contrary to the purposes and principles of the United Nations.

Article 15

(1) Everyone has the right to a nationality.

(2) No one shall be arbitrarily deprived of his nationality nor denied the right to change his nationality.

Article 16

(1) Men and women of full age, without any limitation due to race, nationality or religion, have the right to marry and to found a family. They are entitled to equal rights as to marriage, during marriage and at its dissolution.

(2) Marriage shall be entered into only with the free and full consent of the intending spouses.

(3) The family is the natural and funda-

mental group unit of society and is entitled to protection by society and the State.

Article 17

(1) Everyone has the right to own property alone as well as in association with others.

(2) No one shall be arbitrarily deprived of his property.

Article 18

Everyone has the right to freedom of thought, conscience and religion; this right includes freedom to change his religion or belief, and freedom, either alone or in community with others and in public or private, to manifest his religion or belief in teaching, practice, worship and observance.

Article 19

Everyone has the right to freedom of opinion and expression; this right includes freedom to hold opinions without interference and to seek, receive and impart information and ideas through any media and regardless of frontiers.

Article 20

(1) Everyone has the right to freedom of peaceful assembly and association.

(2) No one may be compelled to belong to an association.

Article 21

(1) Everyone has the right to take part in the government of his country, directly or through freely chosen representatives.

(2) Everyone has the right of equal access to public service in his country.

(3) The will of the people shall be the basis of the authority of government; this will shall be expressed in periodic and genuine elections which shall be by universal and equal suffrage and shall be held by secret vote or by equivalent free voting procedures.

Article 22

Everyone, as a member of society, has the right to social security and is entitled to realization, through national effort and international co-operation and in accordance with the organization and resources of each State, of the economic, social and cultural rights indispensable for his dignity and the free development of his personality.

Article 23

(1) Everyone has the right to work, to free choice of employment, to just and favourable conditions of work and to protection against unemployment.

(2) Everyone, without any discrimination, has the right to equal pay for equal work.

(3) Everyone who works has the right to just and favourable remuneration ensuring for himself and his family an existence worthy of human dignity, and supplemen-

ted, if necessary, by other means of social protection.

(4) Everyone has the right to form and to join trade unions for the protection of his interests.

Article 24

Everyone has the right to rest and leisure, including reasonable limitation of working hours and periodic holidays with pay.

Article 25

(1) Everyone has the right to a standard of living adequate for the health and well-being of himself and of his family, including food, clothing, housing and medical care and necessary social services, and the right to security in the event of unemployment, sickness, disability, widowhood, old age or other lack of livelihood in circumstances beyond his control.

(2) Motherhood and childhood are entitled to special care and assistance. All children, whether born in or out of wedlock, shall enjoy the same social protection.

Article 26

(1) Everyone has the right to education. Education shall be free, at least in the elementary and fundamental stages. Elementary education shall be compulsory. Technical and professional education shall be made generally available and higher education shall be equally accessible to all on the basis of merit.

(2) Education shall be directed to the full development of the human personality and to the strengthening of respect for human rights and fundamental freedoms. It shall promote understanding, tolerance and friendship among all nations, racial or religious groups, and shall further the activities of the United Nations for the maintenance of peace.

(3) Parents have a prior right to choose the kind of education that shall be given to their children.

Article 27

(1) Everyone has the right freely to participate in the cultural life of the community, to enjoy the arts and to share in scientific advancement and its benefits.

(2) Everyone has the right to the protection of the moral and material interests resulting from any scientific, literary or artistic production of which he is the author.

Article 28

Everyone is entitled to a social and international order in which the rights and freedoms set forth in this Declaration can be fully realized.

Article 29

(1) Everyone has duties to the community in which alone the free and full development of his personality is possible.

(2) In the exercise of his rights and freedoms, everyone shall be subject only to such limitations as are determined by law

solely for the purpose of securing due recognition and respect for the rights and freedoms of others and of meeting the just requirements of morality, public order and the general welfare in a democratic society.

(3) These rights and freedoms may in no case be exercised contrary to the purposes and principles of the United Nations.

Article 30

Nothing in this Declaration may be interpreted as implying for any State, group or person any right to engage in any activity or to perform any act aimed at the destruction of any of the rights and freedoms set forth herein.

Study Questions

1. How do the provisions of the Universal Declaration square with Roosevelt's "Four Freedoms"?

   freedom of speech:

   freedom of religion:

   freedom from want:

   freedom from fear:

2. Which guarantees listed in the Universal Declaration flow from the *laissez-faire* tradition and which fit better with the tradition of progressive reform?

3. Compare the reference to "inalienable rights" in the preamble to the limitation stated in Art. 29, para. 3. Does the United Nations adhere to the same sense of "inalienable rights" as America's founders did in the Declaration of Independence?

Harry S. Truman, Inaugural Address (1949)

On election night in November 1948, Harry Truman fell asleep thinking he had lost to Republican candidate Thomas E. Dewey, the governor of New York. He woke up the following morning to discover that the editors of the *Chicago Tribune* had assumed the same, for the front page headline read: "DEWEY DEFEATS TRUMAN." Despite the early prognostications of *Tribune* political analyst Arthur Sears Henning, Truman in fact won the election, 303 electoral votes to 189. In January 1949, Truman placed his hand on two Bibles, one opened to the Ten Commandments and the other to the Beatitudes, as he raised his right hand to take the oath of office. In his inaugural address, he extolled the virtues of American democracy while warning against the threat of Soviet communism.

Mr. Vice President, Mr. Chief Justice, fellow citizens:

I accept with humility the honor which the American people have conferred upon me. I accept it with a resolve to do all that I can for the welfare of this Nation and for the peace of the world.

In performing the duties of my office, I need the help and the prayers of every one of you. I ask for your encouragement and for your support. The tasks we face are difficult. We can accomplish them only if we work together.

Each period of our national history has had its special challenges. Those that confront us now are as momentous as any in the past. Today marks the beginning not only of a new administration, but of a period that will be eventful, perhaps decisive, for us and for the world.

It may be our lot to experience, and in a large measure bring about, a major turning point in the long history of the human race. The first half of this century has been marked by unprecedented and brutal attacks on the rights of man, and by the two most frightful wars in history. The supreme need of our time is for men to learn to live together in peace and harmony.

The peoples of the earth face the future with grave uncertainty, composed almost equally of great hopes and great fears. In this time of doubt, they look to the United States as never before for good will, strength, and wise leadership.

It is fitting, therefore, that we take this occasion to proclaim to the world the essential principles of the faith by which we live, and to declare our aims to all peoples.

The American people stand firm in the faith which has inspired this Nation from the beginning. We believe that all men have a right to equal justice under law and equal opportunity to share in the common good. We believe that all men have a right to freedom of thought and expression. We believe that all men are created equal because they are created in the image of God.

From this faith we will not be moved.

The American people desire, and are determined to work for, a world in which all nations and all peoples are free to govern themselves as they see fit, and to achieve a decent and satisfying life. Above all else, our people desire, and are determined to work for, peace on earth—a just and lasting peace—based on genuine agreement freely arrived at by equals.

In the pursuit of these aims, the United States and other like-minded nations find themselves directly opposed by a regime with contrary aims and a totally different concept of life.

That regime adheres to a false philosophy which purports to offer freedom, security, and greater opportunity to mankind. Misled by that philosophy, many peoples have sacrificed their liberties only to learn to their sorrow that deceit and mockery, poverty and tyranny, are their reward.

That false philosophy is communism.

Communism is based on the belief that man is so weak and inadequate that he is unable to govern himself, and therefore requires the rule of strong masters.

Democracy is based on the conviction that man has the moral and intellectual capacity, as well as the inalienable right, to govern himself with reason and justice.

Communism subjects the individual to arrest without lawful cause, punishment without trial, and forced labor as the chattel of the state. It decrees what information he shall receive, what art he shall produce, what leaders he shall follow, and what thoughts he shall think.

Democracy maintains that government is established for the benefit of the individual, and is charged with the responsibility of protecting the rights of the individual and his freedom in the exercise of those abilities of his.

Communism maintains that social wrongs can be corrected only by violence.

Democracy has proved that social justice can be achieved through peaceful change.

Communism holds that the world is so widely divided into opposing classes that war is inevitable.

Democracy holds that free nations can settle differences justly and maintain a lasting peace.

These differences between communism and democracy do not concern the United States alone. People everywhere are coming to realize that what is involved is material well-being, human dignity, and the right to believe in and worship God.

I state these differences, not to draw issues of belief as such, but because the actions resulting from the Communist philosophy are a threat to the efforts of free nations to bring about world recovery and lasting peace.

Since the end of hostilities, the United States has invested its substance and its energy in a great constructive effort to restore peace, stability, and freedom to the world.

We have sought no territory. We have imposed our will on none. We have asked for no privileges we would not extend to others.

We have constantly and vigorously supported the United Nations and related agencies as a means of applying democratic principles to international relations.

We have consistently advocated and relied upon peaceful settlement of disputes among nations.

We have made every effort to secure agreement on effective international control of our most powerful weapon, and we have worked steadily for the limitation and control of all armaments.

We have encouraged, by precept and example, the expansion of world trade on a sound and fair basis.

Almost a year ago, in company with 16 free nations of Europe, we launched the greatest cooperative economic program in history. The purpose of that unprecedented effort is to invigorate and strengthen democracy in Europe, so that the free people of that continent can resume their rightful place in the forefront of civilization and can contribute once more to the security and welfare of the world.

Our efforts have brought new hope to all mankind. We have beaten back despair and defeatism. We have saved a number of countries from losing their liberty. Hundreds of millions of people all over the world now agree with us, that we need not have war—that we can have peace.

The initiative is ours.

We are moving on with other nations to build an even stronger structure of international order and justice. We shall have as our partners countries which, no longer solely concerned with the problem of national survival, are now working to improve the standards of living of all their people. We are ready to undertake new projects to strengthen a free world.

In the coming years, our program for peace and freedom will emphasize four major courses of action.

First, we will continue to give unfaltering support to the United Nations and related agencies, and we will continue to search for ways to strengthen their authority and increase their effectiveness. We believe that the United Nations will be strengthened by the new nations which are being formed in lands now advancing toward self-government under democratic principles.

Second, we will continue our programs for world economic recovery.

This means, first of all, that we must keep our full weight behind the European recovery program. We are confident of the success of this major venture in world recovery. We believe that our partners in this effort will achieve the status of self-supporting nations once again.

In addition, we must carry out our plans for reducing the barriers to world trade and increasing its volume. Economic recovery and peace itself depend on increased world trade.

Third, we will strengthen freedom-loving nations against the dangers of aggression.

We are now working out with a number of countries a joint agreement designed to strengthen the security of the North Atlantic area. Such an agreement would take the form of a collective defense arrangement within the terms of the United Nations Charter.

We have already established such a defense pact for the Western Hemisphere by the treaty of Rio de Janeiro.

The primary purpose of these agreements is to provide unmistakable proof of the joint determination of the free countries to resist armed attack from any quarter. Every country participating in these arrangements must contribute all it can to the common defense.

If we can make it sufficiently clear, in advance, that any armed attack affecting our national security would be met with overwhelming force, the armed attack might never occur.

I hope soon to send to the Senate a treaty respecting the North Atlantic security plan.

In addition, we will provide military advice and equipment to free nations which will cooperate with us in the maintenance of peace and security.

Fourth, we must embark on a bold new program for making the benefits of our scientific advances and industrial progress available for the improvement and growth of underdeveloped areas.

More than half the people of the world are living in conditions approaching misery. Their food is inadequate. They are victims of disease. Their economic life is primitive and stagnant. Their poverty is a handicap and a threat both to them and to more prosperous areas.

For the first time in history, humanity posesses the knowledge and skill to relieve suffering of these people.

The United States is pre-eminent among nations in the development of industrial and scientific techniques. The material resources which we can afford to use for assistance of other peoples are lim-

ited. But our imponderable resources in technical knowledge are constantly growing and are inexhaustible.

I believe that we should make available to peace-loving peoples the benefits of our store of technical knowledge in order to help them realize their aspirations for a better life. And, in cooperation with other nations, we should foster capital investment in areas needing development.

Our aim should be to help the free peoples of the world, through their own efforts, to produce more food, more clothing, more materials for housing, and more mechanical power to lighten their burdens.

We invite other countries to pool their technological resources in this undertaking. Their contributions will be warmly welcomed. This should be a cooperative enterprise in which all nations work together through the United Nations and its specialized agencies whenever practicable. It must be a worldwide effort for the achievement of peace, plenty, and freedom.

With the cooperation of business, private capital, agriculture, and labor in this country, this program can greatly increase the industrial activity in other nations and can raise substantially their standards of living.

Such new economic developments must be devised and controlled to the benefit of the peoples of the areas in which they are established. Guarantees to the investor must be balanced by guarantees in the interest of the people whose resources and whose labor go into these developments.

The old imperialism—exploitation for

foreign profit—has no place in our plans. What we envisage is a program of development based on the concepts of democratic fair-dealing.

All countries, including our own, will greatly benefit from a constructive program for the better use of the world's human and natural resources. Experience shows that our commerce with other countries expands as they progress industrially and economically.

Greater production is the key to prosperity and peace. And the key to greater production is a wider and more vigorous application of modern scientific and technical knowledge.

Only by helping the least fortunate of its members to help themselves can the human family achieve the decent, satisfying life that is the right of all people.

Democracy alone can supply the vitalizing force to stir the peoples of the world into triumphant action, not only against their human oppressors, but also against their ancient enemies—hunger, misery, and despair.

On the basis of these four major courses of action we hope to help create the conditions that will lead eventually to personal freedom and happiness for all mankind.

If we are to be successful in carrying out these policies, it is clear that we must have continued prosperity in this country and we must keep ourselves strong.

Slowly but surely we are weaving a world fabric of international security and growing prosperity.

We are aided by all who wish to live in freedom from fear—even by those who live today in fear under their own governments.

We are aided by all who want relief from lies and propaganda—those who desire truth and sincerity.

We are aided by all who desire self-government and a voice in deciding their own affairs.

We are aided by all who long for economic security—for the security and abundance that men in free societies can enjoy.

We are aided by all who desire freedom of speech, freedom of religion, and freedom to live their own lives for useful ends.

Our allies are the millions who hunger and thirst after righteousness.

In due time, as our stability becomes manifest, as more and more nations come to know the benefits of democracy and to participate in growing abundance, I believe that those countries which now oppose us will abandon their delusions and join with the free nations of the world in a just settlement of international differences.

Events have brought our American democracy to new influence and new responsibilities. They will test our courage, our devotion to duty, and our concept of liberty.

But I say to all men, what we have achieved in liberty, we will surpass in greater liberty.

Steadfast in our faith in the Almighty, we will advance toward a world where man's freedom is secure.

To that end we will devote our strength, our resources, and our firmness of resolve. With God's help, the future of mankind will be assured in a world of justice, harmony, and peace.

Study Questions

1. Identify the points of contrast that Truman perceived between democracy and communism.

2. What four "courses of action" did Truman propose in his "program for peace and freedom"?

National Security Council, NSC–68 (1950)

On January 31, 1950, President Truman issued a directive to the National Security Council requesting an analysis of U.S.-Soviet relations with recommendations for the future course of U.S. foreign policy. The Council responded on April 7 with National Security Council document 68, a top secret report portraying the United States and Soviet Union as fundamentally at odds.

I. Background of the Present Crisis

Within the past thirty-five years the world has experienced two global wars of tremendous violence. It has witnessed two revolutions—the Russian and the Chinese —of extreme scope and intensity. It has also seen the collapse of five empires—the Ottoman, the Austro-Hungarian, German, Italian, and Japanese—and the drastic decline of two major imperial systems, the British and the French. During the span of one generation, the international distribution of power has been fundamentally altered. For several centuries it had proved impossible for any one nation to gain such preponderant strength that a coalition of other nations could not in time face it with greater strength. The international scene was marked by recurring periods of violence and war, but a system of sovereign and independent states was maintained, over which no state was able to achieve hegemony.

Two complex sets of factors have now basically altered this historic distribution of power. First, the defeat of Germany and Japan and the decline of the British and French Empires have interacted with the development of the United States and the Soviet Union in such a way that power increasingly gravitated to these two centers. Second, the Soviet Union, unlike previous aspirants to hegemony, is animated by a new fanatic faith, anti-thetical to our own, and seeks to impose its absolute authority over the rest of the world. Conflict has, therefore, become endemic and is waged, on the part of the Soviet Union, by violent or non-violent methods in accordance with the dictates of expediency. With the development of increasingly terrifying weapons of mass destruction, every individual faces the ever-present possibility of annihilation should the conflict enter the phase of total war.

On the one hand, the people of the world yearn for relief from the anxiety arising from the risk of atomic war. On the other hand, any substantial further extension of the area under the domination of the Kremlin would raise the possibility that no coalition adequate to confront the Kremlin with greater strength could be assembled. It is in this context that this Republic and its citizens in the ascendancy of their strength stand in their deepest peril.

The issues that face us are momentous, involving the fulfillment or destruction not only of this Republic but of civilization itself. They are issues which will not await our deliberations. With conscience and resolution this Government and the people it represents must now take new and fateful decisions.

II. Fundamental Purpose of the United States

The fundamental purpose of the United States is laid down in the Preamble to the Constitution: "... to form a more perfect Union, establish justice, insure domestic Tranquility, provide for the common defence, promote the general Welfare, and secure the Blessings of Liberty to ourselves and our Posterity." In essence, the fundamental purpose is to assure the integrity and vitality of our free society, which is founded upon the dignity and worth of the individual.

Three realities emerge as a consequence of this purpose: Our determination to maintain the essential elements of individual freedom, as set forth in the Constitution and Bill of Rights; our determination to create conditions under which our free and democratic system can live and prosper; and our determination to fight if necessary to defend our way of life, for which as in the Declaration of Independence, "with a firm reliance on the protection of Divine Providence, we mutually pledge to each other our lives, our Fortunes, and our sacred Honor."

III. Fundamental Design of the Kremlin

The fundamental design of those who control the Soviet Union and the international communist movement is to retain and solidify their absolute power, first in the Soviet Union and second in the areas now under their control. In the minds of the Soviet leaders, however, achievement of this design requires the dynamic exten-

sion of their authority and the ultimate elimination of any effective opposition to their authority.

The design, therefore, calls for the complete subversion or forcible destruction of the machinery of government and structure of society in the countries of the non-Soviet world and their replacement by an apparatus and structure subservient to and controlled from the Kremlin. To that end Soviet efforts are now directed toward the domination of the Eurasian land mass. The United States, as the principal center of power in the non-Soviet world and the bulwark of opposition to Soviet expansion, is the principal enemy whose integrity and vitality must be subverted or destroyed by one means or another if the Kremlin is to achieve its fundamental design.

IV. The Underlying Conflict in the Realm of Ideas and Values between the U.S. Purpose and the Kremlin Design

A. NATURE OF CONFLICT

The Kremlin regards the United States as the only major threat to the conflict between idea of slavery under the grim oligarchy of the Kremlin, which has come to a crisis with the polarization of power described in Section I, and the exclusive possession of atomic weapons by the two protagonists. The idea of freedom, moreover, is peculiarly and intolerably subversive of the idea of slavery. But the converse is not true. The implacable purpose of the slave state to eliminate the challenge of freedom has placed the two great powers at opposite poles. It is this fact which gives the present polarization of power the quality of crisis.

The free society values the individual as an end in himself, requiring of him only that measure of self-discipline and self-restraint which make the rights of each individual compatible with the rights of every other individual. The freedom of the individual has as its counterpart, therefore, the negative responsibility of the individual not to exercise his freedom in ways inconsistent with the freedom of other individuals and the positive responsibility to make constructive use of his freedom in the building of a just society.

From this idea of freedom with responsibility derives the marvelous diversity, the deep tolerance, the lawfulness of the free society. This is the explanation of the strength of free men. It constitutes the integrity and the vitality of a free and democratic system. The free society attempts to create and maintain an environment in which every individual has the opportunity to realize his creative powers. It also explains why the free society tolerates those within it who would use their freedom to destroy it. By the same token, in relations between nations, the prime reliance of the free society is on the strength and appeal of its idea, and it feels no compulsion sooner or later to bring all societies into conformity with it.

For the free society does not fear, it welcomes, diversity. It derives its strength from its hospitality even to antipathetic ideas. It is a market for free trade in ideas, secure in its faith that free men will take the best wares, and grow to a fuller and better realization of their powers in exercising their choice.

The idea of freedom is the most contagious idea in history, more contagious than the idea of submission to authority. For the breadth of freedom cannot be tolerated in a society which has come under the domination of an individual or group of individuals with a will to absolute power. Where the despot holds absolute power—the absolute power of the absolutely powerful will—all other wills must be subjugated in an act of willing submission, a degradation willed by the individual upon himself under the compulsion of a perverted faith. It is the first article of this faith that he finds and can only find the meaning of his existence in serving the ends of the system. The system becomes God, and submission to the will of God becomes submission to the will of the system. It is not enough to yield outwardly to the system—even Gandhian nonviolence is not acceptable—for the spirit of resistance and the devotion to a higher authority might then remain, and the individual would not be wholly submissive.

The same compulsion which demands total power over all men within the Soviet state without a single exception, demands total power over all Communist Parties and all states under Soviet domination. Thus Stalin has said that the theory and tactics of Leninism as expounded by the Bolshevik party are mandatory for the proletarian parties of all countries. A true internationalist is defined as one who unhesitatingly upholds the position of the Soviet Union and in the satellite states true patriotism is love of the Soviet Union. By the same token the "peace policy" of the Soviet Union, described at a Party Congress as "a more advantageous form of fighting capitalism," is a device to divide and immobilize the non-Communist world, and the peace the Soviet Union seeks is the peace of total conformity to Soviet policy.

The antipathy of slavery to freedom explains the iron curtain, the isolation, the autarchy of the society whose end is absolute power. The existence and persistence of the idea of freedom is a permanent and continuous threat to the foundation of the slave society; and it therefore regards as intolerable the long continued existence of freedom in the world. What is new, what makes the continuing crisis, is the polarization of power which now inescapably confronts the slave society with the free.

The assault on free institutions is world-wide now, and in the context of the present polarization of power a defeat of free institutions anywhere is a defeat everywhere. The shock we sustained in the destruction of Czechoslovakia was not in the measure of Czechoslovakia's material importance to us. In a material sense, her capabilities were already at Soviet disposal. But when the integrity of Czechoslovak institutions was destroyed, it was in the intangible scale of values that we registered a loss more damaging than the material loss we had already suffered.

Thus unwillingly our free society finds itself mortally challenged by the Soviet system. No other value system is so wholly irreconcilable with ours, so implacable in its purpose to destroy ours, so capable of turning to its own uses the most dangerous and divisive trends in our own society, no other so skillfully and powerfully evokes the elements of irrationality in human nature everywhere, and no other has the support of a great and growing center of military power.

B. OBJECTIVES

The objectives of a free society are determined by its fundamental values and by the necessity for maintaining the material environment in which they flourish. Logically and in fact, therefore, the Kremlin's challenge to the United States is directed not only to our values but to our physical capacity to protect their environment. It is a challenge which encompasses both peace and war and our objectives in peace and war must take account of it.

1. Thus we must make ourselves strong, both in the way in which we affirm our values in the conduct of our national life, and in the development of our military and economic strength.

2. We must lead in building a successfully functioning political and economic system in the free world. It is only by practical affirmation, abroad as well as at home, of our essential values, that we can preserve our own integrity, in which lies the real frustration of the Kremlin design.

3. But beyond thus affirming our values our policy and actions must be such as to foster a fundamental change in the nature of the Soviet system, a change toward which the frustration of the design is the first and perhaps the most important step. Clearly it will not only be less costly but more effective if this change occurs to a maximum extent as a result of internal forces in Soviet society.

In a shrinking world, which now faces

the threat of atomic warfare, it is not an adequate objective merely to seek to check the Kremlin design, for the absence of order among nations is becoming less and less tolerable. This fact imposes on us, in our own interests, the responsibility of world leadership. It demands that we make the attempt, and accept the risks inherent in it, to bring about order and justice by means consistent with the principles of freedom and democracy. We should limit our requirement of the Soviet Union to its participation with other nations on the basis of equality and respect for the rights of others. Subject to this requirement, we must with our allies and the former subject peoples seek to create a world society based on the principle of consent. Its framework cannot be inflexible. It will consist of many national communities of great and varying abilities and resources, and hence of war potential. The seeds of conflicts will inevitably exist or will come into being. To acknowledge this is only to acknowledge the impossibility of a final solution. Not to acknowledge it can be fatally dangerous in a world in which there are no final solutions.

All these objectives of a free society are equally valid and necessary in peace and war. But every consideration of devotion to our fundamental values and to our national security demands that we seek to achieve them by the strategy of the cold war. It is only by developing the moral and material strength of the free world that the Soviet regime will become convinced of the falsity of its assumptions and that the preconditions for workable agreements can be created. By practically demonstrating the integrity and vitality of our system the free world widens the area of possible agreement and thus can hope gradually to bring about a Soviet acknowledgment of realities which in sum will eventually constitute a frustration of the Soviet design. Short of this, however, it might be possible to create a situation which will induce the Soviet Union to accommodate itself, with or without the conscious abandonment of its design, to coexistence on tolerable terms with the non-Soviet world. Such a development would be a triumph for the idea of freedom and democracy. It must be an immediate objective of United States policy.

There is no reason, in the event of war, for us to alter our overall objectives. They do not include unconditional surrender, the subjugation of the Russian peoples or a Russia shorn of its economic potential. Such a course would irrevocably unite the Russian people behind the regime which enslaves them. Rather these objectives contemplate Soviet acceptance of the specific and limited conditions requisite to an international environment in which free institutions can flourish, and in which the Russian peoples will have a new chance to work out their own destiny. If we can make the Russian people our allies in the enterprise we will obviously have made our task easier and victory more certain. . . .

VII. *Present Risks*

A. GENERAL

It is apparent from the preceding sections that the integrity and vitality of our system is in greater jeopardy than ever before in our history. Even if there were no Soviet Union we would face the great problem of the free society, accentuated many fold in this industrial age, of reconciling order, security, the need for participation, with the requirement of freedom. We would face the fact that in a shrinking world the absence of order among nations is becoming less and less tolerable. The Kremlin design seeks to impose order among nations by means which would destroy our free and democratic system. The Kremlin's possession of atomic weapons puts new power behind its design, and increases the jeopardy to our system. It adds new strains to the uneasy equilibrium-without-order which exists in the world and raises new doubts in men's minds whether the world will long tolerate this tension without moving toward some kind of order, on somebody's terms.

The risks we face are of a new order of magnitude, commensurate with the total struggle in which we are engaged. For a free society there is never total victory, since freedom and democracy are never wholly attained, are always in the process of being attained. But defeat at the hands of the totalitarian is total defeat. These risks crowd in on us, in a shrinking world of polarized power, so as to give us no choice, ultimately, between meeting them effectively or being overcome by them.

B. SPECIFIC

It is quite clear from Soviet theory and practice that the Kremlin seeks to bring the free world under its dominion by the methods of the cold war. The preferred technique is to subvert by infiltration and intimidation. Every institution of our society is an instrument which it is sought to stultify and turn against our purposes.

Those that touch most closely our material and moral strength arc obviously the prime targets[:] labor unions, civic enterprises, schools, churches, and all media for influencing opinion. The effort is not so much to make them serve obvious Soviet ends as to prevent them from serving our ends, and thus to make them sources of confusion in our economy, our culture, and our body politic. The doubts and diversities that in terms of our values are part of the merit of a free system, the weaknesses and the problems that are peculiar to it, the rights and privileges that free men enjoy, and the disorganization and destruction left in the wake of the last attack on our freedoms, all are but opportunities for the Kremlin to do its evil work. Every advantage is taken of the fact that our means of prevention and retaliation are limited by those principles and scruples which are precisely the ones that give our freedom and democracy its meaning for us. None of our scruples deter those whose only code is "morality is that which serves the revolution."

Since everything that gives us or others respect for our institutions is a suitable object for attack, it also fits the Kremlin's design that where, with impunity, we can be insulted and made to suffer indignity the opportunity shall not be missed, particularly in any context which can be used to cast dishonor on our country, our system, our motives, or our methods. Thus the means by which we sought to restore our own economic health in the '30's, and now seek to restore that of the free world, come equally under attack. The military aid by which we sought to help the free world was frantically denounced by the

Communists in the early days of the last war, and of course our present efforts to develop adequate military strength for ourselves and our allies are equally denounced.

At the same time the Soviet Union is seeking to create overwhelming military force, in order to back up infiltration with intimidation. In the only terms in which it understands strength, it is seeking to demonstrate to the free world that force and the will to use it are on the side of the Kremlin, that those who lack it are decadent and doomed. In local incidents it threatens and encroaches both for the sake of local gains and to increase anxiety and defeatism in all the free world.

The possession of atomic weapons at each of the opposite poles of power, and the inability (for different reasons) of either side to place any trust in the other, puts a premium on a surprise attack against us. It equally puts a premium on a more violent and ruthless prosecution of its design by cold war, especially if the Kremlin is sufficiently objective to realize the improbability of our prosecuting a preventive war. It also puts a premium on piecemeal aggression against others, counting on our unwillingness to engage in atomic war unless we are directly attacked. We run all these risks and the added risk of being confused and immobilized by our inability to weigh and choose, and pursue a firm course based on a rational assessment of each.

The risk that we may thereby be prevented or too long delayed in taking all needful measures to maintain the integrity and vitality of our system is great. The risk that our allies will lose their determination is greater. And the risk that in this manner a descending spiral of too little and too late, of doubt and recrimination, may present us with ever narrower and more desperate alternatives, is the greatest risk of all. For example, it is clear that our present weakness would prevent us from offering effective resistance at any of several vital pressure points. The only deterrent we can present to the Kremlin is the evidence we give that we may make any of the critical points which we cannot hold the occasion for a global war of annihilation.

The risk of having no better choice than to capitulate or precipitate a global war at any of a number of pressure points is bad enough in itself, but it is multiplied by the weakness it imparts to our position in the cold war. Instead of appearing strong and resolute we are continually at the verge of appearing and being alternately irresolute and desperate; yet it is the cold war which we must win, because both the Kremlin design, and our fundamental purpose give it the first priority. . . .

MILITARY EVALUATION OF U.S. AND USSR ATOMIC CAPABILITIES

1. The United States now has an atomic capability, including both numbers and deliverability, estimated to be adequate, if effectively utilized, to deliver a serious blow against the war-making capacity of the USSR. It is doubted whether such a blow, even if it resulted in the complete destruction of the contemplated target systems, would cause the USSR to sue for terms or prevent Soviet forces from occupying Western Europe against such

ground resistance as could presently be mobilized. A very serious initial blow could, however, so reduce the capabilities of the USSR to supply and equip its military organization and its civilian population as to give the United States the prospect of developing a general military superiority in a war of long duration.

2. As the atomic capability of the USSR increases, it will have an increased ability to hit at our atomic bases and installations and thus seriously hamper the ability of the United States to carry out an attack such as that outlined above. It is quite possible that in the near future the USSR will have a sufficient number of atomic bombs and a sufficient deliverability to raise a question whether Britain with its present inadequate air defense could be relied upon as an advance base from which a major portion of the U.S. attack could be launched.

It is estimated that, within the next four years, the USSR will attain the capability of seriously damaging vital centers of the United States, provided it strikes a surprise blow and provided further that the blow is opposed by no more effective opposition than we now have programmed. Such a blow could so seriously damage the United States as to greatly reduce its superiority in economic potential.

Effective opposition to this Soviet capability will require among other measures greatly increased air warning systems, air defenses, and vigorous development and implementation of a civilian defense program which has been thoroughly integrated with the military defense systems.

In time the atomic capability of the USSR can be expected to grow to a point where, given surprise and no more effective opposition than we now have programmed, the possibility of a decisive initial attack cannot be excluded.

3. In the initial phases of an atomic war, the advantages of initiative and surprise would be very great. A police state living behind an iron curtain has an enormous advantage in maintaining the necessary security and centralization of decision required to capitalize on this advantage.

4. For the moment our atomic retaliatory capability is probably adequate to deter the Kremlin from a deliberate direct military attack against ourselves or other free peoples. However, when it calculates that it has a sufficient atomic capability to make a surprise attack on us, nullifying our atomic superiority and creating a military situation decisively in its favor, the Kremlin might be tempted to strike swiftly and with stealth. The existence of two large atomic capabilities in such a relationship might well act, therefore, not as a deterrent, but as an incitement to war.

5. A further increase in the number and power of our atomic weapons is necessary in order to assure the effectiveness of any U.S. retaliatory blow, but would not of itself seem to change the basic logic of the above points. Greatly increased general air, ground, and sea strength, and increased air defense and civilian defense programs would also be necessary to provide reasonable assurance that the free world could survive an initial surprise atomic attack of the weight which it is

estimated the USSR will be capable of delivering by 1954 and still permit the free world to go on to the eventual attainment of its objectives. Furthermore, such a build-up of strength could safeguard and increase our retaliatory power, and thus might put off for some time the date when the Soviet Union could calculate that a surprise blow would be advantageous. This would provide additional time for the effects of our policies to produce a modification of the Soviet system.

6. If the USSR develops a thermonuclear weapon ahead of the U.S., the risks of greatly increased Soviet pressure against all the free world, or an attack against the U.S., will be greatly increased.

7. If the U.S. develops a thermonuclear weapon ahead of the USSR, the U.S. should for the time being be able to bring increased pressure on the USSR. . . .

Study Questions

1. Based upon what specific reasons did the National Security Council conclude that the differences between the United States and the Soviet Union were irreconcilable?

2. What risks, according to the NSC, made it so necessary for the United States to build its nuclear weapons capacity?

3. Would you have analyzed the geopolitical climate differently than Churchill (pp. 423–24) or the NSC? Explain.

Twenty-Second Amendment (1951)

In 1796, George Washington declined to be elected to a third term as president for three reasons. First, he had already served the United States as a long-term military and political leader and longed to retire to private life with his wife in Virginia. Second, he did not wish to set a precedent of treating the presidency as a life-long office, like the British monarchy. Third, the nation was at peace and a smooth transition in power could be effected. Every president since Washington followed his example until Franklin D. Roosevelt sought election to a third term in 1940. Moreover, Roosevelt was elected yet again in 1944. Some might argue that if the people will it, a president should be able to be reelected indefinitely. On the other hand, recent history had warned of the dangers associated with maintaining leadership in the hands of the same person for long periods of time. Adolph Hitler had strong support from the German people, but popular support did not prevent abuse of power. Americans, therefore, considered a constitutional safeguard that would prevent future presidents from continuing their tenure beyond limits that seemed appropriate to a republic.

(proposed, 1947; ratified, 1951)

Section 1. No person shall be elected to the office of the President more than twice, and no person who has held the office of President, or acted as President, for more than two years of a term to which some other person was elected President shall be elected to the office of the President more than once. But this Article shall not apply to any person holding the office of President when this Article was proposed by the Congress, and shall not prevent any person who may be holding the office of President, or acting as President, during the term within which this Article becomes operative from holding the office of President or acting as President during the remainder of such term.

Section 2. This article shall be inoperative unless it shall have been ratified as an amendment to the Constitution by the legislatures of three-fourths of the several States within seven years from the date of its submission to the States by the Congress.

Study Questions

1. Debate: Term limits betray the will of the people and therefore have no place in a democracy.

2. Repeat the same debate, only this time replace "democracy" with "republic."

The Korean Conflict, 1950–1953

The Division of Korea at the Onset of the Cold War

During World War II, Soviet and U.S. troops positioned themselves on the Korean peninsula against Japan. At the close of the war, neither the Americans nor the Soviets were willing to abandon their footholds. Under supervision of the United Nations, an election was held to establish a new government for Korea. However, two rival governments emerged, dividing the nation at the 38th parallel. Kim Il Sung, a Soviet-backed leader of Korea's communist party, became the head of the Democratic People's Republic of Korea (North Korea). Syngman Rhee, a staunch anti-communist, became president of the Republic of Korea (South Korea), supported by the United States. The United Nations recognized South Korea as the only legitimate government at that time.

Attempted Reunification

Both Syngman Rhee and Kim Il Sung desired to reunify Korea, each wanting his own government to encompass the entire peninsula. Sporadic fighting occurred along the 38th parallel, emerging into a civil war. On June 25, 1950, the North Korean army launched a surprise attack, transgressing the 38th parallel. Kim Il Sung and Joseph Stalin both expected the United States would avoid getting entangled in this attempted reunification of Korea.

Responses by the United States and the United Nations

President Truman immediately called for U.N. "police action" against North Korea. Truman's motivations were unmistakable: he feared that "if we let Asia go [into the hands of the communists], the Near East would collapse and no telling what would happen in Europe."

For the United Nations to act, the Security Council would have to pass a resolution. This required that a majority of all member nations on that council agreed, but a negative vote by any of the five permanent-member nations would effectively veto the resolution. The Soviet Union, though a permanent-member nation, did not exercise that veto. Instead, the Soviets boycotted the meeting, protesting that the United Nations had failed to recognize the legitimacy of the People's Republic of China, a communist regime that had assumed power in 1949 under Mao Zedong.

With no Soviet voice at the table, the United Nations authorized a peace-keeping mission, designating the United States to take the lead in coordinating the use of military force. About twenty nations participated, but the U.S. military comprised nearly 90% of the troops committed on behalf of South Korea. The United Nations authorized Truman to select a commander, and he chose Gen. Douglas MacArthur who had victoriously led American troops in the Pacific Theater against Japan in World War II.

Military Engagements

Initially, North Korea had a tremendous advantage. Their opening surprise attack brought the majority of South Korea's territory under northern occupation. MacArthur's forces launched a surprise counter-offensive by amphibious landing at Inchon, far beyond the land front. Within two weeks, the U.N. coalition recaptured South Korea's capital city of Seoul as well as most of the territory south of the 38th parallel.

Truman initially had set no other goal than to reestablish the postwar *status quo* of two Koreas divided at the 38th parallel. Encouraged by MacArthur's early success, Truman secured U.N. approval for a second objective: the creation of a unified and independent Korea under a democratic government.

China warned that it would not tolerate South Korea's northward expansion, but the U.N. coalition elected to call the bluff. By October 1950, the coalition forces had reached the Chinese border at the Yalu River; nearly the entire Korean peninsula was under southern occupation.

In late November, China made good on its threat, counter-attacking with such success that communist troops recaptured Seoul by January 1951. Then the coalition forces responded again, pushing the communists back to the 38th parallel by March.

Sensing a perpetual stalemate, Gen. MacArthur's ambitions began to look beyond Korea. He desired to cross the Yalu River, neutralize the communists in China, and restore the Chinese nationalist government—now exiled in Taiwan—that had preceded Mao Zedong's revolution. Truman, however, did not wish to antagonize Red China or the Soviets any further. In April 1951, he relieved MacArthur from duty for insubordination.

Armistice

The Korean Conflict dragged on for another two years. Technically speaking, it was not a war, since Congress never declared it a war. Rather, the president committed U.S. troops in fulfillment of U.S. treaty obligations through the United Nations. After two years of stalemate, an armistice confirmed the border between North and South Korea essentially where it had been before, but now with a demilitarized zone patrolled jointly by North Korean, South Korean, U.S., and U.N. forces. With no peace treaty ever being signed, the future of the two Koreas would remain uncertain even into the twenty-first century.

Study Questions

1. Explain what was at stake in the Korean conflict for the Korean people, China, the Soviet Union, and the United States.

2. Why did Gen. MacArthur desire to expand the war north of the Yalu River, and why did President Truman disallow this strategy?

3. How consistent was U.S. intervention in the Korea with the policy of NSC-68?

Harry S. Truman, "The Recall of Gen. Douglas MacArthur" (1951)

In mid 1950, over three-fourths of the American people supported Truman's commitment of U.S. troops to Korea. By January 1951, however, two-thirds of Americans desired that the troops be withdrawn. Gen. Omar N. Bradley, Chairman of the Joint Chiefs of Staff, warned President Truman that an extended Korean conflict could erupt into outright war with China, which he considered "the wrong war, at the wrong place, at the wrong time, with the wrong enemy." Gen. Douglas MacArthur, commander of the U.S.-led coalition in the Pacific, disagreed. MacArthur not only desired to liberate all of Korea, but also to support Taiwanese nationalists in reclaiming their Chinese homeland from the Maoists who had taken over in 1949. MacArthur even suggested the use of atomic force, stating, "There is no substitute for victory." Truman did not want the situation in Asia to escalate. With the consent of the Joint Chiefs, Truman fired MacArthur in April 1951.

My fellow Americans:

I want to talk to you plainly tonight about what we are doing in Korea and about our policy in the Far East.

In the simplest terms, what we are doing in Korea is this: We are trying to prevent a third world war.

I think most people in this country recognized that fact last June. And they warmly supported the decision of the Government to help the Republic of Korea against the Communist aggressors. Now, many persons, even some who applauded our decision to defend Korea, have forgotten the basic reason for our action.

It is right for us to be in Korea now. It was right last June. It is right today.

I want to remind you why this is true.

The Communists in the Kremlin are engaged in a monstrous conspiracy to stamp out freedom all over the world. If they were to succeed, the United States would be numbered among their principal victims. It must be clear to everyone that the United States cannot—and will not—sit idly by and await foreign conquest. The only question is: What is the best time to meet the threat and how is the best way to meet it?

The best time to meet the threat is in the beginning. It is easier to put out a fire in the beginning when it is small than after it has become a roaring blaze.

And the best way to meet the threat of aggression is for the peace-loving nations to act together. If they don't act together, they are likely to be picked off, one by one.

If they had followed the right policies in the 1930's—if the free countries had acted together to crush the aggression of the dictators, and if they had acted in the beginning when the aggression was small —there probably would have been no World War II.

If history has taught us anything, it is that aggression anywhere in the world is a threat to the peace everywhere in the world. When that aggression is supported by the cruel and selfish rulers of a powerful nation who are bent on conquest, it becomes a dear and present danger to the security and independence of every free nation.

This is a lesson that most people in this country have learned thoroughly. This is the basic reason why we joined in creating the United Nations. And, since the end of World War II, we have been putting that lesson into practice—we have been working with other free nations to check the aggressive designs of the Soviet Union before they can result in a third world war.

That is what we did in Greece, when that nation was threatened by the aggression of international communism.

The attack against Greece could have led to general war. But this country came to the aid of Greece. The United Nations supported Greek resistance. With our help, the determination and efforts of the Greek people defeated the attack on the spot.

Another big Communist threat to peace was the Berlin blockade. That too could have led to war. But again it was settled because free men would not back down in an emergency.

The aggression against Korea is the boldest and most dangerous move the Communists have yet made.

The attack on Korea was part of a greater plan for conquering all of Asia.

I would like to read to you from a secret intelligence report which came to us after the attack on Korea. It is a report of a speech a Communist army officer in North Korea gave to a group of spies and saboteurs last May, one month before South Korea was invaded. The report shows in great detail how this invasion was part of a carefully prepared plot. Here, in part, is what the Communist officer, who had been trained in Moscow, told his men: "Our forces," he said, "are scheduled to attack South Korean forces about the middle of June. ... The coming attack on South Korea marks the first step toward the liberation of Asia."

Notice that he used the word "liberation." This is Communist double-talk meaning "conquest."

I have another secret intelligence report here. This one tells what another Communist officer in the Far East told his men several months before the invasion of Korea. Here is what he said: "In order to successfully undertake the long-awaited world revolution, we must first unify Asia ... Java, Indochina, Malaya, India, Tibet, Thailand, Philippines, and Japan are our ultimate targets. ... The United States is the only obstacle on our road for the liberation of all the countries in southeast Asia. In other words, we must unify the people of Asia and crush the United States." Again, "liberation" in "commie" language means conquest.

That is what the Communist leaders are telling their people, and that is what they have been trying to do.

They want to control all Asia from the Kremlin.

This plan of conquest is in flat contradiction to what we believe. We believe that Korea belongs to the Koreans, we believe that India belongs to the Indians, we believe that all the nations of Asia should be free to work out their affairs in their own way. This is the basis of peace in the

Far East, and it is the basis of peace everywhere else.

The whole Communist imperialism is back of the attack on peace in the Far East. It was the Soviet Union that trained and equipped the North Koreans for aggression. The Chinese Communists massed 44 well-trained and well-equipped divisions on the Korean frontier. These were the troops they threw into battle when the North Korean Communists were beaten.

The question we have had to face is whether the Communist plan of conquest can be stopped without a general war. Our Government and other countries associated with us in the United Nations believe that the best chance of stopping it without a general war is to meet the attack in Korea and defeat it there.

That is what we have been doing. It is a difficult and bitter task.

But so far it has been successful.

So far, we have prevented world war III.

So far, by fighting a limited war in Korea, we have prevented aggression from succeeding, and bringing on a general war. And the ability of the whole free world to resist Communist aggression has been greatly improved.

We have taught the enemy a lesson. He has found that aggression is not cheap or easy. Moreover, men all over the world who want to remain free have been given new courage and new hope. They know now that the champions of freedom can stand up and fight, and that they will stand up and fight.

Our resolute stand in Korea is helping the forces of freedom now fighting in Indochina and other countries in that part of the world. It has already slowed down the timetable of conquest.

In Korea itself there are signs that the enemy is building up his ground forces for a new mass offensive. We also know that there have been large increases in the enemy's available air forces.

If a new attack comes, I feel confident it will be turned back. The United Nations fighting forces are tough and able and well equipped. They are fighting for a just cause. They are proving to all the world that the principle of collective security will work. We are proud of all these forces for the magnificent job they have done against heavy odds. We pray that their efforts may succeed, for upon their success may hinge the peace of the world.

The Communist side must now choose its course of action. The Communist rulers may press the attack against us. They may take further action which will spread the conflict. They have that choice, and with it the awful responsibility for what may follow. The Communists also have the choice of a peaceful settlement which could lead to a general relaxation of the tensions in the Far East. The decision is theirs, because the forces of the United Nations will strive to limit the conflict if possible.

We do not want to see the conflict in Korea extended. We are trying to prevent a world war—not to start one. And the best way to do that is to make it plain that we and the other free countries will continue to resist the attack.

But you may ask, why can't we take other steps to punish the aggressor? Why don't we bomb Manchuria and China itself? Why don't we assist the Chinese Nationalist troops to land on the mainland of China?

If we were to do these things we would be running a very grave risk of starting a general war. If that were to happen, we would have brought about the exact situation we are trying to prevent.

If we were to do these things, we would become entangled in a vast conflict on the continent of Asia and our task would become immeasurably more difficult all over the world.

What would suit the ambitions of the Kremlin better than for our military forces to be committed to a full-scale war with Red China?

It may well be that, in spite of our best efforts, the Communists may spread the war. But it would be wrong—tragically wrong—for us to take the initiative in extending the war.

The dangers are great. Make no mistake about it. Behind the North Koreans and Chinese Communists in the front lines stand additional millions of Chinese soldiers. And behind the Chinese stand the tanks, the planes, the submarines, the soldiers, and the scheming rulers of the Soviet Union.

Our aim is to avoid the spread of the conflict.

The course we have been following is the one best calculated to avoid an all-out war. It is the course consistent with our obligation to do all we can to maintain international peace and security. Our experience in Greece and Berlin shows that it is the most effective course of action we can follow.

First of all, it is clear that our efforts in Korea can blunt the will of the Chinese Communists to continue the struggle. The United Nations forces have put up a tremendous fight in Korea and have inflicted very heavy casualties on the enemy. Our forces are stronger now than they have been before. These are plain facts which may discourage the Chinese Communists from continuing their attack.

Second, the free world as a whole is growing in military strength every day. In the United States, in Western Europe, and throughout the world, free men are alert to the Soviet threat and are building their defenses. This may discourage the Communist rulers from continuing the war in Korea—and from undertaking new acts of aggression elsewhere.

If the Communist authorities realize that they cannot defeat us in Korea, if they realize it would be foolhardy to widen the hostilities beyond Korea, then they may recognize the folly of continuing their aggression. A peaceful settlement may then be possible. The door is always open.

Then we may achieve a settlement in Korea which will not compromise the principles and purposes of the United Nations.

I have thought long and hard about this question of extending the war in Asia. I have discussed it many times with the ablest military advisers in the country. I believe with all my heart that the course we are following is the best course.

I believe that we must try to limit the war to Korea for these vital reasons: to make sure that the precious lives of our fighting men are not wasted; to see that the security of our country and the free world is not needlessly jeopardized; and to prevent a third world war.

A number of events have made it evident that General MacArthur did not agree with that policy. I have therefore considered it essential to relieve General MacArthur so that there would be no doubt or confusion as to the real purpose and aim of our policy.

It was with the deepest personal regret that I found myself compelled to take this action. General MacArthur is one of our greatest military commanders. But the cause of world peace is much more important than any individual.

The change in commands in the Far East means no change whatever in the policy of the United States. We will carry on the fight in Korea with vigor and determination in an effort to bring the war to a speedy and successful conclusion. The new commander, Lt. Gen. Matthew Ridgway, has already demonstrated that he has the great qualities of military leadership needed for this task.

We are ready, at any time, to negotiate for a restoration of peace in the area. But we will not engage in appeasement. We are only interested in real peace.

Real peace can be achieved through a settlement based on the following factors:

One: The fighting must stop.

Two: Concrete steps must be taken to insure that the fighting will not break out again.

Three: There must be an end to the aggression.

A settlement founded upon these elements would open the way for the unification of Korea and the withdrawal of all foreign forces.

In the meantime, I want to be clear about our military objective. We are fighting to resist an outrageous aggression in Korea. We are trying to keep the Korean conflict from spreading to other areas. But at the same time we must conduct our military activities so as to insure the security of our forces. This is essential if they are to continue the fight until the enemy abandons its ruthless attempt to destroy the Republic of Korea.

That is our military objective—to repel attack and to restore peace.

In the hard fighting in Korea, we are proving that collective action among nations is not only a high principle but a workable means of resisting aggression. Defeat of aggression in Korea may be the turning point in the world's search for a practical way of achieving peace and security.

The struggle of the United Nations in Korea is a struggle for peace.

Free nations have united their strength in an effort to prevent a third world war.

That war can come if the Communist rulers want it to come. But this Nation and its allies will not be responsible for its coming.

We do not want to widen the conflict. We will use every effort to prevent that disaster. And in so doing, we know that we are following the great principles of peace, | freedom, and justice.

Study Question

1. For what reasons did Truman insist upon limiting the Asian war, begun in 1950, to the Korean peninsula?

2. What strategy did Truman offer for achieving a peaceful settlement in Korea?

3. Why did Truman relieve Gen. Douglas MacArthur of his duty?

Douglas MacArthur, "American Policy in the Pacific" (1951)

Not every American supported President Truman's decision to fire Gen. Douglas MacArthur. Within weeks of being relieved of his duties in the Pacific, MacArthur spoke to Congress and via television broadcast he won the hearts of the American people. His 37-minute address concluded poignantly with the aphorism, "old soldiers never die; they just fade away." The larger significance of the Truman-MacArthur episode does not concern which of these two men was in the right in this instance, but which of their respective offices had the authority to determine the foreign policy of the United States. Where have We the People placed the constitutional power to command the military—in the hands of generals or in the delicate balance between the President, as commander-in-chief, and the Congress, as the war-declaring body?

Mr. President, Mr. Speaker and Distinguished Members of the Congress:

I stand on this rostrum with a sense of deep humility and pride—humility in the weight of those great architects of our history who have stood here before me, pride in the reflection that this home of legislative debate represents human liberty in the purest form yet devised.

Here are centered the hopes and aspirations and faith of the entire human race.

I do not stand here as advocate for any partisan cause, for the issues are fundamental and reach quite beyond the realm of partisan considerations. They must be resolved on the highest plane of national interest if our course is to prove sound and our future protected.

I trust, therefore, that you will do me the justice of receiving that which I have to say as solely expressing the considered viewpoint of a fellow American.

I address you with neither rancor nor bitterness in the fading twilight of life, with but one purpose in mind: to serve my country.

The issues are global, and so interlocked that to consider the problems of one sector oblivious to those of another is to court disaster for the whole. While Asia is commonly referred to as the Gateway to Europe, it is no less true that Europe is the Gateway to Asia, and the broad influence of the one cannot fail to have its impact upon the other. There are those who claim our strength is inadequate to protect on both fronts, that we cannot divide our effort. I can think of no greater expression of defeatism.

If a potential enemy can divide his strength on two fronts, it is for us to counter his effort. The Communist threat is a global one.

Its successful advance in one sector threatens the destruction of every other sector. You can not appease or otherwise surrender to communism in Asia without simultaneously undermining our efforts to halt its advance in Europe.

Beyond pointing out these general truisms, I shall confine my discussion to the general areas of Asia. Before one may objectively assess the situation now existing there, he must comprehend something of Asia's past and the revolutionary changes which have marked her course up to, the present. Long exploited by the so-called colonial powers, with little opportunity to achieve any degree of social justice, individual dignity or a higher standard life such as guided our own noble administration in the Philippines, the people of Asia found their opportunity in the war just past to throw off the shackles of colonialism and now see the dawn of new opportunity and heretofore unfelt dignity, and the self-respect of political freedom.

Mustering half of the earth's population, and 60 percent of its natural resources these peoples are rapidly consolidating a new force, both moral and material, with which to raise the living standard and erect adaptations of the design of modern progress to their own distinct cultural environments.

Whether one adheres to the concept of colonialization or not, this is the direction of Asian progress and it may not be stopped. It is a corollary to the shift of the world economic frontiers as the whole epicenter of world affairs rotates back toward the area whence it started.

In this situation, it becomes vital that our own country orient its policies in consonance with this basic evolutionary condition rather than pursue a course blind to reality that the colonial era is now past and the Asian peoples covet the right to shape their own free destiny. What they seek now is friendly guidance, understanding and support, not imperious direction, the dignity of equality and not the shame of subjugation.

Their pre-war standard of life, pitifully low, is infinitely lower now in the devastation left in war's wake. World ideologies play little part in Asian thinking and are little understood.

What the peoples strive for is the opportunity for a little more food in their stomachs, a little better clothing on their backs and a little firmer roof over their heads, and the realization of the normal nationalist urge for political freedom.

These political-social conditions have but an indirect bearing upon our own national security, but do form a backdrop to contemporary planning which must be thoughtfully considered if we are to avoid the pitfalls of unrealism.

Of more direct and immediately bearing upon our national security are the changes wrought in the strategic potential of the Pacific Ocean in the course of the past war.

Prior thereto the western strategic frontier of the United States lay on the literal line of the Americas, with an exposed island salient extending out through Hawaii, Midway and Guam to the Philippines. That salient proved not an outpost of strength but an avenue of weakness along which the enemy could and did attack. The Pacific was a potential area of advance for any predatory force intent upon striking at the bordering land areas.

All this was changed by our Pacific victory[:] our strategic frontier then shifted to embrace the entire Pacific Ocean, which became a vast moat to protect us as long as we hold it. Indeed, it acts as a protective shield for all of the Americas and all free lands of the Pacific Ocean area. We control it to the shores of Asia by a chain of islands extending in an arc from the Aleutians to the Mariannas held by us and our free allies.

From this island chain we can dominate with sea and air power every Asiatic port from Vladivostok to Singapore—with sea and air power every port, as I said, from Vladivostok to Singapore—and prevent any hostile movement into the Pacific.

Any predatory attack from Asia must be an amphibious effort. No amphibious force can be successful without control of the sea lanes and the air over those lanes in its avenue of advance. With naval and air supremacy and modest ground elements to defend bases, any major attack from continental Asia toward us or our friends in the Pacific would be doomed to failure.

Under such conditions, the Pacific no longer represents menacing avenues of approach for a prospective invader. It assumes, instead, the friendly aspect of a peaceful lake.

Our line of defense is a natural one and can be maintained with a minimum of military effort and expenses. It envisions no attack against anyone, nor does it provide the bastions essential for offensive operations, but properly maintained, would be an invincible defense against aggression.

The holding of this defense line in the western Pacific is entirely dependent upon holding all segments thereof, for any major breach of that line by an unfriendly power would render vulnerable to determined attack every other major segment. This is a military estimate as to which I have yet to find a military leader who will take exception.

For that reason, I have strongly recommended in the past, as a matter of military urgency, that under no circumstances must Formosa fall under Communist control. Such an eventuality would at once threaten the freedom of the Philippines and the loss of Japan and might well force our western frontier back to the coast of California, Oregon, and Washington.

To understand the changes which now appear upon the Chinese mainland, one must understand the changes in Chinese character and culture over the past 50 years. China up to 50 years ago was completely non-homogenous, being compartmented into groups divided against each other. The war-making tendency was almost non-existent as they still followed the tenets of the Confucian ideal of pacifist culture.

At the turn of the century under the regime of Chang Tso Lin efforts toward greater homogenity produced the start of a nationalist urge. This was further and more successfully developed under the leadership of Chiang Kai-Shek, but has been brought to its greatest fruition under the present regime to the point that it has now taken on the character of a united nationalism of increasingly dominant aggressive tendencies.

Through these past 50 years the Chinese people have thus become militarize in their concepts and in their ideals. They now constitute excellent soldiers, with competent staffs, and commanders. This has produced a new and dominant power in Asia, which, for its own purposes, is allied with Soviet Russia but which in its own concepts and methods has become aggressively imperialistic, with a lust for expansions and increased power normal to this type of imperialism.

There is little of the ideological concept either one way or another in the Chinese make-up. The standard of living is so low and the capital accumulation has been so thoroughly dissipated by war that the masses are desperate and eager to follow any leadership which seems to promise the alleviation of woeful stringencies.

I have from the beginning believed that the Chinese Communists' support of the North Koreans was the dominant one. Their interests are at present parallel with those of the Soviet, but I believe that the aggressiveness recently displayed not only in Korea but also in Indo-China and Tibet and pointing potentially toward the South reflects predominantly the same lust for the expansion of power which has animated every would-be conqueror since the beginning of time.

The Japanese people since the war have undergone the greatest reformation recorded in modern history. With a commendable will, eagerness to learn, and marked capacity to understand, they have from the ashes left in war's wake erected in Japan an edifice dedicated to the supremacy of individual liberty and personal dignity and in the ensuing process there has been created a truly representative government committed to the advance of political morality, freedom of economic enterprise, and social justice.

Politically, economically, and socially Japan is now abreast of many free nations of the earth and will not again fail the universal trust. That it may be counted upon to wield a profoundly beneficial influence over the course of events in Asia is attested by the magnificent manner in which the Japanese people have met the recent challenge of war, unrest and confusion surrounding them from the outside and checked communism within their own frontiers without the slightest slackening in their forward progress.

I sent all four of our occupation divisions to the Korean battlefront, without the slightest qualms as to the effect of the resulting power vacuum upon Japan. The results fully justified my faith.

I know of no nation more serene, orderly and industrious, nor in which higher hopes can be entertained for future constructive service in the advance of the human race.

Of our former ward, the Philippines, we can look forward in confidence that the existing unrest will be corrected and a strong and healthy nation will grow in the longer aftermath of war's terrible destructiveness. We must be patient and understanding and never fail them. As in our hour of need, they did not fail us.

A Christian nation, the Philippines stand as a mighty bulwark of Christianity in the Far East, and its capacity for high moral leadership in Asia is unlimited.

On Formosa the government of the Republic of China has had the opportunity to refute by action much of the malicious gossip which so undermined the strength of its leadership on the Chinese mainland. The Formosan people are receiving a just and enlightened administration with majority representation in the organs of government, and politically, economically and socially they appear to be advancing along sound and constructive lines.

With this brief insight into the surrounding area, I now turn to the Korean conflict.

While I was not consulted prior to the President's decision to intervene in support of the Republic of Korea, that decision from a military standpoint, proved a sound one. As I said, it proved to be a sound one, as we hurled back the invader and decimated his forces. Our victory was complete, and our objectives within reach, when Red China intervened with numerically superior ground forces.

This created a new war and an entirely new situation, a situation not contemplated when our forces were committed against the North Korean invaders; a situation which called for new decisions in the diplomatic sphere to permit the realistic adjustment of military strategy. Such decisions have not been forthcoming.

While no man in his right mind would advocate sending our ground forces into continental China, and such was never given a thought, the new situation did urgently demand a drastic revision of strategic planning if our political aim was to defeat this new enemy as we had defeated the old one.

Apart from the military need, as I saw it, to neutralize sanctuary protection given the enemy north of the Yalu, I felt that military necessity in the conduct of the war made necessary the intesification of our economic blockade against China, the imposition of a naval blockade against the China coast, removal of restrictions on air reconnaissance of China's coastal area and of Manchuria, removal of restrictions on the forces of the Republic of China on Formosa, with logistical support to contribution to their effective operations against the Chinese mainland.

For entertaining these views, all professionally designed to support our forces in Korea and to bring hostilities to an end with the least possible delay and at a saving of countless American and allied lives, I have been severely criticized in lay circles, principally abroad, despite my understanding that from a military standpoint the above views have been fully shared in the past by practically every military leader concerned with the Korean campaign, including our own Joint Chiefs of Staff.

I called for reinforcements, but was informed that reinforcements were not available. I made clear that if not permitted to destroy the enemy built-up bases north of the Yalu, if not permitted to utilize the friendly Chinese Force of some 600,000 men on Formosa, if not permitted to blockade the China coast to prevent the Chinese Reds from getting succor from without, and if there was to be no hope of major reinforcements, the position of the command from the military standpoint forbade victory.

We could hold in Korea by constant maneuver and in an approximate area where our supply line advantages were in balance with the supply line disadvantages of the enemy, but we could hope at best for only an indecisive campaign with its terrible and constant attrition upon our forces if the enemy utilized its full military potential.

I have constantly called for the new political decisions essential to a solution.

Efforts have been made to distort my position. It has been said in effect that I was a warmonger. Nothing could be further from the truth.

I know war as few other men now living know it, and nothing to me—and nothing to me is more revolting. I have long advocated its complete abolition, as its very destructiveness on both friend and foe has rendered it useless as a means of settling international disputes.

Indeed, the Second Day of September, 1945, just following the surrender of the Japanese nation on the Battleship Missouri, I formally cautioned as follows:

Men since the beginning of time have sought peace. Various methods through the ages have been attempted to devise an international process to prevent or settle disputes between nations. From the very start workable methods were found in so far as individual citizens were concerned, but the mechanics of an instrumentality of larger international scope have never been successful. Military alliances, balances of power, Leagues of Nations, all in turn failed, leaving the only path to be by way of the crucible of war. The utter destructiveness of war now blocks out, this alternative. We have had our last chance. If we will not devise some greater and more equitable system, Armageddon will be at our door. The problem basically is theological and involves a spiritual recrudescence and improvement of human character that will synchronize with our almost matchless advances in science, art, literature and all the material and cultural developments of the past 2000 years. It must be of the spirit if we are to save the flesh.

But once war is forced upon us, there is no other alternative than to apply every available means to bring it to a swift end. War's very object is victory, not prolonged indecision.

In war there can be no substitute for victory.

There are some who for varying reasons would appease Red China. They are blind to history's clear lesson, for history teaches with unmistakable emphasis that appeasement but begets new and bloodier wars. It points to no single instance where this end has justified that means, where appeasement has led to more than a sham peace. Like blackmail, it lays the basis for new and successively greater demands until, as in blackmail, violence becomes the only other alternative. Why, my soldiers asked me, surrender military advantages to an enemy in the field? I could not answer.

Some, may say to avoid spread of the conflict into an all-out war with China, Others, to avoid Soviet intervention. Neither explanation seems valid, for China is already engaging with the maximum power it can commit, and the Soviet will not necessarily mesh its actions with our moves. Like a cobra, any new enemy, will more likely strike whenever it feels that the relativity of military and other potentialities is in its favor on a world-wide basis.

The tragedy of Korea is further heightened by the fact that its military action was confined to its territorial limits. It condemns that nation, which it is our purpose to save, to suffer the devastating impact of full naval and air bombardment while the enemy's sanctuaries are fully protected from such attack and devastation.

Of the nations of the world, Korea alone, up to now, is the sole one which has risked its all against communism. The magnificence of the courage and fortitude of the Korean people defies description. They have chosen to risk death rather than slavery. Their last words to me were: "Don't scuttle the Pacific."

I have just left your fighting sons in Korea. They have done their best there, and I can report to you without reservation that they are splendid in every way.

It was my constant effort to preserve them and end this savage conflict honorably and with the least loss of time and a minimum sacrifice of life. Its growing bloodshed has caused me the deepest anguish and anxiety. Those gallant men will remain often in my thoughts and in my prayers always.

I am closing my 52 years of military service. When I joined the Army, even before the turn of the century, it was the fullfillment of all of my boyish hopes and dreams. The world has turned over many times since I took the oath at West Point, and the hopes and dreams have all since vanished, but I still remember the refrain of one of the most popular barracks ballads of that day which proclaimed most proudly that old soldiers never die; they just fade away. And like the old soldier of that ballad, I now close my military career and just fade away, an old soldier who tried to do his duty as God gave him the light to see that duty.

Good-bye.

Study Question

1. What four courses of action did MacArthur think necessary?

2. What "tragedy of Korea" did he fear would ensue if his recommendations were not followed?

PART 4:

The Cold War and Civil Rights

1953–1981

A Cold War Abroad, Civil Rights Protests at Home

With the Korean Conflict (1950–1953) concluded in a stalemate, it appeared that the Cold War would continue indefinitely. Indeed, just as tensions settled down to a simmer in Korea, the Cold War turned hot in Vietnam. The Vietnam War (1955–1975) was worse than a stalemate; it was a slow and painful defeat for the United States. Meanwhile, other challenges surfaced on the home front. Encouraged by the 1954 Supreme Court ruling in *Brown v. Board of Education*, African Americans rallied for civil rights. During the 1960s, the civil rights movement achieved great success—mobilizing the black community, winning over the hearts of northern whites, commandeering the national leadership of the Democratic Party, and accomplishing legislative victories in Congress. When President Lyndon B. Johnson signed the Civil Rights of Act of 1964, it became federal policy that blacks and whites would have equal access to education, employment, and public accommodations nationwide. The simultaneity of the Cold War and the civil rights movement brought two questions to the forefront of American identity: Are you a communist? Where do you stand on the "negro question"?

Interestingly, there was no clear correlation between civil rights and the Cold War. On the one hand, opposition to communism abroad suggested a commitment to liberty and democracy at home, thus reinforcing the civil rights movement. On the other hand, some civil rights leaders rejected the American creed and embraced communism instead, since the latter philosophy emphasized socioeconomic equality.

Additional nuances in American policy had to do with how strictly one should pursue the containment of communism. In 1948, a former Soviet spy named Whittaker Chambers accused U.S. State Department official Alger Hiss of espionage. Hiss was convicted of perjury charges two years later. In 1951, Julius and Ethel Rosenberg were convicted of selling secrets to the Soviets from the U.S. nuclear laboratory at Los Alamos. The Rosebergs got the electric chair. The "Red Scare" reached its zenith in the early 1950s when Senator Joseph McCarthy led investigations of State Department workers whom he claimed were communists. Despite making hundreds of accusations, McCarthy never produced sufficient evidence for even a single conviction. When he broadened his attack to the U.S. Army, claiming the military had been infiltrated by Soviet agents, public opinion shifted. "Have you no decency, sir?" asked one respected witness. The Senate censured McCarthy into silence in 1954.

In a similar manner, the civil rights movement also reached a peak and then fell into disarray. In 1965, Johnson signed the Voting Rights Act, which authorized the federal government to enforce the Fifteenth Amendment so that southern blacks would not be deprived of the opportunity to vote. In the years that followed, in-fighting among civil rights leaders, racial violence in the streets, and a judicial challenge to affirmative action—which whites branded as reverse discrimination—indicated that the movement had declined.

Chronological Overview: The Cold War and Civil Rights

1954   In *Brown v. Board of Education*, the Supreme Court declares racial segregation in public schools to be unconstitutional, reversing the "separate but equal" doctrine of the *Plessy* (1896) court.

1955   At the Geneva Conference, American and Soviet leaders appear to be making progress in diplomacy.

1955–1956   After Rosa Parks refuses to yield her seat to a white man, Martin Luther King, Jr., inspires the year-long Montgomery Bus Boycott in protest to racial segregation.

1956   Soviet tanks roll into Hungary to crush a democratic revolution and secure the nation as part of the Soviet bloc in eastern Europe.

1957   The Soviet Union takes the lead in the "space race" by placing Sputnik, the first artificial satellite, into orbit around the earth.

When Arkansas Governor Orval Faubus tries to prevent black students from enrolling at Central High in Little Rock, President Dwight D. Eisenhower sends in the 101st Airborne Division to escort the students safely onto campus.

1960   The Soviet Union discovers an American U-2 spy plane over its airspace and shoots the plane down.

Voters narrowly select John F. Kennedy over Richard Nixon as president.

1961   Kennedy fumbles his first foreign policy challenge, as he withdraws U.S. support from Cuban nationals in the Bay of Pigs who seek to overthrow communist leader Fidel Castro.

1962   America and the Soviet Union narrowly avert nuclear war when the Americans discover a Soviet plan to install nuclear missiles in Cuba.

1963   President Kennedy is assassinated, but not before establishing a legacy for civil rights reform that his successor, Lyndon B. Johnson, later fulfills.

1964   The Civil Rights Act expands federal power into southern states to end segregation.

Johnson launches the Great Society, a program of progressive reform that declares war against poverty by promising federal aid.

Congress passes the Gulf of Tonkin Resolution, authorizing President Johnson to take any action necessary against North Vietnamese attacks upon U.S. personnel and their South Vietnamese allies.

1965   Johnson begins sending ground troops to serve in Vietnam.

The Voting Rights Act expands federal power into southern states to ensure that African Americans will not be denied their Fifteenth Amendment right to vote.

1966–1968   U.S. involvement in Vietnam's civil war escalates, and U.S. pacifists take to the streets in protest.

1968   The U.S. military suffers humiliation in Vietnam, as North Vietnam's Tet Offensive sends raiding parties deep into South Vietnam. Johnson, recognizing the war can never be won, announces he will not seek reelection.

1969   In his first year as president, Richard Nixon implements a plan for gradually withdrawing American troops from Vietnam while continuing to support South Vietnam economically and diplomatically against North Vietnam.

1970   Ohio National Guardsmen at Kent State University open fire on students who are protesting a bombing campaign that Nixon has authorized in Cambodia.

1973   The Supreme Court, in *Roe v. Wade*, rules that the Fourteenth Amendment guarantees women a "right to privacy" and that this right includes a right to abortion.

The Paris Accords formally conclude U.S. military involvement in Vietnam. President Richard Nixon withdrawals all American troops while North and South Vietnam maintain a cease fire agreement.

1974   Nixon resigns from the presidency after the House threatens to pass charges of impeachment regarding his alleged involvement in the Watergate campaign conspiracy.

Violating the Paris Accords, North Vietnam renews its invasion of South Vietnam.

1975   President Gerald Ford tries to re-establish confidence in American government, but the economy stalls under heavy inflation.

1976   Americans elect Jimmy Carter, who campaigns as a "Washington outsider" and promises to restore integrity to the White House.

1978   The Supreme Court, in *Bakke v. Regents of the University of California*, prohibits affirmative action programs that involve strict quotas.

1979   With unemployment and inflation both on the rise, and the specters of Vietnam and Watergate still haunting the American psyche, President Carter strives to give the nation hope but finds his own popularity plummeting.

1980   A coalition of economically and religiously frustrated conservatives elect Ronald Reagan to the presidency. After taking office in 1981, Reagan boosts national defense but cuts social programs and lowers taxes in hopes of rejuvenating the economy through "trickle-down" economics.

Presidents of from the Korean War to the Iran Hostage Crisis, 1953–1981

Dwight D. Eisenhower (Republican—Pennsylvania), 1953–1961

"I like Ike!" read the campaign buttons supporting the Republican presidential candidate of 1952. Gen. Dwight D. Eisenhower had been courted by both the Democrats and the Republicans in 1948, with Truman even offering to step aside if Eisenhower would accept the Democratic Party's nomination for the presidency. Saying no to both parties, Eisenhower instead settled upon the presidency of Columbia University in New York. In 1950, he took a leave of absence from that post to serve as the Supreme Commander of NATO troops in Europe. Meanwhile, wealthy New York Republicans drew him back toward politics, easily securing the Republican nomination for him.

The Democrats nominated Adlai E. Stevenson, a New Deal liberal. Eisenhower's campaign discredited Stevenson as a Washington "egghead" who lacked the ability to handle Cold War diplomacy. Eisenhower for his part offered to personally go to Korea to finish off the war, a promise he kept in December 1952, just after winning the election with a handsome 56% popular-vote majority that carried the electoral votes in all but nine states.

As a military hero from World War II, Eisenhower knew enough about Pentagon tactics to keep the military on a short leash, and a tight budget. Just months into his presidency, "Truman's War"—the Korean Conflict—gave way to "Ike's peace" as the Cold War turned onto a less belligerent tack. American GIs settled into suburbs and the "Happy Days" era commenced. On the homefront, Eisenhower did not expand the New Deal, as Truman had sought to do, but nor did he contract it; he held the course as a moderate Republican—the sort of Republican whom the Democrats had plausibly thought could lead their own party. Historians correspondingly refer to the Eisenhower years as a time of national "consensus."

In other ways, however, the 1950s represent a time of great division. Certainly that became apparent in the politics of race. It was under Eisenhower's watch that the modern civil rights movement was born, and it was Eisenhower who deployed the 101st Airborne Division in 1957 to protect black students who were integrating Central High School in Little Rock, Arkansas. Still, compared to the turbulence that would come in the 1960s, the Eisenhower years offered a calm recuperation following World War II and Korea.

Ike's wife, Mary "Mamie" Eisenhower, played hostess to an unprecedented number of foreign dignitaries. Her charm also had assisted in her husband's election, as "Mamie for First Lady" buttons complemented the "I Like Ike" campaign. It was Mamie who encouraged her husband to begin his inaugural address with a word of prayer.

Though a Presbyterian himself, President Eisenhower promoted a generic civic religion for the American public. With the Nazi holocaust in recent memory and an atheistic thrust of communism running strong in the eastern hemisphere, America during the Eisenhower years stood firm for the Judeo-Christian tradition.

John F. Kennedy (Democrat—Massachusetts), 1961–1963

Few American presidents of the twentieth century have been memorialized so nostalgically as John F. Kennedy—the young, handsome, vibrant representative of a new generation whose life ended abruptly at the gunshot of an assassin. His widow Jacqueline primed an editor at *Life* magazine to publish a memorial article emphasizing the uniquely hopeful years of Kennedy's brief presidency: "Don't let it be forgot, that once there was a spot, for one brief shining moment that was known as Camelot."

JFK came from a lineage of powerfully influential Boston families. His paternal grandfather, P.J. Kennedy was a wealthy banker, while his maternal grandfather, John E. Fitzgerald, was a politician. His father, Joseph Kennedy, made a fortune on the stock market in the 1920s and served as Chairman of the Security and Exchange Commission as well as Ambassador to Great Britain under Franklin D. Roosevelt. Old "Joe" Kennedy had even higher ambitions for his children, attempting to position his sons for election to federal offices. In the end, John became president and appointed his brother Robert as attorney general. Robert later served as a U.S. senator, but the longest political career in the family was that of their brother Ted, who served in the Senate from 1967 until 2009.

With Eisenhower old enough to be his grandfather, John F. Kennedy brought to the White House a youthful confidence, spurred on by the camaraderie of his brother Robert. Behind the television-ready poise, however, the president suffered serious back pain. A private doctor concocted a special mix of drugs to take the edge off before the president gave any important speeches. Even so, JFK suffered serious embarrassment at times, for no medication could overcome the foreign policy fumble he committed during his first few months in office. From Eisenhower's administration, Kennedy had inherited a CIA plot to overthrow Fidel Castro, the communist leader of Cuba. When the State Department expressed concern that the CIA's plan was too aggressive, and would exasperate America's tense relations with the Soviet Union, Kennedy agreed to downscale the mission. The result was that the United States abandoned the CIA-trained Cubans in 1961, depriving them of necessary air support when Castro's troops killed, captured, or expelled the freedom fighters from the beach at the Bay of Pigs.

Fortunately for Kennedy's record, his administration handled the Cuban missile crisis of 1962 more favorably, averting the near outbreak of nuclear war. As for domestic matters, Kennedy accepted tax cuts under the realization that greater business efficiency would lead to greater profits and hence greater tax revenues in the future—much as the Coolidge administration had discovered in the 1920s. A greater challenge came from the civil rights movement, which Kennedy increasingly supported, particularly when he realized the political advantage that he could obtain for the Democratic Party. In June 1963, Kennedy announced on television that the desegregation of public universities in the South "is not a sectional issue. This is not even a legal or a legislative issue alone. . . . We are confronted primarily with a moral issue." Although Kennedy had stifled civil rights legislation while serving in the Senate, he now championed the cause as president.

How far Kennedy would have taken the civil rights movement, one cannot say for sure. On November 22, 1963, while riding in an open car through Dallas as part of his campaign for re-election, he was shot. Within a half hour, he was pronounced dead at Parkland Memorial Hospital. About an hour after that, police arrested Lee Harvey Oswald as the murder suspect. Was Oswald in fact the assassin? If so, why? And had he acted alone or as part of a conspiracy? Americans long would ponder these questions, but meanwhile Vice President Lyndon B. Johnson was sworn in to succeed Kennedy as president. The nation mourned, but the nation also had to continue on.

Lyndon Baines Johnson (Democrat—Texas), 1963–1969

Lyndon B. Johnson had one of the most successful political careers of the twentieth century, and yet even he had to admit that he had no chance of being re-elected to a second full term as president. Even more paradoxical, Johnson's presidency stood not only at a high point of liberalism, but also became the inspiration for a conservative resurgence. Beginning as a teacher and a rancher from Texas, Johnson became his state's leading senator, then vice president under Kennedy, until finally emerging into his comfort zone, the U.S. presidency. "I never think about politics more than eighteen hours a day," he once quipped. Both as a senator and as president, Johnson was a phenomenal deal-maker. He knew how to get things accomplished on Capitol Hill. But in the end, the problems that he tried to solve—and the problems that his proposed solutions created—got the best of Johnson.

Just as Franklin D. Roosevelt had his New Deal, Johnson advocated the Great Society. Medicare, Medicaid, student loans, food stamps, Head Start, National Public Radio, and PBS television all date back to the Johnson administration, as do the National Endowment for the Arts, the National Endowment for the Humanities, and the Civil Rights and Voting Rights Acts. To effect such sweeping change, Johnson had to be persuasive. When necessary, he knew how to give people "the Johnson Treatment": towering at six-feet, three-inches, he stood toe-to-toe with policy makers, leaning down into their faces, whispering his wishes down their throats.

The president's wife, Claudia Alta "Lady Bird" Johnson, also had a strong political presence. Touring the southern states in celebration of the Civil Rights Act, a train called "The Lady Bird Special" brought her to several speaking engagements independently of her husband, where she urged women voters in particular to support LBJ for the 1964 election. Lady Bird set a new standard for first ladies by assuming so prominent a part in her husband's campaign.

Even as Lyndon Johnson basked in the glory of his civil rights achievements and electoral victory of 1964, he concealed from the American people his true strategy—or perhaps his lack thereof—in Vietnam. In July 1965, Johnson committed 100,000 additional troops to the war, but understated the number in his press conference by half. In January 1966, when escalating the war by another 120,000 troops, Johnson again tried to equivocate as to the number of American lives he was placing on the line, focusing on the per month commitment rather than the aggregate number of troops. In the Vietnam War, Johnson at last had met his match. No amount of political savvy could extricate the nation from the quagmire of despondency. By March of 1968, Johnson's popularity had plummeted so deeply that he knew he could not pursue re-election.

Johnson would go down in history as the only U.S. president ever to loose a war. Worse than that, he lost two wars, for his so-called War on Poverty failed to eliminate economic suffering and arguably exasperated the conditions that put people at risk for poverty, since welfare reform under the Great Society discouraged marital parenthood in favor of cohabitation and divorce. In this way, Johnson's liberalism became a favorite example among conservatives of how not to run the nation. Not only would the supporters of Johnson's conservative opponent from the 1964 election—Barry Goldwater—become a formidable political force behind Ronald Reagan in the 1980s, but even Democrats would have to take a similar lesson from Johnson's track record. For example, in 1992, Bill Clinton explicitly repudiated aspects of the Great Society in order to win election as a "New Democrat."

Richard Milhous Nixon (Republican—California), 1969–1974

Many Americans may have thought they had seen the end of Richard Nixon when John F. Kennedy defeated him in the 1960 presidential election. Attempting a rebound, Nixon ran for governor of California two years later, but that effort also failed. In reply to the criticism he received by the media, Nixon held one final press conference, conceding his loss and suggesting that the journalists were the real losers: "You won't have Dick Nixon to kick around any more."

This was not the first time Nixon had toyed with the press, and it would not be the last. While running for vice president on Dwight Eisenhower's ticket in 1952, Nixon had been accused of receiving inappropriate campaign contributions. Nixon boomeranged the accusation right back, staring into a television camera to admit forthrightly to accepting one gift in particular:

You know what it was? It was a little cocker spaniel dog in a crate that he'd sent all the way from Texas, black and white, spotted. And our little girl Tricia, the six year old, named it "Checkers." And you know, the kids, like all kids, love the dog, and I just want to say this, right now, that regardless of what they say about it, we're gonna keep it.

Having won the sympathy of the American people in this "Checkers Speech," Nixon and Eisenhower claimed an electoral victory that November. Rebounding from his 1960 loss against Kennedy, Nixon eventually won an eight-year residency in the White House by sweeping majorities in 1968 and in 1972. Maintaining popular support would, however, prove much more difficult during Nixon's second term.

Like Lyndon Johnson before him, Nixon experienced periods of extreme success and periods of devastating failure. On the positive side, Nixon withdrew America from the Vietnam War and normalized relations with communist China. Following a plan developed by National Security Advisor Henry Kissinger, Nixon exploited the emerging tension between China and the Soviet Union and capitalized on his own career history as a demonstrated anti-communist. Frustrations with the Soviet Union gave the United States and China some common ground on which to build diplomatic relations; meanwhile, Nixon could be congenial to China's communist government while minimizing the offense to the Taiwanese anti-communists since everyone knew Nixon to be an anti-communist, too.

Nixon also celebrated America's scientific triumph over the Soviets. In 1957, the Soviets became the first to put an artificial satellite in orbit around the earth—Sputnik. During Nixon's first year as president, U.S. astronaut Neil Armstrong demonstrated America's superiority by becoming the first person to walk on the moon. During Nixon's first term, at least, America seemed to be recovering from the troubles of Johnson's second term. Appealing to the "silent majority" of Americans who were not riotous war-protestors, Nixon spoke calmly and promised a path toward peace, both at home and abroad.

From a distance, it may have appeared that Nixon had every reason to be confident as he entered his second term in 1973, able to boast of an electoral victory in every state but Massachusetts. Soon, however, news reports of a burglary attempt at the Democratic National Committee office in the Watergate complex in Washington, DC, changed Nixon's career forever. As investigations pointed ever closer to Nixon's staff and eventually to Nixon himself, the president determined that his best option was to resign. In August 1974, Nixon handed over the reins to Gerald Ford, whom he had appointed vice president about a year earlier, following the resignation of Spiro T. Agnew.

Gerald Ford (Republican—Michigan), 1974–1977

Only once has a man served as president who never was elected either to the presidency or the vice presidency: Leslie Lynch King, Jr. Of course, most American know him not by his birth name, but by his adopted name: Gerald Ford. After playing football for the University of Michigan, Ford turned down a National Football League contract to attend Yale University for law school. Elected to Congress in 1948, Ford won enough respect from his fellow Republicans to become House Minority Leader in 1965. His consistent pattern of supporting President Nixon's policies paved an unforeseeable path into the vice presidency in December 1973 and the presidency in August 1974 after each of these offices became vacant due to scandal-induced resignations.

Historians sometimes refer to the Ford administration as a "caretaker presidency," implying that Ford offered no bold initiatives for either foreign or domestic policy, but simply held the course. Even if this were true, holding a steady course in the 1970s would have been a remarkable feat. Ford, however, did offer some ideas of his own. To combat inflation, he proposed a voluntary system of wage and price controls under the slogan WIN—"whip inflation now." Despite the clever acronym, which appeared on red, white, and blue buttons, the movement failed to deliver and soon became the subject of ridicule.

Ford's greatest accomplishment was that he preserved the nation from further ruin. Yes, America's final evacuation from Vietnam in April 1975 was an embarrassment, as thousands of South Vietnamese soldiers and civilians who had supported the United States were left to fend for themselves against the encroaching North Vietnamese communists. Yes, the domestic economy sputtered and stalled under the joint pressures of unemployment and inflation. Yes, the Watergate scandal had left Americans suspicious of national leadership in general. But even so, Ford stood steadily at the helm until the 1976 election, when the American people peacefully chose a new leader—by a process sketched out by James Madison, Alexander Hamilton, and John Jay nineteen decades earlier and still working on the 200th anniversary of America's independence. Compared to the violent regime transitions occurring elsewhere in the world, America still had reason to be thankful.

Jimmy Carter (Democrat—Georgia), 1977–1981

"My name is Jimmy Carter, and I'm running for president." With these words James Earl Carter, Jr., introduced himself to the American people in the 1976 presidential campaign. Although he had been elected as governor in Georgia, Carter was not well known nationally. This fact worked to his advantage. Jaded by the Watergate scandal, voters eagerly took to a Washington outsider who had grown up working on a southern peanut farm. "I will never lie to you," Carter assured them, and as a Bible-believing Baptist Sunday School teacher he held their confidence—even going so far as to confess that he once committed the sin of lust in his heart. As for a political agenda, Carter spoke common sense:

> All I want is the same thing you want: to have a nation with a government that is good and honest and decent and competent and compassionate and as filled with love as are the American people.

Once elected, however, Carter struggled to accomplish anything noteworthy in domestic affairs. Preferring to remain a Washington outsider even while in the White House, he failed to obtain the cooperation of even his own party's leadership within Congress. Meanwhile, the ominous combination of rising inflation and stagnant economic growth—"stagflation"—left workers underpaid if not unemployed.

The Organization of Petrolium Exporting Countries (OPEC) had cut shipments of oil to America in 1973. By 1979, OPEC production had dropped so low that the resulting oil scarcity sent prices to the stratosphere while gas stations across America closed down for a lack of anything to sell at the pumps. Carter called this energy crisis "the moral equivalent to war," but it was a war he had no way to win. Retreating to Camp David for an eight-day reprieve, he sought advice from pollster Pat Caddell, who suggested that he stop focusing on policy and instead speak to the American people directly about the "crisis of confidence." This plan ultimately backfired, for the televised address he delivered on July 15, 1979, became known as Carter's "malaise speech"—a bleak confession that America had fallen from greatness and the president had nothing but wishful thinking to offer as a remedy.

When Soviet troops invaded Afghanistan in December 1979, President Carter responded first with a grain embargo and second with a boycott of the 1980 Olympics, to be held in Moscow. Then a dark Iranian cloud overshadowed the final year of Carter's administration as fifty-three American citizens were held hostage for 444 days by Islamic fundamentalists led by Ayatolah Ruhollah Khomeini. The Khomeini faction had wrested control of the Iranian government from the pro-American Shah. When President Carter granted permission for the Shah to come to America to receive medical treatment for cancer, protesters in Iran burned American flags, raided the U.S. embassy at Tehran, and took American civilians hostage. Carter's attempt to rescue them resulted in the deaths of eight U.S. servicemen.

Perhaps the greatest accomplishment during Carter's administration was the 1978 Camp David Accord he negotiated between between Egyptian President Anwar el-Sedat and Israeli Prime Minister Menachem Begin. These national leaders agreed that Israel would withdraw from the Sinai Peninsula (which it had occupied since 1967) and Egypt would recognize the sovereignty of the State of Israel, which had been established under U.S. sponsorship in 1948.

Only after leaving office, however, did Carter's record clear of the "malaise" surrounding his policies of 1979 and 1980. In 1982, the former president founded the

Carter Center as a nonprofit organization for promoting global health, democracy, and human rights. Carter also mediated peace between the communist-backed Sandinistas and the U.S.-supported Contras in Nicaragua in 1989, as well as fostered dialogue for the de-nuclearization and reunification of Korea in the 1990s. In 2002, Carter was awarded the Nobel Peace Prize. While historians today may paint Carter in favorable light in view of these post-presidency accomplishments, voters in 1980 could not rid themselves of Carter soon enough; even blue collar workers—the core of the New Deal Democratic coalition—went to the polls to vote for Carter's Republican opponent, Ronald Reagan.

Study Questions

1. In what sense was Dwight Eisenhower considered a "moderate" Republican?

2. Which contributed more to John F. Kennedy's positive reputation—the accomplishments of his lifetime or the stories told of him after his death?

3. Lyndon Johnson and Richard Nixon both celebrated great accomplishments and suffered tremendous defeats. Which of them, on balance, led the nation more effectively?

4. What was the greatest challenge Americans faced from 1974 through 1980, and who handled it better—Ford or Carter?

Dwight D. Eisenhower, First Inaugural Address (1953)

Like many other American presidents, Dwight D. Eisenhower publicly acknowledged his dependence upon God for guidance and strength to lead the nation aright. He began his inaugural address with a prayer. During Eisenhower's administration, Congress formally adopted "In God We Trust" as a second national motto. (The original motto, adopted in 1782, was "*e pluribus unum*," Latin for "from many, one.") In the Soviet Union, atheism was the official state religion, but America had always had "a firm reliance on the protection of divine Providence," as the Declaration of Independence phrased it. During the "consensus" years of Eisenhower's presidency, Americans united around a shared civic theology broad enough to encompass both Protestants and Catholics, plus, in the wake of the Nazi holocaust, Jews as well. In 1957, U.S. paper bills began carrying the motto "In God We Trust," a practice the U.S. Mint previously had applied to all coins.

My friends, before I begin the expression of those thoughts that I deem appropriate to this moment, would you permit me the privilege of uttering a little private prayer of my own. And I ask that you bow your heads:

Almighty God, as we stand here at this moment my future associates in the Executive branch of Government join me in beseeching that Thou will make full and complete our dedication to the service of the people in this throng, and their fellow citizens everywhere.

Give us, we pray, the power to discern clearly right from wrong, and allow all our words and actions to be governed thereby, and by the laws of this land. Especially we pray that our concern shall be for all the people regardless of station, race or calling.

May cooperation be permitted and be the mutual aim of those who, under the concepts of our Constitution, hold to differing political faiths; so that all may work for the good of our beloved country and Thy glory. Amen.

My fellow citizens:

The world and we have passed the midway point of a century of continuing challenge. We sense with all our faculties that forces of good and evil are massed and armed and opposed as rarely before in history.

This fact defines the meaning of this day. We are summoned by this honored and historic ceremony to witness more than the act of one citizen swearing his oath of service, in the presence of God. We are called as a people to give testimony in the sight of the world to our faith that the future shall belong to the free.

Since this century's beginning, a time of tempest has seemed to come upon the continents of the earth. Masses of Asia have awakened to strike off shackles of the past. Great nations of Europe have fought their bloodiest wars. Thrones have toppled and their vast empires have disappeared. New nations have been born.

For our own country, it has been a time of recurring trial. We have grown in power and in responsibility. We have passed through the anxieties of depression and of war to a summit unmatched in man's history. Seeking to secure peace in the world, we have had to fight through the forests of the Argonne to the shores of Iwo Jima, and to the cold mountains of Korea.

In the swift rush of great events, we find ourselves groping to know the full sense and meaning of these times in which we live. In our quest of understanding, we beseech God's guidance. We summon all our knowledge of the past and we scan all signs of the future. We bring all our wit and all our will to meet the question:

How far have we come in man's long pilgrimage from darkness toward the light? Are we nearing the light—a day of freedom and of peace for all mankind? Or are the shadows of another night closing in upon us?

Great as are the preoccupations absorbing us at home, concerned as we are with matters that deeply affect our livelihood today and our vision of the future, each of these domestic problems is dwarfed by, and often even created by, this question that involves all humankind.

This trial comes at a moment when man's power to achieve good or to inflict evil surpasses the brightest hopes and the sharpest fears of all ages. We can turn rivers in their courses, level mountains to the plains. Oceans and land and sky are avenues for our colossal commerce. Disease diminishes and life lengthens.

Yet the promise of this life is imperiled by the very genius that has made it possible. Nations amass wealth. Labor sweats to create—and turns out devices to level not only mountains but also cities. Science seems ready to confer upon us, as its final gift, the power to erase human life from this planet.

At such a time in history, we who are free must proclaim anew our faith. This faith is the abiding creed of our fathers. It is our faith in the deathless dignity of man, governed by eternal moral and natural laws.

This faith defines our full view of life. It establishes, beyond debate, those gifts of the Creator that are man's inalienable rights, and that make all men equal in His sight.

In the light of this equality, we know that the virtues most cherished by free people—love of truth, pride of work, devotion to country—all are treasures equally precious in the lives of the most humble and of the most exalted. The men who mine coal and fire furnaces, and balance ledgers, and turn lathes, and pick cotton, and heal the sick and plant corn—all serve as proudly and as profitably for America as the statesmen who draft treaties and the legislators who enact laws.

This faith rules our whole way of life. It decrees that we, the people, elect leaders not to rule but to serve. It asserts that we have the right to choice of our own work and to the reward of our own toil. It inspires the initiative that makes our productivity the wonder of the world. And it warns that any man who seeks to deny equality among all his brothers betrays the spirit of the free and invites the mockery of the tyrant.

It is because we, all of us, hold to these principles that the political changes accomplished this day do not imply turbulence, upheaval or disorder. Rather this change expresses a purpose of strengthening our dedication and devotion to the precepts of our founding documents, a conscious renewal of faith in our country and in the watchfulness of a Divine Providence.

The enemies of this faith know no god but force, no devotion but its use. They tutor men in treason. They feed upon the hunger of others. Whatever defies them, they torture, especially the truth.

Here, then, is joined no argument between slightly differing philosophies. This conflict strikes directly at the faith of our fathers and the lives of our sons. No principle or treasure that we hold, from the spiritual knowledge of our free schools and churches to the creative magic of free labor and capital, nothing lies safely beyond the reach of this struggle.

Freedom is pitted against slavery; lightness against the dark

The faith we hold belongs not to us alone but to the free of all the world. This common bond binds the grower of rice in Burma and the planter of wheat in Iowa, the shepherd in southern Italy and the mountaineer in the Andes. It confers a common dignity upon the French soldier who dies in Indo-China, the British soldier killed in Malaya, the American life given in Korea.

We know, beyond this, that we are linked to all free peoples not merely by a noble idea but by a simple need. No free people can for long cling to any privilege or enjoy any safety in economic solitude. For all our own material might, even we need markets in the world for the surpluses of our farms and our factories. Equally, we need for these same farms and factories vital materials and products of distant lands. This basic law of interdependence, so manifest in the commerce of peace, applies with thousand-fold intensity in the event of war.

So we are persuaded by necessity and by belief that the strength of all free peoples lies in unity; their danger, in discord.

To produce this unity, to meet the challenge of our time, destiny has laid upon our country the responsibility of the free world's leadership.

So it is proper that we assure our friends once again that, in the discharge of this responsibility, we Americans know and we observe the difference between world leadership and imperialism; between firmness and truculence; between a thoughtfully calculated goal and spasmodic reaction to the stimulus of emergencies.

We wish our friends the world over to know this above all: we face the threat—not with dread and confusion—but with confidence and conviction.

We feel this moral strength because we know that we are not helpless prisoners of history. We are free men. We shall remain free, never to be proven guilty of the one capital offense against freedom, a lack of stanch faith.

In pleading our just cause before the bar of history and in pressing our labor for world peace, we shall be guided by certain fixed principles. These principles are:

1. Abhorring war as a chosen way to balk the purposes of those who threaten us, we hold it to be the first task of statesmanship to develop the strength that will

deter the forces of aggression and promote the conditions of peace. For, as it must be the supreme purpose of all free men, so it must be the dedication of their leaders, to save humanity from preying upon itself.

In the light of this principle, we stand ready to engage with any and all others in joint effort to remove the causes of mutual fear and distrust among nations, so as to make possible drastic reduction of armaments. The sole requisites for undertaking such effort are that—in their purpose—they be aimed logically and honestly toward secure peace for all; and that—in their result—they provide methods by which every participating nation will prove good faith in carrying out its pledge.

2. Realizing that common sense and common decency alike dictate the futility of appeasement, we shall never try to placate an aggressor by the false and wicked bargain of trading honor for security. Americans, indeed, all free men, remember that in the final choice a soldier's pack is not so heavy a burden as a prisoner's chains.

3. Knowing that only a United States that is strong and immensely productive can help defend freedom in our world, we view our Nation's strength and security as a trust upon which rests the hope of free men everywhere. It is the firm duty of each of our free citizens and of every free citizen everywhere to place the cause of his country before the comfort, the convenience of himself.

4. Honoring the identity and the special heritage of each nation in the world, we shall never use our strength to try to impress upon another people our own cherished political and economic institutions.

5. Assessing realistically the needs and capacities of proven friends of freedom, we shall strive to help them to achieve their own security and well-being. Likewise, we shall count upon them to assume, within the limits of their resources, their full and just burdens in the common defense of freedom.

6. Recognizing economic health as an indispensable basis of military strength and the free world's peace, we shall strive to foster everywhere, and to practice ourselves, policies that encourage productivity and profitable trade. For the impoverishment of any single people in the world means danger to the well-being of all other peoples.

7. Appreciating that economic need, military security and political wisdom combine to suggest regional groupings of free peoples, we hope, within the framework of the United Nations, to help strengthen such special bonds the world over. The nature of these ties must vary with the different problems of different areas.

In the Western Hemisphere, we enthusiastically join with all our neighbors in the work of perfecting a community of fraternal trust and common purpose.

In Europe, we ask that enlightened and inspired leaders of the Western nations strive with renewed vigor to make the unity of their peoples a reality. Only as free Europe unitedly marshals its strength can it effectively safeguard, even with our help, its spiritual and cultural heritage.

8. Conceiving the defense of freedom, like freedom itself, to be one and indivisible, we hold all continents and peoples in equal regard and honor. We reject any insinuation that one race or another, one people or another, is in any sense inferior or expendable.

9. Respecting the United Nations as the living sign of all people's hope for peace, we shall strive to make it not merely an eloquent symbol but an effective force. And in our quest for an honorable peace, we shall neither compromise, nor tire, nor ever cease.

By these rules of conduct, we hope to be known to all peoples.

By their observance, an earth of peace may become not a vision but a fact.

This hope—this supreme aspiration—must rule the way we live.

We must be ready to dare all for our country. For history does not long entrust the care of freedom to the weak or the timid. We must acquire proficiency in defense and display stamina in purpose.

We must be willing, individually and as a Nation, to accept whatever sacrifices may be required of us. A people that values its privileges above its principles soon loses both.

These basic precepts are not lofty abstractions, far removed from matters of daily living. They are laws of spiritual strength that generate and define our material strength. Patriotism means equipped forces and a prepared citizenry.

Moral stamina means more energy and more productivity, on the farm and in the factory. Love of liberty means the guarding of every resource that makes freedom possible—from the sanctity of our families and the wealth of our soil to the genius of our scientists.

And so each citizen plays an indispensable role. The productivity of our heads, our hands and our hearts is the source of all the strength we can command, for both the enrichment of our lives and the winning of the peace.

No person, no home, no community can be beyond the reach of this call. We are summoned to act in wisdom and in conscience, to work with industry, to teach with persuasion, to preach with conviction, to weigh our every deed with care and with compassion. For this truth must be clear before us: whatever America hopes to bring to pass in the world must first come to pass in the heart of America.

The peace we seek, then, is nothing less than the practice and fulfillment of our whole faith among ourselves and in our dealings with others. This signifies more than the stilling of guns, casing the sorrow of war. More than escape from death, it is a way of life. More than a haven for the weary, it is a hope for the brave.

This is the hope that beckons us onward in this century of trial. This is the work that awaits us all, to be done with bravery, with charity, and with prayer to Almighty God.

My citizens—I thank you.

Study Questions

1. Eisenhower defined the "dignity of man" in terms of "eternal, moral and natural laws." Explain how he applied this concept to America's role in the twentieth century.

2. Eisenhower stated that "destiny has laid upon our country the responsibility of the free world's leadership." What guiding principles did he propose for how America should fulfill this responsibility?

Dwight D. Eisenhower, "The Korean Armistice" (1953)

The Korean Conflict (1950–1953) demonstrated that the Truman Doctrine—containing communism by assisting nations that struggle against it—could not always be pursued by mere diplomacy or through economic sanctions. The Cold War had turned hot. Whereas U.S. military involvement in both World War I and World War II led to decisive victory, U.S. military deployment during the Cold War seldom resulted in more than a stalemate. Such was the case in Korea, but in the summer of 1953 at least the killing came to stop as the two factions agreed to split their differences near the 38th parallel, essentially where the fighting had begun three years earlier.

My fellow citizens:

Tonight we greet, with prayers of thanksgiving, the official news that an armistice was signed almost an hour ago in Korea. It will quickly bring to an end the fighting between the United Nations forces and the Communist armies. For this Nation the cost of repelling aggression has been high. In thousands of homes it has been incalculable. It has been paid in terms of tragedy.

With special feelings of sorrow—and of solemn gratitude—we think of those who were called upon to lay down their lives in that far-off land to prove once again that only courage and sacrifice can keep freedom alive upon the earth. To the widows and orphans of this war, and to those veterans who bear disabling wounds, America renews tonight her pledge of lasting devotion and care.

Our thoughts turn also to those other Americans wearied by many months of imprisonment behind the enemy lines. The swift return of all of them will bring joy to thousands of families. It will be evidence of good faith on the part of those with whom we have signed this armistice.

Soldiers, sailors, and airmen of 16 different countries have stood as partners beside us throughout these long and bitter months. America's thanks go to each. In this struggle we have seen the United Nations meet the challenge of aggression—not with pathetic words of protest, but with deeds of decisive purpose. It is proper that we salute particularly the valorous armies of the Republic of Korea, for they have done even more than prove their right to freedom. Inspired by President Syngman Rhee, they have given an example of courage and patriotism which again demonstrates that men of the West and men of the East can fight and work and live together side by side in pursuit of a just and noble cause.

And so at long last the carnage of war is to cease and the negotiations of the conference table is to begin. On this Sabbath evening each of us devoutly prays that all nations may come to see the wisdom of composing differences in this fashion before, rather than after, there is resort to brutal and futile battle.

Now as we strive to bring about that wisdom, there is, in this moment of sober satisfaction, one thought that must discipline our emotions and steady our resolution. It is this: we have won an armistice on a single battleground—not peace in the world. We may not now relax our guard nor cease our quest.

Throughout the coming months, during the period of prisoner screening and exchange, and during the possibly longer period of the political conference which looks toward the unification of Korea, we and our United Nations Allies must be vigilant against the possibility of untoward developments.

And as we do so, we shall fervently strive to insure that this armistice will, in fact, bring free peoples one step nearer to their goal of a world at peace.

My friends, almost 90 years ago, Abra-ham Lincoln at the end of a war delivered his second Inaugural Address. At the end of that speech he spoke some words that I think more nearly express the true feelings of America tonight than would any other words ever spoken or written. You will recall them:

> With malice toward none; with charity for all; with firmness in the right as God gives us to see the right, let us strive on to finish the work we are in . . . to do all which may achieve and cherish a just and a lasting peace, among ourselves, and with all nations.

This is our resolve and our dedication.

Study Question

1. What "sober satisfaction" did Eisenhower derive from the cease-fire achieved in Korea?

2. What hope did Eisenhower express for the future of Korea and the United States?

Dwight D. Eisenhower, "Atoms for Peace" (1953)

Following the death of Joseph Stalin in March 1953, Georgi Malenkov served as interim leader of the Soviet Union. Malenkov appeared willing to pursue diplomatic agreements with the West in order to steer the course of the Cold War toward a peaceful coexistence. Eisenhower replied with the following speech to the United Nations, requesting that an international agency oversee the nuclear operations of all nations.

Madame President [Vijaya Pandit, President of the U.N. General Assembly], Members of the General Assembly:

. . . Never before in history has so much hope for so many people been gathered together in a single organization. Your deliberations and decisions during these somber years have already realized part of those hopes.

But the great tests and the great accomplishments still lie ahead. And in the confident expectation of those accomplishments, I would use the office which, for the time being, I hold, to assure you that the Government of the United States will remain steadfast in its support of this body. This we shall do in the conviction that you will provide a great share of the wisdom, the courage, and the faith which can bring to this world lasting peace for all nations, and happiness and well-being for all men.

Clearly, it would not be fitting for me to take this occasion to present to you a unilateral American report on Bermuda. Nevertheless, I assure you that in our deliberations on that lovely island we sought to invoke those same great concepts of universal peace and human dignity which are so clearly etched in your Charter.

Neither would it be a measure of this great opportunity merely to recite, however hopefully, pious platitudes.

I therefore decided that this occasion warranted my saying to you some of the things that have been on the minds and hearts of my legislative and executive associates and on mine for a great many months—thoughts I had originally planned to say primarily to the American people.

I know that the American people share my deep belief that if a danger exists in the world, it is a danger shared by all—and equally, that if hope exists in the mind of one nation, that hope should be shared by all.

Finally, if there is to be advanced any proposal designed to ease even by the smallest measure the tensions of today's world, what more appropriate audience could there be than the members of the General Assembly of the United Nations?

I feel impelled to speak today in a language that in a sense is new—one which I, who have spent so much of my life in the military profession, would have preferred never to use.

That new language is the language of atomic warfare.

The atomic age has moved forward at such a pace that every citizen of the world should have some comprehension, at least in comparative terms, of the extent of this development of the utmost significance to every one of us. Clearly, if the peoples of the world are to conduct an intelligent search for peace, they must be armed with the significant facts of today's existence.

My recital of atomic danger and power is necessarily stated in United States terms, for these are the only incontrovertible facts that I know. I need hardly point out to this Assembly, however, that this subject is global, not merely national in character.

On July 16, 1945, the United States set off the world's first atomic explosion. Since that date in 1945, the United States of America has conducted 42 test explosions.

Atomic bombs today are more than 25 times as powerful as the weapons with which the atomic age dawned, while hydrogen weapons are in the ranges of millions of tons of TNT equivalent.

Today, the United States' stockpile of atomic weapons, which, of course, increases daily, exceeds by many times the explosive equivalent of the total of all bombs and all shells that came from every plane and every gun in every theatre of war in all of the years of World War II.

A single air group, whether afloat or land-based, can now deliver to any reachable target a destructive cargo exceeding in power all the bombs that fell on Britain in all of World War II.

In size and variety, the development of atomic weapons has been no less remarkable. The development has been such that atomic weapons have virtually achieved conventional status within our armed services. In the United States, the Army, the Navy, the Air Force, and the Marine Corps are all capable of putting this weapon to military use.

But the dread secret, and the fearful engines of atomic might, are not ours alone.

In the first place, the secret is possessed by our friends and allies, Great Britain and Canada, whose scientific genius made a tremendous contribution to our original discoveries, and the designs of atomic bombs.

The secret is also known by the Soviet Union.

The Soviet Union has informed us that, over recent years, it has devoted extensive resources to atomic weapons. During this period, the Soviet Union has exploded a series of atomic devices, including at least one involving thermo-nuclear reactions.

If at one time the United States possessed what might have been called a monopoly of atomic power, that monopoly ceased to exist several years ago. Therefore, although our earlier start has permitted us to accumulate what is today a great quantitative advantage, the atomic realities of today comprehend two facts of even greater significance.

First, the knowledge now possessed by several nations will eventually be shared by others—possibly all others.

Second, even a vast superiority in numbers of weapons, and a consequent capability of devastating retaliation, is no preventive, of itself, against the fearful material damage and toll of human lives that would be inflicted by surprise aggression.

The free world, at least dimly aware of these facts, has naturally embarked on a large program of warning and defense systems. That program will be accelerated and expanded.

But let no one think that the expenditure of vast sums for weapons and systems of defense can guarantee absolute safety for the cities and citizens of any nation. The awful arithmetic of the atomic bomb does not permit of any such easy solution. Even against the most powerful defense, an aggressor in possession of the effective minimum number of atomic bombs for a surprise attack could probably place a sufficient number of his bombs on the chosen targets to cause hideous damage.

Should such an atomic attack be launched against the United States, our reactions would be swift and resolute. But for me to say that the defense capabilities of the United States are such that they could inflict terrible losses upon an aggressor—for me to say that the retaliation capabilities of the United States are so great that such an aggressor's land would be laid waste—all this, while fact, is not the true expression of the purpose and the hope of the United States.

To pause there would be to confirm the hopeless finality of a belief that two atomic colossi are doomed malevolently to eye each other indefinitely across a trembling world. To stop there would be to accept helplessly the probability of civilization destroyed—the annihilation of the irreplaceable heritage of mankind handed down to us generation from generation—and the condemnation of mankind to begin all over again the age-old struggle upward from savagery toward decency, and right, and justice.

Surely no sane member of the human race could discover victory in such desolation. Could anyone wish his name to be coupled by history with such human degradation and destruction?

Occasional pages of history do record the faces of the "Great Destroyers" but the whole book of history reveals mankind's never-ending quest for peace, and mankind's God-given capacity to build.

It is with the book of history, and not with isolated pages, that the United States will ever wish to be identified. My country wants to be constructive, not destructive. It wants agreements, not wars, among nations. It wants itself to live in freedom, and in the confidence that the people of every other nation enjoy equally the right of choosing their own way of life.

So my country's purpose is to help us move out of the dark chamber of horrors into the light, to find a way by which the minds of men, the hopes of men, the souls of men everywhere, can move forward toward peace and happiness and well being.

In this quest, I know that we must not lack patience.

I know that in a world divided, such as ours today, salvation cannot be attained by one dramatic act.

I know that many steps will have to be taken over many months before the world can look at itself one day and truly realize that a new climate of mutually peaceful confidence is abroad in the world.

But I know, above all else, that we must start to take these steps—now.

The United States and its allies, Great Britain and France, have over the past months tried to take some of these steps. Let no one say that we shun the conference table.

On the record has long stood the request of the United States, Great Britain, and France to negotiate with the Soviet Union the problems of a divided Germany.

On that record has long stood the request of the same three nations to negotiate an Austrian Peace Treaty.

On the same record still stands the request of the United Nations to negotiate the problems of Korea.

Most recently, we have received from the Soviet Union what is in effect an expression of willingness to hold a Four Power Meeting. Along with our allies, Great Britain and France, we were pleased to see that this note did not contain the unacceptable preconditions previously put forward.

As you already know from our joint Bermuda communique, the United States, Great Britain, and France have agreed promptly to meet with the Soviet Union.

The Government of the United States approaches this conference with hopeful sincerity. We will bend every effort of our minds to the single purpose of emerging from that conference with tangible results toward peace—the only true way of lessening international tension.

We never have, we never will, propose or suggest that the Soviet Union surrender what is rightfully theirs.

We will never say that the peoples of Russia are an enemy with whom we have no desire ever to deal or mingle in friendly and fruitful relationship.

On the contrary, we hope that this coming Conference may initiate a relationship with the Soviet Union which will eventually bring about a free intermingling of the peoples of the East and of the West—the one sure, human way of developing the understanding required for confident and peaceful relations.

Instead of the discontent which is now settling upon Eastern Germany, occupied Austria, and the countries of Eastern Europe, we seek a harmonious family of free European nations, with none a threat to the other, and least of all a threat to the peoples of Russia.

Beyond the turmoil and strife and misery of Asia, we seek peaceful opportunity for these peoples to develop their natural resources and to elevate their lives.

These are not idle words or shallow visions. Behind them lies a story of nations lately come to independence, not as a result of war, but through free grant or peaceful negotiation. There is a record, already written, of assistance gladly given by nations of the West to needy peoples, and to those suffering the temporary effects of famine, drought, and natural disaster.

These are deeds of peace. They speak more loudly than promises or protestations of peaceful intent.

But I do not wish to rest either upon the reiteration of past proposals or the restatement of past deeds. The gravity of the time is such that every new avenue of peace, no matter how dimly discernible, should be explored.

There is at least one new avenue of peace which has not yet been well explored —an avenue now laid out by the General Assembly of the United Nations.

In its resolution of November 18th, 1953, this General Assembly suggested— and I quote—"that the Disarmament Commission study the desirability of establishing a sub-committee consisting of representatives of the Powers principally involved, which should seek in private an acceptable solution . . . and report on such a solution to the General Assembly and to the Security Council not later than 1 September 1954."

The United States, heeding the suggestion of the General Assembly of the United Nations, is instantly prepared to meet privately with such other countries as may be "principally involved," to seek "an acceptable solution" to the atomic armaments race which overshadows not only the peace, but the very life, of the world.

We shall carry into these private or diplomatic talks a new conception.

The United States would seek more than the mere reduction or elimination of atomic materials for military purposes.

It is not enough to take this weapon out of the hands of the soldiers. It must be put into the hands of those who will know how to strip its military casing and adapt it to the arts of peace.

The United States knows that if the fearful trend of atomic military buildup can be reversed, this greatest of destructive forces can be developed into a great boon, for the benefit of all mankind.

The United States knows that peaceful power from atomic energy is no dream of the future. That capability, already proved, is here—now—today. Who can doubt, if the entire body of the world's scientists and engineers had adequate amounts of fissionable material with which to test and develop their ideas, that this capability would rapidly be transformed into universal, efficient, and economic usage.

To hasten the day when fear of the atom will begin to disappear from the minds of people, and the governments of the East and West, there are certain steps that can be taken now.

I therefore make the following proposals:

The Governments principally involved, to the extent permitted by elementary prudence, to begin now and continue to make joint contributions from their stockpiles of normal uranium and fissionable materials to an International Atomic Energy Agency. We would expect that such an agency would be set up under the aegis of the United Nations.

The ratios of contributions, the procedures and other details would properly be within the scope of the "private conversations" I have referred to earlier.

The United States is prepared to undertake these explorations in good faith. Any partner of the United States acting in the same good faith will find the United States a not unreasonable or ungenerous associate.

Undoubtedly initial and early contributions to this plan would be small in quantity. However, the proposal has the great virtue that it can be undertaken without the irritations and mutual suspicions incident to any attempt to set up a completely acceptable system of world-wide inspection and control.

The Atomic Energy Agency could be made responsible for the impounding, storage, and protection of the contributed fissionable and other materials. The ingenuity of our scientists will provide special safe conditions under which such a bank of fissionable material can be made essentially immune to surprise seizure.

The more important responsibility of this Atomic Energy Agency would be to devise methods whereby this fissionable material would be allocated to serve the peaceful pursuits of mankind. Experts would be mobilized to apply atomic energy to the needs of agriculture, medicine, and other peaceful activities. A special purpose would be to provide abundant electrical energy in the power-starved areas of the world. Thus the contributing powers would be dedicating some of their strength to serve the needs rather than the fears of mankind.

The United States would be more than willing—it would be proud to take up with others "principally involved" the development of plans whereby such peaceful use of atomic energy would be expedited.

Of those "principally involved" the Soviet Union must, of course, be one.

I would be prepared to submit to the Congress of the United States, and with every expectation of approval, any such plan that would:

First—encourage world-wide investigation into the most effective peacetime uses of fissionable material, and with the certainty that they had all the material needed for the conduct of all experiments that were appropriate;

Second—begin to diminish the potential destructive power of the world's atomic stockpiles;

Third—allow all peoples of all nations to see that, in this enlightened age, the great powers of the earth, both of the East and of the West, are interested in human aspirations first, rather than in building up the armaments of war;

Fourth—open up a new channel for peaceful discussion, and initiate at least a new approach to the many difficult problems that must be solved in both private and public conversations, if the world is to shake off the inertia imposed by fear, and is to make positive progress toward peace.

Against the dark background of the atomic bomb, the United States does not wish merely to present strength, but also the desire and the hope for peace.

The coming months will be fraught with fateful decisions. In this Assembly; in the capitals and military headquarters of the world; in the hearts of men everywhere, be they governors or governed, may they be the decisions which will lead this world out of fear and into peace.

To the making of these fateful decisions, the United States pledges before you—and therefore before the world—its determination to help solve the fearful atomic dilemma—to devote its entire heart and mind to find the way by which the miraculous inventiveness of man shall not be dedicated to his death, but consecrated to his life.

I again thank the delegates for the great honor they have done me, in inviting me to appear before them, and in listening to me so courteously. Thank you.

Study Question

1. What dangers did Eisenhower perceive in "the awful arithmetic of the atomic bomb"?

2. How did Eisenhower respond to the U.N. proposal of nuclear disarmament?

Supreme Court Decisions under Chief Justice Earl Warren

President Dwight D. Eisenhower appointed California Governor Earl Warren to serve as Chief Justice of the Supreme Court in 1953. Warren carefully arranged for the Court to issue a unanimous ruling in the controversial *Brown v. Board of Education* school segregation case of 1954. Other rulings during his tenure tended to expand individual rights in a manner contrary to the traditions of previous generations: prayer and Bible reading would be prohibited in school, but criminals would have more explicit guarantees of justice. Based on these examples, the Warren Court marks a turn toward liberalism.

1954   In *Brown v. Board of Education*, the Court overruled *Plessy v. Ferguson* (1896) and required that all public schools become racially integrated.

1962   The Court declared state-mandated prayer in public schools unconstitutional in *Engel v. Vitale*.

1963   The Court declared state-organized Bible reading in public schools unconstitutional in *Abington School District v. Schempp*.

In *Gideon v. Wainwright*, the Court held that a person accused of a felony has a the right to an attorney, even if he cannot afford one himself.

1964   The Court upheld the Civil Rights Act of 1964 as constitutional in *Heart of Atlanta Motel v. U.S.*

1965   In *Griswold v. Connecticut*, the Court discovered a "right to privacy" in the "penumbras, formed by emanations" from guarantees stated in the Bill of Rights. The Court then concluded that this implicit "right to privacy" includes the right of married persons to purchase and use contraception.

1966   The Court required that law enforcement agents inform suspects of their constitutional rights before interrogating them in *Miranda v. Arizona*.

1969   In *Brandenburg v. Ohio*, the Court struck down an Ohio law limiting freedom of speech, unanimously ruling that the First Amendment protects even hateful speech unless it incites people to "imminent lawless action."

Study Question

1. In what respects did the Warren Court depart from a conservation of America's Judeo-Christian heritage and embrace a philosophy of individualism?

2. How did the Warren Court reinforce the Fifth and Sixth Amendments?

The Origins of the Civil Rights Movement, 1870–1960

Jim Crow in Southern Society (ca. 1870–ca. 1900)

In 1870, Americans likely would not have foreseen the need for the civil rights movement of the 1950s and 1960s. In 1870, the Fifteenth Amendment guaranteed African Americans the right to vote. Two years earlier, the Fourteenth Amendment had guaranteed them full rights of citizenship. Three years before that, the Thirteenth Amendment had abolished slavery in America forever. A new era clearly had begun, an era known as Reconstruction. Not only were African Americans permitted to vote in theory, but they were in actuality elected to public office as well. About six hundred were elected to state legislatures, fourteen to the U.S. House of Representatives, and two to the U.S. Senate during the years following the Civil War. But after a few decades, most of this progress in racial equality was erased.

After the last federal troops left the South following the compromise election of Rutherford B. Hayes in 1877, southern whites wrestled control of their states from the influence of black voters. Social customs and legal codes, known as "Jim Crow," imposed a strict separation of the races throughout society. Blacks could not sit in the same train cars as whites, seek employment in the same jobs as whites, enroll their children in the same schools as whites, live in the same neighborhoods as whites, or be buried in the same cemeteries as whites. Some black men who crossed the color line— particularly in those instances involving communication with a white woman—suffered torture and death at the hands of lynch mobs. Although most black men were never lynched, the mere possibility paralyzed many of them with fear.

If intimidation by groups such as the Ku Klux Klan was not enough to keep blacks from voting, a series of new laws targeted blacks for disqualification. For example, poll taxes prevented poorer blacks from voting, and literacy tests were rigged in such a manner that even well-educated blacks failed to satisfy the white administrators. For all practical purposes, southern blacks had been relegated to second-class citizenship by the early twentieth century, with no one in the federal government willing to enforce the Fourteenth or Fifteenth Amendment.

African American Activism before Brown (early to mid 1900s)

By the 1930s, a new generation of African Americans was poised to make a difference. The cultural innovations of the Harlem Renaissance during the 1920s had given artistic expression to a new black consciousness, dubbed the "New Negro." Blacks who came of age during the mid century increasingly aspired to something greater than the second-class citizenship they had inherited from Jim Crow. The National Association for the Advancement of Colored People (NAACP), founding in 1909, established a platform for articulating social reform and provided assistance in urban communities.

African Americans also were laying the foundation for a civil rights revolution in the courtroom. Charles H. Houston, a black graduate of Harvard Law School, served as dean of Howard University's School of Law from 1929 to 1935. Howard, an all-black university located in Washington, DC, produced a number of strong graduates, including Thurgood Marshall (Law School class of 1933), who later served on the U.S. Supreme Court. In 1935, Houston became the legal advisor to the NAACP. Thus began a series of court victories culminating in the landmark school desegregation decision, *Brown v. Board of Education* (1954).

Brown v. Board of Education *(1954)*

In 1952, five similar cases came before the U.S. Supreme Court for combined oral argument. The lead case involved Linda Brown, a young school child who had to cross railroad tracks in Topeka, Kansas, to get to an all-black school since the closer, all-white school prohibited her from enrolling. In a second case, twenty black parents in South Carolina sued the local government for not providing adequate funding or staffing to the black schools. The other three cases likewise brought grievances concerning public school segregation, so the Court arranged to consider them together as a group.

Thurgood Marshall, by now an NAACP attorney, represented the black students. He argued not merely that the school districts failed to meet the "separate but equal" standard the Court had established in *Plessy v. Ferguson* (1896), but furthermore that not even complete equality in funding, staffing, and other tangible factors would guarantee an equal educational opportunity. To prove this last point, Marshall relied upon psychological research by Kenneth and Mamie Clark. The Clarks had interviewed children who were asked to play with black and white dolls. Black children identified themselves with the black dolls, but expressed a strong preference for the white dolls as the "nice" or "good" dolls that they would rather play with. From these reports, the Clarks inferred that even at a young age children internalize the value structure of racial segregation; black children accordingly develop a sense of racial inferiority. Segregated schooling therefore causes psychological harm that hinders classroom learning, which is to say, black students confined to a segregated school do not learn as well as those who are permitted to attend an integrated school.

The Supreme Court agreed. "We conclude that, in the field of public education, the doctrine of 'separate but equal' has no place," wrote the Court in an unanimous opinion, issued in May 1954. "Separate educational facilities are inherently unequal." The Court further explained that the guarantee of equal citizenship provided by Fourteenth Amendment is broad enough to include a right to education, since education itself is fundamental to democratic citizenship. A subsequent ruling, known as *Brown II*

(1955), called upon local governments to integrate their schools "with all deliberate speed," but gave those local governments considerable discretion as to how to do so. With no firm deadline being set, many southern school districts dragged their feet. Meanwhile, about one hundred members of Congress signed a Southern Manifesto (1956), decrying the *Brown v. Board of Education* ruling as an overreach of federal authority. Even President Dwight D. Eisenhower thought the Court had been unwise to force school integration upon the South rather than permit race relations to work themselves out more gradually.

The Murder of Emmett Till (1955)

Emmett Till, a fourteen-year-old black Chicago boy, learned a lesson about Jim Crow that cost him his life while visiting his relatives in Mississippi in August 1955. Emmett bragged to his southern cousin about dating a white girl in the North and then proceeded to say something flirtatious to Carolyn Bryant, a white married woman who worked at a Mississippi grocery store. Her husband Roy and his brother-in-law J.W. Milam kidnapped Emmett from his grandfather's house. Three days later, a fisherman found the child's disfigured body in the Tallahatchie River. An all-white jury found both Roy Bryant and J.W. Milam not guilty. With the Fifth Amendment protecting them from being tried for the same crime twice, they sold their story to a *Look* magazine journalist for $4000, confessing to the boy's murder.

Despite the injustice, two factors suggested that times were starting to change. First, the trial of Bryant and Milam was the first instance in Mississippi history of a black man—in this case, Emmett's grandfather—testifying in court against a white man. Second, Emmett's mother arranged an open-casket funeral and *Jet* magazine published a gruesome picture of the boy's remains, drawing the sympathy of northern whites. In the years that followed, similar mixtures of southern black activism and northern white sympathy would fan a flame of civil rights reform that nobody could extinguish.

The Montgomery Bus Boycott (1955–1956)

Although the *Brown* decision required that public schools be integrated, it did nothing for public transportation. In November 1955, the Interstate Commerce Commission prohibited racially segregated seating on buses and trains crossing state lines, but left local transportation unaffected. On December 1, however, a black woman named Rosa Parks refused to yield her seat to white passengers on a Montgomery, Alabama, bus service. Parks was well liked and well connected in the community, serving as secretary to E.D. Nixon, the president of the local NAACP chapter. Other members of the black community soon rallied around her cause, including college professor Jo Ann Robinson and the Rev. Martin Luther King, Jr. Robinson mimeographed fliers to organize a boycott. King delivered a rousing speech that encouraged the community to extend the boycott. The result was a 381-day boycott involving fifty thousand volunteers. In 1956 the Supreme Court ordered the City of Montgomery to integrate its bus seats. Encouraged by this victory, King and other ministers established the Southern Christian Leadership Conference (SCLC) to organize civil rights projects in other communities as well.

The Little Rock Nine (1957)

When a local school board developed a plan for integrating Central High School of Little Rock, Arkansas, the nation discovered just how divisive race could be in southern communities. Governor Orval Faubus spoke against integration, claiming that the vast majority of the state's citizens favored segregation and, in any case, the matter should be decided locally, not by federal interference. The NAACP filed a lawsuit urging that the Brown ruling be implemented. The school board sought a compromise to maintain the peace, reducing the number of proposed black pupils from twenty-five to nine. Then the county chancellor ordered a stop to the plan in the name of public safety. The NAACP again took the matter to court, securing a judge's order to integrate without delay. In response, Governor Faubus deployed the National Guard to prevent the black students from entering the campus.

So who would have the final say? The scene became ripe for disaster. Elizabeth Eckford, one of the nine black school children, was engulfed by an angry white mob of parents and students who shouted racial epithets. A federal judge ordered Faubus to recall the National Guard, but this only left the black school children at the mercy of the white mob. Mayor Woodrow Mann urged President Eisenhower to intervene. Reluctantly, the president agreed. So long as local authorities continued to defy the Supreme Court's Brown ruling, it was the president's duty to uphold the rule of law by intervention. Though patient until now, Eisenhower felt forced into acting decisively to ensure the safety of the nine school children and also to defend the constitutional principle that a federal court order trumps the wishes of a state governor. The president federalized the Arkansas National Guard and deployed the 101st Airborne Division to escort the "Little Rock Nine" from their homes to their classrooms at Central High School.

The Sit-In Movements (1960)

In February 1960, four students from North Carolina Agricultural and Technical College, an all-black school located in Greensboro, sat down at the all-white lunch counter in a local Woolworth's shop to order lunch. They felt emboldened to challenge the color line by their activities in NAACP youth groups and by some presentations they had heard from both Martin Luther King and the Little Rock Nine. Their strategy was to remain calm, polite, and peaceful, asking simply to be treated with respect in return. Their example caught on like wildfire. In the weeks that followed, over ninety percent of their classmates participated in sit-ins—that is, remained seated in the "white" section until served or arrested.

By the year's end, sit-ins had occurred in 130 cities, spread throughout every southern state except Mississippi. Some 70,000 youth participated, being organized and guided by the Student Nonviolent Coordinating Commission (SNCC, pronounced "snick"). Drawing inspiration from Mahatma Gandhi, SNCC leader James Lawson hosted workshops for coaching college students to remain calm even when attacked by white mobs or brutalized by the police. As presidential candidate John F. Kennedy mused, the sit-ins came out of "the American tradition to stand up for one's rights—even if the new way is to sit down."

Study Questions

1. On what basis did the Supreme Court decide that segregated schooling is unconstitutional?

2. What was the long-term significance of the Montgomery Bus Boycott?

3. Did Eisenhower make the right decision regarding the Little Rock crisis? Explain.

4. By 1960, the civil rights movement had achieved success both in the courtroom and in the White House. Total participants of mass events numbered well over 100,000, including both middle-aged adults (Montgomery Bus Boycott) and college students (sit-ins). What would a contemporary observer reasonably predict to happen during the coming years?

Dwight D. Eisenhower, Second Inaugural Address (1957)

During the 1950s, Americans embraced television. Invented in 1939, the TV remained a hobbyist's toy until after World War II. From 1950 to 1952, the number of TV sets sold per year more than quadrupled. About 450 channels were broadcasting in America by 1956. Although Eisenhower became the first president to campaign on the new medium, viewers were even more entranced by entertainment than by current events—and especially by a new genre: the Western. In 1957, one-third of prime time programming consisted of sheriffs, rustlers, saloon girls, and horses. *Gunsmoke* alone aired over 600 episodes, with a quarter of the world's population viewing at least one show. Perhaps the stories of justice on the wild frontier captivated Americans because they saw a parallel to their own lives. The United States stood ready at high noon to face off against the Soviet Union, willing to use force if necessary but hoping to resolve the conflict peacefully. Eisenhower's second inaugural address focused on this Cold War tension and offered a honorable, gentlemanly peace—if only the world would be willing to accept it.

Mr. Chairman [i.e., Robert V. Fleming, chairman of the Inaugural Committee], Mr. Vice President, Mr. Chief Justice, Mr. Speaker, members of my family and friends, my countrymen, and the friends of my country wherever they may be:

We meet again, as upon a like moment four years ago, and again you have witnessed my solemn oath of service to you.

I, too, am a witness, today testifying in your name to the principles and purposes to which we, as a people, are pledged.

Before all else, we seek, upon our common labor as a nation, the blessings of Almighty God. And the hopes in our hearts fashion the deepest prayers of our whole people.

May we pursue the right—without self-righteousness.

May we know unity—without conformity.

May we grow in strength—without pride in self.

May we, in our dealings with all peoples of the earth, ever speak truth and serve justice.

And so shall America—in the sight of all men of good will—prove true to the honorable purposes that bind and rule us as a people in all this time of trial through which we pass.

We live in a land of plenty, but rarely has this earth known such peril as today.

In our nation work and wealth abound. Our population grows. Commerce crowds our rivers and rails, our skies, harbors and highways. Our soil is fertile, our agriculture productive. The air rings with the song of our industry—rolling mills and blast furnaces, dynamos, dams and assembly lines—the chorus of America the bountiful.

Now this is our home—yet this is not the whole of our world. For our world is where our full destiny lies—with men, of all peoples and all nations, who are or would be free. And for them—and so for us—this is no time of ease or of rest.

In too much of the earth there is want, discord, danger. New forces and new nations stir and strive across the earth, with power to bring, by their fate, great good or great evil to the free world's future. From the deserts of North Africa to the islands of the South Pacific one third of all mankind has entered upon an historic struggle for a new freedom: freedom from grinding poverty. Across all continents, nearly a billion people seek, sometimes almost in desperation, for the skills and knowledge and assistance by which they may satisfy from their own resources, the material wants common to all mankind.

No nation, however old or great, escapes this tempest of change and turmoil. Some, impoverished by the recent World War, seek to restore their means of livelihood. In the heart of Europe, Germany still stands tragically divided. So is the whole continent divided. And so, too, all the world.

The divisive force is International Communism and the power that it controls.

The designs of that power, dark in purpose, are clear in practice. It strives to seal forever the fate of those it has enslaved. It strives to break the ties that unite the free. And it strives to capture—to exploit for its own greater power—all forces of change in the world, especially the needs of the hungry and the hopes of the oppressed.

Yet the world of International Communism has itself been shaken by a fierce and mighty force: the readiness of men who love freedom to pledge their lives to that love. Through the night of their bondage, the unconquerable will of heroes has struck with the swift, sharp thrust of light-ning. Budapest is no longer merely the name of a city; henceforth it is a new and shining symbol of man's yearning to be free.

Thus across all the globe there harshly blow the winds of change. And, we—though fortunate be our lot—know that we can never turn our backs to them.

We look upon this shaken earth, and we declare our firm and fixed purpose—the building of a peace with justice in a world where moral law prevails.

The building of such a peace is a bold and solemn purpose. To proclaim it is easy. To serve it will be hard. And to attain it, we must be aware of its full meaning—and ready to pay its full price.

We know clearly what we seek, and why.

We seek peace, knowing that peace is the climate of freedom. And now, as in no other age, we seek it because we have been warned, by the power of modern weapons, that peace may be the only climate possible for human life itself.

Yet this peace we seek cannot be born of fear alone: it must be rooted in the lives of nations. There must be justice, sensed and shared by all peoples, for, without justice the world can know only a tense and unstable truce. There must be law, steadily invoked and respected by all nations, for without law, the world promises only such meager justice as the pity of the strong upon the weak. But the law of which we speak, comprehending the values of freedom, affirms the equality of all nations, great and small.

Splendid as can be the blessings of such

a peace, high will be its cost: in toil patiently sustained, in help honorably given, in sacrifice calmly borne.

We are called to meet the price of this peace.

To counter the threat of those who seek to rule by force, we must pay the costs of our own needed military strength, and help to build the security of others.

We must use our skills and knowledge and, at times, our substance, to help others rise from misery, however far the scene of suffering may be from our shores. For wherever in the world a people knows desperate want, there must appear at least the spark of hope, the hope of progress or there will surely rise at last the flames of conflict.

We recognize and accept our own deep involvement in the destiny of men everywhere. We are accordingly pledged to honor, and to strive to fortify, the authority of the United Nations. For in that body rests the best hope of our age for the assertion of that law by which all nations may live in dignity.

And beyond this general resolve, we are called to act a responsible role in the world's great concerns or conflicts—whether they touch upon the affairs of a vast region, the fate of an island in the Pacific, or the use of a canal in the Middle East. Only in respecting the hopes and cultures of others will we practice the equality of all nations. Only as we show willingness and wisdom in giving counsel in receiving counsel—and in sharing burdens, will we wisely perform the work of peace.

For one truth must rule all we think and all we do. No people can live to itself alone. The unity of all who dwell in freedom is their only sure defense. The economic need of all nations—in mutual dependence —makes isolation an impossibility: not even America's prosperity could long survive if other nations did not also prosper. No nation can longer be a fortress, lone and strong and safe. And any people, seeking such shelter for themselves, can now build only their own prison.

Our pledge to these principles is constant, because we believe in their rightness.

We do not fear this world of change. America is no stranger to much of its spirit. Everywhere we see the seeds of the same growth that America itself has known. The American experiment has, for generations, fired the passion and the courage of millions elsewhere seeking freedom, equality, opportunity. And the American story of material progress has helped excite the longing of all needy peoples for some satisfaction of their human wants. These hopes that we have helped to inspire, we can help to fulfill.

In this confidence, we speak plainly to all peoples.

We cherish our friendship with all nations that are or would be free. We respect, no less, their independence. And when, in time of want or peril, they ask our help, they may honorably receive it; for we no more seek to buy their sovereignty than we would sell our own. Sovereignty is never bartered among free men.

We honor the aspirations of those nations which, now captive, long for freedom. We seek neither their military alliance nor any artificial imitation of our society. And they can know the warmth of the welcome that awaits them when, as must be, they join again the ranks of freedom.

We honor, no less in this divided world than in a less tormented time, the people of Russia. We do not dread, rather do we welcome, their progress in education and industry. We wish them success in their demands for more intellectual freedom, greater security before their own laws, fuller enjoyment of the rewards of their own toil. For as such things come to pass, the more certain will be the coming of that day when our peoples may freely meet in friendship.

So we voice our hope and our belief that we can help to heal this divided world.

Thus may the nations cease to live in trembling before the menace of force. Thus may the weight of fear and the weight of arms be taken from the burdened shoulders of mankind.

This, nothing less, is the labor to which we are called and our strength dedicated.

And so the prayer of our people carries far beyond our own frontiers, to the wide world of our duty and our destiny.

May the light of freedom, coming to all darkened lands, flame brightly—until at last the darkness is no more.

May the turbulence of our age yield to a true time of peace, when men and nations shall share a life that honors the dignity of each, the brotherhood of all.

Thank you very much.

Study Questions

1. To what extent did Eisenhower agree with the Truman Doctrine?

2. How are law and justice related in Eisenhower's view—in other words, what was his conception of ordered liberty?

Dwight D. Eisenhower, "Military-Industrial Complex Speech" (1961)

As the nation awaited the inauguration of President-elect John F. Kennedy in January 1961, the current president, Dwight D. Eisenhower, spoke one last time to the American people. One sentence has echoed through the years to the present day, a solemn warning that "we must guard against the acquisition of unwarranted influence, whether sought or unsought, by the military-industrial complex." Eisenhower was referring to the triangular cooperation among university science departments, defense contract industries, and the federal government—a combination powerful enough to take a firm stand against the Soviet Union, but also powerful enough wreak havoc in America and throughout the world.

My fellow Americans:

Three days from now, after half a century in the service of our country, I shall lay down the responsibilities of office as, in traditional and solemn ceremony, the authority of the Presidency is vested in my successor.

This evening I come to you with a message of leave-taking and farewell, and to share a few final thoughts with you, my countrymen.

Like every other citizen, I wish the new President, and all who will labor with him, Godspeed. I pray that the coming years will be blessed with peace and prosperity for all.

Our people expect their President and the Congress to find essential agreement on issues of great moment, the wise resolution of which will better shape the future of the Nation.

My own relations with the Congress, which began on a remote and tenuous basis when, long ago, a member of the Senate appointed me to West Point, have since ranged to the intimate during the war and immediate post-war period, and,

finally, to the mutually interdependent during these past eight years.

In this final relationship, the Congress and the Administration have, on most vital issues, cooperated well, to serve the national good rather than mere partisanship, and so have assured that the business of the Nation should go forward. So, my official relationship with the Congress ends in a feeling, on my part, of gratitude that we have been able to do so much together.

II.

We now stand ten years past the midpoint of a century that has witnessed four major wars among great nations. Three of these involved our own country. Despite these holocausts America is today the strongest, the most influential and most productive nation in the world. Understandably proud of this pre-eminence, we yet realize that America's leadership and prestige depend, not merely upon our unmatched material progress, riches and military strength, but on how we use our power in the interests of world peace and human betterment.

III.

Throughout America's adventure in free government, our basic purposes have been to keep the peace; to foster progress in human achievement, and to enhance liberty, dignity and integrity among people and among nations. To strive for less would be unworthy of a free and religious people. Any failure traceable to arrogance, or our lack of comprehension or readiness to sacrifice would inflict upon us grievous hurt both at home and abroad.

Progress toward these noble goals is persistently threatened by the conflict now engulfing the world. It commands our whole attention, absorbs our very beings. We face a hostile ideology—global in scope, atheistic in character, ruthless in purpose, and insidious in method. Unhappily the danger is poses promises to be of indefinite duration. To meet it successfully, there is called for, not so much the emotional and transitory sacrifices of crisis, but rather those which enable us to carry forward steadily, surely, and without complaint the burdens of a prolonged and complex struggle—with liberty the stake. Only thus shall we remain, despite every provocation, on our charted course toward permanent peace and human betterment.

Crises there will continue to be. In meeting them, whether foreign or domestic, great or small, there is a recurring temptation to feel that some spectacular and costly action could become the miraculous solution to all current difficulties. A huge increase in newer elements of our defense; development of unrealistic programs to cure every ill in agriculture; a dramatic expansion in basic and applied research—these and many other possibilities, each possibly promising in itself, may be suggested as the only way to the road we wish to travel.

But each proposal must be weighed in the light of a broader consideration: the need to maintain balance in and among national programs—balance between the private and the public economy, balance between cost and hoped for advantage—balance between the clearly necessary and the comfortably desirable; balance between our essential requirements as a nation and the duties imposed by the nation upon the individual; balance between actions of the moment and the national welfare of the future. Good judgment seeks balance and progress; lack of it eventually finds imbalance and frustration.

The record of many decades stands as proof that our people and their government have, in the main, understood these truths and have responded to them well, in the face of stress and threat. But threats, new in kind or degree, constantly arise. I mention two only.

IV.

A vital element in keeping the peace is our military establishment. Our arms must be mighty, ready for instant action, so that no potential aggressor may be tempted to risk his own destruction.

Our military organization today bears little relation to that known by any of my predecessors in peacetime, or indeed by the fighting men of World War II or Korea.

Until the latest of our world conflicts, the United States had no armaments industry. American makers of plowshares could, with time and as required, make swords as well. But now we can no longer risk emergency improvisation of national defense; we have been compelled to create a permanent armaments industry of vast proportions. Added to this, three and a half million men and women are directly engaged in the defense establishment. We annually spend on military security more than the net income of all United States corporations.

This conjunction of an immense military establishment and a large arms industry is new in the American experience. The total influence—economic, political, even spiritual—is felt in every city, every State house, every office of the Federal government. We recognize the imperative need for this development. Yet we must not fail to comprehend its grave implications. Our toil, resources and livelihood are all involved; so is the very structure of our society.

In the councils of government, we must guard against the acquisition of unwarranted influence, whether sought or unsought, by the military-industrial complex. The potential for the disastrous rise of misplaced power exists and will persist.

We must never let the weight of this combination endanger our liberties or democratic processes. We should take nothing for granted. Only an alert and knowledgeable citizenry can compel the proper meshing of the huge industrial and military machinery of defense with our peaceful methods and goals, so that security and liberty may prosper together.

Akin to, and largely responsible for the sweeping changes in our industrial-military posture, has been the technological revolution during recent decades.

In this revolution, research has become central; it also becomes more formalized, complex, and costly. A steadily increasing share is conducted for, by, or at the direction of, the Federal government.

Today, the solitary inventor, tinkering in his shop, has been overshadowed by task forces of scientists in laboratories and testing fields. In the same fashion, the free university, historically the fountainhead of free ideas and scientific discovery, has experienced a revolution in the conduct of research. Partly because of the huge costs involved, a government contract becomes virtually a substitute for intellectual curiosity. For every old blackboard there are now hundreds of new electronic computers.

The prospect of domination of the nation's scholars by Federal employment, project allocations, and the power of money is ever present and is gravely to be regarded. Yet, in holding scientific research and discovery in respect, as we should, we must also be alert to the equal and opposite danger that public policy could itself become the captive of a scientific-technological elite.

It is the task of statesmanship to mold, to balance, and to integrate these and other forces, new and old, within the principles of our democratic system—ever aiming toward the supreme goals of our free society.

V.

Another factor in maintaining balance

involves the element of time. As we peer into society's future, we—you and I, and our government—must avoid the impulse to live only for today, plundering, for our own ease and convenience, the precious resources of tomorrow. We cannot mortgage the material assets of our grandchildren without risking the loss also of their political and spiritual heritage. We want democracy to survive for all generations to come, not to become the insolvent phantom of tomorrow.

VI.

Down the long lane of the history yet to be written America knows that this world of ours, ever growing smaller, must avoid becoming a community of dreadful fear and hate, and be instead, a proud confederation of mutual trust and respect.

Such a confederation must be one of equals. The weakest must come to the conference table with the same confidence as do we, protected as we are by our moral, economic, and military strength. That table, though scarred by many past frustrations, cannot be abandoned for the certain agony of the battlefield.

Disarmament, with mutual honor and confidence, is a continuing imperative. Together we must learn how to compose differences, not with arms, but with intellect and decent purpose. Because this need is so sharp and apparent I confess that I lay down my official responsibilities in this field with a definite sense of disappointment. As one who has witnessed the horror and the lingering sadness of war— as one who knows that another war could utterly destroy this civilization which has been so slowly and painfully built over

thousands of years—I wish I could say tonight that a lasting peace is in sight.

Happily, I can say that war has been avoided. Steady progress toward our ultimate goal has been made. But, so much remains to be done. As a private citizen, I shall never cease to do what little I can to help the world advance along that road.

VII.

So—in this my last good night to you as your President—I thank you for the many opportunities you have given me for public service in war and peace. I trust that in that service you find some things worthy; as for the rest of it, I know you will find ways to improve performance in the future.

You and I—my fellow citizens—need to be strong in our faith that all nations, under God, will reach the goal of peace with justice. May we be ever unswerving in devotion to principle, confident but humble with power, diligent in pursuit of the Nation's great goals.

To all the peoples of the world, I once more give expression to America's prayerful and continuing aspiration:

We pray that peoples of all faiths, all races, all nations, may have their great human needs satisfied; that those now denied opportunity shall come to enjoy it to the full; that all who yearn for freedom may experience its spiritual blessings; that those who have freedom will understand, also, its heavy responsibilities; that all who are insensitive to the needs of others will learn charity; that the scourges of poverty, disease and ignorance will be made to disappear from the earth, and that, in the goodness of time, all peoples will come to live together in a peace guaranteed by the binding force of mutual respect and love.

Study Questions

1. What was the "military-industrial complex" and why did Eisenhower warn against it?

2. What, according to Eisenhower, was the "task of statesmanship" in this Cold War context as applied to economic progress and technological advancement?

John F. Kennedy, Inaugural Address (1961)

The 1960 presidential contest centered on two candidates who superficially had much in common even though the media drew sharp contrasts between them. Both were young, both had served in the military, both had served in Congress, and both had strong followings among their constituents. Indeed, both received 50% of the popular vote—or more precisely, Kennedy received 49.7% and Nixon received 49.5%. The slight edge in the popular vote translated into a clear margin in the electoral vote, with Kennedy defeating Nixon 303 to 219. The close decision may have tilted on the perceptions of television viewers who watched a debate between the candidates shortly before election day. Nixon, suffering from a cold, appeared nervous on camera, whereas Kennedy held his poise throughout the program. Those who listened on radio, however, did not give Kennedy such an advantage, as both candidates ably presented their views orally. Henceforth campaign managers would recognize that in order to win the American people, one must score a victory with the television cameras.

Vice President Johnson, Mr. Speaker, Mr. Chief Justice, President Eisenhower, Vice President Nixon, President Truman, Reverend Clergy [i.e., His Eminence Richard Cardinal Cushing, Archbishop of Boston; His Eminence Archbishop Iakovos, head of the Greek Archdiocese of North and South America; the Reverend Dr. John Barclay, pastor of the Central Christian Church, Austin, Tex.; and Rabbi Dr. Nelson Glueck, President of the Hebrew Union College, Cincinnati, Ohio], fellow citizens:

We observe today not a victory of party but a celebration of freedom—symbolizing an end as well as a beginning—signifying renewal as well as change. For I have sworn before you and Almighty God the same solemn oath our forebears prescribed nearly a century and three quarters ago.

The world is very different now. For man holds in his mortal hands the power to abolish all forms of human poverty and all forms of human life. And yet the same revolutionary beliefs for which our fore-bears fought are still at issue around the globe—the belief that the rights of man come not from the generosity of the state but from the hand of God.

We dare not forget today that we are the heirs of that first revolution. Let the word go forth from this time and place, to friend and foe alike, that the torch has been passed to a new generation of Americans—born in this century, tempered by war, disciplined by a hard and bitter peace, proud of our ancient heritage—and unwilling to witness or permit the slow undoing of those human rights to which this nation has always been committed, and to which we are committed today at home and around the world.

Let every nation know, whether it wishes us well or ill, that we shall pay any price, bear any burden, meet any hardship, support any friend, oppose any foe to assure the survival and the success of liberty.

This much we pledge—and more.

To those old allies whose cultural and

spiritual origins we share, we pledge the loyalty of faithful friends. United, there is little we cannot do in a host of cooperative ventures. Divided, there is little we can do —for we dare not meet a powerful challenge at odds and split asunder.

To those new states whom we welcome to the ranks of the free, we pledge our word that one form of colonial control shall not have passed away merely to be replaced by a far more iron tyranny. We shall not always expect to find them supporting our view. But we shall always hope to find them strongly supporting their own freedom—and to remember that, in the past, those who foolishly sought power by riding the back of the tiger ended up inside.

To those peoples in the huts and villages of half the globe struggling to break the bonds of mass misery, we pledge our best efforts to help them help themselves, for whatever period is required—not because the communists may be doing it, not because we seek their votes, but because it is right. If a free society cannot help the many who are poor, it cannot save the few who are rich.

To our sister republics south of our border, we offer a special pledge—to convert our good words into good deeds—in a new alliance for progress—to assist free men and free governments in casting off the chains of poverty. But this peaceful revolution of hope cannot become the prey of hostile powers. Let all our neighbors know that we shall join with them to oppose aggression or subversion anywhere in the Americas. And let every other power know that this Hemisphere intends to remain the master of its own house.

To that world assembly of sovereign states, the United Nations, our last best hope in an age where the instruments of war have far outpaced the instruments of peace, we renew our pledge of support—to prevent it from becoming merely a forum for invective—to strengthen its shield of the new and the weak—and to enlarge the area in which its writ may run.

Finally, to those nations who would make themselves our adversary, we offer not a pledge but a request: that both sides begin anew the quest for peace, before the dark powers of destruction unleashed by science engulf all humanity in planned or accidental self-destruction.

We dare not tempt them with weakness. For only when our arms are sufficient beyond doubt can we be certain beyond doubt that they will never be employed.

But neither can two great and powerful groups of nations take comfort from our present course—both sides overburdened by the cost of modern weapons, both rightly alarmed by the steady spread of the deadly atom, yet both racing to alter that uncertain balance of terror that stays the hand of mankind's final war.

So let us begin anew—remembering on both sides that civility is not a sign of weakness, and sincerity is always subject to proof. Let us never negotiate out of fear. But let us never fear to negotiate.

Let both sides explore what problems unite us instead of belaboring those problems which divide us.

Let both sides, for the first time, formulate serious and precise proposals for the inspection and control of arms—and bring the absolute power to destroy other nations under the absolute control of all nations.

Let both sides seek to invoke the wonders of science instead of its terrors. Together let us explore the stars, conquer the deserts, eradicate disease, tap the ocean depths and encourage the arts and commerce.

Let both sides unite to heed in all corners of the earth the command of Isaiah—to "undo the heavy burdens . . . (and) let the oppressed go free."

And if a beach-head of cooperation may push back the jungle of suspicion, let both sides join in creating a new endeavor, not a new balance of power, but a new world of law, where the strong are just and the weak secure and the peace preserved.

All this will not be finished in the first one hundred days. Nor will it be finished in the first one thousand days, nor in the life of this Administration, nor even perhaps in our lifetime on this planet. But let us begin.

In your hands, my fellow citizens, more than mine, will rest the final success or failure of our course. Since this country was founded, each generation of Americans has been summoned to give testimony to its national loyalty. The graves of young Americans who answered the call to service surround the globe.

Now the trumpet summons us again—not as a call to bear arms, though arms we need—not as a call to battle, though embattled we are—but a call to bear the burden of a long twilight struggle, year in and year out, "rejoicing in hope, patient in tribulation"—a struggle against the common enemies of man: tyranny, poverty, disease and war itself.

Can we forge against these enemies a grand and global alliance, North and South, East and West, that can assure a more fruitful life for all mankind? Will you join in that historic effort?

In the long history of the world, only a few generations have been granted the role of defending freedom in its hour of maximum danger. I do not shrink from this responsibility—I welcome it. I do not believe that any of us would exchange places with any other people or any other generation. The energy, the faith, the devotion which we bring to this endeavor will light our country and all who serve it—and the glow from that fire can truly light the world.

And so, my fellow Americans: ask not what your country can do for you—ask what you can do for your country.

My fellow citizens of the world: ask not what America will do for you, but what together we can do for the freedom of man.

Finally, whether you are citizens of America or citizens of the world, ask of us here the same high standards of strength and sacrifice which we ask of you. With a good conscience our only sure reward, with history the final judge of our deeds, let us go forth to lead the land we love, asking His blessing and His help, but knowing that here on earth God's work must truly be our own.

Study Questions

1. Where, according to Kennedy, do the rights of men originate?

2. List three challenges that Kennedy identified for the American people. How, specifically, did he propose that Americans respond to those challenges?

3. What did Kennedy ask of his fellow Americans, and what did he ask of his fellow citizens of the world?

John F. Kennedy, "The Berlin Crisis" (1961)

In 1955, President Eisenhower met with leaders from the Soviet Union, Great Britain, and France at Geneva, Switzerland. The "Big Four" convened this Geneva Summit for the purpose of reducing international tensions and fostering global security. They discussed free trade, arms reductions, and the possibility of reunifying Germany. Although no promises were made, the press reported that a fresh "spirit of Geneva" was reshaping the Cold War for the better. Soon, however, the Americans and the Soviets each had reason to suspect one another of duplicity. In November 1956, Soviet tanks rolled into Budapest to prevent a democratic government from ousting the Soviet influence from that country. But there also was another side to the Cold War story. In May 1960, the Soviets discovered and shot down an American U–2 spy plan flying in their air space. Soviet Premier Nikita Khrushchev was alarmed that the CIA was conducting covert surveillance of the Soviet Union. With the U–2 incident preceding a Paris Summit of the Big Four by just two weeks, the spirit of optimism inherited from the Geneva Summit evaporated. Eisenhower and Khrushchev faced off in a tense debate, with Khrushchev rescinding his earlier offer for Eisenhower to visit the Soviet Union. When John F. Kennedy assumed the presidency in the following year, the responsibility of dealing with Khrushchev continued. Kennedy delivered the following address in July 1961; within a month, East Germany constructed the Berlin Wall—a barrier that would separate East and West Berlin until 1989.

Good evening:

Seven weeks ago tonight I returned from Europe to report on my meeting with Premier Khrushchev and the others. His grim warnings about the future of the world, his aide memoire on Berlin, his subsequent speeches and threats which he and his agents have launched, and the increase in the Soviet military budget that he has announced, have all prompted a series of decisions by the Administration and a series of consultations with the members of the NATO organization. In Berlin, as you recall, he intends to bring to an end, through a stroke of the pen, first our legal rights to be in West Berlin—and secondly our ability to make good on our commitment to the two million free people of that city. That we cannot permit.

We are clear about what must be done —and we intend to do it. I want to talk frankly with you tonight about the first steps that we shall take. These actions will require sacrifice on the part of many of our citizens. More will be required in the future. They will require, from all of us, courage and perseverance in the years to come. But if we and our allies act out of strength and unity of purpose—with calm determination and steady nerves—using restraint in our words as well as our weapons. I am hopeful that both peace and freedom will be sustained.

The immediate threat to free men is in West Berlin. But that isolated outpost is not an isolated problem. The threat is worldwide. Our effort must be equally wide and strong, and not be obsessed by any single manufactured crisis. We face a challenge in Berlin, but there is also a challenge in Southeast Asia, where the borders are less guarded, the enemy harder to find, and the dangers of communism less apparent to those who have so little. We face a challenge in our own hemisphere, and indeed wherever else the freedom of human beings is at stake.

Let me remind you that the fortunes of war and diplomacy left the free people of West Berlin, in 1945, 110 miles behind the Iron Curtain.

This map makes very dear the problem that we face. The white is West Germany— the East is the area controlled by the Soviet Union, and as you can see from the chart, West Berlin is 110 miles within the area which the Soviets now dominate— which is immediately controlled by the so-called East German regime.

We are there as a result of our victory over Nazi Germany—and our basic rights to be there, deriving from that victory, include both our presence in West Berlin and the enjoyment of access across East Germany. These rights have been repeatedly confirmed and recognized in special agreements with the Soviet Union. Berlin is not a part of East Germany, but a separate territory under the control of the allied powers. Thus our rights there are clear and deep-rooted. But in addition to those rights is our commitment to sustain —and defend, if need be—the opportunity for more than two million people to determine their own future and choose their own way of life.

II.

Thus, our presence in West Berlin, and our access thereto, cannot be ended by any act of the Soviet government. The NATO shield was long ago extended to cover West Berlin—and we have given our word that an attack upon that city will be regarded as an attack upon us all.

For West Berlin lying exposed 110 miles inside East Germany, surrounded by Soviet troops and close to Soviet supply lines, has many roles. It is more than a showcase of liberty, a symbol, an island of freedom in a Communist sea. It is even more than a link with the Free World, a beacon of hope behind the Iron Curtain, an escape hatch for refugees.

West Berlin is all of that. But above all it has now become—as never before—the great testing place of Western courage and will, a focal point where our solemn commitments stretching back over the years since 1945, and Soviet ambitions now meet in basic confrontation.

It would be a mistake for others to look upon Berlin, because of its location, as a tempting target. The United States is there; the United Kingdom and France are there; the pledge of NATO is there—and the people of Berlin are there. It is as secure, in that sense, as the rest of us—for we cannot separate its safety from our own.

I hear it said that West Berlin is militarily untenable. And so was Bastogne. And so, in fact, was Stalingrad. Any dangerous spot is tenable if men—brave men—will make it so.

We do not want to fight—but we have fought before. And others in earlier times have made the same dangerous mistake of assuming that the West was too selfish and too soft and too divided to resist invasions of freedom in other lands. Those who threaten to unleash the forces of war on a dispute over West Berlin should recall the words of the ancient philosopher: "A man who causes fear cannot be free from fear."

We cannot and will not permit the Communists to drive us out of Berlin, either gradually or by force. For the fulfillment of our pledge to that city is essential to the morale and security of Western Germany, to the unity of Western Europe, and to the faith of the entire Free World. Soviet strategy has long been aimed, not merely at Berlin, but at dividing and neutralizing all of Europe, forcing us back on our own shores. We must meet our oft-stated pledge to the free peoples of West Berlin—and maintain our rights and their safety, even in the face of force—in order to maintain the confidence of other free peoples in our word and our resolve. The strength of the alliance on which our security depends is dependent in turn on our willingness to meet our commitments to them.

III.

So long as the Communists insist that they are preparing to end by themselves unilaterally our rights in West Berlin and our commitments to its people, we must be prepared to defend those rights and those commitments. We will at all times be ready to talk, if talk will help. But we must also be ready to resist with force, if force is used upon us. Either alone would fail. Together, they can serve the cause of freedom and peace.

The new preparations that we shall make to defend the peace are part of the long-term build-up in our strength which has been underway since January. They are based on our needs to meet a worldwide threat, on a basis which stretches far beyond the present Berlin crisis. Our primary purpose is neither propaganda nor provocation—but preparation.

A first need is to hasten progress toward the military goals which the North Atlantic allies have set for themselves. In Europe today nothing less will suffice. We will put even greater resources into fulfilling those goals, and we look to our allies to do the same.

The supplementary defense build-ups that I asked from the Congress in March and May have already started moving us toward these and our other defense goals. They included an increase in the size of the Marine Corps, improved readiness of our reserves, expansion of our air and sea lift, and stepped-up procurement of needed weapons, ammunition, and other items. To insure a continuing invulnerable capacity to deter or destroy any aggressor, they provided for the strengthening of our missile power and for putting 50% of our B–52 and B–47 bombers on a ground alert which would send them on their way with 15 minutes' warning.

These measures must be speeded up, and still others must now be taken. We must have sea and air lift capable of moving our forces quickly and in large numbers to any part of the world.

But even more importantly, we need the capability of placing in any critical area at the appropriate time a force which, combined with those of our allies, is large enough to make clear our determination and our ability to defend our rights at all costs—and to meet all levels of aggressor pressure with whatever levels of force are required. We intend to have a wider choice than humiliation or all-out nuclear action. While it is unwise at this time either to call up or send abroad excessive numbers of these troops before they are needed, let me make it clear that I intend to take, as time goes on, whatever steps are necessary to make certain that such forces can be deployed at the appropriate time without lessening our ability to meet our commitments elsewhere.

Thus, in the days and months ahead, I shall not hesitate to ask the Congress for additional measures, or exercise any of the executive powers that I possess to meet this threat to peace. Everything essential to the security of freedom must be done; and if that should require more men, or more taxes, or more controls, or other new powers, I shall not hesitate to ask them. The measures proposed today will be constantly studied, and altered as necessary. But while we will not let panic shape our policy, neither will we permit timidity to direct our program.

Accordingly, I am now taking the following steps:

(1) I am tomorrow requesting the Congress for the current fiscal year an additional $3,247,000,000 of appropriations for the Armed Forces.

(2) To fill out our present Army Divisions, and to make more men available for prompt deployment, I am requesting an increase in the Army's total authorized strength from 875,000 to approximately 1 million men.

(3) I am requesting an increase of 29,000 and 63,000 men respectively in the active duty strength of the Navy and the Air Force.

(4) To fulfill these manpower needs, I am ordering that our draft calls be doubled and tripled in the coming months; I am asking the Congress for authority to order to active duty certain ready reserve units and individual reservists, and to extend tours of duty; and, under that authority, I am planning to order to active duty a number of air transport squadrons and Air National Guard tactical air squadrons, to give us the airlift capacity and protection that we need. Other reserve forces will be called up when needed.

(5) Many ships and planes once headed for retirement are to be retained or reactivated, increasing our airpower tactically and our sealift, airlift, and anti-submarine warfare capability. In addition, our strategic air power will be increased by delaying the deactivation of B–47 bombers.

(6) Finally, some $1.8 billion—about half of the total sum—is needed for the procurement of non-nuclear weapons, ammunition and equipment.

The details on all these requests will be presented to the Congress tomorrow. Subsequent steps will be taken to suit subsequent needs. Comparable efforts for the common defense are being discussed with our NATO allies. For their commitment and interest are as precise as our own.

And let me add that I am well aware of the fact that many American families will bear the burden of these requests. Studies or careers will be interrupted; husbands and sons will be called away; incomes in some cases will be reduced. But these are burdens which must be borne if freedom is to be defended—Americans have willingly borne them before—and they will not flinch from the task now.

IV.

We have another sober responsibility. To recognize the possibilities of nuclear war in the missile age, without our citizens knowing what they should do and where they should go if bombs begin to fall, would be a failure of responsibility. In May, I pledged a new start on Civil Defense. Last week, I assigned, on the recommendation of the Civil Defense Director, basic responsibility for this program to the Secretary of Defense, to make certain it is administered and coordinated with our continental defense efforts at the highest civilian level. Tomorrow, I am requesting of the Congress new funds for the following immediate objectives: to identify and mark space in existing structures—public and private—that could be used for fall-out shelters in case of attack; to stock those shelters with food, water, first-aid kits and other minimum essentials for survival; to increase their capacity; to improve our air-raid warning and fall-out detection systems, including a new household warning system which is now under development; and to take other measures that will be effective at an early date to save millions of lives if needed.

In the event of an attack, the lives of those families which are not hit in a nuclear blast and fire can still be saved—if they can be warned to take shelter and if that shelter is available. We owe that kind of insurance to our families—and to our country. In contrast to our friends in Europe, the need for this kind of protection is new to our shores. But the time to start is now. In the coming months, I hope to let every citizen know what steps he can take without delay to protect his family in case of attack. I know that you will want to do no less.

V.

The addition of $207 million in Civil Defense appropriations brings our total new defense budget requests to $3.454 billion, and a total of $47.5 billion for the year. This is an increase in the defense budget of $6 billion since January, and has resulted in official estimates of a budget deficit of over $5 billion. The Secretary of the Treasury and other economic advisers assure me, however, that our economy has the capacity to bear this new request.

We are recovering strongly from this year's recession. The increase in this last quarter of our year of our total national output was greater than that for any postwar period of initial recovery. And yet, wholesale prices are actually lower than they were during the recession, and consumer prices are only 1/4 of 1% higher than they were last October. In fact, this last quarter was the first in eight years in which our production has increased without an increase in the overall-price index. And for the first time since the fall of 1959, our gold position has improved and the dollar is more respected abroad. These gains, it should be stressed, are being accomplished with Budget deficits far smaller than those of the 1958 recession.

This improved business outlook means

improved revenues; and I intend to submit to the Congress in January a budget for the next fiscal year which will be strictly in balance. Nevertheless, should an increase in taxes be needed—because of events in the next few months—to achieve that balance, or because of subsequent defense rises, those increased taxes will be requested in January.

Meanwhile, to help make certain that the current deficit is held to a safe level, we must keep down all expenditures not thoroughly justified in budget requests. The luxury of our current post-office deficit must be ended. Costs in military procurement will be closely scrutinized—and in this effort I welcome the cooperation of the Congress. The tax loopholes I have specified—on expense accounts, overseas income, dividends, interest, cooperatives and others—must be closed.

I realize that no public revenue measure is welcomed by everyone. But I am certain that every American wants to pay his fair share, and not leave the burden of defending freedom entirely to those who bear arms. For we have mortgaged our very future on this defense—and we cannot fail to meet our responsibilities.

VI.

But I must emphasize again that the choice is not merely between resistance and retreat, between atomic holocaust and surrender. Our peace-time military posture is traditionally defensive; but our diplomatic posture need not be. Our response to the Berlin crisis will not be merely military or negative. It will be more than merely standing firm. For we do not intend to leave it to others to choose and monopolize the forum and the framework of discussion. We do not intend to abandon our duty to mankind to seek a peaceful solution.

As signers of the UN Charter, we shall always be prepared to discuss international problems with any and all nations that are willing to talk—and listen—with reason. If they have proposals—not demands—we shall hear them. If they seek genuine understanding—not concessions of our rights—we shall meet with them. We have previously indicated our readiness to remove any actual irritants in West Berlin, but the freedom of that city is not negotiable. We cannot negotiate with those who say "What's mine is mine and what's yours is negotiable." But we are willing to consider any arrangement or treaty in Germany consistent with the maintenance of peace and freedom, and with the legitimate security interests of all nations.

We recognize the Soviet Union's historical concern about their security in Central and Eastern Europe, after a series of ravaging invasions, and we believe arrangements can be worked out which will help to meet those concerns, and make it possible for both security and freedom to exist in this troubled area.

For it is not the freedom of West Berlin which is "abnormal" in Germany today, but the situation in that entire divided country. If anyone doubts the legality of our rights in Berlin, we are ready to have it submitted to international adjudication. If anyone doubts the extent to which our presence is desired by the people of West Berlin, compared to East German feelings about their regime, we are ready to have that question submitted to a free vote in Berlin and, if possible, among all the German people. And let us hear at that time from the two and one-half million refugees who have fled the Communist regime in East Germany—voting for Western-type freedom with their feet.

The world is not deceived by the Communist attempt to label Berlin as a hot-bed of war. There is peace in Berlin today. The source of world trouble and tension is Moscow, not Berlin. And if war begins, it will have begun in Moscow and not Berlin.

For the choice of peace or war is largely theirs, not ours. It is the Soviets who have stirred up this crisis. It is they who are trying to force a change. It is they who have opposed free elections. It is they who have rejected an all-German peace treaty, and the rulings of international law. And as Americans know from our history on our own old frontier, gun battles are caused by outlaws, and not by officers of the peace.

In short, while we are ready to defend our interests, we shall also be ready to search for peace—in quiet exploratory talks—in formal or informal meetings. We do not want military considerations to dominate the thinking of either East or West. And Mr. Khrushchev may find that his invitation to other nations to join in a meaningless treaty may lead to their inviting him to join in the community of peaceful men, in abandoning the use of force, and in respecting the sanctity of agreements.

VII.

While all of these efforts go on, we must not be diverted from our total responsibil-ities, from other dangers, from other tasks. If new threats in Berlin or elsewhere should cause us to weaken our program of assistance to the developing nations who are also under heavy pressure from the same source, or to halt our efforts for realistic disarmament, or to disrupt or slow down our economy, or to neglect the education of our children, then those threats will surely be the most successful and least costly maneuver in Communist history. For we can afford all these efforts, and more but we cannot afford not to meet this challenge.

And the challenge is not to us alone. It is a challenge to every nation which asserts its sovereignty under a system of liberty. It is a challenge to all those who want a world of free choice. It is a special challenge to the Atlantic Community—the heartland of human freedom.

We in the West must move together in building military strength. We must consult one another more closely than ever before. We must together design our proposals for peace, and labor together as they are pressed at the conference table. And together we must share the burdens and the risks of this effort.

The Atlantic Community, as we know it, has been built in response to challenge: the challenge of European chaos in 1947, of the Berlin blockade in 1948, the challenge of Communist aggression in Korea in 1950. Now, standing strong and prosperous, after an unprecedented decade of progress, the Atlantic Community will not forget either its history or the principles which gave it meaning.

The solemn vow each of us gave to West

Berlin in time of peace will not be broken in time of danger. If we do not meet our commitments to Berlin, where will we later stand? If we are not true to our word there, all that we have achieved in collective security, which relies on these words, will mean nothing. And if there is one path above all others to war, it is the path of weakness and disunity.

Today, the endangered frontier of freedom runs through divided Berlin. We want it to remain a frontier of peace. This is the hope of every citizen of the Atlantic Community; every citizen of Eastern Europe; and, I am confident, every citizen of the Soviet Union. For I cannot believe that the Russian people—who bravely suffered enormous losses in the Second World War —would now wish to see the peace upset once more in Germany. The Soviet government alone can convert Berlin's frontier of peace into a pretext for war.

The steps I have indicated tonight are aimed at avoiding that war. To sum it all up: we seek peace—but we shall not surrender. That is the central meaning of this crisis, and the meaning of your government's policy.

With your help, and the help of other free men, this crisis can be surmounted. Freedom can prevail—and peace can endure.

I would like to close with a personal word. When I ran for the Presidency of the United States, I knew that this country faced serious challenges, but I could not realize—nor could any man realize who does not bear the burdens of this office— how heavy and constant would be those burdens.

Three times in my life-time our country and Europe have been involved in major wars. In each case serious misjudgments were made on both sides of the intentions of others, which brought about great devastation.

Now, in the thermonuclear age, any misjudgment on either side about the intentions of the other could rain more devastation in several hours than has been wrought in all the wars of human history.

Therefore I, as President and Commander-in-Chief, and all of us as Americans, are moving through serious days. I shall bear this responsibility under our Constitution for the next three and one-half years, but I am sure that we all, regardless of our occupations, will do our very best for our country, and for our cause. For all of us want to see our children grow up in a country at peace, and in a world where freedom endures.

I know that sometimes we get impatient, we wish for some immediate action that would end our perils. But I must tell you that there is no quick and easy solution. The Communists control over a billion people, and they recognize that if we should falter, their success would be imminent.

We must look to long days ahead, which if we are courageous and persevering can bring us what we all desire.

In these days and weeks I ask for your help, and your advice. I ask for your suggestions, when you think we could do better.

All of us, I know, love our country, and we shall all do our best to serve it.

In meeting my responsibilities in these coming months as President, I need your good will, and your support—and above all, your prayers.

Thank you, and good night.

Study Question

1. What did Kennedy mean when he called West Berlin "the great testing place of Western courage and will"?

2. What was Kennedy planning to ask of Congress in response to the Berlin crisis?

3. What, to Kennedy, was the "central meaning of this crisis"?

The Expansion of the Civil Rights Movement, 1961–1963

In the mid 1960s, the African American civil rights movement reached its zenith. Northern whites increasingly sympathized with southern blacks, while southern whites who resisted the movement fell behind the changing times. When local law enforcement failed to keep the peace, the federal government had little choice but to act. The movement's mainstream followed the leadership of Martin Luther King, who celebrated the guarantees of personal liberty and equal rights before the law as contained in the nation's founding documents—the Declaration of Independence and the U.S. Constitution. A reformer more than a revolutionary, King knew how to rally white politicians to his people's cause. Indeed, he knew how to frame the issue as all humanity's cause. But King did not act alone. Other leaders emerged with ambitions of their own.

The Freedom Riders (1961)

When blacks in the Deep South wrote letters to the Chicago-based Congress for Racial Equality (CORE) to complain about segregation on interstate buses and at bus stations, CORE planned an interracial "freedom ride." Blacks and whites would ride through the South side-by-side in friendship, ignoring Jim Crow. Starting in Washington, DC, the freedom riders aimed to arrive in New Orleans on May 17, 1961—the anniversary of the *Brown* ruling. Like King's followers in the Montgomery Bus Boycott of 1955–1956 and the sit-in participants of 1960, the freedom riders committed themselves to the principle of nonviolence, borrowed both from Jesus Christ and Mahatma Ghandi. CORE's national director, James Farmer, took encouragement from recent Supreme Court decisions prohibiting racial discrimination in interstate transportation. Having federal law on their side, the freedom riders sought to make a spectacle of southern whites who might harass them along their journey.

Harassment was not the half of it. In Anniston, Alabama—sixty miles east of Birmingham—the bus driver himself used the n-word and delivered the freedom riders into the hands of a white mob. Windows were smashed, tires were slashed, and a smoke bomb forced the riders out, resulting in serious wounds to several riders whom the mob pummeled as they exited. One of the white freedom riders suffered such trauma that he was confined to a wheelchair for life. After an Alabama state patrolmen called the attackers off, the Rev. Fred Shuttlesworth of the Southern Christian Leadership Conference sent rescue cars.

When the freedom riders resumed their journey, more trouble broke out. As FBI director J. Edgar Hoover, Attorney General Robert Kennedy, and local government officials negotiated by telephone, the riders fled from one ambush to another until finally being carted off to a state prison in Mississippi. With the riders behind bars, under pretentious charges of "disorderly conduct," thousands of other southern blacks took their places to integrate bus terminals. Finally, the attorney general directed the Interstate Commerce Commission to require that all interstate terminals display signs clearly stating that seating was available without regard to race. Thus, the Supreme Court ruling to desegregate interstate transportation was implemented at last.

The Albany Movement (1961–1962)

Following the success of the freedom rides, a young Baptist preacher named Charles Sherrod mobilized the Student Nonviolent Coordinating Committee (SNCC) to recruit other civil rights groups into a partnership known as the Albany Movement. Founded by two locals—a pharmacist and a realtor—the Albany Movement first tried to sway city officials into desegregating downtown businesses by organizing boycotts. The next phase involved sit-ins that targeted hotels, restaurants, and theaters. Chief of Police Laurie Pritchett, meanwhile, had been doing his homework. He knew that the earlier civil rights victories had depended upon the sympathy that northern whites had for southern blacks who suffered violence from local whites. Pritchett therefore planned to arrest and jail the demonstrators in as peaceful a manner as possible. When more volunteers arrived, thinking Pritchett could not possibly arrest all of them, the police chief trucked them off to jails in other towns. Before long, no one was left on the streets to protest segregation. The Albany Movement had failed, but black leaders would learn from this experience.

James Meredith and the Battle of Oxford (1962)

When Air Force veteran James Meredith sought to enroll at the University of Mississippi, he knew he was asking for trouble. He desired nothing less than for the federal government—the same government that had stationed him in Japan to promote freedom in Asia—to protect his right to go to college regardless of the color of his skin. "Ole Miss," the pride of Mississippi's white ruling class, was just the place to stage this drama. Not surprisingly, the registrar rejected Meredith's application, choosing one technicality after another in what became a twenty-month-long battle. Governor Ross Barnett, who had campaigned on a segregationist platform, rallied support for the southern cause in the university football stadium. Playing the crowd with his political savvy, Barnett promised, "No school will be integrated in Mississippi while I am your governor. . . . Never!"

In the end, Meredith received a seat in the classroom, but not before the biggest fight of his life. A federal court ruled in his favor—that was the easy part. With southern leaders refusing to honor the court order, U.S. marshals prepared to escort Meredith onto campus. Suddenly, decades of pent-up frustration broke lose all across the South. As if the Civil War had not yet ended, as if there was one more opportunity for the South to show its sovereignty over the federal government, volunteers from neighboring states joined local residents in armed opposition against the U.S. marshals. In the ensuing mayhem, a foreign journalist was killed and all footage of the event was destroyed. Bricks landed on people's heads, tear gas filled the air, and a desperate U.S. marshal stuck a coin into a payphone to call for reinforcements. With negotiations between Jackson, Mississippi, and Washington, DC, getting nowhere fast, Attorney General Robert Kennedy sent in the 503rd Marine Battalion to restore order. Recalling Eisenhower's dealings with Little Rock, President John F. Kennedy federalized the Mississippi National Guard. Meredith finally got what he wanted, but at a price few others would be willing to pay.

Birmingham (1963)

Drawing lessons from the failure in Albany, the SCLC planned Project C for Birmingham, Alabama. "C" stood for "Confrontation" through sit-ins, city hall marches, and the Children's Crusade. Until this point, King had been careful never to disobey a federal court order. In Albany, for example, he relaxed his protest when a federal judge set limits. King's strategy was always to win the approval of the federal government in order to trump the local government. Now King began to think differently. In defiance of a federal judge's order, King led a march to Birmingham's city hall, promising not to disperse until "Pharaoh lets God's people go." Not surprisingly, he was arrested.

Scribbling on scraps of paper from his jail cell, King wrote an eloquent appeal, known as his Letter from a Birmingham Jail. "I am in Birmingham because injustice is here," he explained, and then broadened his vision into a universal principle: "Injustice anywhere is a threat to justice everywhere." King proceeded to argue, in the spirit of St. Augustine, that "an unjust law is no law at all." He therefore advocated civil disobedience, emphasizing all the while that any protest for justice must remain nonviolent. "The purpose of our direct-action campaign is to create a situation so crisis-packed that it will inevitably open the door to negotiation," explained King. He also made a passionate appeal to white moderates, faulting them for not supporting the civil rights campaign: "Shallow understanding from people of good will is more frustrating than absolute misunderstanding from people of ill will. Lukewarm acceptance is much more bewildering than outright rejection."

As the nation pondered King's moralizing from the newspaper pages that reprinted his letter, the final phase of the Birmingham movement began. Hundreds of children walked in a campaign for desegregation. When news cameras recorded the peaceful children being carted off to jail, more children came to take their place. At his wit's end, public safety commissioner Bull Connor ordered the police to spray fire hoses to disperse the crowd of children. As Connor had hoped, the crowd dispersed, but to his horror, the media took pictures of the trauma that the powerful hoses inflicted upon the children. "The civil rights movement," noted President Kennedy, "should thank God for

Bull Connor." With southern whites appearing cruel, northern political sympathy for the civil rights movement reached new heights.

The March on Washington (1963)

In May 1963, Robert Kennedy met in a New York City apartment with black leaders to learn firsthand about their experiences with racial injustice. Kennedy discovered that all blacks—not just impoverished southern blacks—longed for freedom from the oppression of Jim Crow. Afterward, Kennedy testified before Congress that something needed to change. In reference to blacks who served in the military, he pleaded, "How can you say to a man that in a time of war, you're an American citizen, but the rest of the time you're a citizen of the state of Mississippi, and we can't protect you?"

Meanwhile, A. Philip Randolph, who had attempted to hold a mass rally in Washington, DC, in 1941, thought the time had come to try once more. The leadership of every major civil rights organization—including the SCLC, SNCC, the NAACP, CORE, and the National Urban League—coordinated a "March on Washington for Jobs and Freedom," to be held in August 1963. Although President Kennedy had promised civil rights legislation in his June 11 television address, he worried that a mass rally might take a radical turn against his administration. FBI Director J. Edgar Hoover, who suspected King of communism, found the proposed march threatening as well. Randolph's dream nearly evaporated when word leaked about the criticism that SNCC speaker John Lewis was planning to voice against the Justice Department. Pleading with tears in his eyes, Randolph persuaded Lewis to soften up his language just moments before he took the stage.

In the end, Lewis's speech was hardly memorable. Martin Luther King's voice boomed "I have a dream" from the Lincoln Memorial to a crowd of some 250,000 people, plus innumerable more via television broadcast. Masterfully, King united the highest ambitions of America's political tradition—yes, even the tradition of white men—with biblical prophecy in a poetic cadence of freedom for all:

> When the architects of our great republic wrote the magnificent words of the Constitution and the Declaration of Independence, they were signing a promissory note to which every American was to fall heir. . . .

> This note was a promise that all men, yes, black men as well as white men, would be guaranteed to the inalienable rights of life, liberty, and the pursuit of happiness. . . .

> I have a dream that my four little children will one day live in a nation where they will not be judged by the color of their skin but by the content of their character. . . .

I have a dream that one day every valley shall be exalted, and every hill and every mountain shall be made low, the rough places will be made plains and the crooked places will be made straight and the glory of the Lord shall be revealed and all flesh shall see it together. . . .

And when this happens, when we let freedom ring, when we let it ring from every tenement and every hamlet, from every state and every city, we will be able to speed up that day when all of God's children, black men and white men, Jews and Gentiles, Protestants and Catholics, will be able to join hands and sing in the words of the old negro spiritual, "Free at last, free at last. Thank God Almighty, we are free at last."

King succeeded where Lewis had nearly failed: the civil rights movement would henceforth be grafted into the mainstream of American political identity, as the Kennedy and Johnson administrations pushed Congress to enact the Civil Rights Act of 1964 and the Voting Rights Act of 1965. Even so, these victories for civil rights would come at a cost. The Democratic Party alienated its southern white constituents when endorsing the civil rights movement. More significantly, since the South failed to implement local solutions for ensuring racial justice, the federal government filled the void with an expansion of power that would not easily contract in more benevolent times.

Study Questions

1. What injustices were civil rights activists seeking to correct in the early 1960s?

2. What role did the federal government have in the civil rights movement?

3. What features characterized the worldview promoted by Martin Luther King?

Overview of Civil Rights and Voting Rights Acts, 1957–1965

The Civil Rights Act of 1957

The Civil Rights Act of 1957 established a six-member Civil Rights Commission and a Civil Rights Division within the Justice Department. Congress authorized the Attorney General to seek district court injunctions against local governments who deprived persons of the right to vote. Senator Strom Thurmond, a South Carolina Dixiecrat, attempted to block the measure by filibustering for twenty-four hours and eighteen minutes (the longest filibuster ever recorded), August 28–29, 1957.

Two amendments drastically limited the potential of the 1957 act: the Attorney General could not seek court injunctions against Jim Crow; and, cases of criminal contempt concerning voting rights would be heard by local juries—which in practice meant all-white juries. Senator Lyndon B. Johnson, a Texas Democrat with aspirations for the presidency, orchestrated the adoption of both amendments, thereby establishing political support among southern Democrats. Vice President Richard Nixon, a Republican, opposed these changes, but with support from Democratic Senator John F. Kennedy of Massachusetts, Johnson had his way.

Political Realignment

Ironically, Kennedy, Johnson, and the national Democratic Party reversed their stance on civil rights during the 1960s. The transition occurred gradually. In the 1960 presidential campaign, Kennedy applauded the sit-ins and suggested that, if elected, he would end housing discrimination by executive order. In October, Kennedy also made a courtesy call to Coretta Scott King, offering sympathy while her husband, Martin Luther King, Jr., was jailed during an Atlanta sit-in protest. Nixon, meanwhile, remained silent on civil rights. Once elected, Kennedy proceeded cautiously. His brother Robert, whom he appointed attorney general, negotiated by phone with southern government leaders in an effort to contain the civil rights movement before it became too much of a political nuisance. Ultimately, the Kennedy brothers concluded that the most prudent political move would be to channel the energy of the movement into their own political party, even if this meant alienating southern whites.

The Civil Rights Act of 1964

The Civil Rights Act of 1964 is the most comprehensive civil rights legislation Congress has ever passed. Calling civil rights a "moral crisis" that necessitated federal action, President Kennedy announced on June 11, 1963 that he would send a civil rights bill to Congress. The August 28 "March on Washington for Jobs and Freedom" rallied support for the bill. After Kennedy's assassination in November, President Johnson urged Congress to enact the proposed legislation. He signed the bill into law on June 2, 1964, solidifying the Democratic Party as the party of civil rights.

The new law authorized the Attorney General to file desegregation suits relating to public accommodations and public education; outlawed employment discrimination based on race, color, religion, sex, or national origin; outlawed discrimination in federally funded institutions (including universities); established the Equal Employment Opportunity Commission; declared that a sixth-grade education suffices for any voting registration literacy test; and, prohibited the denial of voting registration based on filing errors.

Mississippi Freedom Democratic Party

Barred from participating in their state's Democratic Party, blacks in Mississippi mobilized to form their own organization, the Mississippi Freedom Democratic Party. Electing delegates to the 1964 national convention, they hoped to be received as equals among white delegates from other states. When the credentials committee, under pressure from southern whites, blocked their registration, a political disaster erupted on national television. President Johnson's supporters worked out a compromise by allowing the black delegation to fill some at-large seats in 1964 and guaranteeing blacks full participation in the 1968 convention.

The Voting Rights Act of 1965

Calling out "We shall overcome"—the refrain of a popular civil rights song—President Johnson urged Congress to pass the Voting Rights Act. This law authorized the Justice Department to suspend literacy and related tests in districts where fewer than half the persons of sufficient age had been registered to vote and to place those districts under federal supervision. The Justice Department invoked this authority over seven states on August 7, 1965, the day after the bill was signed.

Study Questions

1. What were the chief provisions of the Civil Rights Act of 1964 and the Voting Rights Act of 1965?

2. How did the Democratic Party become the party of civil rights?

American Interventions in Vietnam, 1945–1975

The Vietnam War (1955–1975) began and ended gradually. The United States never appeared to have a clear plan for entering the war for victory, nor for exiting the war with honor. An undeniable fact is that whatever happened in the middle did not turn out well for the United States. The ordeal struck the Vietnamese and their neighbors in Cambodia even more tragically. Future foreign policy decisions, such as what course of action to take against Iraq following the September 11 terrorist attacks in 2001, would be articulated always with a caution that Americans wanted to avoid "another Vietnam."

French Indochina and U.S. Foreign Aid

During World War II, Vietnamese nationalist leader Ho Chi Minh organized a guerrilla movement within Vietnam, known as the Viet Minh, to push back Japanese invaders. After Japan surrendered to the Allies, Ho Chi Minh declared himself the ruler of the Democratic Republic of Vietnam. However, the Allies had agreed at the 1945 Potsdam Conference to return Vietnam to France, which had governed Indochina (Vietnam, Laos, and Cambodia) since 1887. Ho therefore retreated with his Viet Minh guerrillas to the jungles and rice paddies while U.S. policy advisors warned that the Viet Minh did not seek merely independence, but also a communist takeover of the country. In 1950, the U.S. began sending financial and advisory aid to the French regime in Vietnam in an effort to contain communism, even as the U.S. began sending troops to Korea for the same purpose.

In 1954, the Viet Minh defeated French colonial forces in Vietnam and assumed control of North Vietnam. The U.S. helped Ngo Dinh Diem, a Catholic anti-communist, become Prime Minister of South Vietnam, in hopes of preventing the Viet Minh from controlling the entire country. An election was to be held in 1956 to determine the future leadership of the nation, but Diem canceled the election when he realized that Ho Chi Minh easily would defeat him. In 1960, Diem's opponents formed the National Liberation Front (NLF), which launched a series of raids against his army. Although not all members of the NLF were communists, Diem called the movement the Viet Cong—Vietnamese communists. This naming game reinforced U.S. support for his regime, given the dynamics of the Cold War.

The selection of Diem as prime minister proved problematic. Diem was a Catholic who opposed Buddhism, the religion to which 90% of the Vietnamese people adhered. Protesting Diem's harsh regime, several Buddhist monks lit themselves on fire. The United States awkwardly supported Diem, supposing his governance, however unsettling, to be preferable to communism. During the early 1960s, President John F. Kennedy increased U.S. aid to Vietnam. By 1963, U.S. personnel there numbered 16,000. Kennedy also dispatched 3,000 Green Berets, specialists in unconventional warfare and counter-insurgency, to train Diem's Army of the Republic of Vietnam.

The Gulf of Tonkin Incident and Escalation

Already in 1954, President Einsenhower had warned that the nations of southeast Asia were like dominoes. "You knock over the first one, and what will happen to the last one is the certainty that it will go over very quickly." The containment policy therefore required that communist influences in North Vietnam not be permitted to spread into South Vietnam. By the mid 1960s, however, it almost was too late. The Viet Cong consisted of South Vietnamese rebels supplied by Ho Chi Minh's North Vietnamese government via a network of delivery routes known as the Ho Chi Minh Trail. Although Ho may not have been strictly speaking a communist, he had sought assistance from both the Soviets and the Chinese in view of the fact that communism was the most readily available alternative to European colonialism. The United States meanwhile found itself in a quandary: to surrender Vietnam to Ho and the Viet Cong meant risking the loss of all Asia to communism, but to persist in Vietnam meant getting dragged down further into a quagmire of geopolitical forces that few Americans understood and none could control.

In August 1964, just months before a U.S. presidential election, the military reported that North Vietnamese patrol boats had opened fire on American destroyers in the Gulf of Tonkin. In retaliation, Congress passed the Gulf of Tonkin Resolution, authorizing President Johnson "to take all necessary means to repel any armed attack against the forces of the United States and to prevent further aggression." Such broad language empowered the president to take military action against Vietnam. Military strategy and political necessity became closely intertwined, as Johnson realized that he must demonstrate a tough stance against communism if he was to defeat Senator Barry Goldwater's militantly anti-communist campaign for the presidency.

When the Viet Cong attacked an American base in South Vietnam in February 1965, Johnson committed the first official ground troops (as compared to supposed "advisors") by dispatching 3,500 U.S. Marines to Da Nang. By summer, monthly draft calls reached 35,000, resulting in a full deployment of 200,000 troops by the end of the year. Meanwhile, a bombing campaign called Operation Rolling Thunder began in March 1965.

Over the next three years, bombing campaigns continued and the troop numbers swelled. By 1967, 500,000 American servicemen were serving in Vietnam. Defense Secretary Robert McNamara continued to re-calculate the numbers, urging the president to step up the commitment of U.S. troops in a process known as "escalation." Each time Johnson believed he had enough force to overpower the Viet Cong, America was surprised by another setback. Johnson then had to wrestle with the decision of whether to answer Gen. William Westmoreland's requests for more troops or to cater to war protesters and draft-dodgers in the states who severely challenged the president's leadership.

The War Protestor Movement and the Tet Offensive

As the escalation policy failed to deliver the intended effect, Johnson wearied of waging war on two fronts, and losing in both contests. Angry Americans protested the war at home, while the North Vietnamese continued to hold the upper hand in a long war of attrition. War protestors rallied in New York, Chicago, Philadelphia, Boston, and San Francisco, as well as the nation's capital. Angry Americans defiantly burned their draft cards. A student movement swept the nation under the banner of the New Left, calling for peaceful withdrawal from Vietnam.

In January 1968, the United States suffered a humiliating series of attacks coordinated by the Viet Cong. Shortly after Gen. Westmoreland announced that victory was in reach, some 70,000 North Vietnamese soldiers and Viet Cong guerrillas launched a bold offensive on multiple fronts, targeting thirty South Vietnamese cities simultaneously. Although eventually repelled by U.S. and South Vietnamese forces, the communists managed to strike the U.S. embassy in Saigon. The surprising show of force coincided with Tet, the Vietnamese lunar new year, and thus became known as the Tet Offensive.

With 543,000 U.S. troops in Vietnam, and $70 million spent each day, the war no longer appeared sustainable. Nor did Johnson's political career. In March 1968, the president announced that he would not seek re-election that November. Anti-war Democrats rallied support for Eugene McCarthy, a Senator from Minnesota. Johnson's successor, Richard Nixon, took a different approach: rather than cater to war protesters, brand them as "un-American" and then find an honorable way to extricate American troops from the Vietnam disaster.

Vietnamization and the Peace Accords

In 1969, President Nixon announced a policy of "Vietnamization." America would continue to support South Vietnam as an ally, but U.S. ground troops would be withdrawn and replaced by Vietnamese soldiers. By 1972, only 24,000 U.S. troops remained in Vietnam, essentially the same number as in 1964, before Johnson's escalation policy had commenced.

The most challenging days for America still lay ahead. In November 1969, an investigative reporter broke the story that U.S. soldiers under command of Lt. William Calley had massacred innocent Vietnamese civilians in the village of My Lai in March 1968. Calley was later court martialed, but the spirit of suspicion spread beyond just his platoon. In 1970, President Nixon authorized a bombing campaign against Cambodia, which led war-protestors to question the sincerity of Nixon's earlier commitment to downsize U.S. military involvement in southeast Asia. Student protestors at Kent State University were particularly outraged at Nixon. When the crowd refused to disperse,

Ohio National Guardsman opened fire, killing four students and injuring several others—including innocent bystanders trying to get to class. The Kent State incident gave Americans a small taste of My Lai. When would the killing end?

Finally, after an intense bombing campaign in the fall of 1972, the North Vietnamese agreed to peace talks with the United States. In January 1973, the Paris Accords went into effect, requiring the United States to withdraw fully within sixty days and the North Vietnamese to release all prisoners of war. In February, nearly 600 U.S. POWs left Hanoi. Meanwhile, Vietnam was to remain split under two governments, north and south, until further diplomacy could arrange for a long-term solution. The situation cooled to a simmer for the next two years.

In December 1974, North Vietnam transgressed the Paris Accords by renewing its invasion of South Vietnam. The U.S. military, meanwhile, had its hands tied by a 1973 congressional ban on further intervention. In April 1975, communist forces entered Saigon as frantic crowds stormed the U.S. embassy in hopes of being airlifted to freedom. Vietnam was now reunited under a communist regime.

Although America's involvement in Vietnam ended in 1973, Vietnam's involvement in America lingered on. The families of the 58,000 servicemen killed in action now had a lonely seat at the dining room table. The survivors hardly fared better. Hundreds of thousands of U.S. veterans returned home to angry war protestors. For decades to come, post-traumatic stress disorder left the vets with nightmares, depression, and anxiety. Agent Orange, a toxic defoliant used by the U.S. military in the jungles of Vietnam, induced cancer. For many veterans, the war is still not over.

Study Questions

1. How did the containment doctrine shape U.S. involvement in Vietnam from World War II through the early 1960s?

2. Explain the significance of the Gulf of Tonkin Resolution, Johnson's escalation policy, and Nixon's Vietnamization policy.

Youth Movements of the 1960s

In 1787, the framers of the U.S. Constitution began their work with the words "We the People of the United States of America." In the 1960s, a small but vocal minority of American youth began to reject America as a nation of hypocrites who merely played lip-service to the ideals of liberty and equality. In 1962, for example, one group of college students formulated a new charter, beginning with words that separated them from their parents and grandparents: "We are people of *this generation.* . . ."

The youth movements of the 1960s often bring to mind images of young idealists pushing liberalism to the extreme. Some of them rightly are called "radicals" for their rejection of America's roots. Others were radical in a different sense, for they desired to restore America's roots. Young Americans for Freedom, for example, rallied around the conservative presidential candidacy of Barry Goldwater and the right-wing journalism of William F. Buckley Jr., even as others from their generation flirted with communism and championed the New Left.

The youth movements of the 1960s, despite their diversity, all had one thing in common: the participants were young. In 1960, more Americans attended college than worked on farms. The baby boom generation was about to enter adulthood, transforming the nation even as they transformed themselves.

Students for a Democratic Society

In 1960, student activists gathered at the University of Michigan in Ann Arbor to establish Students for a Democratic Society (SDS), which adopted the *Port Huron Statement* two years later:

> We are people of this generation, bred in at least modest comfort, housed now in universities, looking uncomfortably to the world we inherit. . . . First, the permeating and victimizing fact of human degradation, symbolized by the Southern struggle against racial bigotry, compelled most of us from silence to activism. Second, the enclosing fact of the Cold War, symbolized by the presence of the Bomb, brought awareness that we ourselves, and our friends, and millions of abstract "others" we knew more directly because of our common peril, might die at any time. . . .

Critical of the military industrial complex, against which Eisenhower also had warned, SDS faulted both Republicans and Democrats for hypocrisy. America claimed to be fighting for freedom in Vietnam, and yet the only result thus far was death for both the Vietnamese and the American GIs. Moreover, African Americans lacked freedom right here in America, so who did Americans think they were to tell other countries how to treat their citizens? As a remedy, SDS called for "participatory democracy," by which they meant that the people most closely impacted by policy-making should have a voice in the process. As U.S. deployment in Vietnam escalated during the mid 1960s, SDS members held "teach-ins" at American universities in opposition to the war, as well as rallies at the nation's capitol.

Berkeley Free Speech Movement

At the University of California in Berkeley, student groups commonly distributed pamphlets to recruit members in a plaza that the university regents had agreed to transfer to the City of Berkeley. Treating the space as public property, the students—including conservatives as well as liberals—felt they had a First Amendment right to advocate their causes there. In September 1964, the administration announced that student groups no longer could engage in political activities in that plaza. When negotiations failed to satisfy the students, they organized the Free Speech Movement and called for strikes and a mass protest, culminating in a sit-in that December. Addressing a crowd of thousands, a college junior named Mario Savio stated the students' cause:

> Now, I ask you to consider: if this is a firm, and if the Board of Regents are the board of directors, and if President Kerr in fact is the manager, then I'll tell you something: the faculty are a bunch of employees, and we're the raw material! But we're a bunch of raw material that don't mean to have any process upon us, don't mean to be made into any product, don't mean to end up being bought by some clients of the University, be they the government, be they industry, be they organized labor, be they anyone! We're human beings! There is a time when the operation of the machine becomes so odious, makes you so sick at heart, that you can't take part; you can't even passively take part, and you've got to put your bodies upon the gears and upon the wheels, upon the levers, upon all the apparatus, and you've got to make it stop. And you've got to indicate to the people who run it, to the people who own it, that unless you're free, the machine will be prevented from working at all!

Following a mass arrest of student protesters, the administration agreed to relax its restrictions on student speech. Student groups on other campuses confidently followed the example from Berkeley, while newly elected California Governor Ronald Reagan called for President Clark Kerr's dismissal for failing to keep the protesters in line.

Young Americans for Freedom

Not all student activists supported the New Left. In 1960, the same year that SDS was founded, conservatives established Young Americans for Freedom (YAF). Whereas the radical left rejected America's founding roots, YAF members affirmed in their Sharon Statement of 1960 that "the Constitution of the United States is the best arrangement yet devised for empowering government to fulfill its proper role, while restraining it from the concentration and abuse of power." The students received encouragement from William F. Buckley, Jr., the founding editor of the *National Review*, a conservative counterpoint to the progressive-liberal bias he perceived in the press. YAF supported Republican presidential candidate Barry Goldwater against Lyndon Johnson in 1964 as well as Ronald Reagan, who delivered an endorsement speech for Goldwater at the national convention and himself won the California gubernatorial election two years later.

Youth International Party

On New Year's Eve 1967, several young, disgruntled leftists brainstormed about a supplement to the term "hippie," which referred to the youth culture obsessed with rock-'n'-roll music and psychedelic drugs. Some hippies also sought to change America politically, and these became known as "yippies," which also served as an abbreviation of the Youth International Party. In March 1968, the Yippies held a press conference to announce their vision for reform. Calling for food co-ops and free medical clinics, they criticized American institutions for being too cold and formal. Yippies demanded that hostilities in Vietnam should cease, marijuana should be legalized, and money should be abolished. Peace, love, and community were all that America really needed.

In August 1968, the Yippies staged a protest against the Democratic National Convention in Chicago. Television viewers witnessed the protestors clashing with Chicago police officers, who used tear gas and billy clubs to disperse the crowd. Seven of the New Left activists were arrested and tried for conspiracy, including Yippie founder Jerry Rubin who unabashedly said getting arrested was precisely his goal. He hoped the government would spend a billion dollars convicting him so that the Department of Defense would have one billion fewer dollars to spend on the Vietnam War.

Woodstock

A year after the Chicago convention, half a million hippies converged on a farm in Woodstock, New York, for a week-long music festival to celebrate "Peace, Love, and Rock 'n' Roll." By peace, they meant an end of the Vietnam War and a surrender of nuclear arms. By love, they meant so-called "free love," the separation of sexual intimacy from marital commitment. In addition to rock music, the festival also featured drugs and, by the end of the week, the largest heap of garbage any mass gathering had ever produced. Of course, at some point these young people would have to learn to clean up after themselves and pay their bills. What America would be like then, was anybody's guess.

Study Questions

1. Why, specifically, were the youthful members of Students for a Democratic Society so frustrated with their parent's generation of Americans?

2. How did SDS define "participatory democracy"?

3. What was the "military-industrial complex," and why were SDS members so concerned about it?

4. Against what were Savio and other participants in the Free Speech Movement protesting?

5. Who were the hippies and the yippies?

6. Why would it be a mistake to suppose that the entire youth culture of the 1960s supported New Left radicalism?

Lyndon B. Johnson, "Great Society Speech" (1964)

On May 7, 1964, President Lyndon B. Johnson introduced the term "Great Society" in a speech delivered at Ohio University in Athens, Ohio. "It is a Society where no child will go unfed, and no youngster will go unschooled," said Johnson. Two weeks later, on May 22, Johnson gave fuller expression to his vision for a renewed America while delivering the following commencement address at the University of Michigan in Ann Arbor. Johnson intended this speech as a launching pad for his 1964 presidential campaign. In April, he called two of his top aids to join him for a swim in the White House pool, where they brainstormed together about "the Great Society," which was to become the signature legislative program of Johnson's presidency.

President Hatcher, Governor Romney, Senators McNamara and Hart, Congressmen Meader and Staebler, and other members of the fine Michigan delegation, members of the graduating class, my fellow Americans:

It is a great pleasure to be here today. This university has been coeducational since 1870, but I do not believe it was on the basis of your accomplishments that a Detroit high school girl said, "In choosing a college, you first have to decide whether you want a coeducational school or an educational school."

Well, we can find both here at Michigan, although perhaps at different hours.

I came out here today very anxious to meet the Michigan student whose father told a friend of mine that his son's education had been a real value. It stopped his mother from bragging about him.

I have come today from the turmoil of your Capital to the tranquility of your campus to speak about the future of your country.

The purpose of protecting the life of our Nation and preserving the liberty of our citizens is to pursue the happiness of our people. Our success in that pursuit is the test of our success as a Nation.

For a century we labored to settle and to subdue a continent. For half a century we called upon unbounded invention and untiring industry to create an order of plenty for all of our people.

The challenge of the next half century is whether we have the wisdom to use that wealth to enrich and elevate our national life, and to advance the quality of our American civilization.

Your imagination, your initiative, and your indignation will determine whether we build a society where progress is the servant of our needs, or a society where old values and new visions are buried under unbridled growth. For in your time we have the opportunity to move not only toward the rich society and the powerful society, but upward to the Great Society.

The Great Society rests on abundance and liberty for all. It demands an end to poverty and racial injustice, to which we are totally committed in our time. But that is just the beginning.

The Great Society is a place where every

child can find knowledge to enrich his mind and to enlarge his talents. It is a place where leisure is a welcome chance to build and reflect, not a feared cause of boredom and restlessness. It is a place where the city of man serves not only the needs of the body and the demands of commerce but the desire for beauty and the hunger for community.

It is a place where man can renew contact with nature. It is a place which honors creation for its own sake and for what is adds to the understanding of the race. It is a place where men are more concerned with the quality of their goals than the quantity of their goods.

But most of all, the Great Society is not a safe harbor, a resting place, a final objective, a finished work. It is a challenge constantly renewed, beckoning us toward a destiny where the meaning of our lives matches the marvelous products of our labor.

So I want to talk to you today about three places where we begin to build the Great Society—in our cities, in our countryside, and in our classrooms.

Many of you will live to see the day, perhaps 50 years from now, when there will be 400 million Americans—four-fifths of them in urban areas. In the remainder of this century urban population will double, city land will double, and we will have to build homes, highways, and facilities equal to all those built since this country was first settled. So in the next 40 years we must re-build the entire urban United States.

Aristotle said: "Men come together in cities in order to live, but they remain together in order to live the good life." It is harder and harder to live the good life in American cities today.

The catalog of ills is long: there is the decay of the centers and the despoiling of the suburbs. There is not enough housing for our people or transportation for our traffic. Open land is vanishing and old landmarks are violated.

Worst of all expansion is eroding the precious and time honored values of community with neighbors and communion with nature.

The loss of these values breeds loneliness and boredom and indifference.

Our society will never be great until our cities are great. Today the frontier of imagination and innovation is inside those cities and not beyond their borders.

New experiments are already going on. It will be the task of your generation to make the American city a place where future generations will come, not only to live but to live the good life.

I understand that if I stayed here tonight I would see that Michigan students are really doing their best to live the good life.

This is the place where the Peace Corps was started. It is inspiring to see how all of you, while you are in this country, are trying so hard to live at the level of the people.

A second place where we begin to build the Great Society is in our countryside. We have always prided ourselves on being not only America the strong and America the free, but America the beautiful. Today that beauty is in danger. The water we drink, the food we eat, the very air that we breathe, are threatened with pollution. Our parks are overcrowded, our seashores overburdened. Green fields and dense forests are disappearing.

A few years ago we were greatly concerned about the "Ugly American." Today we must act to prevent an ugly America.

For once the battle is lost, once our natural splendor is destroyed, it can never be recaptured. And once man can no longer walk with beauty or wonder at nature his spirit will wither and his sustenance be wasted.

A third place to build the Great Society is in the classrooms of America. There your children's lives will be shaped. Our society will not be great until every young mind is set free to scan the farthest reaches of thought and imagination. We are still far from that goal.

Today, 8 million adult Americans, more than the entire population of Michigan, have not finished 5 years of school. Nearly 20 million have not finished 8 years of school. Nearly 54 million—more than one quarter of all America—have not even finished high school.

Each year more than 100,000 high school graduates, with proved ability, do not enter college because they cannot afford it. And if we cannot educate today's youth, what will we do in 1970 when elementary school enrollment will be 5 million greater than 1960? And high school enrollment will rise by 5 million. College enrollment will increase by more than 3 million.

In many places, classrooms are overcrowded and curricula are outdated. Most of our qualified teachers are underpaid, and many of our paid teachers are unqualified. So we must give every child a place to sit and a teacher to learn from. Poverty must not be a bar to learning, and learning must offer an escape from poverty.

But more classrooms and more teachers are not enough. We must seek an educational system which grows in excellence as it grows in size. This means better training for our teachers. It means preparing youth to enjoy their hours of leisure as well as their hours of labor. It means exploring new techniques of teaching, to find new ways to stimulate the love of learning and the capacity for creation.

These are three of the central issues of the Great Society. While our Government has many programs directed at those issues, I do not pretend that we have the full answer to those problems.

But I do promise this: We are going to assemble the best thought and the broadest knowledge from all over the world to find those answers for America. I intend to establish working groups to prepare a series of White House conferences and meetings—on the cities, on natural beauty, on the quality of education, and on other emerging challenges. And from these meetings and from this inspiration and from these studies we will begin to set our course toward the Great Society.

The solution to these problems does not rest on a massive program in Washington, nor can it rely solely on the strained resources of local authority. They require us to create new concepts of cooperation, a creative federalism, between the National Capital and the leaders of local communities.

Woodrow Wilson once wrote: "Every man sent out from his university should be a man of his Nation as well as a man of his time."

Within your lifetime powerful forces, already loosed, will take us toward a way of life beyond the realm of our experience, almost beyond the bounds of our imagination.

For better or for worse, your generation has been appointed by history to deal with those problems and to lead America toward a new age. You have the chance never before afforded to any people in any age. You can help build a society where the demands of morality, and the needs of the spirit, can be realized in the life of the Nation.

So, will you join in the battle to give every citizen the full equality which God enjoins and the law requires, whatever his belief, or race, or the color of his skin?

Will you join in the battle to give every citizen an escape from the crushing weight of poverty?

Will you join in the battle to make it possible for all nations to live in enduring peace—as neighbors and not as mortal enemies?

Will you join in the battle to build the Great Society, to prove that our material progress is only the foundation on which we will build a richer life of mind and spirit?

There are those timid souls who say this battle cannot be won; that we are condemned to a soulless wealth. I do not agree. We have the power to shape the civilization that we want. But we need your will, your labor, your hearts, if we are to build that kind of society.

Those who came to this land sought to build more than just a new country. They sought a new world. So I have come here today to your campus to say that you can make their vision our reality. So let us from this moment begin our work so that in the future men will look back and say: It was then, after a long and weary way, that man turned the exploits of his genius to the full enrichment of his life.

Thank you. Good-bye.

Study Questions

1. What chief features characterize the "Great Society" that Johnson imagined?

2. What roles did Johnson envision for the government and for the people in order to achieve the Great Society? (See also "Great Society Programs" on the next page.)

Great Society Programs, 1964–1969

Between 1964 and 1969, the Johnson administration recommended some 250 policy reforms under the banner of the "Great Society," roughly 90% of which received the approval of Congress. The resulting collage of progressive reform dwarfed FDR's New Deal as the federal government expanded its reach in the realm of the states, transforming individuals into three classes: taxpayers who funded federal programs, welfare recipients who received that aid, and bureaucrats who made a career out of the administration of these programs. Never before had a president been so ambitious.

The War on Poverty

In his 1964 State of the Union address, Johnson declared an "unconditional war on poverty." Congress delivered by enacting several programs aimed at relief for the poor:

1. **The Economic Opportunity Act of 1964** established the Office of Economic Opportunity to oversee "community action" programs that funneled federal dollars into local anti-poverty projects.
2. The **Job Corps** sought to assist young people in developing marketable skills, while **Head Start** subsidized preschool education for impoverished children.
3. Amendments to **Social Security** in 1965 and 1967 expanded benefit levels.
4. **Aid for Families with Dependent Children (AFDC)** payments increased, with 1968 aid exceeding the 1960 level by 35%.

However, despite the statistics indicating broader participation in federal anti-poverty programs, the middle class in fact declined as the poverty line covered a growing proportion of Americans in the decades that followed. African Americans experienced the brunt of this economic tragedy, largely because AFDC payments privileged single parents and thereby discouraged marriage. Whereas African American family structure during the 1950s had been on par with the white community, by the 1980s, blacks were significantly more likely to cohabit and bear children out of wedlock —two significant risk factors for poverty.

Education

In 1965, the **Elementary and Secondary Education Act** infused federal funding into local public schools while also expanding Head Start into a permanent program. Meanwhile, the **Higher Education Act of 1965** increase federal aid to universities and established federally subsidized student loans. As a result, college became more affordable but also more expensive, since the same federal dollars that empowered low-income students to pay tuition also increased the demand for higher education, thus driving prices higher.

Healthcare

The Social Security Act of 1965 established **Medicare**, a government health insurance program for people over 65 years of age who had paid in employment taxes. Title XIX of the same act created **Medicaid**, which provided health coverage for impoverished people of all ages. Medicaid involved a mixture of federal and state funding, with states administering the program within federal guidelines.

Arts and Culture

In 1965, Congress also established both the **National Endowment for the Arts (NEA)** and the **National Endowment for the Humanities (NEH)**. These programs channeled taxpayer dollars into artistic and literary projects, sponsoring university research in the name of the public good—clearly a progressive ideal. The **Public Broadcasting Act of 1967** chartered the Corporation for Public Broadcasting, which led to the creation of both the Public Broadcasting Service for television as well as National Public Radio. As in the case of the NEA and NEH, the federal government sponsored an alternative to the free market at taxpayers' expense, all with the promise of delivering quality programming that otherwise might not have been valued among entrepreneurs.

Housing

The **Housing and Urban Development Act of 1965** offered rental subsidies to low-income families while also providing a stimulus to real estate developers for renewing urban areas and establishing affordable housing. HUD guidelines also reshaped the kind of housing that would be available to Americans, shifting away from homes that had productive spaces (large kitchens for homemade meals or large garages that could accommodate carpentry projects) toward homes that would serve primarily for consumption of ready-made products, as people commuted to work from the suburbs.

Study Question

Identify the chief benefits and drawbacks of the Great Society.

Lyndon B. Johnson, Inaugural Address (1965)

As Lyndon B. Johnson took the presidential oath of office for the second time, he reflected on the challenges of governing a changing nation, expressing his hopes and fears concerning the future. Soberly, Johnson acknowledged that "we have no promise from God that our greatness will endure." To achieve and sustain greatness would require, Johnson claimed, broad-based cooperation between the government and all its citizens. Indeed, Johnson even went so far as to say that the American people must take the oath of office together with him. In the coming years, the Great Society would blur another distinction as well: the growing federal bureaucracy brought legislative and judicial functions under the purview of new executive agencies, departing from the "separation of powers" doctrine that the framers of the U.S. Constitution had established.

My fellow countrymen:

On this occasion the oath I have taken before you and before God is not mine alone, but ours together. We are one nation and one people. Our fate as a nation and our future as a people rest not upon one citizen but upon all citizens.

That is the majesty and the meaning of this moment.

For every generation there is a destiny. For some, history decides. For this generation the choice must be our own.

Even now, a rocket moves toward Mars. It reminds us that the world will not be the same for our children, or even for ourselves in a short span of years. The next man to stand here will look out on a scene that is different from our own.

Ours is a time of change—rapid and fantastic change—bearing the secrets of nature, multiplying the nations, placing in uncertain hands new weapons for mastery and destruction, shaking old values and uprooting old ways.

Our destiny in the midst of change will rest on the unchanged character of our people and on their faith.

The American Covenant

They came here—the exile and the stranger, brave but frightened—to find a place where a man could be his own man. They made a covenant with this land. Conceived in justice, written in liberty, bound in union, it was meant one day to inspire the hopes of all mankind. And it binds us still. If we keep its terms we shall flourish.

Justice and Change

First, justice was the promise that all who made the journey would share in the fruits of the land.

In a land of great wealth, families must not live in hopeless poverty. In a land rich in harvest, children just must not go hungry. In a land of healing miracles, neighbors must not suffer and die untended. In a great land of learning and scholars, young people must be taught to read and write.

For more than 30 years that I have served this Nation I have believed that this injustice to our people, this waste of our resources, was our real enemy. For 30 years or more, with the resources I have had, I have vigilantly fought against it. I have learned and I know that it will not surrender easily.

But change has given us new weapons. Before this generation of Americans is finished, this enemy will not only retreat, it will be conquered.

Justice requires us to remember: when any citizen denies his fellow, saying, "His color is not mine or his beliefs are strange and different" in that moment he betrays America, though his forebears created this Nation.

Liberty and Change

Liberty was the second article of our covenant. It was self-government. It was our Bill of Rights. But it was more. America would be a place where each man could be proud to be himself: stretching his talents, rejoicing in his work, important in the life of his neighbors and his nation.

This has become more difficult in a world where change and growth seem to tower beyond the control and even the judgment of men. We must work to provide the knowledge and the surroundings which can enlarge the possibilities of every citizen.

The World and Change

The American covenant called on us to help show the way for the liberation of man. And that is today our goal. Thus, if as a nation, there is much outside our control, as a people no stranger is outside our hope.

Change has brought new meaning to that old mission. We can never again stand aside, prideful in isolation. Terrific dangers and troubles that we once called "foreign" now constantly live among us. If American lives must end, and American treasure be spilled, in countries that we barely know, then that is the price that change has demanded of conviction and of our enduring covenant.

Think of our world as it looks from that rocket that is heading toward Mars. It is like a child's globe, hanging in space, the continent stuck to its side like colored maps. We are all fellow passengers on a dot of earth. And each of us, in the span of time, has really only a moment among our companions.

How incredible it is that in this fragile existence we should hate and destroy one another. There are possibilities enough for all who will abandon mastery over others to pursue mastery over nature. There is world enough for all to seek their happiness in their own way.

Our Nation's course is abundantly clear. We aspire to nothing that belongs to others. We seek no dominion over our fellow man, but man's dominion over tyranny and misery.

But more is required. Men want to be part of a common enterprise, a cause greater than themselves. And each of us must find a way to advance the purpose of the Nation, thus finding new purpose for ourselves. Without this, we will simply become a nation of strangers.

Union and Change

The third article is union. To those who

were small and few against the wilderness, the success of liberty demanded the strength of union. Two centuries of change have made this true again.

No longer need capitalist and worker, farmer and clerk, city and countryside, struggle to divide our bounty. By working shoulder to shoulder together we can increase the bounty of all. We have discovered that every child who learns, and every man who finds work, and every sick body that is made whole—like a candle added to an altar—brightens the hope of all the faithful.

So let us reject any among us who seek to reopen old wounds and rekindle old hatreds. They stand in the way of a seeking nation.

Let us now join reason to faith and action to experience, to transform our unity of interest into a unity of purpose. For the hour and the day and the time are here to achieve progress without strife, to achieve change without hatred; not without difference of opinion but without the deep and abiding divisions which scar the union for generations.

The American Belief

Under this covenant of justice, liberty, and union we have become a nation—prosperous, great, and mighty. And we have kept our freedom. But we have no promise from God that our greatness will endure. We have been allowed by Him to seek greatness with the sweat of our hands and the strength of our spirit.

I do not believe that the Great Society is the ordered, changeless, and sterile battalion of the ants. It is the excitement of becoming—always becoming, trying, probing, falling, resting, and trying again—but always trying and always gaining.

In each generation, with toil and tears, we have had to earn our heritage again. If we fail now then we will have forgotten in abundance what we learned in hardship: that democracy rests on faith, that freedom asks more than it gives, and the judgment of God is harshest on those who are most favored.

If we succeed it will not be because of what we have, but it will be because of what we are; not because of what we own, but rather because of what we believe.

For we are a nation of believers. Underneath the clamor of building and the rush of our day's pursuits, we are believers in justice and liberty and in our own union. We believe that every man must some day be free. And we believe in ourselves.

And that is the mistake that our enemies have always made. In my lifetime, in depression and in war they have awaited our defeat. Each time, from the secret places of the American heart, came forth the faith that they could not see or that they could not even imagine. And it brought us victory. And it will again.

For this is what America is all about. It is the uncrossed desert and the unclimbed ridge. It is the star that is not reached and the harvest that is sleeping in the unplowed ground. Is our world gone? We say farewell. Is a new world coming? We welcome it, and we will bend it to the hopes of man.

And to these trusted public servants

and to my family, and those close friends of mine who have followed me down a long winding road, and to all the people of this Union and the world, I will repeat today what I said on that sorrowful day in November last year: I will lead and I will do the best I can.

But you, you must look within your own hearts to the old promises and to the old dreams. They will lead you best of all.

For myself, I ask only in the words of an ancient leader [King Solomon]: "Give me now wisdom and knowledge, that I may go out and come in before this people: for who can judge this thy people, that is so great?" [2 Chronicles 1:10].

Study Questions

1. Johnson expressed the American covenant in term of justice, liberty, and union. Explain what he meant by these words.

2. What did Johnson mean when he said, "the judgment of God is harshest on those who are most favored"?

U.S. Dept. of Labor, "The Negro Family: The Case for National Action" (1965)

In March 1965, the Office of Policy Planning and Research, a division of the U.S. Department of Labor, issued a policy recommendation that by summer's end had become a political hot potato. Chiefly authored by Daniel Patrick Moynihan, the so-called "Moynihan Report" identified weak family structure as the chief impediment to African American progress. This problem, in turn, was traced to a history of oppression during the eras of slavery, Reconstruction, and Jim Crow, compounded more recently by racial discrimination that blocked African American males from higher education and middle-class careers. Although Moynihan intended his report to encourage government support for educating and employing black males, in order that they may serve as stable heads of their families, critics ridiculed him for blaming the victims. The Johnson administration therefore chose to divert its efforts away from restoring black families and toward a group-rights strategy known as "affirmative action."

Introduction

The United States is approaching a new crisis in race relations.

In the decade that began with the school desegregation decision of the Supreme Court, and ended with the passage of the Civil Rights Act of 1964, the demand of Negro Americans for full recognition of their civil rights was finally met.

The effort, no matter how savage and brutal, of some State and local governments to thwart the exercise of those rights is doomed. The nation will not put up with it—least of all the Negroes. The present moment will pass. In the meantime, a new period is beginning.

In this new period the expectations of the Negro Americans will go beyond civil rights. Being Americans, they will now expect that in the near future equal opportunities for them as a group will produce roughly equal results, as compared with other groups. This is not going to happen. Nor will it happen for generations to come unless a new and special effort is made.

There are two reasons. First, the racist virus in the American blood stream still afflicts us: Negroes will encounter serious personal prejudice for at least another generation. Second, three centuries of sometimes unimaginable mistreatment have taken their toll on the Negro people. The harsh fact is that as a group, at the present time, in terms of ability to win out in the competitions of American life, they are not equal to most of those groups with which they will be competing. Individually, Negro Americans reach the highest peaks of achievement. But collectively, in the spectrum of American ethnic and religious and regional groups, where some get plenty and some get none, where some send eighty percent of their children to college and others pull them out of school at the 8th grade, Negroes are among the weakest.

The most difficult fact for white Americans to understand is that in these terms the circumstances of the Negro American community in recent years has probably been getting worse, not better.

Indices of dollars of income, standards of living, and years of education deceive. The gap between the Negro and most other groups in American society is widening.

The fundamental problem, in which this is most clearly the case, is that of family structure. The evidence—not final, but powerfully persuasive—is that the Negro family in the urban ghettos is crumbling. A middle class group has managed to save itself, but for vast numbers of the unskilled, poorly educated city working class the fabric of conventional social relationships has all but disintegrated. There are indications that the situation may have been arrested in the past few years, but the general post war trend is unmistakable. So long as this situation persists, the cycle of poverty and disadvantage will continue to repeat itself.

The thesis of this paper is that these events, in combination, confront the nation with a new kind of problem. Measures that have worked in the past, or would work for most groups in the present, will not work here. A national effort is required that will give a unity of purpose to the many activities of the Federal government in this area, directed to a new kind of national goal: the establishment of a stable Negro family structure. . . .

Chapter 2—The Negro American Family

At the heart of the deterioration of the fabric of Negro society is the deterioration of the Negro family.

It is the fundamental source of the weakness of the Negro community at the present time.

There is probably no single fact of Negro American life so little understood by whites. The Negro situation is commonly perceived by whites in terms of the visible manifestation of discrimination and poverty, in part because Negro protest is directed against such obstacles, and in part, no doubt, because these are facts which involve the actions and attitudes of the white community as well. It is more difficult, however, for whites to perceive the effect that three centuries of exploitation have had on the fabric of Negro society itself. Here the consequences of the historic injustices done to Negro Americans are silent and hidden from view. But here is where the true injury has occurred: unless this damage is repaired, all the effort to end discrimination and poverty and injustice will come to little.

The role of the family in shaping character and ability is so pervasive as to be easily overlooked. The family is the basic social unit of American life; it is the basic socializing unit. By and large, adult conduct in society is learned as a child.

A fundamental insight of psychoanalytic theory, for example, is that the child learns a way of looking at life in his early years through which all later experience is viewed and which profoundly shapes his adult conduct.

It may be hazarded that the reason family structure does not loom larger in public discussion of social issues is that people tend to assume that the nature of family life is about the same throughout American society. The mass media and the development of suburbia have created an image of the American family as a highly standardized phenomenon. It is therefore easy to assume that whatever it is that makes for differences among individuals or groups of individuals, it is not a different family structure.

There is much truth to this; as with any other nation, Americans are producing a recognizable family system. But that process is not completed by any means. There are still, for example, important differences in family patterns surviving from the age of the great European migration to the United States, and these variations account for notable differences in the progress and assimilation of various ethnic and religious groups. A number of immigrant groups were characterized by unusually strong family bonds; these groups have characteristically progressed more rapidly than others.

But there is one truly great discontinuity in family structure in the United States at the present time: that between the white world in general and that of the Negro American.

The white family has achieved a high degree of stability and is maintaining that stability.

By contrast, the family structure of lower class Negroes is highly unstable, and in many urban centers is approaching complete breakdown.

N.B. There is considerable evidence that the Negro community is in fact dividing between a stable middle class group that is steadily growing stronger and more successful, and an increasingly disorganized and disadvantaged lower class group. There are indications, for example, that the middle class Negro family puts a higher premium on family stability and the conserving of family resources than does the white middle class family. The discussion of this paper is not, obviously, directed to the first group excepting as it is affected by the experiences of the second— an important exception. ... Nearly a Quarter of Urban Negro Marriages are Dissolved. ... Nearly One-Quarter of Negro Births are now Illegitimate. ... Almost One-Fourth of Negro Families are Headed by Females. ... The Breakdown of the Negro Family Has Led to a Startling Increase in Welfare Dependency....

Chapter 4—The Tangle of Pathology

That the Negro American has survived at all is extraordinary—a lesser people might simply have died out, as indeed others have. That the Negro community has not only survived, but in this political generation has entered national affairs as a moderate, humane, and constructive national force is the highest testament to the healing powers of the democratic ideal and the creative vitality of the Negro people.

But it may not be supposed that the Negro American community has not paid a fearful price for the incredible mistreatment to which it has been subjected over the past three centuries.

In essence, the Negro community has been forced into a matriarchal structure which, because it is so out of line with the rest of the American society, seriously retards the progress of the group as a whole, and imposes a crushing burden on the Negro male and, in consequence, on a great many Negro women as well. . . .

It might be estimated that as much as half of the Negro community falls into the middle class. However, the remaining half is in desperate and deteriorating circumstances. Moreover, because of housing segregation it is immensely difficult for the stable half to escape from the cultural influences of the unstable one. The children of middle class Negroes often as not must grow up in, or next to the slums, an experience almost unknown to white middle class children. They are therefore constantly exposed to the pathology of the disturbed group and constantly in danger of being drawn into it. It is for this reason that the propositions put forth in this study may be thought of as having a more or less general application.

In a word, most Negro youth are in danger of being caught up in the tangle of pathology that affects their world, and probably a majority are so entrapped. Many of those who escape do so for one generation only: as things now are, their children may have to run the gauntlet all over again. That is not the least vicious aspect of the world that white America has made for the Negro. . . .

The term alienation may by now have been used in too many ways to retain a clear meaning, but it will serve to sum up the equally numerous ways in which large numbers of Negro youth appear to be withdrawing from American society.

One startling way in which this occurs is that the men are just not there when the Census enumerator comes around. . . . Along with the diminution of white middle class contacts for a large percentage of Negroes, observers report that the Negro churches have all but lost contact with men in the Northern cities as well. This may be a normal condition of urban life, but it is probably a changed condition for the Negro American and cannot be a socially desirable development.

The only religious movement that appears to have enlisted a considerable number of lower class Negro males in Northern cities of late is that of the Black Muslims: a movement based on total rejection of white society, even though it emulates whites more.

In a word: the tangle of pathology is tightening.

Chapter 5—The Case for National Action

The object of this study has been to define a problem, rather than propose solutions to it. We have kept within these confines for three reasons.

First, there are many persons, within and without the Government, who do not feel the problem exists, at least in any serious degree. These persons feel that, with the legal obstacles to assimilation out of the way, matters will take care of themselves in the normal course of events. This is a fundamental issue, and requires a decision within the government.

Second, it is our view that the problem is so inter-related, one thing with another, that any list of program proposals would necessarily be incomplete, and would distract attention from the main point of inter-relatedness. We have shown a clear relation between male employment, for example, and the number of welfare dependent children. Employment in turn reflects educational achievement, which depends in large part on family stability, which reflects employment. Where we should break into this cycle, and how, are the most difficult domestic questions facing the United States. We must first reach agreement on what the problem is, then we will know what questions must be answered.

Third, it is necessary to acknowledge the view, held by a number of responsible persons, that this problem may in fact be out of control. This is a view with which we emphatically and totally disagree, but the view must be acknowledged. The persistent rise in Negro educational achievement is probably the main trend that belies this thesis. On the other hand our study has produced some clear indications that the situation may indeed have begun to feed on itself. It may be noted, for example, that for most of the post-war period male Negro unemployment and the number of new AFDC [Aid for Families with Dependent Children] cases rose and fell together as if connected by a chain from 1948 to 1962. The correlation between the two series of data was an astonishing .91. (This would mean that 83 percent of the rise and fall in AFDC cases can be statistically ascribed to the rise and fall in the unemployment rate.) In 1960, however, for the first time, unemployment declined, but the number of new AFDC cases rose. In 1963 this happened a second time. In 1964 a third. The possible implications of these and other data are serious enough that they, too, should be understood before program proposals are made.

However, the argument of this paper does lead to one central conclusion: Whatever the specific elements of a national effort designed to resolve this problem, those elements must be coordinated in terms of one general strategy.

What then is that problem? We feel the answer is clear enough. Three centuries of injustice have brought about deep-seated structural distortions in the life of the Negro American. At this point, the present tangle of pathology is capable of perpetuating itself without assistance from the white world. The cycle can be broken only if these distortions are set right.

In a word, a national effort towards the problems of Negro Americans must be directed towards the question of family structure. The object should be to strengthen the Negro family so as to enable it to raise and support its members as do other families. After that, how this group of Americans chooses to run its affairs, take advantage of its opportunities, or fail to do so, is none of the nation's business.

The fundamental importance and urgency of restoring the Negro American Family structure has been evident for some time. E. Franklin Frazier put it most succinctly in 1950:

As the result of family disorganization a large proportion of Negro children and youth have not undergone the socialization which only the family can provide. The disorganized families have failed to provide for their emotional needs and have not provided the discipline and habits which are necessary for personality development. Because the disorganized family has failed in its function as a socializing agency, it has handicapped the children in their relations to the institutions in the community. Moreover, family disorganization has been partially responsible for a large amount of juvenile delinquency and adult crime among Negroes. Since the widespread family disorganization among Negroes has resulted from the failure of the father to play the role in family life required by American society, the mitigation of this problem must await those changes in the Negro and American society which will enable the Negro father to play the role required of him.

Nothing was done in response to Fra-

zier's argument. Matters were left to take care of themselves, and as matters will, grew worse not better. The problem is now more serious, the obstacles greater. There is, however, a profound change for the better in one respect. The President has committed the nation to an all out effort to eliminate poverty wherever it exists, among whites or Negroes, and a militant, organized, and responsible Negro movement exists to join in that effort.

Such a national effort could be stated thus:

The policy of the United States is to bring the Negro American to full and equal sharing in the responsibilities and rewards of citizenship. To this end, the programs of the Federal government bearing on this objective shall be designed to have the effect, directly or indirectly, of enhancing the stability and resources of the Negro American family.

Study Questions

1. What relationships—historical, economic, and psychological—did the Moynihan Report identify between poverty and family structure?

2. Is blaming poverty on weak family structure the same as blaming poverty on individual family members, or might broader social forces be at work?

Report of the National Advisory Commission on Civil Disorders (1968)

In July 1967, President Lyndon Johnson established an eleven-member National Advisory Commission on Civil Disorders to probe the causes of urban race riots that had been occurring since the summer of 1964. Chaired by Illinois Governor Otto Kerner, Jr., the "Kerner Commission," as it was familiarly known, concluded that the nation was "moving toward two societies, one black, one white—separate and unequal." Despite apparent progress in race relations forged by the civil rights movement, the inner cities of major metropolitan areas suffered poverty and violence along a sharp racial division.

Introduction

The summer of 1967 again brought racial disorders to American cities, and with them shock, fear and bewilderment to the nation.

The worst came during a two-week period in July, first in Newark and then in Detroit. Each set off a chain reaction in neighboring communities.

On July 28, 1967, the President of the United States established this Commission and directed us to answer three basic questions:

What happened? Why did it happen? What can be done to prevent it from happening again?

To respond to these questions, we have undertaken a broad range of studies and investigations. We have visited the riot cities; we have heard many witnesses; we have sought the counsel of experts across the country.

This is our basic conclusion: Our nation is moving toward two societies, one black, one white—separate and unequal.

Reaction to last summer's disorders has quickened the movement and deepened the division. Discrimination and segregation have long permeated much of American life; they now threaten the future of every American.

This deepening racial division is not inevitable. The movement apart can be reversed. Choice is still possible. Our principal task is to define that choice and to press for a national resolution.

To pursue our present course will involve the continuing polarization of the American community and, ultimately, the destruction of basic democratic values.

The alternative is not blind repression or capitulation to lawlessness. It is the realization of common opportunities for all within a single society.

This alternative will require a commitment to national action—compassionate, massive and sustained, backed by the resources of the most powerful and the richest nation on this earth. From every American it will require new attitudes, new understanding, and, above all, new will.

The vital needs of the nation must be met; hard choices must be made, and, if necessary, new taxes enacted.

Violence cannot build a better society. Disruption and disorder nourish repression, not justice. They strike at the freedom of every citizen. The community cannot—it will not—tolerate coercion and mob rule.

Violence and destruction must be ended—in the streets of the ghetto and in the lives of people.

Segregation and poverty have created in the racial ghetto a destructive environment totally unknown to most white Americans.

What white Americans have never fully understood—but what the Negro can never forget—is that white society is deeply implicated in the ghetto. White institutions created it, white institutions maintain, and white society condones it.

It is time now to turn with all the purpose at our command to the major unfinished business of this nation. It is time to adopt strategies for action that will produce quick and visible progress. It is time to make good the promises of American democracy to all citizens—urban and rural, white and black, Spanish-surname, American Indian, and every minority group.

Our recommendations embrace three basic principles:

To mount programs on a scale equal to the dimension of the problems;

To aim these programs for high impact in the immediate future in order to close the gap between promise and performance;

To undertake new initiatives and experiments that can change the system of failure and frustration that now dominates the ghetto and weakens our society.

These programs will require unprecedented levels of funding and performance, but they neither probe deeper nor demand more than the problems which called them forth. There can be no higher priority for national action and no higher claim on the nation's conscience. . . .

PART I—WHAT HAPPENED?
Chapter 1—Profiles of Disorder

The report contains profiles of a selection of the disorders that took place during the summer of 1967. These profiles are designed to indicate how the disorders happened, who participated in them, and how local officials, police forces, and the National Guard responded. Illustrative excerpts follow:

NEWARK

. . . On Saturday, July 15, [Director of Police Dominick] Spina received a report of snipers in a housing project. When he arrived he saw approximately 100 National Guardsmen and police officers crouching behind vehicles, hiding in corners and lying on the ground around the edge of the courtyard.

Since everything appeared quiet and it was broad daylight, Spina walked directly down the middle of the street. Nothing happened. As he came to the last building of the complex, he heard a shot. All around him the troopers jumped, believing themselves to be under sniper fire. A moment later a young Guardsman ran from behind a building.

The Director of Police went over and asked him if he had fired the shot. The soldier said yes, he had fired to scare a man away from a window; that his orders were to keep everyone away from windows.

Spina said he told the soldier: "Do you know what you just did? You have now created a state of hysteria. Every Guardsman up and down this street and every state policeman and every city policeman that is present thinks that somebody just fired a shot and that it is probably a sniper."

A short time later more "gunshots" were heard. Investigating, Spina came upon a Puerto Rican sitting on a wall. In reply to a question as to whether he knew "where the firing is coming from?" the man said:

"That's no firing. That's fireworks. If you look up to the fourth floor, you will see the people who are throwing down these cherry bombs."

By this time four truckloads of National Guardsmen had arrived and troopers and policemen were again crouched everywhere looking for a sniper. The Director of Police remained at the scene for three hours, and the only shot fired was the one by the Guardsmen.

Nevertheless, at six o'clock that evening two columns of National Guardsmen and state troopers were directing mass fire at the Hayes Housing Project in response to what they believed were snipers. . . .

DETROIT

. . . A spirit of carefree nihilism was taking hold. To riot and destroy appeared more and more to become ends in themselves. Late Sunday afternoon it appeared to one observer that the young people were "dancing amidst the flames."

A Negro plainclothes officer was standing at an intersection when a man threw a Molotov cocktail into a business establishment at the corner. In the heat of the afternoon, fanned by the 20 to 25 m.p.h. winds of both Sunday and Monday, the fire reached the home next door within minutes. As residents uselessly sprayed the flames with garden hoses, the fire jumped from roof to roof of adjacent two- and three-story buildings. Within the hour the entire block was in flames. The ninth house in the burning row belonged to the arsonist who had thrown the Molotov cocktail. . . .

. . . Employed as a private guard, 55-year-old Julius L. Dorsey, a Negro, was standing in front of a market when accosted by two Negro men and a woman. They demanded he permit them to loot the market. He ignored their demands. They began to berate him. He asked a neighbor to call the police. As the argument grew more heated, Dorsey fired three shots from his pistol into the air.

The police radio reported: "Looters, they have rifles." A patrol car driven by a police officer and carrying three National Guardsmen arrived. As the looters fled, the law enforcement personnel opened fire. When the firing ceased, one person lay dead.

He was Julius L. Dorsey. . . .

As the riot alternatively waxed and waned, one area of the ghetto remained insulated. On the northeast side the residents of some 150 square blocks inhabited by 21,000 persons had, in 1966, banded together in the Positive Neighborhood Action Committee (PNAC). With professional help from the Institute of Urban Dynamics, they had organized block clubs and made plans for the improvement of the neighborhood. . . .

When the riot broke out, the residents, through the block clubs, were able to organize quickly. Youngsters, agreeing to stay in the neighborhood, participated in detouring traffic. While many persons reportedly sympathized with the idea of a rebellion against the "system," only two small fires were set—one in an empty building. . . .

According to Lt. Gen. Throckmorton and Col. Bolling, the city, at this time, was saturated with fear. The National Guardsmen were afraid, the residents were afraid, and the police were afraid. Numerous persons, the majority of them Negroes, were being injured by gunshots of undetermined origin. The general and his staff felt that the major task of the troops was to reduce the fear and restore an air of normalcy.

In order to accomplish this, every effort was made to establish contact and rapport between the troops and the residents. The soldiers—20 percent of whom were Negro—began helping to clean up the streets, collect garbage, and trace persons who had disappeared in the confusion. Residents in the neighborhoods responded with soup and sandwiches for the troops. In areas where the National Guard tried to establish rapport with the citizens, there was a smaller response.

NEW BRUNSWICK

... A short time later, elements of the crowd—an older and rougher one than the night before—appeared in front of the police station. The participants wanted to see the mayor.

Mayor [Patricia] Sheehan went out onto the steps of the station. Using a bullhorn, she talked to the people and asked that she be given an opportunity to correct conditions. The crowd was boisterous. Some persons challenged the mayor. But, finally, the opinion, "She's new! Give her a chance!" prevailed.

A demand was issued by people in the crowd that all persons arrested the previous night be released. Told that this already had been done, the people were suspicious. They asked to be allowed to inspect the jail cells.

It was agreed to permit representatives of the people to look in the cells to satisfy themselves that everyone had been released.

The crowd dispersed. The New Brunswick riot had failed to materialize.

Chapter 2—Patterns of Disorder

The "typical" riot did not take place. The disorders of 1967 were unusual, irregular, complex and unpredictable social processes. Like most human events, they did not unfold in an orderly sequence. However, an analysis of our survey information leads to some conclusions about the riot process.

In general:

The civil disorders of 1967 involved Negroes acting against local symbols of white American society, authority and property in Negro neighborhoods—rather than against white persons.

Of 164 disorders reported during the first nine months of 1967, eight (5 percent) were major in terms of violence and damage; 33 (20 percent) were serious but not major; 123 (75 percent) were minor and undoubtedly would not have received national attention as "riots" had the nation not been sensitized by the more serous outbreaks.

In the 75 disorders studied by a Senate subcommittee, 83 deaths were reported. Eighty-two percent of the deaths and more than half the injuries occurred in Newark and Detroit. About 10 percent of the dead and 38 percent of the injured were public employees, primarily law officers and firemen. The overwhelming majority of the persons killed or injured in all the disorders were Negro civilians.

Initial damage estimates were greatly exaggerated. In Detroit, newspaper damage estimates at first ranged from $200 million to $500 million; the highest recent estimate is $45 million. In Newark, early estimates ranged from $15 to $25 million. A month later damage was estimated at $10.2 million, over 80 percent in inventory losses.

In the 24 disorders in 23 cities which we surveyed:

The final incident before the outbreak of disorder, and the initial violence itself, generally took place in the evening or at night at a place in which it was normal for many people to be on the streets.

Violence usually occurred almost immediately following the occurrence of the final precipitating incident, and then escalated rapidly. With but few exceptions, violence subsided during the day, and flared rapidly again at night. The night-day cycles continued through the early period of the major disorders.

Disorder generally began with rock and bottle throwing and window breaking. Once store windows were broken, looting usually followed.

Disorder did not erupt as a result of a single "triggering" or "precipitating" incident. Instead, it was generated out of an increasingly disturbed social atmosphere, in which typically a series of tension-heightening incidents over a period of weeks or months became linked in the minds of many in the Negro community with a reservoir of underlying grievances.

At some point in the mounting tension, a further incident—in itself often routine or trivial—became the breaking point and the tension spilled over into violence.

"Prior" incidents, which increased tensions and ultimately led to violence, were police actions in almost half the cases; police actions were "final" incidents before the outbreak of violence in 12 of the 24 surveyed disorders.

No particular control tactic was successful in every situation. The varied effectiveness of control techniques emphasizes the need for advance training, planning, adequate intelligence systems, and knowledge of the ghetto community.

Negotiations between Negroes—including your militants as well as older Negro leaders—and white officials concerning "terms of peace" occurred during virtually all the disorders surveyed. In many cases, these negotiations involved discussion of underlying grievances as well as the handling of the disorder by control authorities.

The typical rioter was a teenager or young adult, a lifelong resident of the city in which he rioted, a high school dropout; he was, nevertheless, somewhat better educated than his nonrioting Negro neighbor, and was usually underemployed or employed in a menial job. He was proud of his race, extremely hostile to both whites and middle-class Negroes and, although informed about politics, highly distrustful of the political system.

A Detroit survey revealed that approximately 11 percent of the total residents of two riot areas admitted participation in the rioting, 20 to 25 percent identified themselves as "bystanders," over 16 percent identified themselves as "counter-ri- oters" who urged rioters to "cool it," and the remaining 48 to 53 percent said they were at home or elsewhere and did not participate. In a survey of Negro males between the ages of 15 and 35 residing in the disturbance area in Newark, about 45 percent identified themselves as rioters, and about 55 percent as "noninvolved."

Most rioters were young Negro males. Nearly 53 percent of arrestees were between 15 and 24 years of age; nearly 81 percent between 15 and 35.

In Detroit and Newark about 74 percent of the rioters were brought up in the North. In contrast, of the noninvolved, 36 percent in Detroit and 52 percent in Newark were brought up in the North.

What the rioters appeared to be seeking was fuller participation in the social order and the material benefits enjoyed by the majority of American citizens. Rather than rejecting the American system, they were anxious to obtain a place for themselves in it.

Numerous Negro counter-rioters walked the streets urging rioters to "cool it." The typical counter-rioter was better educated and had higher income than either the rioter or the noninvolved.

The proportion of Negroes in local government was substantially smaller than the Negro proportion of population. Only three of the 20 cities studied had more than one Negro legislator; none had ever had a Negro mayor or city manager. In only four cities did Negroes hold other important policy-making positions or serve as heads of municipal departments.

Although almost all cities had some sort of formal grievance mechanism for handling citizen complaints, this typically was regarded by Negroes as ineffective and was generally ignored.

Although specific grievances varied from city to city, at least 12 deeply held grievances can be identified and ranked into three levels of relative intensity:

First Level of Intensity
1. Police practices
2. Unemployment and underemployment
3. Inadequate housing
Second Level of Intensity
4. Inadequate education
5. Poor recreation facilities and programs
6. Ineffectiveness of the political structure and grievance mechanisms.
Third Level of Intensity
7. Disrespectful white attitudes
8. Discriminatory administration of justice
9. Inadequacy of federal programs
10. Inadequacy of municipal services
11. Discriminatory consumer and credit practices
12. Inadequate welfare programs

The results of a three-city survey of various federal programs—manpower, education, housing, welfare and community action—indicate that, despite substantial expenditures, the number of persons assisted constituted only a fraction of those in need.

The background of disorder is often as complex and difficult to analyze as the disorder itself. But we find that certain general conclusions can be drawn:

Social and economic conditions in the riot cities constituted a clear pattern of severe disadvantage for Negroes compared with whites, whether the Negroes lived in the area where the riot took place or outside it. Negroes had completed fewer years of education and fewer had attended high school. Negroes were twice as likely to be unemployed and three times as likely to be in unskilled and service jobs. Negroes averaged 70 percent of the income earned by whites and were more than twice as likely to be living in poverty. Although housing cost Negroes relatively more, they had worse housing—three times as likely to be overcrowded and substandard. When compared to white suburbs, the relative disadvantage is even more pronounced.

A study of the aftermath of disorder leads to disturbing conclusions. We find that, despite the institution of some post-riot programs:

Little basic change in the conditions underlying the outbreak of disorder has taken place. Actions to ameliorate Negro grievances have been limited and sporadic; with but few exceptions, they have not significantly reduced tensions.

In several cities, the principal official response has been to train and equip the police with more sophisticated weapons.

In several cities, increasing polarization is evident, with continuing breakdown of inter-racial communication, and growth of white segregationist or black separatist groups. . . .

PART II—WHY DID IT HAPPEN? Chapter 4—The Basic Causes

In addressing the question "Why did it happen?" we shift our focus from the local to the national scene, from the particular events of the summer of 1967 to the factors within the society at large that created a mood of violence among many urban Negroes.

These factors are complex and interacting; they vary significantly in their effect from city to city and from year to year; and the consequences of one disorder, generating new grievances and new demands, become the causes of the next. Thus was created the "thicket of tension, conflicting evidence and extreme opinions" cited by the President.

Despite these complexities, certain fundamental matters are clear. Of these, the most fundamental is the racial attitude and behavior of white Americans toward black Americans.

Race prejudice has shaped our history decisively; it now threatens to affect our future.

White racism is essentially responsible for the explosive mixture which has been accumulating in our cities since the end of World War II. Among the ingredients of this mixture are:

Pervasive discrimination and segregation in employment, education and housing, which have resulted in the continuing exclusion of great numbers of Negroes from the benefits of economic progress.

Black in-migration and white exodus, which have produced the massive and growing concentrations of impoverished Negroes in our major cities, creating a growing crisis of deteriorating facilities and services and unmet human needs.

The black ghettos where segregation

and poverty converge on the young to destroy opportunity and enforce failure. Crime, drug addiction, dependency on welfare, and bitterness and resentment against society in general and white society in particular are the result.

At the same time, most whites and some Negroes outside the ghetto have prospered to a degree unparalleled in the history of civilization. Through television and other media, this affluence has been flaunted before the eyes of the Negro poor and the jobless ghetto youth.

Yet these facts alone cannot be said to have caused the disorders. Recently, other powerful ingredients have begun to catalyze the mixture:

Frustrated hopes are the residue of the unfulfilled expectations aroused by the great judicial and legislative victories of the Civil Rights Movement and the dramatic struggle for equal rights in the South.

A climate that tends toward approval and encouragement of violence as a form of protest has been created by white terrorism directed against nonviolent protest; by the open defiance of law and federal authority by state and local officials resisting desegregation; and by some protest groups engaging in civil disobedience who turn their backs on nonviolence, go beyond the constitutionally protected rights of petition and free assembly, and resort to violence to attempt to compel alteration of laws and policies with which they disagree.

The frustrations of powerlessness have led some Negroes to the conviction that there is no effective alternative to violence as a means of achieving redress of grievances, and of "moving the system." These frustrations are reflected in alienation and hostility toward the institutions of law and government and the white society which controls them, and in the reach toward racial consciousness and solidarity reflected in the slogan "Black Power."

A new mood has sprung up among Negroes, particularly among the young, in which self-esteem and enhanced racial pride are replacing apathy and submission to "the system."

The police are not merely a "spark" factor. To some Negroes police have come to symbolize white power, white racism and white repression. And the fact is that many police do reflect and express these white attitudes. The atmosphere of hostility and cynicism is reinforced by a widespread belief among Negroes in the existence of police brutality and in a "double standard" of justice and protection —one for Negroes and one for whites.

To this point, we have attempted to identify the prime components of the "explosive mixture." In the chapters that follow we seek to analyze them in the perspective of history. Their meaning, however, is clear:

In the summer of 1967, we have seen in our cities a chain reaction of racial violence. If we are heedless, none of us shall escape the consequences.

Study Questions

1. What basic causes did the Kerner Commission assign to the race riots of 1967?

2. What kinds of solutions would be necessary, if those causes have been correctly identified?

Lyndon B. Johnson, "Steps to Limit the War in Vietnam and Decision Not To Seek Reelection" (1968)

By the late 1960s, Johnson found himself waging two wars, one of his own choosing and the other a result of poorly coordinated choices made by himself and others. The war of his own choosing was the "War on Poverty," a vast array of aid programs for which he struggled to secure funding because the other war—the one waged in Vietnam—was draining national resources. The roots of the Vietnam War extended back to the Truman Doctrine of containment and President Eisenhower's decision to provide aid to South Vietnam in the late 1950s. During Kennedy's administration, U.S. involvement expanded to include not merely aid but also personnel. President Johnson served as commander-in-chief during a new phase of the war, known as "escalation": bombing campaigns, ground troops, more bombing, and more ground troops. Each attempt to step up America's commitment to the war failed to deliver the intended result; the North Vietnamese not only persisted, but they started to gain the upper hand. In January 1968, North Vietnamese forces launched a series of attacks, known as the Tet Offensive, which humbled any American hopes for victory. After CBS News anchor Walter Cronkite announced his opinion that the United States could not achieve anything better than a stalemate in Vietnam, Johnson realized public opinion could not be recovered in his favor. He decided to reverse the escalation policy and to step aside from the next presidential election.

Good evening, my fellow Americans:

Tonight I want to speak to you of peace in Vietnam and Southeast Asia.

No other question so preoccupies our people. No other dream so absorbs the 250 million human beings who live in that part of the world. No other goal motivates American policy in Southeast Asia.

For years, representatives of our Government and others have traveled the world—seeking to find a basis for peace talks.

Since last September, they have carried the offer that I made public at San Antonio. That offer was this:

That the United States would stop its bombardment of North Vietnam when that would lead promptly to productive discussions—and that we would assume that North Vietnam would not take military advantage of our restraint.

Hanoi denounced this offer, both privately and publicly. Even while the search for peace was going on, North Vietnam rushed their preparations for a savage assault on the people, the government, and the allies of South Vietnam.

Their attack—during the Tet holidays—failed to achieve its principal objectives.

It did not collapse the elected government of South Vietnam or shatter its army—as the Communists had hoped.

It did not produce a "general uprising" among the people of the cities as they had predicted.

The Communists were unable to maintain control of any of the more than 30 cities that they attacked. And they took very heavy casualties.

But they did compel the South Vietnamese and their allies to move certain forces from the countryside into the cities.

They caused widespread disruption and suffering. Their attacks, and the battles that followed, made refugees of half a million human beings.

The Communists may renew their attack any day.

They are, it appears, trying to make 1968 the year of decision in South Vietnam —the year that brings, if not final victory or defeat, at least a turning point in the struggle. This much is clear:

If they do mount another round of heavy attacks, they will not succeed in destroying the fighting power of South Vietnam and its allies.

But tragically, this is also clear: Many men—on both sides of the struggle—will be lost. A nation that has already suffered 20 years of warfare will suffer once again. Armies on both sides will take new casualties. And the war will go on.

There is no need for this to be so.

There is no need to delay the talks that could bring an end to this long and this bloody war.

Tonight, I renew the offer I made last August—to stop the bombardment of North Vietnam. We ask that talks begin promptly, that they be serious talks on the substance of peace. We assume that during those talks Hanoi will not take advantage of our restraint.

We are prepared to move immediately toward peace through negotiations.

So, tonight, in the hope that this action will lead to early talks, I am taking the first step to deescalate the conflict. We are reducing—substantially reducing—the present level of hostilities.

And we are doing so unilaterally, and at once.

Tonight, I have ordered our aircraft and our naval vessels to make no attacks on North Vietnam, except in the area north of the demilitarized zone where the continuing enemy buildup directly threatens allied forward positions and where the movements of their troops and supplies are clearly related to that threat.

The area in which we are stopping our attacks includes almost 90 percent of North Vietnam's population, and most of its territory. Thus there will be no attacks around the principal populated areas, or in the food-producing areas of North Vietnam.

Even this very limited bombing of the North could come to an early end—if our restraint is matched by restraint in Hanoi. But I cannot in good conscience stop all bombing so long as to do so would immediately and directly endanger the lives of our men and our allies. Whether a complete bombing halt becomes possible in the future will be determined by events.

Our purpose in this action is to bring about a reduction in the level of violence that now exists.

It is to save the lives of brave men—and to save the lives of innocent women and children. It is to permit the contending forces to move closer to a political settlement.

And tonight, I call upon the United Kingdom and I call upon the Soviet Union —as cochairmen of the Geneva Conferences, and as permanent members of the United Nations Security Council—to do all they can to move from the unilateral act of deescalation that I have just announced toward genuine peace in Southeast Asia.

Now, as in the past, the United States is ready to send its representatives to any forum, at any time, to discuss the means of bringing this ugly war to an end.

I am designating one of our most distinguished Americans, Ambassador Averell Harriman, as my personal representative for such talks. In addition, I have asked Ambassador Llewellyn Thompson, who returned from Moscow for consultation, to be available to join Ambassador Harriman at Geneva or any other suitable place—just as soon as Hanoi agrees to a conference.

I call upon President Ho Chi Minh to respond positively, and favorably, to this new step toward peace.

But if peace does not come now through negotiations, it will come when Hanoi understands that our common resolve is unshakable, and our common strength is invincible.

Tonight, we and the other allied nations are contributing 600,000 fighting men to assist 700,000 South Vietnamese troops in defending their little country.

Our presence there has always rested on this basic belief: The main burden of preserving their freedom must be carried out by them—by the South Vietnamese themselves.

We and our allies can only help to provide a shield behind which the people of South Vietnam can survive and can grow and develop. On their efforts—on their determination and resourcefulness— the outcome will ultimately depend.

That small, beleaguered nation has suffered terrible punishment for more than 20 years.

I pay tribute once again tonight to the great courage and endurance of its people. South Vietnam supports armed forces tonight of almost 700,000 men—and I call your attention to the fact that this is the equivalent of more than 10 million in our own population. Its people maintain their firm determination to be free of domination by the North.

There has been substantial progress, I think, in building a durable government during these last 3 years. The South Vietnam of 1965 could not have survived the enemy's Tet offensive of 1968. The elected government of South Vietnam survived that attack—and is rapidly repairing the devastation that it wrought.

The South Vietnamese know that further efforts are going to be required:

—to expand their own armed forces,

—to move back into the countryside as quickly as possible,

—to increase their taxes,

—to select the very best men that they have for civil and military responsibility,

—to achieve a new unity within their

constitutional government, and

—to include in the national effort all those groups who wish to preserve South Vietnam's control over its own destiny. Last week President Thieu ordered the mobilization of 135,000 additional South Vietnamese. He plans to reach—as soon as possible—a total military strength of more than 800,000 men.

To achieve this, the Government of South Vietnam started the drafting of 19-year-olds on March 1st. On May 1st, the Government will begin the drafting of 18-year-olds.

Last month, 10,000 men volunteered for military service—that was two and a half times the number of volunteers during the same month last year. Since the middle of January, more than 48,000 South Vietnamese have joined the armed forces—and nearly half of them volunteered to do so.

All men in the South Vietnamese armed forces have had their tours of duty extended for the duration of the war, and reserves are now being called up for immediate active duty.

President Thieu told his people last week: "We must make greater efforts and accept more sacrifices because, as I have said many times, this is our country. The existence of our nation is at stake, and this is mainly a Vietnamese responsibility."

He warned his people that a major national effort is required to root out corruption and incompetence at all levels of government.

We applaud this evidence of determination on the part of South Vietnam. Our first priority will be to support their effort.

We shall accelerate the reequipment of South Vietnam's armed forces—in order to meet the enemy's increased firepower. This will enable them progressively to undertake a larger share of combat operations against the Communist invaders.

On many occasions I have told the American people that we would send to Vietnam those forces that are required to accomplish our mission there. So, with that as our guide, we have previously authorized a force level of approximately 525,000.

Some weeks ago—to help meet the enemy's new offensive—we sent to Vietnam about 11,000 additional Marine and airborne troops. They were deployed by air in 48 hours, on an emergency basis. But the artillery, tank, aircraft, medical, and other units that were needed to work with and to support these infantry troops in combat could not then accompany them by air on that short notice.

In order that these forces may reach maximum combat effectiveness, the Joint Chiefs of Staff have recommended to me that we should prepare to send—during the next 5 months—support troops totaling approximately 13,500 men.

A portion of these men will be made available from our active forces. The balance will come from reserve component units which will be called up for service.

The actions that we have taken since the beginning of the year

—to reequip the South Vietnamese forces,

—to meet our responsibilities in Korea, as well as our responsibilities in Vietnam,

—to meet price increases and the cost of activating and deploying reserve forces,

—to replace helicopters and provide the other military supplies we need, all of these actions are going to require additional expenditures.

The tentative estimate of those additional expenditures is $2.5 billion in this fiscal year, and $2.6 billion in the next fiscal year.

These projected increases in expenditures for our national security will bring into sharper focus the Nation's need for immediate action: action to protect the prosperity of the American people and to protect the strength and the stability of our American dollar.

On many occasions I have pointed out that, without a tax bill or decreased expenditures, next year's deficit would again be around $20 billion. I have emphasized the need to set strict priorities in our spending. I have stressed that failure to act and to act promptly and decisively would raise very strong doubts throughout the world about America's willingness to keep its financial house in order.

Yet Congress has not acted. And tonight we face the sharpest financial threat in the postwar era—a threat to the dollar's role as the keystone of international trade and finance in the world.

Last week, at the monetary conference in Stockholm, the major industrial countries decided to take a big step toward creating a new international monetary asset that will strengthen the international monetary system. I am very proud of the very able work done by Secretary Fowler and Chairman Martin of the Federal Reserve Board.

But to make this system work the United States just must bring its balance of payments to—or very close to—equilibrium. We must have a responsible fiscal policy in this country. The passage of a tax bill now, together with expenditure control that the Congress may desire and dictate, is absolutely necessary to protect this Nation's security, to continue our prosperity, and to meet the needs of our people.

What is at stake is 7 years of unparalleled prosperity. In those 7 years, the real income of the average American, after taxes, rose by almost 30 percent—a gain as large as that of the entire preceding 19 years.

So the steps that we must take to convince the world are exactly the steps we must take to sustain our own economic strength here at home. In the past 8 months, prices and interest rates have risen because of our inaction.

We must, therefore, now do everything we can to move from debate to action— from talking to voting. There is, I believe— I hope there is—in both Houses of the Congress—a growing sense of urgency that this situation just must be acted upon and must be corrected.

My budget in January was, we thought, a tight one. It fully reflected our evaluation of most of the demanding needs of this Nation.

But in these budgetary matters, the President does not decide alone. The Congress has the power and the duty to determine appropriations and taxes.

The Congress is now considering our proposals and they are considering reductions in the budget that we submitted.

As part of a program of fiscal restraint that includes the tax surcharge, I shall approve appropriate reductions in the January budget when and if Congress so decides that that should be done.

One thing is unmistakably clear, however: Our deficit just must be reduced. Failure to act could bring on conditions that would strike hardest at those people that all of us are trying so hard to help.

These times call for prudence in this land of plenty. I believe that we have the character to provide it, and tonight I plead with the Congress and with the people to act promptly to serve the national interest, and thereby serve all of our people.

Now let me give you my estimate of the chances for peace:

—the peace that will one day stop the bloodshed in South Vietnam,

—that will permit all the Vietnamese people to rebuild and develop their land,

—that will permit us to turn more fully to our own tasks here at home.

I cannot promise that the initiative that I have announced tonight will be completely successful in achieving peace any more than the 30 others that we have undertaken and agreed to in recent years.

But it is our fervent hope that North Vietnam, after years of fighting that have left the issue unresolved, will now cease its efforts to achieve a military victory and will join with us in moving toward the peace table.

And there may come a time when South Vietnamese—on both sides—are able to work out a way to settle their own differences by free political choice rather than by war.

As Hanoi considers its course, it should be in no doubt of our intentions. It must not miscalculate the pressures within our democracy in this election year.

We have no intention of widening this war.

But the United States will never accept a fake solution to this long and arduous struggle and call it peace.

No one can foretell the precise terms of an eventual settlement.

Our objective in South Vietnam has never been the annihilation of the enemy. It has been to bring about a recognition in Hanoi that its objective—taking over the South by force—could not be achieved.

We think that peace can be based on the Geneva Accords of 1954—under political conditions that permit the South Vietnamese—all the South Vietnamese—to chart their course free of any outside domination or interference, from us or from anyone else.

So tonight I reaffirm the pledge that we made at Manila—that we are prepared to withdraw our forces from South Vietnam as the other side withdraws its forces to the north, stops the infiltration, and the level of violence thus subsides.

Our goal of peace and self-determination in Vietnam is directly related to the future of all of Southeast Asia—where much has happened to inspire confidence during the past 10 years. We have done all that we knew how to do to contribute and to help build that confidence.

A number of its nations have shown what can be accomplished under conditions of security. Since 1966, Indonesia, the fifth largest nation in all the world, with a population of more than 100 million people, has had a government that is dedicated to peace with its neighbors and improved conditions for its own people. Political and economic cooperation between nations has grown rapidly.

I think every American can take a great deal of pride in the role that we have played in bringing this about in Southeast Asia. We can rightly judge—as responsible Southeast Asians themselves do—that the progress of the past 3 years would have been far less likely—if not completely impossible—if America's sons and others had not made their stand in Vietnam.

At Johns Hopkins University, about 3 years ago, I announced that the United States would take part in the great work of developing Southeast Asia, including the Mekong Valley, for all the people of that region. Our determination to help build a better land—a better land for men on both sides of the present conflict—has not diminished in the least. Indeed, the ravages of war, I think, have made it more urgent than ever.

So, I repeat on behalf of the United States again tonight what I said at Johns Hopkins—that North Vietnam could take its place in this common effort just as soon as peace comes.

Over time, a wider framework of peace and security in Southeast Asia may become possible. The new cooperation of the nations of the area could be a foundation-stone. Certainly friendship with the nations of such a Southeast Asia is what the United States seeks—and that is all that the United States seeks.

One day, my fellow citizens, there will be peace in Southeast Asia.

It will come because the people of Southeast Asia want it—those whose armies are at war tonight, and those who, though threatened, have thus far been spared.

Peace will come because Asians were willing to work for it—and to sacrifice for it —and to die by the thousands for it.

But let it never be forgotten: Peace will come also because America sent her sons to help secure it.

It has not been easy—far from it. During the past four and a half years, it has been my fate and my responsibility to be Commander in Chief. I have lived—daily and nightly—with the cost of this war. I know the pain that it has inflicted. I know, perhaps better than anyone, the misgivings that it has aroused.

Throughout this entire, long period, I have been sustained by a single principle: that what we are doing now, in Vietnam, is vital not only to the security of Southeast Asia, but it is vital to the security of every American.

Surely we have treaties which we must respect. Surely we have commitments that we are going to keep. Resolutions of the Congress testify to the need to resist aggression in the world and in Southeast Asia.

But the heart of our involvement in South Vietnam—under three different presidents, three separate administrations —has always been America's own security.

And the larger purpose of our involvement has always been to help the nations of Southeast Asia become independent and stand alone, self-sustaining, as members of a great world community—at peace with themselves, and at peace with all others.

With such an Asia, our country—and the world—will be far more secure than it is tonight.

I believe that a peaceful Asia is far nearer to reality because of what America has done in Vietnam. I believe that the men who endure the dangers of battle— fighting there for us tonight—are helping the entire world avoid far greater conflicts, far wider wars, far more destruction, than this one.

The peace that will bring them home someday will come. Tonight I have offered the first in what I hope will be a series of mutual moves toward peace.

I pray that it will not be rejected by the leaders of North Vietnam. I pray that they will accept it as a means by which the sacrifices of their own people may be ended. And I ask your help and your support, my fellow citizens, for this effort to reach across the battlefield toward an early peace.

Finally, my fellow Americans, let me say this:

Of those to whom much is given, much is asked. I cannot say and no man could say that no more will be asked of us.

Yet, I believe that now, no less than when the decade began, this generation of Americans is willing to "pay any price, bear any burden, meet any hardship, support any friend, oppose any foe to assure the survival and the success of liberty."

Since those words were spoken by John F. Kennedy, the people of America have kept that compact with mankind's noblest cause.

And we shall continue to keep it.

Yet, I believe that we must always be mindful of this one thing, whatever the trials and the tests ahead. The ultimate strength of our country and our cause will lie not in powerful weapons or infinite resources or boundless wealth, but will lie in the unity of our people.

This I believe very deeply.

Throughout my entire public career I have followed the personal philosophy that I am a free man, an American, a public servant, and a member of my party, in that order always and only.

For 37 years in the service of our Nation, first as a Congressman, as a Senator, and as Vice President, and now as your President, I have put the unity of the people first. I have put it ahead of any divisive partisanship.

And in these times as in times before, it is true that a house divided against itself by the spirit of faction, of party, of region, of religion, of race, is a house that cannot stand.

There is division in the American house now. There is divisiveness among us all tonight. And holding the trust that is mine, as President of all the people, I cannot disregard the peril to the progress of the American people and the hope and the prospect of peace for all peoples.

So, I would ask all Americans, whatever their personal interests or concern, to guard against divisiveness and all its ugly consequences.

Fifty-two months and 10 days ago, in a moment of tragedy and trauma, the duties of this office fell upon me. I asked then for your help and God's, that we might continue America on its course, binding up our wounds, healing our history, moving forward in new unity, to clear the American agenda and to keep the American commitment for all of our people.

United we have kept that commitment. United we have enlarged that commitment.

Through all time to come, I think America will be a stronger nation, a more just society, and a land of greater opportunity and fulfillment because of what we have all done together in these years of unparalleled achievement.

Our reward will come in the life of freedom, peace, and hope that our children will enjoy through ages ahead.

What we won when all of our people united just must not now be lost in suspicion, distrust, selfishness, and politics among any of our people.

Believing this as I do, I have concluded that I should not permit the Presidency to become involved in the partisan divisions that are developing in this political year.

With America's sons in the fields far away, with America's future under challenge right here at home, with our hopes and the world's hopes for peace in the balance every day, I do not believe that I should devote an hour or a day of my time to any personal partisan causes or to any duties other than the awesome duties of this office—the Presidency of your country.

Accordingly, I shall not seek, and I will not accept, the nomination of my party for another term as your President.

But let men everywhere know, however, that a strong, a confident, and a vigilant America stands ready tonight to seek an honorable peace—and stands ready tonight to defend an honored cause—whatever the price, whatever the burden, whatever the sacrifice that duty may require.

Thank you for listening. Good night and God bless all of you.

Study Question

1. Previously, Johnson had offered to stop bombing North Vietnam if the North Vietnamese government would agree to hold diplomatic talks. Although that government refused the offer, Johnson announced a substantial reduction in U.S. bombing anyway. What did he hope to accomplish by this?

2. Why did Johnson refuse to seek or accept his party's renomination to the presidency?

The Fragmentation and Legacies of the Civil Rights Movement, 1961–1978

Rivalries and Dissensions among Civil Rights Activists

Civil rights leaders did not all speak with one voice. In the Albany Movement (1961–1962), for example, the National Association for the Advancement of Colored People (NAACP), the Southern Christian Leadership Conference (SCLC), and the Student Nonviolent Coordinating Committee (SNCC) each had distinct plans. Charles Sherrod of SNCC was particularly frustrated with Martin Luther King and the SCLC. According to Sherrod, King's presence at rallies helped to draw large crowds, but as soon as King left town, SNCC had trouble maintaining enthusiasm. As jealousy led to rivalry, the young leaders of SNCC sought to go about things their own way. In time, this meant rejecting the interracial cooperation favored by both King and the Congress for Racial Equality (CORE). By 1966, SNCC's Stokely Carmichael would be shouting "Black Power!"—a slogan more consistent with the views of Malcolm X than Martin Luther King.

Malcolm X and Elijah Muhammad's Black Nationalism (1963–1965)

Malcolm X was King's greatest rival for national leadership of the civil rights movement. Malcolm's home had been burned down when he was four years old and his father was killed two years later. In both cases the cause apparently was racially motivated violence. As a young adult, Malcolm peddled illicit drugs, pimped prostitutes, and ran gambling operations—a path of crime that landed him in jail from 1946 to 1952. Behind bars he learned of the Nation of Islam (NOI), a religious movement led by the Rev. Elijah Muhammad. Converting, Malcolm dropped the surname of his birth parents and assumed the title "X," indicating that his true heritage had been obscured by the white culture in which he lived.

Mixing aspects of traditional Islam with a racist doctrine of black supremacy, the NOI blamed the white man for all of the problems that blacks suffered in America. Whereas King called upon whites to make good on the promises of equal rights that their ancestors had made in the nation's founding documents, the NOI rejected the American creed and called for the establishment of a pure black state, hoping eventually to repatriate Africa. Malcolm X therefore rejected the integrationist agenda of King and sought to separate the races—only for black supremacy rather than the white supremacy promoted by certain southern whites. "God wants us to separate ourselves from the wicked white race here in America," wrote Malcolm in *The Black Revolution* (1963), "because this American House of Bondage is number one on God's list for divine destruction today." Malcolm X also rejected King's principle of nonviolence. "Be nonviolent only with those who are nonviolent to you," he wrote in *The Afro-American's*

Right to Self-Defense (1964). Whereas King campaigned for the Voting Rights Act as a constitutional right, Malcolm offered a bluntly practical warning: "If the black man doesn't get the ballot, then you are going to be faced with another man who forgets the ballot and starts using the bullet."

In 1964, Malcolm X made a pilgrimage to Mecca, returning with a changed perspective. He now realized that some white men adhered to the Muslim religion as well as black men. Malcolm relaxed his earlier insistence on black supremacy and began suggesting a more cooperative approach to civil rights. Malcolm also parted ways from his mentor, Elijah Muhammad, after discovering that "the Prophet" was a hypocritical adulterer. Malcolm now appeared a traitor to the NOI, and in 1965 a disgruntled NOI member fatally shot him.

The Emergence of Black Power (1966)

As Malcolm's black separatist rhetoric reverberated across the nation, the younger generation of civil rights activists began to question how much wisdom King and his fellow SCLC clergymen had. Stokely Carmichael, SNCC's new leader, picked up the torch that Malcolm had dropped, shouting "Black Power!" to sharecroppers along a Mississippi highway in a 1966 march. The crowds had already been primed by an advance messenger who had tested the new slogan the evening before. With television cameras rolling, people made fists in the air as they raised their voices in unison.

Black power manifested itself in a variety of ways during the late 1960s. Howard University students urged the faculty to establish a black studies program. "Afro" hairstyles became more popular. Rather than seeking an equal place within the white culture, African Americans sought to celebrate their own unique heritage. For the civil rights movement, this meant that integration no longer could be assumed as the main objective. Indeed, it was now questionable whether such a thing as "the" civil rights movement still existed.

Challenges in the Urban North (1966–1967)

Decades before the Civil War, the French analyst Alexis de Tocqueville had observed that "Race prejudice seems stronger in those states that have abolished slavery than in those where it still exists, and nowhere is it more intolerant than in those states where it has never been known" (*Democracy in America*, 1835). A century after the Civil War, Tocqueville's observation remained accurate. Civil rights activists discovered that the techniques that had been successful in the South would not work in Chicago or Detroit. Although slavery had never been permitted in either of these northern cities, Jim Crow was deeply entrenched.

In January 1966, the SCLC developed the Chicago Plan, a nonviolent direct-action movement for greater Chicago. Jobs and housing were top priorities, for in 1960 blacks represented 23% of Chicago's population but 43% of the unemployed, an economic disparity that was compounded by real estate discrimination. Unlike in the South, where discrimination was visible and often violent, Chicago was characterized by what movement leaders came to call "institutional racism"—an impersonal form of discrimination that could not be exposed so easily. City officials offered tokens of appeasement, leaving the movement's participants uncertain of how to proceed. Against the wishes of veteran civil rights leaders, a young black minister named Jesse Jackson boldly led a march into Cicero, a white neighborhood where few blacks would dare step foot. The marchers were met by angry whites hurling bottles and bricks. Unlike the marchers led by King, these marchers had not been trained in nonviolence and so some of the blacks returned blow for blow. The Chicago Plan failed to measure up to the earlier standard of peaceful success set by the Montgomery Bus Boycott.

The following year, a police raid on an unlicensed bar sparked a race riot in Detroit that persisted for days. Shootings and lootings ravished several city blocks under the shroud of darkness after city lights had been shot out. As in previous instances, local and federal authorities negotiated a response. Once again, federal troops arrived to restore order. Ironically, some of those soldiers had just returned home from Vietnam only to find their own nation in just as much turmoil as southeast Asia.

The Paradoxes of Vietnam (1966–1968)

Although only one in nine Americans were black in 1967, they accounted for one out of every five combat troops stationed in Vietnam and nearly one out of every four casualties. In fact, 45% of the U.S. Airborne Infantry troops—those facing front-line combat—were African Americans. The disproportionate rate of service in dangerous military positions resulted from several factors. First, blacks generally were less-educated, so they were less likely to be recruited for specialized training and more likely to be assigned to combat. Second, blacks had fewer legal mechanisms than whites for avoiding the draft. Third, blacks who were drafted from the ghetto were more likely than middle-class whites to take dangerous assignments in search of higher pay. Whatever the causes of black military service, the effect was to intensify the agitation for civil rights at home. After all, why should a black man from Mississippi risk his life to liberate Southeast Asia only to return and find no freedom for himself in America?

In 1964, a black boxer named Cassius Clay won the world heavyweight boxing championship. With his name still fresh on Americans' minds, he joined the Nation of Islam. Elijah Muhammad renamed him Muhammad Ali. In April 1967, Muhammad Ali refused to be drafted into the U.S. Army, claiming a conscientious objection as a pacifist. A judge sentenced him to five years in prison. Meanwhile, that same April, Martin Luther

King denounced America's involvement in Vietnam when visiting Riverside Church in New York City. In a rousing speech, King called the Vietnam War a "demoniacal destructive suction tube" that takes public money away from education and rehabilitation programs that would serve America's poor people, especially blacks.

"I could never again raise my voice against the violence of the oppressed in the ghettos without having first spoken clearly to the greatest purveyor of violence in the world today—my own government," charged King in a statement that put a rift between himself and white politicians who previously had assisted the civil rights movement. But even King's increasingly radical stance still seemed calm compared to the growing array of civil rights activists and war protesters who rallied in the streets of New York City and Washington, DC.

From Black Power to the Black Panther Party (1966–1972)

In 1964, Stokely Carmichael organized a black voter registration drive in Lowndes County, Alabama, which adopted the black panther as its logo. Two years later, Huey Newton and Bobby Seale founded an organization borrowing the same image, the Black Panther Party for Self-Defense. Based in Oakland, California, the Black Panther Party "policed the police" in order to prevent and report police brutality against blacks. The Panthers, which soon numbered some 2,000, also adopted humanitarian causes, such as providing lunches for black children.

After a shootout with the police, Newton was convicted and jailed for killing a white police officer. For a time, the "Free Huey" campaign gave strength to the Panther movement, but by the end of the decade internal squabbles over leadership led to the group's demise. Some Pathers faulted the federal government for infiltrating the organization in order to plant seeds of rivalry among its members. As Panther veteran Mumia Abu-Jamal wrote, while serving a sentence on death row, "the nation's premier law enforcement agency, one said to be investigating hate crimes, had itself been committing crimes motivated by hatred against Black Americans for decades" (*We Want Freedom*, 2004).

On the one hand, the Panthers stood for traditional American values, such as the Second Amendment right to bear arms. On the other hand, the Panthers rejected the constitutional pathway that King trod and followed instead the communist writings of Mao Zedong and anti-colonial revolutionaries in the Third World. In the end, the Panthers failed to steer America's political leaders toward their cause.

The Legacies of Dr. Martin Luther King, Jr. (1968)

In 1968, sanitation workers in Memphis organized a strike to protest low wages and racial discrimination. Even though many black sanitation workers also held second jobs, their wages were so low that they still qualified for welfare. The strikers adopted a simple slogan—"I am a Man"—which they printed in bold letters on signs across their chests. Supporting their effort at an April 3 rally, Martin Luther King cried out, "We are tired of our men being emasculated so that our wives and daughters have to go out and work in the white lady's kitchen, leaving us unable to be with our children and give them the time and attention that they need." The next day, King was assassinated as he exited his room of a Memphis hotel.

Perhaps King had seen it coming. The evening before, he had told the crowd, "I've seen the promised land. I may not get there with you. But I want you to know, that we, as a people will get to the promised land." The Rev. Ralph Abernathy, preaching for King's funeral in Atlanta, likened the civil rights leader to Christ, saying, "There has been a crucifixion in our nation, but here in this spring season . . . we know that the Resurrection will shortly appear." Others were less nostalgic, having labeled King as a communist and an adulterer. No one, however, could deny that the civil rights movement had drawn much of its stability—a commitment to nonviolent protest—from King's leadership.

Affirmative Action and the End of the Civil Rights Movement (1965–1978)

The civil rights movement had begun as a quest for procedural equality, pleading that government policy should apply to blacks the same as it does to whites. In the late 1960s, the goal shifted toward substantive equality—not merely an equality of opportunity, but also an equality of attainment. Speaking at Howard University in June 1965, President Lyndon Johnson said that the Civil Rights Act only marked the beginning of reform. Blacks had gained many freedoms in recent years, but to attain success would require something more. As Johnson explained:

> But freedom is not enough. You do not wipe away the scars of centuries by saying: Now you are free to go where you want, and do as you desire, and choose the leaders you please.

> You do not take a person who for years has been hobbled by chains and liberate him, bring him up to the starting line of a race and then say, "you are free to compete with all the others," and still justly believe that you have been completely fair.

> Thus it is not enough just to open the gates of opportunity. All our citizens must have the ability to walk through those gates.

In September, Johnson issued an executive order directing the Equal Employment Opportunity Commission to take "affirmative action" in ensuring that blacks receive the same level of employment and compensation as whites. The phrase "affirmative action" had also appeared in a 1961 executive order issued by President Kennedy. Although no such policy appeared in the 1964 Civil Rights Act, President Johnson directed his administration to enforce the act as if it did, and the courts generally supported this interpretation during the 1970s.

Not until 1978 did the U.S. Supreme Court begin to put the breaks on affirmative action. The case involved an American of Norwegian ancestry who twice was rejected for admission to the medical school of the University of California at Berkeley. Allan Bakke sued the university for admitting minority students—blacks and Hispanics—who had scored lower than he on standardized tests. The university policy allowed minorities to be considered twice: once with the general pool of applicants that included Bakke, competing for 84 slots, and again with a special minority pool that competed for 16 other slots, regardless of how they ranked compared to the 84th placement in the general pool. Bakke, because he was not considered a minority, was denied the chance to compete for the second pool of 16 slots. His attorney argued that this was a violation of Bakke's Fourteenth Amendment right to equal protection with respect to Sec. 601 of Title VI of the Civil Rights Act of 1964, which provides that no person shall be excluded for reason of race or color from participating in any program receiving federal financial assistance.

In a 5–4 majority opinion, the U.S. Supreme Court declared that university's quota system was unconstitutional and therefore Bakke should be granted admission. However, one of the five justices voting in the majority on that point also swung his vote to join with the other four justices for another aspect of the ruling, producing a secondary 5–4 majority opinion that allowed race to be a factor in admissions policies, so long as the quota system operates more flexibly than it had in Bakke's situation.

By this time, the civil rights movement no longer existed as such. A new generation of politicians began debating affirmative action, with liberals arguing that the policy "leveled the playing field" for minorities, while conservatives objected that such a policy amounted to "reverse discrimination" against whites. Gender equality also became increasingly wrapped up in questions of social justice. SNCC and the Panthers disintegrated in the late 1960s and early 1970s as a result of internal contests between men and women for leadership of the movement. Meanwhile, a broader feminist movement was forming nationwide.

Study Questions

1. How did the political philosophies of Martin Luther King, Jr., and Malcolm X differ, and which of these two men proved more successful in accomplishing his goals?

2. Explain the relation of the Vietnam War to the civil rights movement.

3. Define "affirmative action" and explain why it was controversial in the 1970s.

The Modern Feminist Movement

Historians generally refer to feminist reform efforts of the 1960s through the 1980s as the "second wave" of American feminism. The "first wave," beginning in the mid 1800s and continuing through the early 1900s, emphasized property rights and voting rights. Feminists of that earlier tradition generally were "maternalists," rather than feminists in the modern sense. Recall, for example, that Jane Addams and Florence Kelley had taken on "mothering" roles in society as they advocated progressive reforms to improve the lots of families. Similarly, Frances Perkins, as Secretary of State under Franklin D. Roosevelt, shaped the Social Security Act of 1935 as a care-taking safety net for families, assuming the marital household with a male breadwinner as the norm. Thus, a widowed wife could receive retirement income based on the prior employment of her deceased husband. In this sense, public policy recognized the family—a husband and wife with their children—rather than the individual as the basic unit of society.

Following World War II, Americans became increasingly focused on their rights as individuals, rather than their well-being as families. Public policy shifted, with federal aid programs under the Great Society preferring to subsidize daycare and requiring that single mothers work, rather than the New Deal model of providing a replacement income for a disabled or deceased husband so that a mother could remain in the home with her children. Meanwhile, women themselves began to look for fulfillment beyond the family. First, however, they would need a new vocabulary for expressing these dreams.

Many historians regard Betty Friedan's 1963 book *The Feminine Mystique* as the launching pad for the "second wave" of American feminism. Henceforth, the new generation of feminists would focus on access to contraception and abortion plus affirmative action policies for achieving gender equality in both education and employment. Friedan supplied the language for this new agenda by detailing, in her opening chapter, "The Problem That Has No Name." According to Friedan, countless American women were not content to have the American dream of the 1950s: marriage to a gainfully employed man, children, and a nice house in the suburbs. Friedan went so far as to compare this domestic lifestyle to a Nazi concentration camp. She argued that women wanted, and deserved, something more—the same thing men already had: careers outside the home. Friedan thus opened a conversation and gave women a way to talk about their desire for higher education and full-time careers. The book became a bestseller, with women often meeting in groups to discuss its implications for their lives. Over the next few decades, the rate of full-time employment for women increased, as did the rates of cohabitation, divorce, contraception, and abortion and, for those children who were born, the rate of daycare enrollment.

Unknown to most American readers, the German psychologist Alexander Mitscherlich had published *Society without the Father* the same year as Friedan's book appeared. Mitscherlich warned that the removal of the "working, teaching father" from the home, where he could model for children what meaningful labor is like, was already having a devastating impact upon children. For women also to leave the home, consigning children to daycare and all-day schooling, would deny children of both their parents for most hours of the day. Industrialization, in other words, had separated men's work from family, thus separating working fathers from their children and delaying the natural process of social maturation. For women to leave the home as well would only compound the difficulty, especially when women discovered that paid employment outside the home seldom is as fulfilling as it may look from a distance.

Even as the second wave of feminism challenged earlier understandings of the parent-child relationship, it also offered a transformed vision for gender relations. Rather than celebrating the differences between men and women, feminism called for total equality. In 1966, Friedan founded the National Organization for Women, which advocated for the ratification of the Equal Rights Amendment (ERA), proposed in 1972:

> Section 1. Equality of rights under the law shall not be denied or abridged by the United States or by any State on account of sex.

> Section 2. The Congress shall have the power to enforce, by appropriate legislation, the provisions of this article.

> Section 3. This amendment shall take effect two years after the date of ratification.

The states have never ratified the ERA. Instead, it became a wedge issue that divided liberal feminists in the Democratic Party from conservative guardians of family values in the Republican Party. On the one hand, the ERA echoed a longstanding American commitment to the principle of equality. On the other hand, one implication that troubled many women—and their husbands, fathers, and brothers—was the military draft. With the Vietnam War still fresh in people's minds, were they really willing to demand that the federal government treat young women exactly like young men, sending them to risk their lives in combat?

Study Questions

1. How were the first and second waves of feminism different?

2. What was the most insightful claim that Betty Friedan made in her book *The Feminine Mystique*—and why did some people, both men and women, disagree with her?

Constitutional Amendments of the 1960s and 1970s

During the 1960s and 1970s, the states ratified four amendments to the U.S. Constitution. The Twenty-Third Amendment enabled residents of the District of Columbia to participate in presidential elections. Two amendments had to do with voter eligibility. The Twenty-Fourth Amendment removed the poll tax requirement, which particularly in southern states had been deployed to deprive African Americans of their Fifteenth Amendment right to suffrage. The Twenty-Sixth Amendment reduced the voting age to eighteen nationwide, largely in response to frustrations over the fact that eighteen-year-olds could be drafted into military service even though they were not old enough in some states to elect the congressmen who instituted the draft. The Twenty-Fifth Amendment modified the procedure by which vacancies in the presidency or vice presidency are filled. When President Woodrow Wilson suffered a stroke in 1919, his wife Edith assumed many of his presidential duties, a practice that drew much criticism. The Twenty-Fifth Amendment provided a means for declaring a president incompetent and assigning a replacement. The vice presidency remained vacant during the forty-five months that Harry S. Truman assumed the presidency following the death of Franklin D. Roosevelt in 1945. This amendment would ensure that future vacancies of the vice presidency would be filled in due time. As history would have it, the Twenty-Fifth Amendment shaped the succession of both the vice president and the president during the Watergate scandal surrounding the Nixon administration during 1973–1974.

Twenty-Third Amendment

(proposed, 1960; ratified 1961)

Section 1. The District constituting the seat of Government of the United States shall appoint in such manner as the Congress may direct:

A number of electors of President and Vice President equal to the whole number of Senators and Representatives in Congress to which the District would be entitled if it were a State, but in no event more than the least populous State; they shall be in addition to those appointed by the States, but they shall be considered, for the purposes of the election of President and Vice President, to be electors appointed by a State; and they shall meet in the District and perform such duties as provided by the twelfth article of amendment.

Section 2. The Congress shall have power to enforce this article by appropriate legislation.

Twenty-Fourth Amendment

(proposed, 1962; ratified, 1964)

Section 1. The right of citizens of the United States to vote in any primary or other election for President or Vice President, for electors for President or Vice President, or for Senator or Representative in Congress, shall not be denied or abridged by the United States or any State by reason of failure to pay any poll tax or other tax.

Section 2. The Congress shall have power to enforce this article by appropriate legislation.

Twenty-Fifth Amendment

(proposed, 1965; ratified, 1967)

Section 1. In case of the removal of the President from office or of his death or resignation, the Vice President shall become President.

Section 2. Whenever there is a vacancy in the office of the Vice President, the President shall nominate a Vice President who shall take office upon confirmation by a majority vote of both Houses of Congress.

Section 3. Whenever the President transmits to the President pro tempore of the Senate and the Speaker of the House of Representatives his written declaration that he is unable to discharge the powers and duties of his office, and until he transmits to them a written declaration to the contrary, such powers and duties shall be discharged by the Vice President as Acting President.

Section 4. [1] Whenever the Vice President and a majority of either the principal officers of the executive departments or of such other body as Congress may by law provide, transmit to the President pro tempore of the Senate and the Speaker of the House of Representatives their written declaration that the President is unable to discharge the powers and duties of his office, the Vice President shall immediately assume the powers and duties of the office as Acting President.

[2] Thereafter, when the President transmits to the President pro tempore of the Senate and the Speaker of thc House of Representatives his written declaration that no inability exists, he shall resume the powers and duties of his office unless the Vice President and a majority of either the principal officers of the executive department or of such other body as Congress may by law provide, transmit within four days to the President pro tempore of the Senate and the Speaker of the House of Representatives their written declaration that the President is unable to discharge the powers and duties of his office. Thereupon Congress shall decide the issue, assembling within forty-eight hours for that purpose if not in session. If the Congress, within twenty-one days after receipt of the latter written declaration, or, if Congress is not in session, within twenty-one days after Congress is required to assemble, determines by two-thirds vote of both Houses that the President is unable to discharge the powers and duties of his office, the Vice President shall continue to discharge the same as Acting President; otherwise, the President shall resume the powers and duties of his office.

Twenty-Sixth Amendment

(proposed, 1971; ratified, 1971)

Section 1. The right of citizens of the United States, who are eighteen years of age or older, to vote shall not be denied or abridged by the United States or by any State on account of age.

Section 2. The Congress shall have power to enforce this article by appropriate legislation.

Study Questions

1. How did the Twenty-Third, Twenty-Fourth, and Twenty-Sixth Amendments, each in its own way, seek to make the federal government more representative of all citizens?

2. Under what conditions, according to the Twenty-Fifth Amendment, may a person not elected as president serve as president?

3. Conduct some independent research to discover actual situations in which the Twenty-Fifth Amendment has determined who served as president or vice president.

Richard Nixon, First Inaugural Address (1969)

With the Youth International Party demonstrating outside of the Democratic National Convention in Chicago in the summer of 1968, the Republican Party seized the opportunity to clothe itself with a mantle of law and order. By electing Richard M. Nixon to the presidency, the American people sought to reclaim the more tranquil years of the Eisenhower consensus, when Nixon had served as Vice President and the civil rights movement had not yet spawned a radical generation of New Left activists. President Nixon hinted that the Vietnam Conflict could be resolved at last; the "long night" was now over and "the first rays of dawn" were appearing on the horizon. It was time for Americans to recommit themselves to the virtues of individual liberty while recognizing "the limits of what government alone can do."

Senator Dirksen, Mr. Chief Justice, Mr. Vice president, President Johnson, Vice president Humphrey, my fellow Americans —and my fellow citizens of the world community:

I ask you to share with me today the majesty of this moment. In the orderly transfer of power, we celebrate the unity that keeps us free.

Each moment in history is a fleeting time, precious and unique. But some stand out as moments of beginning, in which courses are set that shape decades or centuries.

This can be such a moment.

Forces now are converging that make possible, for the first time, the hope that many of man's deepest aspirations can at last be realized. The spiraling pace of change allows us to contemplate, within our own lifetime, advances that once would have taken centuries.

In throwing wide the horizons of space, we have discovered new horizons on earth.

For the first time, because the people of the world want peace, and the leaders of the world are afraid of war, the times are on the side of peace.

Eight years from now America will celebrate its 200th anniversary as a nation. Within the lifetime of most people now living, mankind will celebrate that great new year which comes only once in a thousand years—the beginning of the third millennium.

What kind of a nation we will be, what kind of a world we will live in, whether we shape the future in the image of our hopes, is ours to determine by our actions and our choices.

The greatest honor history can bestow is the title of peacemaker. This honor now beckons America—the chance to help lead the world at last out of the valley of turmoil and onto that high ground of peace that man has dreamed of since the dawn of civilization.

If we succeed, generations to come will say of us now living that we mastered our moment, that we helped make the world safe for mankind.

This is our summons to greatness.

I believe the American people are ready to answer this call.

The second third of this century has been a time of proud achievement. We have made enormous strides in science and industry and agriculture. We have shared our wealth more broadly than ever. We have learned at last to manage a modern economy to assure its continued growth.

We have given freedom new reach. We have begun to make its promise real for black as well as for white.

We see the hope of tomorrow in the youth of today. I know America's youth. I believe in them. We can be proud that they are better educated, more committed, more passionately driven by conscience than any generation in our history.

No people has ever been so close to the achievement of a just and abundant society, or so possessed of the will to achieve it. And because our strengths are so great, we can afford to appraise our weaknesses with candor and to approach them with hope.

Standing in this same place a third of a century ago, Franklin Delano Roosevelt addressed a nation ravaged by depression and gripped in fear. He could say in surveying the Nation's troubles: "They concern, thank God, only material things." Our crisis today is in reverse.

We find ourselves rich in goods, but ragged in spirit; reaching with magnificent precision for the moon, but failing into raucous discord on earth.

We are caught in war, wanting peace. We are torn by division, wanting unity. We see around us empty lives, wanting fulfillment. We see tasks that need doing, waiting for hands to do them.

To a crisis of the spirit, we need an answer of the spirit.

And to find that answer, we need only look within ourselves.

When we listen to "the better angels of our nature," we find that they celebrate the simple things, the basic things—such as goodness, decency, love, kindness.

Greatness comes in simple trappings. The simple things are the ones most needed today if we are to surmount what divides us, and cement what unites us.

To lower our voices would be a simple thing.

In these difficult years, America has suffered from a fever of words; from inflated rhetoric that promises more than it can deliver; from angry rhetoric that fans discontents into hatreds; from bombastic rhetoric that postures instead of persuading.

We cannot learn from one another until we stop shouting at one another—until we speak quietly enough so that our words can be heard as well as our voices.

For its part, government will listen. We will strive to listen in new ways—to the voices of quiet anguish, the voices that speak without words, the voices of the heart—to the injured voices, the anxious voices, the voices that have despaired of being heard.

Those who have been left out, we will try to bring in.

Those left behind, we will help to catch up.

For all of our people, we will set as our goal the decent order that makes progress possible and our lives secure.

As we reach toward our hopes, our task is to build on what has gone before—not turning away from the old, but turning toward the new.

In this past third of a century, government has passed more laws, spent more money, initiated more programs than in all our previous history.

In pursuing our goals of full employment, better housing, excellence in education; in rebuilding our cities and improving our rural areas; in protecting our environment and enhancing the quality of life—in all these and more, we will and must press urgently forward.

We shall plan now for the day when our wealth can be transferred from the destruction of war abroad to the urgent needs of our people at home.

The American dream does not come to those who fall asleep.

But we are approaching the limits of what government alone can do.

Our greatest need now is to reach beyond government, to enlist the legions of the concerned and the committed.

What has to be done, has to be done by government and people together or it will not be done at all. The lesson of past agony is that without the people we can do nothing—with the people we can do everything.

To match the magnitude of our tasks, we need the energies of our people—enlisted not only in grand enterprises, but more importantly in those small, splendid efforts that make headlines in the neighborhood newspaper instead of the national journal.

With these, we can build a great cathedral of the spirit—each of us raising it one stone at a time, as he reaches out to his neighbor, helping, caring, doing.

I do not offer a life of uninspiring ease. I do not call for a life of grim sacrifice. I ask you to join in a high adventure—one as rich as humanity itself, and exciting as the times we live in.

The essence of freedom is that each of us shares in the shaping of his own destiny.

Until he has been part of a cause larger than himself, no man is truly whole.

The way to fulfillment is in the use of our talents. We achieve nobility in the spirit that inspires that use.

As we measure what can be done, we shall promise only what we know we can produce; but as we chart our goals, we shall be lifted by our dreams.

No man can be fully free while his neighbor is not. To go forward at all is to go forward together.

This means black and white together, as one nation, not two. The laws have caught up with our conscience. What remains is to give life to what is in the law: to insure at last that as all are born equal in dignity before God, all are born equal in dignity before man.

As we learn to go forward together at home, let us also seek to go forward together with all mankind.

Let us take as our goal: Where peace is unknown, make it welcome; where peace is fragile, make it strong; where peace is temporary, make it permanent.

After a period of confrontation, we are entering an era of negotiation.

Let all nations know that during this administration our lines of communication will be open.

We seek an open world—open to ideas, open to the exchange of goods and people —a world in which no people, great or small, will live in angry isolation.

We cannot expect to make everyone our friend, but we can try to make no one our enemy.

Those who would be our adversaries, we invite to a peaceful competition—not in conquering territory or extending dominion, but in enriching the life of man.

As we explore the reaches of space, let us go to the new worlds together—not as new worlds to be conquered, but as a new adventure to be shared.

With those who are willing to join, let us cooperate to reduce the burden of arms, to strengthen the structure of peace, to lift up the poor and the hungry.

But to all those who would be tempted by weakness, let us leave no doubt that we will be as strong as we need to be for as long as we need to be.

Over the past twenty years, since I first came to this Capital as a freshman Congressman, I have visited most of the nations of the world. I have come to know the leaders of the world and the great forces, the hatreds, the fears that divide the world.

I know that peace does not come through wishing for it—that there is no substitute for days and even years of patient and prolonged diplomacy.

I also know the people of the world.

I have seen the hunger of a homeless child, the pain of a man wounded in battle, the grief of a mother who has lost her son. I know these have no ideology, no race.

I know America. I know the heart of America is good.

I speak from my own heart, and the heart of my country, the deep concern we have for those who suffer and those who sorrow.

I have taken an oath today in the presence of God and my countrymen to uphold and defend the Constitution of the United States. To that oath I now add this sacred commitment: I shall consecrate my Office, my energies, and all the wisdom I can summon to the cause of peace among nations.

Let this message be heard by strong and weak alike:

The peace we seek, the peace we seek to win—is not victory over any other people, but the peace that comes "with healing in its wings"; with compassion for those who have suffered; with understanding for those who have opposed us; with the opportunity for all the peoples of this earth to choose their own destiny.

Only a few short weeks ago we shared the glory of man's first sight of the world as God sees it, as a single sphere reflecting light in the darkness.

As the Apollo astronauts flew over the moon's gray surface on Christmas Eve, they spoke to us of the beauty of earth—and in that voice so clear across the lunar distance, we heard them invoke God's blessing on its goodness.

In that moment, their view from the moon moved poet Archibald MacLeish to write:

> To see the earth as it truly is, small and blue and beautiful in that eternal silence where it floats, is to see ourselves as riders on the earth together, brothers on that bright loveliness in the eternal cold—brothers who know now they are truly brothers.

In that moment of surpassing technological triumph, men turned their thoughts toward home and humanity—seeing in that far perspective that man's destiny on earth is not divisible; telling us that however far we reach into the cosmos, our destiny lies not in the stars but on earth itself, in our own hands, in our own hearts.

We have endured a long night of the American spirit. But as our eyes catch the dimness of the first rays of dawn, let us not curse the remaining dark. Let us gather the light.

Our destiny offers not the cup of despair, but the chalice of opportunity. So let us seize it not in fear, but in gladness—and "riders on the earth together," let us go forward, firm in our faith, steadfast in our purpose, cautious of the dangers, but sustained by our confidence in the will of God and the promise of man.

Study Questions

1. To whom was Nixon referring when he said, "We cannot learn from one another until we stop shouting at one another"? What was Nixon proposing?

2. Compare Nixon's view of government to that of Lyndon Johnson. Did Nixon support Johnson's Great Society program?

Supreme Court Decisions under Chief Justice Warren E. Burger

Although some legal analysts expected that President Nixon's appointment of Warren E. Burger as Chief Justice in 1969 would reverse the liberal trends of the Warren court, many of Burger's decisions held the course. The Court increasingly saw itself as the guardian of individual rights, including rights not specifically mentioned in the Constitution. Against traditional family values, the Court championed abortion rights. Despite national security concerns, the Court favored freedom of the press. However, the Court's approach to affirmative action gradually became more moderate, and in Burger's final year on the bench he upheld a prohibition of homosexual behavior as consistent with the Christian tradition and the legal codes of Western Civilization.

1971   The Supreme Court ruled in *New York Times v. U.S.* that the newspaper had a First Amendment right to publish the Pentagon Papers, despite the government's objection that this would compromise national security. (The Pentagon Papers, leaked to the press in 1971, consisted of internal government reports indicating that the Johnson administration had lied to the American people by understating the extent of U.S. military involvement in Vietnam.)

In *Lemon v. Kurtzman*, the Court adopted a three-part test for determining whether cooperation between church and state violates the First Amendment. First, the government's policy must have a secular purpose. Second, the primary effect of the policy must neither support nor hinder religion. Third, the policy must avoid excessive entanglement with religion.

1972   The Court extended the "privacy right" permitting married couples to use contraception (from *Griswold v. Connecticut*, 1965) to include also unmarried couples in *Eisenstadt v. Baird*.

In *Furman v. Georgia*, the Court ruled the death penalty to be in violation of the Eighth and Fourteenth Amendments because the evolving standards of society now considered it "cruel and unusual."

1973   The Court expanded the "right of privacy," established in *Griswold v. Connecticut* (1965), to include the right of a woman to obtain an abortion in *Roe v. Wade*.

1974   In *U.S. v. Nixon*, the Court unanimously ordered President Richard Nixon to turn over the evidence requested by the special prosecutor in the Watergate scandal. Nixon earlier had refused, claiming an executive privilege for national security.

1978   The Court was closely divided regarding affirmative action in *Regents of the University of California v. Bakke*. One majority of the justices approved of affirmative action in principle, while a separate majority rejected the particular formula that had been employed in this case.

1984   The Court ruled in *Lynch v. Donnelly* that a Christmas display on government property passes the *Lemon* test if it is shown in a secular context.

1986   In *Bowers v. Hardwick*, the Court upheld a state anti-sodomy law as constitutional. Chief Justice Burger concurred in this decision, noting that "Decisions of individuals relating to homosexual conduct have been subject to state intervention throughout the history of Western civilization," with a longstanding consensus that such acts are punishable by death.

Study Questions

1. In what sense does the Burger court represent a continuation of the Warren court?

2. Compare the Court's rulings in *Furman v. Georgia* and *Roe v. Wade*. What paradox appears in the jurisprudence of this time period?

3. Would government aid for a church-operated soup kitchen or homeless shelter violate the First Amendment's No Establishment clause? Consider how the three-part test adopted in *Lemon v. Kurtzman* should apply.

Richard Nixon, "'Silent Majority' Speech" (1969)

During the Johnson administration, the United States committed over half a million ground troops to South Vietnam. Unknown to the American people until 1971, the Pentagon Papers indicated that the United States also had launched bombing campaigns against portions of Laos and Cambodia and invasions into North Vietnam. In November 1969, President Richard Nixon announced that his administration would take a different approach, which he called Vietnamization. He based his decision both on his own moral conscience as well as the consensus of what he called the "great silent majority of my fellow Americans." In a heart-felt appeal, he begged the "vocal minority"— young war protestors associated with the New Left—to give the nation, and the world, a chance to obtain an honorable peace.

Good evening, my fellow Americans:

Tonight I want to talk to you on a subject of deep concern to all Americans and to many people in all parts of the world—the war in Vietnam.

I believe that one of the reasons for the deep division about Vietnam is that many Americans have lost confidence in what their Government has told them about our policy. The American people cannot and should not be asked to support a policy which involves the overriding issues of war and peace unless they know the truth about that policy.

Tonight, therefore, I would like to answer some of the questions that I know are on the minds of many of you listening to me.

How and why did America get involved in Vietnam in the first place?

How has this administration changed the policy of the previous administration?

What has really happened in the negotiations in Paris and on the battlefront in Vietnam?

What choices do we have if we are to end the war?

What are the prospects for peace?

Now, let me begin by describing the situation I found when I was inaugurated on January 20.

–The war had been going on for 4 years.

–31,000 Americans had been killed in action.

–The training program for the South Vietnamese was behind schedule.

–540,000 Americans were in Vietnam with no plans to reduce the number.

–No progress had been made at the negotiations in Paris and the United States had not put forth a comprehensive peace proposal.

–The war was causing deep division at home and criticism from many of our friends as well as our enemies abroad.

In view of these circumstances there were some who urged that I end the war at once by ordering the immediate withdrawal of all American forces.

From a political standpoint this would

have been a popular and easy course to follow. After all, we became involved in the war while my predecessor was in office. I could blame the defeat which would be the result of my action on him and come out as the Peacemaker. Some put it to me quite bluntly: This was the only way to avoid allowing Johnson's war to become Nixon's war.

But I had a greater obligation than to think only of the years of my administration and of the next election. I had to think of the effect of my decision on the next generation and on the future of peace and freedom in America and in the world.

Let us all understand that the question before us is not whether some Americans are for peace and some Americans are against peace. The question at issue is not whether Johnson's war becomes Nixon's war.

The great question is: How can we win America's peace?

Well, let us turn now to the fundamental issue. Why and how did the United States become involved in Vietnam in the first place?

Fifteen years ago North Vietnam, with the logistical support of Communist China and the Soviet Union, launched a campaign to impose a Communist government on South Vietnam by instigating and supporting a revolution.

In response to the request of the Government of South Vietnam, President Eisenhower sent economic aid and military equipment to assist the people of South Vietnam in their efforts to prevent a Communist takeover. Seven years ago,

President Kennedy sent 16,000 military personnel to Vietnam as combat advisers. Four years ago, President Johnson sent American combat forces to South Vietnam.

Now, many believe that President Johnson's decision to send American combat forces to South Vietnam was wrong. And many others—I among them—have been strongly critical of the way the war has been conducted.

But the question facing us today is: Now that we are in the war, what is the best way to end it?

In January I could only conclude that the precipitate withdrawal of American forces from Vietnam would be a disaster not only for South Vietnam but for the United States and for the cause of peace.

For the South Vietnamese, our precipitate withdrawal would inevitably allow the Communists to repeat the massacres which followed their takeover in the North 15 years before.

–They then murdered more than 50,000 people and hundreds of thousands more died in slave labor camps.

–We saw a prelude of what would happen in South Vietnam when the Communists entered the city of Hue last year. During their brief rule there, there was a bloody reign of terror in which 3,000 civilians were clubbed, shot to death, and buried in mass graves.

–With the sudden collapse of our support, these atrocities of Hue would become the nightmare of the entire nation—and particularly for the million and a half Catholic refugees who fled to South Vietnam when the Communists took over in the North.

For the United States, this first defeat in our Nation's history would result in a collapse of confidence in American leadership, not only in Asia but throughout the world.

Three American Presidents have recognized the great stakes involved in Vietnam and understood what had to be done.

In 1963, President Kennedy, with his characteristic eloquence and clarity, said:

> ... we want to see a stable government there, carrying on a struggle to maintain its national independence.
>
> We believe strongly in that. We are not going to withdraw from that effort. In my opinion, for us to withdraw from that effort would mean a collapse not only of South Viet-Nam, but Southeast Asia. So we are going to stay there.

President Eisenhower and President Johnson expressed the same conclusion during their terms of office.

For the future of peace, precipitate withdrawal would thus be a disaster of immense magnitude.

–A nation cannot remain great if it betrays its allies and lets down its friends.

–Our defeat and humiliation in South Vietnam without question would promote recklessness in the councils of those great powers who have not yet abandoned their goals of world conquest.

–This would spark violence wherever our commitments help maintain the peace –in the Middle East, in Berlin, eventually even in the Western Hemisphere.

Ultimately, this would cost more lives.

It would not bring peace; it would bring more war.

For these reasons, I rejected the recommendation that I should end the war by immediately withdrawing all of our forces. I chose instead to change American policy on both the negotiating front and battlefront.

In order to end a war fought on many fronts, I initiated a pursuit for peace on many fronts.

In a television speech on May 14, in a speech before the United Nations, and on a number of other occasions I set forth our peace proposals in great detail.

–We have offered the complete withdrawal of all outside forces within 1 year.

–We have proposed a cease-fire under international supervision.

–We have offered free elections under international supervision with the Communists participating in the organization and conduct of the elections as an organized political force. And the Saigon Government has pledged to accept the result of the elections.

We have not put forth our proposals on a take-it-or-leave-it basis. We have indicated that we are willing to discuss the proposals that have been put forth by the other side. We have declared that anything is negotiable except the right of the people of South Vietnam to determine their own future. At the Paris peace conference, Ambassador Lodge has demonstrated our flexibility and good faith in 40 public meetings.

Hanoi has refused even to discuss our

proposals. They demand our unconditional acceptance of their terms, which are that we withdraw all American forces immediately and unconditionally and that we overthrow the Government of South Vietnam as we leave.

We have not limited our peace initiatives to public forums and public statements. I recognized, in January, that a long and bitter war like this usually cannot be settled in a public forum. That is why in addition to the public statements and negotiations I have explored every possible private avenue that might lead to a settlement.

Tonight I am taking the unprecedented step of disclosing to you some of our other initiatives for peace—initiatives we undertook privately and secretly because we thought we thereby might open a door which publicly would be closed.

I did not wait for my inauguration to begin my quest for peace.

–Soon after my election, through an individual who is directly in contact on a personal basis with the leaders of North Vietnam, I made two private offers for a rapid, comprehensive settlement. Hanoi's replies called in effect for our surrender before negotiations.

–Since the Soviet Union furnishes most of the military equipment for North Vietnam, Secretary of State Rogers, my Assistant for National Security Affairs, Dr. Kissinger, Ambassador Lodge, and I, personally, have met on a number of occasions with representatives of the Soviet Government to enlist their assistance in getting meaningful negotiations started. In addition, we have had extended discussions directed toward that same end with representatives of other governments which have diplomatic relations with North Vietnam. None of these initiatives have to date produced results.

–In mid-July, I became convinced that it was necessary to make a major move to break the deadlock in the Paris talks. I spoke directly in this office, where I am now sitting, with an individual who had known [North Vietnamese President] Ho Chi Minh on a personal basis for 25 years. Through him I sent a letter to Ho Chi Minh.

I did this outside of the usual diplomatic channels with the hope that with the necessity of making statements for propaganda removed, there might be constructive progress toward bringing the war to an end. Let me read from that letter to you now.

Dear Mr. President:

I realize that it is difficult to communicate meaningfully across the gulf of four years of war. But precisely because of this gulf, I wanted to take this opportunity to reaffirm in all solemnity my desire to work for a just peace. I deeply believe that the war in Vietnam has gone on too long and delay in bringing it to an end can benefit no one—least of all the people of Vietnam. . . .

The time has come to move forward at the conference table toward an early resolution of this tragic war. You will find us forthcoming and open-minded in a common effort to bring the blessings of peace to the brave people of Vietnam. Let history record that at this critical juncture, both sides turned their face toward peace rather than toward conflict and war.

I received Ho Chi Minh's reply on

August 30, 3 days before his death. It simply reiterated the public position North Vietnam had taken at Paris and flatly rejected my initiative.

The full text of both letters is being released to the press.

—In addition to the public meetings that I have referred to, Ambassador Lodge has met with Vietnam's chief negotiator in Paris in 11 private sessions.

—We have taken other significant initiatives which must remain secret to keep open some channels of communication which may still prove to be productive.

But the effect of all the public, private, and secret negotiations which have been undertaken since the bombing halt a year ago and since this administration came into office on January 20, can be summed up in one sentence: No progress whatever has been made except agreement on the shape of the bargaining table.

Well now, who is at fault?

It has become clear that the obstacle in negotiating an end to the war is not the President of the United States. It is not the South Vietnamese Government.

The obstacle is the other side's absolute refusal to show the least willingness to join us in seeking a just peace. And it will not do so while it is convinced that all it has to do is to wait for our next concession, and our next concession after that one, until it gets everything it wants.

There can now be no longer any question that progress in negotiation depends only on Hanoi's deciding to negotiate, to negotiate seriously.

I realize that this report on our efforts on the diplomatic front is discouraging to the American people, but the American people are entitled to know the truth—the bad news as well as the good news where the lives of our young men are involved.

Now let me turn, however, to a more encouraging report on another front.

At the time we launched our search for peace I recognized we might not succeed in bringing an end to the war through negotiation. I, therefore, put into effect another plan to bring peace—a plan which will bring the war to an end regardless of what happens on the negotiating front.

It is in line with a major shift in U.S. foreign policy which I described in my press conference at Guam on July 25. Let me briefly explain what has been described as the Nixon Doctrine—a policy which not only will help end the war in Vietnam, but which is an essential element of our program to prevent future Vietnams.

We Americans are a do-it-yourself people. We are an impatient people. Instead of teaching someone else to do a job, we like to do it ourselves. And this trait has been carried over into our foreign policy.

In Korea and again in Vietnam, the United States furnished most of the money, most of the arms, and most of the men to help the people of those countries defend their freedom against Communist aggression.

Before any American troops were committed to Vietnam, a leader of another Asian country expressed this opinion to me when I was traveling in Asia as a private citizen. He said: "When you are trying to assist another nation defend its freedom, U.S. policy should be to help them fight the war but not to fight the war for them."

Well, in accordance with this wise counsel, I laid down in Guam three principles as guidelines for future American policy toward Asia:

—First, the United States will keep all of its treaty commitments.

—Second, we shall provide a shield if a nuclear power threatens the freedom of a nation allied with us or of a nation whose survival we consider vital to our security.

—Third, in cases involving other types of aggression, we shall furnish military and economic assistance when requested in accordance with our treaty commitments. But we shall look to the nation directly threatened to assume the primary responsibility of providing the manpower for its defense.

After I announced this policy, I found that the leaders of the Philippines, Thailand, Vietnam, South Korea, and other nations which might be threatened by Communist aggression, welcomed this new direction in American foreign policy.

The defense of freedom is everybody's business—not just America's business. And it is particularly the responsibility of the people whose freedom is threatened. In the previous administration, we Americanized the war in Vietnam. In this administration, we are Vietnamizing the search for peace.

The policy of the previous administration not only resulted in our assuming the primary responsibility for fighting the war, but even more significantly did not adequately stress the goal of strengthening the South Vietnamese so that they could defend themselves when we left.

The Vietnamization plan was launched following Secretary Laird's visit to Vietnam in March. Under the plan, I ordered first a substantial increase in the training and equipment of South Vietnamese forces.

In July, on my visit to Vietnam, I changed General Abrams' orders so that they were consistent with the objectives of our new policies. Under the new orders, the primary mission of our troops is to enable the South Vietnamese forces to assume the full responsibility for the security of South Vietnam.

Our air operations have been reduced by over 20 percent.

And now we have begun to see the results of this long overdue change in American policy in Vietnam.

—After 5 years of Americans going into Vietnam, we are finally bringing American men home. By December 15, over 60,000 men will have been withdrawn from South Vietnam—including 20 percent of all of our combat forces.

—The South Vietnamese have continued to gain in strength. As a result they have been able to take over combat responsibilities from our American troops.

Two other significant developments have occurred since this administration took office.

—Enemy infiltration, infiltration which

is essential if they are to launch a major attack, over the last 3 months is less than 20 percent of what it was over the same period last year.

—Most important—United States casualties have declined during the last 2 months to the lowest point in 3 years.

Let me now turn to our program for the future.

We have adopted a plan which we have worked out in cooperation with the South Vietnamese for the complete withdrawal of all U.S. combat ground forces, and their replacement by South Vietnamese forces on an orderly scheduled timetable. This withdrawal will be made from strength and not from weakness. As South Vietnamese forces become stronger, the rate of American withdrawal can become greater.

I have not and do not intend to announce the timetable for our program. And there are obvious reasons for this decision which I am sure you will understand. As I have indicated on several occasions, the rate of withdrawal will depend on developments on three fronts.

One of these is the progress which can be or might be made in the Paris talks. An announcement of a fixed timetable for our withdrawal would completely remove any incentive for the enemy to negotiate an agreement. They would simply wait until our forces had withdrawn and then move in.

The other two factors on which we will base our withdrawal decisions are the level of enemy activity and the progress of the training programs of the South Vietnamese forces. And I am glad to be able to

report tonight progress on both of these fronts has been greater than we anticipated when we started the program in June for withdrawal. As a result, our timetable for withdrawal is more optimistic now than when we made our first estimates in June. Now, this clearly demonstrates why it is not wise to be frozen in on a fixed timetable.

We must retain the flexibility to base each withdrawal decision on the situation as it is at that time rather than on estimates that are no longer valid.

Along with this optimistic estimate, I must—in all candor—leave one note of caution.

If the level of enemy activity significantly increases we might have to adjust our timetable accordingly.

However, I want the record to be completely clear on one point.

At the time of the bombing halt just a year ago, there was some confusion as to whether there was an understanding on the part of the enemy that if we stopped the bombing of North Vietnam they would stop the shelling of cities in South Vietnam. I want to be sure that there is no misunderstanding on the part of the enemy with regard to our withdrawal Program.

We have noted the reduced level of infiltration, the reduction of our casualties, and are basing our withdrawal decisions partially on those factors.

If the level of infiltration or our casualties increase while we are trying to scale down the fighting, it will be the result of a conscious decision by the enemy.

Hanoi could make no greater mistake than to assume that an increase in violence will be to its advantage. If I conclude that increased enemy action jeopardizes our remaining forces in Vietnam, I shall not hesitate to take strong and effective measures to deal with that situation.

This is not a threat. This is a statement of policy, which as Commander in Chief of our Armed Forces, I am making in meeting my responsibility for the protection of American fighting men wherever they may be.

My fellow Americans, I am sure you can recognize from what I have said that we really only have two choices open to us if we want to end this war.

–I can order an immediate, precipitate withdrawal of all Americans from Vietnam without regard to the effects of that action.

–Or we can persist in our search for a just peace through a negotiated settlement if possible, or through continued implementation of our plan for Vietnamization if necessary—a plan in which we will withdraw all of our forces from Vietnam on a schedule in accordance with our program, as the South Vietnamese become strong enough to defend their own freedom.

I have chosen this second course.

It is not the easy way.

It is the right way.

It is a plan which will end the war and serve the cause of peace—not just in Vietnam but in the Pacific and in the world.

In speaking of the consequences of a precipitate withdrawal, I mentioned that our allies would lose confidence in America.

Far more dangerous, we would lose confidence in ourselves. Oh, the immediate reaction would be a sense of relief that our men were coming home. But as we saw the consequences of what we had done, inevitable remorse and divisive recrimination would scar our spirit as a people.

We have faced other crises in our history and have become stronger by rejecting the easy way out and taking the right way in meeting our challenges. Our greatness as a nation has been our capacity to do what had to be done when we knew our course was right.

I recognize that some of my fellow citizens disagree with the plan for peace I have chosen. Honest and patriotic Americans have reached different conclusions as to how peace should be achieved.

In San Francisco a few weeks ago, I saw demonstrators carrying signs reading: "Lose in Vietnam, bring the boys home."

Well, one of the strengths of our free society is that any American has a right to reach that conclusion and to advocate that point of view. But as President of the United States, I would be untrue to my oath of office if I allowed the policy of this Nation to be dictated by the minority who hold that point of view and who try to impose it on the Nation by mounting demonstrations in the street.

For almost 200 years, the policy of this Nation has been made under our Constitution by those leaders in the Congress and the White House elected by all of the people. If a vocal minority, however fervent its cause, prevails over reason and the will of the majority, this Nation has no future as a free society.

And now I would like to address a word, if I may, to the young people of this Nation who are particularly concerned, and I understand why they are concerned, about this war.

I respect your idealism.

I share your concern for peace.

I want peace as much as you do.

There are powerful personal reasons I want to end this war. This week I will have to sign 83 letters to mothers, fathers, wives, and loved ones of men who have given their lives for America in Vietnam. It is very little satisfaction to me that this is only one-third as many letters as I signed the first week in office. There is nothing I want more than to see the day come when I do not have to write any of those letters.

–I want to end the war to save the lives of those brave young men in Vietnam.

–But I want to end it in a way which will increase the chance that their younger brothers and their sons will not have to fight in some future Vietnam someplace in the world.

–And I want to end the war for another reason. I want to end it so that the energy and dedication of you, our young people, now too often directed into bitter hatred against those responsible for the war, can be turned to the great challenges of peace, a better life for all Americans, a better life for all people on this earth.

I have chosen a plan for peace. I believe it will succeed.

If it does succeed, what the critics say now won't matter. If it does not succeed, anything I say then won't matter.

I know it may not be fashionable to speak of patriotism or national destiny these days. But I feel it is appropriate to do so on this occasion

Two hundred years ago this Nation was weak and poor. But even then, America was the hope of millions in the world. Today we have become the strongest and richest nation in the world. And the wheel of destiny has turned so that any hope the world has for the survival of peace and freedom will be determined by whether the American people have the moral stamina and the courage to meet the challenge of free world leadership.

Let historians not record that when America was the most powerful nation in the world we passed on the other side of the road and allowed the last hopes for peace and freedom of millions of people to be suffocated by the forces of totalitarianism.

And so tonight—to you, the great silent majority of my fellow Americans—I ask for your support.

I pledged in my campaign for the Presidency to end the war in a way that we could win the peace. I have initiated a plan of action which will enable me to keep that pledge.

The more support I can have from the American people, the sooner that pledge can be redeemed; for the more divided we are at home, the less likey, the enemy is to negotiate at Paris.

Let us be united for peace. Let us also

be united against defeat. Because let us understand: North Vietnam cannot defeat or humiliate the United States. Only Americans can do that.

Fifty years ago, in this room and at this very desk, President Woodrow Wilson spoke words which caught the imagination of a war-weary world. He said: "This is the war to end war." His dream for peace after World War I was shattered on the hard realities of great power politics and Woodrow Wilson died a broken man.

Tonight I do not tell you that the war in Vietnam is the war to end wars. But I do say this: I have initiated a plan which will end this war in a way that will bring us closer to that great goal to which Woodrow Wilson and every American President in our history has been dedicated—the goal of a just and lasting peace.

As President I hold the responsibility for choosing the best path to that goal and then leading the Nation along it.

I pledge to you tonight that I shall meet this responsibility with all of the strength and wisdom I can command in accordance with your hopes, mindful of your concerns, sustained by your prayers.

Thank you and goodnight.

Study Questions

1. How and why had the United States become entangled in Vietnam, according to Nixon?

2. What did Nixon predict would result if America suffered "defeat and humiliation" in Vietnam?

3. Define the Nixon Doctrine in general and explain what Nixon meant in particular by "Vietnamizing the search for peace."

4. Whose opinion should hold greater influence in foreign policy according to Nixon—the "vocal minority" or the "silent majority"? Explain what he meant by these terms.

Richard Nixon, Second Inaugural Address (1973)

With the economy strong, American involvement in Vietnam on the wane, and U.S. relations with China improving, President Richard Nixon had much credit to his record when seeking reelection in 1972. The Democrats mustered Senator George McGovern of South Dakota against him, but the media branded McGovern a leftist who supported "amnesty, abortion, and acid," the last term referring to drugs, which McGovern suggested should be legalized. McGovern promised to guarantee a minimum income to every American and also to end U.S. involvement in Vietnam immediately. Nixon, meanwhile, set a more balanced course, offering a gradual withdrawal of American GIs from southeast Asia amid the progressive "Vietnamization" of combat troops. In one of the widest presidential election margins ever, Nixon carried every state but one.

Mr. Vice President, Mr. Speaker, Mr. Chief Justice, Senator Cook, Mrs. Eisenhower, and my fellow citizens of this great and good country we share together:

When we met here 4 years ago, America was bleak in spirit, depressed by the prospect of seemingly endless war abroad and of destructive conflict at home.

As we meet here today, we stand on the threshold of a new era of peace in the world.

The central question before us is: How shall we use that peace?

Let us resolve that this era we are about to enter will not be what other postwar periods have so often been: a time of retreat and isolation that leads to stagnation at home and invites new danger abroad.

Let us resolve that this will be what it can become: a time of great responsibilities greatly borne, in which we renew the spirit and the promise of America as we enter our third century as a nation.

This past year saw far-reaching results from our new policies for peace. By continuing to revitalize our traditional friendships, and by our missions to Peking and to Moscow, we were able to establish the base for a new and more durable pattern of relationships among the nations of the world. Because of America's bold initiatives, 1972 will be long remembered as the year of the greatest progress since the end of World War II toward a lasting peace in the world.

The peace we seek in the world is not the flimsy peace which is merely an interlude between wars, but a peace which can endure for generations to come.

It is important that we understand both the necessity and the limitations of America's role in maintaining that peace.

Unless we in America work to preserve the peace, there will be no peace.

Unless we in America work to preserve freedom, there will be no freedom.

But let us clearly understand the new nature of America's role, as a result of the new policies we have adopted over these past 4 years.

We shall respect our treaty commitments.

We shall support vigorously the principle that no country has the right to impose its will or rule on another by force.

We shall continue, in this era of negotiation, to work for the limitation of nuclear arms and to reduce the danger of confrontation between the great powers.

We shall do our share in defending peace and freedom in the world. But we shall expect others to do their share.

The time has passed when America will make every other nation's conflict our own, or make every other nation's future our responsibility, or presume to tell the people of other nations how to manage their own affairs.

Just as we respect the right of each nation to determine its own future, we also recognize the responsibility of each nation to secure its own future.

Just as America's role is indispensable in preserving the world's peace, so is each nation's role indispensable in preserving its own peace.

Together with the rest of the world, let us resolve to move forward from the beginnings we have made. Let us continue to bring down the walls of hostility which have divided the world for too long, and to build in their place bridges of understanding—so that despite profound differences between systems of government, the people of the world can be friends.

Let us build a structure of peace in the world in which the weak are as safe as the strong, in which each respects the right of the other to live by a different system, in which those who would influence others will do so by the strength of their ideas and not by the force of their arms.

Let us accept that high responsibility not as a burden, but gladly—gladly because the chance to build such a peace is the noblest endeavor in which a nation can engage; gladly also because only if we act greatly in meeting our responsibilities abroad will we remain a great nation, and only if we remain a great nation will we act greatly in meeting our challenges at home.

We have the chance today to do more than ever before in our history to make life better in America—to ensure better education, better health, better housing, better transportation, a cleaner environment—to restore respect for law, to make our communities more livable—and to ensure the God-given right of every American to full and equal opportunity.

Because the range of our needs is so great, because the reach of our opportunities is so great, let us be bold in our determination to meet those needs in new ways.

Just as building a structure of peace abroad has required turning away from old policies that have failed, so building a new era of progress at home requires turning away from old policies that have failed.

Abroad, the shift from old policies to new has not been a retreat from our responsibilities, but a better way to peace.

And at home, the shift from old policies to new will not be a retreat from our responsibilities, but a better way to progress.

Abroad and at home, the key to those new responsibilities lies in the placing and the division of responsibility. We have lived too long with the consequences of attempting to gather all power and responsibility in Washington.

Abroad and at home, the time has come to turn away from the condescending policies of paternalism—of "Washington knows best."

A person can be expected to act responsibly only if he has responsibility. This is human nature. So let us encourage individuals at home and nations abroad to do more for themselves, to decide more for themselves. Let us locate responsibility in more places. And let us measure what we will do for others by what they will do for themselves.

That is why today I offer no promise of a purely governmental solution for every problem. We have lived too long with that false promise. In trusting too much in government, we have asked of it more than it can deliver. This leads only to inflated expectations, to reduced individual effort, and to a disappointment and frustration that erode confidence both in what government can do and in what people can do.

Government must learn to take less from people so that people can do more for themselves.

Let us remember that America was built not by government, but by people; not by welfare, but by work; not by shirking responsibility, but by seeking responsibility.

In our own lives, let each of us ask—not just what will government do for me, but what can I do for myself?

In the challenges we face together, let each of us ask—not just how can government help, but how can I help?

Your National Government has a great and vital role to play. And I pledge to you that where this Government should act, we will act boldly and we will lead boldly. But just as important is the role that each and every one of us must play, as an individual and as a member of his own community.

From this day forward, let each of us make a solemn commitment in his own heart: to bear his responsibility, to do his part, to live his ideals—so that together we can see the dawn of a new age of progress for America, and together, as we celebrate our 200th anniversary as a nation, we can do so proud in the fulfillment of our promise to ourselves and to the world.

As America's longest and most difficult war comes to an end, let us again learn to debate our differences with civility and decency. And let each of us reach out for that one precious quality government cannot provide—a new level of respect for the rights and feelings of one another, a new level of respect for the individual human dignity which is the cherished birthright of every American.

Above all else, the time has come for us to renew our faith in ourselves and in America.

In recent years, that faith has been challenged.

Our children have been taught to be ashamed of their country, ashamed of their parents, ashamed of America's record at home and its role in the world.

At every turn we have been beset by those who find everything wrong with America and little that is right. But I am confident that this will not be the judgment of history on these remarkable times in which we are privileged to live.

America's record in this century has been unparalleled in the world's history for its responsibility, for its generosity, for its creativity, and for its progress.

Let us be proud that our system has produced and provided more freedom and more abundance, more widely shared, than any system in the history of the world.

Let us be proud that in each of the four wars in which we have been engaged in this century, including the one we are now bringing to an end, we have fought not for our selfish advantage, but to help others resist aggression.

And let us be proud that by our bold, new initiatives, by our steadfastness for peace with honor, we have made a breakthrough toward creating in the world what the world has not known before—a structure of peace that can last, not merely for our time, but for generations to come. We are embarking here today on an era that presents challenges as great as those any nation, or any generation, has ever faced.

We shall answer to God, to history, and to our conscience for the way in which we use these years.

As I stand in this place, so hallowed by history, I think of others who have stood here before me. I think of the dreams they had for America and I think of how each recognized that he needed help far beyond himself in order to make those dreams come true.

Today I ask your prayers that in the years ahead I may have God's help in making decisions that are right for America, and I pray for your help so that together we may be worthy of our challenge.

Let us pledge together to make these next 4 years the best 4 years in America's history, so that on its 200th birthday America will be as young and as vital as when it began, and as bright a beacon of hope for all the world.

Let us go forward from here confident in hope, strong in our faith in one another, sustained by our faith in God who created us, and striving always to serve His purpose.

Study Questions

1. In the midst of the Cold War, which had turned hot in Vietnam, Nixon spoke of "peace." How did he intend for the United States to forge peace throughout the world?

2. Was Nixon turning his back on the Truman Doctrine? Explain.

3. Criticizing the New Left, Nixon said, "Our children have been taught to be ashamed of their country, ashamed of their parents." Why, then, was Nixon proud of America?

Richard M. Nixon, "Resignation Speech" (1974)

In June 1972, seven suspects were arrested for attempted burglary at the Democratic National Committee office in the Watergate complex in Washington, DC. Three of the seven suspects had ties to the Committee to Reelect the President (CREEP), a campaign team serving President Nixon. The other four suspects had been involved in CIA operations against Fidel Castro. Clearly, this was no ordinary burglary. As investigative reporters Carl Bernstein and Bob Woodward of the *Washington Post* pursued story leads, they discovered that key personnel at the White House had been involved in the escapade. By the summer of 1974, televised Senate hearings revealed evidence that implicated President Nixon himself. In October, Vice President Spiro Agnew resigned. When the U.S. House of Representatives prepared impeachment charges and the U.S. Supreme Court ordered Nixon to turn over tape recordings to investigators, the president felt he had no other choice than to resign. His resignation speech, delivered on August 8, 1974, identified the reasons he left office as well as several achievements during his administration.

Good evening:

This is the 37th time I have spoken to you from this office, where so many decisions have been made that shaped the history of this Nation. Each time I have done so to discuss with you some matter that I believe affected the national interest. In all the decisions I have made in my public life, I have always tried to do what was best for the Nation.

Throughout the long and difficult period of Watergate, I have felt it was my duty to persevere, to make every possible effort to complete the term of office to which you elected me. In the past few days, however, it has become evident to me that I no longer have a strong enough political base in the Congress to justify continuing that effort.

As long as there was such a base, I felt strongly that it was necessary to see the constitutional process through to its conclusion, that to do otherwise would be unfaithful to the spirit of that deliberately difficult process and a dangerously destabilizing precedent for the future. But with the disappearance of that base, I now believe that the constitutional purpose has been served, and there is no longer a need for the process to be prolonged.

I would have preferred to carry through to the finish, whatever the personal agony it would have involved, and my family unanimously urged me to do so. But the interests of the Nation must always come before any personal considerations. From the discussions I have had with Congressional and other leaders, I have concluded that because of the Watergate matter, I might not have the support of the Congress that I would consider necessary to back the very difficult decisions and carry out the duties of this office in the way the interests of the Nation will require.

I have never been a quitter. To leave office before my term is completed is abhorrent to every instinct in my body. But as President, I must put the interests of

America first.

America needs a full-time President and a full-time Congress, particularly at this time with problems we face at home and abroad. To continue to fight through the months ahead for my personal vindication would almost totally absorb the time and attention of both the President and the Congress in a period when our entire focus should be on the great issues of peace abroad and prosperity without inflation at home.

Therefore, I shall resign the Presidency effective at noon tomorrow. Vice President Ford will be sworn in as President at that hour in this office.

As I recall the high hopes for America with which we began this second term, I feel a great sadness that I will not be here in this office working on your behalf to achieve those hopes in the next 2 1/2 years.

But in turning over direction of the Government to Vice President Ford, I know, as I told the Nation when I nominated him for that office 10 months ago, that the leadership of America will be in good hands.

In passing this office to the Vice President, I also do so with the profound sense of the weight of responsibility that will fall on his shoulders tomorrow and, therefore, of the understanding, the patience, the cooperation he will need from all Americans. As he assumes that responsibility, he will deserve the help and the support of all of us. As we look to the future, the first essential is to begin healing the wounds of this Nation, to put the bitterness and divisions of the recent past behind us and to rediscover those shared ideals that lie at the heart of our strength and unity as a great and as a free people.

By taking this action, I hope that I will have hastened the start of that process of healing which is so desperately needed in America.

I regret deeply any injuries that may have been done in the course of the events that led to this decision. I would say only that if some of my judgments were wrong —and some were wrong—they were made in what I believed at the time to be the best interest of the Nation.

To those who have stood with me during these past difficult months—to my family, my friends, to many others who joined in supporting my cause because they believed it was right—I will be eternally grateful for your support.

And to those who have not felt able to give me your support, let me say I leave with no bitterness toward those who have opposed me, because all of us, in the final analysis, have been concerned with the good of the country, however our judgments might differ.

So, let us all now join together in affirming that common commitment and in helping our new President succeed for the benefit of all Americans.

I shall leave this office with regret at not completing my term, but with gratitude for the privilege of serving as your President for the past 5 1/2 years. These years have been a momentous time in the history of our Nation and the world. They have been a time of achievement in which we can all be proud, achievements that represent the shared efforts of the Administration, the Congress, and the people.

But the challenges ahead are equally great, and they, too, will require the support and the efforts of the Congress and the people working in cooperation with the new Administration.

We have ended America's longest war, but in the work of securing a lasting peace in the world, the goals ahead are even more far-reaching and more difficult. We must complete a structure of peace so that it will be said of this generation, our generation of Americans, by the people of all nations, not only that we ended one war but that we prevented future wars.

We have unlocked the doors that for a quarter of a century stood between the United States and the People's Republic of China. We must now ensure that the one quarter of the world's people who live in the People's Republic of China will be and remain not our enemies, but our friends.

In the Middle East, 100 million people in the Arab countries, many of whom have considered us their enemy for nearly 20 years, now look on us as their friends. We must continue to build on that friendship so that peace can settle at last over the Middle East and so that the cradle of civilization will not become its grave.

Together with the Soviet Union, we have made the crucial breakthroughs that have begun the process of limiting nuclear arms. But we must set as our goal not just limiting but reducing and, finally, destroying these terrible weapons so that they cannot destroy civilization and so that the threat of nuclear war will no longer hang over the world and the people.

We have opened the new relation with the Soviet Union. We must continue to develop and expand that new relationship so that the two strongest nations of the world will live together in cooperation, rather than confrontation.

Around the world in Asia, in Africa, in Latin America, in the Middle East—there are millions of people who live in terrible poverty, even starvation. We must keep as our goal turning away from production for war and expanding production for peace so that people everywhere on this Earth can at last look forward in their children's time, if not in our own time, to having the necessities for a decent life.

Here in America, we are fortunate that most of our people have not only the blessings of liberty but also the means to live full and good and, by the world's standards, even abundant lives. We must press on, however, toward a goal, not only of more and better jobs but of full opportunity for every American and of what we are striving so hard right now to achieve, prosperity without inflation.

For more than a quarter of a century in public life, I have shared in the turbulent history of this era. I have fought for what I believed in. I have tried, to the best of my ability, to discharge those duties and meet those responsibilities that were entrusted to me.

Sometimes I have succeeded and sometimes I have failed, but always I have taken heart from what Theodore Roosevelt once said about the man in the arena, "whose face is marred by dust and sweat and blood, who strives valiantly, who errs and comes short again and again because there is not effort without error and shortcoming, but who does actually strive to do the deed, who knows the great enthusiasms, the great devotions, who spends himself in a worthy cause, who at the best knows in the end the triumphs of high achievements and who at the worst, if he fails, at least fails while daring greatly."

I pledge to you tonight that as long as I have a breath of life in my body, I shall continue in that spirit. I shall continue to work for the great causes to which I have been dedicated throughout my years as a Congressman, a Senator, Vice President, and President, the cause of peace, not just for America but among all nations— prosperity, justice, and opportunity for all of our people.

There is one cause above all to which I have been devoted and to which I shall always be devoted for as long as I live.

When I first took the oath of office as President 5 1/2 years ago, I made this sac-red commitment: to "consecrate my office, my energies, and all the wisdom I can summon to the cause of peace among nations."

I have done my very best in all the days since to be true to that pledge. As a result of these efforts, I am confident that the world is a safer place today, not only for the people of America but for the people of all nations, and that all of our children have a better chance than before of living in peace rather than dying in war.

This, more than anything, is what I hoped to achieve when I sought the Presidency. This, more than anything, is what I hope will be my legacy to you, to our country, as I leave the Presidency.

To have served in this office is to have felt a very personal sense of kinship with each and every American. In leaving it, I do so with this prayer: May God's grace be with you in all the days ahead.

Study Question

1. Nixon said, "I have never been a quitter." Why, then, did he resign from the presidency?

2. What fears, and what hopes, did Nixon identify for his successor?

Gerald Ford, Inaugural Address (1974)

On August 9, 1974, Chief Justice Warren E. Burger administered the presidential oath of office to Gerald Ford upon the resignation of Richard Nixon. President Ford then delivered the following message as the first, and thus far the only, American president who was never elected to either the presidency or the vice presidency.

Mr. Chief Justice, my dear friends, my fellow Americans:

The oath that I have taken is the same oath that was taken by George Washington and by every President under the Constitution. But I assume the Presidency under extraordinary circumstances never before experienced by Americans. This is an hour of history that troubles our minds and hurts our hearts.

Therefore, I feel it is my first duty to make an unprecedented compact with my countrymen. Not an inaugural address, not a fireside chat, not a campaign speech —just a little straight talk among friends. And I intend it to be the first of many.

I am acutely aware that you have not elected me as your President by your ballots, and so I ask you to confirm me as your President with your prayers. And I hope that such prayers will also be the first of many. If you have not chosen me by secret ballot, neither have I gained office by any secret promises. I have not campaigned either for the Presidency or the Vice Presidency. I have not subscribed to any partisan platform. I am indebted to no man, and only to one woman—my dear wife—as I begin this very difficult job.

I have not sought this enormous responsibility, but I will not shirk it. Those who nominated and confirmed me as Vice President were my friends and are my friends. They were of both parties, elected by all the people and acting under the Constitution in their name. It is only fitting then that I should pledge to them and to you that I will be the President of all the people.

Thomas Jefferson said the people are the only sure reliance for the preservation of our liberty. And down the years, Abraham Lincoln renewed this American article of faith asking, "Is there any better way or equal hope in the world?"

I intend, on Monday next, to request of the Speaker of the House of Representatives and the President pro tempore of the Senate the privilege of appearing before the Congress to share with my former colleagues and with you, the American people, my views on the priority business of the Nation and to solicit your views and their views. And may I say to the Speaker and the others, if I could meet with you right after these remarks, I would appreciate it.

Even though this is late in an election year, there is no way we can go forward except together and no way anybody can win except by serving the people's urgent needs. We cannot stand still or slip backwards. We must go forward now together.

To the peoples and the governments of all friendly nations, and I hope that could encompass the whole world, I pledge an uninterrupted and sincere search for peace. America will remain strong and united, but its strength will remain dedicated to the safety and sanity of the entire family of man, as well as to our own precious freedom. I believe that truth is the glue that holds government together, not only our Government but civilization itself. That bond, though stained, is unbroken at home and abroad.

In all my public and private acts as your President, I expect to follow my instincts of openness and candor with full confidence that honesty is always the best policy in the end.

My fellow Americans, our long national nightmare is over.

Our Constitution works. Our great Republic is a government of laws and not of men. Here, the people rule. But there is a higher Power, by whatever name we honor Him, who ordains not only righteousness but love, not only justice but mercy. As we bind up the internal wounds of Watergate, more painful and more poisonous than those of foreign wars, let us restore the golden rule to our political process, and let brotherly love purge our hearts of suspicion and of hate.

In the beginning, I asked you to pray for me. Before closing, I ask again your prayers, for Richard Nixon and for his family. May our former President, who brought peace to millions, find it for himself. May God bless and comfort his wonderful wife and daughters, whose love and loyalty will forever be a shining legacy to all who bear the lonely burdens of the White House. I can only guess at those burdens, although I have witnessed at close hand the tragedies that befell three Presidents and the lesser trials of others.

With all the strength and all the good sense I have gained from life, with all the confidence of my family, my friends, and my dedicated staff impart to me, and with the good will of countless Americans I have encountered in recent visits to 40 States, I now solemnly reaffirm my promise I made to you last December 6: To uphold the Constitution; to do what is right as God gives me to see the right; and to do the very best I can for America.

God helping me, I will not let you down.

Thank you.

Study Questions

1. What did President Ford mean in saying that "our long national nightmare is over"?

2. In what sense was President Ford referring both to the original U.S. Constitution as ratified in 1788 as well as the Twenty-Fifth Amendment when he said, "our Constitution works"?

Gerald Ford, Announcement to Pardon Richard Nixon (1974)

Thirty days into his presidency, Gerald Ford pardoned Richard Nixon. In the following address, he offered his reasons for doing so. Never before had a president resigned. Never before had his successor pardoned him. Ford was traveling uncharted territory, and yet he spoke with equal measures of candor and confidence—even if he knew his decision was sure to spark controversy.

Ladies and gentlemen:

I have come to a decision which I felt I should tell you and all of my fellow American citizens, as soon as I was certain in my own mind and in my own conscience that it is the right thing to do.

I have learned already in this office that the difficult decisions always come to this desk. I must admit that many of them do not look at all the same as the hypothetical questions that I have answered freely and perhaps too fast on previous occasions.

My customary policy is to try and get all the facts and to consider the opinions of my countrymen and to take counsel with my most valued friends. But these seldom agree, and in the end, the decision is mine. To procrastinate, to agonize, and to wait for a more favorable turn of events that may never come or more compelling external pressures that may as well be wrong as right, is itself a decision of sorts and a weak and potentially dangerous course for a President to follow.

I have promised to uphold the Constitution, to do what is right as God gives me to see the right, and to do the very best that I can for America.

I have asked your help and your prayers, not only when I became President but many times since. The Constitution is the supreme law of our land and it governs our actions as citizens. Only the laws of God, which govern our consciences, are superior to it.

As we are a nation under God, so I am sworn to uphold our laws with the help of God. And I have sought such guidance and searched my own conscience with special diligence to determine the right thing for me to do with respect to my predecessor in this place, Richard Nixon, and his loyal wife and family.

Theirs is an American tragedy in which we all have played a part. It could go on and on and on, or someone must write the end to it. I have concluded that only I can do that, and if I can, I must.

There are no historic or legal precedents to which I can turn in this matter, none that precisely fit the circumstances of a private citizen who has resigned the Presidency of the United States. But it is common knowledge that serious allegations and accusations hang like a sword over our former President's head, threatening his health as he tries to reshape his life, a great part of which was spent in the service of this country and by the mandate of its people.

After years of bitter controversy and divisive national debate, I have been advised, and I am compelled to conclude that many months and perhaps more years will have to pass before Richard Nixon could obtain a fair trial by jury in any jurisdiction of the United States under governing decisions of the Supreme Court.

I deeply believe in equal justice for all Americans, whatever their station or former station. The law, whether human or divine, is no respecter of persons; but the law is a respecter of reality.

The facts, as I see them, are that a former President of the United States, instead of enjoying equal treatment with any other citizen accused of violating the law, would be cruelly and excessively penalized either in preserving the presumption of his innocence or in obtaining a speedy determination of his guilt in order to repay a legal debt to society.

During this long period of delay and potential litigation, ugly passions would again be aroused. And our people would again be polarized in their opinions. And the credibility of our free institutions of government would again be challenged at home and abroad.

In the end, the courts might well hold that Richard Nixon had been denied due process, and the verdict of history would even be more inconclusive with respect to those charges arising out of the period of his Presidency, of which I am presently aware.

But it is not the ultimate fate of Richard Nixon that most concerns me, though surely it deeply troubles every decent and every compassionate person. My concern is the immediate future of this great country.

In this, I dare not depend upon my personal sympathy as a longtime friend of the former President, nor my professional judgment as a lawyer, and I do not.

As President, my primary concern must always be the greatest good of all the people of the United States whose servant I am. As a man, my first consideration is to be true to my own convictions and my own conscience.

My conscience tells me clearly and certainly that I cannot prolong the bad dreams that continue to reopen a chapter that is closed. My conscience tells me that only I, as President, have the constitutional power to firmly shut and seal this book. My conscience tells me it is my duty, not merely to proclaim domestic tranquility but to use every means that I have to insure it. I do believe that the buck stops here, that I cannot rely upon public opinion polls to tell me what is right. I do believe that right makes might and that if I am wrong, ten angels swearing I was right would make no difference. I do believe, with all my heart and mind and spirit, that I, not as President but as a humble servant of God, will receive justice without mercy if I fail to show mercy.

Finally, I feel that Richard Nixon and his loved ones have suffered enough and will continue to suffer, no matter what I do, no matter what we, as a great and good nation, can do together to make his goal of peace come true.

Now, therefore, I, Gerald R. Ford, President of the United States, pursuant to the pardon power conferred upon me by Article II, Section 2, of the Constitution, have granted and by these presents do grant a full, free, and absolute pardon unto Richard Nixon for all offenses against the

United States which he, Richard Nixon, has committed or may have committed or taken part in during the period from January 20, 1969, through August 9, 1974.

In witness whereof, I have hereunto set my hand this eighth day of September, in the year of our Lord nineteen hundred and seventy-four, and of the Independence of the United States of America the one hundred and ninety-ninth.

President Gerald R. Ford

Study Questions:

1. To what authorities did President Ford appeal when making his decision to pardon Nixon, and which of those authorities is the highest?

2. On what basis did Ford conclude that the best interests of both Nixon and the nation would be served by pardoning Nixon? Do you agree with Ford's assessment?

Jimmy Carter, Inaugural Address (1977)

Gerald Ford, who had been appointed Vice President by Richard Nixon and then succeeded to the presidency after Nixon resigned, received the Republican nomination for the election of 1976 by a narrow victory over California Governor Ronald Reagan. The Democrats, meanwhile, turned their attention to a surprise candidate, Washington outsider Jimmy Carter. Although Ford had not directly participated in the Watergate scandal, he did lose popularity among many Americans when granting a pardon to Nixon. Carter, by contrast, brought the fresh air of integrity to the contest. Even so, the election results were close: Ford claimed 27 states over Carter's 23, but Carter carried 297 electoral votes to Ford's 240.

For myself and for our Nation, I want to thank my predecessor for all he has done to heal our land.

In this outward and physical ceremony, we attest once again to the inner and spiritual strength of our Nation. As my high school teacher, Miss Julia Coleman, used to say, "We must adjust to changing times and still hold to unchanging principles."

Here before me is the Bible used in the inauguration of our first President, in 1789, and I have just taken the oath of office on the Bible my mother gave me just a few years ago, opened to a timeless admonition from the ancient prophet Micah: "He hath showed thee, O man, what is good; and what doth the Lord require of thee, but to do justly, and to love mercy, and to walk humbly with thy God."

This inauguration ceremony marks a new beginning, a new dedication within our Government, and a new spirit among us all. A President may sense and proclaim that new spirit, but only a people can provide it.

Two centuries ago, our Nation's birth was a milestone in the long quest for freedom. But the bold and brilliant dream which excited the founders of this Nation still awaits its consummation. I have no new dream to set forth today, but rather urge a fresh faith in the old dream.

Ours was the first society openly to define itself in terms of both spirituality and human liberty. It is that unique self-definition which has given us an exceptional appeal, but it also imposes on us a special obligation to take on those moral duties which, when assumed, seem invariably to be in our own best interests.

You have given me a great responsibility—to stay close to you, to be worthy of you, and to exemplify what you are. Let us create together a new national spirit of unity and trust. Your strength can compensate for my weakness, and your wisdom can help to minimize my mistakes.

Let us learn together and laugh together and work together and pray together, confident that in the end we will triumph together in the right.

The American dream endures. We must once again have full faith in our country—and in one another. I believe America can be better. We can be even stronger than before.

Let our recent mistakes bring a resurgent commitment to the basic principles of our Nation, for we know that if we despise our own government, we have no future. We recall in special times when we have stood briefly, but magnificently, united. In those times no prize was beyond our grasp.

But we cannot dwell upon remembered glory. We cannot afford to drift. We reject the prospect of failure or mediocrity or an inferior quality of life for any person. Our Government must at the same time be both competent and compassionate.

We have already found a high degree of personal liberty, and we are now struggling to enhance equality of opportunity. Our commitment to human rights must be absolute, our laws fair, our national beauty preserved; the powerful must not persecute the weak, and human dignity must be enhanced.

We have learned that more is not necessarily better, that even our great Nation has its recognized limits, and that we can neither answer all questions nor solve all problems. We cannot afford to do everything, nor can we afford to lack boldness as we meet the future. So, together, in a spirit of individual sacrifice for the common good, we must simply do our best.

Our Nation can be strong abroad only if it is strong at home. And we know that the best way to enhance freedom in other lands is to demonstrate here that our democratic system is worthy of emulation.

To be true to ourselves, we must be true to others. We will not behave in foreign places so as to violate our rules and standards here at home, for we know that the trust which our Nation earns is essential to our strength.

The world itself is now dominated by a new spirit. Peoples more numerous and more politically aware are craving, and now demanding, their place in the sun—not just for the benefit of their own physical condition, but for basic human rights.

The passion for freedom is on the rise. Tapping this new spirit, there can be no nobler nor more ambitious task for America to undertake on this day of a new beginning than to help shape a just and peaceful world that is truly humane.

We are a strong nation, and we will maintain strength so sufficient that it need not be proven in combat—a quiet strength based not merely on the size of an arsenal but on the nobility of ideas.

We will be ever vigilant and never vulnerable, and we will fight our wars against poverty, ignorance, and injustice, for those are the enemies against which our forces can be honorably marshaled.

We are a proudly idealistic nation, but let no one confuse our idealism with weakness.

Because we are free, we can never be indifferent to the fate of freedom elsewhere. Our moral sense dictates a clearcut preference for those societies which share with us an abiding respect for individual human rights. We do not seek to intimidate, but it is clear that a world which others can dominate with impunity would be inhospitable to decency and a threat to the well-being of all people.

The world is still engaged in a massive armaments race designed to ensure continuing equivalent strength among potential adversaries. We pledge perseverance and wisdom in our efforts to limit the world's armaments to those necessary for each nation's own domestic safety. And we will move this year a step toward our ultimate goal—the elimination of all nuclear weapons from this Earth. We urge all other people to join us, for success can mean life instead of death.

Within us, the people of the United States, there is evident a serious and purposeful rekindling of confidence. And I join in the hope that when my time as your President has ended, people might say this about our Nation:

—that we had remembered the words of Micah and renewed our search for humility, mercy, and justice;

—that we had torn down the barriers that separated those of different race and region and religion, and where there had been mistrust, built unity, with a respect for diversity;

—that we had found productive work for those able to perform it;

—that we had strengthened the American family, which is the basis of our society;

—that we had ensured respect for the law and equal treatment under the law, for the weak and the powerful, for the rich and the poor; and

—that we had enabled our people to be proud of their own Government once again.

I would hope that the nations of the world might say that we had built a lasting peace, based not on weapons of war but on international policies which reflect our own most precious values.

These are not just my goals—and they will not be my accomplishments—but the affirmation of our Nation's continuing moral strength and our belief in an undiminished, ever-expanding American dream.

Thank you very much.

Study Questions

1. Carter said, "Ours was the first society openly to define itself in terms of both spirituality and of human liberty." Explain what he meant, both as to America's earlier history and as to Carter's own vision for the future.

2. How did Carter's foreign policy program compare to the Truman Doctrine?

Jimmy Carter, "Crisis of Confidence Speech" (1979)

A June 1979 poll indicated that merely 28% of the American people approved of President Jimmy Carter's leadership. Economic hardship, Cold War fears, the oil crisis, a perpetuation of racial tension, and lingering memories of the Watergate scandal and the Vietnam War all contributed to a general feeling of malaise—a vague sense of illness with no cure in sight. Historians, in fact, would later label the following speech, delivered by Carter in July 1979, his "Malaise Speech." Although he did not use that term, he did use the word "confidence" fifteen times, primarily to acknowledge that Americans no longer had much confidence in anything. (It is telling that Carter used the term "crisis" nearly as frequently.) The immediate impact of this speech was to boost Carter's approval rating, albeit only to 37%. As weeks passed into months, Carter's reputation continued to languish in uncertainty. The national crisis truly was his own.

Good evening. This is a special night for me. Exactly three years ago, on July 15, 1976, I accepted the nomination of my party to run for president of the United States.

I promised you a president who is not isolated from the people, who feels your pain, and who shares your dreams and who draws his strength and his wisdom from you.

During the past three years I've spoken to you on many occasions about national concerns, the energy crisis, reorganizing the government, our nation's economy, and issues of war and especially peace. But over those years the subjects of the speeches, the talks, and the press conferences have become increasingly narrow, focused more and more on what the isolated world of Washington thinks is important. Gradually, you've heard more and more about what the government thinks or what the government should be doing and less and less about our nation's hopes, our dreams, and our vision of the future.

Ten days ago I had planned to speak to you again about a very important subject— energy. For the fifth time I would have described the urgency of the problem and laid out a series of legislative recommendations to the Congress. But as I was preparing to speak, I began to ask myself the same question that I now know has been troubling many of you. Why have we not been able to get together as a nation to resolve our serious energy problem?

It's clear that the true problems of our Nation are much deeper—deeper than gasoline lines or energy shortages, deeper even than inflation or recession. And I realize more than ever that as president I need your help. So I decided to reach out and listen to the voices of America.

I invited to Camp David people from almost every segment of our society—business and labor, teachers and preachers, governors, mayors, and private citizens. And then I left Camp David to listen to other Americans, men and women like you.

It has been an extraordinary ten days, and I want to share with you what I've heard. First of all, I got a lot of personal advice. Let me quote a few of the typical comments that I wrote down.

This from a southern governor: "Mr. President, you are not leading this nation —you're just managing the government."

"You don't see the people enough any more."

"Some of your Cabinet members don't seem loyal. There is not enough discipline among your disciples."

"Don't talk to us about politics or the mechanics of government, but about an understanding of our common good."

"Mr. President, we're in trouble. Talk to us about blood and sweat and tears."

"If you lead, Mr. President, we will follow."

Many people talked about themselves and about the condition of our nation.

This from a young woman in Pennsylvania: "I feel so far from government. I feel like ordinary people are excluded from political power."

And this from a young Chicano: "Some of us have suffered from recession all our lives."

"Some people have wasted energy, but others haven't had anything to waste."

And this from a religious leader: "No material shortage can touch the important things like God's love for us or our love for one another."

And I like this one particularly from a black woman who happens to be the mayor of a small Mississippi town: "The big-shots are not the only ones who are important. Remember, you can't sell anything on Wall Street unless someone digs it up somewhere else first."

This kind of summarized a lot of other statements: "Mr. President, we are confronted with a moral and a spiritual crisis."

Several of our discussions were on energy, and I have a notebook full of comments and advice. I'll read just a few.

"We can't go on consuming 40 percent more energy than we produce. When we import oil we are also importing inflation plus unemployment."

"We've got to use what we have. The Middle East has only five percent of the world's energy, but the United States has 24 percent."

And this is one of the most vivid statements: "Our neck is stretched over the fence and OPEC has a knife."

"There will be other cartels and other shortages. American wisdom and courage right now can set a path to follow in the future."

This was a good one: "Be bold, Mr. President. We may make mistakes, but we are ready to experiment."

And this one from a labor leader got to the heart of it: "The real issue is freedom. We must deal with the energy problem on a war footing."

And the last that I'll read: "When we enter the moral equivalent of war, Mr. President, don't issue us BB guns."

These ten days confirmed my belief in the decency and the strength and the wisdom of the American people, but it also bore out some of my long-standing concerns about our nation's underlying problems.

I know, of course, being president, that government actions and legislation can be very important. That's why I've worked hard to put my campaign promises into law—and I have to admit, with just mixed success. But after listening to the American people I have been reminded again that all the legislation in the world can't fix what's wrong with America. So, I want to speak to you first tonight about a subject even more serious than energy or inflation. I want to talk to you right now about a fundamental threat to American democracy.

I do not mean our political and civil liberties. They will endure. And I do not refer to the outward strength of America, a nation that is at peace tonight everywhere in the world, with unmatched economic power and military might.

The threat is nearly invisible in ordinary ways. It is a crisis of confidence. It is a crisis that strikes at the very heart and soul and spirit of our national will. We can see this crisis in the growing doubt about the meaning of our own lives and in the loss of a unity of purpose for our nation.

The erosion of our confidence in the future is threatening to destroy the social and the political fabric of America.

The confidence that we have always had as a people is not simply some romantic dream or a proverb in a dusty book that we read just on the Fourth of July.

It is the idea which founded our nation and has guided our development as a people. Confidence in the future has supported everything else—public institutions and private enterprise, our own families, and the very Constitution of the United States. Confidence has defined our course and has served as a link between generations. We've always believed in something called progress. We've always had a faith that the days of our children would be better than our own.

Our people are losing that faith, not only in government itself but in the ability as citizens to serve as the ultimate rulers and shapers of our democracy. As a people we know our past and we are proud of it. Our progress has been part of the living history of America, even the world. We always believed that we were part of a great movement of humanity itself called democracy, involved in the search for freedom, and that belief has always strengthened us in our purpose. But just as we are losing our confidence in the future, we are also beginning to close the door on our past.

In a nation that was proud of hard work, strong families, close-knit communities, and our faith in God, too many of us now tend to worship self-indulgence and consumption. Human identity is no longer defined by what one does, but by what one owns. But we've discovered that owning things and consuming things does not satisfy our longing for meaning. We've learned that piling up material goods cannot fill the emptiness of lives which have no confidence or purpose.

The symptoms of this crisis of the American spirit are all around us. For the first time in the history of our country a majority of our people believe that the next five years will be worse than the past five years. Two-thirds of our people do not even vote. The productivity of American workers is actually dropping, and the willingness of Americans to save for the future has fallen below that of all other people in the Western world.

As you know, there is a growing disrespect for government and for churches and for schools, the news media, and other institutions. This is not a message of happiness or reassurance, but it is the truth and it is a warning.

These changes did not happen overnight. They've come upon us gradually over the last generation, years that were filled with shocks and tragedy.

We were sure that ours was a nation of the ballot, not the bullet, until the murders of John Kennedy and Robert Kennedy and Martin Luther King, Jr. We were taught that our armies were always invincible and our causes were always just, only to suffer the agony of Vietnam. We respected the presidency as a place of honor until the shock of Watergate.

We remember when the phrase "sound as a dollar" was an expression of absolute dependability, until ten years of inflation began to shrink our dollar and our savings. We believed that our nation's resources were limitless until 1973, when we had to face a growing dependence on foreign oil.

These wounds are still very deep. They have never been healed. Looking for a way out of this crisis, our people have turned to the Federal government and found it isolated from the mainstream of our nation's life. Washington, D.C., has become an island. The gap between our citizens and our government has never been so wide. The people are looking for honest answers, not easy answers; clear leadership, not false claims and evasiveness and politics as usual.

What you see too often in Washington and elsewhere around the country is a system of government that seems incapable of action. You see a Congress twisted and pulled in every direction by hundreds of well-financed and powerful special interests. You see every extreme position defended to the last vote, almost to the last breath by one unyielding group or another. You often see a balanced and a fair approach that demands sacrifice, a little sacrifice from everyone, abandoned like an orphan without support and without friends.

Often you see paralysis and stagnation and drift. You don't like it, and neither do I. What can we do?

First of all, we must face the truth, and then we can change our course. We simply must have faith in each other, faith in our ability to govern ourselves, and faith in the future of this nation. Restoring that faith and that confidence to America is now the most important task we face. It is a true challenge of this generation of Americans.

One of the visitors to Camp David last week put it this way: "We've got to stop crying and start sweating, stop talking and start walking, stop cursing and start praying. The strength we need will not come from the White House, but from every house in America."

We know the strength of America. We are strong. We can regain our unity. We can regain our confidence. We are the heirs of generations who survived threats much more powerful and awesome than those that challenge us now. Our fathers and mothers were strong men and women who shaped a new society during the Great Depression, who fought world wars, and who carved out a new charter of peace for the world.

We ourselves are the same Americans who just ten years ago put a man on the Moon. We are the generation that dedicated our society to the pursuit of human rights and equality. And we are the generation that will win the war on the energy problem and in that process rebuild the unity and confidence of America.

We are at a turning point in our history. There are two paths to choose. One is a path I've warned about tonight, the path that leads to fragmentation and self-interest. Down that road lies a mistaken idea of freedom, the right to grasp for ourselves some advantage over others. That path would be one of constant conflict between narrow interests ending in chaos and immobility. It is a certain route to failure.

All the traditions of our past, all the lessons of our heritage, all the promises of our future point to another path, the path of common purpose and the restoration of American values. That path leads to true freedom for our nation and ourselves. We can take the first steps down that path as we begin to solve our energy problem.

Energy will be the immediate test of our ability to unite this nation, and it can also be the standard around which we rally. On the battlefield of energy we can win for our nation a new confidence, and we can seize control again of our common destiny.

In little more than two decades we've gone from a position of energy independence to one in which almost half the oil we use comes from foreign countries, at prices that are going through the roof. Our excessive dependence on OPEC has already taken a tremendous toll on our economy and our people. This is the direct cause of the long lines which have made millions of you spend aggravating hours waiting for gasoline. It's a cause of the increased inflation and unemployment that we now face. This intolerable dependence on foreign oil threatens our economic independence and the very security of our nation. The energy crisis is real. It is worldwide. It is a clear and present danger to our nation. These are facts and we simply must face them.

What I have to say to you now about energy is simple and vitally important.

Point one: I am tonight setting a clear goal for the energy policy of the United States. Beginning this moment, this nation will never use more foreign oil than we did in 1977—never. From now on, every new addition to our demand for energy will be met from our own production and our own conservation. The generation-long growth in our dependence on foreign oil will be stopped dead in its tracks right now and then reversed as we move through the 1980s, for I am tonight setting the further goal of cutting our dependence on foreign oil by one-half by the end of the next decade—a saving of over 4-1/2 million barrels of imported oil per day.

Point two: To ensure that we meet these targets, I will use my presidential authority to set import quotas. I'm announcing tonight that for 1979 and 1980, I will forbid the entry into this country of one drop of foreign oil more than these goals allow. These quotas will ensure a reduction in imports even below the ambitious levels we set at the recent Tokyo summit.

Point three: To give us energy security, I am asking for the most massive peacetime commitment of funds and resources in our nation's history to develop America's own alternative sources of fuel—from coal, from oil shale, from plant products for gasohol, from unconventional gas, from the sun.

I propose the creation of an energy security corporation to lead this effort to replace 2-1/2 million barrels of imported oil per day by 1990. The corporation I will issue up to $5 billion in energy bonds, and I especially want them to be in small denominations so that average Americans can invest directly in America's energy security.

Just as a similar synthetic rubber corporation helped us win World War II, so will we mobilize American determination and ability to win the energy war. Moreover, I will soon submit legislation to Congress calling for the creation of this nation's first solar bank, which will help us achieve the crucial goal of 20 percent of our energy coming from solar power by the year 2000.

These efforts will cost money, a lot of money, and that is why Congress must enact the windfall profits tax without delay. It will be money well spent. Unlike the billions of dollars that we ship to foreign countries to pay for foreign oil, these funds will be paid by Americans to Americans. These funds will go to fight, not to increase, inflation and unemployment.

Point four: I'm asking Congress to mandate, to require as a matter of law, that our nation's utility companies cut their massive use of oil by 50 percent within the next decade and switch to other fuels, especially coal, our most abundant energy source.

Point five: To make absolutely certain that nothing stands in the way of achieving these goals, I will urge Congress to create an energy mobilization board which, like the War Production Board in World War II, will have the responsibility and authority to cut through the red tape, the delays, and the endless roadblocks to completing key energy projects.

We will protect our environment. But when this nation critically needs a refinery or a pipeline, we will build it.

Point six: I'm proposing a bold conservation program to involve every state, county, and city and every average American in our energy battle. This effort will permit you to build conservation into your homes and your lives at a cost you can afford.

I ask Congress to give me authority for mandatory conservation and for standby gasoline rationing. To further conserve energy, I'm proposing tonight an extra $10 billion over the next decade to strengthen our public transportation systems. And I'm asking you for your good and for your nation's security to take no unnecessary trips, to use carpools or public transportation whenever you can, to park your car one extra day per week, to obey the speed limit, and to set your thermostats to save fuel. Every act of energy conservation like this is more than just common sense—I tell you it is an act of patriotism.

Our nation must be fair to the poorest among us, so we will increase aid to needy Americans to cope with rising energy prices. We often think of conservation only in terms of sacrifice. In fact, it is the most painless and immediate way of rebuilding our nation's strength. Every gallon of oil each one of us saves is a new form of production. It gives us more freedom, more confidence, that much more control over our own lives.

So, the solution of our energy crisis can also help us to conquer the crisis of the spirit in our country. It can rekindle our sense of unity, our confidence in the future, and give our nation and all of us individually a new sense of purpose.

You know we can do it. We have the natural resources. We have more oil in our shale alone than several Saudi Arabias. We have more coal than any nation on Earth. We have the world's highest level of technology. We have the most skilled work force, with innovative genius, and I firmly believe that we have the national will to win this war.

I do not promise you that this struggle for freedom will be easy. I do not promise a quick way out of our nation's problems, when the truth is that the only way out is an all-out effort. What I do promise you is that I will lead our fight, and I will enforce fairness in our struggle, and I will ensure honesty. And above all, I will act. We can manage the short-term shortages more effectively and we will, but there are no short-term solutions to our long-range problems. There is simply no way to avoid sacrifice.

Twelve hours from now I will speak again in Kansas City, to expand and to explain further our energy program. Just as the search for solutions to our energy shortages has now led us to a new awareness of our Nation's deeper problems, so our willingness to work for those solutions in energy can strengthen us to attack those deeper problems.

I will continue to travel this country, to hear the people of America. You can help me to develop a national agenda for the 1980s. I will listen and I will act. We will act together. These were the promises I made three years ago, and I intend to keep them.

Little by little we can and we must rebuild our confidence. We can spend until we empty our treasuries, and we may summon all the wonders of science. But we can succeed only if we tap our greatest resources—America's people, America's values, and America's confidence.

I have seen the strength of America in the inexhaustible resources of our people. In the days to come, let us renew that strength in the struggle for an energy secure nation.

In closing, let me say this: I will do my best, but I will not do it alone. Let your voice be heard. Whenever you have a chance, say something good about our country. With God's help and for the sake of our nation, it is time for us to join hands in America. Let us commit ourselves together to a rebirth of the American spirit. Working together with our common faith we cannot fail.

Thank you and good night.

Study Questions

1. What factors did President Carter identify as the sources of America's "crisis of confidence"?

2. Summarize the six recommendations that Carter made for revitalizing America.

3. Ultimately, what did Carter conclude was the only way to renew American prosperity?

The President Campaign of 1980

The presidential election of 1980 marked a significant turning point in American politics. To the surprise of many political analysts, the regime of liberalism—in both its New Deal and Great Society varieties—suffered a serious blow. The American people overwhelmingly favored Ronald Reagan, the most *laissez-faire* president since Calvin Coolidge. Even union workers, the backbone of FDR's Democratic coalition, defected from their party to become "Reagan Democrats." Moreover, Reagan solidified a transformation that had begun in 1964 when another small-government Republican, Barry Goldwater, captured votes within the Democratic "solid South." Southern whites continued to switch from Democratic—the party they had supported ever since the Civil War—to Republican when Richard Nixon was elected in 1968 and again in 1972, but it was Reagan's 1980 landslide (a 489-to-49 electoral victory) that dealt a death blow to the old order and established a new tradition, the "Republican L": a band of states stretching from Montana and North Dakota down to Arizona and Texas and across the southeast to the Atlantic coast.

The Democratic Party, meanwhile, shifted its center of gravity away from southern whites—including the southern evangelicals who had championed Jimmy Carter in 1976—toward a collage of special-interest groups. African Americans had discovered during the Kennedy and Johnson administrations that the Democratic Party would support their quest for civil rights. Feminists then followed suit, persuading the Democratic Party to adopt abortion rights as a defining plank of their national platform in 1980, after securing a modest support for *Roe v. Wade* in the 1976 platform. Rights for immigrants, for the handicapped, for gays and lesbians, and other minority groups soon would characterize the Democratic Party, together with a vision for progressive reform reminiscent of the Johnson administration.

Two factors, especially, favored Republicans over Democrats as the parties realigned in 1980. The first was economic. In 1976, Carter had coined the term "misery index" as a composite of the unemployment rate and the inflation rate. In 1980, Reagan could point out that the misery index had only increased during Carter's administration. In a televised debate a week before the election, Reagan frankly advised the American people: "I think when you make that decision, it might be well if you would ask yourself, are you better off than you were four years ago?" Clearly, they were worse off; blaming Carter, they voted for Reagan. The second factor was moral and religious. The Warren and Burger courts had expanded rights for accused criminals and for women seeking abortions while removing prayer and Bible reading from public schools. America had been founded on Christian principles, but it appeared now that America's own government was rejecting that foundation. Evangelical minister Jerry Falwell founded the Moral Majority in 1979 to correct America's course. Politically, that meant voting Republican, especially after Reagan announced "I endorse you" to 15,000 activists assembled by the Moral Majority shortly before the 1980 election.

Study Questions

1. Which groups of voters switched from Republican to Democrat during the 1960s and 1970s, and why?

2. Which groups of voters switched from Democrat to Republican during the 1960s and 1970s, and why?

PART 5:

The Triumph and the Vulnerability of the World's Only Superpower

1981–Present

America's Triumph and Vulnerability in the New World Order

Under the leadership of Woodrow Wilson, Franklin D. Roosevelt, Harry S. Truman, and Lyndon B. Johnson, the federal government had adopted progressivism with increasing enthusiasm. Some presidents, such as Dwight D. Eisenhower and Richard M. Nixon, had merely held the course. Others, like Jimmy Carter, had tried to advance a progressive agenda, but accomplished little. No one since Calvin Coolidge had seriously tried to revert the American political economy to the *laissez-faire* doctrines of the nineteenth century. Twentieth-century leaders instead committed themselves to government regulation of the economy in the name of the common good—or for the sake of "the Great Society," as Johnson termed it. Quite ironically, the United States was thereby drifting toward socialism in its domestic policy even while taking a firm stand against Soviet communism in its foreign policy.

Then suddenly economic policy reverted to a *laissez-faire* posture during Ronald Reagan's two terms as president (1981–1989). Reagan's foreign policy also became more aggressive against the Soviet Union, which he dubbed an "evil empire." Meanwhile, a parallel resurgence of conservative economic theory transformed Great Britain, where Margaret Thatcher served as prime minister from 1979 to 1990. A Soviet journalist attempted to smear her with the eponym "Iron Lady," but she wore that title with pride—standing resolutely with Reagan for free markets. Both Thatcher and Reagan set to work dismantling the regulatory burdens imposed on businesses and streamlining the welfare bureaucracies that bloated their national balance sheets with debt. With two major world leaders together heralding a new era of economic opportunity, even the Soviet Union could not ignore the signs of the times. In 1985, a new Soviet leader, Mikhail Gorbachev, showed a greater willingness than any of his predecessors to dialogue with the free world about ending the Cold War.

Gorbachev faced the facts: a communist economy stifles the production of wealth and therefore the Soviet Union could sustain neither its military build-up nor its welfare distributions much longer. The Iron Curtain receded steadily from 1989 to 1991 as the Soviet Union forfeited its empire and self-destructed into multiple distinct states. Communism had collapsed from within, even as the entrepreneurial spirit of the United States soared to new heights. With the Soviet Union gone, America now stood alone as the world's only superpower. However, new challenges loomed on the horizon—both at home and abroad.

In foreign policy, the United States soon discovered that decisions made for short-term advantage during the Cold War could have devastating long-term repercussions stretching well beyond the Cold War. During the 1980s, for example, the U.S. Central Intelligence Agency buttressed Mujahideen rebels in Afghanistan against the threat of Soviet invasion, only to discover that a radical faction among those rebels came to support the Taliban, an emerging regime which allied itself with al-Qaeda terrorists led by Saudi Arabian refugee Osama bin Laden. Meanwhile, the United States also was supporting the regime of Saddam Hussein in Iraq during a decade-long conflict between Iraq and Iran. When the balance of geopolitical power shifted in the 1990s, both Hussein and bin Laden turned against the United States. The United States fought two wars against Hussein's Iraq (first in 1991 and starting again in 2003) and suffered humiliating terrorist attacks sponsored by al Qaeda (including several small attacks in the 1990s followed by major blows delivered on September 11, 2001).

On the home front, Americans struggled to retain the integrity of their Judeo-Christian tradition amid a "culture war" between conservatives who championed family values and liberals who favored individual liberty in matters of sexuality. The debate turned personal in 1998, when the U.S. House of Representatives adopted impeachment charges against President Bill Clinton (1993–2001) for lying under oath concerning allegations of sexual misconduct. Theodore Roosevelt, Calvin Coolidge, Harry S. Truman, Dwight D. Eisenhower, and Jimmy Carter all presented themselves as men of character—models of honesty, goodness, and virtue worthy of emulation by the young. Even Richard Nixon paid lip service to such traits and, upon being accused of wrongdoing in the Watergate scandal, resigned to retain the dignity of the presidential office. In the Clinton scandal, however, heroes seemed to be lacking altogether: Clinton craftily redefined the word "sex" in order to claim he had done nothing wrong, while Kenneth Starr—the special counsel leading the investigation against him—exceeded the bounds of decency in his aggressive pursuit, much like Senator Joseph McCarthy had done in his anti-communist crusade during the 1950s.

The presidential election of 2000 failed to deliver America from this sense of moral confusion. Due to controversies surrounding the counting of ballots in Florida, the U.S. Supreme Court ultimately chose the winner, and did so along lines that appeared partisan to many observers. Attempting to revive the ethos of the civil rights movement, several members of Congress formally objected that African American voters in Florida had effectively been disenfranchised by the Court's decision. Liberals who had supported the presidential candidacy of Al Gore—vice president under Clinton—were not the only ones to suffer defeat. Although President-elect George W. Bush hailed from the Republican Party, he represented one particular brand of conservatism at a time when another group of conservatives increasingly felt alienated by the party.

President George W. Bush (2001–2009), like his father George H. W. Bush who had served as president a decade earlier (1989–1993), envisioned the United States as the guardian of democracy throughout the world and was willing to commit the nation to unilateral military action when needed. This "neo-conservative" foreign policy correlated with a domestic outlook that would deploy the federal government to prop up large corporations in order to prevent unemployment. Maintaining a balanced budget was not a priority for neo-conservatives. "Paleo-conservatives," by contrast, cherished a strict reading of the U.S. Constitution and therefore saw a more limited role for government.

Reagan, and especially Coolidge, rather than Nixon or either of the Bushes, were the paleo-conservatives' heroes. Keep government small, keep spending low, and maintain national sovereignty rather than forging international coalitions in a global crusade for human rights. In the 2008 and 2012 presidential elections, paleo-conservatives rallied behind Republican Senator Ron Paul, who criticized Bush's interventionist foreign policy and called for a balanced budget. In each case, however, the Republic Party instead endorsed a neoconservative if not an outright moderate—John McCain in 2008 and Mitt Romney four years later. To the chagrin of both kinds of "conservatives," neither of these candidates could prevail against the Democratic nominee Barack Obama, who starting in 2009 proved himself to be the most liberal-progressive president the nation had ever seen.

Although it is too early at present to tell, the dramatic shift from Reagan to Obama may be signaling a fundamental realignment of American politics. In late 2008, Republican President George W. Bush signed off on a $700 billion bailout program by which the federal government offered to rescue the economy from a recession. In early 2009, Democratic President Barack Obama signed a similar stimulus bill, this time budgeted at $800 billion. Neither president seemed particularly troubled that the national debt was mushrooming out of proportion with the gross domestic product. Neither president seemed to recall that the Soviet Union's unsustainable fiscal policies had resulted in its downfall twenty years earlier. Progressivism, which critics of the New Deal long ago had called "creeping socialism," had now become the consensus of both parties, no matter the financial cost.

Oddly, the only area in which *laissez-faire* ideals carried much weight was the one area in which traditional Americans had been slowest to embrace *laissez faire*: family values. American public policy long had cherished the natural family—a husband and wife together with their children—as the bedrock of civilization. Although family policy turned against the natural family in the 1960s, even as recently as 2003 some states continued to outlaw deviations from the natural norm, such as homosexuality. By 2013, however, fifteen states (encompassing over one third of the nation's population) had revised their laws to permit same-sex couples to marry. Libertarian conservatives supported this radical transformation in social policy under the pretense that individuals should be free to choose whom to marry—even someone of the same sex. In other words, the state should have a *laissez-faire* posture toward marriage.

However, not liberty but rather government coercion followed in the wake of liberalized marriage regulations. School children were required to undergo indoctrination into the new standard, even against the conscientious objections of their parents. Entrepreneurs were forbidden from choosing whether or not to serve as florists, photographers, or food caterers for same-sex ceremonies; if they provided such services to opposite-sex couples, then the state required them to do the same for same-sex couples, regardless of personal religious objections. Even when the majority of California voters supported a state constitutional amendment defining marriage as the union of one man and one woman, a federal court ordered the state to permit same-sex couples to marry after all. But if marriage is, in fact, fundamental to civilization, then what befalls a nation that forcibly redefines marriage? Americans therefore found themselves wondering, once again, what the proper recipe for ordered liberty must be.

Chronological Overview:
The End of the Cold War to the Present Day

1981   Congress passes the Economic Recovery Tax Act, reducing the highest income tax rate from 70% to 50%.

1983   Labeling the Soviet Union an "evil empire," President Reagan calls for a military build up, including MX missiles (nuclear warheads capable of reaching intercontinental targets) and a Strategic Defense Initiative (familiarly known as "Star Wars"), consisting of space satellites capable of intercepting Soviet missiles.

1985   As leadership in the Soviet Union shifts to Mikhail Gorbachev, relations with the United States improve. Reagan and Gorbachev negotiate plans for mutual disarmament and an end to the Cold War.

1986   Congress reduces the highest income tax rate from 50% to 28% and the highest corporate rate from 46% to 34% while also entirely eliminating income taxes for low-income Americans.

1986–1987   A Lebanese newspaper reveals that the United States has been secretly selling arms to Iran; Senate hearings then reveal that profits from these arms sales have been funding the Contras against the Soviet-backed Sandinistas in Nicaragua, despite a congressional prohibition.

1989   The Soviet Union stops supporting the East German government, leaving it to collapse. German citizens tear down the Berlin Wall as the Iron Curtain recedes.

1991   The Soviet Union disintegrates, marking the conclusion of the Cold War.

President George H. W. Bush assembles an international coalition to liberate Kuwait from Iraq.

1993   The U.S. Senate ratifies the North American Free Trade Agreement (NAFTA), linking the United States economically to Mexico and Canada while favoring large-scale agricultural producers over small family farms.

1998   Congress adopts a balanced budget for the first time in thirty years.

The House of Representatives impeaches President Bill Clinton for perjury before a grand jury concerning allegations of sexual misconduct.

2001   Congress enacts the No Child Left Behind Act, requiring public schools to submit to federal standards for the continuance of federal funding.

Terrorists strike New York City and Washington, DC, on September 11. Congress responds with the Patriot Act, which limits individual liberties for the sake of promoting national security.

2002   The Homeland Security Act restructures the federal government and links local law enforcement into a national security task force.

2003   The War on Terrorism expands into Iraq, as President George W. Bush accuses Saddam Hussein of developing weapons of mass destruction.

2008   Congress passes the Emergency Economic Stabilization Act, authorizing the Treasury Department to purchase failing investments (primarily, mortgage-backed securities) in order to inject fresh credit into banks. About $700 billion is allocated for the Troubled Asset Relief Program (TARP).

2009   The American Recovery and Reinvestment Act allocates an additional $800 billion for infrastructure, education, healthcare, and renewable energy programs aimed collectively at lifting the economy out of a recession. Meanwhile, the Federal Reserve Board covertly commits $7.8 trillion to the bailout program—more than half the gross domestic product.

2010   Congress passes the Patient Protection and Affordable Care Act ("Obamacare"), which mandates what all health insurance policies must cover (including controversial coverage for abortion and contraception), requires that nearly every American purchase such insurance, and imposes new taxes on the rich to subsidize insurance for the poor.

2013   The federal government temporarily lays off 800,000 workers and shuts down several operations while Congress faces a two-week impasse in the debate of whether to lift the debt ceiling beyond $16.4 trillion.

Presidents of the Last Surviving Superpower, 1981–Present

Ronald Reagan (Republican—California), 1981–1989

Conservatism never ceases to surprise people, particularly liberals. Who would have imagined that a Democrat of the New Deal vintage who headed the liberal Screen Actors Guild in the 1950s and also participated actively in the California chapter of Americans for Democratic Action would become the most conservative Republican president of the late twentieth century? Indeed, the very name "Ronald Reagan" would become the Republican gold standard against whom conservatives in the party judged all other candidates for an entire generation. The story of Reagan's political transformation is instructive not only because it reveals an intriguing dimension of his own life, but because it points to a broader pattern that characterized America as a nation during the 1980s: a resurgence of conservatism.

Raised by an alcoholic shoe salesman who depended upon a federal relief agency to survive the Great Depression, Ronald Reagan found work as a sports announcer in Des Moines during the mid 1930s before moving to Hollywood to attempt a career as an actor. He managed to appear in over fifty movies, generally as supporting roles in B-grade films. A bigger break came in 1954 when General Electric hired Reagan as a corporate spokesman. For eight years, he hosted General Electric Theatre on television. Though unforeseen as the time, he was preparing to become "the great communicator" who not only would win two landslide presidential victories in America but also would herald the fall of communism worldwide.

Meanwhile, Reagan's marriage to Nancy Davis, the daughter of a conservative physician, in 1952 linked him to a new side of politics. In 1964, Reagan delivered a televised convention speech for presidential candidate Barry Goldwater. Critical of the welfare bureaucracy, militantly anti-communist, and staunchly for states' rights, Goldwater envisioned a smaller federal government and a return of political power to the local people. Goldwater's conservatism received particularly strong support in Orange County, California, where grass-roots efforts rallied behind Reagan's bid for the governor's office in 1966. After twice being elected as governor, Reagan nearly defeated President Gerald Ford in the contest for the Republican Party's presidential endorsement in 1976. Although Ford received the nomination that year, he lost to Jimmy Carter in the general election. Therefore, in 1980 the Republicans were ready to choose Ronald Reagan.

Reagan had a particular gift for humorously simplifying the complex issues of the day. For choosing a president, Reagan recommended that people simply ask, "Are you better off than you were four years ago?" Against Jimmy Carter's statistics—which Reagan found to be inaccurate—the great communicator simply said, "Now there you go again." About three months into his presidency, Reagan was wounded by a would-be assassin. As he looked up from his hospital bed to the attending surgeon, the president joked, "I hope you're all Republicans." The surgeon, though a Democrat, playfully assured him, "We're all Republicans today."

All joking aside, Reagan had serious intentions to reform the nation's economy. Rejecting the demand-side theory of economics which calls upon the government to prime the pump by putting money into the hands of consumers, Reagan championed supply-side economics, which calls for tax cuts so that business owners have more cash on hand for expanding operations. According to "Reaganomics," wealth will then "trickle down" to the lower classes as business owners expand employment and increase wages. After a decade of stagflation, Congress was ready at least to give this idea a try.

On social issues, Reagan's record was less consistent. On the one hand, he had as California governor signed into law a no-fault divorce bill as well as the legalization of abortion. Nevertheless, the Moral Majority supported his presidential candidacy in 1980. Once elected, Reagan wrote a book entitled *Abortion and the Conscience of a Nation*, which exposed *Roe v. Wade* as an immoral and unconstitutional ruling. Nevertheless, Reagan's first appointee to the Supreme Court, Sandra Day O'Connor, proved to be one of the strongest proponents of abortion on demand that the Court has known.

Perhaps Reagan's most memorable statement came in June 1987, when he addressed a crowd of 20,000 people in West Berlin, saying, "Mr. Gorbachev, tear down this wall!" The Berlin Wall in fact came down two years later, the same year Reagan left office. After twenty-eight years of separation, the people of East and West Germany were able to reconcile as friends and family in a post-communist age. Reagan retired to California following his presidency. For a few years, he gave speeches in favor of a balanced budget and a line-item veto, but in 1994 he withdrew from public life under a diagnosis of Alzheimer's disease. Reagan died of pneumonia ten years later, at the age of 93.

George H. W. Bush (Republican—Texas), 1989–1993

Campaigning against Ronald Reagan in the race for the 1980 Republican presidential nomination, George Herbert Walker Bush criticized Reagan's supply-side theory as "voodoo economics." When, however, Reagan took the lead, Bush found himself accepting the party's offer to be the vice presidential candidate and learning to keep quiet about his disagreements with Reagan. Bush brought to the administration a wealth of experience in foreign relations, for he had served as both the director of the Central Intelligence Agency and the U.S. ambassador to the United Nations. In 1988, Bush again set his eyes on the presidency. Knowing why the Republican Party loved Reagan, Bush promised more of the same, vowing "no new taxes."

Inheriting the foreign policy victories of his predecessor, Bush presided over America while the Berlin Wall toppled and the Soviet Union disintegrated. However, just when the Iron Curtain was lifted in Eastern Europe, the Middle East took center stage in a new phase of foreign relations. Iraq invaded Kuwait in 1990 and threatened to takeover Saudi Arabia next. With American oil interests at stake, as well as a desire to protect the right of nations to govern themselves, the United States led a coalition in early 1991 to liberate Kuwait from Iraq.

Despite a quick and decisive victory in the Gulf War, Bush's popularity ratings in America were falling. Some speculated that the president had led the nation into war because his own family fortune depended upon oil trade. Others faulted Bush for backpedaling on his no-new-taxes pledge when agreeing with congressional Democrats to increase tax rates in 1990. Political analysts came to recognize that Bush represented a different kind of conservative than Reagan—less committed to supply-side economics at home and more committed to forging a new world order abroad with the United States taking the lead in restructuring the Middle East.

Bush also sought to improve educational standards in America, urging that national standards be adopted for a variety of subject areas across multiple grade levels by the year 2000. Here, too, he showed his neoconservative colors. Whereas the paleo-conservative Reagan had vowed in the 1980 campaign to abolish the U.S. Department of Education (which had been established on doubtful constitutional grounds just a year earlier), Bush sought to extend the role of this federal bureau in shaping curriculum nationwide. However, the Bush family also recognized a role for charitable organizations in the advancement of learning. Upon learning that some thirty-five million adult Americans in the 1980s could not read at a high school level, President Bush's wife Barbara devoted her service as first lady to the promotion of literacy. This campaign led to the establishment of the Barbara Bush Foundation for Family Literacy, aimed at helping parents and children to learn to read together.

After his presidency, George H. W. Bush continued to make public appearances. In addition to supporting the candidacy of his son, George W., he also teamed with Democrat Bill Clinton in 2005 to encourage charitable donations to a relief fund for helping people recover from Hurricane Katrina, which ravaged the New Orleans region that August.

Bill Clinton (Democrat—Arkansas), 1993–2001

Situated between the presidencies of the two Bushes, Bill Clinton filled a peculiar chapter in American history. He was a Democrat, but not the kind of Democrat Americans had come to expect. Personally, he had deep flaws, and yet many people loved him anyway. History remembers Clinton as the last American president to have a balanced budget, and yet it had been the avowedly anti-Clinton Republicans who launched the balanced budget effort in their 1994 ploy for a "Contract with America." Clinton proved once again that politics never disappoints people's craving for surprises.

Clinton's ascendancy began as the 1992 presidential election approached, when Democrats were desperately wondering what had gone wrong. Theirs was the party of FDR and the New Deal. Theirs was the party of JFK and LBJ and the Great Society. From 1933 to 1981, the White House had been occupied by a Democrat twice as often as by a Republican. Moreover, the rare Republican tenants—Eisenhower, Nixon, and Ford—had been moderates who only slowed, but did not reverse, the twentieth-century trend of liberal progressivism. How, then, had Ronald Reagan won not just one, but two, landslide victories as a paleo-conservative in the 1980s? And how had the Democrats failed to win back the presidency when Reagan's second term was winding down in 1988?

As the Democratic Leadership Council reviewed the course of presidential history, they realized that their party had lost the vital center of American politics. Starting in the 1960s, the Democrats had become the party of special-interest groups, not of the "silent majority" of which Nixon had spoken. African Americans, feminists, the disabled, and other minorities had each won a piece of the Democratic Party, but the nation as a whole slipped out of the party's hand because Average Joe America was tired of paying taxes to support other people's special interests. Even union workers—the bread and butter of the Democratic New Deal coalition—had bolted from the party of FDR to support Reagan's promises of tax relief.

Learning from their past mistakes, the Democrat Leadership Council centered their attention on Arkansas Governor William Jefferson Clinton, who became the poster child for the "New Democrat" image of the 1990s. Whereas Republicans had branded Democrats as "tax and spend liberals" who doled out "welfare handouts," Clinton called for fiscal responsibility and welfare reform. Campaigning for the presidency in 1992, he promoted, for example, the earned income tax credit, whereby poor families would receive government aid but only if they found employment first. Similarly, New Democrats promoted a 1997 welfare reform program known as Temporary Assistance for Needy Families (TANF). Unlike the Johnson-era programs, TANF provided government aid only during the first two years of unemployment. After that, people had to get a job, rather than depend indefinitely on welfare. By raising taxes, drastically cutting back on military expenditures, and ensuring a more responsible use of welfare dollars, the Clinton administration worked with Congress to achieve a balanced budget by 1998.

Clinton's success in welfare reform demonstrated that the New Democrats had in fact found the pulse of the American people. More radical proposals, such as the nationalization of healthcare, flopped. First Lady Hillary Rodham Clinton had hoped to expand the federal bureaucracy to guarantee healthcare for everyone under the banner of an African proverb, "It takes a village to raise a child." Enough Americans realized that there was a great difference between a village community and Washington, DC, so the Clintons' healthcare proposal was shelved to gather dust until a more charismatic leader could revive the cause.

In December 1998, Bill Clinton became the second president ever to face impeachment charges passed by the House of Representatives. Andrew Johnson had been the first, in 1868; Richard Nixon likely would have been impeached in 1974 as well, but he resigned just before the House took action. Like Johnson, Clinton was acquitted by the Senate, but not until a tumultuous controversy saturated the news media for months. The impeachment charges centered around Clinton's denial, under oath before a grand jury, concerning an alleged sexual affair with White House intern Monica Lewinski. This accusation, in turn, related to a civil suit brought against Clinton by Paula Jones claiming $850,000 in damages for sexual harassment back in the days when he was governor of Arkansas. Similarly, Gennifer Flowers had sought to discredit Clinton during the 1992 presidential election by publicizing her long-term affair with him. In the end, evidence strongly indicated that Clinton had an embarrassingly consistent track record of impropriety and that he also lied in court to protect himself from Jones's lawsuit. Technically, that is called perjury, which is a felony. Nevertheless, the U.S. Senate voted to acquit the president. America's attention then turned to Vice President Al Gore, who sought the presidency in 2000.

George W. Bush (Republican—Texas), 2001–2009

The 2000 presidential election came down to a contest between George W. Bush, son of the former president, and Al Gore. With Bush being a neo-conservative and Gore being a New Democrat, the candidates did not differ as starkly on economic policy as Reagan and Carter had twenty years earlier. Bush, however, clearly represented social conservatives in the culture war concerning family values. In the wake of Clinton's infidelity, Bush offered to bring respectability back into the White House. Even so, the contest was close—so close that victory hinged on the ballot count in several Florida precincts. As a recount was attempted, the two candidates also faced off in court, eventually ascending to the nation's highest court. In December 2000, the nine justices of the U.S. Supreme Court voted 7–2 that the Florida recount was conducted in an unconstitutional manner and 5–4 that no constitutional recount was possible in the time allotted by the election statute. Therefore, the initial count, with Bush leading Gore, had to be respected as final.

During the 1990s, George Walker Bush had served as governor of Texas (being the first governor in that state to be elected to four consecutive terms) and as managing partner of the Texas Rangers baseball team. Previously, he had operated an oil business. Just as the Democrats were refashioning themselves as "New Democrats," Bush set forth the concept of "compassionate conservatism." A strict formula of *laissez faire* might leave some people slipping through the cracks, but the government could provide a safety net to catch them. Bush, a Methodist who became "born again" in the early 1980s, especially desired to foster cooperation between religious organizations and government social services. Liberals, however, objected that his "faith-based initiatives" improperly mixed church and state.

Bush's neo-conservatism became apparent in one of the first major bills he signed into law: the No Child Left Behind Act of 2001. It hardly mattered whether Gore or Bush had won the 2000 election, since either of them would have supported this legislative reform that imposed federal guidelines upon local schools, threatening a loss of funding for schools that failed to perform. Supporters hailed the legislation as a responsible stewardship of federal dollars and a guarantee of equal educational opportunity nationwide. Critics objected that the federal bureaucracy was limiting local decision-making and that the standards did not accommodate the variations among school populations that might account for lower performance in some districts.

A Republican who shared more in common with Teddy Roosevelt than with Ronald Reagan, Bush supported the expansion of Medicare prescription drug coverage for seniors even while also suggesting the privatization of Social Security. But just nine months into his presidency, "Dubya" (as he was nicknamed for his middle initial and Texan accent) began to wrestle with the single issue that defined his political career: the terrorist attacks of September 11, 2001. Calling for a "war on terrorism," Bush urged Congress to pass the Providing Appropriate Tools Required to Intercept and Obstruct Terrorists (PATRIOT) Act of 2001, which expanded the government's surveillance authority. In 2002, Congress established the Department of Homeland Security for coordinating federal, state, and local security efforts. Citizens found their individual liberties diminished as the state expanded its authority in the name of national security— a controversial balance that continues to be debated today. As for foreign policy, the president set forth the Bush Doctrine, by which he vowed that the United States would take pro-active, even pre-emptive, measures to root out terrorist groups from any nation that harbored them. Supporters thanked the president for ensuring their security, while opponents warned that Bush had effectively committed the nation to a perpetual state of war. Time will tell which version of the story Americans will remember longer.

Barack Obama (Democrat—Illinois), 2009–

In July 2004, a state senator from Illinois who was campaigning for the U.S. Senate delivered a keynote address at the Democratic National Convention in Boston. His name was Barack Obama. Although hardly known beyond Illinois until that year, he won election to the U.S. Senate and quickly rose to national prominence within the Democratic Party. In 2008, he became the first African American ever to be elected president of the United States.

Obama embodied the melting-pot image of American identity: born in Hawaii to a Kenyan father and Kansan mother, raised in Indonesia by his mother and step-father, pursuing higher education in both California and Massachusetts, and claiming a mixture of Christian and Islamic religious roots. In his 2004 address to the Democratic convention, he argued that individualism is not enough to sustain the American community:

> It's not enough for just some of us to prosper—for alongside our famous individualism, there's another ingredient in the American saga, a belief that we're all connected as one people. If there is a child on the south side of Chicago who can't read, that matters to me, even if it's not my child. If there is a senior citizen somewhere who can't pay for their prescription drugs, and having to choose between medicine and the rent, that makes my life poorer, even if it's not my grandparent. If there's an Arab American family being rounded up without benefit of an attorney or due process, that threatens my civil liberties.

> It is that fundamental belief—I am my brother's keeper; I am my sister's keeper—that makes this country work. It's what allows us to pursue our individual dreams and yet still come together as one American family.

During the early 1990s, Obama served as a law professor at the University of Chicago while also engaging in community development programs that spring-boarded his career into local, and eventually national, politics. The titles of two of his books, *Dreams of My Father* and *The Audacity of Hope*, reveal his ambition and determination to make something of himself despite a difficult past. In order for other people to fulfill the same dream, Obama believed that the government must act to elevate the oppressed into prosperity. He called for progressive reform in the tradition of Lyndon Johnson, although with an even broader perspective that encompassed the development of third-world nations abroad and the enshrinement of homosexuality at home. Savvy enough not to get too far ahead of public opinion, Obama gently hinted at his pro-gay agenda during his first term and then boldly endorsed same-sex marriage as he entered his second term.

For his signature accomplishment, Obama finished what Truman and the Clintons had sought, but failed, even to begin: establish a universal national healthcare program. Officially called the Patient Protection and Affordable Care Act of 2010, "Obamacare" likely will long be known by the name of its chief spokesperson, even as "FDR" remains synonymous with "the New Deal." Liberals hailed Obamacare as a compassionate program that would ensure healthcare for the poor, while conservatives objected ethically to its provisions for abortion and contraception and prudentially to its impact on the national debt. Meanwhile, First Lady Michele Obama launched a "Let's Move!" campaign to encourage exercise in order to combat childhood obesity.

In the 2012 presidential election, Republican challenger Mitt Romney warned that 47% of Americans now were recipients of government payments, whereas the other half were paying taxes into the system. With socialism creeping into the American Republic, a growing number of voters acquired a vested interest in perpetuating the bureaucracy that promised to feed, house, clothe, and educate them—and now pay for their medical care, too. Romney's own proposals, however, did not offer any reprieve from the growing national debt, and as Massachusetts governor he had overseen the implementation of a state healthcare program not unlike the federal program that Obama signed into law. Overlooking the paleo-conservative candidacy of Ron Paul, the Republican leadership simply refused to support a clear alternative to the incumbent president. Obama defeated Romney by five million popular votes, or 332–206 in the electoral college.

Obama confidently took the podium for both his second inaugural address and the 2013 state of the union address. Quoting from the Declaration of Independence, the U.S. Constitution, and the Gettysburg Address, he redefined American heritage in a manner that would justify a renewal of the liberal tradition begun in the New Deal and expanded in the Great Society. Unlike the New Deal, however, Obama's agenda did not rest on the foundation of the natural family, but rather envisioned a redefinition of marriage that would accommodate same-sex couples and a redefinition of parenthood that would potentially make all of America's children wards of the state through universal enrollment in federally subsidized preschools and daycare centers. In the Obama administration, progressivism could see no limits.

Study Questions

1. Distinguish between paleo- and neo-conservatives and identify which Republican presidents most clearly exemplified each category.

2. What lasting impact did Ronald Reagan have upon American policy—both foreign and domestic?

3. On what basis may it be concluded that Barack Obama has carried the liberal-progressive tradition further than any of his predecessors?

Ronald Reagan, First Inaugural Address (1981)

At twelve noon on January 20, 1981, Ronald Reagan delivered his first inaugural address. At that very moment, just minutes after Chief Justice Warren E. Burger had administered the presidential oath of office to Reagan, Iranian officials released the fifty-two American hostages who had been held for the past 444 days. The Iranians had selected this timing in order to spite Jimmy Carter. Although the moment certainly gave Reagan cause for celebration, he graciously appointed Carter as a special U.S. envoy to meet the released hostages in Algeria. Meanwhile, on the home front Republicans regained control of the U.S. Senate for the first time since 1954 while also significantly closing the gap between the Democratic majority and the Republican minority in the House of Representatives. A new era was dawning for the American people; conservatism had experienced a rebirth.

Senator Hatfield, Mr. Chief Justice, Mr. President, Vice President Bush, Vice President Mondale, Senator Baker, Speaker O'Neill, Reverend Moomaw, and my fellow citizens:

To a few of us here today this is a solemn and most momentous occasion, and yet in the history of our nation it is a commonplace occurrence. The orderly transfer of authority as called for in the Constitution routinely takes place, as it has for almost two centuries, and few of us stop to think how unique we really are. In the eyes of many in the world, this every 4-year ceremony we accept as normal is nothing less than a miracle.

Mr. President, I want our fellow citizens to know how much you did to carry on this tradition. By your gracious cooperation in the transition process, you have shown a watching world that we are a united people pledged to maintaining a political system which guarantees individual liberty to a greater degree than any other, and I thank you and your people for all your help in maintaining the continuity which is the bulwark of our Republic.

The business of our nation goes forward. These United States are confronted with an economic affliction of great proportions. We suffer from the longest and one of the worst sustained inflations in our national history. It distorts our economic decisions, penalizes thrift, and crushes the struggling young and the fixed-income elderly alike. It threatens to shatter the lives of millions of our people.

Idle industries have cast workers into unemployment, human misery, and personal indignity. Those who do work are denied a fair return for their labor by a tax system which penalizes successful achievement and keeps us from maintaining full productivity.

But great as our tax burden is, it has not kept pace with public spending. For decades we have piled deficit upon deficit, mortgaging our future and our children's future for the temporary convenience of the present. To continue this long trend is to guarantee tremendous social, cultural, political, and economic upheavals.

You and I, as individuals, can, by borrowing, live beyond our means, but for only a limited period of time. Why, then, should we think that collectively, as a nation, we're not bound by that same limitation? We must act today in order to preserve tomorrow. And let there be no misunderstanding: We are going to begin to act, beginning today.

The economic ills we suffer have come upon us over several decades. They will not go away in days, weeks, or months, but they will go away. They will go away because we as Americans have the capacity now, as we've had in the past, to do whatever needs to be done to preserve this last and greatest bastion of freedom.

In this present crisis, government is not the solution to our problem; government is the problem. From time to time we've been tempted to believe that society has become too complex to be managed by self-rule, that government by an elite group is superior to government for, by, and of the people. Well, if no one among us is capable of governing himself, then who among us has the capacity to govern someone else? All of us together, in and out of government, must bear the burden. The solutions we seek must be equitable, with no one group singled out to pay a higher price.

We hear much of special interest groups. Well, our concern must be for a special interest group that has been too long neglected. It knows no sectional boundaries or ethnic and racial divisions, and it crosses political party lines. It is made up of men and women who raise our food, patrol our streets, man our mines and factories, teach our children, keep our homes, and heal us when we're sick—professionals, industrialists, shopkeepers,

clerks, cabbies, and truck drivers. They are, in short, "We the people." this breed called Americans.

Well, this administration's objective will be a healthy, vigorous, growing economy that provides equal opportunities for all Americans, with no barriers born of bigotry or discrimination. Putting America back to work means putting all Americans back to work. Ending inflation means freeing all Americans from the terror of runaway living costs. All must share in the productive work of this "new beginning." and all must share in the bounty of a revived economy. With the idealism and fair play which are the core of our system and our strength, we can have a strong and prosperous America, at peace with itself and the world.

So, as we begin, let us take inventory. We are a nation that has a government—not the other way around. And this makes us special among the nations of the Earth. Our government has no power except that granted it by the people. It is time to check and reverse the growth of government, which shows signs of having grown beyond the consent of the governed.

It is my intention to curb the size and influence of the Federal establishment and to demand recognition of the distinction between the powers granted to the Federal Government and those reserved to the States or to the people. All of us need to be reminded that the Federal Government did not create the States; the States created the Federal Government.

Now, so there will be no misunderstanding, it's not my intention to do away with government. It is rather to make it work—work with us, not over us; to stand by our side, not ride on our back. Government can and must provide opportunity, not smother it; foster productivity, not stifle it.

If we look to the answer as to why for so many years we achieved so much, prospered as no other people on Earth, it was because here in this land we unleashed the energy and individual genius of man to a greater extent than has ever been done before. Freedom and the dignity of the individual have been more available and assured here than in any other place on Earth. The price for this freedom at times has been high, but we have never been unwilling to pay that price.

It is no coincidence that our present troubles parallel and are proportionate to the intervention and intrusion in our lives that result from unnecessary and excessive growth of government. It is time for us to realize that we're too great a nation to limit ourselves to small dreams. We're not, as some would have us believe, doomed to an inevitable decline. I do not believe in a fate that will fall on us no matter what we do. I do believe in a fate that will fall on us if we do nothing. So, with all the creative energy at our command, let us begin an era of national renewal. Let us renew our determination, our courage, and our strength. And let us renew our faith and our hope.

We have every right to dream heroic dreams. Those who say that we're in a time when there are not heroes, they just don't know where to look. You can see heroes every day going in and out of factory gates.

Others, a handful in number, produce enough food to feed all of us and then the world beyond. You meet heroes across a counter, and they're on both sides of that counter. There are entrepreneurs with faith in themselves and faith in an idea who create new jobs, new wealth and opportunity. They're individuals and families whose taxes support the government and whose voluntary gifts support church, charity, culture, art, and education. Their patriotism is quiet, but deep. Their values sustain our national life.

Now, I have used the words "they" and "their" in speaking of these heroes. I could say "you" and "your" because I'm addressing the heroes of whom I speak—you, the citizens of this blessed land. Your dreams, your hopes, your goals are going to be the dreams, the hopes, and the goals of this administration, so help me God.

We shall reflect the compassion that is so much a part of your makeup. How can we love our country and not love our countrymen; and loving them, reach out a hand when they fall, heal them when they're sick, and provide opportunity to make them self-sufficient so they will be equal in fact and not just in theory?

Can we solve the problems confronting us? Well, the answer is an unequivocal and emphatic "yes." To paraphrase Winston Churchill, I did not take the oath I've just taken with the intention of presiding over the dissolution of the world's strongest economy.

In the days ahead I will propose removing the roadblocks that have slowed our economy and reduced productivity. Steps will be taken aimed at restoring the balance between the various levels of government. Progress may be slow, measured in inches and feet, not miles, but we will progress. It is time to reawaken this industrial giant, to get government back within its means, and to lighten our punitive tax burden. And these will be our first priorities, and on these principles there will be no compromise.

On the eve of our struggle for independence a man who might have been one of the greatest among the Founding Fathers, Dr. Joseph Warren, president of the Massachusetts Congress, said to his fellow Americans, "Our country is in danger, but not to be despaired of . . . . On you depend the fortunes of America. You are to decide the important questions upon which rests the happiness and the liberty of millions yet unborn. Act worthy of yourselves."

Well, I believe we, the Americans of today, are ready to act worthy of ourselves, ready to do what must be done to ensure happiness and liberty for ourselves, our children, and our children's children. And as we renew ourselves here in our own land, we will be seen as having greater strength throughout the world. We will again be the exemplar of freedom and a beacon of hope for those who do not now have freedom.

To those neighbors and allies who share our freedom, we will strengthen our historic ties and assure them of our support and firm commitment. We will match loyalty with loyalty. We will strive for mutually beneficial relations. We will not use our friendship to impose on their sovereignty, for our own sovereignty is not for sale.

As for the enemies of freedom, those who are potential adversaries, they will be reminded that peacc is the highest aspiration of the American people. We will negotiate for it, sacrifice for it; we will not surrender for it, now or ever.

Our forbearance should never be misunderstood. Our reluctance for conflict should not be misjudged as a failure of will. When action is required to preserve our national security, we will act. We will maintain sufficient strength to prevail if need be, knowing that if we do so we have the best chance of never having to use that strength.

Above all, we must realize that no arsenal or no weapon in the arsenals of the world is so formidable as the will and moral courage of free men and women. It is a weapon our adversaries in today's world do not have. It is a weapon that we as Americans do have. Let that be understood by those who practice terrorism and prey upon their neighbors.

I'm told that tens of thousands of prayer meetings are being held on this day, and for that I'm deeply grateful. We are a nation under God, and I believe God intended for us to be free. It would be fitting and good, I think, if on each Inaugural Day in future years it should be declared a day of prayer.

This is the first time in our history that this ceremony has been held, as you've been told, on this West Front of the Capitol. Standing here, one faces a magnificent vista, opening up on this city's special beauty and history. At the end of this open mall are those shrines to the giants on whose shoulders we stand.

Directly in front of me, the monument to a monumental man, George Washington, father of our country. A man of humility who came to greatness reluctantly. He led America out of revolutionary victory into infant nationhood. Off to one side, the stately memorial to Thomas Jefferson. The Declaration of Independence flames with his eloquence. And then, beyond the Reflecting Pool, the dignified columns of the Lincoln Memorial. Whoever would understand in his heart the meaning of America will find it in the life of Abraham Lincoln.

Beyond those monuments to heroism is the Potomac River, and on the far shore the sloping hills of Arlington National Cemetery, with its row upon row of simple white markers bearing crosses or Stars of David. They add up to only a tiny fraction of the price that has been paid for our freedom.

Each one of those markers is a monument to the kind of hero I spoke of earlier. Their lives ended in places called Belleau Wood, the Argonne, Omaha Beach, Salerno, and halfway around the world on Guadalcanal, Tarawa, Pork Chop Hill, the Chosin Reservoir, and in a hundred rice paddies and jungles of a place called Vietnam.

Under one such marker lies a young man, Martin Treptow, who left his job in a small town barbershop in 1917 to go to France with the famed Rainbow Division. There, on the western front, he was killed trying to carry a message between battalions under heavy artillery fire.

We're told that on his body was found a diary. On the flyleaf under the heading, "My Pledge," he had written these words: "America must win this war. Therefore I will work, I will save, I will sacrifice, I will endure, I will fight cheerfully and do my utmost, as if the issue of the whole struggle depended on me alone."

The crisis we are facing today does not require of us the kind of sacrifice that Martin Treptow and so many thousands of others were called upon to make. It does require, however, our best effort and our willingness to believe in ourselves and to believe in our capacity to perform great deeds, to believe that together with God's help we can and will resolve the problems which now confront us.

And after all, why shouldn't we believe that? We are Americans.

God bless you, and thank you.

Study Questions

1. Reagan said, "We must act today in order to preserve tomorrow." What dangers to the American way of life did he identify? And what did he mean when he said, "government is not the solution to our problem"?

2. Recall President Carter's "malaise" speech and contrast Reagan's statement that "We have every right to dream heroic dreams." Who were the heroes that Reagan identified?

3. In what respect did Martin Treptow represent Reagan's ideal American?

The "Misery Index" during the Carter and Reagan Years

As a presidential candidate in 1976, Jimmy Carter introduced the term "misery index" to refer to the combined effects of inflation and unemployment. Through the 1980s, this remained a common measure of the nation's economic health.

Source: Bureau of Labor Statistics, *www.bls.gov/data*.

Study Questions

1. Compare the misery index in 1976, when Carter was elected, to the misery index in 1980, when Reagan defeated Carter. How might this comparison explain why Carter lost the election?

2. Calculate the decline in the misery index during Reagan's presidency. Which factor accounted for the bulk of that decline—inflation or unemployment?

National Commission on Excellence in Education, "A Nation at Risk: The Imperative for Educational Reform" (1983)

In 1981, the U.S. Department of Education established the National Commission on Excellence in Education, assigned with the task of evaluating the quality of education in America. In April 1983, the commission published its report under the alarming title, "A Nation at Risk." The commission found that American high school graduates of the 1980s performed at substantially lower levels than those of the 1960s, and also were falling behind students of other developed nations. For example, the nation's average scores on the Scholastic Aptitude Test (SAT) had declined 40 points for the mathematics section and 50 points for the verbal section from 1963 to 1980. In 19 academic tests compared across developed nations, Americans ranked last seven times; never once did Americans rank first or second. The commission found the following conclusion especially disturbing: "Each generation of Americans has outstripped its parents in education, in literacy, and in economic attainment. For the first time in the history of our country, the educational skills of one generation will not surpass, will not equal, will not even approach, those of their parents."

Introduction

Our Nation is at risk. Our once unchallenged preeminence in commerce, industry, science, and technological innovation is being overtaken by competitors throughout the world. This report is concerned with only one of the many causes and dimensions of the problem, but it is the one that undergirds American prosperity, security, and civility. We report to the American people that while we can take justifiable pride in what our schools and colleges have historically accomplished and contributed to the United States and the well-being of its people, the educational foundations of our society are presently being eroded by a rising tide of mediocrity that threatens our very future as a

Nation and a people. What was unimaginable a generation ago has begun to occur—others are matching and surpassing our educational attainments.

If an unfriendly foreign power had attempted to impose on America the mediocre educational performance that exists today, we might well have viewed it as an act of war. As it stands, we have allowed this to happen to ourselves. We have even squandered the gains in student achievement made in the wake of the Sputnik challenge. Moreover, we have dismantled essential support systems which helped make those gains possible. We have, in effect, been committing an act of unthinking, unilateral educational disarmament.

Our society and its educational institutions seem to have lost sight of the basic purposes of schooling, and of the high expectations and disciplined effort needed to attain them. This report, the result of 18 months of study, seeks to generate reform of our educational system in fundamental ways and to renew the Nation's commitment to schools and colleges of high quality throughout the length and breadth of our land.

That we have compromised this commitment is, upon reflection, hardly surprising, given the multitude of often conflicting demands we have placed on our Nation's schools and colleges. They are routinely called on to provide solutions to personal, social, and political problems that the home and other institutions either will not or cannot resolve. We must understand that these demands on our schools and colleges often exact an educational cost as well as a financial one.

On the occasion of the Commission's first meeting, President Reagan noted the central importance of education in American life when he said: "Certainly there are few areas of American life as important to our society, to our people, and to our families as our schools and colleges." This report, therefore, is as much an open letter to the American people as it is a report to the Secretary of Education. We are confident that the American people, properly informed, will do what is right for their children and for the generations to come.

The Risk

History is not kind to idlers. The time is long past when America's destiny was assured simply by an abundance of natural resources and inexhaustible human enthusiasm, and by our relative isolation from the malignant problems of older civilizations. The world is indeed one global village. We live among determined, well-educated, and strongly motivated competitors. We compete with them for international standing and markets, not only with products but also with the ideas of our laboratories and neighborhood workshops. America's position in the world may once have been reasonably secure with only a few exceptionally well-trained men and women. It is no longer.

The risk is not only that the Japanese make automobiles more efficiently than Americans and have government subsidies for development and export. It is not just that the South Koreans recently built the world's most efficient steel mill, or that American machine tools, once the pride of the world, are being displaced by German products. It is also that these developments signify a redistribution of trained capability throughout the globe. Knowledge, learning, information, and skilled intelligence are the new raw materials of international commerce and are today spreading throughout the world as vigorously as miracle drugs, synthetic fertilizers, and blue jeans did earlier. If only to keep and improve on the slim competitive edge we still retain in world markets, we must dedicate ourselves to the reform of our educational system for the benefit of all—old and young alike, affluent and poor, majority and minority. Learning is the indispensable investment required for success in the "information age" we are entering.

Our concern, however, goes well beyond matters such as industry and commerce. It also includes the intellectual, moral, and spiritual strengths of our people which knit together the very fabric of our society. The people of the United States need to know that individuals in our society who do not possess the levels of skill, literacy, and training essential to this new era will be effectively disenfranchised, not simply from the material rewards that accompany competent performance, but also from the chance to participate fully in our national life. A high level of shared education is essential to a free, democratic society and to the fostering of a common culture, especially in a country that prides itself on pluralism and individual freedom.

For our country to function, citizens must be able to reach some common understandings on complex issues, often on short notice and on the basis of conflicting or incomplete evidence. Education helps form these common understandings, a point Thomas Jefferson made long ago in his justly famous dictum:

> I know no safe depository of the ultimate powers of the society but the people themselves; and if we think them not enlightened enough to exercise their control with a wholesome discretion, the remedy is not to take it from them but to inform their discretion.

Part of what is at risk is the promise first made on this continent: All, regardless of race or class or economic status, are entitled to a fair chance and to the tools for developing their individual powers of mind and spirit to the utmost. This promise means that all children by virtue of their own efforts, competently guided, can hope to attain the mature and informed judgment needed to secure gainful employment, and to manage their own lives, thereby serving not only their own interests but also the progress of society itself. . . .

The Learning Society

In a world of ever-accelerating competition and change in the conditions of the workplace, of ever-greater danger, and of ever-larger opportunities for those prepared to meet them, educational reform should focus on the goal of creating a Learning Society. At the heart of such a society is the commitment to a set of values and to a system of education that affords all members the opportunity to stretch their minds to full capacity, from early childhood through adulthood, learning more as the world itself changes. Such a society has as a basic foundation the idea that education is important not only because of what it contributes to one's career goals but also because of the value it adds to the general quality of one's life. Also at the heart of the Learning Society are educational opportunities extending far beyond the traditional institutions of learning, our schools and colleges. They extend into homes and workplaces; into libraries, art galleries, museums, and science centers; indeed, into every place where the individual can develop and mature in work and life. In our view, formal schooling in youth is the essential foundation for learning throughout one's life. But without life-long learning, one's skills will become rapidly dated.

In contrast to the ideal of the Learning Society, however, we find that for too many people education means doing the minimum work necessary for the moment, then coasting through life on what may have been learned in its first quarter. But this should not surprise us because we tend to express our educational standards and expectations largely in terms of "minimum requirements." And where there should be a coherent continuum of learning, we have none, but instead an often incoherent, outdated patchwork quilt. Many individual, sometimes heroic, examples of schools and colleges of great merit do exist. Our findings and testimony confirm the vitality of a number of notable schools and programs, but their very distinction stands out against a vast mass shaped by tensions and pressures that inhibit systematic academic and vocational achievement for the majority of students. In some metropolitan areas basic literacy has become the goal rather than the starting point. In some colleges maintaining enrollments is of greater day-to-day concern than maintaining rigorous academic standards. And the ideal of academic excellence as the primary goal of schooling seems to be fading across the board in American education.

Thus, we issue this call to all who care about America and its future: to parents and students; to teachers, administrators, and school board members; to colleges and industry; to union members and military leaders; to governors and State legislators; to the President; to members of Congress and other public officials; to members of learned and scientific societies; to the print and electronic media; to concerned citizens everywhere. America is at risk. . . .

Study Questions

1. What historical conditions made education so critical in the 1980s—and why was America "at risk" in this regard?

2. What is "the Learning Society," and what does it take to maintain such a culture?

Ronald Reagan, Second Inaugural Address (1985)

The economy worsened during Ronald Reagan's first few years in office. Democrats blamed "Reaganomics" for deepening the recession. Republicans continued to blame Jimmy Carter, saying that it would take time for Reagan's new policies to undo the damage of the previous administration. From 1981 through 1983, Congress phased in tax cuts while also reducing government outlays for school lunches, student loans, job training, and other social programs. By 1984, the economy showed signs of improvement, enabling Reagan to boast that Americans were better off now than four years ago. On the other hand, some Americans were worse off, particularly those who had become dependent upon government welfare programs begun under Lyndon Johnson and continued by Carter. The Democratic National Convention nominated Walter Mondale, who had served as Carter's vice president. Delivering the keynote address at that convention, New York Governor Mario Cuomo told "a tale of two cities," stating that under Reaganomics the rich had gotten richer but the poor had gotten poorer. American voters then chose between Mondale's plan of boosting the lower class through government aid and Reagan's plan of liberating investors and entrepreneurs to expand the economy with the hope that benefits would "trickle down" to the lower classes as well. The voters overwhelmingly favored Reagan, awarding him 525 of the nation's 538 electoral votes. Even in Mondale's home state of Minnesota, Reagan came within 3,800 votes of victory.

Senator Mathias, Chief Justice Burger, Vice President Bush, Speaker O'Neill, Senator Dole, reverend clergy, and members of my family and friends and my fellow citizens:

This day has been made brighter with the presence here of one who, for a time, has been absent. Senator John Stennis, God bless you and welcome back.

There is, however, one who is not with us today. Representative Gillis Long of Louisiana left us last night. And I wonder if we could all join in a moment of silent prayer.

[The President resumed speaking after a moment of silence.]

Amen.

There are no words adequate to express my thanks for the great honor that you've bestowed on me. I'll do my utmost to be deserving of your trust.

This is, as Senator Mathias told us, the 50th time that we, the people, have celebrated this historic occasion. When the first President, George Washington, placed his hand upon the Bible, he stood less than a single day's journey by horseback from raw, untamed wilderness. There were 4 million Americans in a union of 13 States. Today, we are 60 times as many in a union of 50 States. We've lighted the world with our inventions, gone to the aid of mankind wherever in the world there was a cry for help, journeyed to the Moon and safely returned. So much has changed, and yet we stand together as we did two centuries ago.

When I took this oath 4 years ago, I did so in a time of economic stress. Voices were raised saying that we had to look to our past for the greatness and glory. But we, the present-day Americans, are not given to looking backward. In this blessed land, there is always a better tomorrow.

Four years ago, I spoke to you of a New Beginning, and we have accomplished that. But in another sense, our New Beginning is a continuation of that beginning created two centuries ago when, for the first time in history, government, the people said, was not our master, it is our servant; its only power that which we the people allow it to have.

That system has never failed us, but for a time we failed the system. We asked things of government that government was not equipped to give. We yielded authority to the National Government that properly belonged to States or to local governments or to the people themselves. We allowed taxes and inflation to rob us of our earnings and savings and watched the great industrial machine that had made us the most productive people on Earth slow down and the number of unemployed increase.

By 1980 we knew it was time to renew our faith, to strive with all our strength toward the ultimate in individual freedom, consistent with an orderly society.

We believed then and now: There are no limits to growth and human progress when men and women are free to follow their dreams. And we were right to believe that. Tax rates have been reduced, inflation cut dramatically, and more people are employed than ever before in our history.

We are creating a nation once again vibrant, robust, and alive. But there are many mountains yet to climb. We will not rest until every American enjoys the fullness of freedom, dignity, and opportunity as our birthright. It is our birthright as citizens of this great Republic.

And if we meet this challenge, these will be years when Americans have restored their confidence and tradition of progress; when our values of faith, family, work, and neighborhood were restated for a modern age; when our economy was finally freed from government's grip; when we made sincere efforts at meaningful arms reductions and by rebuilding our defenses, our economy, and developing new technologies, helped preserve peace in a troubled world; when America courageously supported the struggle for individual liberty, self-government, and free enterprise throughout the world and turned the tide of history away from totalitarian darkness and into the warm sunlight of human freedom.

My fellow citizens, our nation is poised for greatness. We must do what we know is right, and do it with all our might. Let history say of us: "These were golden years —when the American Revolution was reborn, when freedom gained new life, and America reached for her best."

Our two-party system has solved us-served us, I should say, well over the years, but never better than in those times of great challenge when we came together not as Democrats or Republicans, but as Americans united in a common cause.

Two of our Founding Fathers, a Boston lawyer named Adams and a Virginia planter named Jefferson, members of that remarkable group who met in Independence Hall and dared to think they could start the world over again, left us an important lesson. They had become, in the years then in government, bitter political rivals in the Presidential election of 1800. Then, years later, when both were retired and age had softened their anger, they began to speak to each other again through letters. A bond was reestablished between those two who had helped create this government of ours.

In 1826, the 50th anniversary of the Declaration of Independence, they both died. They died on the same day, within a few hours of each other, and that day was the Fourth of July.

In one of those letters exchanged in the sunset of their lives, Jefferson wrote: "It carries me back to the times when, beset with difficulties and dangers, we were fellow laborers in the same cause, struggling for what is most valuable to man, his right of self-government. Laboring always at the same oar, with some wave ever ahead threatening to overwhelm us, and yet passing harmless ... we rode through the storm with heart and hand."

Well, with heart and hand let us stand as one today—one people under God, determined that our future shall be worthy of our past. As we do, we must not repeat the well-intentioned errors of our past. We must never again abuse the trust of working men and women by sending their earnings on a futile chase after the spiraling demands of a bloated Federal Establishment. You elected us in 1980 to end this prescription for disaster, and I don't believe you reelected us in 1984 to reverse course.

At the heart of our efforts is one idea vindicated by 25 straight months of economic growth: Freedom and incentives unleash the drive and entrepreneurial genius that are the core of human progress. We have begun to increase the rewards for work, savings, and investment; reduce the increase in the cost and size of government and its interference in people's lives.

We must simplify our tax system, make it more fair and bring the rates down for all who work and earn. We must think anew and move with a new boldness, so every American who seeks work can find work, so the least among us shall have an equal chance to achieve the greatest things —to be heroes who heal our sick, feed the hungry, protect peace among nations, and leave this world a better place.

The time has come for a new American emancipation—a great national drive to tear down economic barriers and liberate the spirit of enterprise in the most distressed areas of our country. My friends, together we can do this, and do it we must, so help me God.

From new freedom will spring new opportunities for growth, a more productive, fulfilled, and united people, and a stronger America—an America that will lead the technological revolution and also open its mind and heart and soul to the treasures of literature, music, and poetry, and the values of faith, courage, and love.

A dynamic economy, with more citizens working and paying taxes, will be our strongest tool to bring down budget deficits. But an almost unbroken 50 years of deficit spending has finally brought us to a time of reckoning. We've come to a turning point, a moment for hard decisions. I have asked the Cabinet and my staff a question and now I put the same question to all of you. If not us, who? And if not now, when? It must be done by all of us going forward with a program aimed at reaching a balanced budget. We can then begin reducing the national debt.

I will shortly submit a budget to the Congress aimed at freezing government program spending for the next year. Beyond this, we must take further steps to permanently control government's power to tax and spend. We must act now to protect future generations from government's desire to spend its citizens' money and tax them into servitude when the bills come due. Let us make it unconstitutional for the Federal Government to spend more than the Federal Government takes in.

We have already started returning to the people and to State and local governments responsibilities better handled by them. Now, there is a place for the Federal Government in matters of social compassion. But our fundamental goals must be to reduce dependency and upgrade the dignity of those who are infirm or disadvantaged. And here, a growing economy and support from family and community offer our best chance for a society where compassion is a way of life, where the old and infirm are cared for, the young and, yes, the unborn protected, and the unfortunate looked after and made self-sufficient.

Now, there is another area where the Federal Government can play a part. As an older American, I remember a time when people of different race, creed, or ethnic origin in our land found hatred and prejudice installed in social custom and, yes, in law. There's no story more heartening in our history than the progress that we've made toward the brotherhood of man that God intended for us. Let us resolve there will be no turning back or hesitation on the road to an America rich in dignity and abundant with opportunity for all our citizens.

Let us resolve that we, the people, will build an American opportunity society in which all of us—white and black, rich and poor, young and old—will go forward together, arm in arm. Again, let us remember that though our heritage is one of blood lines from every corner of the Earth, we are all Americans, pledged to carry on this last, best hope of man on Earth.

I've spoken of our domestic goals and the limitations we should put on our National Government. Now let me turn to a task that is the primary responsibility of National Government—the safety and security of our people.

Today, we utter no prayer more fervently than the ancient prayer for peace on Earth. Yet history has shown that peace does not come, nor will our freedom be preserved, by good will alone. There are those in the world who scorn our vision of human dignity and freedom. One nation, the Soviet Union, has conducted the greatest military buildup in the history of man, building arsenals of awesome offensive weapons.

We've made progress in restoring our

defense capability. But much remains to be done. There must be no wavering by us, nor any doubts by others, that America will meet her responsibilities to remain free, secure, and at peace.

There is only one way safely and legitimately to reduce the cost of national security, and that is to reduce the need for it. And this we're trying to do in negotiations with the Soviet Union. We're not just discussing limits on a further increase of nuclear weapons; we seek, instead, to reduce their number. We seek the total elimination one day of nuclear weapons from the face of the Earth.

Now, for decades, we and the Soviets have lived under the threat of mutual assured destruction—if either resorted to the use of nuclear weapons, the other could retaliate and destroy the one who had started it. Is there either logic or morality in believing that if one side threatens to kill tens of millions of our people our only recourse is to threaten killing tens of millions of theirs?

I have approved a research program to find, if we can, a security shield that will destroy nuclear missiles before they reach their target. It wouldn't kill people; it would destroy weapons. It wouldn't militarize space; it would help demilitarize the arsenals of Earth. It would render nuclear weapons obsolete. We will meet with the Soviets, hoping that we can agree on a way to rid the world of the threat of nuclear destruction.

We strive for peace and security, heartened by the changes all around us. Since the turn of the century, the number of democracies in the world has grown fourfold. Human freedom is on the march, and nowhere more so than in our own hemisphere. Freedom is one of the deepest and noblest aspirations of the human spirit. People, worldwide, hunger for the right of self-determination, for those inalienable rights that make for human dignity and progress.

America must remain freedom's staunchest friend, for freedom is our best ally and it is the world's only hope to conquer poverty and preserve peace. Every blow we inflict against poverty will be a blow against its dark allies of oppression and war. Every victory for human freedom will be a victory for world peace.

So, we go forward today, a nation still mighty in its youth and powerful in its purpose. With our alliances strengthened, with our economy leading the world to a new age of economic expansion, we look to a future rich in possibilities. And all of this is because we worked and acted together, not as members of political parties but as Americans.

My friends, we live in a world that's lit by lightning. So much is changing and will change, but so much endures and transcends time.

History is a ribbon, always unfurling. History is a journey. And as we continue our journey, we think of those who traveled before us. We stand again at the steps of this symbol of our democracy—well, we would have been standing at the steps if it hadn't gotten so cold. [Laughter] Now we're standing inside this symbol of our democracy, and we see and hear again the echoes of our past: a general falls to his knees in the hard snow of Valley Forge; a lonely President paces the darkened halls and ponders his struggle to preserve the Union; the men of the Alamo call out encouragement to each other; a settler pushes west and sings a song, and the song echoes out forever and fills the unknowing air.

It is the American sound. It is hopeful, big-hearted, idealistic, daring, decent, and fair. That's our heritage, that's our song. We sing it still. For all our problems, our differences, we are together as of old. We raise our voices to the God who is the Author of this most tender music. And may He continue to hold us close as we fill the world with our sound—in unity, affection, and love—one people under God, dedicated to the dream of freedom that He has placed in the human heart, called upon now to pass that dream on to a waiting and hopeful world.

God bless you, and God bless America.

Study Questions

1. Reagan said that America's system of government "has never failed us, but, for a time, we failed the system." Explain what he meant.

2. Outline Reagan's economic policies, based on his summary of the preceding four years and the vision he cast for the next four years.

3. What did Reagan hope to accomplish through his negotiations with the Soviet Union, and how?

Supreme Court Decisions under Chief Justice William H. Rehnquist

President Ronald Reagan appointed three associate justices to the U.S. Supreme Court plus elevated William H. Rehnquist, a Nixon appointee, to serve as chief justice following the retirement of Warren E. Burger in 1986. Reagan's first appointment, in 1981, went to Sandra Day O'Connor, the first woman ever to serve on the nation's highest court. Regan appointed Antonin Scalia in 1986 and Anthony Kennedy in 1988. Scalia has consistently proven himself to be a strict constructionist—always inquiring what the Constitution says and interpreting those words at face value; O'Connor and Kennedy, by contrast, have taken into consideration contemporary social concerns as they expand upon the principles written in the U.S. Constitution. For example, both O'Connor and Kennedy have supported the ever-broadening "right to privacy," a phrase nowhere found in the Constitution but enshrined into case law as a defense of abortion and homosexuality. The Rehnquist Court defies simple classification, since the majority oscillated between liberal and conservative decisions depending upon swing votes by O'Connor and Kennedy.

1992   The Supreme Court ruled that a woman has a right to an abortion without seeking or obtaining permission from her husband (or the father of the child, if not her husband) in *Planned Parenthood v. Casey*. O'Connor's majority decision rests largely on two claims: career women would be inconvenienced and the Supreme Court would suffer a credibility blow if the Court were to overturn *Roe v. Wade* at this point in history.

1996   In *U.S. v. Virginia*, the Supreme Court ordered the all-male Virginia Military Institute to accept female applicants.

2000   In *Stenberg v. Carhardt*, the Court struck down a Nebraska law that prohibited partial-birth abortions, ruling that it is within a woman's constitutional right to ask her doctor to induce labor and crush her baby's skull before the rest of the child'd body is born.

        In *Bush v. Gore*, the nation's highest court settled an election dispute in Florida, awarding to George W. Bush the votes necessary for his victory.

2002   The Court ruled in *Zelman v. Simmons-Harris* that an Ohio voucher program, whereby parents received state aid to pay for private school tuition, did not violate the No Establishment clause of the First Amendment since the parents, not the state, chose whether to use the money at a religious school.

2003   The Supreme Court overturned the *Bowers* (1986) decision, declaring homosexual acts to be legal among consenting adults nationwide in *Lawrence v. Texas*.

2004   The Supreme Court upheld the campaign fund-raising restrictions imposed by the McCain-Feingold Act in *McConnell v. Federal Elections Commission.*

2005   In *Kelo v. City of New London,* the Court denied private property owners the protection they sought under the Fifth Amendment when city planners imposed the right of eminent domain to acquire their properties for developers that would establish businesses to generate more tax revenue for the city.

Study Question

1. Define "strict construction" and explain how it relates to the constitutional duties of a Supreme Court justice.

2. Which Supreme Court rulings during the Rehnquist years followed the trajectory of progressive reform?

George H. W. Bush, Inaugural Address (1989)

Early in the 1988 presidential campaign, two popular Christian ministers each sought his own party's nomination. Pat Robertson, a white conservative Republican who had served as a Southern Baptist pastor, drew support from the same crowd that had supported Jerry Falwell's Moral Majority a decade earlier. Promoting a conservative agenda of family values—against the liberal culture that tolerated, if not sponsored, divorce, abortion, and drug use—Robertson offered to return America to its Christian roots. Meanwhile, another Baptist minister, Jesse Jackson, emphasized a different strain of the Christian tradition: social justice, particularly as applied to racial harmony. An African American who had worked with Martin Luther King, Jr., during the civil rights movement of the 1960s, Jackson assembled a "rainbow coalition" of Democrats who favored the liberal tradition of progressive reform. Ultimately, however, both the Democrats and the Republicans favored more moderate candidates, with Republicans nominating Vice President George H. W. Bush rather than Robertson for the presidency and Democrats nominating Massachusetts Governor Michael Dukakis rather than Jackson. Riding on Reagan's *laissez-faire* coattails, Bush secured electoral victory when his campaign criticized the big-government liberalism of "Michael Do-Taxes" and Bush himself vowed to an enthusiastic crowed at the Republican National Convention: "Read my lips: no new taxes!"

Mr. Chief Justice, Mr. President, Vice President Quayle, Senator Mitchell, Speaker Wright, Senator Dole, Congressman Michel, and fellow citizens, neighbors, and friends:

There is a man here who has earned a lasting place in our hearts and in our history. President Reagan, on behalf of our nation, I thank you for the wonderful things that you have done for America.

I've just repeated word for word the oath taken by George Washington 200 years ago, and the Bible on which I placed my hand is the Bible on which he placed his. It is right that the memory of Washington be with us today not only because this is our bicentennial inauguration but because Washington remains the Father of our Country. And he would, I think, be gladdened by this day; for today is the con-crete expression of a stunning fact: our continuity, these 200 years, since our government began.

We meet on democracy's front porch. A good place to talk as neighbors and as friends. For this is a day when our nation is made whole, when our differences, for a moment, are suspended. And my first act as President is a prayer. I ask you to bow your heads.

Heavenly Father, we bow our heads and thank You for Your love. Accept our thanks for the peace that yields this day and the shared faith that makes its continuance likely. Make us strong to do Your work, willing to heed and hear Your will, and write on our hearts these words: "Use power to help people." For we are given power not to advance our own purposes, nor to make a great show in the world, nor a name. There is but one just use of power, and it is to serve people. Help us remember, Lord. Amen.

I come before you and assume the Presidency at a moment rich with promise. We live in a peaceful, prosperous time, but we can make it better. For a new breeze is blowing, and a world refreshed by freedom seems reborn. For in man's heart, if not in fact, the day of the dictator is over. The totalitarian era is passing, its old ideas blown away like leaves from an ancient, lifeless tree. A new breeze is blowing, and a nation refreshed by freedom stands ready to push on. There is new ground to be broken and new action to be taken. There are times when the future seems thick as a fog; you sit and wait, hoping the mists will lift and reveal the right path. But this is a time when the future seems a door you can walk right through into a room called tomorrow.

Great nations of the world are moving toward democracy through the door to freedom. Men and women of the world move toward free markets through the door to prosperity. The people of the world agitate for free expression and free thought through the door to the moral and intellectual satisfactions that only liberty allows.

We know what works: Freedom works. We know what's right: Freedom is right. We know how to secure a more just and prosperous life for man on Earth: through free markets, free speech, free elections, and the exercise of free will unhampered by the state.

For the first time in this century, for the first time in perhaps all history, man does not have to invent a system by which to live. We don't have to talk late into the night about which form of government is better. We don't have to wrest justice from the kings. We only have to summon it from within ourselves. We must act on what we know. I take as my guide the hope of a saint: In crucial things, unity; in important things, diversity; in all things, generosity.

America today is a proud, free nation, decent and civil, a place we cannot help but love. We know in our hearts, not loudly and proudly but as a simple fact, that this country has meaning beyond what we see, and that our strength is a force for good. But have we changed as a nation even in our time? Are we enthralled with material things, less appreciative of the nobility of work and sacrifice?

My friends, we are not the sum of our possessions. They are not the measure of our lives. In our hearts we know what matters. We cannot hope only to leave our children a bigger car, a bigger bank account. We must hope to give them a sense of what it means to be a loyal friend; a loving parent; a citizen who leaves his home, his neighborhood, and town better than he found it. And what do we want the men and women who work with us to say when we're no longer there? That we were more driven to succeed than anyone around us? Or that we stopped to ask if a sick child had gotten better and stayed a moment there to trade a word of friendship?

No President, no government can teach us to remember what is best in what we are. But if the man you have chosen to lead this government can help make a difference; if he can celebrate the quieter, deeper successes that are made not of gold and silk but of better hearts and finer souls; if he can do these things, then he must.

America is never wholly herself unless she is engaged in high moral principle. We as a people have such a purpose today. It is to make kinder the face of the Nation and gentler the face of the world. My friends, we have work to do. There are the homeless, lost and roaming. There are the children who have nothing, no love and no normalcy. There are those who cannot free themselves of enslavement to whatever addiction—drugs, welfare, the demoralization that rules the slums. There is crime to be conquered, the rough crime of the streets. There are young women to be helped who are about to become mothers of children they can't care for and might not love. They need our care, our guidance, and our education, though we bless them for choosing life.

The old solution, the old way, was to think that public money alone could end these problems. But we have learned that that is not so. And in any case, our funds are low. We have a deficit to bring down. We have more will than wallet, but will is what we need. We will make the hard choices, looking at what we have and perhaps allocating it differently, making our decisions based on honest need and prudent safety. And then we will do the wisest thing of all. We will turn to the only resource we have that in times of need always grows: the goodness and the courage of the American people.

And I am speaking of a new engage-ment in the lives of others, a new activism, hands-on and involved, that gets the job done. We must bring in the generations, harnessing the unused talent of the elderly and the unfocused energy of the young. For not only leadership is passed from generation to generation but so is stewardship. And the generation born after the Second World War has come of age.

I have spoken of a Thousand Points of Light, of all the community organizations that are spread like stars throughout the Nation, doing good. We will work hand in hand, encouraging, sometimes leading, sometimes being led, rewarding. We will work on this in the White House, in the Cabinet agencies. I will go to the people and the programs that are the brighter points of light, and I'll ask every member of my government to become involved. The old ideas are new again because they're not old, they are timeless: duty, sacrifice, commitment, and a patriotism that finds its expression in taking part and pitching in.

We need a new engagement, too, between the Executive and the Congress. The challenges before us will be thrashed out with the House and the Senate. And we must bring the Federal budget into balance. And we must ensure that America stands before the world united, strong, at peace, and fiscally sound. But of course things may be difficult. We need to compromise; we've had dissension. We need harmony; we've had a chorus of discordant voices.

For Congress, too, has changed in our time. There has grown a certain divisiveness. We have seen the hard looks and heard the statements in which not each other's ideas are challenged but each other's motives. And our great parties have too often been far apart and untrusting of each other. It's been this way since Vietnam. That war cleaves us still. But, friends, that war began in earnest a quarter of a century ago, and surely the statute of limitation has been reached. This is a fact: The final lesson of Vietnam is that no great nation can long afford to be sundered by a memory. A new breeze is blowing, and the old bipartisanship must be made new again.

To my friends, and, yes, I do mean friends—in the loyal opposition and, yes, I mean loyal—I put out my hand. I am putting out my hand to you, Mr. Speaker. I am putting out my hand to you, Mr. Majority Leader. For this is the thing: This is the age of the offered hand. And we can't turn back clocks, and I don't want to. But when our fathers were young, Mr. Speaker, our differences ended at the water's edge. And we don't wish to turn back time, but when our mothers were young, Mr. Majority Leader, the Congress and the Executive were capable of working together to produce a budget on which this nation could live. Let us negotiate soon and hard. But in the end, let us produce. The American people await action. They didn't send us here to bicker. They ask us to rise above the merely partisan. "In crucial things, unity"—and this, my friends, is crucial.

To the world, too, we offer new engagement and a renewed vow: We will stay strong to protect the peace. The offered hand is a reluctant fist; once made—strong, and can be used with great effect. There are today Americans who are held against their will in foreign lands and Americans who are unaccounted for. Assistance can be shown here and will be long remembered. Good will begets good will. Good faith can be a spiral that endlessly moves on.

Great nations like great men must keep their word. When America says something, America means it, whether a treaty or an agreement or a vow made on marble steps. We will always try to speak clearly, for candor is a compliment; but subtlety, too, is good and has its place. While keeping our alliances and friendships around the world strong, ever strong, we will continue the new closeness with the Soviet Union, consistent both with our security and with progress. One might say that our new relationship in part reflects the triumph of hope and strength over experience. But hope is good, and so is strength and vigilance.

Here today are tens of thousands of our citizens who feel the understandable satisfaction of those who have taken part in democracy and seen their hopes fulfilled. But my thoughts have been turning the past few days to those who would be watching at home, to an older fellow who will throw a salute by himself when the flag goes by and the woman who will tell her sons the words of the battle hymns. I don't mean this to be sentimental. I mean that on days like this we remember that we are all part of a continuum, inescapably connected by the ties that bind.

Our children are watching in schools throughout our great land. And to them I say, Thank you for watching democracy's big day. For democracy belongs to us all, and freedom is like a beautiful kite that can go higher and higher with the breeze. And to all I say, No matter what your circumstances or where you are, you are part of this day, you are part of the life of our great nation.

A President is neither prince nor pope, and I don't seek a window on men's souls. In fact, I yearn for a greater tolerance, and easygoingness about each other's attitudes and way of life.

There are few clear areas in which we as a society must rise up united and express our intolerance. The most obvious now is drugs. And when that first cocaine was smuggled in on a ship, it may as well have been a deadly bacteria, so much has it hurt the body, the soul of our country. And there is much to be done and to be said, but take my word for it: This scourge will stop!

And so, there is much to do. And tomorrow the work begins. And I do not mistrust the future. I do not fear what is ahead. For our problems are large, but our heart is larger. Our challenges are great, but our will is greater. And if our flaws are endless, God's love is truly boundless.

Some see leadership as high drama and the sound of trumpets calling, and sometimes it is that. But I see history as a book with many pages, and each day we fill a page with acts of hopefulness and meaning. The new breeze blows, a page turns, the story unfolds. And so, today a chapter begins, a small and stately story of unity, diversity, and generosity—shared, and written, together.

Thank you. God bless you. And God bless the United States of America

Study Questions

1. What did Bush mean when he said that "the totalitarian era is passing"?

2. Why did Bush think it essential that Americans exhibit "high moral principle," and how did his concept of "a Thousand Points of Light" fit this vision?

3. What did Bush mean when he said that "a president is neither prince nor pope"? Do you see Bush as a weak leader or a strong leader in this regard?

George H. W. Bush, "Announcing the U.S. Attack against Iraq" (1991)

In August 1990, Iraq invaded oil-rich Kuwait. Iraq had been at war with Iran for a decade and desperately needed oil. Iraq also sought an economic boost to survive its mushrooming national debt. Within days of capturing Kuwait, Iraq positioned its army along the border of another oil-rich nation: Saudi Arabia. The United States depended heavily upon oil imports from that nation. President Bush acted quickly, invoking principles of national self-determination and international law, but also pursuing America's own interests in the Middle East. Assembling about thirty nations into a coalition, Bush announced Operation Desert Shield as air, land, and naval forces arrived to defend Saudi Arabia from Iraq. By early January 1991, over 400,000 U.S. troops had been deployed—a number proportionate to U.S. forces in Vietnam in 1967. When Saddam Hussein failed to satisfy the coalition's ultimatum and withdraw from Kuwait, Operation Desert Shield became Operation Desert Storm: commencing on January 17, a forty-day air raid destroyed military targets, refineries, and power plants. A massive ground assault began on February 23 with a decisive show of force. One hundred hours later, Hussein agreed to surrender his hold over Kuwait. Bush announced on March 1, "We've kicked the Vietnam syndrome once and for all."

Just two hours ago, Allied air forces began an attack on military targets in Iraq and Kuwait. These attacks continue as I speak. Ground forces are not engaged. This conflict started Aug. 2, when the dictator of Iraq invaded a small and helpless neighbor. Kuwait, a member of the Arab League and a member of the United Nations, was crushed, its people brutalized. Five months ago, Saddam Hussein started this cruel war against Kuwait; tonight, the battle has been joined.

This military action, taken in accord with United Nations resolutions and with the consent of the United States Congress, follows months of constant and virtually endless diplomatic activity on the part of the United Nations, the United States and many, many other countries.

Arab leaders sought what became known as an Arab solution, only to conclude that Saddam Hussein was unwilling to leave Kuwait. Others traveled to Baghdad in a variety of efforts to restore peace and justice. Our Secretary of State, James Baker, held an historic meeting in Geneva, only to be totally rebuffed.

This past weekend, in a last-ditch effort, the Secretary General of the United Nations went to the Middle East with peace in his heart—his second such mission. And he came back from Baghdad with no progress at all in getting Saddam Hussein to withdraw from Kuwait.

While the world waited, Saddam Hussein systematically raped, pillaged, and plundered a tiny nation no threat to his own.

Now, the 28 countries with forces in the Gulf area have exhausted all reasonable efforts to reach a peaceful resolution, and have no choice but to drive Saddam from

Kuwait by force. We will not fail.

As I report to you, air attacks are under way against military targets in Iraq. We are determined to knock out Saddam Hussein's nuclear bomb potential. We will also destroy his chemical weapons facilities. Much of Saddam's artillery and tanks will be destroyed. Our operations are designed to best protect the lives of all the coalition forces by targeting Saddam's vast military arsenal.

Initial reports from General Schwartzkopf are that our operations are proceeding according to plan. Our objectives are clear: Saddam Hussein's forces will leave Kuwait. The legitimate government of Kuwait will be restored to its rightful place, and Kuwait will once again be free.

Iraq will eventually comply with all relevant United Nations resolutions, and then, when peace is restored, it is our hope that Iraq will live as a peaceful and cooperative member of the family of nations, thus enhancing the security and stability of the Gulf.

Some may ask, why act now? Why not wait? The answer is clear. The world could wait no longer. Sanctions, though having some effect, showed no signs of accomplishing their objective. Sanctions were tried for well over five months, and we and our allies concluded that sanctions alone would not force Saddam from Kuwait.

While the world waited, Saddam Hussein systematically raped, pillaged, and plundered a tiny nation no threat to his own. He subjected the people of Kuwait to unspeakable atrocities, and among those, maimed and murdered innocent children.

While the world waited, Saddam sought to add to the chemical weapons arsenal he now possesses an infinitely more dangerous weapon of mass destruction—a nuclear weapon. And while the world waited, while the world talked peace and withdrawal, Saddam Hussein dug in and moved massive forces into Kuwait.

While the world waited, while Saddam stalled, more damage was being done to the fragile economies of the Third World, emerging democracies of Eastern Europe, to the entire world, including to our own economy.

The United States, together with the United Nations, exhausted every means at our disposal to bring this crisis to a peaceful end. However, Saddam clearly felt that by stalling and threatening and defying the United Nations, he could weaken the forces arrayed against him.

While the world waited, Saddam Hussein met every overture of peace with open contempt.

While the world prayed for peace, Saddam prepared for war.

I had hoped that when the United States Congress, in historic debate, took its resolute action, Saddam would realize he could not prevail, and would move out of Kuwait in accord with the United Nations resolutions. He did not do that. Instead, he remained intransigent, certain that time was on his side.

Saddam was warned over and over again to comply with the will of the United Nations: Leave Kuwait or be driven out. Saddam has arrogantly rejected all warnings. Instead, he tried to make this a dispute between Iraq and the United States of America.

Well, he failed. Tonight 28 nations—countries from five continents, Europe and Asia, Africa and the Arab League—have forces in the Gulf area standing shoulder-to-shoulder against Saddam Hussein. These countries had hoped the use of force could be avoided. Regrettably, we now believe that only force will make him leave.

Prior to ordering our forces into battle, I instructed our military commanders to take every necessary step to prevail, as quickly as possible, and with the greatest degree of protection possible for American and Allied service men and women.

I've told the American people before that this will not be another Vietnam, and I repeat this here tonight. Our troops will have the best possible support in the entire world, and they will not be asked to fight with one hand tied behind their back. I'm hopeful that this fighting will not go on for long, and that casualties will be held to an absolute minimum.

This is an historic moment. We have in this past year made great progress in ending the long era of conflict and cold war. We have before us the opportunity to forge for ourselves and for future generations a new world order, a world where the rule of law, not the law of the jungle, governs the conduct of nations.

When we are successful, and we will be, we have a real chance at this new world order, an order in which a credible United Nations can use its peace-keeping role to fulfill the promise and vision of the U.N.'s founders.

We have no argument with the people of Iraq. Indeed, for the innocents caught in this conflict, I pray for their safety.

Our goal is not the conquest of Iraq. It is the liberation of Kuwait. It is my hope that somehow the Iraqi people can, even now, convince their dictator that he must lay down his arms, leave Kuwait, and let Iraq itself rejoin the family of peace-loving nations.

Thomas Paine wrote many years ago: "These are the times that try men's souls." Those well-known words are so very true today. But even as planes of the multi-national forces attack Iraq, I prefer to think of peace, not war. I am convinced not only that we will prevail, but that out of the horror of combat will come the recognition that no nation can stand against a world united. No nation will be permitted to brutally assault its neighbor.

No President can easily commit our sons and daughters to war. They are the nation's finest. Ours is an all-volunteer force, magnificently trained, highly motivated. The troops know why they're there. And listen to what they say, because they've said it better than any President or Prime Minister ever could. Listen to 'Hollywood' Huddleston, Marine lance corporal. He says: "Let's free these people so we can go home and be free again." And he's right. The terrible crimes and tortures committed by Saddam's henchmen against the innocent people of Kuwait are an affront to mankind and a challenge to the freedom of all.

Listen to one of our great officers out there, Marine Lieutenant-General Walter Boomer. He said:

"There are things worth fighting for. A world in which brutality and lawlessness are allowed to go unchecked isn't the kind of world we're going to want to live in."

Listen to Master Sergeant J.P. Kendall of the 82nd Airborne:

"We're here for more than just the price of a gallon of gas. What we're doing is going to chart the future of the world for the next hundred years. It's better to deal with this guy now than five years from now."

And finally, we should all sit up and listen to Jackie Jones, an Army Lieutenant, when she says, "If we let him get away with this, who knows what's going to be next."

I've called upon Hollywood and Walter and J.P. and Jackie, and all their courageous comrades-in-arms, to do what must be done. Tonight, America and the world are deeply grateful to them and to their families.

And let me say to everyone listening or watching tonight: When the troops we've sent in finish their work, I'm determined to bring them home as soon as possible. Tonight, as our forces fight, they and their families are in our prayers.

May God bless each and every one of them, and the coalition forces at our side in the Gulf, and may He continue to bless our nation, the United States of America.

Study Questions

1. What reasons did President George H. W. Bush give to support the U.S. military invasion of Iraq in January 1991?

2. Do you feel the invasion was justified? Why or why not?

Twenty-Seventh Amendment (1992)

When the first Congress convened in 1789, twelve proposed amendments were submitted to the states. The states ratified ten of these as the Bill of Rights in 1791. One of the original twelve proposals, calling for a reformulation of representation in the House, never received enough support to be ratified. The other, likewise, faded into the annals of the past—hardly to be noticed until an undergraduate student at the University of Texas at Austin rediscovered it in 1982. Gregory D. Wilson wrote up a research paper explaining the rationale behind the amendment when it was proposed and arguing that those reasons should be supported again today. Observing that the proposed amendment did not have a time expiration (as other proposals have had), Wilson concluded that it was not too late for the states to ratify it. His professor thought otherwise, and graded his paper with a "C." But Wilson did not give up. Ten years later, as a result of Wilson's politicking, the requisite three-fourths majority of the states ratified the Congressional Pay Amendment, making it part of the U.S. Constitution 203 years after it was first proposed.

Twenty-Seventh Amendment

(proposed, 1789; ratified, 1992)

No law, varying the compensation for the services of the Senators and Representatives, shall take effect, until an election of Representatives shall have intervened.

Study Question

How did the Twenty-Seventh Amendment ensure that congressional representatives would be held accountable for their attempts to increase their salaries?

William J. Clinton, First Inaugural Address (1993)

Branding himself as a "New Democrat," Arkansas Governor William J. ("Bill") Clinton managed to recapture the vital center of the American political spectrum for a presidential victory in 1992. He faced off against two strong candidates. There was, of course, incumbent George H. W. Bush, but he had alienated conservatives in his own Republican party by breaking his "no new taxes" pledge and endorsing a tax increase. In 1992, many fiscally conservative voters gave serious attention to an independent candidate named H. Ross Perot, who promised to run the nation like a corporation—with a lean and productive budget. Clinton carefully steered a middle course. On the one hand, he acknowledged that the Johnson-vintage welfare programs should be streamlined, announcing in Reagan-speak that "the age of big government is over." On the other hand, Clinton clearly sided with the feminist end of the spectrum in the social values debate, endorsing both a woman's right to an abortion and, upon being elected, the right of homosexuals to serve in the military.

My fellow citizens, today we celebrate the mystery of American renewal. This ceremony is held in the depth of winter, but by the words we speak and the faces we show the world, we force the spring, a spring reborn in the world's oldest democracy that brings forth the vision and courage to reinvent America. When our Founders boldly declared America's independence to the world and our purposes to the Almighty, they knew that America, to endure, would have to change; not change for change's sake but change to preserve America's ideals: life, liberty, the pursuit of happiness. Though we marched to the music of our time, our mission is timeless. Each generation of Americans must define what it means to be an American.

On behalf of our Nation, I salute my predecessor, President Bush, for his half-century of service to America. And I thank the millions of men and women whose steadfastness and sacrifice triumphed over depression, fascism, and communism.

Today, a generation raised in the shadows of the cold war assumes new responsibilities in a world warmed by the sunshine of freedom but threatened still by ancient hatreds and new plagues. Raised in unrivaled prosperity, we inherit an economy that is still the world's strongest but is weakened by business failures, stagnant wages, increasing inequality, and deep divisions among our own people.

When George Washington first took the oath I have just sworn to uphold, news traveled slowly across the land by horseback and across the ocean by boat. Now, the sights and sounds of this ceremony are broadcast instantaneously to billions around the world. Communications and commerce are global. Investment is mobile. Technology is almost magical. And ambition for a better life is now universal.

We earn our livelihood in America today in peaceful competition with people all across the Earth. Profound and powerful forces are shaking and remaking our world. And the urgent question of our time is whether we can make change our friend and not our enemy. This new world has already enriched the lives of millions of

Americans who are able to compete and win in it. But when most people are working harder for less; when others cannot work at all; when the cost of health care devastates families and threatens to bankrupt our enterprises, great and small; when the fear of crime robs law-abiding citizens of their freedom; and when millions of poor children cannot even imagine the lives we are calling them to lead, we have not made change our friend.

We know we have to face hard truths and take strong steps, but we have not done so; instead, we have drifted. And that drifting has eroded our resources, fractured our economy, and shaken our confidence. Though our challenges are fearsome, so are our strengths. Americans have ever been a restless, questing, hopeful people. And we must bring to our task today the vision and will of those who came before us. From our Revolution to the Civil War, to the Great Depression, to the civil rights movement, our people have always mustered the determination to construct from these crises the pillars of our history. Thomas Jefferson believed that to preserve the very foundations of our Nation, we would need dramatic change from time to time. Well, my fellow Americans, this is our time. Let us embrace it.

Our democracy must be not only the envy of the world but the engine of our own renewal. There is nothing wrong with America that cannot be cured by what is right with America. And so today we pledge an end to the era of deadlock and drift, and a new season of American renewal has begun.

To renew America, we must be bold.

We must do what no generation has had to do before. We must invest more in our own people, in their jobs, and in their future, and at the same time cut our massive debt. And we must do so in a world in which we must compete for every opportunity. It will not be easy. It will require sacrifice, but it can be done and done fairly, not choosing sacrifice for its own sake but for our own sake. We must provide for our Nation the way a family provides for its children.

Our Founders saw themselves in the light of posterity. We can do no less. Anyone who has ever watched a child's eyes wander into sleep knows what posterity is. Posterity is the world to come: the world for whom we hold our ideals, from whom we have borrowed our planet, and to whom we bear sacred responsibility. We must do what America does best: offer more opportunity to all and demand more responsibility from all. It is time to break the bad habit of expecting something for nothing from our Government or from each other. Let us all take more responsibility not only for ourselves and our families but for our communities and our country.

To renew America, we must revitalize our democracy. This beautiful Capital, like every capital since the dawn of civilization, is often a place of intrigue and calculation. Powerful people maneuver for position and worry endlessly about who is in and who is out, who is up and who is down, forgetting those people whose toil and sweat sends us here and pays our way. Americans deserve better. And in this city today there are people who want to do better. And so I say to all of you here: Let us resolve to reform our politics so that power and privilege no longer shout down the voice of the people. Let us put aside personal advantage so that we can feel the pain and see the promise of America. Let us resolve to make our Government a place for what Franklin Roosevelt called bold, persistent experimentation, a Government for our tomorrows, not our yesterdays. Let us give this Capital back to the people to whom it belongs.

To renew America, we must meet challenges abroad as well as at home. There is no longer a clear division between what is foreign and what is domestic. The world economy, the world environment, the world AIDS crisis, the world arms race: they affect us all. Today, as an older order passes, the new world is more free but less stable. Communism's collapse has called forth old animosities and new dangers. Clearly, America must continue to lead the world we did so much to make.

While America rebuilds at home, we will not shrink from the challenges nor fail to seize the opportunities of this new world. Together with our friends and allies, we will work to shape change, lest it engulf us. When our vital interests are challenged or the will and conscience of the international community is defied, we will act, with peaceful diplomacy whenever possible, with force when necessary. The brave Americans serving our Nation today in the Persian Gulf, in Somalia, and wherever else they stand are testament to our resolve. But our greatest strength is the power of our ideas, which are still new in many lands. Across the world we see them embraced, and we rejoice. Our hopes, our hearts, our hands are with those on every continent who are building

democracy and freedom. Their cause is America's cause.

The American people have summoned the change we celebrate today. You have raised your voices in an unmistakable chorus. You have cast your votes in historic numbers. And you have changed the face of Congress, the Presidency, and the political process itself. Yes, you, my fellow Americans, have forced the spring. Now we must do the work the season demands. To that work I now turn with all the authority of my office. I ask the Congress to join with me. But no President, no Congress, no Government can undertake this mission alone.

My fellow Americans, you, too, must play your part in our renewal. I challenge a new generation of young Americans to a season of service: to act on your idealism by helping troubled children, keeping company with those in need, reconnecting our torn communities. There is so much to be done; enough, indeed, for millions of others who are still young in spirit to give of themselves in service, too. In serving, we recognize a simple but powerful truth: We need each other, and we must care for one another.

Today we do more than celebrate America. We rededicate ourselves to the very idea of America, an idea born in revolution and renewed through two centuries of challenge; an idea tempered by the knowledge that, but for fate, we, the fortunate, and the unfortunate might have been each other; an idea ennobled by the faith that our Nation can summon from its myriad diversity the deepest measure of unity; an idea infused with the conviction that America's long, heroic journey must go forever upward.

And so, my fellow Americans, as we stand at the edge of the 21st century, let us begin anew with energy and hope, with faith and discipline. And let us work until our work is done. The Scripture says, "And let us not be weary in well doing: for in due season we shall reap, if we faint not" [Galatians 6:9]. From this joyful mountaintop of celebration we hear a call to service in the valley. We have heard the trumpets. We have changed the guard. And now, each in our own way and with God's help, we must answer the call.

Thank you, and God bless you all.

Study Questions

1. What did Clinton mean when he said, "We must provide for our nation the way a family provides for its children"?

2. In what ways did Clinton see himself as another Franklin Roosevelt? Do you think that this comparison was accurate?

William J. Clinton, Second Inaugural Address (1997)

During Clinton's first term as president, the economy recovered from the recession of the early 1990s to reach its most productive level since the Eisenhower administration of the 1950s. Neither Republican challenger Bob Dole nor third-party candidate H. Ross Perot could unseat him in 1996. Although Dole promised to reduce income tax rates significantly, Clinton boasted of a strong economy with a reduced federal deficit, persuading many Americans to hold the course. Leading by eight million popular votes, Clinton secured his re-election with a 379–159 victory in the electoral college.

My fellow citizens, at this last Presidential Inauguration of the 20th century, let us lift our eyes toward the challenges that await us in the next century. It is our great good fortune that time and chance have put us not only at the edge of a new century, in a new millennium, but on the edge of a bright new prospect in human affairs, a moment that will define our course and our character for decades to comes. We must keep our old democracy forever young. Guided by the ancient vision of a promised land, let us set our sights upon a land of new promise.

The promise of America was born in the 18th century out of the bold conviction that we are all created equal. It was extended and preserved in the 19th century, when our Nation spread across the continent, saved the Union, and abolished the awful scourge of slavery.

Then, in turmoil and triumph, that promise exploded onto the world stage to make this the American Century. And what a century it has been. America became the world's mightiest industrial power, saved the world from tyranny in two World Wars and a long cold war, and time and again reached out across the globe to millions who, like us, longed for the blessings of liberty.

Along the way, Americans produced a great middle class and security in old age, built unrivaled centers of learning and opened public schools to all, split the atom and explored the heavens, invented the computer and the microchip, and deepened the wellspring of justice by making a revolution in civil rights for African-Americans and all minorities and extending the circle of citizenship, opportunity, and dignity to women.

Now, for the third time, a new century is upon us and another time to choose. We began the 19th century with a choice: to spread our Nation from coast to coast. We began the 20th century with a choice: to harness the industrial revolution to our values of free enterprise, conservation, and human decency. Those choices made all the difference. At the dawn of the 21st century, a free people must now choose to shape the forces of the information age and the global society, to unleash the limitless potential of all our people, and yes, to form a more perfect Union.

When last we gathered, our march to this new future seemed less certain than it does today. We vowed then to set a clear course to renew our Nation. In these 4 years, we have been touched by tragedy, exhilarated by challenge, strengthened by achievement. America stands alone as the world's indispensable nation. Once again, our economy is the strongest on Earth. Once again, we are building stronger families, thriving communities, better educational opportunities, a cleaner environment. Problems that once seemed destined to deepen, now bend to our efforts. Our streets are safer, and record numbers of our fellow citizens have moved from welfare to work. And once again, we have resolved for our time a great debate over the role of Government. Today we can declare: Government is not the problem, and Government is not the solution. We—the American people—we are the solution. Our Founders understood that well and gave us a democracy strong enough to endure for centuries, flexible enough to face our common challenges and advance our common dreams in each new day.

As times change, so Government must change. We need a new Government for a new century, humble enough not to try to solve all our problems for us but strong enough to give us the tools to solve our problems for ourselves, a Government that is smaller, lives within its means, and does more with less. Yet where it can stand up for our values and interests around the world, and where it can give Americans the power to make a real difference in their everyday lives, Government should do more, not less. The preeminent mission of our new Government is to give all Americans an opportunity, not a guarantee but a real opportunity, to build better lives.

Beyond that, my fellow citizens, the future is up to us. Our Founders taught us that the preservation of our liberty and our Union depends upon responsible citizenship. And we need a new sense of responsibility for a new century. There is work to do, work that Government alone cannot do: teaching children to read, hiring people off welfare rolls, coming out from behind locked doors and shuttered windows to help reclaim our streets from drugs and gangs and crime, taking time out of our own lives to serve others.

Each and every one of us, in our own way, must assume personal responsibility not only for ourselves and our families but for our neighbors and our Nation. Our greatest responsibility is to embrace a new spirit of community for a new century. For any one of us to succeed, we must succeed as one America. The challenge of our past remains the challenge of our future: Will we be one Nation, one people, with one common destiny, or not? Will we all come together, or come apart?

The divide of race has been America's constant curse. And each new wave of immigrants gives new targets to old prejudices. Prejudice and contempt cloaked in the pretense of religious or political conviction are no different. These forces have nearly destroyed our Nation in the past. They plague us still. They fuel the fanaticism of terror. And they torment the lives of millions in fractured nations all around the world.

These obsessions cripple both those who hate and of course those who are hated, robbing both of what they might become. We cannot, we will not, succumb to the dark impulses that lurk in the far regions of the soul everywhere. We shall overcome them. And we shall replace them with the generous spirit of a people who feel at home with one another. Our rich texture of racial, religious, and political diversity will be a godsend in the 21st century. Great rewards will come to those who can live together, learn together, work together, forge new ties that bind together.

As this new era approaches, we can already see its broad outlines. Ten years ago, the Internet was the mystical province of physicists; today, it is a commonplace encyclopedia for millions of schoolchildren. Scientists now are decoding the blueprint of human life. Cures for our most feared illnesses seem close at hand. The world is no longer divided into two hostile camps. Instead, now we are building bonds with nations that once were our adversaries. Growing connections of commerce and culture give us a chance to lift the fortunes and spirits of people the world over. And for the very first time in all of history, more people on this planet live under democracy than dictatorship.

My fellow Americans, as we look back at this remarkable century, we may ask, can we hope not just to follow but even to surpass the achievements of the 20th century in America and to avoid the awful bloodshed that stained its legacy? To that question, every American here and every American in our land today must answer a resounding, "Yes." This is the heart of our task. With a new vision of Government, a new sense of responsibility, a new spirit of community, we will sustain America's journey.

The promise we sought in a new land, we will find again in a land of new promise. In this new land, education will be every citizen's most prized possession. Our schools will have the highest standards in the world, igniting the spark of possibility in the eyes of every girl and every boy. And the doors of higher education will be open to all. The knowledge and power of the information age will be within reach not just of the few but of every classroom, every library, every child. Parents and children will have time not only to work but to read and play together. And the plans they make at their kitchen table will be those of a better home, a better job, the certain chance to go to college.

Our streets will echo again with the laughter of our children, because no one will try to shoot them or sell them drugs anymore. Everyone who can work, will work, with today's permanent under class part of tomorrow's growing middle class. New miracles of medicine at last will reach not only those who can claim care now but the children and hard-working families too long denied.

We will stand mighty for peace and freedom and maintain a strong defense against terror and destruction. Our children will sleep free from the threat of nuclear, chemical, or biological weapons. Ports and airports, farms and factories will thrive with trade and innovation and ideas. And the world's greatest democracy will lead a whole world of democracies.

Our land of new promise will be a nation that meets its obligations, a nation that balances its budget but never loses the balance of its values, a nation where our grandparents have secure retirement and health care and their grandchildren know we have made the reforms necessary to sustain those benefits for their time, a nation that fortifies the world's most productive economy even as it protects the great natural bounty of our water, air, and majestic land. And in this land of new promise, we will have reformed our politics so that the voice of the people will always speak louder than the din of narrow interests, regaining the participation and deserving the trust of all Americans.

Fellow citizens, let us build that America, a nation ever moving forward toward realizing the full potential of all its citizens. Prosperity and power, yes, they are important, and we must maintain them. But let us never forget, the greatest progress we have made and the greatest progress we have yet to make is in the human heart. In the end, all the world's wealth and a thousand armies are no match for the strength and decency of the human spirit.

Thirty-four years ago, the man whose life we celebrate today spoke to us down there, at the other end of this Mall, in words that moved the conscience of a nation. Like a prophet of old, he told of his dream that one day America would rise up and treat all its citizens as equals before the law and in the heart. Martin Luther King's dream was the American dream. His quest is our quest: the ceaseless striving to live out our true creed. Our history has been built on such dreams and labors. And by our dreams and labors, we will redeem the promise of America in the 21st century.

To that effort I pledge all my strength and every power of my office. I ask the Members of Congress here to join in that pledge. The American people returned to office a President of one party and a Con-

gress of another. Surely they did not do this to advance the politics of petty bickering and extreme partisanship they plainly deplore. No, they call on us instead to be repairers of the breach and to move on with America's mission. America demands and deserves big things from us, and nothing big ever came from being small. Let us remember the timeless wisdom of Cardinal Bernardin, when facing the end of his own life. He said, "It is wrong to waste the precious gift of time on acrimony and division."

Fellow citizens, we must not waste the precious gift of this time. For all of us are on that same journey of our lives, and our journey, too, will come to an end. But the journey of our America must go on.

And so, my fellow Americans, we must be strong, for there is much to dare. The demands of our time are great, and they are different. Let us meet them with faith and courage, with patience and a grateful, happy heart. Let us shape the hope of this day into the noblest chapter in our history. Yes, let us build our bridge, a bridge wide enough and strong enough for every American to cross over to a blessed land of new promise.

May those generations whose faces we cannot yet see, whose names we may never know, say of us here that we led our beloved land into a new century with the American dream alive for all her children, with the American promise of a more perfect Union a reality for all her people, with America's bright flame of freedom spreading throughout all the world.

From the height of this place and the summit of this century, let us go forth.

May God strengthen our hands for the | our America.
good work ahead, and always, always bless |

Study Questions

1. In his first inaugural address, Ronald Reagan had said, "government is not the solution to our problem; government is the problem." In his second inaugural address, William J. Clinton said, "Government is not the problem, and Government is not the solution." Explain Clinton's reworking of Reagan's phrase in terms of the "New Democrat" image he had molded for himself.

2. What level of importance did Clinton assign to education in America's future, and what role did he envision the government should have in education?

3. What sort of "bridge" to the twenty-first century did Clinton urge Americans to build?

George W. Bush, First Inaugural Address (2001)

George W. Bush campaigned in 2000 as a "compassionate conservative." That is, he sought to steer the nation away from the government-based welfare system of the liberal-progressive tradition while at the same time avoiding the cut-throat competition of the free market. Bush believed that religious organizations working in partnership with the government could serve communities more efficiently than either private philanthropists acting alone or the government expanding its own bureaucracy. In the wake of President Bill Clinton's impeachment scandal, Bush also campaigned as a candidate who would restore integrity to the nation's highest office. Al Gore, who served as Vice President under Clinton, received the Democratic Party's nomination and a slightly greater share of popular votes than Bush, but neither candidate emerged with a clear electoral victory due to a confusion in counting the ballots for Florida. Ultimately, the U.S. Supreme Court decided the matter, declaring Bush the winner of Florida's votes and therefore of the national election.

Thank you, all. Chief Justice Rehnquist, President Carter, President Bush, President Clinton, distinguished guests, and my fellow citizens. The peaceful transfer of authority is rare in history, yet common in our country. With a simple oath, we affirm old traditions and make new beginnings.

As I begin, I thank President Clinton for his service to our Nation, and I thank Vice President Gore for a contest conducted with spirit and ended with grace.

I am honored and humbled to stand here where so many of America's leaders have come before me, and so many will follow. We have a place, all of us, in a long story, a story we continue but whose end we will not see. It is a story of a new world that became a friend and liberator of the old, the story of a slaveholding society that became a servant of freedom, the story of a power that went into the world to protect but not possess, to defend but not to conquer.

It is the American story, a story of flawed and fallible people united across the generations by grand and enduring ideals. The grandest of these ideals is an unfolding American promise that everyone belongs, that everyone deserves a chance, that no insignificant person was ever born.

Americans are called to enact this promise in our lives and in our laws. And though our Nation has sometimes halted and sometimes delayed, we must follow no other course.

Through much of the last century, America's faith in freedom and democracy was a rock in a raging sea. Now it is a seed upon the wind, taking root in many nations. Our democratic faith is more than the creed of our country. It is the inborn hope of our humanity, an ideal we carry but do not own, a trust we bear and pass along. Even after nearly 225 years, we have a long way yet to travel.

While many of our citizens prosper, others doubt the promise, even the justice of our own country. The ambitions of some Americans are limited by failing schools and hidden prejudice and the circumstances of their birth. And sometimes our differences run so deep, it seems we share a continent but not a country. We do not accept this, and we will not allow it.

Our unity, our Union, is a serious work of leaders and citizens and every generation. And this is my solemn pledge: I will work to build a single nation of justice and opportunity. I know this is in our reach because we are guided by a power larger than ourselves, who creates us equal, in His image, and we are confident in principles that unite and lead us onward.

America has never been united by blood or birth or soil. We are bound by ideals that move us beyond our backgrounds, lift us above our interests, and teach us what it means to be citizens. Every child must be taught these principles. Every citizen must uphold them. And every immigrant, by embracing these ideals, makes our country more, not less, American.

Today we affirm a new commitment to live out our Nation's promise through civility, courage, compassion, and character. America at its best matches a commitment to principle with a concern for civility. A civil society demands from each of us good will and respect, fair dealing and forgiveness.

Some seem to believe that our politics can afford to be petty because in a time of peace the stakes of our debates appear small. But the stakes for America are never small. If our country does not lead the cause of freedom, it will not be led. If we do not turn the hearts of children toward knowledge and character, we will lose their gifts and undermine their idealism. If we permit our economy to drift and decline,

the vulnerable will suffer most.

We must live up to the calling we share. Civility is not a tactic or a sentiment; it is the determined choice of trust over cynicism, of community over chaos. And this commitment, if we keep it, is a way to shared accomplishment.

America at its best is also courageous. Our national courage has been clear in times of depression and war, when defeating common dangers defined our common good. Now we must choose if the example of our fathers and mothers will inspire us or condemn us. We must show courage in a time of blessing by confronting problems instead of passing them on to future generations.

Together we will reclaim America's schools before ignorance and apathy claim more young lives. We will reform Social Security and Medicare, sparing our children from struggles we have the power to prevent. And we will reduce taxes to recover the momentum of our economy and reward the effort and enterprise of working Americans.

We will build our defenses beyond challenge, lest weakness invite challenge. We will confront weapons of mass destruction, so that a new century is spared new horrors. The enemies of liberty and our country should make no mistake: America remains engaged in the world, by history and by choice, shaping a balance of power that favors freedom.

We will defend our allies and our interests. We will show purpose without arrogance. We will meet aggression and bad faith with resolve and strength. And to all nations, we will speak for the values that gave our Nation birth.

America at its best is compassionate. In the quiet of American conscience, we know that deep, persistent poverty is unworthy of our Nation's promise. And whatever our views of its cause, we can agree that children at risk are not at fault.

Abandonment and abuse are not acts of God; they are failures of love. And the proliferation of prisons, however necessary, is no substitute for hope and order in our souls. Where there is suffering, there is duty. Americans in need are not strangers; they are citizens—not problems but priorities. And all of us are diminished when any are hopeless.

Government has great responsibilities for public safety and public health, for civil rights and common schools. Yet, compassion is the work of a nation, not just a government. And some needs and hurts are so deep they will only respond to a mentor's touch or a pastor's prayer. Church and charity, synagogue and mosque lend our communities their humanity, and they will have an honored place in our plans and in our laws.

Many in our country do not know the pain of poverty. But we can listen to those who do. And I can pledge our Nation to a goal: When we see that wounded traveler on the road to Jericho, we will not pass to the other side.

America at its best is a place where personal responsibility is valued and expected. Encouraging responsibility is not a search for scapegoats; it is a call to conscience. And though it requires sacrifice, it brings a deeper fulfillment. We find the fullness of life not only in options but in commitments. And we find that children and community are the commitments that set us free.

Our public interest depends on private character, on civic duty and family bonds and basic fairness, on uncounted, unhonored acts of decency, which give direction to our freedom.

Sometimes in life we're called to do great things. But as a saint of our times has said, "Every day we are called to do small things with great love." The most important tasks of a democracy are done by everyone.

I will live and lead by these principles: to advance my convictions with civility, to serve the public interest with courage, to speak for greater justice and compassion, to call for responsibility and try to live it, as well. In all these ways, I will bring the values of our history to the care of our times.

What you do is as important as anything Government does. I ask you to seek a common good beyond your comfort, to defend needed reforms against easy attacks, to serve your Nation, beginning with your neighbor. I ask you to be citizens: Citizens, not spectators; citizens, not subjects; responsible citizens building communities of service and a nation of character.

Americans are generous and strong and decent, not because we believe in ourselves but because we hold beliefs beyond ourselves. When this spirit of citizenship is missing, no Government program can replace it. When this spirit is present, no wrong can stand against it.

After the Declaration of Independence was signed, Virginia statesman John Page wrote to Thomas Jefferson, "We know the race is not to the swift, nor the battle to the strong. Do you not think an angel rides in the whirlwind and directs this storm?"

Much time has passed since Jefferson arrived for his inauguration. The years and changes accumulate, but the themes of this day, he would know: our Nation's grand story of courage and its simple dream of dignity.

We are not this story's author, who fills time and eternity with his purpose. Yet, his purpose is achieved in our duty. And our duty is fulfilled in service to one another. Never tiring, never yielding, never finishing, we renew that purpose today, to make our country more just and generous, to affirm the dignity of our lives and every life. This work continues, the story goes on, and an angel still rides in the whirlwind and directs this storm.

God bless you all, and God bless America.

Study Questions

1. What did George W. Bush pledge to the American people, and what gave him confidence that he could fulfill this pledge?

2. What, according to Bush, was the meaning unfolding in America's ongoing story, and who authors that story?

3. What relationship did Bush propose between the government and individuals? Between the government and religious organizations?

George W. Bush, "September 20th Address" (2001)

On Tuesday, September 11, 2001, at 8:46 a.m., American Airlines Flight 11 from Boston crashed into the North Tower of the World Trade Center in New York City. At 9:03 a.m., United Airlines Flight 117, also from Boston, crashed into the South Tower. Forty-two minutes later, a third plane, American Airlines Flight 77 from Dulles International Airport in Washington, DC, crashed into the Pentagon Building. At 10:05 a.m., the South Tower of the World Trade Center collapsed. Twenty-three minutes later, the North Tower collapsed as well. A fourth plan, presumably headed for the White House, crashed into rural Pennsylvania when passengers acted to thwart the hijackers' conspiracy. Nine days later, President Bush addressed a joint session of Congress to identify the causes behind these terrorist attacks and to set the course for America's response.

Mr. Speaker, Mr. President Pro Tempore, members of Congress, and fellow Americans:

In the normal course of events, Presidents come to this chamber to report on the state of the Union. Tonight, no such report is needed. It has already been delivered by the American people.

We have seen it in the courage of passengers, who rushed terrorists to save others on the ground—passengers like an exceptional man named Todd Beamer. And would you please help me to welcome his wife, Lisa Beamer, here tonight. (Applause.)

We have seen the state of our Union in the endurance of rescuers, working past exhaustion. We have seen the unfurling of flags, the lighting of candles, the giving of blood, the saying of prayers—in English, Hebrew, and Arabic. We have seen the decency of a loving and giving people who have made the grief of strangers their own.

My fellow citizens, for the last nine days, the entire world has seen for itself the state of our Union—and it is strong. (Applause.)

Tonight we are a country awakened to danger and called to defend freedom. Our grief has turned to anger, and anger to resolution. Whether we bring our enemies to justice, or bring justice to our enemies, justice will be done. (Applause.)

I thank the Congress for its leadership at such an important time. All of America was touched on the evening of the tragedy to see Republicans and Democrats joined together on the steps of this Capitol, singing "God Bless America." And you did more than sing; you acted, by delivering $40 billion to rebuild our communities and meet the needs of our military.

Speaker Hastert, Minority Leader Gephardt, Majority Leader Daschle and Senator Lott, I thank you for your friendship, for your leadership and for your service to our country. (Applause.)

And on behalf of the American people, I thank the world for its outpouring of support. America will never forget the sounds of our National Anthem playing at Buckingham Palace, on the streets of Paris, and at Berlin's Brandenburg Gate.

We will not forget South Korean children gathering to pray outside our embassy in Seoul, or the prayers of sympathy offered at a mosque in Cairo. We will not forget moments of silence and days of mourning in Australia and Africa and Latin America.

Nor will we forget the citizens of 80 other nations who died with our own: dozens of Pakistanis; more than 130 Israelis; more than 250 citizens of India; men and women from El Salvador, Iran, Mexico and Japan; and hundreds of British citizens. America has no truer friend than Great Britain. (Applause.) Once again, we are joined together in a great cause—so honored the British Prime Minister has crossed an ocean to show his unity of purpose with America. Thank you for coming, friend. (Applause.)

On September the 11th, enemies of freedom committed an act of war against our country. Americans have known wars—but for the past 136 years, they have been wars on foreign soil, except for one Sunday in 1941. Americans have known the casualties of war—but not at the center of a great city on a peaceful morning. Americans have known surprise attacks—but never before on thousands of civilians. All of this was brought upon us in a single day—and night fell on a different world, a world where freedom itself is under attack.

Americans have many questions tonight. Americans are asking: Who attacked our country? The evidence we have gathered all points to a collection of loosely affiliated terrorist organizations known as al Qaeda. They are the same murderers indicted for bombing American embassies in Tanzania and Kenya, and responsible for bombing the *U.S.S. Cole*.

Al Qaeda is to terror what the mafia is to crime. But its goal is not making money; its goal is remaking the world—and imposing its radical beliefs on people everywhere.

The terrorists practice a fringe form of Islamic extremism that has been rejected by Muslim scholars and the vast majority of Muslim clerics—a fringe movement that perverts the peaceful teachings of Islam. The terrorists' directive commands them to kill Christians and Jews, to kill all Americans, and make no distinction among military and civilians, including women and children.

This group and its leader—a person named Osama bin Laden—are linked to many other organizations in different countries, including the Egyptian Islamic Jihad and the Islamic Movement of Uzbekistan. There are thousands of these terrorists in more than 60 countries. They are recruited from their own nations and neighborhoods and brought to camps in places like Afghanistan, where they are trained in the tactics of terror. They are sent back to their homes or sent to hide in countries around the world to plot evil and destruction.

The leadership of al Qaeda has great influence in Afghanistan and supports the Taliban regime in controlling most of that country. In Afghanistan, we see al Qaeda's vision for the world.

Afghanistan's people have been brutalized—many are starving and many have fled. Women are not allowed to attend school. You can be jailed for owning a television. Religion can be practiced only as their leaders dictate. A man can be jailed in Afghanistan if his beard is not long enough.

The United States respects the people of Afghanistan—after all, we are currently its largest source of humanitarian aid—but we condemn the Taliban regime. (Applause.) It is not only repressing its own people, it is threatening people everywhere by sponsoring and sheltering and supplying terrorists. By aiding and abetting murder, the Taliban regime is committing murder.

And tonight, the United States of America makes the following demands on the Taliban: Deliver to United States authorities all the leaders of al Qaeda who hide in your land. (Applause.) Release all foreign nationals, including American citizens, you have unjustly imprisoned. Protect foreign journalists, diplomats and aid workers in your country. Close immediately and permanently every terrorist training camp in Afghanistan, and hand over every terrorist, and every person in their support structure, to appropriate authorities. (Applause.) Give the United States full access to terrorist training camps, so we can make sure they are no longer operating.

These demands are not open to negotiation or discussion. (Applause.) The Taliban must act, and act immediately. They will hand over the terrorists, or they will share in their fate.

I also want to speak tonight directly to Muslims throughout the world. We respect your faith. It's practiced freely by many millions of Americans, and by millions more in countries that America counts as friends. Its teachings are good and peaceful, and those who commit evil in the name of Allah blaspheme the name of Allah. (Applause.) The terrorists are traitors to their own faith, trying, in effect, to hijack Islam itself. The enemy of America is not our many Muslim friends; it is not our many Arab friends. Our enemy is a radical network of terrorists, and every government that supports them. (Applause.)

Our war on terror begins with al Qaeda, but it does not end there. It will not end until every terrorist group of global reach has been found, stopped and defeated. (Applause.)

Americans are asking, why do they hate us? They hate what we see right here in this chamber—a democratically elected government. Their leaders are self-appointed. They hate our freedoms—our freedom of religion, our freedom of speech, our freedom to vote and assemble and disagree with each other.

They want to overthrow existing governments in many Muslim countries, such as Egypt, Saudi Arabia, and Jordan. They want to drive Israel out of the Middle East. They want to drive Christians and Jews out of vast regions of Asia and Africa.

These terrorists kill not merely to end lives, but to disrupt and end a way of life. With every atrocity, they hope that America grows fearful, retreating from the world and forsaking our friends. They stand against us, because we stand in their way.

We are not deceived by their pretenses to piety. We have seen their kind before. They are the heirs of all the murderous ideologies of the 20th century. By sacrificing human life to serve their radical visions—by abandoning every value except the will to power—they follow in the path of fascism, and Nazism, and totalitarianism. And they will follow that path all the way, to where it ends: in history's unmarked grave of discarded lies. (Applause.)

Americans are asking: How will we fight and win this war? We will direct every resource at our command—every means of diplomacy, every tool of intelligence, every instrument of law enforcement, every financial influence, and every necessary weapon of war—to the disruption and to the defeat of the global terror network.

This war will not be like the war against Iraq a decade ago, with a decisive liberation of territory and a swift conclusion. It will not look like the air war above Kosovo two years ago, where no ground troops were used and not a single American was lost in combat.

Our response involves far more than instant retaliation and isolated strikes. Americans should not expect one battle, but a lengthy campaign, unlike any other we have ever seen. It may include dramatic strikes, visible on TV, and covert operations, secret even in success. We will starve terrorists of funding, turn them one against another, drive them from place to place, until there is no refuge or no rest. And we will pursue nations that provide aid or safe haven to terrorism. Every nation, in every region, now has a decision to make. Either you are with us, or you are with the terrorists. (Applause.) From this day forward, any nation that continues to harbor or support terrorism will be regarded by the United States as a hostile regime.

Our nation has been put on notice: We are not immune from attack. We will take defensive measures against terrorism to protect Americans. Today, dozens of federal departments and agencies, as well as state and local governments, have responsibilities affecting homeland security. These efforts must be coordinated at the highest level. So tonight I announce the creation of a Cabinet-level position reporting directly to me—the Office of Homeland Security.

And tonight I also announce a distinguished American to lead this effort, to strengthen American security: a military veteran, an effective governor, a true patriot, a trusted friend—Pennsylvania's Tom Ridge. (Applause.) He will lead, oversee and coordinate a comprehensive national strategy to safeguard our country against terrorism, and respond to any attacks that may come.

These measures are essential. But the only way to defeat terrorism as a threat to our way of life is to stop it, eliminate it, and destroy it where it grows. (Applause.)

Many will be involved in this effort, from FBI agents to intelligence operatives to the reservists we have called to active duty. All deserve our thanks, and all have our prayers. And tonight, a few miles from the damaged Pentagon, I have a message for our military: Be ready. I've called the Armed Forces to alert, and there is a reason. The hour is coming when America will act, and you will make us proud. (Applause.)

This is not, however, just America's

fight. And what is at stake is not just America's freedom. This is the world's fight. This is civilization's fight. This is the fight of all who believe in progress and pluralism, tolerance and freedom.

We ask every nation to join us. We will ask, and we will need, the help of police forces, intelligence services, and banking systems around the world. The United States is grateful that many nations and many international organizations have already responded—with sympathy and with support. Nations from Latin America, to Asia, to Africa, to Europe, to the Islamic world. Perhaps the NATO Charter reflects best the attitude of the world: An attack on one is an attack on all.

The civilized world is rallying to America's side. They understand that if this terror goes unpunished, their own cities, their own citizens may be next. Terror, unanswered, can not only bring down buildings, it can threaten the stability of legitimate governments. And you know what—we're not going to allow it. (Applause.)

Americans are asking: What is expected of us? I ask you to live your lives, and hug your children. I know many citizens have fears tonight, and I ask you to be calm and resolute, even in the face of a continuing threat.

I ask you to uphold the values of America, and remember why so many have come here. We are in a fight for our principles, and our first responsibility is to live by them. No one should be singled out for unfair treatment or unkind words because of their ethnic background or religious faith. (Applause.)

I ask you to continue to support the victims of this tragedy with your contributions. Those who want to give can go to a central source of information, *libertyunites.org*, to find the names of groups providing direct help in New York, Pennsylvania, and Virginia.

The thousands of FBI agents who are now at work in this investigation may need your cooperation, and I ask you to give it.

I ask for your patience, with the delays and inconveniences that may accompany tighter security; and for your patience in what will be a long struggle.

I ask your continued participation and confidence in the American economy. Terrorists attacked a symbol of American prosperity. They did not touch its source. America is successful because of the hard work, and creativity, and enterprise of our people. These were the true strengths of our economy before September 11th, and they are our strengths today. (Applause.)

And, finally, please continue praying for the victims of terror and their families, for those in uniform, and for our great country. Prayer has comforted us in sorrow, and will help strengthen us for the journey ahead.

Tonight I thank my fellow Americans for what you have already done and for what you will do. And ladies and gentlemen of the Congress, I thank you, their representatives, for what you have already done and for what we will do together.

Tonight, we face new and sudden national challenges. We will come together to improve air safety, to dramatically expand the number of air marshals on domestic flights, and take new measures to prevent hijacking. We will come together to promote stability and keep our airlines flying, with direct assistance during this emergency. (Applause.)

We will come together to give law enforcement the additional tools it needs to track down terror here at home. (Applause.) We will come together to strengthen our intelligence capabilities to know the plans of terrorists before they act, and find them before they strike. (Applause.)

We will come together to take active steps that strengthen America's economy, and put our people back to work.

Tonight we welcome two leaders who embody the extraordinary spirit of all New Yorkers: Governor George Pataki, and Mayor Rudolph Giuliani. (Applause.) As a symbol of America's resolve, my administration will work with Congress, and these two leaders, to show the world that we will rebuild New York City. (Applause.)

After all that has just passed—all the lives taken, and all the possibilities and hopes that died with them—it is natural to wonder if America's future is one of fear. Some speak of an age of terror. I know there are struggles ahead, and dangers to face. But this country will define our times, not be defined by them. As long as the United States of America is determined and strong, this will not be an age of terror; this will be an age of liberty, here and across the world. (Applause.)

Great harm has been done to us. We have suffered great loss. And in our grief and anger we have found our mission and our moment. Freedom and fear are at war.

The advance of human freedom—the great achievement of our time, and the great hope of every time—now depends on us. Our nation—this generation—will lift a dark threat of violence from our people and our future. We will rally the world to this cause by our efforts, by our courage. We will not tire, we will not falter, and we will not fail. (Applause.)

It is my hope that in the months and years ahead, life will return almost to normal. We'll go back to our lives and routines, and that is good. Even grief recedes with time and grace. But our resolve must not pass. Each of us will remember what happened that day, and to whom it happened. We'll remember the moment the news came—where we were and what we were doing. Some will remember an image of a fire, or a story of rescue. Some will carry memories of a face and a voice gone forever.

And I will carry this: It is the police shield of a man named George Howard, who died at the World Trade Center trying to save others. It was given to me by his mom, Arlene, as a proud memorial to her son. This is my reminder of lives that ended, and a task that does not end. (Applause.)

I will not forget this wound to our country or those who inflicted it. I will not yield; I will not rest; I will not relent in waging this struggle for freedom and security for the American people.

The course of this conflict is not known, yet its outcome is certain. Freedom and fear, justice and cruelty, have always been at war, and we know that God is not neutral between them. (Applause.)

Fellow citizens, we'll meet violence with patient justice—assured of the rightness of our cause, and confident of the victories to come. In all that lies before us, may God grant us wisdom, and may He watch over the United States of America.

Thank you. (Applause.)

Study Questions

1. How did President George W. Bush's September 20th address compare to President Roosevelt's "Four Freedoms" (p. 387)?

2. Did Bush's policy of eradicating terrorism wherever it may be found mark a continuation of, or a departure from, U.S. foreign policy as defined by NSC–68 (p. 439) during the Cold War?

U.S. Congress, "Authorization for the Use of Military Force against Iraq" (2002)

In the wake of the September 11, 2001, terrorist attacks, President George W. Bush advanced a new national security principle, known as the Bush Doctrine. Whereas the Truman Doctrine called for vigilant containment of communism by assisting any people at risk being overrun by the Soviets, the Bush Doctrine advocated a more proactive effort. Bush aimed to prevent future terrorist attacks by ensuring that terrorist-sponsoring regimes would not acquire, develop, or use weapons of mass destruction. Having traced the September 11 attacks to al Qaeda, and al Qaeda to Saddam Hussein's Iraq, Bush urged Congress to authorize military action against Iraq.

Joint Resolution: To authorize the use of United States Armed Forces against Iraq

Whereas in 1990 in response to Iraq's war of aggression against and illegal occupation of Kuwait, the United States forged a coalition of nations to liberate Kuwait and its people in order to defend the national security of the United States and enforce United Nations Security Council resolutions relating to Iraq;

Whereas after the liberation of Kuwait in 1991, Iraq entered into a United Nations sponsored cease-fire agreement pursuant to which Iraq unequivocally agreed, among other things, to eliminate its nuclear, biological, and chemical weapons programs and the means to deliver and develop them, and to end its support for international terrorism;

Whereas the efforts of international weapons inspectors, United States intelligence agencies, and Iraqi defectors led to the discovery that Iraq had large stockpiles of chemical weapons and a large scale biological weapons program, and that Iraq had an advanced nuclear weapons devel-

opment program that was much closer to producing a nuclear weapon than intelligence reporting had previously indicated;

Whereas Iraq, in direct and flagrant violation of the cease-fire, attempted to thwart the efforts of weapons inspectors to identify and destroy Iraq's weapons of mass destruction stockpiles and development capabilities, which finally resulted in the withdrawal of inspectors from Iraq on October 31, 1998;

Whereas in Public Law 105-235 (August 14, 1998), Congress concluded that Iraq's continuing weapons of mass destruction programs threatened vital United States interests and international peace and security, declared Iraq to be in "material and unacceptable breach of its international obligations" and urged the President "to take appropriate action, in accordance with the Constitution and relevant laws of the United States, to bring Iraq into compliance with its international obligations";

Whereas Iraq both poses a continuing threat to the national security of the United States and international peace and security in the Persian Gulf region and remains in material and unacceptable breach of its international obligations by, among other things, continuing to possess and develop a significant chemical and biological weapons capability, actively seeking a nuclear weapons capability, and supporting and harboring terrorist organizations;

Whereas Iraq persists in violating resolution of the United Nations Security Council by continuing to engage in brutal repression of its civilian population thereby threatening international peace and security in the region, by refusing to release, repatriate, or account for non-Iraqi citizens wrongfully detained by Iraq, including an American serviceman, and by failing to return property wrongfully seized by Iraq from Kuwait;

Whereas the current Iraqi regime has demonstrated its capability and willingness to use weapons of mass destruction against other nations and its own people;

Whereas the current Iraqi regime has demonstrated its continuing hostility toward, and willingness to attack, the United States, including by attempting in 1993 to assassinate former President Bush and by firing on many thousands of occasions on United States and Coalition Armed Forces engaged in enforcing the resolutions of the United Nations Security Council;

Whereas members of al Qaeda, an organization bearing responsibility for attacks on the United States, its citizens, and interests, including the attacks that occurred on September 11, 2001, are known to be in Iraq;

Whereas Iraq continues to aid and harbor other international terrorist organizations, including organizations that threaten the lives and safety of United States citizens;

Whereas the attacks on the United States of September 11, 2001, underscored the gravity of the threat posed by the acquisition of weapons of mass destruction by international terrorist organizations;

Whereas Iraq's demonstrated capability and willingness to use weapons of mass destruction, the risk that the current Iraqi regime will either employ those weapons to launch a surprise attack against the United States or its Armed Forces or provide them to international terrorists who would do so, and the extreme magnitude of harm that would result to the United States and its citizens from such an attack, combine to justify action by the United States to defend itself;

Whereas United Nations Security Council Resolution 678 (1990) authorizes the use of all necessary means to enforce United Nations Security Council Resolution 660 (1990) and subsequent relevant resolutions and to compel Iraq to cease certain activities that threaten international peace and security, including the development of weapons of mass destruction and refusal or obstruction of United Nations weapons inspections in violation of United Nations Security Council Resolution 687 (1991), repression of its civilian population in violation of United Nations Security Council Resolution 688 (1991), and threatening its neighbors or United Nations operations in Iraq in violation of United Nations Security Council Resolution 949 (1994);

Whereas in the Authorization for Use of

Military Force Against Iraq Resolution (Public Law 102-1), Congress has authorized the President "to use United States Armed Forces pursuant to United Nations Security Council Resolution 678 (1990) in order to achieve implementation of Security Council Resolution 660, 661, 662, 664, 665, 666, 667, 669, 670, 674, and 677";

Whereas in December 1991, Congress expressed its sense that it "supports the use of all necessary means to achieve the goals of United Nations Security Council Resolution 687 as being consistent with the Authorization of Use of Military Force Against Iraq Resolution (Public Law 102-1)," that Iraq's repression of its civilian population violates United Nations Security Council Resolution 688 and "constitutes a continuing threat to the peace, security, and stability of the Persian Gulf region," and that Congress, "supports the use of all necessary means to achieve the goals of United Nations Security Council Resolution 688";

Whereas the Iraq Liberation Act of 1998 (Public Law 105-338) expressed the sense of Congress that it should be the policy of the United States to support efforts to remove from power the current Iraqi regime and promote the emergence of a democratic government to replace that regime;

Whereas on September 12, 2002, President Bush committed the United States to "work with the United Nations Security Council to meet our common challenge" posed by Iraq and to "work for the necessary resolutions," while also making clear that "the Security Council resolutions will be enforced, and the just demands of peace and security will be met, or action will be unavoidable";

Whereas the United States is determined to prosecute the war on terrorism and Iraq's ongoing support for international terrorist groups combined with its development of weapons of mass destruction in direct violation of its obligations under the 1991 cease-fire and other United Nations Security Council resolutions make clear that it is in the national security interests of the United States and in furtherance of the war on terrorism that all relevant United Nations Security Council resolutions be enforced, including through the use of force if necessary;

Whereas Congress has taken steps to pursue vigorously the war on terrorism through the provision of authorities and funding requested by the President to take the necessary actions against international terrorists and terrorist organizations, including those nations, organizations, or persons who planned, authorized, committed, or aided the terrorist attacks that occurred on September 11, 2001, or harbored such persons or organizations;

Whereas the President and Congress are determined to continue to take all appropriate actions against international terrorists and terrorist organizations, including those nations, organizations, or persons who planned, authorized, committed, or aided the terrorist attacks that occurred on September 11, 2001, or harbored such persons or organizations;

Whereas the President has authority under the Constitution to take action in order to deter and prevent acts of international terrorism against the United States, as Congress recognized in the joint resolution on Authorization for Use of Military Force (Public Law 107-40); and

Whereas it is in the national security interests of the United States to restore international peace and security to the Persian Gulf region:

Now, therefore, be it Resolved by the Senate and House of Representatives of the United States of America in Congress assembled,

Section 1. Short Title.

This joint resolution may be cited as the "Authorization for Use of Military Force Against Iraq Resolution of 2002."

Sec. 2. Support for United States Diplomatic Efforts.

The Congress of the United States supports the efforts by the President to—

(1) Strictly enforce through the United Nations Security Council all relevant Security Council resolutions regarding Iraq and encourages him in those efforts; and

(2) Obtain prompt and decisive action by the Security Council to ensure that Iraq abandons its strategy of delay, evasion and noncompliance and promptly and strictly complies with all relevant Security Council resolutions regarding Iraq.

Sec. 3. Authorization for Use of United States Armed Forces.

(a) Authorization.—The President is authorized to use the Armed Forces of the United States as he determines to be necessary and appropriate in order to—

(1) Defend the national security of the United States against the continuing threat posed by Iraq; and

(2) Enforce all relevant United Nations Security Council resolutions regarding Iraq.

(b) Presidential Determination.—In connection with the exercise of the authority granted in subsection (a) to use force the President shall, prior to such exercise or as soon thereafter as may be feasible, but no later than 48 hours after exercising such authority, make available to the Speaker of the House of Representatives and the President pro tempore of the Senate his determination that—

(1) Reliance by the United States on further diplomatic or other peaceful means alone either (A) will not adequately protect the national security of the United States against the continuing threat posed by Iraq or (B) is not likely to lead to enforcement of all relevant United Nations Security Council resolutions regarding Iraq; and

(2) Acting pursuant to this joint resolution is consistent with the United States and other countries continuing to take the necessary actions against international terrorist and terrorist organizations, including those nations, organizations, or persons who planned, authorized, committed or aided the terrorist attacks that occurred on September 11, 2001.

(c) War Powers Resolution Requirements.—

(1) Specific statutory authorization.—Consistent with section 8(a)(1) of the War Powers Resolution, the Congress declares that this section is intended to constitute specific statutory authorization within the meaning of section 5(b) of the War Powers Resolution.

(2) Applicability of other requirements.—Nothing in this joint resolution supersedes any requirement of the War Powers Resolution.

Sec. 4. Reports to Congress.

(a) Reports.—The President shall, at least once every 60 days, submit to the Congress a report on matters relevant to this joint resolution, including actions taken pursuant to the exercise of authority granted in section 3 and the status of planning for efforts that are expected to be required after such actions are completed, including those actions described in section 7 of the Iraq Liberation Act of 1998 (Public Law 105-338).

(b) Single Consolidated Report.—To the extent that the submission of any report described in subsection (a) coincides with the submission of any other report on matters relevant to this joint resolution otherwise required to be submitted to Congress pursuant to the reporting requirements of the War Powers Resolution (Public Law 93-148), all such reports may be submitted as a single consolidated report to the Congress.

(c) Rule of Construction.—To the extent that the information required by section 3 of the Authorization for Use of Military Force Against Iraq Resolution (Public Law 102-1) is included in the report required by this section, such report shall be considered as meeting the requirements of section 3 of such resolution.

Approved October 16, 2002.

Study Questions

1. What reasons did Congress give for authorizing President George W. Bush to use military force against Iraq in 2002? How do these reasons compare to those listed by Bush's father in 1991 (p. 669)?

2. Do you believe that Congress made the right decision in authorizing a pre-emptive strike? Why or why not?

George W. Bush, Second Inaugural Address (2005)

In the 2004 presidential election, Senator John Kerry, a Democrat from Massachusetts, challenged incumbent George W. Bush. Both candidates focused considerable attention on foreign policy, with Kerry criticizing Bush's handling of the War on Terrorism. As for domestic issues, Bush labeled Kerry a "Massachusetts liberal," arguing that the Democratic senator was out of touch with mainstream America. For his own agenda, Bush advocated an "ownership society"—for example, allowing individuals to invest their Social Security contributions into the stock market while also sponsoring federal housing policies that would increase home ownership. Although these suggestions may have boosted his ratings enough to defeat Kerry in 2004, the housing market took a nose dive, as did stocks, toward the end of Bush's second term. By 2008, Bush found himself choosing a new kind of "ownership society": he signed into law a government bailout plan allocating trillions of dollars to salvage failing companies.

Vice President Cheney, Mr. Chief Justice, President Carter, President Bush, President Clinton, Members of the United States Congress, reverend clergy, distinguished guests, fellow citizens:

On this day, prescribed by law and marked by ceremony, we celebrate the durable wisdom of our Constitution and recall the deep commitments that unite our country. I am grateful for the honor of this hour, mindful of the consequential times in which we live, and determined to fulfill the oath that I have sworn and you have witnessed.

At this second gathering, our duties are defined not by the words I use but by the history we have seen together. For a half a century, America defended our own freedom by standing watch on distant borders. After the shipwreck of communism came years of relative quiet, years of repose, years of sabbatical, and then there came a day of fire.

We have seen our vulnerability, and we have seen its deepest source. For as long as whole regions of the world simmer in resentment and tyranny, prone to ideologies that feed hatred and excuse murder, violence will gather and multiply in destructive power and cross the most defended borders and raise a mortal threat. There is only one force of history that can break the reign of hatred and resentment and expose the pretensions of tyrants and reward the hopes of the decent and tolerant, and that is the force of human freedom.

We are led, by events and common sense, to one conclusion: The survival of liberty in our land increasingly depends on the success of liberty in other lands. The best hope for peace in our world is the expansion of freedom in all the world.

America's vital interests and our deepest beliefs are now one. From the day of our founding, we have proclaimed that every man and woman on this Earth has rights and dignity and matchless value, because they bear the image of the Maker of heaven and Earth. Across the generations, we have proclaimed the imperative of self-government, because no one is fit to be a master and no one deserves to be a slave. Advancing these ideals is the mission that created our Nation. It is the honorable achievement of our fathers. Now, it is the urgent requirement of our Nation's security and the calling of our time.

So it is the policy of the United States to seek and support the growth of democratic movements and institutions in every nation and culture, with the ultimate goal of ending tyranny in our world. This is not primarily the task of arms, though we will defend ourselves and our friends by force of arms when necessary. Freedom, by its nature, must be chosen and defended by citizens and sustained by the rule of law and the protection of minorities. And when the soul of a nation finally speaks, the institutions that arise may reflect customs and traditions very different from our own. America will not impose our own style of government on the unwilling. Our goal instead is to help others find their own voice, attain their own freedom, and make their own way.

The great objective of ending tyranny is the concentrated work of generations. The difficulty of the task is no excuse for avoiding it. America's influence is not unlimited, but fortunately for the oppressed, America's influence is considerable and we will use it confidently in freedom's cause.

My most solemn duty is to protect this Nation and its people from further attacks and emerging threats. Some have unwisely chosen to test America's resolve and have found it firm. We will persistently clarify the choice before every ruler and every nation, the moral choice between oppression, which is always wrong, and freedom, which is eternally right.

America will not pretend that jailed dissidents prefer their chains or that women welcome humiliation and servitude or that any human being aspires to live at the mercy of bullies. We will encourage reform in other governments by making clear that success in our relations will require the decent treatment of their own people. America's belief in human dignity will guide our policies. Yet rights must be more than the grudging concessions of dictators. They are secured by free dissent and the participation of the governed. In the long run, there is no justice without freedom and there can be no human rights without human liberty.

Some, I know, have questioned the global appeal of liberty, though this time in history, four decades defined by the swiftest advance of freedom ever seen, is an odd time for doubt. Americans, of all people, should never be surprised by the power of our ideals. Eventually, the call of freedom comes to every mind and every soul. We do not accept the existence of permanent tyranny because we do not accept the possibility of permanent slavery. Liberty will come to those who love it.

Today, America speaks anew to the peoples of the world. All who live in tyranny and hopelessness can know: The United States will not ignore your oppression or excuse your oppressors. When you stand for your liberty, we will stand with you.

Democratic reformers facing repression, prison, or exile can know: America sees you for who you are, the future leaders of your free country.

The rulers of outlaw regimes can know that we still believe as Abraham Lincoln did: "Those who deny freedom to others deserve it not for themselves and, under the rule of a just God, cannot long retain it."

The leaders of governments with long habits of control need to know: To serve your people, you must learn to trust them. Start on this journey of progress and justice, and America will walk at your side.

And all the allies of the United States can know: We honor your friendship; we rely on your counsel; and we depend on your help. Division among free nations is a primary goal of freedom's enemies. The concerted effort of free nations to promote democracy is a prelude to our enemies' defeat.

Today I also speak anew to my fellow citizens. From all of you I have asked patience in the hard task of securing America, which you have granted in good measure. Our country has accepted obligations that are difficult to fulfill and would be dishonorable to abandon. Yet because we have acted in the great liberating tradition of this Nation, tens of millions have achieved their freedom. And as hope kindles hope, millions more will find it. By our efforts, we have lit a fire as well, a fire in the minds of men. It warms those who feel its power. It burns those who fight its progress. And one day this untamed fire of freedom will reach the darkest corners of our world.

A few Americans have accepted the hardest duties in this cause, in the quiet work of intelligence and diplomacy, the idealistic work of helping raise up free governments, the dangerous and necessary work of fighting our enemies. Some have shown their devotion to our country in deaths that honored their whole lives, and we will always honor their names and their sacrifice.

All Americans have witnessed this idealism and some for the first time. I ask our youngest citizens to believe the evidence of your eyes. You have seen duty and allegiance in the determined faces of our soldiers. You have seen that life is fragile and evil is real and courage triumphs. Make the choice to serve in a cause larger than your wants, larger than yourself, and in your days you will add not just to the wealth of our country but to its character.

America has need of idealism and courage because we have essential work at home, the unfinished work of American freedom. In a world moving toward liberty, we are determined to show the meaning and promise of liberty.

In America's ideal of freedom, citizens find the dignity and security of economic independence instead of laboring on the edge of subsistence. This is the broader definition of liberty that motivated the Homestead Act, the Social Security Act, and the GI bill of rights. And now we will extend this vision by reforming great institutions to serve the needs of our time. To give every American a stake in the promise and future of our country, we will bring the highest standards to our schools and build an ownership society. We will widen the ownership of homes and businesses, retirement savings, and health insurance, preparing our people for the challenges of life in a free society. By making every citizen an agent of his or her own destiny, we will give our fellow Americans greater freedom from want and fear and make our society more prosperous and just and equal.

In America's ideal of freedom, the public interest depends on private character, on integrity and tolerance toward others and the rule of conscience in our own lives. Self-government relies, in the end, on the governing of the self. That edifice of character is built in families, supported by communities with standards, and sustained in our national life by the truths of Sinai, the Sermon on the Mount, the words of the Koran, and the varied faiths of our people. Americans move forward in every generation by reaffirming all that is good and true that came before, ideals of justice and conduct that are the same yesterday, today, and forever.

In America's ideal of freedom, the exercise of rights is ennobled by service and mercy and a heart for the weak. Liberty for all does not mean independence from one another. Our Nation relies on men and women who look after a neighbor and surround the lost with love. Americans, at our best, value the life we see in one another and must always remember that even the unwanted have worth. And our country must abandon all the habits of racism, because we cannot carry the message of freedom and the baggage of bigotry at the same time.

From the perspective of a single day, including this day of dedication, the issues and questions before our country are many. From the viewpoint of centuries, the questions that come to us are narrowed and few: Did our generation advance the cause of freedom? And did our character bring credit to that cause?

These questions that judge us also unite us, because Americans of every party and background, Americans by choice and by birth are bound to one another in the cause of freedom. We have known divisions, which must be healed to move forward in great purposes, and I will strive in good faith to heal them. Yet those divisions do not define America. We felt the unity and fellowship of our Nation when freedom came under attack, and our response came like a single hand over a single heart. And we can feel that same unity and pride whenever America acts for good and the victims of disaster are given hope and the unjust encounter justice and the captives are set free.

We go forward with complete confidence in the eventual triumph of freedom, not because history runs on the wheels of inevitability—it is human choices that move events; not because we consider ourselves a chosen nation—God moves and chooses as He wills. We have confidence because freedom is the permanent hope of mankind, the hunger in dark places, the longing of the soul. When our Founders declared a new order of the ages, when soldiers died in wave upon wave for a union based on liberty, when citizens marched in peaceful outrage under the banner "Freedom Now," they were acting on an ancient hope that is meant to be fulfilled. History has an ebb and flow of justice, but history also has a visible direction, set by liberty and the Author of Liberty.

When the Declaration of Independence was first read in public and the Liberty Bell was sounded in celebration, a witness said, "It rang as if it meant something." In our time, it means something still. America, in this young century, proclaims liberty throughout all the world and to all the inhabitants thereof. Renewed in our strength, tested but not weary, we are ready for the greatest achievements in the history of freedom.

May God bless you, and may He watch over the United States of America.

Study Questions

1. What, according to Bush, was the best strategy for preserving freedom in America?

2. When Bush defined "the dignity and security of economic independence," did he sound more like Calvin Coolidge and Ronald Reagan, or more like Theodore Roosevelt and Franklin Roosevelt? Explain.

3. In the Eisenhower era, Americans forged a consensus identity as Protestants, Catholics, and Jews. Bush, on the other hand, spoke of "the truths of Sinai, the Sermon on the Mount, and the words of the Koran." What was he attempting to communicate, and why did he feel this message was so necessary in the year 2005?

Supreme Court Decisions under Chief Justice John Roberts

With Associate Justice Sandra Day O'Connor retiring, President George W. Bush nominated John Roberts to succeed her in 2005. When Chief Justice William Rehnquist died before the Senate had confirmed Roberts, Bush re-nominated him to fill the position of chief justice and selected Samuel Alito to replace O'Connor. Legal scholars anticipated that both Roberts and Alito would tilt the Court toward a more conservative jurisprudence, joining with Antonin Scalia and Clarence Thomas plus the moderate Anthony Kennedy against liberals on the bench. However, not all "conservatives" are woven of the same thread. Scalia, for example, has strictly followed the text of the Constitution even if this means withholding an endorsement for conservative social values. Meanwhile, the appointments of Sonia Sotomayor and Elena Kagan to the Court by President Barack Obama in 2009 and 2010 shifted the balance back toward the liberal end of the spectrum, both as to social values and as to how loosely one might interpret the Constitution. The result has been a continuation under Chief Justice John Roberts of the unpredictable roller-coaster ride that began under William Rehnquist.

2006   In *Gonzales v. Oregon* the Court ruled that physicians prescribing lethal drugs in a state where physician-assisted suicide is legal cannot be prosecuted for violating the federal Controlled Substances Act.

2007   The Court upheld a 2003 congressional ban on partial-birth abortion, departing from the course set in *Stenberg v. Carhardt* (2000) since the 2003 law had been carefully crafted to escape the *Stenberg* provisions.

2008   Striking down a gun control law, the Court ruled in *District of Columbia v. Heller* that the Second Amendment guarantees individuals a right to keep guns in their homes.

2011   In *Dukes v. Wal-Mart Stores*, the largest class-action civil rights case in history, the Court rejected the attempt of women across the nation to claim that they had jointly suffered gender discrimination as employees.

2012   The Court unanimously ruled that the First Amendment grants a church sole discretion over employment decisions regarding its ministers, despite government regulations of employment, in *Hosanna-Tabor Evangelical Lutheran Church v. EEOC*.

2012   The Court ruled in *National Federation of Independent Business v. Sebelius* that Congress has the authority to impose a tax penalty on persons who fail to purchase health insurance. Roberts wrote the majority opinion, whereas Scalia authored a sharp dissent.

Study Question

How should the Roberts Court be characterized?

Barack Obama, First Inaugural Address (2009)

The presidential election of 2008 stands out in history for several reasons. Never before had two sitting senators run against each other—in this case, Senator Barack Obama from Illinois and Senator John McCain from Arizona. This election also was the first time since 1952 that neither the current president nor the current vice president ran for office. For the first time ever, the Republican Party nominated a woman for vice president, Alaska Governor Sarah Palin. The Democratic Party became the first major party to nominate an African American for the presidency. Although McCain claimed in a televised debate that Obama's economic proposals would ruin the livelihood of "Joe the Plumber" (a representative of the average American), Obama held the lead by ten million popular votes, securing a 365–173 victory in the electoral college.

My fellow citizens:

I stand here today humbled by the task before us, grateful for the trust you have bestowed, mindful of the sacrifices borne by our ancestors. I thank President Bush for his service to our nation, as well as the generosity and co-operation he has shown throughout this transition.

Forty-four Americans have now taken the presidential oath. The words have been spoken during rising tides of prosperity and the still waters of peace. Yet, every so often the oath is taken amidst gathering clouds and raging storms. At these moments, America has carried on not simply because of the skill or vision of those in high office, but because we, the people, have remained faithful to the ideals of our forbearers, and true to our founding documents.

So it has been. So it must be with this generation of Americans.

That we are in the midst of crisis is now well understood. Our nation is at war, against a far-reaching network of violence and hatred. Our economy is badly weakened, a consequence of greed and irresponsibility on the part of some, but also our collective failure to make hard choices and prepare the nation for a new age. Homes have been lost; jobs shed; businesses shuttered. Our health care is too costly; our schools fail too many; and each day brings further evidence that the ways we use energy strengthen our adversaries and threaten our planet.

These are the indicators of crisis, subject to data and statistics. Less measurable but no less profound is a sapping of confidence across our land—a nagging fear that America's decline is inevitable, and that the next generation must lower its sights.

Today I say to you that the challenges we face are real. They are serious and they are many. They will not be met easily or in a short span of time. But know this, America—they will be met.

On this day, we gather because we have chosen hope over fear, unity of purpose over conflict and discord.

On this day, we come to proclaim an end to the petty grievances and false promises, the recriminations and worn out dogmas, that for far too long have strangled our politics.

We remain a young nation, but in the words of scripture, the time has come to set aside childish things. The time has come to reaffirm our enduring spirit; to choose our better history; to carry forward that precious gift, that noble idea, passed on from generation to generation: the God-given promise that all are equal, all are free, and all deserve a chance to pursue their full measure of happiness.

In reaffirming the greatness of our nation, we understand that greatness is never a given. It must be earned. Our journey has never been one of short-cuts or settling for less. It has not been the path for the faint-hearted—for those who prefer leisure over work, or seek only the pleasures of riches and fame. Rather, it has been the risk-takers, the doers, the makers of things—some celebrated but more often men and women obscure in their labor, who have carried us up the long, rugged path towards prosperity and freedom.

For us, they packed up their few worldly possessions and traveled across oceans in search of a new life.

For us, they toiled in sweatshops and settled the West; endured the lash of the whip and ploughed the hard earth.

For us, they fought and died, in places like Concord and Gettysburg; Normandy and Khe Sahn.

Time and again these men and women struggled and sacrificed and worked till their hands were raw so that we might live a better life. They saw America as bigger than the sum of our individual ambitions; greater than all the differences of birth or wealth or faction.

This is the journey we continue today. We remain the most prosperous, powerful nation on earth. Our workers are no less productive than when this crisis began. Our minds are no less inventive, our goods and services no less needed than they were last week or last month or last year. Our capacity remains undiminished. But our time of standing pat, of protecting narrow interests and putting off unpleasant decisions—that time has surely passed. Starting today, we must pick ourselves up, dust ourselves off, and begin again the work of remaking America.

For everywhere we look, there is work to be done. The state of the economy calls for action, bold and swift, and we will act—not only to create new jobs, but to lay a new foundation for growth. We will build the roads and bridges, the electric grids and digital lines that feed our commerce and bind us together. We will restore science to its rightful place, and wield technology's wonders to raise health care's quality and lower its cost. We will harness the sun and the winds and the soil to fuel our cars and run our factories. And we will transform our schools and colleges and universities to meet the demands of a new age. All this we can do. All this we will do.

Now, there are some who question the scale of our ambitions—who suggest that our system cannot tolerate too many big plans. Their memories are short. For they have forgotten what this country has already done; what free men and women can achieve when imagination is joined to common purpose, and necessity to courage.

What the cynics fail to understand is

that the ground has shifted beneath them —that the stale political arguments that have consumed us for so long no longer apply. The question we ask today is not whether our government is too big or too small, but whether it works—whether it helps families find jobs at a decent wage, care they can afford, a retirement that is dignified. Where the answer is yes, we intend to move forward. Where the answer is no, programs will end. And those of us who manage the public's dollars will be held to account—to spend wisely, reform bad habits, and do our business in the light of day—because only then can we restore the vital trust between a people and their government.

Nor is the question before us whether the market is a force for good or ill. Its power to generate wealth and expand freedom is unmatched, but this crisis has reminded us that without a watchful eye, the market can spin out of control—that a nation cannot prosper long when it favors only the prosperous. The success of our economy has always depended not just on the size of our gross domestic product, but on the reach of our prosperity; on the ability to extend opportunity to every willing heart—not out of charity, but because it is the surest route to our common good.

As for our common defense, we reject as false the choice between our safety and our ideals. Our founding fathers, faced with perils we can scarcely imagine, drafted a charter to assure the rule of law and the rights of man, a charter expanded by the blood of generations. Those ideals still light the world, and we will not give them up for expedience's sake. And so to all other peoples and governments who are

watching today, from the grandest capitals to the small village where my father was born: know that America is a friend of each nation and every man, woman, and child who seeks a future of peace and dignity, and we are ready to lead once more.

Recall that earlier generations faced down fascism and communism not just with missiles and tanks, but with the sturdy alliances and enduring convictions. They understood that our power alone cannot protect us, nor does it entitle us to do as we please. Instead, they knew that our power grows through its prudent use; our security emanates from the justness of our cause, the force of our example, the tempering qualities of humility and restraint.

We are the keepers of this legacy. Guided by these principles once more, we can meet those new threats that demand even greater effort—even greater cooperation and understanding between nations. We will begin to responsibly leave Iraq to its people, and forge a hard-earned peace in Afghanistan. With old friends and former foes, we will work tirelessly to lessen the nuclear threat, and roll back the specter of a warming planet. We will not apologize for our way of life, nor will we waver in its defense, and for those who seek to advance their aims by inducing terror and slaughtering innocents, we say to you now that our spirit is stronger and cannot be broken; you cannot outlast us, and we will defeat you.

For we know that our patchwork heritage is a strength, not a weakness. We are a nation of Christians and Muslims, Jews and Hindus—and non-believers. We are shaped by every language and culture, drawn from every end of this earth; and because we have tasted the bitter swill of civil war and segregation, and emerged from that dark chapter stronger and more united, we cannot help but believe that the old hatreds shall someday pass; that the lines of tribe shall soon dissolve; that as the world grows smaller, our common humanity shall reveal itself; and that America must play its role in ushering in a new era of peace.

To the Muslim world, we seek a new way forward, based on mutual interest and mutual respect. To those leaders around the globe who seek to sow conflict, or blame their society's ills on the West— know that your people will judge you on what you can build, not what you destroy. To those who cling to power through corruption and deceit and the silencing of dissent, know that you are on the wrong side of history; but that we will extend a hand if you are willing to unclench your fist.

To the people of poor nations, we pledge to work alongside you to make your farms flourish and let clean waters flow; to nourish starved bodies and feed hungry minds. And to those nations like ours that enjoy relative plenty, we say we can no longer afford indifference to suffering outside our borders; nor can we consume the world's resources without regard to effect. For the world has changed, and we must change with it.

As we consider the road that unfolds before us, we remember with humble gratitude those brave Americans who, at this very hour, patrol far-off deserts and dis-

tant mountains. They have something to tell us, just as the fallen heroes who lie in Arlington whisper through the ages. We honor them not only because they are guardians of our liberty, but because they embody the spirit of service; a willingness to find meaning in something greater than themselves. And yet, at this moment—a moment that will define a generation—it is precisely this spirit that must inhabit us all.

For as much as government can do and must do, it is ultimately the faith and determination of the American people upon which this nation relies. It is the kindness to take in a stranger when the levees break, the selflessness of workers who would rather cut their hours than see a friend lose their job which sees us through our darkest hours. It is the firefighter's courage to storm a stairway filled with smoke, but also a parent's willingness to nurture a child, that finally decides our fate.

Our challenges may be new. The instruments with which we meet them may be new. But those values upon which our success depends—honesty and hard work, courage and fair play, tolerance and curiosity, loyalty and patriotism—these things are old. These things are true. They have been the quiet force of progress throughout our history. What is demanded then is a return to these truths. What is required of us now is a new era of responsibility—a recognition, on the part of every American, that we have duties to ourselves, our nation, and the world, duties that we do not grudgingly accept but rather seize gladly, firm in the knowledge that there is nothing so satisfying to the spirit, so defining of our character, than giving our all to a difficult task.

This is the price and the promise of citizenship.

This is the source of our confidence—the knowledge that God calls on us to shape an uncertain destiny.

This is the meaning of our liberty and our creed—why men and women and children of every race and every faith can join in celebration across this magnificent mall, and why a man whose father less than 60 years ago might not have been served at a local restaurant can now stand before you to take a most sacred oath.

So let us mark this day with remembrance, of who we are and how far we have traveled. In the year of America's birth, in the coldest of months, a small band of patriots huddled by dying campfires on the shores of an icy river. The capital was abandoned. The enemy was advancing. The snow was stained with blood. At a moment when the outcome of our revolution was most in doubt, the father of our nation ordered these words be read to the people:

"Let it be told to the future world . . . that in the depth of winter, when nothing but hope and virtue could survive . . . that the city and the country, alarmed at one common danger, came forth to meet [it]."

America. In the face of our common dangers, in this winter of our hardship, let us remember these timeless words. With hope and virtue, let us brave once more the icy currents, and endure what storms may come. Let it be said by our children's children that when we were tested we refused to let this journey end, that we did not turn back nor did we falter; and with eyes fixed on the horizon and God's grace upon us, we carried forth that great gift of freedom and delivered it safely to future generations.

Thank you. God bless you. And God bless the United States of America.

Study Question

Contextualize Barack Obama's inaugural address in American history. For example, identify two key themes that he emphasized and indicate the history behind them.

Barack Obama, "A New Beginning" (2009)

On June 4, 2009, President Barack Obama delivered an address at Cairo University aimed at reconciling the United States to the Muslim world. Following the September 11, 2001 terrorist attacks, President George W. Bush had said:

> The terrorists are traitors to their own faith, trying, in effect, to hijack Islam itself. The enemy of America is not our many Muslim friends; it is not our many Arab friends. Our enemy is a radical network of terrorists, and every government that supports them.

In 2009, President Obama took even bolder steps to appease Muslims. He claimed that the Judeo-Christian heritage of the United States and the Islamic heritage of the Middle East are fundamentally compatible. Indeed, Obama even suggested that several American heroes of the past had subscribed to Islamic ideals. The following transcript, released by the White House, indicates statements to which the audience in Egypt applauded. In America, however, critics charged Obama with endorsing internationalism rather than American sovereignty and cherishing multiculturalism rather than the natural law values upon which America was founded. Some even suggested that Obama was America's first Muslim president.

Thank you very much. Good afternoon. I am honored to be in the timeless city of Cairo, and to be hosted by two remarkable institutions. For over a thousand years, Al-Azhar has stood as a beacon of Islamic learning; and for over a century, Cairo University has been a source of Egypt's advancement. And together, you represent the harmony between tradition and progress. I'm grateful for your hospitality, and the hospitality of the people of Egypt. And I'm also proud to carry with me the goodwill of the American people, and a greeting of peace from Muslim communities in my country: *Assalaamu alaykum.* (Applause.)

We meet at a time of great tension between the United States and Muslims around the world—tension rooted in historical forces that go beyond any current policy debate. The relationship between Islam and the West includes centuries of coexistence and cooperation, but also conflict and religious wars. More recently, tension has been fed by colonialism that denied rights and opportunities to many Muslims, and a Cold War in which Muslim-majority countries were too often treated as proxies without regard to their own aspirations. Moreover, the sweeping change brought by modernity and globalization led many Muslims to view the West as hostile to the traditions of Islam.

Violent extremists have exploited these tensions in a small but potent minority of Muslims. The attacks of September 11, 2001 and the continued efforts of these extremists to engage in violence against civilians has led some in my country to view Islam as inevitably hostile not only to America and Western countries, but also to human rights. All this has bred more fear and more mistrust.

So long as our relationship is defined by our differences, we will empower those who sow hatred rather than peace, those who promote conflict rather than the cooperation that can help all of our people achieve justice and prosperity. And this cycle of suspicion and discord must end.

I've come here to Cairo to seek a new beginning between the United States and Muslims around the world, one based on mutual interest and mutual respect, and one based upon the truth that America and Islam are not exclusive and need not be in competition. Instead, they overlap, and share common principles—principles of justice and progress; tolerance and the dignity of all human beings.

I do so recognizing that change cannot happen overnight. I know there's been a lot of publicity about this speech, but no single speech can eradicate years of mistrust, nor can I answer in the time that I have this afternoon all the complex questions that brought us to this point. But I am convinced that in order to move forward, we must say openly to each other the things we hold in our hearts and that too often are said only behind closed doors. There must be a sustained effort to listen to each other; to learn from each other; to respect one another; and to seek common ground. As the Holy Koran tells us, "Be conscious of God and speak always the truth." (Applause.) That is what I will try to do today—to speak the truth as best I can, humbled by the task before us, and firm in my belief that the interests we share as human beings are far more powerful than the forces that drive us apart.

Now part of this conviction is rooted in my own experience. I'm a Christian, but my father came from a Kenyan family that includes generations of Muslims. As a boy, I spent several years in Indonesia and heard the call of the *azaan* at the break of dawn and at the fall of dusk. As a young man, I worked in Chicago communities where many found dignity and peace in their Muslim faith.

As a student of history, I also know civilization's debt to Islam. It was Islam—at places like Al-Azhar—that carried the light of learning through so many centuries, paving the way for Europe's Renaissance and Enlightenment. It was innovation in Muslim communities—(applause)—it was innovation in Muslim communities that developed the order of algebra; our magnetic compass and tools of navigation; our mastery of pens and printing; our understanding of how disease spreads and how it can be healed. Islamic culture has given us majestic arches and soaring spires; timeless poetry and cherished music; elegant calligraphy and places of peaceful contemplation. And throughout history, Islam has demonstrated through words and deeds the possibilities of religious tolerance and racial equality. (Applause.)

I also know that Islam has always been a part of America's story. The first nation to recognize my country was Morocco. In signing the Treaty of Tripoli in 1796, our second President, John Adams, wrote, "The United States has in itself no character of enmity against the laws, religion or tranquility of Muslims." And since our founding, American Muslims have enriched the United States. They have fought in our wars, they have served in our government, they have stood for civil rights, they have started businesses, they have taught at our universities, they've excelled in our sports arenas, they've won Nobel Prizes, built our tallest building, and lit the Olympic Torch. And when the first Muslim American was recently elected to Congress, he took the oath to defend our Constitution using the same Holy Koran that one of our Founding Fathers—Thomas Jefferson—kept in his personal library. (Applause.)

So I have known Islam on three continents before coming to the region where it was first revealed. That experience guides my conviction that partnership between America and Islam must be based on what Islam is, not what it isn't. And I consider it part of my responsibility as President of the United States to fight against negative stereotypes of Islam wherever they appear. (Applause.)

But that same principle must apply to Muslim perceptions of America. (Applause.) Just as Muslims do not fit a crude stereotype, America is not the crude stereotype of a self-interested empire. The United States has been one of the greatest sources of progress that the world has ever known. We were born out of revolution against an empire. We were founded upon the ideal that all are created equal, and we have shed blood and struggled for centuries to give meaning to those words—within our borders, and around the world. We are shaped by every culture, drawn from every end of the Earth, and dedicated to a simple concept: *E pluribus unum*—"Out of many, one."

Now, much has been made of the fact that an African American with the name Barack Hussein Obama could be elected President. (Applause.) But my personal story is not so unique. The dream of opportunity for all people has not come true for everyone in America, but its promise exists for all who come to our shores—and that includes nearly seven million American Muslims in our country today who, by the way, enjoy incomes and educational levels that are higher than the American average. (Applause.)

Moreover, freedom in America is indivisible from the freedom to practice one's religion. That is why there is a mosque in every state in our union, and over 1,200 mosques within our borders. That's why the United States government has gone to court to protect the right of women and girls to wear the hijab and to punish those who would deny it. (Applause.)

So let there be no doubt: Islam is a part of America. And I believe that America holds within her the truth that regardless of race, religion, or station in life, all of us share common aspirations—to live in peace and security; to get an education and to work with dignity; to love our families, our communities, and our God. These things we share. This is the hope of all humanity.

Of course, recognizing our common humanity is only the beginning of our task. Words alone cannot meet the needs of our people. These needs will be met only if we act boldly in the years ahead; and if we understand that the challenges we face are shared, and our failure to meet them will hurt us all.

For we have learned from recent experience that when a financial system weakens in one country, prosperity is hurt everywhere. When a new flu infects one human being, all are at risk. When one nation pursues a nuclear weapon, the risk of nuclear attack rises for all nations. When violent extremists operate in one stretch of mountains, people are endangered across an ocean. When innocents in Bosnia and Darfur are slaughtered, that is a stain on our collective conscience. (Applause.) That is what it means to share this world in the 21st century. That is the responsibility we have to one another as human beings.

And this is a difficult responsibility to embrace. For human history has often been a record of nations and tribes—and, yes, religions—subjugating one another in pursuit of their own interests. Yet in this new age, such attitudes are self-defeating. Given our interdependence, any world order that elevates one nation or group of people over another will inevitably fail. So whatever we think of the past, we must not be prisoners to it. Our problems must be dealt with through partnership; our progress must be shared. (Applause.)

Now, that does not mean we should ignore sources of tension. Indeed, it suggests the opposite: We must face these tensions squarely. And so in that spirit, let me speak as clearly and as plainly as I can about some specific issues that I believe we must finally confront together.

The first issue that we have to confront is violent extremism in all of its forms.

In Ankara, I made clear that America is not—and never will be—at war with Islam. (Applause.) We will, however, relentlessly confront violent extremists who pose a grave threat to our security—because we reject the same thing that people of all faiths reject: the killing of innocent men, women, and children. And it is my first duty as President to protect the American people.

The situation in Afghanistan demonstrates America's goals, and our need to work together. Over seven years ago, the United States pursued al Qaeda and the Taliban with broad international support. We did not go by choice; we went because of necessity. I'm aware that there's still some who would question or even justify the events of 9/11. But let us be clear: Al Qaeda killed nearly 3,000 people on that day. The victims were innocent men, women and children from America and many other nations who had done nothing to harm anybody. And yet al Qaeda chose to ruthlessly murder these people, claimed credit for the attack, and even now states their determination to kill on a massive scale. They have affiliates in many countries and are trying to expand their reach. These are not opinions to be debated; these are facts to be dealt with.

Now, make no mistake: We do not want to keep our troops in Afghanistan. We see no military—we seek no military bases there. It is agonizing for America to lose our young men and women. It is costly and politically difficult to continue this conflict. We would gladly bring every single one of our troops home if we could be confident that there were not violent extremists in Afghanistan and now Pakistan determined to kill as many Americans as they possibly can. But that is not yet the case.

And that's why we're partnering with a

coalition of forty-six countries. And despite the costs involved, America's commitment will not weaken. Indeed, none of us should tolerate these extremists. They have killed in many countries. They have killed people of different faiths —but more than any other, they have killed Muslims. Their actions are irreconcilable with the rights of human beings, the progress of nations, and with Islam. The Holy Koran teaches that whoever kills an innocent is as—it is as if he has killed all mankind. (Applause.) And the Holy Koran also says whoever saves a person, it is as if he has saved all mankind. (Applause.) The enduring faith of over a billion people is so much bigger than the narrow hatred of a few. Islam is not part of the problem in combating violent extremism—it is an important part of promoting peace.

Now, we also know that military power alone is not going to solve the problems in Afghanistan and Pakistan. That's why we plan to invest $1.5 billion each year over the next five years to partner with Pakistanis to build schools and hospitals, roads and businesses, and hundreds of millions to help those who've been displaced. That's why we are providing more than $2.8 billion to help Afghans develop their economy and deliver services that people depend on.

Let me also address the issue of Iraq. Unlike Afghanistan, Iraq was a war of choice that provoked strong differences in my country and around the world. Although I believe that the Iraqi people are ultimately better off without the tyranny of Saddam Hussein, I also believe that events in Iraq have reminded America of the need to use diplomacy and build international consensus to resolve our problems whenever possible. (Applause.) Indeed, we can recall the words of Thomas Jefferson, who said: "I hope that our wisdom will grow with our power, and teach us that the less we use our power the greater it will be."

Today, America has a dual responsibility: to help Iraq forge a better future—and to leave Iraq to Iraqis. And I have made it clear to the Iraqi people—(applause)—I have made it clear to the Iraqi people that we pursue no bases, and no claim on their territory or resources. Iraq's sovereignty is its own. And that's why I ordered the removal of our combat brigades by next August. That is why we will honor our agreement with Iraq's democratically elected government to remove combat troops from Iraqi cities by July, and to remove all of our troops from Iraq by 2012. (Applause.) We will help Iraq train its security forces and develop its economy. But we will support a secure and united Iraq as a partner, and never as a patron.

And finally, just as America can never tolerate violence by extremists, we must never alter or forget our principles. Nine-eleven was an enormous trauma to our country. The fear and anger that it provoked was understandable, but in some cases, it led us to act contrary to our traditions and our ideals. We are taking concrete actions to change course. I have unequivocally prohibited the use of torture by the United States, and I have ordered the prison at Guantanamo Bay closed by early next year. (Applause.)

So America will defend itself, respectful of the sovereignty of nations and the rule of law. And we will do so in partnership with Muslim communities which are also threatened. The sooner the extremists are isolated and unwelcome in Muslim communities, the sooner we will all be safer.

The second major source of tension that we need to discuss is the situation between Israelis, Palestinians and the Arab world.

America's strong bonds with Israel are well known. This bond is unbreakable. It is based upon cultural and historical ties, and the recognition that the aspiration for a Jewish homeland is rooted in a tragic history that cannot be denied.

Around the world, the Jewish people were persecuted for centuries, and anti-Semitism in Europe culminated in an unprecedented Holocaust. Tomorrow, I will visit Buchenwald, which was part of a network of camps where Jews were enslaved, tortured, shot and gassed to death by the Third Reich. Six million Jews were killed—more than the entire Jewish population of Israel today. Denying that fact is baseless, it is ignorant, and it is hateful. Threatening Israel with destruction—or repeating vile stereotypes about Jews—is deeply wrong, and only serves to evoke in the minds of Israelis this most painful of memories while preventing the peace that the people of this region deserve.

On the other hand, it is also undeniable that the Palestinian people—Muslims and Christians—have suffered in pursuit of a homeland. For more than sixty years they've endured the pain of dislocation. Many wait in refugee camps in the West Bank, Gaza, and neighboring lands for a life of peace and security that they have never been able to lead. They endure the daily humiliations—large and small—that come with occupation. So let there be no doubt: The situation for the Palestinian people is intolerable. And America will not turn our backs on the legitimate Palestinian aspiration for dignity, opportunity, and a state of their own. (Applause.)

For decades then, there has been a stalemate: two peoples with legitimate aspirations, each with a painful history that makes compromise elusive. It's easy to point fingers—for Palestinians to point to the displacement brought about by Israel's founding, and for Israelis to point to the constant hostility and attacks throughout its history from within its borders as well as beyond. But if we see this conflict only from one side or the other, then we will be blind to the truth: The only resolution is for the aspirations of both sides to be met through two states, where Israelis and Palestinians each live in peace and security. (Applause.)

That is in Israel's interest, Palestine's interest, America's interest, and the world's interest. And that is why I intend to personally pursue this outcome with all the patience and dedication that the task requires. (Applause.) The obligations—the obligations that the parties have agreed to under the road map are clear. For peace to come, it is time for them—and all of us—to live up to our responsibilities.

Palestinians must abandon violence. Resistance through violence and killing is wrong and it does not succeed. For centuries, black people in America suffered the lash of the whip as slaves and the humiliation of segregation. But it was not violence that won full and equal rights. It was a peaceful and determined insistence upon the ideals at the center of America's founding. This same story can be told by people from South Africa to South Asia; from Eastern Europe to Indonesia. It's a story with a simple truth: that violence is a dead end. It is a sign neither of courage nor power to shoot rockets at sleeping children, or to blow up old women on a bus. That's not how moral authority is claimed; that's how it is surrendered.

Now is the time for Palestinians to focus on what they can build. The Palestinian Authority must develop its capacity to govern, with institutions that serve the needs of its people. Hamas does have support among some Palestinians, but they also have to recognize they have responsibilities. To play a role in fulfilling Palestinian aspirations, to unify the Palestinian people, Hamas must put an end to violence, recognize past agreements, recognize Israel's right to exist.

At the same time, Israelis must acknowledge that just as Israel's right to exist cannot be denied, neither can Palestine's. The United States does not accept the legitimacy of continued Israeli settlements. (Applause.) This construction violates previous agreements and undermines efforts to achieve peace. It is time for these settlements to stop. (Applause.)

And Israel must also live up to its obligation to ensure that Palestinians can live and work and develop their society. Just as it devastates Palestinian families, the continuing humanitarian crisis in Gaza does not serve Israel's security; neither does the continuing lack of opportunity in the West Bank. Progress in the daily lives of the Palestinian people must be a critical part of a road to peace, and Israel must take concrete steps to enable such progress.

And finally, the Arab states must recognize that the Arab Peace Initiative was an important beginning, but not the end of their responsibilities. The Arab-Israeli conflict should no longer be used to distract the people of Arab nations from other problems. Instead, it must be a cause for action to help the Palestinian people develop the institutions that will sustain their state, to recognize Israel's legitimacy, and to choose progress over a self-defeating focus on the past.

America will align our policies with those who pursue peace, and we will say in public what we say in private to Israelis and Palestinians and Arabs. (Applause.) We cannot impose peace. But privately, many Muslims recognize that Israel will not go away. Likewise, many Israelis recognize the need for a Palestinian state. It is time for us to act on what everyone knows to be true.

Too many tears have been shed. Too much blood has been shed. All of us have a responsibility to work for the day when the mothers of Israelis and Palestinians can see their children grow up without fear; when the Holy Land of the three great faiths is the place of peace that God intended it to be; when Jerusalem is a secure and lasting home for Jews and Christians and Muslims, and a place for all of the children of Abraham to mingle peacefully together as in the story of Isra—(applause) —as in the story of Isra, when Moses,

Jesus, and Mohammed, peace be upon them, joined in prayer.[4] (Applause.)

The third source of tension is our shared interest in the rights and responsibilities of nations on nuclear weapons.

This issue has been a source of tension between the United States and the Islamic Republic of Iran. For many years, Iran has defined itself in part by its opposition to my country, and there is in fact a tumultuous history between us. In the middle of the Cold War, the United States played a role in the overthrow of a democratically elected Iranian government. Since the Islamic Revolution, Iran has played a role in acts of hostage-taking and violence against U.S. troops and civilians. This history is well known. Rather than remain trapped in the past, I've made it clear to Iran's leaders and people that my country is prepared to move forward. The question now is not what Iran is against, but rather what future it wants to build.

I recognize it will be hard to overcome decades of mistrust, but we will proceed with courage, rectitude, and resolve. There will be many issues to discuss between our two countries, and we are willing to move

---

[4]President Obama was referring to the *hadith* (or traditional story) that expounds upon two brief passage in the Koran, chapters 17 and 53, alluding to a night journey taken by Muhammad into heaven. In the *hadith*, as collected in *Sahih al-Bukhari* (the most authoritative Sunni account), Moses and Jesus each greet Muhammad with the words, "You are welcome, O brother and a prophet." However, Moses and Jesus do this at separate times in separate parts of heaven, so the president's reference to a group prayer does not seem to follow the *hadith* faithfully. In fact, the main point of the story is that Moses guided Muhammad in negotiating with Allah to reduce the required number of daily prayers from fifty down to five.

forward without preconditions on the basis of mutual respect. But it is clear to all concerned that when it comes to nuclear weapons, we have reached a decisive point. This is not simply about America's interests. It's about preventing a nuclear arms race in the Middle East that could lead this region and the world down a hugely dangerous path.

I understand those who protest that some countries have weapons that others do not. No single nation should pick and choose which nation holds nuclear weapons. And that's why I strongly reaffirmed America's commitment to seek a world in which no nations hold nuclear weapons. (Applause.) And any nation—including Iran—should have the right to access peaceful nuclear power if it complies with its responsibilities under the Nuclear Non-Proliferation Treaty. That commitment is at the core of the treaty, and it must be kept for all who fully abide by it. And I'm hopeful that all countries in the region can share in this goal.

The fourth issue that I will address is democracy. (Applause.)

I know—I know there has been controversy about the promotion of democracy in recent years, and much of this controversy is connected to the war in Iraq. So let me be clear: No system of government can or should be imposed by one nation by any other.

That does not lessen my commitment, however, to governments that reflect the will of the people. Each nation gives life to this principle in its own way, grounded in the traditions of its own people. America does not presume to know what is best for everyone, just as we would not presume to pick the outcome of a peaceful election. But I do have an unyielding belief that all people yearn for certain things: the ability to speak your mind and have a say in how you are governed; confidence in the rule of law and the equal administration of justice; government that is transparent and doesn't steal from the people; the freedom to live as you choose. These are not just American ideas; they are human rights. And that is why we will support them everywhere. (Applause.)

Now, there is no straight line to realize this promise. But this much is clear: Governments that protect these rights are ultimately more stable, successful and secure. Suppressing ideas never succeeds in making them go away. America respects the right of all peaceful and law-abiding voices to be heard around the world, even if we disagree with them. And we will welcome all elected, peaceful governments—provided they govern with respect for all their people.

This last point is important because there are some who advocate for democracy only when they're out of power; once in power, they are ruthless in suppressing the rights of others. (Applause.) So no matter where it takes hold, government of the people and by the people sets a single standard for all who would hold power: You must maintain your power through consent, not coercion; you must respect the rights of minorities, and participate with a spirit of tolerance and compromise; you must place the interests of your people and the legitimate workings of the political process above your party. Without these ingredients, elections alone do not make true democracy.

AUDIENCE MEMBER: Barack Obama, we love you!

PRESIDENT OBAMA: Thank you. (Applause.) The fifth issue that we must address together is religious freedom.

Islam has a proud tradition of tolerance. We see it in the history of Andalusia and Cordoba during the Inquisition. I saw it firsthand as a child in Indonesia, where devout Christians worshiped freely in an overwhelmingly Muslim country. That is the spirit we need today. People in every country should be free to choose and live their faith based upon the persuasion of the mind and the heart and the soul. This tolerance is essential for religion to thrive, but it's being challenged in many different ways.

Among some Muslims, there's a disturbing tendency to measure one's own faith by the rejection of somebody else's faith. The richness of religious diversity must be upheld—whether it is for Maronites in Lebanon or the Copts in Egypt. (Applause.) And if we are being honest, fault lines must be closed among Muslims, as well, as the divisions between Sunni and Shia have led to tragic violence, particularly in Iraq.

Freedom of religion is central to the ability of peoples to live together. We must always examine the ways in which we protect it. For instance, in the United States, rules on charitable giving have made it harder for Muslims to fulfill their religious obligation. That's why I'm committed to working with American Muslims to ensure that they can fulfill zakat.

Likewise, it is important for Western countries to avoid impeding Muslim citizens from practicing religion as they see fit—for instance, by dictating what clothes a Muslim woman should wear. We can't disguise hostility towards any religion behind the pretense of liberalism.

In fact, faith should bring us together. And that's why we're forging service projects in America to bring together Christians, Muslims, and Jews. That's why we welcome efforts like Saudi Arabian King Abdullah's interfaith dialogue and Turkey's leadership in the Alliance of Civilizations. Around the world, we can turn dialogue into interfaith service, so bridges between peoples lead to action—whether it is combating malaria in Africa, or providing relief after a natural disaster.

The sixth issue—the sixth issue that I want to address is women's rights. (Applause.) I know—I know—and you can tell from this audience, that there is a healthy debate about this issue. I reject the view of some in the West that a woman who chooses to cover her hair is somehow less equal, but I do believe that a woman who is denied an education is denied equality. (Applause.) And it is no coincidence that countries where women are well educated are far more likely to be prosperous.

Now, let me be clear: Issues of women's equality are by no means simply an issue for Islam. In Turkey, Pakistan, Bangladesh, Indonesia, we've seen Muslim-majority countries elect a woman to lead. Meanwhile, the struggle for women's equality continues in many aspects of American life, and in countries around the world.

I am convinced that our daughters can contribute just as much to society as our sons. (Applause.) Our common prosperity will be advanced by allowing all humanity—men and women—to reach their full potential. I do not believe that women must make the same choices as men in order to be equal, and I respect those women who choose to live their lives in traditional roles. But it should be their choice. And that is why the United States will partner with any Muslim-majority country to support expanded literacy for girls, and to help young women pursue employment through micro-financing that helps people live their dreams. (Applause.)

Finally, I want to discuss economic development and opportunity.

I know that for many, the face of globalization is contradictory. The Internet and television can bring knowledge and information, but also offensive sexuality and mindless violence into the home. Trade can bring new wealth and opportunities, but also huge disruptions and change in communities. In all nations—including America—this change can bring fear. Fear that because of modernity we lose control over our economic choices, our politics, and most importantly our identities—those things we most cherish about our communities, our families, our traditions, and our faith.

But I also know that human progress cannot be denied. There need not be contradictions between development and tradition. Countries like Japan and South Korea grew their economies enormously while maintaining distinct cultures. The same is true for the astonishing progress within Muslim-majority countries from Kuala Lumpur to Dubai. In ancient times and in our times, Muslim communities have been at the forefront of innovation and education.

And this is important because no development strategy can be based only upon what comes out of the ground, nor can it be sustained while young people are out of work. Many Gulf states have enjoyed great wealth as a consequence of oil, and some are beginning to focus it on broader development. But all of us must recognize that education and innovation will be the currency of the 21st century—(applause)—and in too many Muslim communities, there remains underinvestment in these areas. I'm emphasizing such investment within my own country. And while America in the past has focused on oil and gas when it comes to this part of the world, we now seek a broader engagement.

On education, we will expand exchange programs, and increase scholarships, like the one that brought my father to America. (Applause.) At the same time, we will encourage more Americans to study in Muslim communities. And we will match promising Muslim students with internships in America; invest in online learning for teachers and children around the world; and create a new online network, so a young person in Kansas can communicate instantly with a young person in Cairo.

On economic development, we will create a new corps of business volunteers to partner with counterparts in Muslim-majority countries. And I will host a Summit on Entrepreneurship this year to identify how we can deepen ties between business leaders, foundations and social entrepreneurs in the United States and Muslim communities around the world.

On science and technology, we will launch a new fund to support technological development in Muslim-majority countries, and to help transfer ideas to the marketplace so they can create more jobs. We'll open centers of scientific excellence in Africa, the Middle East and Southeast Asia, and appoint new science envoys to collaborate on programs that develop new sources of energy, create green jobs, digitize records, clean water, grow new crops. Today I'm announcing a new global effort with the Organization of the Islamic Conference to eradicate polio. And we will also expand partnerships with Muslim communities to promote child and maternal health.

All these things must be done in partnership. Americans are ready to join with citizens and governments; community organizations, religious leaders, and businesses in Muslim communities around the world to help our people pursue a better life.

The issues that I have described will not be easy to address. But we have a responsibility to join together on behalf of the world that we seek—a world where extremists no longer threaten our people, and American troops have come home; a world where Israelis and Palestinians are each secure in a state of their own, and nuclear energy is used for peaceful purposes; a world where governments serve their citizens, and the rights of all God's children are respected. Those are mutual interests. That is the world we seek. But we can only achieve it together.

I know there are many—Muslim and non-Muslim—who question whether we can forge this new beginning. Some are eager to stoke the flames of division, and to stand in the way of progress. Some suggest that it isn't worth the effort—that we are fated to disagree, and civilizations are doomed to clash. Many more are simply skeptical that real change can occur. There's so much fear, so much mistrust that has built up over the years. But if we choose to be bound by the past, we will never move forward. And I want to particularly say this to young people of every faith, in every country—you, more than anyone, have the ability to reimagine the world, to remake this world.

All of us share this world for but a brief moment in time. The question is whether we spend that time focused on what pushes us apart, or whether we commit ourselves to an effort—a sustained effort—to find common ground, to focus on the future we seek for our children, and to respect the dignity of all human beings.

It's easier to start wars than to end them. It's easier to blame others than to look inward. It's easier to see what is different about someone than to find the things we share. But we should choose the right path, not just the easy path. There's

one rule that lies at the heart of every religion—that we do unto others as we would have them do unto us. (Applause.) This truth transcends nations and peoples—a belief that isn't new; that isn't black or white or brown; that isn't Christian or Muslim or Jew. It's a belief that pulsed in the cradle of civilization, and that still beats in the hearts of billions around the world. It's a faith in other people, and it's what brought me here today.

We have the power to make the world we seek, but only if we have the courage to make a new beginning, keeping in mind what has been written.

The Holy Koran tells us: "O mankind! We have created you male and a female; and we have made you into nations and tribes so that you may know one another."

The Talmud tells us: "The whole of the Torah is for the purpose of promoting peace."

The Holy Bible tells us: "Blessed are the peacemakers, for they shall be called sons of God." (Applause.)

The people of the world can live together in peace. We know that is God's vision. Now that must be our work here on Earth.

Thank you. And may God's peace be upon you. Thank you very much. Thank you. (Applause.)

Study Questions

1. On what basis did Obama claim that "Islam has always been a part of America's story"? Does your own knowledge of history support his conclusion?

2. List the seven issues that Obama said must be confronted in order for the Muslim World and the West to achieve a sustainable cooperation. Which of these issues do you expect can be settled most easily, and which issue do you perceive to be the most controversial?

3. Referring to Jews, Christians, and Muslims as "all of the children of Abraham," Obama promised that "faith should bring us together." Historically, these three groups have never acknowledged each other as "children of Abraham" in the same sense, precisely because they disagree concerning the fundamental question: What does it mean to have faith in God as Abraham did? In order to foster unity, the president sought to sidestep both history and theology by redefining "faith" in these words: "It's a faith in other people, and it's what brought me here today. We have the power to make the world we seek." Upon what foundation, then, did Obama propose to re-establish world civilization, and how does that differ from the foundation upon which the founding fathers built the American Republic?

The Patient Protection and Affordable Care Act (2010)

Background

In 2010, Congress passed and President Obama signed the Patient Protection and Affordable Care Act (PPACA). This comprehensive reform bill requires that all large companies provide health insurance to their employees, that all persons (with a few exceptions) obtain health insurance (whether through their employer or on their own), that all insurance programs satisfy ten core standards of coverage, and that wealthier Americans subsidize poorer Americans so that no person will lack healthcare for reason of cost.

President Harry S. Truman had proposed a nationalized healthcare program as part of his Fair Deal of the 1940s, but Congress was unwilling. In the 1960s, President Lyndon B. Johnson did persuade Congress to establish Medicare for the elderly and Medicaid for the poor, but most Americans still remained responsible for their own healthcare costs. In the 1990s, President Bill Clinton, together with his wife Hillary, sought approval for nationalized healthcare, but once again Congress rejected the plan. In 2003, President George W. Bush signed into law the Medicare Prescription Drug, Improvement, and Modernization Act, expanding the benefits provided to the elderly through Medicare. In the 2008 presidential campaign, nationalized healthcare again received prominent attention, with both of the leading Democratic candidates—Hillary Clinton and Barack Obama—promising to deliver this progressive reform.

Following Obama's election, Democrats held the majority in both the House and the Senate. Obama claimed the electoral victory of his party as a popular mandate to enact comprehensive healthcare reform. Despite strong objections from congressional Republicans, the PPACA passed in the Senate by a vote of 60–39 and in the House by a vote of 219–212. Prior to the vote, a bill to expand student loans was merged with the proposed healthcare legislation to increase its chances of passing. Another factor that may have assisted the bill's passage was that most members of Congress relied on second-hand reports as to what the proposal, known as Obamacare, would accomplish and how. Few had read the thousand-page bill in its entirety; in fact, the final language was not even available to be read in time for the vote. As Speaker of the House Nancy Pelosi, a Democrat from California, explained, rather cryptically, at a legislative conference, "But we have to pass the bill so that you can find out what is in it, away from the fog of controversy."

Provisions, Requirements, and Exemptions

Under Obamacare, insurance companies are required to provide coverage to persons regardless of pre-existing conditions and insurers also are forbidden from limiting benefits by a lifetime dollar cap. Co-payments, co-insurance, and deductibles are eliminated for "preventative care," a term which also includes FDA-approved birth control methods. All insurance plans must cover dependent children through age twenty-six. The law also classifies insurance plans into four categories—bronze, silver, gold, and platinum—based on the percentage of eligible healthcare costs that the insurance company pays on behalf of the patient (ranging from 60% to 90%).

An "individual responsibility mandate" requires that all persons obtain insurance. Employers generally are required to provide insurance for their workers, but for the self-employed or for those who work for small businesses, individuals must do so themselves. People who cannot afford to purchase insurance may shop at a government-exchange "marketplace" developed in cooperation between federal and state governments. In these "marketplaces," taxpayers subsidize insurance premiums for the poor—an odd use of the term "market" for an arrangement that fits the definition of socialism rather than *laissez faire*.

Individuals and families desiring to opt out of Obamacare have few legal options. One of them is to participate in a medical cost-sharing ministry, an exception allowed under 26 U.S.C. 5000a(d)(2)(B):

> The term "health care sharing ministry" means an organization . . . members of which share a common set of ethical or religious beliefs and share medical expenses among members in accordance with those beliefs and without regard to the State in which a member resides or is employed, . . . [and] which (or a predecessor of which) has been in existence at all times since December 31, 1999, and medical expenses of its members have been shared continuously and without interruption since at least December 31, 1999.

It appears that only three organizations satisfy the grandfather clause regarding a continual existence since December 31, 1999: Samaritan Ministries International, Medi-Share, and Christian Healthcare Ministries. With Samaritan, for example, a family agrees to share about $400 per month with any family having a healthcare need assigned to the first family. So, if Mr. Jones has a medical bill for $4,000, Samaritan Ministries asks ten of its member families each to send a check to Mr. Jones for $400 that month. Unlike traditional insurance, medical cost-sharing is charity-based, not contract-driven. Samaritan members do not pay premiums to the central office, but instead pay their shares directly to families in need. Moreover, biblical morality shapes the entire process, including both a prohibition of sponsoring immorality (such as abortion) as well as a positive command to bear the burdens of one's neighbor: "Bear one another's burdens, and so fulfill the law of Christ" (Galatians 6:2).

Controversy

No legislation of the early-twenty-first century has attracted as much controversy as the PPACA—or "Obamacare," as especially its critics call it. Objections arise from moral, economic, political, and legal concerns.

On the moral front, conservatives object to the "marriage penalty" that the marketplace exchange imposes upon couples: under Obamacare, insurance is less expensive if a man and a woman cohabit out of wedlock than if they are married. Much like welfare under Johnson's Great Society program, the PPACA offers a financial *dis*incentive to become or to remain married. Moreover, the PPACA mandates that all insurance companies provide coverage for contraception, including abortifacient forms of contraception.

Economic forecasters also have expressed great alarm over Obamacare. By requiring that all insurance companies provide a high benefit level even to unhealthy populations, the PPACA necessarily will drive up the cost of private insurance plans. As these cost increases are passed to patients in the form of premium hikes, more people are likely to leave the private market and seek a subsidized plan in the government-run exchanges. The likely result is that private insurance plans will fold, being replaced by socialized healthcare. Premium increases will be compounded by tax increases, with wealthier Americans purchasing not only their own insurance at a higher price but also footing the bill for those who participate in subsidized exchanges. From the providers' standpoint, Obamacare increases the complexity of what already was a burdensome maze of paperwork. Some doctors, in fact, switched to a cash-only policy as Obamacare was scheduled to come into full effect on January 1, 2014.

Politically, congressional Republicans have attempted to use the controversy surrounding the PPACA to force Democrats to the negotiating table on broader concerns about the growing national debt. In October 2013, the government experienced a partial shutdown because the two parties in Congress reached an impasse concerning the debt ceiling—the upper limit of how much money the U.S. Treasury Department is able to borrow in order to pay for government programs.

Philosophically, the whole debate echoes many American voices from the past who championed *laissez-faire* economics versus the advocates of progressive reform. The PPACA represents the greatest triumph of progressivism that the nation has ever witnessed, which from a *laissez-faire* perspective means the greatest menace the government has ever produced.

Critics of Obamacare have advanced two basic legal arguments against the PPACA in court. On the first issue, the U.S. Supreme Court held in *National Federation of Independent Business v. Sebelius* (2012) that the individual mandate falls under Congress's power to tax and therefore is constitutional. (The mandate imposes a tax penalty for individuals who fail to obtain insurance and also do not qualify for an exemption, such as by participating in a medical cost-sharing ministry.) The second issue has to do with religious freedom, and remains to be determined by the nation's highest court: Does the PPACA violate the right to religious liberty, protected by the First Amendment, by requiring that a Christian business owner provide insurance to employees that funds procedures contrary to the owner's Christian convictions, such as abortifacient contraception?

Study Questions

1. What does the PPACA require, and why?

2. What are the chief objections that critics of the PPACA have voiced?

3. Consider the notion of "ordered liberty" as it has been explored in this book from the Gilded Age to the present. Where does the PPACA fit in this narrative?

Barack Obama, Second Inaugural Address (2013)

In 2012, the Democratic Party eagerly re-nominated President Barack Obama. A dozen Republican candidates competed against each other in a long campaign season, with delegates for the libertarian Ron Paul trying to wrest control of the Republican National Convention from the party insiders who supported Mitt Romney, a moderate on economic reform. Although the margin of victory was closer than in 2008, Obama again captured the lead. In his second inaugural address, the president quoted from the Declaration of Independence, the U.S. Constitution, and the Gettysburg Address to suggest that the founding fathers would be proud of the liberal tradition flowing from the Roosevelt's New Deal and Johnson's Great Society. Like his Democratic predecessors, Obama called for collective action toward economic recovery. Unlike any president before him, he also advocated state recognition of same-sex "marriage," as if to prompt the U.S. Supreme Court in how to handle two pending cases on that topic.

Thank you. Thank you so much.

Vice President Biden, Mr. Chief Justice, Members of the United States Congress, distinguished guests, and fellow citizens:

Each time we gather to inaugurate a President we bear witness to the enduring strength of our Constitution. We affirm the promise of our democracy. We recall that what binds this Nation together is not the colors of our skin or the tenets of our faith or the origins of our names. What makes us exceptional—what makes us American—is our allegiance to an idea articulated in a declaration made more than two centuries ago:

> We hold these truths to be self-evident, that all men are created equal; that they are endowed by their Creator with certain unalienable rights; that among these are life, liberty, and the pursuit of happiness.

Today we continue a never-ending journey to bridge the meaning of those words with the realities of our time. For history tells us that while these truths may be self-evident, they've never been self-executing; that while freedom is a gift from God, it must be secured by His people here on Earth. The patriots of 1776 did not fight to replace the tyranny of a king with the privileges of a few or the rule of a mob. They gave to us a republic, a government of and by and for the people, entrusting each generation to keep safe our founding creed.

And for more than 200 years, we have.

Through blood drawn by lash and blood drawn by sword, we learned that no union founded on the principles of liberty and equality could survive half-slave and half-free. We made ourselves anew, and vowed to move forward together.

Together, we determined that a modern economy requires railroads and highways to speed travel and commerce, schools and colleges to train our workers.

Together, we discovered that a free market only thrives when there are rules to ensure competition and fair play.

Together, we resolved that a great nation must care for the vulnerable and protect its people from life's worst hazards and misfortune.

Through it all, we have never relinquished our skepticism of central authority nor have we succumbed to the fiction that all society's ills can be cured through government alone. Our celebration of initiative and enterprise, our insistence on hard work and personal responsibility, these are constants in our character.

But we have always understood that when times change, so must we; that fidelity to our founding principles requires new responses to new challenges; that preserving our individual freedoms ultimately requires collective action. For the American people can no more meet the demands of today's world by acting alone than American soldiers could have met the forces of fascism or communism with muskets and militias. No single person can train all the math and science teachers we'll need to equip our children for the future, or build the roads and networks and research labs that will bring new jobs and businesses to our shores. Now more than ever, we must do these things together, as one nation and one people.

This generation of Americans has been tested by crises that steeled our resolve and proved our resilience. A decade of war is now ending. An economic recovery has begun. America's possibilities are limitless, for we possess all the qualities that this world without boundaries demands: youth and drive; diversity and openness; an endless capacity for risk and a gift for reinvention. My fellow Americans, we are made for this moment and we will seize it —so long as we seize it together.

For we, the people, understand that our country cannot succeed when a shrinking few do very well and a growing many barely make it. We believe that America's prosperity must rest upon the broad shoulders of a rising middle class. We know that America thrives when every person can find independence and pride in their work; when the wages of honest labor liberate families from the brink of hardship. We are true to our creed when a little girl born into the bleakest poverty knows that she has the same chance to succeed as anybody else, because she is an American; she is free and she is equal, not just in the eyes of God, but also in our own.

We understand that outworn programs are inadequate to the needs of our time. So we must harness new ideas and technology to remake our government, revamp our Tax Code, reform our schools, and empower our citizens with the skills they need to work harder, learn more, reach higher. But while the means will change, our purpose endures: a nation that rewards the effort and determination of every single American. That is what this moment requires. That is what will give real meaning to our creed.

We, the people, still believe that every citizen deserves a basic measure of security and dignity. We must make the hard choices to reduce the cost of health care and the size of our deficit. But we reject the belief that America must choose between caring for the generation that built this country and investing in the generation that will build its future. For we remember the lessons of our past, when twilight years were spent in poverty and parents of a child with a disability had nowhere to turn.

We do not believe that in this country freedom is reserved for the lucky, or happiness for the few. We recognize that no matter how responsibly we live our lives, any one of us at any time may face a job loss or a sudden illness or a home swept away in a terrible storm. The commitments we make to each other through Medicare and Medicaid and Social Security, these things do not sap our initiative, they strengthen us. They do not make us a nation of takers; they free us to take the risks that make this country great.

We, the people, still believe that our obligations as Americans are not just to ourselves, but to all posterity. We will respond to the threat of climate change, knowing that the failure to do so would betray our children and future generations. Some may still deny the overwhelming judgment of science, but none can avoid the devastating impact of raging fires and crippling drought and more powerful storms.

The path towards sustainable energy sources will be long and sometimes difficult. But America cannot resist this transition, we must lead it. We cannot cede to other nations the technology that will power new jobs and new industries, we must claim its promise. That's how we will maintain our economic vitality and our national treasure—our forests and waterways, our crop lands and snow-capped peaks. That is how we will preserve our planet, commanded to our care by God. That's what will lend meaning to the creed our fathers once declared.

We, the people, still believe that enduring security and lasting peace do not require perpetual war. Our brave men and women in uniform, tempered by the flames of battle, are unmatched in skill and courage. Our citizens, seared by the memory of those we have lost, know too well the price that is paid for liberty. The knowledge of their sacrifice will keep us forever vigilant against those who would do us harm. But we are also heirs to those who won the peace and not just the war; who turned sworn enemies into the surest of friends—and we must carry those lessons into this time as well.

We will defend our people and uphold our values through strength of arms and rule of law. We will show the courage to try and resolve our differences with other nations peacefully—not because we are naive about the dangers we face, but because engagement can more durably lift suspicion and fear.

America will remain the anchor of strong alliances in every corner of the globe. And we will renew those institutions that extend our capacity to manage crisis abroad, for no one has a greater stake in a peaceful world than its most powerful nation. We will support democracy from Asia to Africa, from the Americas to the Middle East, because our interests and our conscience compel us to act on behalf of those who long for freedom. And we must be a source of hope to the poor, the sick, the marginalized, the victims of prejudice —not out of mere charity, but because peace in our time requires the constant advance of those principles that our common creed describes: tolerance and opportunity, human dignity and justice.

We, the people, declare today that the

most evident of truths—that all of us are created equal—is the star that guides us still; just as it guided our forebears through Seneca Falls and Selma and Stonewall; just as it guided all those men and women, sung and unsung, who left footprints along this great Mall, to hear a preacher say that we cannot walk alone; to hear a King proclaim that our individual freedom is inextricably bound to the freedom of every soul on Earth.

It is now our generation's task to carry on what those pioneers began. For our journey is not complete until our wives, our mothers and daughters can earn a living equal to their efforts. Our journey is not complete until our gay brothers and sisters are treated like anyone else under the law—for if we are truly created equal, then surely the love we commit to one another must be equal as well. Our journey is not complete until no citizen is forced to wait for hours to exercise the right to vote. Our journey is not complete until we find a better way to welcome the striving, hopeful immigrants who still see America as a land of opportunity—until bright young students and engineers are enlisted in our workforce rather than expelled from our country. Our journey is not complete until all our children, from the streets of Detroit to the hills of Appalachia, to the quiet lanes of Newtown, know that they are cared for and cherished and always safe from harm.

That is our generation's task—to make these words, these rights, these values of life and liberty and the pursuit of happiness real for every American. Being true to our founding documents does not require us to agree on every contour of life. It does not mean we all define liberty in exactly the same way or follow the same precise path to happiness. Progress does not compel us to settle centuries-long debates about the role of government for all time, but it does require us to act in our time.

For now decisions are upon us and we cannot afford delay. We cannot mistake absolutism for principle or substitute spectacle for politics or treat name-calling as reasoned debate. We must act, knowing that our work will be imperfect. We must act, we must act knowing that today's victories will be only partial and that it will be up to those who stand here in 4 years and 40 years and 400 years hence to advance the timeless spirit once conferred to us in a spare Philadelphia hall.

My fellow Americans, the oath I have sworn before you today, like the one recited by others who serve in this Capitol, was an oath to God and country, not party or faction. And we must faithfully execute that pledge during the duration of our service. But the words I spoke today are not so different from the oath that is taken each time a soldier signs up for duty or an immigrant realizes her dream. My oath is not so different from the pledge we all make to the flag that waves above and that fills our hearts with pride.

They are the words of citizens and they represent our greatest hope. You and I, as citizens, have the power to set this country's course. You and I, as citizens, have the obligation to shape the debates of our time—not only with the votes we cast, but with the voices we lift in defense of our most ancient values and enduring ideals.

Let us, each of us, now embrace with

solemn duty and awesome joy what is our lasting birthright. With common effort and common purpose, with passion and dedication, let us answer the call of history and carry into an uncertain future that precious light of freedom.

Thank you. God bless you, and may He forever bless these United States of America.

Study Questions

1. What did President Obama say in his second inaugural address to defend the Patient Protection and Affordable Care Act (which at the time was being phased into implementation)?

2. What did Obama mean in referring to "Seneca Falls and Selma and Stonewall"? (Consult an historical encyclopedia if needed.)

3. What are "our most ancient values and enduring ideals," according to Obama, and how did Republicans at the time disagree with his characterization of American principles?

The Debt Crisis

In October 2013, segments of the federal government closed as Congress cut off funding because a deadline had lapsed for raising the debt ceiling. In other words, the government was forbidden from borrowing more money, and therefore could not spend what was necessary to maintain all federal programs. By the middle of the month, lawmakers agreed to resume the pattern of borrowing. The debt immediately jumped $300 billion, reaching $17 trillion by October 18. Few Americans can conceptualize what such large numbers mean. As a standard measure, economists calculate the public debt in proportion to the gross domestic product, as illustrated in the following chart.

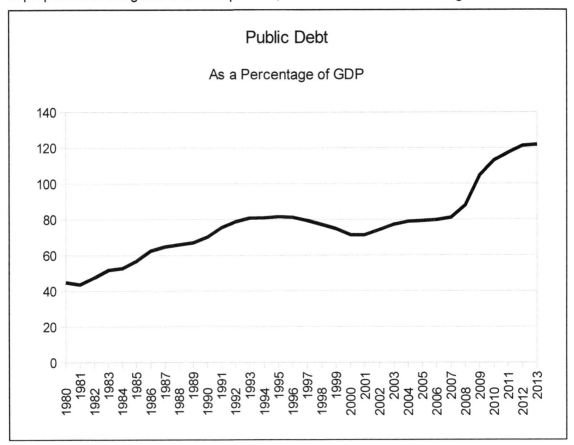

Study Question

Which appears to have had the greatest impact upon the nation's debt load—Cold War military expenditures (in in the 1980s), the War on Terrorism (announced in September 2001), or the government bailouts of Wall Street (2008–2009)?

Epilogue

Advice for Keeping Your Republic

The following has been adapted from a Constitution Day address delivered by Ryan C. MacPherson, Ph.D., in Mankato, Minnesota, on September 17, 2011. It also serves as a suitable epilogue for this textbook, which has explored the principles of ordered liberty upon which the American Republic was founded and has been sustained.

Introduction

On September 17, 1787, the Philadelphia Convention finished drafting the Constitution. It was a revolutionary document for its time. It remains a radical document today. The principles that the Constitution embodies run deep in the human spirit.

Congress and the state legislatures had charged the Philadelphia Convention with recommending amendments to the current system of government, known as the Articles of Confederation. But even before the convention met in May of 1787, delegates were drafting plans for a complete overhaul of America's government. For the next four months, the convention conducted its business in a closed chamber, sealing the windows for secrecy. Just imagine: fifty-five men of portly stature gathered in a small room all summer long without ever opening a window for fresh air.

Tempers sometimes ran hot, but several crucial compromises prevented the assembly from dissolving. At last, it was finished. The delegates had produced a new constitution for the largest republic in world history. The delegates also had invented the first political system in which the courts would be reserved in a special branch separate from the legislature and the executive. Gleaning all they could from the musings of political philosophers and the lessons of history, the delegates had established, as they phrased it, "a more perfect union."

But what kind of union was it? Dr. James McHenry, a delegate from Maryland, recorded the following exchange in his notes from the convention. A lady asked Benjamin Franklin, "Well, Doctor, what have we got: a republic or a monarchy?" To this Franklin replied, "a republic, if you can keep it."

This conversation begs two important questions. First, what is a republic? Second, how can you go about keeping it?

What a Republic Is

A republic, to imperial officials and colonists who had been loyal to the Crown, was a terrifying idea. It reminded them of the chaos England had experience a century earlier during the bloody English Civil War and the short-lived Commonwealth under Oliver Cromwell. Society must be orderly to sustain itself, and the monarch—thought many learned men—provided that necessary stability.

Britain was proud to have a mixed constitution, consisting of a monarchy (the king), an aristocracy (the House of Lords), and a democracy (the House of Commons). In theory, those three layers of government balanced each other out for the good of the empire.

Even as late as December 1775, most American colonists, no matter how disgruntled they were over taxation without representation, still treasured the concept of a monarchy. Their complaint was not so much with Britain's form of government, but with the failure of King George III to listen to their pleas for colonial representation. Although Parliament had turned a deaf ear to the colonists' concerns, they had been hoping that at least the king would listen.

But in January 1776 American sentiments quickly shifted. The change was prompted by the publication of Thomas Paine's *Common Sense*. Paine ridiculed the very idea of monarchy and in its place cast before the American colonists a vision of government by elected representatives. Six months later came the Declaration of Independence, by which the American colonists forever severed their ties to the British crown.

Even so, the stability afforded by a monarchy still appealed to many American patriots. John Adams and Alexander Hamilton feared that in rejecting monarchy America would drift too far in the direction of democracy, resulting in mob rule. Hamilton, in fact, had proposed that the U.S. Constitution establish long, monarch-like terms for the presidency, rather than the four-year terms that the majority of the convention favored.

Fearing the tyranny of a monarch at one extreme and the tyranny of the masses at the other, the framers of the Constitution chartered what Franklin aptly identified as a republic. The term derives from the Latin phrase *res publica*, which often is translated "commonwealth"—the good of the people. Representation by elected officials is the first ingredient of a republic; balance of power among multiple portions of the government is the second.

The republican principle of representative government rests upon a foundation of popular sovereignty. In the Declaration of Independence, Thomas Jefferson had asserted that "governments are instituted among men, deriving their just powers from the consent of the governed." The purpose of government was to secure people's "unalienable rights" to "life, liberty, and the pursuit of happiness"—or, to borrow John Locke's phrasing in place of Jefferson's: life, liberty, and property. The Declaration of Independence offered a justification for popular rebellion with these words:

> whenever any form of Government becomes destructive of these ends, it is the right of the People to alter or to abolish it, and to institute new Government, laying its foundation on such principles, and organizing its powers in such form, as to them shall seem most likely to effect their safety and happiness.

Consistent with the Declaration's assertion of popular sovereignty, the Constitution began with three key words: "We the People." As Ronald Reagan later would say, "Let us take inventory. We are a nation that has a government—not the other way around. And this makes us special among the nations of the earth." But in 1787, the words "We the People" meant more than "popular sovereignty," or what Abraham Lincoln later described as "government of the people, by the people, for the people." In 1787, "We the People" also meant that the people within the states, and not merely their state legislatures, had the authority to change the form of government by which those states were joined into a confederation.

Virginia's Patrick Henry smelled a rat. Patrick Henry—who on the eve of the American Revolution had cried, "Give me liberty, or give me death!"—now spoke against the Constitution with vehemence. Under the existing Articles of Confederation, the state legislatures held most of the reigns of government, especially that power which the people feared the most: taxation. The American Revolution had been waged under the banner of "No Taxation without Representation," and Henry believed that the state legislatures represented the people better than any federal government ever could. Therefore, Henry wanted power to stay where the Articles of Confederation had kept it: with the states.

But Henry lost that debate, and the Constitution won acceptance in all thirteen states. The Constitution's supporters argued that a stronger federal government was necessary in order to protect both the people and their states. Whereas the Constitution's opponents feared that the federal government would have too much power, the Constitution's supporters thought the Constitution itself would prevent the federal government from abusing its power. An intricate system of checks and balances and a regular schedule of elections would ensure that no single person or group of people would wield too much power for too long.

James Madison was among the chief architects of those checks and balances, and also one of the Constitution's most eloquent supporters. "What is government itself," he asked in Federalist No. 51, "but the greatest of all reflections on human nature? If men were angels, no government would be necessary." Madison knew as well as you do that people are not angels. Government is necessary.

But governments are not angelic, either. In politics, it seems that no one can be trusted; everyone is prone to selfish ambition. How, then, to prevent the corruption in government that craves and abuses power? Madison's answer was brilliant: distribute a limited amount of authority from the people and their states to the federal government, and divide the federal government into three distinct branches, each with separate powers (the legislative, the executive, and the judicial).

Thus emerged the American Republic—a representative form of government in which powers were balanced to minimize corruption and avoid tyranny. At least that is how it looked on paper. But what about in practice? Had not Franklin himself alluded to danger when saying, "a republic, if you can keep it"?

How to Keep a Republic

Republics foster liberty, and that is what makes them vulnerable to political sabotage by one faction seeking to dominate others. Madison admitted as much in Federalist No. 10, where he wrote, "Liberty is to faction what air is to fire." Abolishing liberty would eliminate the threat of factions, but, of course, it also would eradicate the republic itself. Rather than eliminate faction, Madison concluded that a republic must instead limit its effects.

There are two basic ways to limit the effects of faction. The first is to balance one faction against the other. That is why the Constitution established a Congress consisting of both the House of Representatives and the Senate. That is why any law must be adopted in like form by both the House and the Senate, and usually also signed by the President. That is why a law can nonetheless be passed over the President's veto if a two-thirds majority in each chamber of Congress agrees. And that is why all of these government officials are subject to popular approval through a regular schedule of elections. In short, the rules of the game are designed to prevent any one person or group of people from wielding too much power for too long.

Some political theorists believe that a balancing of interests suffices to preserve a republic. In a free market of ideas, whatever wins general approval deserves to carry the day. This democratic doctrine once was known as "liberalism," but, as that word now has new connotations, it generally is called "libertarianism" today.

"Republicanism," by contrast, traditionally has held that the nation requires something more than checks and balances within an environment of free speech. In order to serve the public good, a republic must also limit faction by a second means: virtue.

George Washington, in his first inaugural address, acknowledged that "there is no truth more thoroughly established than that there exists an indissoluble union between virtue and happiness." Or, as King Solomon expressed it, "Righteousness exalts a nation."

Civic virtue includes a willingness of each citizen to answer the call that President John F. Kennedy sounded in his 1961 inaugural address: "Ask not what your country can do for you—ask what you can do for your country." Civic virtue means that citizens live their lives not demanding what they can get, but asking what they can offer to others. Civic virtue keeps government small and efficient by sustaining communities through the voluntarism of the private sector. Civic virtue therefore safeguards both the people and their government from corruption and its bitter fruit: tyranny.

Civic virtue, unfortunately, does not come naturally. Recall that men are not angels. That is why Congress adopted, in the Northwest Land Ordinance of 1787, the following provision: "Religion, morality, and knowledge, being necessary to good government and the happiness of mankind, schools and the means of education shall forever be encouraged."

Benjamin Rush, a signer of the Declaration of Independence, similarly identified the connection between education and civic virtue. He promoted schools that would shape young ladies into republican mothers who, he said, "should be qualified to a certain degree, by a peculiar and suitable education, to concur in instructing their sons in the principles of liberty and government."

Pause for a moment to ponder Rush's image of a woman instructing her child in civic virtue. For any civilization to remain stable, it must rest upon the natural bedrock of society: the family. For nowhere but the natural family—a man and a woman united for life, together with their children, whether begotten or adopted—nowhere but the natural family are the basic lessons of life more effectively taught. The home is both a person's first schoolhouse and first statehouse.

And the family cultivates civic virtue like nothing else can. Nowhere are the weak more securely protected, the hungry more efficiently fed, or the wealthy more compassionately directed to the needs of others than in the relationships between husband and wife, parent and child, brother and sister. The trust, cooperation, and friendship germinated in the home later blossom into civic virtues that sustain the state. President Barack Obama rightly said in his 2009 inaugural address that it is "a parent's willingness to nurture a child, that finally decides our fate."

How, then, to keep your republic? It begins with you. It begins in your home and your neighborhood. As former Speaker of the House Tip O'Neill once observed, "all politics is local." Examine where your feet are planted and begin to take ownership of your homeland.

So I encourage you today to learn your nation's history. Educate yourselves in the principles of liberty and statecraft. Form a political science book club. Start a blog to stir up conversation of current events. I encourage you to mentor your children by example, remembering that the opposite of civic virtue is not vice but apathy. Therefore, call or write your elected officials. Send a letter to the editor of your local newspaper. Assist in a political campaign. Keep your republic and pass it on to the rising generation.

If you choose not to keep your republic, then know this: alternatives are available. This past century we have witnessed several of them. Communism. Fascism. Totalitarianism. Terrorism. Pork barrelism.

Those alternatives, and others beside them, all succeed or fail according to the degree to which they understand who we are and why we need government. As our

Declaration of Independence recognizes, human nature is not of our own making. Rather, we are "endowed by our Creator with certain unalienable rights." No government, nor even We the People acting collectively, can create or destroy an inalienable right to life, liberty, or property. A just government will protect these rights; an unjust government will trample upon them. But these rights remain ours for the claiming either way. As for governments, they remain good only as long as the people whom they serve remain vigilant and virtuous.

Therefore, keep watch.

Alexander Hamilton, in Federalist No. 78, portrayed the Supreme Court as "the least dangerous" branch of our government. If you suspect that the Supreme Court has become more dangerous than Hamilton foresaw, then encourage the young people in your midst to study hard and go to law school.

The Constitution authorizes Congress to enact any laws "necessary and proper" to the powers explicitly delegated to Congress. If you find some of our laws today to be unnecessary or improper, then it is high time you have a conversation with your legislators—and with your neighbors who voted them into office.

The Constitution requires the President to take an oath to "preserve, protect and defend the Constitution of the United States." As you consider the candidates seeking that office in the next election, hold them to that standard.

But if you find the Constitution itself to be inadequate, then campaign for its amendment. A change in regime, when it becomes necessary, best begins in the hearts and minds of We the People—that means you and your fellow Americans.

"Freedom," said President George W. Bush, "is the hope of every human heart, the right of every person, and the future of every nation." This does not come easily. Battles must be fought—sometimes in the fields of operation overseas, but always and especially in the classrooms, cafés, and courthouses of this nation. And I understand some of you are in the habit of attending tea parties where no one actually drinks tea.

Our history has demonstrated time and again that ideas have consequences. In the twenty-first century we have discovered that the text message and the tweet, like the pens of olden days, are mightier than the sword. Our nation, like our home towns and our families, has always depended upon ordinary people dreaming and doing extraordinary things.

But if you discover that the generation before you has neglected any of these responsibilities, then it falls to you to pick up the pieces and carry on. History provides you with many examples. Consider Martin Luther King, Jr., who in the last speech of his life said:

Somewhere I read of the freedom of assembly. Somewhere I read of the freedom of speech. Somewhere I read of the freedom of press. Somewhere I read that the greatness of America is the right to protest for right.

Yes, these rights belong to you. To preserve these rights for your children and your children's children, you have a republic—if you can keep it.

Study Questions

1. Define "republic" and explain how it differs from other forms of government.

2. Define "civic virtue" and explain its role in the preservation of a republic.

3. Which of America's leaders have done the most to preserve the American Republic, and how?

About the Author / Speaking Engagements

Ryan C. MacPherson holds a Ph.D. in History and Philosophy of Science from the University of Notre Dame. He currently serves as Chair of the History Department at Bethany Lutheran College in Mankato, Minnesota. He also has served as a featured instructor for Rich in American History, a continuing education program for middle school teachers of social studies. Dr. MacPherson's publications span the fields of history, theology, law, and public policy.

Dr. MacPherson is a nationally featured speaker for academic associations, religious organizations, and public policy forums. Starting in 2012, he has served as senior editor for *The Family in America: A Journal of Public Policy*. He also is a member of the Lutherans for Life speakers bureau and has been interviewed on Pastor Todd Wilken's "Issues, Etc." radio program. Dr. MacPherson's expertise includes Christian education, religion and politics, religion and science, bioethics, and the family in public policy.

A homeschool parent who has taught both children's Sunday school and adult Bible classes, Dr. MacPherson also is the founding president of the Hausvater Project (www.hausvater.org), a nonprofit organization promoting a biblical vision for family, church, and society in the spirit of the Lutheran confessions. His publications include *Telling the Next Generation: The Evangelical Lutheran Synod's Vision for Christian Education, 1918–2011 and Beyond* (managing editor, 2011); *The Culture of Life: Ten Essential Principles for Christian Bioethics* (2012); and *Studying Luther's Large Catechism: A Workbook for Christian Discipleship* (2012).

For more information, visit:

www.ryancmacpherson.com

To schedule Dr. MacPherson for a speaking engagement:

www.ryancmacpherson.com/contact

Follow Dr. MacPherson online:

www.facebook.com/ryancmacphersonphd

www.linkedin.com/in/ryancmacpherson

www.twitter.com/ryancmacpherson

About the Publisher

Into Your Hands LLC specializes in research, consulting, publishing, training, and advocacy consistent with the natural law tradition upon which the American Republic was founded.

Ordering Information

Rediscovering the American Republic is available for individual purchase at Amazon.com and other reputable booksellers.

Contents of Volume 1 (1492–1877)

Part 1: From Pre-Columbian to British North America, 1492–1763

Part 2: The Creation of the American Republic, 1763–1789

Part 3: The Power of Political Parties, 1789–1836

Part 4: Liberty, Slavery, and American Destiny, 1836–1860

Part 5: The Civil War and Reconstruction, 1860–1877

Contents of Volume 2 (1877–Present)

Part 1: America in the Gilded Age, 1877–1901

Part 2: Progressive Reform and Human Nature, 1901–1929

Part 3: The Emergence of the American Superpower, 1929–1953

Part 4: The Cold War and Civil Rights, 1953–1981

Part 5: The Triumph and the Vulnerability of the World's Only Superpower, 1981–Present

To inquire about bulk discounts for schools and home school organizations, visit:

www.intoyourhandsllc.com

CPSIA information can be obtained
at www.ICGtesting.com
Printed in the USA
LVOW03s0825311216
519357LV00005B/280/P